Robert Graves

and the

HEBREW MYTHS

Graves and Patai conferring on the *Hebrew Myths*. (Photo courtesy of Leni Iselin.)

Robert Graves
and the
HEBREW
MYTHS

A Collaboration

RAPHAEL PATAI

 Wayne State University Press   Detroit

Jewish Folklore and Anthropology Series

General Editor
Raphael Patai

Advisory Editors

Books in this series

The Myth of the Jewish Race,
revised edition, by Raphael Patai and Jennifer Patai, 1989

The Hebrew Goddess,
third enlarged edition, by Raphael Patai, 1990

Robert Graves and the Hebrew Myths:
A Collaboration, by Raphael Patai, 1992

Library of Congress Cataloging-in-Publication Data

Patai, Raphael, 1910–
    Robert Graves and the Hebrew myths : a collaboration / Raphael
Patai.
        p.   cm. — (Jewish folklore and anthropology series)
    Includes bibliographical references and index.
    ISBN 0–8143–2114–3 (alk. paper)
    1. Graves, Robert, 1895– Hebrew myths.   2. Bible. O.T.
Genesis—Criticism, interpretation, etc.   3. Mythology, Jewish.
4. Mythology, Semitic.   5. Graves, Robert, 1895–   —Correspondence.
6. Authors, English—20th century—Correspondence.   7. Patai,
Raphael, 1910–   —Correspondence.   8. Scholars, Jewish–
–Correspondence.   I. Title.   II. Series.
BS1236.G7K54   1992
222'.11068—dc20
                                                              91–20963

Principal publications by Raphael Patai

Shire Yisrael Berekhya Fontanella (In Hebrew: *The Poems of I.B.F.*)
HaMayim (In Hebrew: *Water: A Study in Palestinology and Palestinian Folklore*)
HaSappanut haʿIvrith blme Qedem (In Hebrew: *Ancient Jewish Seafaring*)
Adam waʾAdama (In Hebrew: *Man and Earth in Hebrew Custom,*
Belief, and Legend)
Madaʿ haʾAdam (In Hebrew: *The Science of Man: An Introduction to Anthropology*)
Man and Temple in Ancient Jewish Myth and Ritual
On Culture Contact and Its Working in Modern Palestine
Israel between East and West
Jordan
Annotated Bibliography of Syria, Lebanon and Jordan
The Kingdom of Jordan
Current Jewish Social Research
Cultures in Conflict
Sex and Family in the Bible and the Middle East
Golden River to Golden Road: Society, Culture and Change in the Middle East
Hebrew Myths (with Robert Graves)
Tents of Jacob: The Diaspora Yesterday and Today
The Hebrew Goddess
Myth and Modern Man
The Arab Mind
The Myth of the Jewish Race (with Jennifer Patai)
The Messiah Texts
Gates to the Old City
The Vanished Worlds of Jewry
The Seed of Abraham
Ignaz Goldziher and His Oriental Diary
Nahum Goldmann: His Missions to the Gentiles
Apprentice in Budapest
The Hebrew Goddess, third enlarged edition

Raphael Patai also edited these works:

Mivḥar haSippur haArtziYisrʾeli (with Zevi Wohlmut) (In Hebrew:
Anthology of Palestinian Short Stories)
EDOTH (Communities): A Quarterly for Folklore and
Ethnology (with Joseph J. Rivlin) (In Hebrew and English)
Sifriya ʾFolqlor vʾEtnologia (with Joseph J. Rivlin) (In Hebrew:
Studies in Folklore and Ethnology)
Meḥqarim Ḥevrutiyyim (with Roberto Bachi) (In Hebrew and
English: *Social Studies*)
Erich Brauer: Yʾhude Kurdistan (In Hebrew; translated and edited by R.P.)
The Hashemite Kingdom of Jordan
The Republic of Syria
The Republic of Lebanon
Herzl Year Book
The Complete Diaries of Theodor Herzl
Angelo S. Rappoport: Myth and Legend of Ancient Israel
Women in the Modern Wrold
Encyclopaedia of Zionism and Israel

Contents

Photographs: frontispiece and pages 197, 260, 319, 328

Preface

THE CENTRAL THEME of this book is my friendship with Robert Graves and the literary collaboration that culminated in our joint authorship of the book *Hebrew Myths: The Book of Genesis.*

The relationship between Graves and me spanned almost three decades: it commenced in 1947 and continued until 1975, when his deteriorating health made it increasingly difficult for him to carry on correspondence. He died ten years later, at the age of ninety.

The Graves-Patai contact is documented not only in the *Hebrew Myths*, but also in other books written by him, which contain quotations—often lengthy—from my letters and works, or references to them. However, the most detailed, and I believe most interesting, record of our friendship and collaboration is found in the two hundred or so letters we exchanged in the course of more than a quarter of a century, in our taped discussion that took place on May 20, 1961, in my home in New York, in our joint lecture on May 15, 1963, at the 92d Street Y, and in our radio-interview taped on February 25, 1964. This material, printed here in full and for the first time, shows the extent to which both Graves and I, despite living an ocean apart, were concerned about each other's work, participated in it, and furthered it. Our letters are reprinted here exactly as we wrote them, with no attempt made to correct inconsistencies of punctuation or spelling.

As far as the letters generated by our collaboration on the myth book are concerned, the reader interested in the final version of that book, which resulted from the process of gestation reflected in these letters, may read them with the *Hebrew Myths* in hand.

9

Inseparable from our joint literary efforts was the work in which each of us was individually engaged during those years. Occasionally there was an implicit or explicit connection between what we were working on separately and the writing we did in collaboration. More frequently, our individual writing, lecturing, teaching, and other commitments took us away from our joint undertakings which, consequently, had to take second place in our schedules.

For my part, I always felt that my scholarly work, even though it branched out into diverse fields—ranging as it did from biblical Hebrew religious developments and rituals to anthropological problems of the modern Muslim Middle East, from talmudic folklore to the royal rites of twentieth-century black Africa, from ancient Jewish seafaring to modern Arab attitudes, from the Hebrew Goddess to the position of women in the modern world—always constituted one indivisible whole, and that each of the studies on which I embarked was based, whether it was apparent or not, on all my writings that had preceded it. This awareness of the basic unity in my scholarly work made it practically impossible for me to tell the story of my collaboration and friendship with Robert Graves without, in the same context, telling also of my other scholarly activities during those years. And, in order to balance what I had to say about my work, I felt I had to tell also, albeit more briefly, about Robert Graves's literary achievements, much richer and more wide-ranging than mine, in which I sensed the same internal unity. Hence, this book is something of a hybrid: the central theme running through it is my work with Robert Graves, but at the same time it also presents and analyzes much of the work each of us separately did over a major part of our lives.

The life and work of Robert Graves have been the subject of several books, most recently of Martin Seymour-Smith's thorough 1983 study. As for me, not being a celebrated man of letters of the stature of Graves, who attracted the interest of biographers and literary critics, when I came to feel that there was something worth telling about my own life and works, I had to be my own chronicler. In 1988 I published the first volume of my autobiography, entitled *Apprentice in Budapest,* which deals with the first twenty-two years of my life. I hope to be able to complete before long a second volume, to be titled *Journeyman in Jerusalem,* which will cover my fifteen years (1933–1947) in that city, coinciding with the last fifteen years of British mandatory rule over Palestine. The present book, beginning as it does with 1947, constitutes a kind of sequel to that second volume, and will have to substitute for the third, which I do not intend to write. It contains enough references to some of the highlights and lowlights of my life since 1947, and with it I feel I have laid to rest the ghosts of my past. More importantly, I also hope that it is a contribution to the still incomplete literary portrait of that remarkable poet and writer, Robert Graves.

The account of my collaboration with Graves contained in this book has much to say about his approach to historical problems and mythological issues, but only very little about his poetry. This, however, should not be taken to mean that I am not fully aware that the position of Graves in literature has been, and will be, judged by his poetry. Although he did characterize himself as a writer—hence the title of one of his books, *Occupation Writer*—Graves considered himself first and foremost a poet. He expressed more than once in writing, and told me in conversation on several occasions, that he wrote prose pieces only to provide a livelihood for his family and himself, and to be able to continue writing poetry whenever the Muse beckoned and called upon him to serve her. This, however, does not mean that Graves's prose writings are inferior in quality to, or lesser in value than, his poems. I must therefore disagree with the facile judgment of the critic J. M. Cohen, who wrote in his 1961 book on Graves that "it is as a poet that he ranks highest, and that he is likely to be read by future generations, who may find his other productions no more than entertaining." Having become closely acquainted with Graves's prose writings before, during and after our collaboration on the *Hebrew Myths,* I feel that they deserve more credit than this.

My view, which I have repeatedly expressed in this book, is that Graves made an important and original contribution to the genre of historical fiction and to myth interpretation by demonstrating that there is a more direct, more spontaneous, and more instantaneous way of grasping the meaning of historical documents and mythical accounts—the two major modes in which human beings have left behind a record of their past—than patiently working through to rigorous scholarly conclusions. That way, he has shown, is poetic insight. One may disagree with a detail, or even with the entire portrait of a scene, an event, a process limned by this method, one may even be sure that it is faulty or that it contains false features, but one cannot deny the value of the approach itself, its originality, its status as a first attempt at moving in an entirely new direction toward getting a hold on that most elusive of past phenomena—the way people thought and felt in remote ages.

This is why, although in this book I barely touch on Graves the poet, I still feel that the detailed presentation it contains of his grappling with the difficult task of collaborating with a biblical scholar, mythologist, and anthropologist on a book on Hebrew myths enriches our comprehension of Graves's literary stature.

As for me, to know Graves and to work with him was a great experience. It was not always easy, not because serious and hard-to-reconcile differences of opinion arose between us, but rather on account of a feature of his personality that somewhere in the present book I call his Michelangeloesque *terribilità,* faced with which I often had difficulty maintaining what I believed and knew was the right conclusion on this or that point. Graves was fifteen years older than I, which at the ages of fifty and sixty-five still made quite a difference (at a later age the significance of such a disparity in age tends to diminish), and he had, of course, the great prestige of world fame as a poet and novelist behind him, while I was but a scholar of modest accomplishments with my most important books still in the future. Thus I felt that I always had to be on guard lest I fall into the trap of accepting Graves's contributions to the *Hebrew Myths* for the wrong reason: not because I recognized that they were correct once I brought my considered scholarly scrutiny to bear upon them, but because they were made by him, that is, were persuasively propounded products of his poetic imagination. But I believe I did hold my own as best I could in the circumstances, and today, almost thirty years later, I still think that the *Hebrew Myths*—despite occasional lapses—is an original study of lasting value.

I wish to thank Beryl Graves, Lucia Graves, and William Graves for their help in locating Gravesiana I needed for writing this book, and for their permission to print letters, lectures, and conversations by Robert Graves. I thank the trustees of the Robert Graves Copyright Trust for their permission to reproduce the letters of Robert Graves. My thanks are due also to Ken McCormick of Doubleday who, twenty-five years after his enthusiastic acceptance for publication of the *Hebrew Myths* when it was nothing more than an idea, evinced a most helpful interest in the making of the present book.

1.

Man and Temple and the First Graves Letter

O N DECEMBER 11, 1947, some two months after my arrival from Jerusalem in New York, I got a letter from Robert Graves. He had written it on November 21 and addressed it to the Edinburgh office of my publishers, Thomas Nelson, who forwarded it to me in Jerusalem. From there my wife Naomi sent it on to me to New York.

The letter was a complete surprise to me. Needless to say, it was an extremely pleasant one. The name Robert Graves was well known to me. I knew that he was the author of the celebrated historical novel *I, Claudius,* which had been published in 1934, and which I had read soon thereafter with great enjoyment in the few hours of leisure I permitted myself as a relaxation from the strain of working on my doctoral thesis for the Hebrew University. Being myself involved in reconstructing certain aspects of the mental world of the ancient Hebrews—my dissertation dealt with the role of water in Palestinian custom and legend in the biblical and mishnaic periods—I was fascinated by the masterly hand with which Graves brought to life the world of ancient Rome as seen through the eyes of Claudius. To receive a letter from the famous author of that book was both a thrill and an honor. I had some difficulty in deciphering Graves's handwriting, and read the letter two or three times to make sure I absorbed and understood the numerous references it contained to Greek and related mythologies. Here is what Graves wrote:

from Señor Don Robert Graves*
Canellun Deya
Mallorca
Spain

*Brother of R. M. Graves
who is mayor of Jerusalem
at the moment

Dear Mr. Patai

I have just read your beautifully argued but too brief Man and Temple. *Do you recall the water sacrifice at Anaphe mentioned in Ap. Rhodius's Argonautica IV 1717 ff? There you have just the same ceremony as at the Tabernacles, including the lightheadedness, in a ritual which was probably Minoan. Anaphe was famous for its partridges, which of course are connected with Jewish folk-lore because of Beth-hoglah where there was a mourning for Jacob and also a round dance mentioned by Jerome; in my view the* pesach *on Carmel was a hobbling dance in imitation of the partridges' love and war dance, and with Minoan affinities c.f. the myths of Talus and Perdix.*

In my White Goddess *(Faber & Faber) now in page proof I have a lot to say about Palestinian tree-myths, and about the* calendar *values of the ethrog, willow & myrtle. The system runs N.W. across Europe, the canon of trees changing with the climate. Each represents a calendar period of fifteen ogdoads— hence the fifteen Ascents, though I have not mentioned this—and of course the palm was the birth tree of the Sun god (Apollo, Dusares etc) The* ethrog *of course superseded the quince in Roman times; in Celtic Europe it was the apple, or the sorb.*

Solomon's 'house of the forest of Lebanon' was, I believe, a 'green lady' bower. It had 3 times 15 pillars, by the way. The same number 15 x 3 occurs in the dimensions of the Ark, if they are multiplied by 8 the number of solar increase: 5 x 3 x 3. Marduk's ziggurat was of course planted with trees. I don't think there was much difference between the worship in Solomon's temple and that in Hierapolis in Luc[i]an's day: including the orgies of the sodomitic priests. I am sure that the Deuteronomic order: 'thou shalt not bring into the House of the Lord . . . the price of a dog' refers to the kelebite *priests or* enareae *in the Green Lady's service who dedicated their earnings to her. The order in fact means: 'this practice must now cease.'*

About Jachin & Boaz: I think they correspond with the green and gold pillars in Hercules's temple—at Byblos wasnt it?—described by Herodotus. One represents the waxing year and is specially carved, one the waning year and is fluted, to judge from votive objects showing the temple facade.

Yours v. sincerely
Robert Graves

I wish all ethnologists wrote as well as you do!

14

Years later I learned that at the time Graves wrote me this letter he was involved in writing the book *The Nazarene Gospel Restored* in collaboration with the Jewish scholar Joshua Podro, and in a selection of letters of Graves published in 1984 I found that three weeks after he wrote the above letter to me he wrote to Podro: "I have just bought a remarkably clear and sensible and original book *Man and Temple* by Raphael Patai. It is first class and I agree with almost every word."[1] The amount of scholarly comment and association contained in Graves's opening letter of the correspondence between him and me certainly testifies to the close attention he paid to my book, and to the stimulus it gave him to recall a variety of data that, he felt, had a bearing on certain points I touched upon in my book.

The book *Man and Temple in Ancient Jewish Myth and Ritual,*[2] which thus aroused Graves's admiration, was a small volume (226 pages) and the first book of mine to be published in English. In it I presented the gist of, and carried further, the argument I first developed in my two-volume Hebrew book *Man and Earth in Jewish Custom, Belief and Legend,* published in 1942–43 by the Hebrew University Press. My argument, as I summarized it twenty years later in the postscript to the second edition,[3] ran as follows:

> At various levels of cultural and religious sophistication, man has developed sets of rituals performed with a view to influencing nature or natural forces and elements in his favor, by showing them what he expected them to do, or by cajoling them into fulfilling his wishes. The mythical correlate of this type of ritual is the attribution of human-like qualities, acts and behavior to the forces and elements of nature (Chapter I).
>
> The greatest and most popular annual feast performed in the Second Temple of Jerusalem, the so-called "Joy of the House of Water Drawing," was a fine example of such a ritual. All the acts performed, and first and foremost the ceremony of water libation, had one central purpose: to bring about the onset of the autumnal rains on which depended the welfare and the very existence of the people. This purpose was subserved by the performance of a rich array of rites which symbolically but unmistakably indicated the natural phenomena they were supposed to bring about: favorable winds, thunder and lightning, and, most importantly, rain—good, rich and soft rain. One of the many rites performed was that of "lightheadedness," i.e. the indulgence in general sexual license, whose ritual purpose was to induce the rain to copulate with the earth (Chapter II).
>
> The mythological counterpart of these rituals was twofold: one type of myth told about the creation of the world, about the primal separation by God of the Upper Male Waters from the Lower Female Waters, and the ceaseless yearning of these two lustful elements to reunite: when it rained their desire was actually achieved. The other told about the place and role of the Temple in the great divine cosmogonical and cosmological scheme: the Temple was the center of the whole universe, the navel of the earth; its foundations pressed down upon the Female Waters of Tehom, the primeval abyss, and its underground shafts reached down into its very depths. Also, the Temple was located on the highest peak on earth, very

near heaven, and facing its heavenly counterpart, the Sanctuary On High. Therefore, the ritual performed in the Temple, not only the ritual of Water Libation and its attendant ceremonies, but any ritual, had an unfailing, direct and immediate effect on the world, on the order and functioning of nature (Chapter III).

Moreover, the Temple symbolically represented the entire universe, and each and every rite performed in it affected that part of nature of which the rite itself was reminiscent. In fact, the function of the Temple was of such basic importance that the very existence of the entire world depended on it. According to the Talmud, the destruction of the Second Temple (70 C.E.) resulted in the gravest disturbances in the natural order, and thereafter the fertility of Palestine was reduced to a mere fraction of its former riches (Chapter IV).

However, the functioning of the natural order was believed to have depended not solely on the regular and precise performance of the Temple ritual, but also on the conduct of the people, particularly of its leaders, outside the sacred precincts. There existed, it was believed, an inner, sympathetic connection between human conduct and the behavior of the natural forces. Sins, i.e. improper or illicit human acts, brought about improper or illicit occurrences in nature—it was in this view that the original, basic sanctions that made for religious conformity were anchored. In the earliest form of this religious imperative, the assumption was that the greatest of all sins was fornication, that is to say, any form of illicit sexual intercourse, because by the inexorable law of sympathy such transgressions caused similar irregular interactions between the male and the female elements of nature: droughts, floods or other natural calamities which can, and in the days of the Deluge actually did, destroy the world (Chapter V).

The other side of the coin was the complementary notion that a central personality, such as a patriarch, a king, or a pious and saintly man, had it in his power to influence the weather and thereby to insure the well-being of his people, either directly, through the working of the same laws of sympathy, or indirectly, through the intermediacy of God. Either way, the merit possessed by the pious and righteous men was of such force that what they ordained had to come to pass. The culmination of this trend of thought was the idea that the coming of the Messiah would usher in a period of great fertility in the vegetable and animal kingdoms, and an era of peace and general welfare for mankind. Once this type of thinking was achieved, man was assumed to influence nature no longer through ties of magical sympathy, but through a spiritual and moral sympathy in which God served as the supreme catalyst between man and nature (Chapter VI).

Much later, when I got acquainted with the writings of Graves other than his Claudius novels, I understood that a book presenting the above argument could not fail to strike a responsive chord in him.

When I received Graves's letter I was still in the midst of the rather difficult process of adjusting to life in New York. I had lived for fifteen years in Jerusalem, which was in those days a very small town within whose heterogeneous population the Jews of European extraction constituted but a small minority. That minority, in turn, comprised no more than a few hundred intellectuals, many of them affiliated with the Hebrew University, and this small group was the society of which I became a member soon after my arrival in the spring of 1933 and my admission as a graduate student at the university. This meant that I got to know personally, and had contact with, at least on and off, practically all the faculty and officials of the university, and with the writers, scholars, rabbis, publishers, physicians, lawyers, and so forth, of Jewish Jerusalem, who formed several small interlocking circles. Among the friends I acquired were students of the university, several of whom later were to make a name for themselves in various scholarly, literary, and public pursuits. I also got to know, and became friendly with, a limited number of Arab teachers, shaykhs, journalists, etc., whose attitudes toward their Jewish neighbors were in most cases those of polite friendliness.

Now, upon my arrival in New York, I found myself not only in a strange world, but also in a world frightening, or at least intimidating, by its sheer size. I still remember the difficulty I had in getting used to the inordinately long time it took to get from the place where I lived to the places where I had to go to meet somebody or to take care of some errand. In Jerusalem, I could get practically anywhere by walking a few minutes; the only place to reach which one had to take a bus was the Hebrew University campus on Mount Scopus—it was a "long" bus ride of all of ten minutes. In New York, going somewhere inevitably meant a long subway ride, so that any visit took up half a day if not more. To adjust to the atmosphere and tempo of New York was in itself an almost full-time job, complicated by the fact that, after having for seven years taken all my meals at home—my wife was a good cook—living alone in New York I found it was annoying and time-consuming to have to go to a restaurant or cafeteria three times a day. These circumstances were, I believe, partly or mostly responsible for the fact that almost six weeks passed before I replied to Graves's letter.

As for the contents of my response, when I finally got around to writing it, rereading it today I must say that I did not rise to the challenge Graves's letter represented. I did not reply to any of the dozen or so suggestions he threw out, the parallels he drew, the ideas he jotted down. I was too involved with efforts to find my footing not only in a new social and academic environment, but also in a new field of scholarly specialization, that of the anthropological study of the contemporary Middle East, which, as I could not help recognizing even before I set out for the United States, was a much more promising field as far as academic employment was concerned than the religious history of ancient Israel. In fact, in the last three or four years before I left Jerusalem I had already veered toward the study of the modern Middle East, as shown by the record of most of my published work from those years. My study accepted by Prof. Alden Mason, editor of the Memoir Series of the American Anthropological Association, dealt with culture change in modern Palestine; another, scheduled for publication in the *American Anthropologist*, dealt with

17

problems of agricultural cooperation among the Arabs of Palestine; a programmatic paper on "Problems and Tasks of Jewish Folklore and Ethnology" was published in 1946 in the *Journal of American Folklore;* several others on the Marrano Jewish community of Meshhed, Iran I published myself in Hebrew and English in *Edoth: A Quarterly for Folklore and Ethnology,* which I edited together with my friend Prof. Joseph J. Rivlin of the Hebrew University, and which in its totality was devoted to contemporary studies; the book on the ethnology of the Kurdish Jews, left behind in an incomplete English manuscript by my late friend Dr. Erich Brauer, was published in Hebrew in 1947 completed, translated, and edited by me. It was on the strength of these anthropological studies of the contemporary Middle East that I received a Viking Fund (later Wenner-Gren Foundation for Anthropological Research) fellowship that brought me to America, and they were the basis for my being invited to teach Middle Eastern anthropology first at Columbia University, and then at the University of Pennsylvania and the Dropsie College for Hebrew and Cognate Learning, a graduate institution, both in Philadelphia.

However, when I began to prepare my first course on the subject, that was to start on February 1, 1948, at Columbia, I found that, despite all the studies I had carried out in Palestine, and the papers I had written on specific topics of the anthropology of the modern Middle East, I was not yet well enough prepared to give a survey course on the subject. I therefore spent most of my time that fall and winter reading studies on the contemporary Middle East and attending the anthropology classes given by Ruth Benedict, Julian Stewart, William Duncan Strong, and others at Columbia, for the double purpose of learning from them substantively and of acquiring a familiarity with American methods of teaching anthropology in universities. In addition, much of my time had to be devoted to intensive correspondence and reading in preparation for my visit to Mexico, where I planned to study (with a grant from the Viking Fund) the "Indios Israelitas" of the village of Venta Prieta, Mexico City, and other localities in the summer of 1948.

All this meant that, in the course of the eighteen or twenty months that had passed since the completion of the manuscript of my book *Man and Temple,* the focus of my scholarly interest had definitely shifted from the historical to the contemporary aspect of Middle Eastern anthropology. This was the reason why, when I finally got around to answering Graves's letter, I was not able to give it the attention it deserved, and certainly not to follow up the many leads it contained. This is what I wrote him in answer:

> *January 20, 1948*
> *c/o The Viking Fund*
> *14 East 71st Street*
> *New York 21, N.Y.*

Dear Mr. Graves,

Your remarkable letter reached me quite some time after you sent it, because it was forwarded to me to America where I am spending this year as a

Viking Fund Fellow and Visiting Lecturer in Anthropology in Columbia University. Circumstances being what they are at present in Palestine, the mail is very irregular.

I cannot tell you how surprised I was and how impressed to receive comments of such erudition as those your letter contained. I am very grateful to you for drawing my attention to the western affinities of the ancient Jewish temple ritual. My interest when writing the book was focussed on the East and I tried to elucidate an interesting and hitherto neglected chapter in ancient Jewish ritual and symbolism by placing it against the background of the ancient Near East. A work dealing comprehensively with these aspects in Mediterranean culture has yet to be written. I am looking forward eagerly to reading your White Goddess *when it appears. I am quite certain that I shall find in your book much that will parallel and complement the material I gathered in my* Man and Temple, *and in particular in my Hebrew "Man and Earth," chapter "Man and Tree."*

Your remarks confirm my impression that Greek religion owed a lot more to the East than is generally conceded. Future studies will no doubt shed much light on this point.

By ordinary mail I am sending you two papers of mine (in English) one of which deals with "Hebrew Installation Rites" and is a study in the culture contact between the ancient Near East and Negro Africa; while the second is a study of culture contact in modern Palestine and appeared as the latest title in the Memoir Series of the American Anthropological Association. Should you have any remarks to make on these papers, I shall be very happy to receive them. Comments from such a learned critic are indeed a rare treat.

> *Yours sincerely*
> *Raphael Patai*

Rereading today, more than forty years later, that memorable first letter of Graves and my rather lame answer to it, I regret I could not, or in any case did not, give it fuller attention. I do not believe that in the time left to me I shall be able to return to that book, although it is, I believe, one of the most original studies I ever wrote, and would deserve to be updated and expanded. Looking at it today I think Graves was right when he wrote that it was "too brief." Let me therefore put down here, albeit belatedly, some observations on the main points Graves raised in his letter which at the time I overlooked.

The first point made by Graves is a reference to the *Argonautica* of Apollonius Rhodius. This is the only lead I followed up and incorporated into the Postscript to the second edition of *Man and Temple*. Apollonius of Rhodes (c. 295–215 B.C.E.) was a Greek epic poet of considerable renown who served as

19

director of the great Alexandrian library from c. 260 to 247 B.C.E. His best known work is the *Argonautica,* in which he retells the legend of the Argonauts in a simple, Homeric style. The passage to which Graves refers (IV:171ff.) reads as follows in E. V. Rieu's translation:

> Dawn came soon after and showed them the low island on which they had landed. They called it Anaphe, or Revelation, because Apollo had revealed it to them when they were benighted. In the shelter of some trees they consecrated ground and built him an altar in the shade calling him the Lord of Light, whose beacon fire had lit them from afar. On that lonely coast they had little to offer him, but they offered what they could, with the result that when Medea's Phaeacian maids, who were accustomed to the rich sacrifices made in Alcinous' palace, saw them using water for libations on the burning logs, they could no longer refrain from laughing. The men, seeing the joke themselves, retaliated with some ribaldry, which was the signal for a light-hearted exchange of insult and repartee. This frolic of the Argonauts is commemorated by the island women, who chaff the men whenever they are sacrificing to Apollo, Lord of Light and protector of the Isle of Revelation.[4]

Were it not for the last sentence, one would not suspect that the events on Anaphe were anything but the mythical validation of a ritual. But that last sentence gives the story away: it makes it clear that Graves was right in interpreting the passage as referring to a ceremony of water sacrifice accompanied by "lightheadedness." If a ritual is said to "commemorate" a past event, and especially an event from the early, mythical past, we can be sure that we are dealing with what could be called a myth-and-ritual syndrome. Unfortunately, Apollonius's account of the ritual on Anaphe is most laconic, but adding features from the myth one can reconstruct it as probably having consisted of the following rites:

1. The consecration of a piece of ground in the woods to Apollo.
2. Building an altar in its midst, shaded by trees.
3. Lighting of fire on the altar.
4. Pouring water upon the fire.
5. "Frolicking" between the men and the women touched off by the reaction of the latter to the water libation.

That the intent of this ritual was rain-making cannot be doubted. Points 1–4 are quite similar to the rites performed by Elijah in his rain-making competition with the prophets of Baal on Mt. Carmel, although Elijah did not light the wood on the altar he built, but waited until a fire from heaven consumed the sacrifice, burned the wood, and dried up the water (1 Kings 18:38). As to point 5, the "frolicking," this certainly parallels closely the "lightheadedness" of the "Joy of the House of Water Drawing" in the Jerusalem Temple, and must have had the same underlying motivation.

Next Graves refers in his letter to partridges, the mourning of Jacob at Bet-Hogla, the round-dance mentioned by Jerome, and the *pesah,* or hobbling dance, on Mt. Carmel. His statements are a brief summary of what he wrote on these subjects just a short time earlier in *The White Goddess.*[5] Let me take up his reference one by one.

The obsequies for Jacob were held by his sons on "the threshing-floor of Atad (*Goren haAtad*) which is beyond the Jordan": "There they wailed with a very great and sore wailing." When the Canaanites, who perceived the family of Jacob as Egyptians (could they have assimilated so quickly the Egyptian garb and language?) "saw the mourning in the floor of Atad, they said, 'This is a grievous mourning for the Egyptians.' Wherefore the name of it was called *Abel-mizrayim* ["mourning of Egypt"], which is beyond the Jordan" (Gen. 50:10–11).

From the context in Genesis 50 it is apparent that this "threshing-floor of Atad" was located to the east of the Jordan, and that only after the sons of Jacob concluded their seven-day mourning ritual at that place did they cross the Jordan and carry the body of their father for burial in the Cave of Machpelah (v. 13). Still, Eusebius in his *Onomasticon* (8, lines 17–19), identifies *Goren haAtad* with Bet Hogla, which, he says, was located at a distance of two miles from the Jordan and three miles to the north of Jericho, that is, to the west of the Jordan. Eusebius (260–339 C.E.), it should be noted, lived in Caesaria on the Palestinian coast, and his book *On the Names of Places in the Divine Book* (usually referred to as *Onomasticon*) was for centuries the only source from which those interested in the Holy Land drew information. It contains, in alphabetical order, a list of the cities and villages mentioned in the Bible, and states their locations and their names in his own times. Among the sources Eusebius used were the writings of Josephus Flavius (c. 37–100 C.E.), the famous Jewish historian, who, like Eusebius, wrote in Greek. The *Onomasticon* was translated into Latin by Jerome (342–420), who also introduced numerous additions and corrections into Eusebius's text, which makes Jerome's version more authentic and reliable.

Bet Hogla is mentioned in the Book of Joshua (15:6; 18:19; 21) as a "city at the north bay of the Salt Sea [i.e., the Dead Sea] at the south end of the Jordan." It is also referred to by Josephus (*Antiquities,* 13:1:5), in the form of Bethalaga, as the place to which Jonathan the Hasmonean fled with his followers before Bacchides.[6]

I do not know on what basis Eusebius (or Jerome) identifies *Goren haAtad* with Bet Hogla, but this is what Jerome says: "The threshing-floor of Atat [i.e., Atad], a place across the Jordan where once they bewailed Jacob, at the third stone from Jericho, two miles from the Jordan, which now is called Bethagla, which is interpreted as 'place of dance,' because there, in the manner of mourners, they went around at the funeral of Jacob."[7] Since the biblical text mentions only "the threshing-floor of Atad" and not Bet Hogla as the

21

place of Jacob's funeral rites, and does not mention at all dancing or circum-ambulation in connection with the seven-day obsequies, Jerome must have based himself on some other tradition that contained these features.

An older contemporary of Jerome, Epiphanius (b. in Palestine c. 315, d. 402), either knew of the same tradition independently or based himself on Eusebius in reporting the same details. Epiphanius was made bishop of Salamis in 367, but before that he had founded a monastery in Palestine and served as its superior for some thirty years, which means that he had ample opportunity to get acquianted with local traditions. In his treatise *On Weights and Measures,* Epiphanius states that the Atad of Genesis 50:10 was identi-fied with the spring and the thornbush of Bet Hogla near Jericho. He writes: "Atat is across the Jordan. There they danced for Jacob when he died. It is at a distance of four miles from Jericho and three miles from the Jordan. And now it is called Bet Hogla which is explained as 'place of circular dance.' "[8]

This statement, as William Robertson Smith remarked, seems to be based on a local tradition of a ritual procession around sacred objects, similar to the *hajj* performed since antiquity around the Ka'ba in Mecca.[9] It is quite likely that Bet Hogla was an ancient religious site and this is why the sons of Jacob chose that spot to halt on their way from Egypt to the ancestral burial cave of Machpelah in Hebron and to perform there what must have been a complex sequence of week-long obsequies.[10]

As is the case with many place names in Palestine, the biblical name Bet Hogla has been preserved in the Arabic names of the spring *'Eyn Ḥajla,* of the fortress next to it called *Qasr Ḥajla,* and the ford across the Jordan also called *Ḥajla.*[11] The explanation of the name Bet Hogla by Eusebius as *topos kyklou,* that is, "place of circle" or "of circumambulation," is based on the meaning of the Aramaic root *hgl,* to draw a circle or to go around.[12] In modern Hebrew the verb *hagal* is still used in precisely the same two meanings.

"The *pesach* on Carmel" which Graves mentions next refers to one ele-ment in the rain-making contest to which Elijah challenged the prophets of Baal on Mt. Carmel. After they placed the carcass of their bullock upon their altar, the prophets of Baal "danced in halting wise (*y'fashu*) about the altar which was made" (1 Kings 18:26)—evidently a rite that formed part of the Phoenician rain-making ritual. It so happens that in a study I had published ten years earlier I dealt with that encounter between Elijah and the prophets of Baal and showed that the point of the contest between the one Yahwist prophet and the 450 Baalist prophets was not so much who would be answered by his god with fire that would consume the proffered sacrifice, but rather who was able to bring rain to the country that had been parched by a long drought. Hence I titled my paper "The 'Control of Rain' in Ancient Palestine." How-ever, I referred to the halting dance of the Baal prophets only briefly.[13]

As for the association of Bet Hogla with partridges, Graves is on the right track. Some scholars explain the name Hogla as "partridge" and the word is still used in the same sense in modern Hebrew. The walk of the partridge certainly makes the impression of a halting, hobbling, or limping gait. The Hebrew term *hogla* for partridge has certainly something to do with the original meaning of the Semitic root *hgl*, which in Arabic (*hajala*) means to hop, to leap, to skip, and from which is derived the Arabic name for partridge, *hajl* or *hijl.*

All this makes it more than likely that the mourning ritual performed by the sons of Jacob was a limping dance, just as a limping or hopping dance seems to accompany the modern Syrian dirge *māʿid.*[14] Moreover, it is known that a limping, hopping, or halting gait has also elsewhere characterized some sacred or ceremonial dances.[15] Both Gunkel and Oesterley suspected that Jacob's limping (Gen. 32:32) may go back to some traditional limping ceremony at the Jordan.[16] The biblical Hebrew verb *pasah* (in the *piʿel* form), describing the dancing of the Baal prophets, is the root from which the noun *pesah* (Passover) is derived, and its use in both the Bible and talmudic literature is well attested in the sense of leaping over (*pasah*), becoming lame (*nifsah*), being lame or limping (*pisseah*).[17] In Syriac the same verb, in different conjugations, means to dance and to mourn.[18]

To understand what Graves means by his reference to "Minoan affinities c.f. the myths of Talus and Perdix," one has to go to *The Greek Myths,* on which he had begun working by 1947 and which was to be published in two volumes in 1955, and reprinted many times thereafter. In that book he speaks of Perdix ("partridge"), the sister of Daedalus the smith and mother of Talos, as well as of Talus the smith who fathered Hephaestus on Hera and whose soul "flew off as a partridge."[19] He mentions that a partridge appeared at the burial of Daedalus's son Icarus; that Hephaestus hobbled when he walked; that "one of Talus's names was Tantalus ('hobbling or lurching')"; that "a cockpartridge hobbles in his love-dance, holding one heel ready to strike at rivals"; that the Latin god Vulcan, whose cult had been introduced from Crete, where he was called Velchanus and had a cock as his emblem, hobbled; and that the cock, which did not reach Crete until the sixth century B.C.E., was "likely to have displaced the partridge as Velchanus's bird." These are interesting observations on the connection between the partridge and burial ceremonies, although they fall short of proving that a hobbling dance was indeed performed at the mourning ritual for Jacob.

The entire first paragraph of Graves's letter is a brief rephrasing of section 92.1 of *The Greek Myths.* In that section he also says that it seems to him that "in the spring an erotic partridge dance was performed in honor of the Moon-goddess, and that the male dancers hobbled and wore wings." Then, in the style that I later learned was typically Gravesian, he states as a fact that "in Palestine this ceremony, called the *Pesah* ('the hobbling') was, according to Jerome still performed at Beth-Hoglah ('the Shrine of the Hobbler'), where the devotees danced in a spiral."

Next in *The Greek Myths* (92.2), Graves goes on to state that at Bet Hogla, identified with the threshing-floor of Atad, mourning was held "for the lame King Jacob, whose name may mean *Jah Aceb* ('the heel-god')." This interpretation appears also in Graves's *The White Goddess*.[20] My comment on this statement must be, I am afraid, rather negative. First of all, Jacob was never a king, but the head of a family or clan. As for the name Jacob (Hebrew *Ya'aqov*), its explanation is a very complex matter in view of the many variants in which it appears in both biblical and extrabiblical sources, such as *'Aqavyah, Ya'aqovah, 'Aqov, 'Aqiva, Ya-akh-qu-ub-il(um), Bal'aqav,* etc. These multiple forms make it likely that originally Ya'aqov was an abridged form of the theophoric name *Ya'aqovel,* which meant "may El (God) protect." Biblical scholars feel that the story in Genesis 25:26 which derives the name *Ya'aqov* from the word *'aqev,* "heel," originally meant to say that since the second of the twins of Rebecca emerged holding on to the heel of the first, he was called by the name which had already existed and was found suitable for the child because of its double meaning, or else it was simply a Midrash explaining the name, the like of which was not unusual.[21] In any case the explanation suggested by Graves is rather unlikely for the simple reason that the biblical theophoric names whose first element is *Yah* take the form *Y'ho,* which is abbreviated to *Yo-,* e.g., *Y'hoahaz-Yoahaz, Y'hoash-Yoash, Y'hohanan-Yohanan, Y'hoyada'-Yoyada', Y'hoyakhim-Yoyakhin,* etc. That is, only if the name form was Yo'aqav would it permit the derivation from a hypothetical theophoric Y'ho'aqav.

Next Graves goes on to say in *The Greek Myths* that Jeremiah warned "the Jews not to take part in those orgiastic Canaanite rites," quoting "the partridge gathereth young that she hath not brought forth." The passage quoted by Graves is from Jeremiah 17:11, and its more accurate translation is, "As the partridge [Hebrew *qore*] that broodeth over young which she hath not brought forth . . ." after which Jeremiah continues,". . . so is he that gathereth riches and not by right; in the midst of his days he shall leave them, and at his end he shall be a fool." This prophetic simile has nothing to do with the reproach of idolatry, of Judah serving the goddess Asherah by leafy trees (Jer. 17:1ff.), that precedes it in the same chapter, but is separated from it by two intervening pericopes containing ethical remonstrations. What we can learn from Jeremiah's reference to the partridge (which he calls not *hogla* but *qore,* translated by the Septuagint as *perdix*) is that the prophet was aware of the zoological fact that occasionally several female partridges lay their eggs into one nest and then one of the birds hatches them.[22]

Finally, still in the same section (92.2), Graves refers to the island of Anaphe, north of Crete, which, he says, "was famous in antiquity as a resting place for migrant partridges." So much for partridges, hobbling, and funeral rites.

The next point Graves touches upon in his November 21 letter is no less intriguing. He refers to *The White Goddess,* which was at the time just about being published by Faber and Faber in London, and calls my attention to the "*calendar* values" of the ethrog, willow, and myrtle, the three species which together constituted the *lulav,* the bundle used ritually by shaking in the course of the Sukkoth (Tabernacles) observances. I pointed out in my *Man and Temple* that the *lulav* was considered in talmudic times a weapon with which Satan could be driven off (p. 38). Graves now noted in his letter that each of the three species "represents a calendar period of fifteen ogdoads," that is, fifteen times eight days, and then connects these ("hence") with the Fifteen Songs of Ascents which were sung by the Levites as part of the ritual of Water Libation. I shall always regret that I did not ask him, while it was still possible, what he meant by these cryptic remarks.

By saying that "of course the palm tree was the birth tree of the Sun god (Apollo, Dusares etc)," Graves seems to intend to indicate that the *lulav* had something to do with a solar deity, although, of course, in the Second Temple, with which I dealt in my *Man and Temple,* no traces of sun worship were left.

Next Graves comments on my reference to Solomon's House of the Forest of Lebanon (1 Kings 7:2ff.), and writes that this structure "was, I believe, a 'green lady's' bower." I can find no reference to the "green lady" either in Graves's *The Greek Myths* or in *The White Goddess.* The "3 times 15 pillars" in the House of the Forest of Lebanon is mentioned in 1 Kings 7:3, where the text says that the roof of this building "lay on forty and five pillars, fifteen in a row." What Graves means by the "number 15×3 occurs in the dimensions of the Ark, if they are multiplied by 8 the number of solar increase: $5 \times 3 \times 3$" is again not clear to me. The dimensions of the Ark, the holiest object in the desert Sanctuary and later in the Solomonic Temple, as given in Exodus 25:10, were: length, 2½ cubits; breadth, 1½ cubits; and height, 1½ cubits. True, multiplied by two this gives $5 \times 3 \times 3$, but I do not see where the multiplication by eight enters.

Graves's next comment, "I don't think there was much difference between the worship in Solomon's temple and that in Hierapolis in Lucian's day: including the orgies of the sodomitic priests," merely approves, and extends backward in time, what I stated in *Man and Temple* about the similarity between the Second Temple ritual of the Water Libation at Sukkoth and the rites carried out at Hierapolis as described by Lucian.[23] The references I found in Lucian's *De Dea Syria* about the Hierapolis temple ritual as paralleling the Jerusalem Temple Water Libation did not include mention of "orgies of the sodomitic priests." Graves contends that "the Deuteronomic order: 'Thou shalt not bring into the House of the Lord . . . the price of a dog' refers to the *kelebite* priests or *enareae* in the Green Lady's service who dedicated their earnings to her. The order in fact means: 'this practice must now cease.' " In

his *White Goddess* (p. 53) Graves says that "the dog-priests," called Enar-
iae . . . attended the Great Goddess of the Eastern Mediterranean and in-
dulged in sodomitic frenzies in the dog days at the rising of the Dog-star,
Sirius." Hence it would seem that by the "green lady" he meant the *Dea
Syria* described by Lucian. The Deuteronomic order Graves quotes in his letter (Deut. 23:18–19), seems to refer to the Canaanite-Phoenician practice of
employing male prostitutes in the temples of Astarte and Asherah, where they
constituted a class of functionaries ranking below that of the priests. They, or
a subdivision of them, were, according to Lucian (21, 26, 51), men who, during a ritual, were seized with an ecstatic frenzy and castrated themselves in
honor of the Great Goddess, after which they donned female garb and lived
among women. They were called *Galli*. Apuleius (c. 123 C.E.), the famous
Latin satirist, mentions in his *Metamorphoses* (published in English as *The
Golden Ass*), that the *Galli* walked about in female dress, gave public performances, and engaged in prophesying, in the course of which they cut themselves until they drew blood, and then collected alms. It also happened, says
Apuleius, that at night they served as sexual partners to men.

Whether the *q'deshim,* who functioned in the Jerusalem Temple, were of
this or of another type of male prostitutes is uncertain. The biblical references
to them do not supply sufficient data (1 Kings 14:24–24; 15:12–13; 22:47; 2
Kings 23:7). However, it is clear that despite the quoted Deuteronomic prohibition which mentions the male sodomites (called "dogs") in one breath
with the female harlots as equal "abominations unto the Lord," the *q'deshim*
practiced their trade in the Temple under several Judahite kings and especially
in association with the worship of the goddess Asherah, whose statue stood in
the sacred precincts for 236 out of the 370 years which were the life span of
the First Temple of Jerusalem.[24]

Incidentally, the term *kelev* ("dog"), by which these male prostitutes or
functionaries of the Temple were called, was not necessarily a derogatory or
contemptuous expression. We can conclude this from the fact that the personal
name Kalev (a slight variant of *kelev*), was borne by a respected leader of
the tribe of Judah in the days of Moses (Num. 13:6), and by others of that tribe
(1 Chron. 2:42). Also among the Arabs the name was an honored one: the
Beni Kalb (literally, "sons of dog") were one of the noble Arab tribes.[25] The
name *kelev* was the official designation of certain temple functionaries according to the Marseille list of sacrifices in which *kelev*s and youths appear
side by side.[26] It would appear that *kelev* and *qadesh* were used as synonyms.
Also in a Phoenician inscription from the fourth century B.C.E., discovered in
the temple of Astarte, the term *kelev* (in plural) appears as one type of temple
functionaries. Jerome, in his commentary on Hosea, identifies the *q'deshim*
with the *Galli*, whom he too describes as *castrati*.[27]

Graves's comments on Jachin and Boaz, the two pillars in Solomon's Temple (1 Kings 7:15–22, 40–42),[28] are in line with the rich archaeological ma-

terial that illuminated the occasionally contradictory biblical references to these two pillars. The conclusion reached is that such two freestanding pillars to the right and left of the entrance, detached from the architectural structure of the building itself were parts of the temples in Palestine and other countries of the ancient Near East. Graves in his letter was not sure where the temple of Hercules, described by Herodotus, stood. He writes, "at Byblos, wasnt it?" In fact the shrine of Hercules was located at Tyre; in it were "two pillars, one of refined gold and one of emerald, a huge pillar that shone by night."[29]

The existence of Herodotus's description of the Tyrian temple of Hercules with its two pillars is especially fortunate since the master craftsman Hiram whom the king of Tyre sent to Solomon to build his temple in Jerusalem was a Tyrian, the son of a Tyrian man and an Israelite woman. This Hiram (or Huram) is described in the Bible as "skilful to work in gold and in silver, in brass, in iron, in stone and in timber, in purple, in blue, and in fine linen and in crimson; also to grave any manner of graving, and to devise any device" (2 Chron. 12–13). Concerning his mother there are two conflicting traditions: one makes her a woman of the tribe of Naphtali, the other of the tribe of Dan (1 Kings 7:14; 2 Chron 2:13). However, both agree that she was a Hebrew woman.

There can be little doubt that in planning and executing the work of "burnished brass" for the Jerusalem Temple Hiram followed styles and patterns with which he was familiar from Tyre, or even reproduced items that he himself, as court architect-decorator, had introduced into the temple of his hometown. Of all of them, the two pillars Jachin and Boaz seem to have been the most important pieces, for the account of Hiram's work in the Book of Kings begins with their description, in considerable detail.

The names of Jachin (Hebrew *Yakhin*) and Boaz (*Boᶜaz*), given by Hiram to the pillars (1 Kings 7:21; 2 Chron. 3:17), are enigmatic. That they should have been named by the master-craftsman who made them, rather than by the king for whom he worked, is in itself not surprising: it is in line with naming practices in ancient Israel.[30] Both *Yakhin* and *Boᶜaz* are well-known Hebrew names: *Yakhin* was the name of a son of Simeon, son of Jacob and that of his clan, the *Yakhini* (Gen. 46:10; Ex. 6:15; Num. 26:12), as well as that of two priests (Neh. 11:10; 1 Chron. 9:10; 24:17). *Boᶜaz* was the name of the well-known Judahites, the husband of Ruth and the great-grandfather of King David (Ruth 2:1, etc.) *Yakhin* means "He [i.e., God] establishes," or "may He establish." *Boᶜaz* may mean "in it is strength," or "in Him is strength."[31] It was on the basis of these meanings that the talmudic sage R. Pinḥas ben Yair (second century C.E.) taught that the first pillar corresponded to the moon and the second to the sun.[32] That the Tyrian Hiram should have given Hebrew names to his pillars indicates that he knew Hebrew: it was his mother's tongue and hence his mother tongue. He also must have had some familiarity with Hebrew culture, of which the two names were part. However, it so happens that the name *Yakhin* is found also in Phoenician.[33] What remains problematic is why Hiram should have given precisely these two names to his pillars, and what he meant by calling them thus.[34]

Equally difficult is to find a satisfactory answer to the question of what was the meaning or function of the two pillars. Graves in his letter quotes Herodotus to the effect that one of the two pillars in Hercules's temple represented the waxing year and was specially carved, the other the waning year and was fluted. Whether the two pillars in Solomon's Temple had a similar meaning is open to question. Since they were made by a Tyrian craftsman, one can assume that he intended to represent the same concept, but the biblical and later Jewish sources are silent on the subject. On the other hand, another feature of the pillars of the Tyrian temple of Hercules seems to have been reproduced by Hiram in Jerusalem: as we have mentioned, Herodotus tells us that one of the Tyrian pillars shone by night, which probably means that it carried a beacon on its top. The biblical description of the two pillars states that they were topped by bowls (*gullot,* sing.; *gulla,* pl.), just as were the golden candlesticks in Solomon's Temple (1 Kings 7:41; Zech. 4:3). This detail definitely indicates that a fire was lit on top of the pillars. It was on this basis that Stanley A. Cook suggested that the two pillars Jachin and Boaz served as two huge lampstands or candlesticks.[35] This explanation is indirectly confirmed by the presence in the Temple of ten extremely tall candelabra, to light which apprentice priests had to climb up ladders, and whose fire lighted up all of Jerusalem.[36]

Yet another explanation is suggested by Sh'muel Yevin in the authoritative Hebrew *Entziqlopediya Miqrait:* the two pillars may have symbolized the pillar of cloud and the pillar of fire, in which, according to Exodus 13:21–22, the Lord himself marched before the Children of Israel in their wanderings in the wilderness. To this I would add that, according to Exodus 33:9–11, when Moses entered the Tent of Meeting (that is, the desert sanctuary), "the pillar of cloud descended and stood at the door of the Tent," and from it the Lord spoke to Moses—that is to say, the pillar in which God was present during the day took up a stationary position before the Sanctuary. Hence a pillar representing this, and a symmetrical one representing the pillar of fire in which God was present at night, were a most appropriate symbolical expression of the divine presence.

I am well aware that in the foregoing discussion of the comments made by Graves in that first letter of his I strayed far and wide from the subject of this chapter—the beginnings of the contact between us. But frankly, rereading that letter of his today, forty years after I received it, I was so fascinated by the issues he raised that I could not resist jotting down what I should have answered him in 1948.

2.

The "Hebrew Installation Rites"

U PON RECEIVING HIS first letter, I determined to find out more about who Robert Graves was and what he had written in addition to *I, Claudius*. I no longer remember to what source or sources I went, but I do recall very clearly that when I read what he had produced I was so impressed, nay, awed, that I responded in a tone of deep respect, and kept my answer to generalities instead of taking the time—however busy I was—to give the letter the thorough going-over that it deserved, and that Graves may have expected from a man whose scholarship he evidently respected. However, simultaneously with answering him I also mailed him (by ship mail) copies of my eighty-three-page study "Hebrew Installation Rites: A Contribution to the Study of Ancient Near Eastern-African Culture Contact,"[1] and my paper *On Culture Contact and Its Working in Modern Palestine*,[2] both of which were published in 1947. Graves responded as soon as he received them:

> *Canellun, Deyá, Mallorca, Spain*
> *March 14, 1948*

Dear Dr Patai

I am most grateful for the two pamphlets you sent me. The Hebrew Installation Rites comes closest to my heart and I agree with your conclusions at every point. In my King Jesus *I assume that Jesus was secretly crowned with these same primitive rites; and also mention that Herod was given a premonitory buffet, when a boy, by an Essene as a prophecy that he was to be king. The events in the story of Jesus's coronation are very close indeed to your argument, beginning with Psalm II, the lustration, & the descent of the ka or double. I assume that he was ritually lamed in the course of the coronation, as Jacob was during his marriage feast to Rachel the local priestess of the Ewe Goddess. That, according to the Toldoth Yeshu, he was pelted with cabbages while trying to fly I take to be another reference to the same ceremony; kings had wings bound to their shoulders at coronations. It's all a very queer business: he wouldn't have been crowned unless he had a title to the throne— and my guess is that he was Herod's grandson. What you say about the subsequent clash of the king and the prophet who anointed him holds good here too: there was a great contention between Jesus & John's disciples.*

The sons of Belial are not just "good for nothings" but attendants of Belili the Canaanite Goddess who controlled all Palestinian marriages. Belial ('that from which one does not come up') was a Hebrew pun on her name. In my view Belili was the important person in that day, more important than Jahweh. She was the mother of Tammuz the pomegranate-hero under whose tree Saul took up his throne: i.e. he acknowledged himself her son. In my King Jesus I point out the importance of the pomegranate, not only in the bell & pomegranate connection of the High Priests robe, but in that of the pomegranate skewer that spits the paschal victim.

I take the "holy hill of Zion" in the 2nd Psalm to be Zin, not Zion, the sacred mountain plateau of the Edomites who provided the original kings caste of Israel: hence 'the dyed garment from Bozrah' worn by the Messiah in his progress from Edom.

Absolom companied in public with his father's wives because the kingdom was (as Hocart points out) conveyed by the local heiress to the king at his marriage with her. It was not inherited directly through the old king. David's technique of getting possession of the kingdom was to steal all the heiresses & turn them into a harem. They were all daughters of Belili, you may say.

Yours v. sincerely
Robert Graves

In the margins of this letter Graves added the following:

The ass was the older mount of kings. It was sacred to Set and all the royal sceptres of all the gods of Egypt have ass's ears usually mistaken for feathers. There was more in that story of Apion's about the golden ass-mask of Dora than Josephus cared to admit. At Rome it was the older royal beast. The patricians introduced the horse; the plebeians had the ass as their own.

Agag & Mephibosheth were both types of lame king; but this is not a Semitic institution: it is Traco-Libyan I think and connected with the partridge cult.

I cannot forego at least a few comments on this letter.

Graves's conjecture about the "sons of Belial" (in Hebrew *b'ne bliyya 'al*) having been "attendants of Belili the Canaanite Goddess" is possibly based on the old suggestion, summarized by T. K. Cheyne,[3] to the effect that "the original word . . . may very possibly have been Belili, which is the name of a goddess of vegetation, and hence of the underworld, the sister of Du'uzu or Tammuz." Cheyne suspected that "the Canaanites and Israelites probably took the name . . . as a synonym for the abyss of Sheol. Afterwards it seems to have become a symbol of insatiable and malignant destructiveness, which is the meaning of *b'liyya'al* in most of its biblical occurrences."[4]

In his very next letter to me (dated March 17, 1948), Graves corrected a minor mistake he had made in his previous letter: Belili, he wrote, was not the mother but the sister of Tammuz. Correct. Belili is described in an Akkadian myth of the descent of Ishtar to the Nether World as entreating Tammuz not to harm her, and expressing the hope that when Tammuz will come up to her "may the dead rise and smell the incense."[5] However, in recent biblical scholarship the Belial-Belili connection has lost credibility to the extent of not even being mentioned by Tur-Sinai in the authoritative *Enztiqlopediya Miqrait.*[6]

That Belili "controlled all Palestinian marriages," that "the sons of Belial" were her "attendants," and that she was "more important than Jahweh," are pure Gravesian conjectures, ingenious but not supported by available evidence. That Saul "took up his throne" under the pomegranate tree is Graves's reinterpretation of 1 Samuel 14:2, which only says that "Saul tarried in the uttermost part of Gibeah under the pomegranate tree which is in Migron." That he thereby "acknowledged himself her [Belili's] son" can, as far as I know, as little be substantiated as Graves's other surmise that the wives of Saul "were all daughters of Belili." In all these assertions, made as if they were established facts, it is Graves the poet and novelist, and not Graves the scholar, speaking.

The same observation must be made on Graves's emendation of "Zion" into "Zin" in view of the fact that Psalm 2:5–6, to which he refers, has the Lord address the nations "in His wrath and affright them" by saying to them, "Truly it is I that have established My king upon Zion My holy mountain." The Hebrew king was established in Zion, not on the Edomite "sacred mountain plateau" of Zin. Yahweh is not known to have considered Zin His "holy mountain." Nor, for that matter, is Zin designated in the Bible as a "mountain plateau": it is called *midbar Zin,* i.e., "wilderness of Zin." Its exact location is still a matter of conjecture, although the biblical references to it make it clear that it was situated to the south of the Dead Sea, west, or northwest of Edom. In any case, there is no basis for the assumption that it was "the sacred mountain plateau of the Edomites."

As for the Edomites having "provided the original kings caste of Israel," I am, frankly, puzzled by this statement, which, to the best of my knowledge, has no factual basis. Ancient Israel had no royal caste: the first two kings of Israel were anointed by the prophet Samuel from among common people: Saul from the tribe of Benjamin (1 Sam. 9:15ff.), and David from Judah (1 Sam.

16:1ff.). In both cases the biblical narrative emphasizes the humble origin of the man chosen by God to be His anointed. Moreover, the relationship between Edom and Israel was one of enmity and almost continuous fighting. David defeated the Edomites (2 Sam. 8:13–14), and David's general Joab "smote every male in Edom" (1 Kings 11:15–16). It was not until some nine centuries later that an Edomite, Herod, became king of the Jews.

Graves found so much interest in the data I assembled in my "Hebrew Installation Rites" that three days later he followed up his letter by another, much longer one, in which he listed brief comments on no fewer than twenty-five points I made in that study. My treatise was based on the hypothetical premise that features of the ancient Near Eastern royal installation ritual, of which the Hebrew installation rites were but variants, were diffused into the Sudan belt of Africa, where they were adapted to local conditions and preserved down to modern times. In examining this hypothesis, I felt I could present a concrete illustration of the more general thesis of A. M. Hocart, C. K. Meek, C. G. and Brenda Seligman, W. Schilde, H. Baumann, Tor Irstam, and others, that ancient Near Eastern culture had penetrated the Sudanic area and suvived there to the present day—that is, into the twentieth century. Next I used the Sudanic ethnographic material gathered by these scholars to elucidate biblical passages that tell about occurrences in connection with the installation of Saul, David, and other Israelite kings. This approach enabled me to isolate more than forty features or rites that were common to the installation of the ancient Hebrew and modern Sudanese kings, and thus to reconstruct the biblical royal installation ritual to which the biblical text itself contains only obscure, and in themselves undecipherable, allusions. The more the number of parallel or equivalent features in the two cultures grew, the greater became the likelihood of a historical connection between them. The Sudanese royal ritual, surviving in an area on the extreme periphery of ancient Near Eastern cultures, preserved features that in ancient Israel, or in the ancient Near East in general, had long disappeared and been replaced by subsequent cultural developments. This phenomenon is well known in the study of cultural diffusion, and is termed "marginal survival." What I did was to use the rites that have survived in the Sudan as keys to a reconstruction of the original meaning of the biblical references to Hebrew installation rites that were no longer understood by the authors or editors of the biblical books which speak of, or allude to, them, and are therefore often "historicized," that is, presented as single historical events instead of rites conforming to an established pattern.

My findings were a veritable treasure trove for Graves, who at the time had already begun to work with Joshua Podro on their joint book *The Nazarene Gospel Restored*. This, of course, I found out only later, when I read the typescript of the first eleven chapters of *The Nazarene Gospel* Graves sent me for critical perusal. In his 1946 novel *King Jesus*, he had described in detail the coronation of Jesus as king of the Jews which, making full use of the fiction writer's licence, he presented as having actually taken place. In *The Nazarene Gospel*, he and Podro retained this idea and made it the cornerstone of their reconstruction of their hypothetical original Gospel. In the ancient Hebrew royal installation ritual as I reconstructed it in my "Hebrew Installation Rites," Graves found numerous individual rites he claimed were reenacted at the coronation of Jesus. So, as he later told me in the course of one of our long conversations in his home in Deyá, it was my "Hebrew Installation Rites" that gave the solid foundation to what he had only suspected years before when he wrote his *King Jesus*. I shall have to return to this subject when speaking of *The Nazarene Gospel* and its critical reception.

In his March 17, 1948 letter, Graves listed his specific comments on my "Hebrew Installation Rites" according to the pages of the offprint I sent him.

Canellun, Deyá, Mallorca, Spain
March 17 48

Dear Dr Patai:

I send you a few notes some of which I hope will interest you, in supplement of the letter I wrote yesterday about your Installation Rites.

p. 154 pulling out the rod. This is paralleled in British folklore where a sword has to be plucked from a rock & only the king-elect can do so.

155. Gunkel should have mentioned the descent of the hawk on the Pharaoh at his coronation: his ka or double.

155. In a fragment of an apocryphal gospel quoted by Epiphanius, 'the Gospel of the Ebionites', a bright light shines over Jordan at the lustration; this is omitted in the canonical gospels. It shows that the 'Father' was pictured as the Sun God. According to Epiphanius the Ebionites held that this was a rebirth; & that Jesus was originally begotten on the seed of man.

155. Absence of bodily blemishes was insisted on in the Irish sacral kingship. A king who lost an eye or hand in battle had to resign.

156. The same taboo on the touching of a dead body by a priest-king was in force at Rome in the case of the Flamen Dialis who took over the functions of the Rex after the Republic was founded.

158. Irish and Scottish kings were crowned on a sacred stone, the most famous of which is the Coronation Stone in Westminster Abbey, stolen from Scone by the English. Most of them had foot prints carved in them.

161. Why thirty? The days of an Egyptian month?

166. The oil was aphrodisiac like the holy incense. The scent attracted the women, the olive oil gave phallic strength. The olive is traditionally connected with Hercules's club.

167. The head of the king was emblematic of the prepuce of the phallus; he was regarded as a walking phallus.

170. The king was really reborn as the son of the Moon Goddess; but by Biblical times Yahu had taken his mother Isis's name and the theory of patrilineal monarchy established. (Ia-hu—'Exalted Dove' in Sumerian)

174. I don't believe it was Rachel's grave, because she was credited with two graves. It was a shrine of Rachel the Ewe Goddess, his mother. The terebinth was sacred to the Cyprian Ewe Goddess, and Tabor was Atabyrius the Calf-God of many changes. In fact Egli-Yahu.

178. In the illustration of the crowning of the king which I print in my King Jesus *(in the U.S. edition it is wrongly captioned) the king is modestly resisting the prophets who come to acclaim him.*

181. In my previous letter I suggest that Beliy ya'al *was Belili 'mother'— but this was a miswriting for 'sister & spouse' of Du-uzu, Tammuz the pomegranate hero under whose tree Saul sat.*

185. This (about the mixed set of traditions) is very well said. My assumption is that the Bible was largely composed to explain a series of ritual pictures. Some of them are correctly explained, some are mixed up with history, some are inconotropically misread: e.g. the obscene story of Lot & his daughters is an iconotropic misreading of a picture showing the ithyphallic dead Osiris in his arbour hung with grapes, mourned over by Isis, Nephthys & their young sons. It had the useful object of libelling Moab & Ammon, Israel's troublesome neighbours.

186. The ritual combat is best illustrated in the case of Jacob & the angel who lamed him.

188. I agree about New Year's Day: Joash, as representative of the sun, was in his weakest condition and shot the arrows as a ceremony to show that he was reborn as the New Sun, that the days would now lengthen and the dragon of darkness not prevail. Hence the Chanukah candles.

192. In Irish mythology the spear is the more ancient royal weapon. This is important, because the spear was brought there about 2500 from Libya via Spain. The sword came in with the bronze-age invasions. I regard Libya as the origin of the whole complex of royal customs here described; they spread N. West; East and South.

193. Why three hundred shields, not 364 or 365? Was this because they omitted January & February from their sacred year like the Etruscans?

197. To 'look on the king while his hair is cut' recalls the story of Samson and all the sacred kings whose lucky hair was cut to their undoing. To 'look at him while he is in his bath' recalls the story of Agamemnon, Minos and various other sacred kings who were killed in a bath. These were ritual *acts, not ordinary murders.*

199. In my White Goddess *I wrote at length on the yearly vicarious death of the king at the winter festival in the person of his son. On p. 201 you mention Saul's attempted sacrifice of Jonathan. I bet that in the original story Jonathan died; as Isaac did on Mount Moriah.*

34

204. In my recent letter I mention Herod's buffeting by the Essene prophet.

208. Beans as the prerogative of the Queen occurs in an Arcadian legend collected by Pausanias. Demeter coming to Arcadia gave the people permission to plant any grain or pulse except beans. (This was because the ghosts of the arbour enter into beans).

210. The midwinter lighting of the Chanukah candlestick is a feast ascribed to Judas Maccabaeus. But Antiochus Epiphanes has sacrificed to Olympian Zeus on the same day at the same place. Zeus's birthday, as that of Mithra, Apollo and Q're (Jehovah) fell on that day. It's safe to say that the candlestick ceremony was as old as the Temple.

216. As mentioned in my recent letter the marriage with the widow or widows of the predecessor is the most important part of the Coronation-ceremony. (I suggest in my King Jesus *that Is-rael, Jacob's new name at marriage, was Ish-rachel—the consort of Rachel.) Hocart is insistent here. But in the Bible we have a carefully edited account which gives no hint that the Queen was of any importance in comparison with the king.*

221. Aaron's two sons destroyed by fire. This was correct procedure. Apollo's son Phaethon; Cretan Dionysus son of Zeus; Icarus son of Daedalus; Aesculapius son of Apollo; Demophoon son of Celeus; Melicertes son of Athamas; Gwern son of Matholwych of Ireland, were all burned in their fathers' honour. I think Herod the Wicked's killing of his sons was really ritual. But I think the account in Leviticus is telescoped; one son was burned at the close of each year of Aaron's reign as a vicarious sacrifice, not both at his original installation.

> *Yours v. sincerely*
> *Robert Graves*

I think you are a very brave man not to 'pull your punches' in writing these books. How dishonest most scholars are!

Again I must insert an explanation of why I did not respond substantially to these two letters. At the time I received them I was unable to subject them to the sharp scrutiny I would have given them in different circumstances. I was too involved, in addition to problems of academic and social readjustment already referred to, with the increasingly difficult relationship between my wife Naomi and myself, and with the worries about the safety of our two little daughters Ofra and Daphne, aged six and four, whom Naomi had left in the care of a German Jewish family in Ramot Hashavim, a village on the Mediterranean coast of Palestine. Although the seashore between Tel Aviv and Haifa was the safest area of Jewish Palestine, Arab terrorist attacks took their toll of Jewish lives everywhere, and Arab-inhabited localities that served as bases for such attacks were at a distance of a mere ten miles from Ramot Hashavim. I also worried about my parents and my sister and her family, who lived in Givatayim, a suburb of Tel Aviv, and my brother Saul and his family, who lived in Jerusalem—all places where terrorist attacks could occur at any moment. The bombing of Ben Yehuda Street, about a mile from my brother's house, took place on February 2, 1948; Arab riots spread to all parts of Palestine; and the *Hagana,* the still "illegal" Jewish defense organization, was able to maintain communications between Jerusalem and the seashore only at the price of heavy casualties. As the American press and radio furnished more and more news about the precarious situation of the 600,000 Jews who constituted the *yishuv* (Jewish community) of Palestine, I became increasingly torn between the feeling that I should instantly return and join my people in their hour of danger, and my sober conviction that my duty was to remain in America and build up a future for myself and my children. In the end, I believe, it was a kind of inertia that made me stay in New York.

In any case, when I received Graves's letters, although I was greatly impressed by the uncommon erudition they displayed, I was psychologically unable to make the effort required to respond to them in a thoroughly scholarly manner. Instead, I felt satisfied with registering in my mind that Graves's letters revealed an approach to problems of religious and cultural history very different from mine, but no less valid, and perhaps even more fruitful. The approach I had learned from my illustrious masters at the universities and seminaries of Budapest and Breslau, and subsequently at the Hebrew University of Jerusalem, was based on an iron rule: if you suspect that there is a connection between item A and item B, or you think you have an explanation for a problem, you can state it as a hypothesis or as a conjecture. But if you want the scholarly world to consider it more than guesswork, you must marshal evidence. "Where is the evidence?" was the question I had heard many times thrown at me, forcing me to go back to the sources again and again until I found it.

Now, in these letters of Graves, and then in the books and articles of his I subsequently read, I got to know—and to appreciate—a different approach. I recognized that the basis of his statements was, as often as not, intuitive insight, which, precisely because it was intuitive, did not require the painstaking, step-by-step process of marshaling evidence. Unless I happened to know that what he stated was wrong, I felt more and more inclined to accept it as right even without proofs. In years to come, in the course of our work on the *Hebrew Myths,* I often had to force myself to overcome this inclination, to look for evidence, and to delete ruthlessly statements for which I found none. This was not easy for him to accept, for he was fond of, or perhaps I would be justified in saying was addicted to, his method of intuitive reasoning. Once he read something, a name that rang a bell, a reference to a fact, an event, a locality—in fact, any item at all—his imagination took over, those wheels in his head began turning, and associations came pouring out, including a profusion of inferences that appeared to him established facts. To point to connections was for him an irresistible challenge, and he never grudged the time needed to put down his ideas in long letters. His two letters dated March 14 and 17, 1948, are fine examples of this. They contain between them some thirty points, each presented as an observation that only has to be made in order to be a fact. When faced with this approach—I came to recognize—it really made little sense to point out that some of these statements had no known factual basis. What difference, in fact, would it make to insist that what Graves writes in the earlier letter, that "Agag & Mephibosheth were both types of lame king," has no basis in the biblical text, the only source in which they are mentioned? Or that the biblical phrase translated in the King James version "And Agag came unto him [Samuel] delicately" (1 Sam. 15:32), which Graves seems to have interpreted as meaning that he walked delicately because of lameness, actually means "And Agag came unto him in chains,"[7] and that not a word in the biblical text says that Agag was lame? And as for Mephibosheth, the unfortunate son of Jonathan and grandson of Saul, true, he became lame in both his legs as a child when his nurse dropped him, but he was never king, not even a pretender to the throne of Israel, which after Saul's death went to David (2 Sam. 4:4; 9:6–13). For Graves's intuitive understanding these two *were* lame kings, whatever is said in the biblical references to them. Whether to have lame kings was a "Thraco-Libyan" institution, I am not in a position to say, but that having lame kings was "connected with the partridge cult" is certainly an original and ingenious suggestion.

Similarly original is the throwaway observation that "all the royal sceptres of all the gods of Egypt have ass's ears usually mistaken for feathers." Whether this is true or not I cannot tell (to check it out would be too lengthy a job), but I seem to remember vaguely having seen statues or paintings (or photographs of them) of Egyptian gods with scepters that did not have this feature.

As against such unprovable and possibly erroneous statements, Graves's letters contain many valuable (I could even say invaluable) suggestions and parallels which strengthened my central argument in the "Hebrew Installation Rites" that in the biblical texts we have allusions to significant elements of an ancient Hebrew royal ritual, disguised in some instances as records of historical events.

Likewise stimulating were the questions, left unanswered, that came to Graves's mind while reading my study. Numbers mentioned in the biblical sources and referred to but left unexplained by me prompted him to pose questions. I mentioned that the numbers thirty, thirty-one, or thirty-two appear constantly in Hebrew tradition: thirty men were assembled by Samuel, David had thirty "mighty men," Jair had thirty sons, Havoth-Jair comprised thirty cities, Judge Ibzan had thirty sons, Judge Abdon had thirty grandsons, thirty companions attended wedding feasts, etc.[8] I did not bother to search for an

37

explanation of this frequently recurring figure, which undoubtedly had some ritual significance. Now Graves threw out the question, "Why thirty? The days of an Egyptian month?" I could have mentioned that the Hebrew lunar month had alternatingly twenty-nine and thirty days, but I could not see any possible connection between them and the thirty sons, cities, etc.

Again, commenting on what I wrote elsewhere in that study (p. 193), Graves asks: "why three hundred shields" (of gold placed by Solomon into the House of the Forest of Lebanon, and replaced by the same number of brazen shields by his son Rehoboam)? Why not 364 or 365, to correspond to the solar year? Why indeed? The suggestion Graves makes that they may have corresponded to the days of the year minus January and February does not seem to be plausible, although I myself mentioned (pp. 193–94) the cosmic significance of these shields. To enter into numerical speculation is an endless and dangerous undertaking.

On pp. 210–11 of my "Hebrew Installation Rites" I tried to show that "the extinguishing and subsequent ceremonial rekindling of fire originally constituted a part of the installation ritual of Hebrew kings." Graves takes this to refer to the midwinter lighting of the Hanukkah candlestick, and hints (though he does not state it clearly) that this kind of lighting a fire at midwinter was part of the birthday celebration of Zeus. Then he says that "Zeus's birthday, as that of Mithra, Apollo, and Q're (Jehovah) fell on that day." Of the four deities he mentions Q're is relatively unknown, although, as Graves informs us in his *Greek Myths,* Q're, or Car, or Carius was "the Great God Ker who seems to have derived his title from his Moon-mother Artemis Caria, or Caryatis," and that "Cer, in fact, whose name (also spelt Car or Q're) came generally to mean 'fate,' 'doom,' or 'destiny'—multiplied into *ceres,* 'spites, plagues, or unseen ills'—must have been the Cretan Bee-goddess, a goddess of Death in Life." He finds the connecting link between Cer and the Cretan Bee-goddess in the Greek word for bee-bread, *cerinthos,* which, he says, is Cretan. He also states that the goddess Car "gave her name to Caria and became the Italian divinatory goddess Carmenta, 'Car the Wise' . . . and the Caryatids are her nut-nymphs." Then he refers to a tradition preserved by Pliny, who says that Car invented augury. Finally he surmises that "The 'Apollo' to whom Theseus dedicated his hair will have been Karu 'son of the goddess Car'.)"[9]

I don't know what is the basis of Graves's assertion that all the four gods he mentioned had their birthday on the same day at midwinter and, again, I am unable to search for verification. However, leaving that question aside, what really puzzled me (and still does) in his comment is the word "Jehovah" added in parentheses after Q're. Since Q're was a goddess, he could not have meant that she was either identical with, or a Greek counterpart of, Jehovah, a male god. I think therefore that by putting "Jehovah" in parentheses after the other four gods he intended to indicate that he felt (or suspected) that the birthday of Jehovah fell on the same day in midwinter. Needless to say, the very idea that God should have a birthday was utterly foreign to biblical Hebrew religion.

As is well known, Graves's orientation was emphatically feminist in more senses than one. Women were much more important in his life than men, goddesses had a much greater role in his reconstruction of ancient religious developments than gods, matriarchy was for him a decisive early phase in human history, and in his poems the Muse and his relations to her temporary earthly incarnations are a recurrent and powerful leitmotif. In view of all this it should not come as a surprise that he was inclined to read "feminist" meanings into biblical passages in which rigorous scholarship can discover nothing of the sort. In both his letters of March 14 and 17 he asserts that the Hebrew kings attained their throne not by inheriting it directly from their royal progenitor, but by marrying the widow of their predecessor. He makes reference in this connection to A. M. Hocart, who in his pioneering book *Kingship* was not only "insistent" that "marriage with the widow or widows of the predecessor [was] a most important part of the Coronation-ceremony," but went a significant step farther in pointing out that in ancient Greece and several other civilizations there seems "to have been a rule that a man to become king must marry his predecessor's widow."[10]

Graves's reference to Hocart struck a responsive chord in me, for in my "Hebrew Installation Rites" I had taken a chapter of Hocart's *Kingship* as my point of departure.[11] (I still remember that when I worked on that study in Jerusalem and felt I had to consult Hocart, neither his *Kingship* nor his later *Kings and Councillors* was in the library of the Hebrew University. I had about resigned myself to the expense of ordering the books from London, as I did many other books in connection with my work. But then, when I next visited Prof. Buber, I asked him whether he had the two Hocart books, and, to my delight, he had them both, and lent them to me most willingly.)

It is against this background that one must view the suggestion made by Graves in connection with my argument that "the taking possession of a king's wives [by his successor or by a pretender] was regarded as equivalent to taking possession of the kingdom," and that marrying the predecessor's wife or wives was part of the royal installation ritual among the Hebrews as it was among other ancient Near Eastern and modern African peoples (see "Hebrew Installation Rites," pp. 164–66). In connection with this Graves notes in his March 17, 1948, letter, under no. 216, that this was "the most important part of the Coronation-ceremony," and that, as he suggested in his *King Jesus,* at marriage a bridegroom received a new name: when Jacob married Rachel, he was renamed "Ish-rachel—the consort of Rachel."

There are several serious problems with this suggestion. One is that Jacob got the new name Israel not at marriage but some fourteen years later, after he left the house of his father-in-law Laban. It was in the course of his encounter

39

and struggle with "the man" at the Ford of Jabbok that he was given this new name. The second is that the derivation of Israel from *Ish-Rachel* is linguistically impossible and mythologically contradicted by the story which tells explicitly that it was the mysterious man with whom Jacob struggled "until the breaking of the day" who told him, "Thy name shall be called no more Jacob but Israel, for thou hast striven with God and with men and hast prevailed" (Gen. 32:29). This explanation of the name Israel is, of course, a classical example of a Midrash in the Bible itself, to which Hosea also (12:4–5) refers, but it indicates the direction in which the derivation of the name Israel must be sought.

As for the original form and meaning of the name, there is a huge literature about it, but still no consensus has been reached. The emendation of the initial syllable *Yis-* into *Ish* ("man") was first suggested by Jerome, who translated Israel as *vir videns deum,* which corresponds to a hypothetical Hebrew *Ish ra'ah el,* that is, "man who saw God" (Gen. 33:10). Although there are a few biblical names beginning with *Ish* (*Ish-Bosheth, Eshbaʿal, Ishhod*) the element *Ish* in them means "man (of)," and not "husband (of)." Hence an original name *Ish-Rachel,* meaning "husband of Rachel" is unlikely. On the other hand there is an abundance of biblical names beginning with the *y* prefix, indicating third person masculine singular in the imperfect, and ending in *-el* ("God"): e.g., Ishmael (*Yishmaʿel,* "God hears"), Jezreel (*Yizrʿel,* "God gives seed"), Jahaziel (*Yahazi'el,* "God sees"), Ezekiel (*Y'hezqel,* "God strengthens"), etc. In listing these names I have given the translation in the third person singular present form, but the names can as well have the optative meaning, such as "may God hear," "may God see," etc. All this makes it very unlikely that the name-form *Yisrael* is the corruption of an original *Ish-Rachel.* In all probability *Yisrael* means "He fights God" (or "God fights"), precisely as explained in Genesis 32:29: "Thy name shall be called no more Jacob but Israel for thou hast stiven with God . . . ."[12]

As for "taking possession of the king's wives," I never drew the inference from the cases of Absalom and Adonijah I quoted that a rule in Hebrew royal succession provided for kingship to be passed on by cohabitation with the deceased king's wives. To marry them may indeed have been a prerogative of the royal successor, but kingship in Judah, and to a lesser extent in the Northern Kingdom of Israel as well, was inherited from father to son, as is made amply clear in the Bible. The patrilineal descent of the Davidic king was a firmly established feature which survived the Judahite monarchy by millennia, and became a cornerstone of Jewish messianism: the expected Messiah was to be "a shoot out of the stock of Jesse" (Isa. 11:1), that is, a scion of the royal House of David.

40

3.

King Jesus and
The White Goddess

I F I HAD the time and the leisure to write a detailed commentary on Graves's 1946 novel *King Jesus,* which unquestionably is a rare blend of historical scholarship and poetic imagination, I am afraid I would feel constrained to point out passages in which the latter faculty led him to make statements either erroneous or not supportable by known facts. But such a critical approach to what is essentially a historical novel would—this I recognize—not be justified. After all, a novelist, however heavy the burden of his erudition, is free to throw it down at any juncture of the road he chooses to follow in his novel. What I can and want to do instead is to point out a few of the insights *King Jesus* shows Graves to have had into the nature of mythology in general and of Hebrew myths in particular, some fifteen or more years before he embarked on writing nonfictional books on these subjects.

Graves was, of course, neither the first nor the only modern author to try his hand at rewriting the Bible. André Gide in his play *Saül,* written in 1896, boldly reinterpreted the biblical story of Saul and David, depicting Saul in love with David, whose beauty is referred to in the Bible. Oscar Wilde chose a similar theme when he showed Salome in love with "Iokanaan," that is, Jochanan, or John the Baptist. Even before him, Heinrich Heine, Gustave Flaubert, Joris-Karl Huysman, and Jules Laforgue all "daringly reconstituted their Salome of the Bible."[1] And, of course, there is the great tetralogy of Thomas Mann, in which an enormous amount of erudition and penetrating familiarity with the world of the ancient Near East is brought to bear on the retelling in great detail of the biblical story of Jacob, Joseph, and his brethren. All of these authors felt that the reinterpretation of, and expatiation on, the biblical stories, told in the original with tantalizing and mystifying terseness,

41

was an irresistible challenge. Yet none of them, to the best of my knowledge, has devoted such a great proportion of his literary output to this, often thankless, task of competing with the Bible. In the case of Graves it is possible that his preoccupation with the Bible goes back to his childhood, when he "not only knew his Bible but also believed in it."[2]

In *King Jesus* Graves makes Agabus the Decapolitan his mouthpiece, and has him tell what Graves himself felt as the proper method of exploring the truth behind the versions in which the biblical stories survived: "By comparison of Hebrew myths with the popular myths of Canaan, and of Jewish history with the history of neighbouring nations, a general working knowledge can be won of the ancient events and legal traditions most relevant to the secret story of Jesus, which is all that need concern us here" (p. 13). No historian, anthropologist, or folklorist could have put this better.

(An incidental remark: on p. 234 of *King Jesus* Graves, with poetic foresight, anticipates the name "Israel" as that of the new Jewish state when he says, "beyond Israel lie Syria, Asia, and the Black Sea.")

Reading *King Jesus,* I was most impressed by Graves's ability to recognize a series of ancient Hebrew coronation rites which he finds were reenacted at the coronation of Jesus. Among them are the "marring," "laming," or "buffeting" of the king (pp. 244, 263), the coronation journey (p. 260), the giving of a new name to the king (p. 244), the partaking of the "sacred shoulder" (p. 264), the ceremonial or ritual battle, the use of the scepter and of the sacred oil (p. 266), and the making of the rounds of the kingdom (p. 269).

No wonder, after all this, that when several years later Graves read my "Hebrew Installation Rites" and found there presented a full reconstruction of the ancient biblical coronation ritual, including practically each and every one of the features he intuitively had asserted were part of the coronation of Jesus, he was more than delighted.

For my part, when I read *King Jesus,* I was intrigued by the manifestation in it of the same Gravesian tendency I had already known by that time from the other works of Graves I had read: the inclination to correct ancient sacred texts, to reestablish the original meaning of stories or references contained in them—in a word, to put them right. In *King Jesus,* where Graves was not hampered by scholarly convention, he (that is, Agabus, who speaks for him) terms some stories in the form transmitted in ancient documents "clumsy forgery," "absurdity," "misrecorded," or, more charitably, "amended story [that] does not make literary sense" (pp. 286–87, 305). Graves himself, again speaking in the guise of Agabus, knows better, of course, and proceeds to restore the story to how it originally must have read.

Graves's masterly blending of scholarship and imagination is most apparent in his use of talmudic and midrashic material for the purpose of elucidating what Jesus really did and said. He uses stories and anecdotes recorded in these rabbinical sources to substantiate scenes from the life of Jesus and to place them in historical perspective and against the contemporary background. He cites, for instance, the story about Hillel, who in his youth almost froze to death while listening outside a skylight to the proceedings of the talmudic academy he was too poor to attend, and the saving of his life by the rabbis despite the prohibition of performing any work on the Sabbath.[3] He uses this story to show that the attitude of Jesus to the Sabbath laws was nothing revolutionary, but rather in keeping with the views of the Pharisees (p. 289).

Elsewhere Graves says that when Jesus proclaimed, "I am the Way, the Truth, and the Life," he was "speaking in Jehovah's name" and the prefatory words, "Thus saith the Lord," must be restored to the text. "Any other interpretation is historically unthinkable" (p. 289). Then, generalizing, he adds, "several well-known sayings of Hillel, Shammai, Simeon the Just and other celebrated Jewish moralists" were attributed to Jesus "by the simple trick of suppressing his humble acknowledgement of them" (p. 290), which anticipates the method he (and Podro) used in *The Nazarene Gospel Restored* seven years later.

In the "Historical Commentary" which concludes *King Jesus* (pp. 419–24), Graves accords some insight into his methods of critically reinterpreting historical sources, and also refers, incidentally, to dozens of them used by him. Most interesting is his interpretation of the *analeptic* (i.e., "restorative") method of writing a historical novel. It is, he says, "the intuitive recovery of forgotten events by a deliberate suspension of time—one must train oneself to think wholly in contemporary terms" (p. 421), that is, in terms contemporary with the characters in the novel. The operative word is "intuitive": here Graves explicitly states that he relies on his novelist's intuition, in addition to, or perhaps even rather than, building on facts that can only be elicited by painstaking and plodding historical research. This, of course, contradicts, and annuls, the solemn promise he makes on the preceding page where he writes: "I undertake to my readers that every important element in my story is based on some tradition" (p. 420). If this were rigorously followed, what room would be left for "intuitive recovery of forgotten events"?

In that "Historical Commentary," Graves explains in some detail his use of "iconotropy," that is, the "deliberate misinterpretation of . . . ancient . . . ritual icons" by later authors, in which, however, "the icons are not defaced or altered, but merely interpreted in a sense hostile to the original cult" (p. 423). We are by now quite familiar with this Gravesian technique and the use he has made of it in his various writings.

One last word about *King Jesus*. In this novel the important characters constantly refer in their conversations to events that took place in biblical times and are recorded in biblical sources, and use those events as guidelines in explaining their own actions or attitudes. This, of course, endows the acts or words in question with a greater significance than they otherwise would have, and the actors in the scenes described gain a historical dimension: by letting themselves be guided by historical or mythical antecedents they become, as it were, larger-than-life figures. A typical example is the long scene (pp. 52–66) in which Simon the High Priest tries (and succeeds) to convince Antipater, the son of King Herod, to marry Mary—it is from this union that Jesus is born, a royal prince with full claim to succeed as king of the Jews. Simon in fact gives Antipater a brief survey of the history of Israel and of Rome, suitably reinterpreted. When Antipater objects and says that he would have to obtain the permission of his father Herod before entering into the marriage advocated by Simon, the latter responds: "You are free to marry without your father's consent, as is proved in the classical case of Esau" (p. 62).

The world in which Jesus moves, as recreated by Graves, is a world of personages who live out their lives in the shadow of their great ancestors, and who are almost like marionettes tied by many invisible as well as visible strings to the hands of great ancestral puppet-masters whose long-past acts and words control their movements.

Graves's *The White Goddess* was written in 1945 and published in 1948, two years after *King Jesus*. Although the focus of this long study is not on the sunny Middle East but on the somber scene of pagan and early Christian Northern Europe, a surprisingly large part of it is devoted to interpretations of biblical stories. *The White Goddess* is not a novel but a historical study—it is subtitled "A Historical Grammar of Poetic Myth"—but the intuitive approach that Graves had developed in his *King Jesus* is much in evidence here as well. Sydney Musgrove, in his thoughtful study *The Ancestry of 'The White Goddess,'* calls the book "a striking mixture of erudition and bravado," and distills the argument advanced in it in two sentences: "The power controlling and inspiring all true poetry at all times in man's history has been that of the feminine principle whom the author calls the 'White Goddess.' Terrible and inscrutably beneficent, she is also the original and residual godhead (though sometimes obscured) in all religious systems."[4]

I am inclined to agree with Musgrove about "erudition and bravado." Bravado is, of course, the product of intuitive fantasy, which can lead the author who possesses it (or who is possessed by it) beyond the narrower paths of scholarly explorations. A few examples, taken from *The White Goddess,* will show the leaps and bounds performed by Graves with the help of his intuitive method.

Genesis 50:11–13 says that the sons of Jacob took the body of their dead father from Egypt to Abel-Mizrayim, where they mourned him, and then carried him on to the Cave of Machpelah for burial. For Graves this becomes: "Genesis 50:11, where it is said that he was buried in Abel-Mizrayim."

Deuteronomy 32:11 has this poetic simile: "As an eagle that stirreth up her nest, hovereth over her young, spreadeth abroad her wings, taketh them, beareth them on her pinions" so did the Lord lead Israel in the wilderness. Here God is explicitly *compared to* an eagle. (Incidentally, the feminine language of the translation is misleading. In the original Hebrew text the noun "eagle" is masculine, and so are all the verb forms describing what the eagle does for his young.) In Graves's reading this simile becomes an identification. He writes: "In the *Song of Moses* (Deut. 32:11) Jehovah is identified with this bird," that is, with "the griffon-vulture sacred to Osiris" (p. 209).

Biblical scholars have devoted much attention to problems presented by the name Samson (in Hebrew, *Shimshon*) and the acts attributed to him in the Book of Judges. For Graves Samson represents no problem: "Samson was a Palestinian Sun-god" (p. 315). He compares Samson to Hercules, King Curoi in the Chuchulain version, King Nisus of Nisa in the Greek version, Achilles of *excidium Troiae,* and a supposed original hero of the Osiris and Isis myth (p. 316).

Least historical and most poetically intuitive are statements in which Graves presents surmises or inferences as if they were established facts. For example, he says that "Jacob was connected with the cult of the Kenite Smith-god" (p. 330), and that this "Kenite Smith-god" was "Elath-Iahu" (p. 337), when there is no proof of the existence of a Kenite Smith-god, or of a deity named "Elath-Iahu," or of any connection between Jacob and any other god except the God of his fathers Isaac and Abraham. Elsewhere he writes, "Dionysus Sabazius was the original Jehovah of the Passover" (p. 336)—again without any basis in known data.

Although Graves points out the difference "between the poetic and prosaic methods of thought," bemoans the atrophy of "the poetic faculty in every educated person who does not privately struggle to cultivate it," and belittles prose in which "one thinks on only one level at a time" (p. 223), I find it difficult to follow him when his poetic method of thought leads him to express himself in statements such as these.

To a different category altogether belong such general observations as this: "The Jews seem always to have based their religious anecdotes on an existing legend, or icon, never to have written fiction in the modern sense" (p. 317). Leaving aside the question of icons, he may have something here, although it would be a major scholarly task to investigate all the biblical religious anecdotes from this point of view. As an illustration of what he has in mind, Graves takes apart the Judith and Holofernes story as recorded in the apocryphal Book of Judith, and "restores" its incidents (with his iconotropic method) to "their natural order," which yields the following:

The queen ties her husband's hair to the bedpost to immobilize him, and beheads him with a sword (based on Jth. 13:6–8); an attendant brings the severed head to the lover whom she has chosen to be the new king (Jth. 14:6); after mourning to appease the ghost of the old king, the Corn-Tammuz, who has died at the barley-harvest (8:2–6), she purifies herself in running water

45

and dresses as a bride (10:3–4). Presently the wedding procession forms up (10:17–21), and the marriage is celebrated with much merriment (12:15–20), bonfires (13:13), religious feasting (16:20), dancing and waving of branches (15:12), many gifts (15:2), killing of victims (15:5), and the ritual circumcision of the bridegroom (14:10). The queen wears a crown of olive as an emblem of fruitfulness (15:13). The head of the old king is put up on the wall of the city as a prophylactic charm (14:11), and the Goddess appears in triad—Hag, Bride, and Maid (16:23)—to bless the union (p. 317).

The reinterpretation is as ingenious as it is fanciful. What makes me dwell on it here is that Graves found it necessary to present precisely this story in such detail, when none of the other parallels did he consider deserving such elaborate presentation. The only explanation I can find for this favored treatment he gives this apocryphal, that is, quasi-biblical, story is that it exerted an attraction on him unmatched by other stories because he found it in a sacred, or, at least, semisacred, ancient Jewish source.

Graves was particularly interested in, or better, fascinated by, the derivation of the Hebrew divine name *Yahweh* (*YHWH,* the famous tetragrammaton), which often appears in an abbreviated, three-letter form as *Yahu (YHW).* This name was so sacred throughout Jewish history that it was not pronounced; the name *Adonai* (''Lord'') was substituted for it. It has remained so sacred to this day that its sanctity attached itself also to its substitute reading, *Adonai,* which is pronounced by religious Jews only in prayer or when reading the Bible in the synagogue; otherwise they substitute *Hashem (''The Name''),* or *Adoshem* (a compound word from the first part of *Adonai* and *Shem,* ''Name''). As for the meaning of *Yahweh,* there is no scholarly consensus, although most experts consider it a verb form derived from the root HWH, and meaning ''He exists,'' or ''He causes to exist,'' or the like.[5]

In his *White Goddess,* Graves offers explanations of his own. He considers *Yahu* as being composed of two parts: ''Ya'' (or, as he spells it, ''Ia''), which, he says, means ''exalted'' in Sumerian, and ''Hu,'' meaning ''dove'' (p. 337). He also speculates, in a manner closely resembling the *Gematria* of the Kabbalists, on the eight-letter (*JEHUOVAO*) and seven-letter (*JIEVOAO*) forms of the name *Iahu,* which he derives from ancient Welsh and ancient Near Eastern sources (pp. 285–87); see also pp. 339–41, 464, 469). He knows that the second H in the tetragrammaton *YHWH* ''is the Shekinah, the Brightness of God, the mystic female emanation of H, the male First Person; with no existence apart from him, but identified with Wisdom'' (p. 468)—a generally adequate description of the kabbalistic view of the Shekhina. He even refers to the forty-two-letter name of God, and explains it with the help of ''the Pythagorean system'' (p. 469). The Pythagorean explanation apart, all this is in keeping with kabbalistic thinking and closely resembles *Gematrias* of divine names found in traditional Jewish prayer-books in use to this day among many a Hasidic and Oriental Jewish community.[6]

In the course of discussing phenomena of which he became aware while searching for the White Goddess, Graves makes observations which attribute far-reaching influences—through the intermediacy of the Pythagoreans—to ancient Jewish myths and concepts. "It seems that the Pythagorean mystics who instigated the change [from a belief in immutable destiny to one in free choice between good and evil] had adopted the Jewish creation myth. . . . I am suggesting, in fact, that the religious revolution which brought about the alphabetic changes in Greece and Britain was a Jewish one initiated by Eze-kiel (622–570 B.C.) which was taken up by the Greek-speaking Jews of Egypt and borrowed from them by the Pythagoreans" (pp. 644, 464–65).

In many places of *The White Goddess,* Graves shows himself to be an es-sential Aggadist, a creator of Midrashim on biblical passages. Thus he com-ments on the Menorah which, he says, "among the Moroccan Jews (whose tradition is the oldest and purest) is surmounted by a small pomegranate," and remarks, "The eighth light must stand for the extra day of the year, the day of the letter J which is intercalated at the winter solstice" (p. 470). Thinking along modern comparative lines, he attributes great familiarity with the In-dian mystics to the talmudic Honi the Circle-drawer (p. 483).

Surprising is the pervasive presence of biblical and Jewish motives in *The White Goddess.* The central subject of this book is the suppositional earliest European deity, the White Goddess of Birth, Love, and Death, who stands for "the single grand theme of poetry: the life, death, and resurrection of the Spirit of the Year, the Goddess's son and lover." Graves postulates an age of matriarchy that preceded patriarchy: this was the golden age of the Goddess. Once patriarchy supplanted it, everything went bad. The language of "poetic myth" (we must not forget the subtitle of the book: "A Historical Grammar of Poetic Myth") celebrates the Goddess who is Mother, Lover, and Crone (Layer-out). The true poet is a "Muse-poet," whose life is devoted to the ser-vice of the Goddess; he is possessed by her. In the chapter "War in Heaven," Graves says: "Poetry began in the matriarchal age, and derives its magic from the moon, not the sun" (p. 448). "The main theme of poetry is, properly, the relations of man and woman" (p. 447). And, again, "The poet is in love with the White Goddess, with truth: his heart breaks with longing and love for her" (p. 448). He is an "obsessed poet," a "woman-poet," and while he is young "has the spell of the White Goddess on him" (p. 455). Graves never raises the question of how, then, can a woman be a true poet? But he does refer, in passing, to Laura Riding as "an ex-poet" (p. 456).

Since the setting of *The White Goddess* is a hypothetical matriarchal Eu-rope of the Old Stone Age, the sources on which Graves builds his throne for the Goddess are, of necessity, old European poetic and other fragments. One would therefore suppose that the Bible and other ancient Near Eastern and Jewish documents would have no place in it. After all, Old Stone Age Europe is not likely to have been touched by influences emanating from the Near

47

East! However, one would be gravely mistaken in such a supposition. For the fact is that, whatever the probable historical connection between Old Stone Age Europe and the ancient Near East, *The White Goddess* abounds in references to the latter, and, in the first place, to the Bible. In fact, these references are so frequent, and occur in contexts so little calling for them, that one cannot but see in them manifestations of the "abiding" (one of Graves's favorite words) attraction the Bible had for Graves as an illimitable hunting ground. And, since the Bible proved irresistible to him, the Jewish speculations centered around it and building on it—Josephus, the Talmud, the Midrashim, the Kabbala—also attracted him, and more than once caught him in their web of interpretations. He became, for instance, fascinated by the Essenes, the Jewish communalistic religious sect which made its appearance in Judea at the end of the Hasmonean revolt (middle of the second century B.C.E.) and existed until after the destruction of the Second Temple of Jerusalem by the Romans, that is, until the end of the first century C.E. The discovery, from 1947 on, of the Dead Sea Scrolls has added much information on the Essenes' rites, practices, and doctrines, although there is still no scholarly consensus on the meaning and derivation of their name.

Graves has much to say about the Essenes, and what he says about them is typically Gravesian: it is based on poetic intuition rather than established fact. Thus, he says, that they "distinguished the historic Moses, who led the Israelites out of Egypt, from the demi-god Moses," and adopted "the Greek formula of Celestial Hercules to their cult of Moses as demi-god." Moreover, "they seem to have been disciples of Pythagoras," although, on the other hand, the Pythagoreans themselves had derived their new sacred name of God "from a sixth-century B.C. Jewish source" (p. 149). The Essenes possessed "a version of the Boibel-Loth letter-names [which] was brought to Ireland in early Christian times by Alexandrian gnostics who were the spiritual heirs of the Essenes after Hadrian had suppressed the Order in 132 A.D." (p. 150). Graves states that "the mystical Essene Ebionites of the first century A.D. believed in a female Holy Spirit" (p. 160), and observes that "spiritually minded men" among them came to regard "the five material senses" represented by the five planets Moon, Mars, Mercury, Jupiter, and Venus, "as sources of error," and

> tried to rise superior to them by pure meditation. This policy was carried to extreme lengths by the God-fearing Essenes, who formed their monkish communities within compounds topped by acacia hedges from which all women were excluded; lived ascetically, cultivated a morbid disgust for their own natural functions and turned their eyes away from World, Flesh and Devil. Though they retained the Bull-calf myth, handed down from Solomon's days, as emblematic of the spiritual life of mortal man and linked it to the seven-letter name of immortal God, it is clear that initiates of the highest Order cultivated the eight-letter name, or the enlarged name of seventy-two letters, and devoted themselves wholly to the

meditative life: ruled by acacia and promegranate, Sunday and Saturday, Illumination and Repose." (p. 465)

It would take much more time than I can afford to subject this passage and the other statements Graves makes on the Essenes to critical analysis. The task is enticing, but I must resist. *The White Goddess* bristles with passages such as this, some just a line or two, others extending over several pages, in which Graves records with abandoned unconcern for verifiable detail what his poetic intuition tells him about biblical and postbiblical Jewish affairs, religious doctrines, secret rituals, symbols, myths, and other products of the mind, whereby it is almost impossible to ascertain whose mind is at work: that of the ancient Hebrews whose workings Graves claims to have uncovered, or that of Graves himself.

Graves himself supplies us with a clue as to the source of the attraction biblical myths had for him. He holds them, together with the Greek and Latin myths, to be the ground upon which Western culture was built, and which was largely lost by the Protestant revolution and the growth of rationalism. "The myths are wearing thin," he writes toward the end of *The White Goddess.* "When the English language was first formed, all educated people were thinking within the framework of the Christian myth cycle, which was Judeo-Greek." Today, however, "Biblical myths no longer serve as a secure base of poetic reference" (p. 459). A few pages later he bemoans the ignorance of the contemporary world which is so great that one may "safely reveal" poetic secrets, "even the Work of the Chariot without fear . . . nobody will be listening" (p. 462). The "Work of the Chariot" is Graves's rendering of the crucial Kabbalistic term *Ma'ase merkavah,* which denotes the secret and dangerous doctrine of the appearance of the Godhead. These comments reveal the extent to which Graves felt himself, in contrast to *hoi polloi,* the mythologically ignorant profane crowd, anchored and grounded in the world of biblical and kabbalistic myth.

And here I must leave *The White Goddess,* but I cannot forego the concluding remark that, contrary to my habit, which is to read everything with pencil in hand and check off passages that appear questionable or remarkable, when I read *The White Goddess* the pencil soon dropped from my hand, and I became victim of a, for me quite unusual, unwilling suspension of disbelief.

4.

"Pharaoh's Chariot Wheels"

I CAN NO longer recall whether I was remiss in answering the March 14 and 17, 1948, letters of Graves, but it would seem that I either did not answer them, or, against my custom, retained no copy of my reply. If I did not answer, it must have been because of my unusually intensive preoccupation with matters that touched me deeply, some of them painfully. In the spring of 1948 my marriage to Naomi broke up, which was for me a traumatic experience, and caused me no little heartache. On a different level, I was very busy with teaching my course at Columbia University—the first course I gave at an American university, and, to boot, on a subject of which I was not a hundred percent sure. Then, in May, I left on a three-month field trip to Mexico where I studied the Jewish Indians. While there I met and fell in love with Irene, who was on a visit in Mexico with an older woman friend.

Upon my return to New York, I started to teach at the Dropsie College and the University of Pennsylvania in Philadelphia, which required much intensive preparation. I also began to work on my book *Israel between East and West,* which became my first book to be published in America (in 1953). All this meant that I was a very busy man with many demanding interests and activities, and neglected most of my correspondence. However, in the fall of 1948 I mailed Graves an offprint of my article "A Survey of Near Eastern Anthropology,"[1] which elicited from him this letter:

Dec 2 1948

Dear Dr Patai:

Many thanks for your pamphlet which interested me a lot; I have an idea that blood-groups are of more importance than skull measurements as indi-

cating cultural propensities and I should like your field-workers to get onto that job one day; their connexion with linguistic trends is already established.

I think it would have been helpful to add to your argument the observation that the sown and the unsown are not stable geographical terms. In Classical times Libya was the granary of Europe, and there was forestland as far south as Thebes, including oaks. And the Negeb flowed with milk and honey, and Edom & Sinai supported sizeable and only semi-nomadic tribes. In Herodotus's time the settlers of the Sirte coast were identical with the nomads of the interior, and were matriarchal not patriarchal. They went inland with their flocks in the pasturing season and returned when the grass dried up to their cool troglodyte burrows. Lowdermilk's book about soil-erosion in Palestine is very helpful.

Do you know any reason for the pomegranate knob on the Feast of Dedication eight-armed candlestick, or for the eight arms? I have a theory about it. (I know the Rabbincial fairy story about the miracle of the oil.) You seem to be one of the few people who think clearly along anthropological lines. . . . And Ill like your opinion on my theory that wherever Pentateuchical moral anecdote smells of the 6th century B.C. rather than of the genuine 1400 B.C. tribal legend or ancient 'maerchen' it is iconotropic, i.e. if you restore it to pictorial form you get a well-known religious icon of a different meaning: e.g. Ithyphallic drunken Lot and his daughters and their misbegotten children at Zoar are really Osiris mourned over by Isis and Nephthys in a grape arbour with the child Horus at Isis's feet.

Yours v. s.

Robert Graves

I add two pp. from additions made to my White Goddess *in further explanation of 'iconotropy'. This story is not a moral anecdote but an aitiological one explaining which the Israelites had disposed [dispossessed?] the Edomites of their ancestral shrines—ingeniously grafted on to an icon of a different sense altogether.*

p. 208 line 7 New Paragraph

The goat-Dionysos, or Pan, was a powerful deity in Palestine. He may have come there from Libya by way of Egypt or taken a roundabout northern route by way of Crete, Thrace, Asia Minor and Syria. The Day of Atonement Scapegoat was a left-handed sacrifice to him under the name of Azazel, and the source of the Jordan was a grotto sacred to him as Baal Gad, the goat king, eponymous ancestor of the tribe of Gad. The prohibition in Deuteronomy xiv against seething a kid in his mother's milk is puzzling only if sentimentally read; it is clearly written in the severe style of the remainder of the chapter, which begins with a prohibition against self-disfigurement at funerals, and directed against a eucharistical rite* [marginal addition: "I hear now that "Ram-Bam" [Rambam, Maimonides] gave this explanation, & he ought to

51

know!"] no longer tolerated by the priesthood of Jehovah. The clue is to be found in the well-known Orphic formula:

Like a kid I have fallen into milk

which was a password for initiates when they reached Hades and were challenged by the guardians of the dead. They had become one with The Kid, that is to say the immortal Dionysus, originally Cretan Zagreus or Zeus, by partaking of his flesh, and with the Goat-goddess, his mother, in whose cauldron and milk he had been seethed.

The prohibition in Deuteronomy *explains the glib and obviously artificial myth of Esau, Jacob, Rebecca and the blessing of Isaac, which is introduced into Genesis* xxvii *to justify the usurpation by the Jacob tribes of priestly and royal prerogatives belonging to the Edomites. The religious picture iconotropically (here insert as a footnote the parenthetical passage,* In my preface . . . and Lot, *in the middle of page 219) advanced in support of that myth seems to have illustrated the kid-eating ceremony in Azazel's honour. Two celebrants wearing goatskin disguises are shown at a seething cauldron presided over by the priestess (Rebeccah), one of them with bow and quiver (Esau) the other (Jacob) being initiated into the mysteries by the old leader of the fraternity (Isaac) who whispers the secret formula into his ear, blesses him and hands him—rather than is handed by him—a piece of the kid to eat. The ceremony probably included a mock-slaughter and resurrection of the initiate, and this would account for the passage at the close of the chapter where Esau murderously pursues Jacob, Rebeccah directs affairs and the orgiastic 'daughters of Heth' in Cretan costume stand by. The 'two' kids are probably an error: the same kid is shown twice in different pictures of the sequence.*

This letter, containing as it did two questions, demanded an immediate answer, and answer it I did within two or three days after its receipt. To my regret I have not preserved the envelope in which it came (it is my custom to this day to discard envelopes and unfold the letters they contain so as to be able to file them away easily), and thus I cannot tell why it took almost eight weeks to reach me. I suspect that Graves must have sent it by ship mail. In the first part of my letter I told him something of my life in America, and of my current interests, which at that time were focused totally on the modern Middle East and the new State of Israel. Then I got down to answering his questions.

January 28, 1949
310 East 15th Street
New York 3, N.Y.

Dear Mr. Graves:

I received your letter of December 2, 1948, a few days ago, with the two pages of additions to your White Goddess. *I must confess to my great shame that to this day I have not read this book, although I am sure it is a "must" for my studies. My chief, but of course inadequate, excuse is that I lead here a very harassed life, teach at three universities (the University of Pennsylvania and the Dropsie College in Philadelpia, and the New School for Social Research in New York), and work in my spare time on a study about the Indian Jews of Mexico among whom I spent three months last summer. My courses in the colleges deal with the ethnology of the Near East, a largely unexplored area (at least scientifically speaking unexplored), concerning which no satisfactory literature exists, so that I have to piece together the information I wish to convey to my classes from a hundred scattered and unsystematic sources which involves a great amount of reading. Also, I have come away lately from that type of historically oriented studies to which my* Man and Temple *belongs, and have concentrated more and more upon the tasks and problems of present-day ethnological and anthropological studies of the Near East. I have been doing this not because I lost interest in the historical aspect of this area—on the contrary, the fascination of historical comparative studies is as great for me as ever—but because the ethnological and anthropological study of the present-day Near East which sheds before our very eyes its age-old leopard-spots is so infinitely more urgent. A man cannot accomplish too much in his lifetime, and although I am only in my 39th year I feel that I must devote my energies to that field the study of which must not suffer delay. It is for this same reason that I endeavour to return as soon as possible to Palestine, that is to Israel, where I can conduct field investigations in this quickly vanishing, or at least changing, field of cultural configurations. I have a very ambitious plan to organize a large-scale research project in the ethnological and general social field in the Near Eastern area as a whole, but I do not yet see my way to securing the necessary financial basis from the Jewish and non-Jewish American scientific and other foundations. In the meantime I also have to battle with my own alma mater the Hebrew University for the recognition of Near Eastern ethnology as at least as important a subject in the curriculum as, say, Near Eastern economics.*

Now let me try to reply in brief to your two questions. The pomegranate decoration on the candlestick should, I think, not be divorced from the candlestick as a whole. Candlelight has always been in Jewish lore a symbol of life, the candlestick in the Temple—a symbol of Israel's life and might over the peoples of the world (see my Man and Temple, *p. 127). The pomegranate is to this day a symbol of fertility among Near Eastern (as well as other) peoples. The candlestick decorated with pomegranates stands for life and fertility. The pomegranate appears also on the priestly robes, and it must have had a similar significance also there, and the connection between the priestly garments and the candelabra was accentuated at the Feast of Water Drawing, when the candelabra's wicks were made of the worn out drawers and girdles of the priests. I feel that this explanation is not quite satisfactory, and I would like to hear your theory.*

53

As to your second question, I would not dare to offer any opinion on such a general problem as the iconotropic theory, without devoting some time to study it. However, the example you mention (Lot and his daughters) is not convincing. There may be other explanations, one of which is the seemingly general tendency to attribute the birth of heroes (in this case the tribal ancestors of Ammon and Moab) to unnatural, or at least unusual, circumstances. The nearest other example I can think of at the moment is that contained in the ancient Arab legend-cycle of the Beni Hillal, in which we are told, i.a., that Abu Zeid did not allow himself complete coition with his wife, whereupon the tribe came privily to his sister and said that the Beni Hillal must have a son from the loins of Abu Zeid. Wherefore one night she went secretly to her brother's bed, and he, not knowing her in the darkness from his wife, lay with her. And as he was about to withdraw himself prematurely, acc. to his habit, she jabbed him with the bodkin that she had kept in her hand in readiness for the moment. The shock achieved its intent, and in the fullness of time she bore a son, who came to be known as ʿAziz bin Khala (ʿAziz, son of his uncle) and became a chief hero of the Beni Hillal (cf. Betram Thomas, Arabia Felix, *pp. 219 sqq.). The similarity between this story and that of Lot is unmistakeable: In both cases a hero is tricked by near blood-relations (sister or daughters) into having (incestuous) sexual relations with them, unknowingly, and the outcome of this union is the birth of a male child, a hero or ancestor of the tribe. This is a type of stories about the birth of heroes, which, as far as I remember, was considered neither by Rank in his psychoanalytical book* Der Mythus von der Geburt des Helden, *nor by Lord Raglan in his* The Hero. *I think it is a safe guess that you will find stories of this type in the Greek, Roman and related oriental literature which you know so much better than I do. I should be glad to hear what you have to say to this.*

Yours very sincerely
Raphael Patai

I sent my letter by airmail. Graves must have received it a few days later, and responded instantly:

Feb 9 1949

Dear Raphael Patai

Many thanks for your careful letter. I very much sympathize with your having to give lectures instead of getting on with research. I remember W. H. R. Rivers whom I knew well, complaining of having to play tutor at St John's

Cambridge; and of the funds collected for 'the conquest of Everest' (in 1921 or so): 'Everest will wait for ever; but Melanesian society is dying out and no funds available for ethnological research there.'

I'm glad you hope to get back to Israel. What a pity that your people were forced to borrow the unpleasant revolutionary technique of the Boston 'Sons of Liberty' and the Sinn Feiners! I agree it was the only way, of course.

I make the pomegranate a symbol of life in death, not just of life; it was that in Greek mysteries. [Marginal addition: "It is most important that the sacrificial lamb at the Passover had to be spitted on a pomegranate spit."] My view of the Chanukah candlestick is that it was long pre-dedication and represented the death of the year at the winter solstice and its revivification by the birth of the Divine Child—eight is the number of increase and winter corn was sprouting about that time.

About Lot and his daughters. In the first place, there is no similar myth in the western world so far as I know: Lot would seduce his daughters perhaps, but not they him. What you report of the Beni Hillal story seems to me a lateish aetiological myth to explain the word 'Aziz ben Khala; it looks as though in the Beni Hillal the chieftain used to marry his niece in order to keep the inheritance-by-mother-right in the family but that the practice fell into desuetude and the tradition having got an incestuous taint had to be accounted for. [Marginal addition: "Query: is uncle-niece an incestuous relationship in the Koran?"] The bodkin story smells of coffee-hearth, not of the genuine myth; but at least it is more plausible than the story of Lot's daughters finding no mate in Zoar and drugging their father into insensibility. The genuine (Lord Raglan type) stories of a hero's peculiar birth are always concerned with ritual objects, such as almonds, pomegranates (as in the Attis story), fish, may-flies, bulls, serpents, with which the mother is impregnated—the bodkin prick is quite another world of ideas. The myth of Onan seems late too, because it is offered as a moral anecdote—how wicked to evade the Levirate law, even before the time of Moses! But since Onan was killed for his act, I should not be surprised if it was not told originally to explain a ritual picture of a dying king under a palm-tree (Tamar) ejaculating on the ground in a fertility act: there's a cave-painting like that in Domboshama. Onan, whose 'mother' was Shuah the Canaanite, was an Edomite-Canaanite tribe absorbed by Judah; my impression is that all the ritual pictures iconotropically used by the redactors of the Pentateuch were found in the shrine of Hebron from which the Edomites were extruded by the Beni Yacob.

Its all a question of smell; some things smell primitive however modern-looking; others smell modern however much patina'd by Biblical tradition of a great age. Your nose in Man and Temple is very acute I find.

Very many thanks and good luck
Robert Graves

Our best friends here are the Arnaldo Rosenstingls. He claims to have known your learned father in Hungary. He's an ex-Vienna ear-specialist, reduced to selling antiques which was his father's trade in Budapesth.

At the top of his letter, Graves had added:

My White Goddess *indicates a new line of scholarly research, rather than being a scholarly book. It suggests that all religious mysteries of Near Eastern Bronze age origin, including the Hebrew, derive from a festal season linked with the 13 month + 1 day calendar and the annual twin-king and Moon Goddess religious system; closely connected with the 13 consonant, 5 vowel 'Orphic' tree-alphabet, and with the seven-day week + the extra day which differentiates the terrestrial 365 day year from the sidereal 364 day one (insisted upon in the* Book of Enoch.*)*

A year or so after I wrote my January 28, 1949, letter to Graves, he sent me a copy of his latest book *Occupation Writer,* [2] in which, as he wrote me on April 28, 1950, he mentioned and quoted me. When I received the book, I went straight to the essay entitled, "Pharaoh's Chariot Wheels: A Study in Iconotropy" (pp. 283–302), which Graves mentioned in his letter, and found that it contained several references to me and my published works. In addition, Graves reprinted in it almost the entire second half of my January 28, 1949, letter.

That highly colorful essay begins with a freewheeling retelling of the story of the Exodus, and then goes on to hypothesize that "the compilers of *Exodus*" disguised the original meaning of the tribal feast at Mount Horeb where "the Midianites seem to have worshipped the Goddess Miriam, identifiable with Cyprian Mari and the Goddess of Amari in Crete" (p. 284), and misinterpreted "the latter half of a sequence of icons preserved in the Temple archives" which were traditionally held to refer to that feast (p. 287). Next Graves proposes the term *iconotropy* for "the misinterpretation of religious pictures or ritual belonging to an earlier faith, in order to establish and justify the new," and contends that "if obviously artificial legends are restored to pictorial form, the original myths they were invented to hide will often leap to the eye" (p. 287). He follows this with an attempt to apply his iconotropy to the Exodus story, which he boldly rewrites by adducing Greek legends, finds that "the same set of icons that underlie the story of the Exodus from Egypt also underlie the legend of Pelops, Hippodamia, Oenomaüs, and Myrtilus," and concludes that it seems "as if the icons on which the *Exodus* narrative is based were originally Greek" (p. 295).

It is in this context that he quotes the Beni Hillal story from my letter of January 28, 1949. He writes: "Dr. Raphael Patai, Director of the Israeli Institute of Folklore and Ethnology, though he insists on the importance of the Goddess in Hebrew history, questions the need of supposing an iconotropic origin for the Lot story. He has written to me . . . " and here follows most of the concluding part of my letter. Following it Graves comments: "Dr. Patai is one of the shrewdest and least inhibited of Biblical scholars, but disclaims any close knowledge of Western mythology; which so far as I am aware, contains no similar story . . . The Beni Hillal story I read as another aetiological myth, reminiscent of the *Genesis* story [of the daughters of Lot], invented to explain the title 'Aziz bin Khala' " (pp. 298–99). Then he continues to repeat almost verbatim what he wrote me about it in his February 9, 1949, letter, including the observation that "the bodkin prick smells of the coffee hearth, not of primitive mythology" (p. 299). (In his letter to me he wrote, "The bodkin story smells of coffee-hearth, not of the genuine myth.") Further on he remarks that "the primitive stories of a hero's peculiar birth, to which Dr. Patai refers, are concerned with ritual objects or creatures, such as almonds, pomegranates, fish, bulls, mayflies, serpents, with which the mother is miraculously impregnated; the bodkin prick belongs to another region of the imagination" (p. 299).

Next Graves quotes what he put into the mouth of Agabus, his fictional first-century narrator, about Solomon's Temple in his book *King Jesus,* and then adds:

> Dr. Patai has taken the argument further in his *Man and Temple* (1947). He holds that the Holy of Holies was originally a nuptial chamber in which a sacred marriage was celebrated between representatives of Jehova and Anatha, like that celebrated by Marduk, on the tree-clad Ziggorath at Babylon, with the most beautiful woman in the land. He shows that the ark was a fertility symbol and quotes several early rabbinic legends in this sense, including one which describes how, when Solomon brought the ark into the Sanctuary, all the trees and cedar beams became green and brought forth fruit: 'Dry wood snuffed the scent of the Life of the World (i.e., the *Shekinah*), blossomed, bore fruit and came to life.' He emphasizes the erotic light-headedness of the women worshippers of the Feast of Tabernacles; and proves that the olive-wood cherubs on the Ark were locked in a sexual embrace quoting Resh Lagish [Laqish]: 'When the heathen entered the Temple and saw the Cherubs whose bodies intertwined they carried them out and said: "These Israelites whose blessing is a blessing and whose curse is a curse occupy themselves with such things!" And immediately they despised them'—though, as the rabbis plaintively pointed out, the group was far from obscene: it represented God's love for Israel, like the love of Solomon for the Shunemite in the *Canticles*. Dr. Patai might have added that the Temple incense was originally an aphrodisiac for use in the nuptial chamber. (p. 301)

When I found these references to my work in Graves's *Occupation Writer,* my reaction was twofold. On the one hand I felt flattered by being quoted and referred to in such detail by the famous writer. On the other, I felt rather uneasy at the liberties Graves had taken in quoting me not literally but rephrasing what I wrote in *Man and Temple*. For instance, nowhere did I say that the

Holy of Holies of the Jerusalem Temple "was originally a nuptial chamber in which a sacred marriage was celebrated between representatives of Jehovah and Anatha." What I said was that in "ancient Jewish legends . . . the Holy of Holies . . . is represented as a Nuptial Chamber, though not until a comparatively late period do we find the express statement that the couple whose Nuptial Chamber it was were God and the Holy Matrona personifying the Community of Israel" (p. 89). A few pages later I state expressly that "the most outspoken description of the Temple as the Nuptial Chamber of God and the Matrona, the symbol of Israel, is found in so late a work as the *Zohar Hadash* [dating from the Middle Ages]" (p. 92).

Also, upon perusing the whole essay, I felt rather uncomfortable with being quoted in one breath with surmises that lacked the rigorous scholarly method of making deductions from quoted sources in a tightly argued manner. When, for instance, I concluded in my *Man and Temple* that the Ark in the Holy of Holies of the Jerusalem Temple was a fertility symbol, that the two Cherubs on the Ark were shown locked in a sexual embrace, that the "light-headedness" engaged in by the men and women in the Temple on the occasion of the Feast of Tabernacles had a ritual basis and was part of the fertility aspect of the great annual celebration of the "Joy of the House of Water Drawing," I based each of these conclusions on a close scrutiny of relevant passages in talmudic and midrashic sources. Graves, on the other hand, proceeded instead in the manner of the historical novelist who feels free to describe events as he sees fit, whether or not the available documentation bears him out.

The essay "Pharaoh's Chariot Wheels" contains many such unproven statements, with assumptions and surmises presented as if they were established facts. To mention only one example: about the biblical story of the birth and naming of Moab and Ammon by their mothers, who bore them after their incestuous union with their own father, Lot (Gen. 19:30–38), Graves writes: "The story in *Genesis* is clearly aetiological: it purports to explain Moab as meaning 'son of my father,' instead of *'The Desired One,' the name of the tribe's goddess mother;* and Ammon as meaning 'son of my kinsmen,' whereas *this is also probably a goddess's name, 'The Mighty One.' The two goddesses were given 'Daughters of Lot' as a geographical title: they were living in the Lotan country, south of the Dead Sea"* (p. 299). The words I put in italics express surmises by Graves, conjectures inspired by intuition or imagination. I, at least, know of no data that would support them, which, of course, does not mean that they are wrong, only that they cannot be presented as statements of facts.

Let me give a quick rundown of what is known about the names Moab and Ammon, which have been the subject of much research. One opinion has it that the name Moab could indeed have the meaning "desirable (people or land)."[3] However, it is a masculine noun, and Graves took the liberty of interpreting it as if it were feminine, which would be required if it were the name of a goddess. Moreover, and more importantly, I know of no evidence that such a goddess ever existed. As for the name Ammon, which according to the biblical story, is derived from *Ben ʿAmmi,* i.e., "Son of my Kinsman," some scholars have indeed related it to the name of the South-Arabian god ʿAmm.[4] However, it is again Graves's own guess that it was originally the name of a goddess, and that its meaning is "Mighty One." Nor is there any documentary basis for the statement that the territories of Moab and Ammon (which, incidentally, lay not south of the Dead Sea, as Graves has it, but to the east and northeast of it) were ever called "Lotan country," even though the two names Lot and Lotan seem to be connected.

I repeat, all this does not mean that what Graves says is wrong, only that it would have been more in line with scholarly practice to insert some qualifying phrase such as "possibly," "could be," or "this suggests." Such hedging would, of course, have weakened the flow and force of his presentation. The biblical etymologies, as T. K. Cheyne pointed out long ago,[5] "are, as they stand, examples of popular paronomasia," or, as we would put it today, of folk etymology—about this there can be no doubt. But it is a far cry from recognizing biblical derivations of names as folk etymologies to presenting alternative explanations as plain facts without any concrete evidence to support them.

I can no longer remember whether what I wrote above actually represents my reaction to reading Graves's "Pharaoh's Chariot Wheels" in 1950, but I suspect that it must have been much along these lines. This could have been the only reason why in letters I wrote Graves at that time I refrained from making any mention of his book *Occupation Writer* or of the essay in which he quoted me. I must have felt that I could not refer to the place he gave me in that essay without also offering my opinion of his approach, his method, and the many unsupported statements he made in the essay—and I was not at all sure at that early stage of our contact how he would take my uninvited criticism of his way of reconstructing lost features of Hebrew antiquity. When he wrote me that he was sending me a copy of *Occupation Writer,* I thanked him in advance of having received it (in my letter of May 6, 1950), but after I received it I never again referred to it. However, as it turned out, the references by Graves to my work in that essay were the introduction to a much more extensive reliance by him on my studies in *The Nazarene Gospel Restored* which he wrote jointly with Joshua Podro, and which ultimately led to the collaboration of Graves and me on the *Hebrew Myths.*

5.

Visit to Israel—1949

I N THE SUMMER of 1949 I went to Israel. I left New York on a chartered plane, on June 26, and after a one-day stopover in Paris arrived in Israel on June 30th. My visit, to which I had looked forward for almost two years, turned out to be a series of trying experiences. First of all, there was my pending divorce from Naomi. Her decision to end our marriage, made in the winter of 1947–48 in New York, was a heavy blow for me, and for months I tried to make her change her mind, but to no avail. Then, by the fall of 1948, I found consolation in my involvement with Irene, and informed Naomi that I was willing to give her the *get*, the letter of divorce, when I next visited Israel. By the time I arrived there, I was eager to end my marriage to her. Still, I was seized with a great sadness, and I understood, for the first time, the talmudic saying that when a man divorces the wife of his youth the altar weeps. I felt that my youth, with all its exuberance, joys, and hopes, had come to an end, and I was entering middle age. I was nearing my thirty-ninth birthday.

Even more painful for me were my visits to my two little daughters, who had been left by Naomi with a German Jewish family in the village of Ramot haShavim, a few miles to the north of Tel Aviv, near the seashore. I rented a car for the duration of my stay in Israel, and drove out to visit Ofra and Daphne two or three times a week. Each time I took one of them along with me to Givatayim, to my parents' house, to stay with us until my next visit when I took her back and brought home the other girl. The house of my parents was not big enough to accommodate me and both of my daughters at the same time. Each time I drove away from Ramot haShavim with one of the girls, the other stood at the gate of the house and cried. I had great difficulty not to cry with them. I promised them that as soon as it was feasible I would bring them to me in New York.

Both Ofra and Daphne told me that their mother came to visit them rarely, perhaps once in two weeks, and that, although they complained of the harsh discipline to which they were subjected by "Doda Trude" ("Aunt T."), and repeatedly begged their mother to take them back to her home, she did not fulfill this, the only request they had. When the time came for me to return to New York, and I said goodbye to Ofra and Daphne, they both stood at the gate, watched me drive away, and cried. Once I was out of their sight I too broke down, and vowed to have them with me as soon as possible whatever obstacles I had to overcome.

That summer in Israel was difficult for other reasons as well. Until that time I had stayed in the United States on a visitor's visa. Now it was necessary to obtain a non-quota immigrant's visa, available for me as a college professor. I submitted my application to the American consulate in Tel Aviv, and was sent by them to their doctor—one of the local Jewish doctors in Tel Aviv—to get a health certificate testifying that I was free of tuberculosis, the one disease that, at the time, made an applicant ineligible for an American immigrant's visa. I went to see the doctor on July 14, and he in turn sent me to have a chest X ray taken. On the 18th I got the results: "probably tbc nodules." To find out whether the case was active or inactive, the doctor told me to go to a medical laboratory to have sputum, gastric content, and blood sedimentation rate examined, and to take my temperature three times daily. Next day I went to the laboratory and was given a glass of water to drink, which then was pumped out of my stomach. Then I was told we had to wait until the culture, or whatever they did with the stomach content, showed the results. In the meantime I started to take my temperature, in the mouth, and found that it was 37.1° centigrade.

Never before had I been as miserable as during the following days. I imagined despairingly what my life would be like if the results were positive: I would lose Irene, I would have to stay in Israel where I had no job, I would be ruined. I took my temperature three times a day—and each time it registered somewhat above 37° centigrade. I was desperate. What the doctor did not tell me was that while the underarm reading of normal body temperature was up to 37°, taken in the mouth the normal range extended up to 37.4°. Not being aware of this, I was convinced I had tuberculosis, indicated by a higher-than-normal temperature, and began to feel all kinds of aches and pains in my chest. Most days I lay about lethargically, unable to do anything. Trying to think positively, I planned, if I could not go back to America, to go to a kibbutz, live there for eight or ten months, and write a study about it somewhat along the lines of my Mexican book, but in a more thorough fashion and more comprehensively. But while thinking about this I remained aware, of course, that I could do even this only if I should be allowed or able to from a medical point of view.

To make sure I did not infect my children I went near them as little as possible, and when I kissed them I did so only on the tops of their heads. To this sorrow was added the need I felt to keep my mother from knowing that anything was wrong with me. She had enough anguish as it was with the initial manifestations of my father's mental deterioration that had set in about that time, and that developed within two years into a severe case of what later became known as Alzheimer's disease. I felt that I must on no account add to her burden by telling her about the serious trouble I believed I was in. The only person in whom I confided was my sister Evi, and she stood by me lovingly, supportingly, and valiantly.

Then, finally, the day of my return visit to the doctor arrived. It was July 28, two weeks after my first visit to him. He told me that all the results were negative, and that the traces the X ray showed in my lungs were found in almost everybody who grew up in an urban environment. And only then did he remember to tell me what body temperature was normal when taken in the mouth. My relief was enormous. I felt reborn, or at least rejuvenated. At the same time I was furious with the doctor who, if he had only told me these things at my earlier visit, could have saved me two weeks of desperation. I told him bitterly, "You know, now I understand the talmudic saying, 'The best of doctors, to hell with him.' " I am not sure he understood what I was talking about. Next day I took the medical report to the American consulate, and on August 3 I was the happy possessor of an immigrant's visa to the United States.

Yet another problem with which I had to cope that summer in Israel was obtaining a new passport and exit permit from the Israeli authorities. I started working on this three days after my arrival, and had to spend an inordinate amount of time getting together the necessary papers. The documents the passport authority wanted me to produce before giving me permission to leave the country included certificates attesting that I owed no income tax, that I owed no War Loan assessment, that I owed no tax to the Givatayim municipality, and that I was exempt from military service. In order to get the last-named document I had to send a cable to the Israeli consulate in New York requesting them to certify that I had received from them such an exemption. I sent off the cable on July 4, and on the 7th I got their reply: "This is to attest that you have received from us exemption from military service until June 1, 1949. Signed: Shomrol, Consul, N.Y." Thus I was "in order" as far as the past was concerned, and all I had to do was to get an extension of that exemption. I had to pay three visits to the Recruiting Office in Jaffa before the matter was finally settled.

To obtain attestations from various governmental and municipal offices to the effect that I owed them no taxes also took numerous visits, each involving long waits in overcrowded, hot, stuffy, antechambers and corridors, and heated arguments with overworked clerks. It was not until August 8 that I finally got my new Israeli passport and had the exit permit duly stamped into it.

Simultaneously I conducted negotiations with Naomi in connection with our divorce. Actually, there was only one issue that had to be discussed and settled: the custody of the children. I had several meetings with her in the offices of S. Z. Abramov, the attorney of the Tolkowsky family (who later became a good friend of mine as my associate in editing the *Encyclopedia of Zionism and Israel*). I was not represented by counsel—I did not feel that I needed one. With Abramov's help we agreed that we should have joint custody, and that as long as I was living in America the children would stay with their mother during the school year, but I could have them with me for the vacation time in the summer. I was not very satisfied with this solution, especially in view of the fact that staying with their mother actually meant for the children remaining with that German-Jewish family in Ramot haShavim and being visited by her once in two weeks. But this was the best I could achieve, and I trusted that time would bring a modification of our agreement.

Once this was settled, we arranged with the Tel Aviv rabbinate to have the *get* take place on August 9, in the apartment of one of its rabbis. When the appointed hour arrived, present were, in addition to the rabbi himself who acted as master of ceremonies, two witnesses who knew both Naomi and me, a scribe, and two other witnesses whose task was to attest that I indeed entrusted the scribe in their presence with the task of writing a *get* to my wife, that the scribe wrote it, and that I personally handed it to Naomi.

The handing of the *get* by husband to wife had to follow the old established and traditional rules. Naomi had to stand facing me, hold out her hands with the palms turned inward, I had to place the *get* between her hands, and she had to lift it up a little and pull it toward her, thereby clearly indicating that she had consented to the divorce and accepted the *get* of her free will. Once this was done, the rabbi made out a Hebrew certificate stating that on that day the divorce had actually taken place according to the *halakha* (the traditional Jewish religious law), and give a copy of it to me and one to Naomi. As for the *get* itself, the rabbi folded it up, took a pair of big scissors, and made two cuts into it, which was the indelible, traditional indication that the *get* had been executed. Thereafter, I was told, the *get* would be placed in the archives of the rabbinate. The whole ceremony lasted two and a half hours, of which the writing of the *get* with black India ink and a quill took up most of the time.

After it was all over, and Naomi and I walked down the stairs to the street, she suggested that we go and sit down at a nearby café. I politely declined, said goodbye to her, and was not to see her again for many years.

Now that my divorce was done and my return to America assured, I felt up to doing some work. A few days before I had left New York I was appointed research associate of the Bureau of Applied Social Research of Columbia University to carry out, while in Israel, two tasks: to arrange for an inquiry on the response of Israeli listeners to broadcasts of the Voice of America, and to explore the possibilities of cooperation on a wider basis between the Bureau and Israeli social research institutions. These ideas came from Kingsley Davis, Paul Lazarsfeld, Leo Srole, and George Wise of Columbia, and Leo Lowenthal of the Voice of America. I met these men several times in June, discussed the Voice of America project in detail, and got a letter of appointment from the bureau. Now I felt ready to tackle the envisaged tasks. I went to see Prof. Louis Guttman (formerly of Cornell University), who headed the Israel Institute of Public Opinion Research, which was sponsored by the Israeli government and headquartered in Jaffa, and his second-in-command, Dr. Uriel Foa, a young Israeli sociologist of Italian-Jewish origin. In the course of several meetings I concluded with them an agreement in regard to the Voice of America project. I was somewhat disturbed when I learned that the opinion (not public, to be sure, but private) of these two fine social scientists about the department of social sciences of the Hebrew University of Jerusalem was very low. Nevertheless, five years later, Guttman, the renowned author of the widely used sociometric "Guttman scale," accepted an appointment to the Hebrew University, not as professor of sociology, but, at the urging of Prof. Martin Buber and other members of the university senate, as professor of "social measurement," or "sociometry." I do not know what happened later to Dr. Foa.

And, of course, I went up to Jerusalem to stay with my brother Saul, who at the time was at the beginning of a distinguished academic career at the Hebrew University, and to find out what, if anything, I could do to obtain an invitation from the university to teach anthropology. I met the rector of the University, Prof. Simha Assaf; numerous professors, including Michael Fekete, who in 1947 had had a crucial role in my coming to America; Joseph J. Rivlin, who coedited with me the journal *Edoth: A Quarterly for Folklore and Ethnology;* Martin Buber and Joseph Klausner, upon whose recommendation my two-volume Hebrew study *Man and Earth in Ancient Jewish Custom, Belief and Legend* was accepted for publication in 1942–43 by the Hebrew University Press; the Middle Eastern economist Alfred A. Bonné; the Jewish demographer Arye Tartakower; and others. I also asked for an appointment with Dr. Selig Brodetsky, president of the university, but he let me know through his secretary that he could not see me because he was too busy, and could not enter into "small details." (I had let him know through his secretary that I wanted to talk to him about the university's department of social sciences and possible cooperation between it and Columbia's Bureau of Applied Social Research.)

With the people who were willing to see me (all of them, except for Brodetsky, were) I discussed the possibilities of such cooperation, and also

64

touched in no uncertain terms upon my desire to come back to Jerusalem and teach at the university. The responses were generally friendly but not enthusiastic, and my feeling that nothing would come from these initiatives eventually proved correct.

More than anything else during those days in Jerusalem I missed the Old City. In the fifteen years I had spent in Jerusalem, periodic visits to the Old City, often in company of my good friend Shaykh Ahmad Fakhr al-Din Al-Kinani, were always exciting, intriguing, and festive occasions for me. Now the Old City, and parts of Jerusalem near it, were in the hands of Jordan, inaccessible to Israelis and Jews. Also inaccessible was the Mount Scopus campus of the Hebrew University from which one could get a wonderful view of the Old City with the Mosque of Omar (the Dome of the Rock) dominating the landscape. Without the Old City, I felt, Jerusalem was incomplete, truncated. I tried to get in touch with Ahmad, who lived on the other side, or at least to find out whether he and his family were alive and well, but found no way. I had always loved Jerusalem, and for many years had not wanted to live anywhere else. But now the attraction of the city had considerably paled for me.

The departure from Israel was not easy emotionally. I had felt that my visit, after an absence of two years during which my work had made considerable progress in America, yet did not yield the results I had hoped for; my academic career, I was forced to recognize, had meager chances to lead me back to Israel. I left my children with a heavy heart because I saw how unhappy they were in Ramot haShavim, and because I was not sure when I would be able to take them to America to live with me. The condition of my father also saddened me—he, who always was such a tower of strength for me and for his whole family, was now frail and increasingly dependent on my mother. The overall conditions in the new state were difficult, the euphoria of the first days after independence had long passed, the large-scale immigration had begun to abate but not the problems of absorption, and the saber-rattling from the Arab countries surrounding Israel was growing more audible. As I was preparing to leave the country it dawned on my that my future lay in America, and that I was to have no share, at least not a direct one, in the life of the Israel whose establishment had been the "head of my hopes" during the fifteen years I had spent in Jerusalem.

After my return I reported to Dr. Massing of the Bureau of Applied Social Research of Columbia about the arrangements I had made with Louis Guttman, and on September 17 Irene and I were married by the deputy town clerk at the Municipal Building of New York. We took a five-day honeymoon trip (to Niagara Falls, of course), and then settled down, for the time being in my furnished room at 310 East 15th Street in Lower Manhattan, near the apartment of Irene's parents, who continued to take care of her daughter Emily. After a few days of house-hunting we rented a two-bedroom apartment in

Kew Gardens, Queens. I resumed my teaching at the Dropsie College, my public lecturing, my research work, and my attendance at conferences. Before the end of the year we moved into our apartment in Kew Gardens.

Now that I had a family and a home to which I could bring my children, I started to organize the technicalities of transporting them from Israel to New York. Since my legal right to have them with me during their summer vacation was assured in the pre-divorce agreement, the only remaining problem was how they should come to New York and who would take care of them on the way. I discussed the matter in correspondence with my sister Evi, and she made arrangements with a woman friend of hers, who planned to visit America, to act as chaperone for the two girls on the ship from Haifa to New York, for which service I paid her fare. A few weeks after their arrival Ofra, who by that time had three years of elementary schooling behind her, wrote to her mother (at my suggestion, and in Hebrew, of course) that she and Daphne would like to stay with me for the coming school year. Daphne knew enough writing to be able to sign her name to the letter. I also wrote to Naomi, asking her to accede to the children's request. She did. Thereafter the question of sending the children back to Israel never arose.

6.

The Nazarene Gospel Restored

T HE ANTECEDENTS OF *The Nazarene Gospel Restored* go back to 1941 when Graves met Joshua Podro, a Jewish scholar of wide reading and liberal views, who held no academic position, instead making a living from a "press cutting business."[1] Had Podro lived in Germany he would, I guess, have been styled a *Privatgelehrter.* He was, as Graves's biographer Martin Seymour-Smith put it, "humble and self-effacing, quite the opposite of Graves; but Graves took much notice of what Joshua told him. . . . He began to tell Graves . . . of his conviction that Jesus was first and foremost a Jew— and of his belief that the Pharisees had been gravely libelled in the Gospels. He convinced Graves."[2]

Collaboration between Graves and Podro on a book about Jesus (in whom Graves retained a keen interest after writing his historical novel *King Jesus*) began in 1949. The project was originally a modest one—to extract from the Gospels and other literature the real sayings of Jesus—but it soon grew into the major undertaking of painting a full panoramic picture of the life and work of Jesus, and of reconstructing his teachings as they originally were prior to being edited and reworked by his disciples, and in the first place by Paul. The task was not an easy one, and at the beginning neither Podro nor Graves felt completely sure of several points they considered crucial to their argument.

Soon after they started their collaboration Graves informed Podro that he was utilizing my "Hebrew Installation Rites" in his work on Jesus. He wrote Podro on September 8, 1949: "This morning . . . I was working at this very point—the quarrel between Jesus and John—and applying Raphael Patai's findings to Jesus's case. He proves that by ancient tradition the prophet who crowned the king never saw him again and often behaved like a personal enemy (*Hebrew Installation Rites* 202–204)."

Then Graves goes on in his letter to summarize my findings: "Patai makes analogy between this relationship and those of African sacred kings and their chief priests. He also stresses the resemblance between Jesus's installation and that of Saul's, though without following up the John the Baptist clue (above), nor two others that I mentioned independently in *King Jesus*."[3]

In fact, the enmity, or at least strained relationship, between prophet and king in ancient Israel was one of the least firmly established conclusions I reached in my study of the Hebrew installation rites. In studying the African rituals I found that in some nations the chief priest and the king could not meet, or the king was buffeted by the chief priest, or was humiliated by those who conducted the installation ceremonies. I also found that at the Babylonian New Year festival, which included a reenactment of the royal installation ritual, the high priest struck the king a blow on the cheek, pulled his ears, and forced him to kneel before the god, while the king had to respond to these humiliations by reciting a sort of "negative confession," that is, "I have not sinned," etc. On the basis of these features I suggested that a similar, ritually determined, strained relationship existed between the Prophet Samuel and the two kings of Israel whom he anointed, Saul and David, and whom he is stated never again to have seen thereafter (1 Sam. 15:35; 16:13); between the Prophet Ahijah and Jeroboam, whom he made king over Israel, and whom Jeroboam could not confront thereafter (1 Kings 11:29–29; 14:1ff.);[4] and between the unnamed prophet who anointed Jehu and "fled" immediately (1 Kings 9:3, 10). I argued that, even though personal factors may have played a role, especially in the relationship between Samuel and Saul, the repetitive character of the events mentioned smacks of conformity with ritual requirements.[5] It was, of course, most astute of Graves to recognize traces of this pattern in the story of Jesus.

As for my not following up various clues to a royal installation ritual contained in the New Testament accounts of the Jesus story, Graves was right. However, my interest in the "Hebrew Installation Rites" was centered on the pre-exilic kings of Israel, and hence I referred to Jesus only tangentially. Were I to edit that paper today, I would certainly follow up the clues referred to by Graves.

Early in 1950 I published in *The Menorah Journal*[6] a paper presenting some of my findings during my 1948 fieldwork in Mexico, where I studied the Indian Jews of the village of Venta Prieta and of Mexico City. It was a brief, popular account titled "The Indios Israelitas of Mexico." In March, 1959 I sent a copy of it to Graves, who responded:

Ap 28 1950

Dear Raphael Patai

Many thanks for the Menorah Journal. *I admire your balances and detachment; and what struck me most was the spiritual connexion between Guillermo Peña and the fresco and mosaic work at Beth Alpha and Doura-Europos. It might be by the same hand, despite the centuries between.*

Listen: I got a clue to the techniques [marginal addition: *"I have isolated twenty-nine main ones!"*] *of textual distortion used by the Evangelists, and with the help of a Talmudist, Joshua Podro, who has been working with me, have been able to get (I think) within a pretty close distance of the original Nazarene tradition of Jesus. (The core of the Nazarenes were a Zadokite apocalyptic group, based on Bethany and Ramathaim-Zophim, akin to the New Covenanters of Damascus, and soaked in contemporary eschatological theory.)*

In my King Jesus, *a novel written as from 99 A.D. by a Decapolitan, I have not removed all the overpainting of the original story and therefore allowed the Alexandrian theory that Jesus was a concealed heir to the throne; in fact a Herodian. In the new book, Podro and I have stripped everything off, down to the real story. I had already, before your 'Installation Rites' appeared, connected the story of Jesus's lustration with Hocart's kingship theory. Since then, with your help, I have been able to push the argument further (and incidentally to supply you with a couple of missing items from Tor Irstam's list) and show that the complete coronation ritual is given in the Gospels, though parts of it have been shifted about to improper contexts. I got the clue to the shifting from a sentence in Irenaeus, who complains (as Celsus also does) of the Alexandrians' indecent juggling about with the tradition in order to prove doctrinal theory.*

The point is: Joshua Podro does not quite feel comfortable with my findings, though I have documented them at all points, but he has a great respect for you and if you could either approve them or point out the flaws I should be most grateful! Please let me know whether I may send you the typescript of the argument, which concerns the Acclamation, Coronation, Royal Marriage and Address from the Throne, in a few weeks' time. There is nobody else but you with the necessary breadth of knowledge and scientific spirit to consult, and if there's no important flaw in the argument, then it's a big discovery.

I never congratulated you on your marriage; forgive me. What's worse, I never sent you a copy of 'Occupation, Writer' in which I mention and quote from you; and offer a new theory about Pharaoh's anachronistic chariot wheels. One's on its way now.

Yours very sincerely
Robert Graves

Are you ever in Europe?

I hurried to answer this letter because I was very interested in seeing the manuscript of the book on which Graves and Podro were collaborating, and because I truly felt I could make a useful contribution to it. At the same time I was glad to be able to tell Graves something about my own work. Incidentally, the book on the Indian Jews of Mexico was never published. I wrote it in Hebrew, and my friends in Mexico who were interested in seeing it published in Yiddish (there was a group of fervent Yiddishists in Mexico City), never managed to take care of the translation into that language. At first I toyed with the idea of translating it myself into English, but as time passed I became increasingly convinced that it needed more work before it could be published in English. The fact is that I never got around to reworking and translating it into English, and the manuscript has remained unpublished to this day. But I did work up several parts of it for articles that were published in Hebrew in *Talpioth*,[7] and in Hungarian in *Mult és Jövö*.[8] On the other hand, the book *Israel Between East and West*, to which I also refer in my letter, was published in 1953, and in a second, enlarged edition, in 1970.

This is what I wrote:

May 6,1950

Dear Don Robert,

By one of those strange coincidences I received your letter just when I was in the very midst of reading—and tremendously enjoying—your King Jesus. *I wanted to read it of course a long time ago, but only these days could I finally find the time to get down to it. Having discovered as soon as I took in my hands that its last few pages contain a "Historical Commentary," I read those first, in true scientific fashion, and thus the name of Joshua Podro whom you mention in your letter was not unknown to me; I only wondered how your neighbor from South Devon was transplanted to Mallorca.*

What you write of having dug down to the real story of Jesus sounds very exciting. The fact that you did this with the help of Joshua Podro indicates that also the scrutiny or even reinterpretation of Rabbinic source-material is involved. It is very flattering that you want me to read the argument; I shall be glad to do it and am looking forward to receiving the typescript.

I have jotted down on the margin of my copy of King Jesus *several remarks; they concern small matters, but I think I will collect them for you after I am through with the book.*

Let me tell you something of my own work. A book of mine is scheduled to be published in Mexico on the Indian Jews of that country (the article in the Menorah Journal was only a brief and popular account). It will be published by a Jewish literary foundation in Mexico City; I am sorry to say I was unable to persuade them to publish the book in Spanish—so that anthropologists specializing in the Latin American field should be able to read it—it will instead be published in Yiddish, a language which is doomed to extinction and which is understood today only by members of the older generation among Jews of East European extraction.

At present I am working on a book called tentatively Israel between East and West. *This will be a study of the cultural processes taking place in the new state of Israel where the relative numbers of Jews from the Middle Eastern countries increase rapidly, causing a serious socio-cultural crisis. I have not yet found a publisher for this book, but I am confident that the actuality of its subject matter will help.*

Thank you in advance for Occupation Writer *the dispatch of which you mention.*

Last summer I was back in Israel for three months, and I do not know yet when I can again get away and across the ocean. I should certainly be very glad to have an opportunity to meet you personally.

Yours very sincerely
Raphael Patai

Graves must have been very pleased with my willingness to read the manuscript of the book on which he was working with Podro, for a day or two after he received my answer he mentioned it in a letter he wrote to T. S. Eliot, whom he admired and with whom he had ties of friendship that spanned decades. "Dr. Patai, the head of the Dept. of Folklore and Ethnology at the Hebrew University at Jerusalem, now in New York, is checking a few specialist chapters concerned with the Nativity and Baptism."[9] Graves mistook the Palestine Institute of Folklore and Ethnology, which I had founded in Jerusalem in 1944, and of which I was director of research until 1948, for the Department of Folklore and Ethnology of the Hebrew University, which did not have, and does not have to this day, such a department.

A few days after he told T. S. Eliot about our collaboration, Graves replied to my letter:

Please return to me, to await arrival:
—c/o Watt & Co 10 Norfolk St
London W. C. 2
(I shall be there from July 1 to Aug 2nd)

Dear Don Rafael:

Many thanks for your letter. Joshua Podro is here on a visit from London where he runs the International Press Cutting Bureau and has the largest private library of Hebraica (I believe) in this continent. He's an authority on Yiddish, in fact you took the chair at one of his lectures—or else it was the

71

other way round—and was once long ago the leading Yiddish journalist in the
States. He's a very good man indeed, and though he knows as little Greek as
I know Aramaic and Syriac, we find that our findings dovetail exactly. From
him I learn that with a few honourable exceptions Jewish scholars are as dis-
honest as Christians about Christian origins—and that takes a lot of doing,
you'll agree.

Sorry that the only chapters of the book which are in triplicate so far are
the ones I send; the later argument affects these, but it can't be helped.

Any addition to, as well as corrections of, the argument will be much
welcomed.

The future of Israel is fascinating: I always think of Israel as a tug-of-war
between the Kassite strain & the Philistine—between Jehovah and the Queen
of Heaven. Urbanization strengthens Jehovah's hand, reclamation of its soil
strengthens the Queen's.

I hope you find a publisher. England is often easier to publish an out-of-
the-way book in than the U.S.A. Gollancz might do it; he did my brother
Dick's book about Jerusalem: "Experiment in Anarchy".

A poet called Sutzkinler has sent me a book in Yiddish about the life in the
Warsaw drain which Podro says is magnificent; but I can't even read the title
page. I am trying to arrange for a translation into English.

> *Yours v. sincerely*
> *Robert Graves*

I got married, too, last week—to the mother of my youngest three chil-
dren—after a ten-year wait for the necessary divorce. But no invitations were
issued, or I'd have sent you one.

Despite what Graves writes, I cannot recall having chaired a lecture of
Joshua Podro, or having met him at all. Why Podro should have judged most
Jewish scholars dishonest about Christian origins, I don't know. The foremost
Jewish scholar prior to 1950 who wrote about Christian origins was Joseph
Klausner, professor at the Hebrew University of Jerusalem, a mentor and
friend of mine, and neither in his *Jesus of Nazareth,* [10] nor in his *From Jesus
to Paul,* [11] could I, as far as I can remember from my reading them many years
ago, discover any signs of dishonesty. As for the dishonesty of Christian
scholars about Christian origins, I shall have to leave that to experts to judge.

The reference to "a tug-of-war between the Kassite strain & the Philistine—between Jehovah and the Queen of Heaven" is a typical Gravesian
comment, introducing a female deity into the least likely places. That the Kassites were the ancestors of the Hebrews was a favorite idea of Graves, who
stated in his 1955 book *Adam's Rib* that "when the Jews decided to disown
the religion which their Cassite ancestors had embraced on first entering Palestine and to adopt a male monotheism, they were obliged to recast all the

72

popular myths concerned with the cult of the immortal, variously-named Cananite Love-Goddess—Bau, Hepa, Belili, Beltis, Ishtar, Isis, Anatha, Neith, Aphrodite, etc.—and her yearly-dying, yearly-resurrected consort, which was no light task."[12]

Most of this is poetic fantasy, for all we know of the Kassites is that they were an ancient non-Semitic people who ruled southern Mesopotamia from the sixteenth to the twelfth century B.C.E. The few written records they left behind are in Babylonian, indicating that they adopted the language of the country they conquered. Their kings honored the Babylonian deities—another sign of their having succumbed to Babylonian culture. The introduction of the horse to Babylonia seems to have been the one major lasting contribution the Kassites made to the culture of Mesopotamia. In the twelfth century B.C.E. their power was broken by the Elamites, and they returned to the Zagros mountains, where they maintained their independence until the time of Alexander the Great. The basis of Graves's attribution of the worship of Jehovah to "the Kassite strain" is unknown to me. The connection between the worship of the Queen of Heaven and the Philistines is clearer: she must have penetrated the religious life of the biblical Hebrews from the Philistines, that is, the polytheistic non-Hebrew inhabitants of Palestine. Years later I came to the conclusion that the Queen of Heaven referred to by the Prophet Jeremiah (7:17–18; 44:15–19) was probably identical with the goddess Anath, who was styled in Egypt "Anath, Lady of Heaven."[13]

The name "Sutzkinler" which appears in Graves's letter is an obvious misspelling for (Abraham) Sutzkever (b. 1913), the Yiddish poet who managed to escape from the Vilna ghetto during World War II, joined the partisans, and was subsequently presented with a high award by the U.S.S.R. The book Graves refers to is the *Geheymshtot* ("Secret Town"), published in 1948, in which Sutzkever describes the life of the Jews in the filth and darkness of the subterranean canals of Vilna, and their dreams of a heroic resurrection of the Jewish people and their peaceful existence in the future.

The marriage Graves refers to in the postscript was to Beryl Hodge, née Pritchard, which took place on May 11, 1950, in Palma de Mallorca. Beryl was the daughter of Sir Harry Pritchard, a distinguished solicitor. She had studied at Oxford, where she met Alan Hodge. Beryl and Hodge were married on January 29, 1938, parted in the late fall of 1939, and Beryl joined Graves. Soon thereafter Beryl and Hodge were divorced. Hodge and Graves remained friends, and collaborated on several literary projects. The first child of Graves and Beryl, William, was born on July 21, 1940; the second, Lucia, on July 21, 1943; the third, Juan, on December 22, 1944. Throughout those years Graves was still married to his first wife, Nancy Nicholson; their divorce took place only on November 18, 1949, which, at long last, made it possible for Graves and Beryl to marry. Their fourth and last child, Tomas, was born on January 27, 1953.

73

Within a week or so after I received the above letter, the typescript of the first eleven chapters of *The Nazarene Gospel Restored* arrived. Since I subsequently returned it with my comments, I no longer remember of how many pages it consisted, but in the printed version those chapters make close to one-hundred tightly set large pages. The whole book runs to 982 pages. It has no index of subjects and names, only a "chapter index," which is a pity, for it makes the critical perusal of so massive a volume very difficult.

At the time I received the typescript I was deeply involved in writing a paper on the complex subject of comparing two types of nomadism: that of the Middle East and that of Central Asia, which was be to a great extent a corrective to a paper written on the culture areas of Asia by the Central Asian anthropologist Elizabeth Bacon.[14] I was also getting more and more involved with my book *Israel between East and West,* to which I devoted most of my time that year and the following, apart from my teaching commitments at the Dropsie College, lecturing, writing book reviews and minor articles. And, of course, I was taking care of my family, which now consisted of my wife Irene and her daughter Emily, aged seven. In addition, in the spring of 1950 I was busy making preparations for my daughters Ofra, aged eight, and Daphne, aged six, who were due to arrive from Haifa on June 28 on the S.S. La Guardia.

As if all this had not been enough, I started to organize The Association for the Study of Jewish Culture and Society (ASJCS). On January 8 I convened a group of interested people who were willing to lend a hand to a meeting in my home. Among those present were Prof. Moshe Perlmann of Dropsie College; Dr. Maurice Zigmond of Yale; Prof. Bessie B. Wessel of Connecticut College; Dr. Nussbaum, a Queens physician; the sociologist Dr. Henrik Infield; Dr. David Bidney of the Viking Fund; and a relative of Irene, Mr. Samuel Backlar of the New York State Attorney General's office. I was elected president of the provisional committee, Dr. Nussbaum secretary-treasurer, and Dr. Infield program chairman. It soon became clear that whatever activities the new society was to engage in had to be initiated by me, and I had to see to their execution. One of the steps I undertook was to go, together with my friend Moshe Perlmann, to see Prof. Salo W. Baron of Columbia University, to win his support for our society. He received us in his office at Columbia on January 18, and we gave him an account of out plans. Baron, in turn, evidently seeing a possible competition for the Conference on Jewish Relations of which he was president, tried to convince us that instead of founding a new society, we should join the conference, whose program, he explained, was to sponsor all kinds of Jewish social studies, so that whatever plans we had for our new group could adequately be carried out within its compass. Although this subdued our enthusiasm, we still held a few meetings, which were quite well attended, and then our association petered out.

A parallel plan I conceived of and discussed repeatedly with Eliezer Liebenstein (who later changed his name to Livneh), a member of the Israeli *Knesset* (parliament), vice-chairman of its Foreign Policy Committee and a frequent visitor to the United States, was to set up a cultural and social research project or institute in one of the *kibbutzim,* communal villages, in Israel. Encouraged by him I wrote about this plan to the large communal settlement of 'Eyn Harod, and to the Center of the K'vutza Organization, in which Liebenstein had considerable influence. I gave the letters to him, and he undertook to add his recommendation and mail them. Some time later (in May, 1950) I sent a memorandum to the Israeli government about the establishment of a Bureau of Applied Anthropology, again giving a copy of it to Liebenstein, who suggested that I send it also to Ben Gurion, with whom, he said, he was ready to speak about it.

In addition to these projects I was kept busy with preparing outlines of books, one of which, titled *Middle East Culture,* I gave to my literary agent, Mrs. Bertha Klausner (on March 13, 1950); another, *The Concept of Jewish Culture,* I sent to Prof. Melville J. Herskovits of Northwestern University (on June 1, 1950). Much of my time was taken up by attending conferences such as that of the Middle East Institute in Washington on March 17, and the founding conference of the Middle East Social Science Committee on March 18, at which I was elected to the organizing committee. Furthermore, I was signed up with the Jewish Center Lecture Bureau, which resulted in about one lecture a week on the average in New York and places within easy distance, had to write some five or six letters daily, visited or invited friends, attended Zionist gatherings, and, of course, gave my weekly courses at the Dropsie College in Philadelphia.

It was in June, 1950 that I wrote a Hebrew article entitled "Is There a Need for a Second University in Israel?" By arguing that, yes, there was, I became one of the first scholars to advocate the breaking of what amounted to a monopoly of higher education in Israel held by the Hebrew University of Jerusalem. I submitted the article to Menahem Ribalow, editor of the American Hebrew weekly *Hadoar;* however, it was not published until 1954, under the changed title, "Is There a Need for a University in Tel Aviv?" [15]

On June 26, just two days before my daughters arrived, Bertha Klausner went with me to the publishers William Morrow, to whom I handed the outline of my planned book on *Middle East Culture,* and to Appleton-Century, to whom we submitted sample chapters of yet another planned book, *Arab Stories,* and the English translation of the table of contents of my two-volume book *The Science of Man: An Introduction to Anthropology,* which had been published in Hebrew in Tel Aviv in 1948.

Despite this extremely busy schedule, I was so interested in the Graves-Podro manuscript that I put aside all other work and devoted many hours to reading it and commenting on what I felt needed correction or change. I took copious notes while reading, and on June 25, 1950, I summarized them in a long letter to Graves.

Dear Don Robert:

I read the MS you sent me with great interest and profound enjoyment. The story of the birth and life of Jesus as you reconstruct it is plausible and I find myself in agreement with the general line of argument. I have nothing important to add or to detract. I have only one general remark to make to the construction of the book as a whole: in contrast to your King Jesus *which was written in the form of a historical novel and in which therefore you could permit yourself to include statements not always supportable by strictly scientific arguments and data, this book, if I understand your intentions correctly, is structured as a scientific study in which the new conclusions it contains are reached by scientific methods only. The methods mainly utilized in the book are those of interpreting the old texts (NT) in the light of roughly contemporary information derived from a considerable number of other sources; and of reconstructing the probable original version of these texts with the help of these same external data, or by arguing from analogies found in the much older OT text. Also, much of your argument is based on the assumption that if any similarity can be discovered between a situation in which Jesus found himself and a presumably corresponding situation alluded to in the OT, he* must have *behaved more or less exactly like the OT prototype; or that he* must have *used, in the form of either direct quotation or indirect allusion or reference, sayings found in the OT.*

Now, my impression is, and I hope you do not mind my saying so—that the arguments and the ways of reaching the conclusions are not in each case water-tight scientifically. Let me illustrate what I mean by picking out an example from the beginning of the MS.

In ch. I, The Nativity, p. 2, you say, " . . . it is most unlikely that a daughter of a priestly house of Jerusalem would have married a Galilean carpenter, even though he came of the house of David, and impossible if she were an only child . . . " "The Mosaic ban on intertribal marriages (Num. xxxvi, 8–9) when the wife was an heiress continued to be strictly enforced." This ban, the purpose of which, as explicitly stated in Num. xxxvi, 9, was, "No inheritance shall pass from one tribe to another," had no meaning for the Tribe of Levi which had no landed inheritance. Therefore this argument cannot be used as a support for the contention that a priestly daughter could not marry a non-Levite. And, even if many centuries previously the ban had been valid also for the landless tribe of the Levites, where is the proof to show that this ban "continued to be strictly enforced" down to the times of Jesus? Your sentence "It may be postulated therefore that two Mary's were concerned in Jesus's nativity . . . " is therefore not sufficiently established.

Even less basis in the written text has the assumption that Solomon had two mothers (ch. vii, The Annunciation, p. 2). The Biblical passage says quite un-equivocally: "And David comforted his wife Bathsheba, and went in unto her and lay with her and she bore a son and she (thus according to the Qeri *of the Massoretic text) called his name Solomon" (2 Sam. xii, 24). The assumption that Bathsheba was merely the adoptive mother of Solomon and that he had another physical mother is therefore contradicted by this passage and cannot be used as a support for the hypothesis that Jesus too had both a physical and an adoptive mother. But, let me repeat, even if Solomon had two mothers it would still remain to be proved that a thousand years later the same customs still survived.*

Let me write down my remarks in the page order of the MS.

Foreword, p. 3. "Apocalytic sect of Zophim." What are the historical data for the existence of such a sect?

p. 4. "Proto-Zoharic." As the Zohar originated in the 13th Century, it is somewhat far-fetched to call by this name any idea current 13 hundred years earlier.

p. 9. Jesus cannot rightly be called a "successor" of Hillel. "Disciple," I think, would more correctly describe the relationship.

Ch. I, The Nativity, p. 2. Lev. xxvii, 6 has nothing to do with a person being dedicated to Temple Service. *It is simply a statement of the varying amounts to be paid to the Sanctuary in fulfillment of a specific kind of vow.*

p. 7. footnote. Human sacrifice cannot be taken for granted as having been practiced by the ancient Hebrews. The story of Abraham and Isaac shows that though known to them from their neighbors, it was rejected by them at a very early date; and rejected, at that, by the popular sentiment and not by an out-standing teacher, like a prophet. To construe i Sam. xiv, 39 etc. as "an ob-vious trick" of Saul to kill Jonathan, is forced.

p. 7. "heir at law." It is not sufficiently established that such an institution existed among the Jews.

p. 12. Matthew ii, 23 does not necessarily show lack of education. The Bib-lical books Joshua-Judges, i & ii Samuel, i & ii Kings, are called in Jewish tradition "the first prophets," while Isaiah through Malachi are called "the last prophets," though I cannot state at the moment the age of this tradition.

It should also be pointed out in this page for the sake of preciseness that nazir *is spelled in Hebrew with a* zayin, *while* nezer, *or more correctly* neṣer, branch; *noṣri, Nazarene, etc. are spelled with a* tsadé *(the accepted translit-eration of which is* ṣ*), and the two Hebrew roots have no connection whatso-ever with each other.*

p. 15. You dismiss, I think, too summarily the ancient equation of the Re-deemer *and Bread. Nor is it sufficient to attribute the ancient Christian ideas concerning Jesus = Bread to Greek influence. This is a thought-pattern which goes back to very old Oriental ideas. Already Osiris was stated to have* said of himself, "I am the barley," and in the Ras Shamra (Ugarit) texts both Alain Baal and Mot are spoken of as of food. The goddess Anat, it is related there, takes Mot, the son of the gods, splits him with her sword, winnows him in her shovel, burns him in fire, grinds him in the mill and sows him in the field; and finally Mot is eaten. Various old Syrian stories tell the same about Tammuz or Adonis: the god of vegetation, the renewer of the youth of the world, is actually but a symbol of the crops or the fruit; his death is merely the harvesting of the field or the descent of the grain into the womb of the earth, and his resurrection—the sprouting of the grain from the soil. In this case the persistence of these ancient thought-patterns is proved for instance by the fact that in Manichaeism Jesus was believed to have a continued existence in the vegetation; the whole vegetable kingdom was for the Manichaeans Jesus patibilis—Jesus perceptible; and as late as the 10th cent. A.D. an Arab writer tells of Tammuz in connection with his description of the festivity celebrated in Haran in Syria in the month of Tammuz, that the women wept for Tammuz (cf. of course Ez. viii, 14), "for his master killed him in the most cruel fashion, ground his bones in the mill and then scattered them to the wind . . ." And, I do not have to remind you of Sir John Barleycorn who was plown into the soil, cut by scythe and sickle, punctuated and pierced by the pitchfork and finally killed by being ground between two stones.

The idea expressed in the Orphic hymn to Adonis, "eternal food . . . Adonis who blossoms constantly, who dies and shines again . . . ," has its counterpart in the ancient Coptic legend on the origin of wheat: God took part of his own body and made a grain of wheat out of it and stamped it with the stamp with which he had stamped the worlds of light, and then gave it to our Lord (Jesus), and told him to give it to the arch-angel Michael who in his turn must give it to Adam and teach him how to sow and reap wheat . . .

In ancient Israelite religion the idea of the "sprouting God" appeared in two forms: in a popular form (Ez. viii, 14) not different from that which obtained all over the ancient Near East; and in a somewhat modified and refined form, as a frequently recurrent prophetic simile in which, however, not God himself but his messenger, his appointed early representative, the Davidic king, was spoken of as the Sprout, the Branch, the Root (Isa. xi, 1; Dan. xi, 7; Isa. xi, 10 and iv, 2; Jer. xxiii, 5; Zach. iii, 8 and vi, 12–13). It was this sublimated type of imagery which contributed its influence on the NT authors (Rev. v, 5; Matthew ii, 23); though the words of Jesus, "I am the Vine" (John, the exact reference escapes me) are too strongly reminiscent of Osiris' "I am the barley." Paul in his Epistle to the Romans xv, 12, of course quotes Isa. xi, 10 directly. The same idea persists to this day in Negro Africa, where among the Jukun of the Sudan the king is addressed as "our Guinea-corn," "Our ground-nuts," "our Beans," or "our crops."

The persistence of these ideas in Christian Europe was greatly facilitated by the presence of the same thought-pattern in Indo-Germanic mythology. Ac-

cording to a Scandinavian legend, for instance, the mystic Scef (or Sceaf = sheaf) was embedded somewhere—nobody knows where—into a sheaf of wheat in a boat, set out onto the sea, and in this boat, without rudder or sail, he arrived safely at Skandia where he grew to become the benefactor of the people. In the Christian Middle Ages Jesus was spoken of as the Wheat which grew out of the "Marien Acker" (the field Mary) or out of the "sheaf Mary." The life of Jesus thus became symbolic of the fate of the crops: Jesus is the grain of wheat which grew up, became an ear, was reaped, tied, threshed (i.e. afflicted), ground (i.e. crucified), put into the oven (i.e. buried), and three days later taken out, when he satisfied as food hundreds of thousands. In Franche Comté the last sheaf, called "la gerbe de la passion," symbolizes Jesus; it is put on a crucifix and thus carried home. And in innumerable pictures Mary is shown with Jesus under her heart and covered by a mantle embroidered with sheafs of wheat.

I have dealt with this subject in some details in my book Man and Earth in Ancient Hebrew Custom, Belief and Legend *(in Hebrew), vol. I, Jerusalem, 1942, pp. 228ff.*

Ch. V, John's Preaching, p. 2. Isa. i, 20 merely says: "If you refuse . . . by the sword (ḥerebh) will you be eaten . . ." Lev. Rabba s. 35 (and elsewhere) plays on this, explaining "carobs (Ḥarubh) will you eat . . ."

*p. 4 top. abanim—stones and banim—children. Not in Aramaic but in He-*brew. *And Matthew iii, 9 is much more than "a play on words." It is a forceful allusion which all his listeners must have understood, to an ancient Jewish folk-idea: Abraham was the Rock whence the people of Israel were hewn (cf. Isa. 1i, 1–2; explicitly explained by Rashi, David Kimhi and others ad loc.; and referred to already in the Pesikta Zutarta, ed. Buber, parashat Balak 128a). The twelve sons of Jacob, i.e. the twelve tribes of Israel, were symbolized by 12 stones: "Jacob took 12 stones from among the stones of the altar upon which his father Isaac was tied, and put them under his head in that place, to show that 12 tribes were to emanate from him in the future . . ." (Pirke diRabbi Eliezer, ch. 35 at the end; Midrash Shoher Tobh, Ps. 91, ed. Buber, 7; in a simpler version already in Gen. Rabba 68, 11, ed. Theodor, p. 782). These and several other midrashic passages show that the idea that the children of Abraham are symbolized by stones was alive both in centuries preceding and following the times of Jesus. What therefore John said was as follows: "Do not be proud of your descent from Abraham the Rock. Just as once God made the twelve stones of Jacob become twelve sons and twelve tribes, so He is able of these stones again to raise up new children unto Abraham." On the subject "Man and Stone" cf. my* Man and Earth *etc., vol. II, Jerusalem, 1943, pp. 3–64.*

p. 4. Beth-nimrah. The name could have been taken as meaning "House of the leopardess" (namēr = leopard in Hebrew). Cf. my remark, to ch. vii, The Annunciation, p. 4.

Vii. The Annunciation, p. 1. Lev. xxvii, 6: cf. my remark above to ch. I, The Nativity, p. 2.

p. 2. I do not see how one can deduce from 1 Kings ii, 19 that the power of the Queen Mother was so great? Bathsheba came with a seemingly small request and was quite rudely refused and even rebuked by her son Solomon (cf. ib. v. 22). In Ps. xlv, 9 (more correctly 10) the reference is to the Shegal, *which seems to mean spouse, consort of the king, not his mother.*

p. 3. The name Moses. This seems simply to mean in Egyptian: Son. Ramses—Son of Ra; Totmes or Tutmosis—Son of Tot; Moses—Son. He could not be called "Son of . . ." by the daughter of Pharaoh who found him, for she did not know whose son he was. ". . . for out of the water have I drawn him" (Ex. ii, 10) is an obvious Hebrew folk-etymology.

p. 4. "Elliptical form." This is merely the usual, *extremely brief Talmudic style. 80% of the Talmud is written in this style.*

Ben Stada. It seems more correct to read Ben Satda.

Ben Pandera. *I have a tentative hypothesis of my own as to the origin of the name Ben Pandera. Jesus was baptized, as you point out, at Beth-nimrah. Baptism was equivalent to rebirth. The name Beth-nimrah must have been popularly taken as meaning "House of the leopardess." Jesus was therefore scornfully referred to as the one who was reborn (baptized) at the House of the leopardess, or in brief, "Son of the Leopardess." Nimrah, however, being a Hebrew word, popular usage soon substituted for it its colloquial Aramaic equivalent, Panthera (spelled* פנתרה *or* פנתרא *) from the Greek* πάνϑηρ, *panther, or leopard. When the origin of this name was forgotten, as it soon must have been, the spelling was changed and became unsteady:* פנטרא, פנדרא *etc. A certain analogy can be found in the story of Jacob and the angel. Jacob crossed the ford of* Yabbok; *a man (angel) wrestled (*yeabbek *in Hebrew) with him. Consequently his name was changed, but not, as we would expect, to something like* Yabbokel, *but to* Yisrael—*explained by another verbal root,* שרה *sarah, also taken to mean "to wrestle" (cf. Gen. xxxi, 23–29).*

p. 5. Rabbenu Tam, a commentator from the Middle Ages, should not be quoted in one line with Talmudic sages.

VIII. The Coronation, p. 1. "King of Israel," better "of the Jews."

p. 2. the last par. I would prefer if it would be phrased more explicitly, like: ". . . shows that modern African coronation ritual is ultimately derived from an ancient Near Eastern prototype, and that of the 27 rites . . ." etc.

p. 3. Solomon—Yedidya: He was called Solomon by his mother (cf. the Qeri *of 2 Sam. xii, 24) while his father called him Yedidya (ib. v. 25). Both names were given to the child at birth. Analogy: Gen. xxxv, 18: The mother, Rachel, calls her son, also at birth, Ben-oni, and the father, Jacob, calls him at the same time Benjamin.*

The footnote on the names Yehoyakim and Zedekia is not convincing.

p. 3, bottom should read: "Ritual combat omitted in case real fighting goes on." (The ritual combat, after all, is merely a symbolical substitute for real fighting. If there is real fighting in which the king can participate, there is no need for staging a ritual combat).

P. 5. Laming of Jesus. In view of the ritual demand that the king be of unblemished body, this seems improbable.

ib. Dead Sea Scrolls. As my friend and colleague, Prof Solomon Zeitlin of the Dropsie College, has conclusively shown, these scrolls are not pre-Christian, but stem from the Middle Ages. However, you do not need these Scrolls to show that the Bible text has not changed or at least not considerably, since the times of Jesus. Talmudic quotations from the Bible show only minor variations, and also these only infrequently, compared to the present Massoretic text.

p. 6 bottom. Instead of "Carricature-word" why not use the accepted term "cacophemism?" I am, however, not convinced that Beliyaal is a cacophemism for Belili. Beliyaal, by the way, means "without use," "availing nothing," like the German "Taugenichts" (good-for-nothing). It is composed of b'li—without; and yaal, from the verbal root meaning, in such forms as mo'il (יַעֲל) etc., use, avail.

p. 9. The reed in 2 Ki xviii, 21, is not emblematic of Egypt but symbolic of its weakness.

ib. bottom. Cant. iii, 11 should not be adduced as evidence that the king was crowned by his mother. The Canticles are marriage-songs, similar to those sung to this day in the Middle East. The groom in these is always referred to as a king.

p. 13. Garush—chaste. cf. my remark on ch. IX, The ointment, pp. 1–2.

Ch. ix. The Address, p. l, bottom. The ten sayings. Mention could be made in this connection of the Ten Commandments.

The Hebrew character for ten a circle?

ch. X. The Water Pots, p. 3. Corban, correct transcr. Qorban.

ib. bottom. Correct transcr. Yayin hameshummar.

ch. XI. The Ointment, p. 1–2. Shimeon Garba: Why not Parush instead of garush, for which the sense chaste is very forced? Parush, or with the Aramaic article Perusha, would be the Aramaic form for Pharisee, thus corroborating Luke vii, 36.

Another general remark, or better, advice: utilize the great work of Strack and Billerbeck, Kommentar zum NT aus Talmud und Midrash—a storehouse of background information!

I could not check the Talmudic and Midrashic quotations contained in the MS though I would have liked to do it. But that is quite a big job for which I would need more time.

I hope you will find some of the above remarks useful.

Yours most cordially
Raphael Patai

P.S. Are you pleased with your present publishers in America? May I recommend to you the services of Mrs. B. Klausner, Literary Agent, 130 East 40th Street, New York City, who told me just the other day that your book could be "pushed" much more than the Creative Age Press does it.

Graves replied within a few days from the Devonshire village where he was spending the summer.

c/o Watt & Co.
10 Norfolk St.
Strand London W C. 2
July, 1950

Dear Don Rafael:

I am most relieved to hear that you are in general agreement with my thesis; and most grateful for your detailed comments, which I will discuss with Joshua Podro next week. He has already made a long list himself, correcting my solecisms, but this part of our joint book has been my work and I naturally wanted to consult you generally on your own specialized field before he and I compared notes and got the thing into final form.

About the inter-tribal marriages. The Levites were surely not landless in the sense of not being able to own or bequeath land? They had their fenced cities and their estates and no exception is made for Levi in Num xxxvi 9. *So far as I can make out, though there are Talmudic regulations for what families can marry their daughters into Levi, there is no regulation for what families can have Levite daughters married into them. But this is a small point.*

About Solomon's two mothers. Either 2 Sam xii 24 is incorrect, or Solomon was a usurper; this rather complicated but watertight argument is found in the Encycl. Biblica *under* Solomon. *That Bathsheba gave Solomon his name at his coronation seems the genuine nucleus of 2 Sam xii 24. That he had previously been called Yededidiah [Yedediah or Yedidya] by his father underlines the importance of the name given by his mother, which became his true name. The Gen xxv parallel is not close; there the father's name sticks, not the mother's. The text apparently accounts for the change of* Benoni *to* Benjamin, *when Benjamin supplied the royal line. Psalm ii: 'My beloved son, sit thou on my right hand.'*

This brings us to the Canticles *as an authority for installation ceremonies. Yes, they are marriage-songs but 'a bridegroom is like unto a king' and they were early enough to be incorporated into the Pharisaic Canon; and if a bridegroom is like unto a king, so is a king unto a bridegroom; and that* the mother of Solomon *crowned him in his espousals seems to me to be a solid tradition.*

Jesus's lameness. The king had to be unblemished when chosen; as I suggest that Jesus was. After all, Jacob was blemished after *his wrestling & remained king; & in the early days circumcision was a marriage rite and a mutilation. If the candidate was unblemished he could be subjected to ritual mutilation.*

Bathsheba's request in 1 Kings II 19 was not at all a small *one. Solomon rightly saw it as a palace plot in Adoniyah's favour; yet though he killed Adoniyah he continued to treat Bathsheba with respect.*

I like your Banim—abanim business very much; it ties up with Jesus's pillar of twelve disciples; & your leopard derivation of Pandara is pretty convincing.

Zeitlin is alone in his dating of the Scrolls. I am not an authority but all the evidence I have read seems to point to the earlier date unless there's a lot of lying being done.

About Abraham & Isaac and human sacrifice. It is clearly a myth of moral intention:—'This practice must cease.' I know how sensitive Israelites are on this subject because of the libel of Passover murder which has injured them so in the past (By the way, the murders seem to have been done in and for the witch-cult—the 'fiend payed to Hell' every seven years—and blamed on the Jews) But there certainly was human sacrifice among the ancient Israelites, e.g. at Aaron's installation, though this is disguised. And Saul was out for Jonathan's blood, that is clear. However, this is not a point of immediate importance.

Joshua Podro has Strack & Billerbeck *under his pillow & brought them out to Mallorca last April.*

About Jesus & bread. Yes, but the Eleusinian mysteries originally come from Libya; and probably 'I am the bread' is Alexandrian Greek, a syncretism of Greek, Syrian & Libyan myth. I certainly should have mentioned the Osirian corn-king. Jesus, I hold, never said: 'I am the vine.' He may have said: 'Israel is the vine & God the husbandman.'

Finally about Jesus: the more we (Joshua & I) study the gospels, the more we find that in the original tradition Jesus moved like an old-world sacred king bound by so many taboos that he has no room for individual thought. Everything has to be in accordance with the Old Testament—'stick strictly to the script'—which he accepted with complete literalness. All his sayings are midrashim on O.T. texts and only make sense as such; but the Paulines cut out the quotations & often twisted the wording of the midrashim. It was apparently this regal capacity that John noted in him: what nowadays would be called 'a complete lack of humour'. He was intent on being a Hezekiah and more than a Hezekiah: not to diverge a nail's breadth from the Will of God; so naturally he had to base everything on the O.T. Perhaps I should have brought this out more clearly.

The Zophim, or Watchers for the kingdom, are deduced from various N.T. passages, but the argument is given later in our book in the chapter about the disciples from Emmaus. They seem to have been an offshoot of the New Covenanters; based on Bethany and Ramathaim.

It will be a great pleasure to show you the completed book; we have solved all the N.T. cruces, just about. Yesterday we uncovered two Aramaic puns of Jesus's; I knew they were there and bullied Joshua until he worked them out, (They are a good deal better than Isaiah's!) We claim to have recaptured Jesus for the Jews.

Many thanks for Mrs Klausner's address. Excuse the pen. I am in a Devonshire village far from typewriters and books.

It is very good indeed of you to take so much trouble and most encouraging; but, after all, we are both in search of the same set of facts and if I can ever help you in any field or my own, youre welcome.

> *Yours v. sincerely*
> *Robert Graves*

Although in this letter Graves argues against my strictures and defends his positions, when *The Nazarene Gospel* was published I found that in most cases he and Podro took my criticisms into account and modified their final text accordingly. Thus, instead of writing, as they originally did in chapter I. The Nativity, p. 2 (see above, the beginning of my letter of June 25) that "the Mosaic ban on intertribal marriages . . . continued to be strictly enforced," they substituted: "and though the Mosaic ban on inter-tribal marriages (Num. 36. 8–9), designed to keep landed property under the same local authority, had now been repealed by the Pharisees (Ta'anith 30b), it seems to have still kept a certain superstitious force . . . " (*The Nazarene Gospel Restored*, p. 49). While I was not quite satisfied with this formulation either, it was certainly an improvement over the original version.

My objection to the assumption that Solomon had two mothers (see my comment to ch. vii. The Annunciation, p. 2) fared less well. The printed text, although somewhat modified, retains the original position: "Dr. Patai does not mention the importance attached to the king's mother in the royal chronicles of Israel and Judah, nor the fact that Solomon, first called Jedidiah, evidently had two mothers: a physical one, probably Abigail the Carmelitess, through whom (despite 2 Samuel 12:24) it seems that he had a better right to the throne by primogeniture than his rival Adonijah (1 Kings 1:11); and his adoptive mother Bathsheba, who gave him his ritual name 'Solomon.' " In my letter I called Graves's attention to 2 Samuel 12:24, which says unequivocally that David begot Solomon on Bathsheba, but he and Podro disregarded that verse, and instead adhered to the suppositional "two mothers" of Solomon.

In the following I mention the dispositions made by Graves and Podro of my comments under the same headings as they appear in my June 25 letter:

In the foreword, on p. 4, the term "proto-Zoharic" was deleted, but on p. 9 the reference to Jesus as a "successor" of Hillel was retained (see *The Nazarene Gospel Restored,* p. xiv) over my objection.

Ch. I, The Nativity, p. 2. My comment that Leviticus 27:6 is "a statement of the varing amounts to be paid to the Sanctuary in fulfillment of a specific kind of vow" has been incorporated verbatim into a footnote on p. 49 of *The Nazarene Gospel Restored,* but with the qualification that "the first eight verses of this chapter are usually read as laying down the varying amounts," etc.

P. 7, footnote. My stricture that "human sacrifice cannot be taken for granted as having been practiced by the ancient Hebrews" resulted in some modification. The revised text of the footnote reads: "Royal sacrifice of an eldest son in times of crisis was a well-attested practice. Abraham was about to sacrifice Isaac (Gen. 22:2) when prevented. Saul tried to kill Jonathan by a trick [no longer "an obvious trick"] but was given another life in ransom (1 Sam. 14:39–45) (p. 55).

P. 12. Despite what I pointed out in this entry about the Book of Judges being termed in Jewish tradition one of "the first prophets," Graves and Podro retained their condemnation of Matthew as "uneducated" because he used this terminology (p. 59).

On the other hand they revised their original text in the light of my comment, and now spoke of "a punning combination of the unrelated words *Nazara, Nazirite,* and *Netzer* (branch)" (p. 59).

P. 15. Most of the material I assembled in this very long comment on the *Redeemer and Bread* I found incorporated in pp. 62–63 of *The Nazarene Gospel Restored,* which caused me considerable satisfaction, although the text does not acknowledge the authors' indebtedness to me for the rich array of data I supplied, which they compressed into twenty lines.

Ch. V. John's Preaching, p. 4 top. My correction that the pun *abanim*—stones, and *banim*—children was not Aramaic but Hebrew was accepted by the authors and so it appears on p. 85 of their book. They also incorporated into their text my reference to *Pirke diRabbi Eliezer* on the twelve stones that symbolized the twelve tribes that were to spring from Jacob (p. 85).

Ch. VII. The Annunciation, p. 3. My reference to the well-known explanation of the name Moses, as being derived from the Egyptian, meaning "son," was included on p. 96.

Ch. VII, p. 4. *Ben Pandera.* My entire note, except for the reference to the analogy in the story of Jacob and the angel, has been reprinted in *The Nazarene Gospel Restored,* p. 97, as a footnote, beginning with the words, "Dr. Patai writes to us . . . " On the same page they also included by suggested emendation of Ben Stada to Ben Satda.

Ch. VII, p. 5. Following my comment, the reference to the medieval Rabbenu Tam was deleted from the context.

Ch. VIII, p. 1. My emendation "King of the Jews" for "King of Israel" was not accepted (p. 105).

Ch. VIII, p. 2. The phrasing as I suggested was accepted (p. 106).

Ch. VIII, p. 3. Solomon—Yedidya. My reminder that, contrary to what the authors say, Solomon was *not* thus renamed at his coronation, but was given *at birth* the name Solomon by his mother Bathsheba, and the name Yedidya by his father (2 Sam. 12:24-25) was diregarded, probably because it did not fit their theory that the physical mother of Solomon was Abigail, and that Bathsheba was merely his adoptive mother (p. 107).

Ch. VIII, p. 3. My suggestion that point eleven in the list of features comprised in the ancient Hebrew royal installation ritual should read, "Ritual combat omitted in case real fighting goes on," was included, p. 107.

Ch. VIII, p. 5. In not accepting my suggestion that the Dead Sea Scrolls were of medieval origin (p. 109), Graves and Podro proved right. At the time I wrote my June 25, 1950, letter to Graves I was under the influence of my friend and colleague Prof. Solomon Zeitlin, who in oral discussion with me often and convincingly defended his view that the Dead Sea Scrolls were of medieval provenance. Since then it has been proven without doubt that he was wrong, and that the Scrolls indeed date from the time of Jesus or even from the first century B.C.E.

Ch. VIII, p. 6. My suggested substitution of "cacophemism" for "carricature" was accepted, and the meaning of the Hebrew *bli-ya'al,* "good-for-nothing," mentioned in a footnote to p. 110.

Ch. VIII, p. 9. Despite my caution that the reed in 2 Kings 18:21 is not "emblematic of Egypt," but is used as a symbol of Egypt's weakness, the original phrasing was left intact on p. 112.

Ch. VIII, p. 9 bot. My correction about the crowning of the bridegroom referred to as "king" was sidestepped (p. 113).

Ch. IX, p. 1. My suggestion to add a reference to the Ten Commandments was heeded (p. 124). The reference to the circle as the Hebrew character for ten was deleted.

Ch. IX, The Ointment, pp. 1–2. My suggestion to read *parush* ("Pharisee") instead of *garosh* ("One who separates himself from his wife") resulted in the addition of a paragraph, according to which the translator in Luke 7:36 (to which I referred) was baffled by *garosh* and guessed *parusha* (I wrote *Perusha*) (p. 135).

Apart from, and in addition to, these modifications, Graves and Podro quote in extenso what I said in my "Hebrew Installation Rites" about the assumed spiritual rebirth of the ancient Hebrew king at the time of his coronation, which, I found, parallelled the rebirth of African kings on the day of their enthronement. I also pointed out that the ancient Hebrew concept that

86

the Davidic king was the son of God reappeared in the Gospels in the story of Jesus's baptism. I wrote:

> It has already been noted by Hocart that the entering of the spirit of God into the newly anointed king, in consequence of which he "turns into another man," closely corresponds to other peoples' ceremonies which symbolize the death and rebirth of the king. According to Hocart the general theory of the installation ritual is that "the king (1) dies; (2) is reborn; (3) as a god." Traces of the existence of this theory in the Hebrew installation ritual can be found in Psalm 2, which puts the following words in the mouth of God: "I have set up my king upon Zion, my sacred mountain." This statement is answered by the king: "I will declare the statute (?), the Lord hath said unto me, Thou art my son, this day I have born thee . . . " To quote only one African example in which the rebirth of the king on the day of his enthronement, referred to in this Psalm, is most strikingly enacted, let us mention the following detail from the coronation ceremonies of the Atah (the king) of Idah, a state lying in the angle formed by the Niger and the Benue. "Two officers, the Onobe Ogbo, 'the oldest man in the world,' and the Oneda, the 'birth giver,' sport together as man and wife; then the Oneda mimics child-birth, and after a diviner has prophesied that the child will be 'a boy . . . lord of the earth,' the Atah appears from beneath the skirts of the Onede . . . " While noting the parallelism between the African enactment and the Hebrew reference, one must not lose sight of the difference between the African king's ritual rebirth by a court-official, and the Hebrew king's rebirth by God. Though, also in the African installation rite the theory seems to be that the king is "reborn as a son of the gods."
>
> As to the ancient Hebrew concept that the Davidic king is the son of God, there is ample evidence to this effect also in addition to Ps. 2, in the Psalter and in other biblical writings. According to later Jewish tradition the king becomes on the day of his coronation "like a one year old babe who has not known the taste of sin," while the concept that the spirit of God enters into the anointed one so that he becomes the son God, reappears in the Gospels in the baptism-story of Jesus.[16]

In addition to all this, practically the entire Chapter VIII, "The Coronation," in *The Nazarene Gospel Restored* is built on my "Hebrew Installation Rites." The authors quote it at length, including my two lists of a total of thirty-six features which, I argued, were comprised in the biblical Hebrew royal installation ritual, and conclude by stating that "Dr. Patai's list of Old Testament rites should be a trustworthy guide to what happened in Jesus's case. The first of those two lists, summarizing the features I found were part of the Hebrew royal installation ritual, reads as follows:

1. The Hebrew king was conceived of as being reborn at the time of his installation as the son of God.
2. He was dressed in purple royal robes.
3. The prophet or the person functioning as his anointed addressed him.
4. A real fight preceded the king's final installation. The king's (ritual) victory over his enemies is often alluded to.

5. After the initial stage the installation ritual was interrupted for the duration of a week.
6. The king received communion by partaking of a sacrificial meal.
7. He was baptized.
8. He mounted a hill, the Bamah, or the "pillar."
9. The king set up for himself a memorial pillar.
10. He was admonished by the prophet and promised to follow the divine instructions.
11. The king was anointed with oil.
12. The king received, as his regalia, a spear, a shield, etc.
13. The king sat on the throne.
14. The king was crowned.
15. A fire rite took place.
16. The king distributed baker's ware among the people.
17. He made the rounds of his domain.
18. Festivities were held.
19. The king was made the butt of the people.
20. Human sacrifices.
21. Substitute king.[17]

To this I added fifteen more ritual features of ancient Hebrew kingship that had their counterparts in Africa:

1. The king is chosen by both electors and oracle.
2. A high official (priest, prophet) functions at the election as well as at the installation.
3. Animosity or incompatibility exists between this official and the king.
4. The king must be of unblemished body, healthy, strong and beautiful.
5. The king must not defile himself with a dead body.
6. Ceremonial marriage in a special hut.
7. The king marries the widow of his predecessor.
8. The king rides a mount.
9. The king hides, is sought, and found.
10. The "shooting of the nations."
11. Ritual combat omitted in case real fighting goes on.
12. Installation ritual very protracted.
13. Periodical (annual, on New Year's day) repetition of installation rites.
14. Monthly new moon festivals.
15. The king is the chief priest of his people.[18]

Graves and Podro reprinted these two lists in full, made several comments on them, and based on them their reconstruction of the coronation of Jesus.

88

7.

A Scholarly Miscellany

FOLLOWING THIS EXCHANGE of letters about *The Nazarene Gospel Restored* there was a hiatus in the correspondence between Graves and me. He was at the time dominated by (or preoccupied with) the idea that individual women can become temporarily the vehicle of the Goddess, and as such prove irresistible to the "obsessed" Muse-poets of whom he himself was the most conspicuous example. Although Graves did not know it at the time, this idea of his echoed in a way the kabbalistic concept of the Shekhina, the female manifestation of God, who had the ability and the habit of making this or that of her devotees "her chariot." However, the human "chariot" ridden by the Shekhina was always a man, completely devoted to her—I hesitate to say enamored of her—and never a woman who, in her state of possession, would arouse the love of men mystics. (It was not until my 1990 revision of my book *The Hebrew Goddess* that I presented this kabbalistic concept with full documentation.) To Graves's mind, the Goddess would choose a woman who, possessed by her, became the poet's Muse, inspiring him with an overwhelming love, and whipping him to a frenzy of poetic creativity. One of Graves's poems—my favorite—expresses this idea in marvelous numbers:

> This they know well: the Goddess yet abides.
> Though each new lovely woman whom she rides,
> Straddling her neck a year or two or three,
> Should sink beneath such weight of majesty
> ....
> Woman is mortal woman. She abides.[1]

How close Graves the poet was to Graves the historian-scholar can be demonstrated by comparing these lines to what he wrote in *The White Goddess:* "No Muse-poet grows conscious of the Muse except by experience of a woman in whom the Goddess is to some degree resident . . . A Muse-poet falls in love, absolutely, and his true love is for him the embodiment of the Muse."[2]

Such an instrument of the Goddess turned up in Majorca in 1950. Her name was Judith, and Graves became totally smitten with her. He wrote hundreds of letters to her.[3] In these circumstances he obviously had no time to write to me.

As for me, I was busy with so many things that I don't know where to begin to describe them. After the arrival of my two daughters, we suddenly were a large family of five with three girls, a veritable Schubertian *Dreimäderlhaus,* and I was the only one able to communicate with all of them: in English with Irene and Emily, and in Hebrew with Ofra and Daphne. For a month or two much of my time was taken up by functioning as translator for the English and Hebrew parts of the family, and by teaching Ofra and Daphne English, which was essential and urgent, since without at least a smattering of the language they could not have started attending elementary school in the fall. Our small apartment in an apartment house in Kew Gardens, just behind the Queens Borough Hall, suddenly proved cramped. It consisted of a combination living-dining room, a bedroom which doubled as my study, and a second, smaller bedroom in which there was barely enough space for the three beds of the girls.

I also felt pressured to finish the manuscript of my book *Israel between East and West,* and to have it published as soon as possible: it would be my first book to be published in America. I worked on it with great concentration, typed it myself, and before the end of September, 1950, delivered a copy of the typescript to Mr. Harry Starr, president of the Lucius N. Littauer Foundation, with whom I had established friendly relations, and who, I hoped, would support the book's publication with a grant from his foundation.

At the same time I continued my efforts to find work in addition to my position as professor of anthropology at the Dropsie College, where my salary was minimal. I got in touch with faculty members of Yeshiva University to suggest courses on subjects such as "Israel and the Middle East," "The Anthropology of the Jews," and "General and Theoretical Anthropology." In Philadelphia I went to see Prof. Wilton M. Krogman, one of the leading American physical anthropologists, who taught at the University of Pennsylvania and was chairman of the Committee on Physical Anthropology of the National Research Council. I asked his help in organizing a research project on physical anthropology in Israel, which country, I explained, with the huge immigration of Jews from all over the world, was a natural laboratory for such research. Krogman's reaction was positive, even enthusiastic, and he promised to do what he could. Nevertheless, nothing came of this plan.

On December 1, 1950, I drove with Irene to Princeton to visit Einstein. I discussed with him the social and anthropological research project I planned for Israel. It was a long and for me fascinating discussion of which Irene sent a detailed account to my parents in Israel (she took shorthand notes during the visit). Because of this I did not bother to make a record of my own. Regrettably that letter is lost. Einstein promised to help, and suggested that I send him a memorandum. Nothing came of this project either. On the same occasion, while I was in Princeton, I went to see Professors Philip K. Hitti and T. Cuyler Young of the university, and suggested to them that they invite me to give a course or courses on the anthropology of the Middle East. This, at least, became realized in 1952. A few days later, on my way back from Philadelphia to New York, I again stopped at Princeton, and went to see Prof. Alfred Kroeber, who, after his retirement from California, served as visiting professor there, and presented to him my plan for an anthropological research project in Israel. He said he was ready to endorse and support the plan, but ultimately nothing came of this either.

About the same time I met David Remez (1886–1951) for the last time in New York. Remez, the well-known Jewish labor leader and Hebrew poet and editor, was, during the last four years prior to the establishment of Israel, chairman of the *Va'ad L'umi*, the National Council of the Jews of Palestine. He was an old acquaintance of mine with whom, on one occasion, I had spent a whole afternoon in the lovely and sleepy Galilean hilltop town of Safed discussing scholarly and literary issues. Now I made strong representations to him about the Israeli anthropological study project. Encouraged by him, I spent all of December 15 trying to obtain the help of American anthropologists for this project. At 10 A.M. I went to see Margaret Mead at the American Museum of Natural History, and then Prof. Harry Shapiro, Dr. Bella Weitzner, and Dr. Alphonse Riesenfeld in their offices in the same building. At 3 P.M. I went to see Prof. Julian Stewart, and at 4 P.M. Prof. Conrad M. Arensberg, both at Columbia University. Similar meetings and efforts took up much of my time on subsequent days as well. And, of course, each meeting had to be followed up with letters, memoranda, project outlines, and the like. Had I known that nothing would result from all these efforts I would have instead devoted my time to my own research and writing.

For several years thereafter my life was to follow the same course: it was dominated by family concerns, teaching at the Dropsie College, trying to find broader fields of activity, writing books and papers, corresponding, lecturing, meetings with colleagues and publishers, and, despite all these preoccupations, attending conferences, theatrical performances, movies, and concerts.

The above sketch of my busy schedule explains, at least in part, why I was rather negligent in answering letters I received from Graves. If he asked something concrete, I responded without delay. But if the letter contained nothing that required a prompt answer, I delayed writing simply because I had so

91

much else to do. Still, in June, 1951, I wrote him—to my regret this was one of my few letters to Graves of which I did not retain a copy, and the family of Graves with whom I communicated about it in 1988 could not locate the original. Thus I know only from Graves's answer, dated December 10, 1951, that I sent him what he refers to as "the Sleyb story," or possibly only a summary of its content. I cannot recall what that story was about or why I sent it to Graves. In the same letter I also apparently mentioned that I had completed the manuscript of my book *Israel between East and West.*

On July 11, 1951, I went with Irene to visit Israel. I found my mother physically well, but greatly depressed because of the deterioration of my father, who by that time suffered from an advance case of Alzheimer's disease. I myself was shaken by seeing my father in such a condition: all my life I knew him as a man of outstanding talent, a poet and a writer, a cultural leader of Hungarian Jewry for many decades, to whom I had always looked for advice and guidance, who had always been full of love and kindness to me, brimming with energy, the provider and protector of our family . . . And now he was a human wreck, an anguish to behold.

I remember especially one painful scene. The Hebrew poet and novelist Avigdor Hameiri, who in his youth had been a protégé and disciple of my father in Hungary, came to visit my parents. All four of us sat around on the terrace and chatted in Hungarian, Avigdor holding forth in his usual spirited, overly lively fashion, while my father sat by silently, his eyes roaming about, evidently incapable of absorbing what was said. Then, suddenly, he turned to Hameiri, saying to him: "Have you seen Hameiri?" Hameiri was taken aback for a brief moment, and then replied: "What are you talking nonsense! I am Hameiri!" My father looked at him in confusion, and remained silent for the balance of Hameiri's visit.

On July 20th, while we were staying in Jerusalem in the house of my brother Saul, King Abdullah of Jordan was assassinated in the *Ḥaram al-Sharīf,* the "Noble Santuary" mosque complex. His adolescent grandson, the future King Hussein, was at his side, but was unharmed.

All the things I did on that visit to Israel, the steps I again took in the hope of obtaining an invitation to a teaching position at my old alma mater, the Hebrew University, or a research job in some other framework, resulted largely in a disappointing repetition of my experiences in 1949, and can be left untold. But I do want to mention that the lack of success of these efforts contributed materially to my growing conviction that I had to envisage my future career not in Israel but in America. We left Lod airport on August 16, and thirty-four hours later arrived at the Idlewild International Airport in New York. A week later our three daughters returned from Camp Ein Harod at Youngsville, New York, where they had spent the summer.

In September, 1951, I began working for the United Nations Secretariat to prepare a report for the U.N. Economic and Social Council on social conditions in the Middle East. This took two days a week, which meant that I was now prevented from doing my own research and writing four days a week: to the two days I had to spend in Philadelphia teaching at the Dropsie College, were now added two more days at the U.N. Since I nevertheless managed to write a number of studies and book reviews, I must conclude that I must have spent all or most of the remaining three days of the week, including Saturdays and Sundays, glued to my desk.

The year 1951 ended for me with an invitation from Dr. Samuel Blumenfield, president of the Chicago College of Jewish Studies, to serve as professor, with the possibility of being also dean of their graduate division. The salary he offered was considerably more than what I received at the Dropsie College and the U.N. together, and I was tempted to accept the invitation. However, just before I gave my final answer, I got an invitation from Prof. Hitti, head of Oriental Studies at Princeton, to teach a course on the anthropology of the Middle East in his department, and this tilted the balance toward remaining in New York and continuing at the Dropsie College.

In December I got a brief note from Graves, which read:

Dec 10 1951

Dear Raphael Patai—

forgive me—it has been a busy, bad year for me. I never answered your letter of last June, but was much interested by the Sleyb story. The Greeks had an occasional festival of complete promiscuity, incest included, in honour of their less inhibited ancestors . . . Looking forward to your Israel between East and West . . . The Nazarene Gospel is not yet in galleys, but being set up. One day I sincerely hope to meet you & Mrs Patai.

Yours v. s.
Robert Graves

Graves wrote the above lines on a "Merry Christmas and Happy New Year" card which carried a printed reproduction of a seal, under it the legend: "Nativity circa B.C. 1953," and on the reverse: "From an unrecorded Cretan Bead-seal in black steatite, showing the death of the Old Year bull and the miraculous birth of the New Year bull-calf from a date-palm. The Goddess is holding a nativity tree." Under this Graves had written: "Call her Tamar & the calf Jah-Egli. The seal was given me the other day."

The name Jah-Egli (its scientific transliteration would be *Yah-ʿEgli*) means "*Yah* [that is, *Yahweh*] my calf." I believe it was an invention of Graves.

To come back to the "Sleyb story" for a moment, I think it may have dealt with some aspect of the women's status among the Sleyb or Solubba, a low-status, vassal tribe dispersed in small groups in the northern half of the Arabian Peninsula. Their women went unveiled, and some of the men tolerated that their wives prostitute themselves. I discussed the Sleyb briefly in several pages of my book *Golden River to Golden Road: Society, Culture and Change in the Middle East,* whose first edition was published in 1962. But I don't find in it any reference to "occasional festival[s] of complete promiscuity" which could have prompted Graves to mention the similar Greek institution.

In April, 1952, the results of my research for the U.N. were published in a condensed form under the title "Social Conditions in the Middle East," as part of the *Preliminary Report on the World Social Situation.* In accordance with the rules of the U.N. Economic and Social Council, it was published anonymously; only those who worked with me in the Secretariat knew that I was its author. Still, I sent a copy of it to Graves, who responded promptly.

> *Ap 19 1952*
> *Deya*
> *Malorca*
> *Spain*

Dear Rafael Patai—

Many thanks for your interesting pamphlet on the Middle East; but I hope that you are not deserting the field of folklore for modern statistical anthropology.

That Nazarene Gospel Restored *is about to be published by Cassell in England & Farrar Straus in New York; it will make a lot of Christian tiles fall off the roof but I hope cause you & your fellow-Israelis a lot of quiet satisfaction. Your* Installation Rites *were a great help.*

I am now working on a dictionary of Greek mythology & much struck by the close connexion between the myths of Corinth & Palestine; I owe you an apology here—there is a Greek parallel for the Daughters of Lot making their father drunk, which I denied in a letter to you.

> *Yours sincerely*
> *Robert Graves*

The troubles Graves had in finding an American publisher for *The Nazarene Gospel Restored* did not end with its acceptance by Farrar Straus. In fact they reneged, and it was not without considerable difficulty that finally Doubleday accepted it. I think the main reason for the publishers' reluctance to accept the manuscript was, in addition to its unwieldly length, its totally unorthodox approach to the problems of the lost text of the "original" gospel on which Matthew, Mark, and Luke are presumed to be based. In fact, the adverse criticism they feared did not fail to materialize. Doubleday's acceptance of the manuscript was due to a great extent to the interest Ken McCormick, Doubleday's editor-in-chief, took in Graves's work. Even so, Graves had to use his powers of persuasion to convince Ken to do so. In a letter to Ken, Graves argued that Podro was "well known in U.S. Jewry—among whom do not forget Dr.

Raphael Patai . . . '' and would be able to give Ken ''a list of Jewish names'' who would ''approve the argument as new, serious and watertight.''[4]

Although the book did not fulfill Graves's hopes as far as sales were concerned, thereafter Doubleday became the almost exclusive American publisher of Graves's books, whether poetry, fiction, or other.

The ''dictionary of Greek mythology'' Graves mentions at the end of his letter became his highly successful and popular two-volume *The Greek Myths*, published by Penguin Books in London and Baltimore in 1955, and reprinted many times thereafter.

I answered Graves's letter some seven weeks later.

June 17 1952

Dear Don Robert:

It was good to hear from you after such a long time. I was beginning to wonder what was happening to your study on Jesus, and I was glad to hear that it will soon be published. I am eagerly looking forward to reading it in its final form. It is a great source of satisfaction for me to know that you found my ''Hebrew Installation Rites'' helpful.

I was much interested in your remark that you found a Greek parallel to the daughters of Lot. Incidentally, I myself have found another Arab story attributing incestuous origin to an outcast group, and thus paralleling quite closely the Lot and his daughters-story explaining the origin of Ammon and Moab. A British gentleman named Lewis Pelly (who I think was later knighted) visited in the middle of the 19th century Central Arabia and saw there something of the life of the pariah-tribe Sleyb (or Solubba or Sulaib). He reports (in the Journal of the Royal Geographical Society, *vol. 35, 1865, pp. 189–191) the following tradition he found among the Bedouin concerning the origin of the Sleyb whom they regarded as outcasts:*

> *The tradition is that, when Nimrod was about to cast Abraham into the fire, some angels appeared and protected him. Eblis or Satan then made his appearance and pointed out to the bystanders that if someone would only commit a shameful crime, the angels would be obliged to depart, and thus Abraham would be left unprotected. Upon this one of the Arabs lay with his own mother, and forthwith the angels fled. Upon this the angel Gabriel came to the rescue, and changed the spot where the fire was kindled into a garden. The descendants of the man who lay with his mother were, thenceforward, called As-Selaib.*

To this I would like to remark that there is a general tendency among the Arabs to slight an enemy or adversary or a despised group, by casting doubt on the legitimacy of their origin. On the other hand, I find in my notes a reference to Strabo xvi, 4, 25, which I cannot check at the moment, and according to which the Nabateans who were an ancestral group of the present-day Arabs, recognized marriage with a widowed mother. The tradition about the origin of the Sleyb could, therefore, merely reflect an old custom which today of course, appears as incestuous.

As you see, even though concentrating on the anthropological study of the Modern Middle East, I occasionally come across folkloristic gems. I am now working on a Handbook of Middle Eastern Anthropology (including North Africa, in accordance with my definition of the area in the Middle East Journal. *Much has been written on the Middle East, but very little on its culture in the wide anthropological sense. I hope my book will fill this lacuna. My book* Israel Between East And West, *a study of the present-day cultural and social problems of Israel, will be published by the Jewish Publication Society of America in January, 1953. Farrar Straus originally planned to publish this book jointly with the Jewish Publ. Soc., but when it came to signing the contract they wanted to take such a small number of copies that the Jewish Publ. Soc. rather kept also the general distribution for itself.*

Last summer my wife and I visited my family in Israel. We flew twice over the Mediterranean and we both would have liked to stop down at Mallorca. This summer we will spend here in New York working, my wife on a novel on the prophet Hosea (you can imagine how much fun I shall have making her stay within historical probabilities), and I working on my Middle East book and preparing my courses for Princeton University where I shall start teaching next fall.

Yours sincerely
Raphael

The handbook of Middle Eastern anthropology I mention in this letter never materialized. In fact, soon thereafter I gave up working on it altogether, and concentrated instead on a number of papers. Among them was a long essay in Hebrew entitled "Birth in Popular Custom," in which I presented part of what I originally intended to form several chapters in the third volume of my Hebrew book, *Man and Earth in Jewish Custom, Belief and Legend,* the first two volumes of which were published by the Hebrew University Press in 1942–43. My birth study was published in three installments in the Hebrew scholarly yearbook *Talpioth,* edited by Samuel K. Mirsky.[5] Late in 1952 was published my paper "The Middle East as a Culture Area,"[6] which was at the time considered a breakthrough in applying to the Middle East the culture area concept originally developed by American anthropologists in connection with studies of American Indian cultures and their spatial distribution over the two American continents. In my paper I outlined the major cultural features that were to be found all over that huge world area loosely called the Middle East, stretching from Morocco and Rio de Oro in the west to Afghanistan and Beluchistan in the east. Later I was to refine this concept, renaming the Middle East a "culture continent," and delimiting twenty-three culture areas I was able to isolate within it. This subsequent paper was published as the lead article in the volume *The Nomadic Alternative: Modes and Models of Inter-*

action in the African-Asian Deserts and Steppes.[7] In addition to these, I also wrote several other papers in Hebrew and English, as well as quite a number of book reviews.

About the same time, at my suggestion, Irene started working on a novel on the Prophet Hosea, whose relationship with his adulterous wife Gomer made him a natural for a historical novel. I gave Irene as much guidance as I could in biblical matters, and it was published in 1956 by Random House under the title *Valley of God*.

Finally, in September, 1953, the printing of *The Nazarene Gospel Restored* was completed, and Jason Epstein, the Doubleday editor in charge of the book, wrote to me to ask whether I was willing to see an advance copy of it. "We would like very much," he wrote, "to have your opinion of it, and naturally we feel that any recommendation you might give would help us present this very important book to the American public." Unfortunately, Epstein did not trouble to find out where I lived, and addressed the letter to "Dr. Raphael Patai, University of Jerusalem, Jerusalem, Israel." The letter was forwarded by the Hebrew University to my New York home address (by that time I lived in Forest Hills). Looking at the date of my reply I see that, surprisingly, it took the letter less than two weeks to make the round trip across the Atlantic and the Mediterranean. I replied to Epstein:

October 11, 1953

Dear Mr. Epstein:

Your letter of September 28 was forwarded to me from Jerusalem to my New York home address. I was very glad to read in it that my friend Robert Graves' The Nazarene Gospel Restored *will be published by you in the early spring.*

As you undoubtedly know, having read the manuscript, a major part of the book's argument is based on an anthropological study of mine published in this country in 1947. I also had some part in shaping the manuscript which was sent to me by Robert Graves some two years ago and on which I commented extensively. All this makes me doubly interested in seeing this important book in its final shape.

Needless to say, I shall be glad to read an advance copy of the book and to let you have my reaction to it in one or two paragraphs which you may wish to utilize for inclusion in a folder or on the dust-cover of the book itself. I shall also be more than willing to review the book. I have in mind especially the New York Times Book Review. *Please feel free to suggest my name as reviewer to its editor, or, for that matter, to the editor of any other forum you may think of.*

Sincerely yours,
Raphael Patai

Please direct all future communications to my New York home address.

97

Epstein replied immediately.

October 13, 1953

Dear Professor Patai:

It was very good to hear from you so soon about Robert Graves' new book, THE NAZARENE GOSPEL RESTORED, *and as soon as we have a reading copy I will send you one. I am writing now to England for bound galleys, which I should receive within a few weeks, and I will send you on of these, too, in the event that you would like to read the book in this form.*

I am sorry to say that publishers have very little influence in placing reviews of their books with journals such as the New York Times Book Review. However, if the occasion does arise to mention your name to the editor of that paper or to the editor of an equally important paper, I will certainly do it. In the meantime I would suggest that you approach an editor on your own with the request the you review Mr. Graves' book. Certainly nothing would please Mr. Graves and us more than to have your comments on his book made public. Thank you very much.

Sincerly yours,
Jason Epstein

Epstein also sent a copy of my October 11 letter to Graves, who thereupon wrote to me.

Oct 28 1953

Dear Raphael Patai:

Doubleday forwarded me a copy of your answer to their propaganda on behalf of the Nazarene Gospel; *thank you very much for your undertakings.*

Joshua Podro & I were glad to avail ourselves of your researches into the sacred kingship at Jerusalem, because it is the most startling suggestion in our whole exegesis that Jesus was installed in the antique style. (You hinted at it very discreetly yourself) Though of course he couldn't have been a Messiah if he hadn't. We are very grateful to you for making our theory respectable, in fact!

The rest of the book will I hope please you. Prof. Moses Hadas has given it a clean bill of health which really is something because he knows his Hebrew antiquities & is also Professor of Classics—a most unusual combination. There may be minor flaws in our argument; there must *be minor flaws in our argument. But it is the first book on this painful subject—and really it is a painful story—to attempt a historical explanation of all the cruces with chapter & verse in every crux case, and we have certainly found a lot of new but obvious things which will be very difficult to set aside historically even though*

*they will remain as small print footnotes to orthodox commentaries for a de-
cade or two. Joshua Podro is a marvel of industry and fortunately has no
chair to lose by speaking plainly: he is the manager of the largest British
Press-cutting agency and turns all the profits into* Hebraica *for his private library.*

*It really is about time that the whole question of the Gospels was cleared
up; & the queer thing is that the editorial forgeries haven't been exposed before. My main intention (to be frank) has been to apologize to the Jews for the
cruel libels fastened on them by my ecclesiastical ancestors; Joshua's has
been to rid his mind of the unhappiness caused to him in childhood by Eastern
European pogroms—by being reasonable, generous and loyal in his statement
of what he thinks really happened. He has several times asked me to moderate
my bitterness in our collaboration, but about St. Paul it has been difficult to
be gentle.*

Yours v. s.
Robert Graves

One day we shall meet.

*I have just completed a dictionary of Greek myths (about 400,000 words)
for Viking Press. My approach has been historical and anthropological. I find
anthropologists my favorite class of scientists: it is in fact the basic science.
And I find books like Eve Meyerowitz's* Akan Kingship *extraordinarily helpful
as a sidelight on Greek myths.*

That I left this generous and revealing letter without an answer I can only
attribute to pressure of work, worries, and the blow or my father's death. On
February 22, 1953, I received a cable from my sister Evi from Israel notifying
my that our father had died the day before. Although I had expected that his
end would come soon after I last saw him in Givatayim in the summer of
1951, I was shaken. The fact that for more than five years prior to his death
I had practically no contact with him, and that his last illness rendered him
less than a shadow of his former self did in no way alleviate the sorrow. I
remembered him then, and still remember him today, nearly forty years later,
as he was before his illness, and what he was for me throughout the first
thirty-seven years of my life: the man to whom I owed not only my existence,
but also my roots, my identification with the Jewish past, and the choice of
my life's work. As soon as I got my sister's cable, I called her and my mother
on the phone, and told my mother that we all wanted her to come to us as soon
as she felt up to the trip. Her visit to America never materialized, but I went
to see her in Israel many times, until she passed away in 1976 at the age
of ninety.

On April 4, 1953, I received the first copy of my *Israel between East and
West*—my first book published in America! The publication of this book

resulted in an increased number of invitations to lecture to universities and Jewish organizations. By this time I had become an experienced and popular speaker, one whose lectures were invariably very well received and more than once greeted with a standing ovation.

On June 7 the psychoanalyst Dr. Warner Muensterberger called me to tell me that our mutual friend Dr. Géza Róheim had died during the night, and that prior to his death he had expressed the wish (or possibly the request was in his will, I no longer remember exactly) that at his funeral somebody should eulogize him in Hungarian. As his joint executors, Muensterberger and Dr. Sándor Lóránd, a leading New York psychoanalyst also of Hungarian origin, wanted me to undertake this function. I, of course, agreed, and on June 10 I spoke at Róheim's funeral, which took place at Campbell's Funeral Church on Madison Avenue.

I had liked Róheim very much. I first met him at a Viking Fund supper conference in 1947 or 1948, and we became friends. He was a rotund man with a large and very round head and even larger and very round embonpoint, with a peculiar stance of chest stuck out, shoulders pulled back, and chin pressed down. He always made the impression on me of looking as the angelic *putti* of Renaissance paintings would look were they allowed to grow up and reach a well-nourished old age. I often visited him in his home on Central Park West, and enjoyed the rich Hungarian cooking of Mrs. Róheim. Róheim was the most devoted husband I ever met. He was, I believe, the first scholar to combine Freudian psychoanalysis and anthropological field techniques, and several of his books are classics to this day. He was a witty and outspoken conversationalist, whose sharp comments were not to everybody's liking. On one occasion, I remember, when I expressed doubt about the universality of the Oedipus complex, he pushed his chin down and said in a stentorian tone: "In every culture where people say, 'Fuck your mother!' there is the Oedipus complex!" Róheim and his wife died within a few days of each other.

On June 17, 1953, after living for almost two years in rather cramped quarters in Kew Gardens, I purchased a seven-room one-family house at 197 Puritan Avenue, in the Forest Hills Gardens.

That summer I worked on a paper for the *American Anthropologist,* and on another for a Colloquium on Islamic Culture that was planned for September by Princeton University jointly with the Library of Congress. I was invited to participate by Dr. Bayard Dodge. About the same time Prof. Abraham Katsh of New York University invited my to give a course on Israel in the fall of 1953. By July 3 I had completed the second installment (one hundred typewritten pages in Hebrew) of my study of Jewish birth customs for the journal *Talpioth.* I spent the week of July 13 to 17 painting the Puritan Avenue house, and a few days later we moved in.

In September, 1953, Irene and I spent a few days as guests of Prof. Bessie B. Wessel in New London, Connecticut. I was invited to lecture at Connecticut College, and while there tried to obtain funds for the establishment of a visiting professorship, and eventually a chair, for Mrs. Wessel at one of the universities of Connecticut, since the date of her retirement from Connecticut College was drawing near. The day after our return home I started out again and drove to Princeton to attend the Colloquium on Islamic Culture, to which I was scheduled to deliver a paper on "Culture Change in the Muslim Town." I stayed in Princeton from September 8 to 12, and then from September 17 to 20, in Washington, where the Colloquium continued at the Library of Congress. I delivered my paper, met quite a number of scholars from various Muslim countries as well as American Arabists and students of the Middle East. Among the former was Prof. Halil Inalcik of the University of Ankara who asked me whether I would be interested in an invitation to teach Middle Eastern anthropology at the University of Ankara as a visiting professor. I was, and at his suggestion I sent him a *vita* which he wanted to forward to Ankara. I also met Dean Mohammad Khalafallah of the University of Alexandria, Egypt, whose idea was that I might come to Alexandria on a Fulbright Scholarship to teach Middle Eastern anthropology there. Subsequently Khalafallah edited the proceedings of the colloquium in an Arabic translation under the title *al-Thaqāfa al-Islāmiyya wal-Ḥayāh al-Muʿāṣira,* which contains my paper in Arabic.[8] My name in Arabic transcription read *Rafāʾīl Bātāy.*

Also that September I began my new teaching assignment at Princeton on Middle East Culture, and at New York University on the ethnic composition of Israel. On the basis of my talk with Dean Khalafallah I wanted to submit an application for a Fulbright Fellowship to enable me to teach at the University of Alexandria, but Prof. Hitti, my chairman at Princeton with whom I discussed the idea, opined that first he would inquire whether I would be granted a visa to Egypt, which was a prerequisite for a Fulbright for that country. A week later Hitti informed me that he had spoken to Muhammad al-Zayyat of the Egyptian Embassy in Washington, who had told him that, to his great regret, the present policies of the Egyptian government did not enable him to grant me a visa. Although by that time I was an American citizen, my Israeli background seemed to have been sufficient for the Egyptian authorities to rule out in advance the possibility of granting me a visa. Thus there was, of course, no point in applying for a Fulbright grant for Egypt.

On October 20, 1953, Dr. Abraham Neuman, president of the Dropsie College, told me that unless the situation improved at the Institute for Israel and the Middle East, the department of Dropsie within which I gave my courses (that is to say, unless the registration increased), the institute would have to be discontinued, which would mean the end of my work. To prevent such a development, he asked me to take care of publicity for the institute. This was very disquieting news, for despite my other teaching assignments, and income from articles and lectures, my main, and only permanent, source of income was from my Dropsie salary, meager though it was. To engage in efforts

101

to publicize the Institute for Israel and the Middle East meant an additional work burden.

Motivated by this glum outlook, I spoke on October 28, 1953, to Hitti, who always was most friendly and forthcoming, and asked him to suggest to the planning committee of the Princeton department of Oriental languages and literatures to add next year an undergraduate course on peoples and cultures of the Middle East. He promised to take up the matter, which he did, but in the event nothing came of this initiative.

About the same time I started to take increasing interest in the embryonic Tel Aviv University, and met with several professors and financial people to discuss what could be done to advance its cause.

While I was in Washington on November 30, 1953, in connection with a lecture I gave at the Library of Congress to a large audience, my friend Allan Lesser asked me whether I would be interested in the position of national director of the B'nai B'rith Institutes for Judaism. I said I would certainly consider it, and he offered to talk about it to the powers that be at the B'nai B'rith. He did, in fact, make his recommendation to Maurice Weinstein, both orally and in writing, but nothing came of this either.

On December 14 I renewed my efforts to be invited to teach an introductory course of anthropology at Yeshiva University, and discussed the matter with Prof. Guterman, Acting Dean of its College department.

I went to see Prof. Baron of Columbia on December 21, after receiving a telephone call from him, and he offered me a course on the anthropology of Israel and the Middle East within the framework of Columbia's Center of Israeli Studies, which he headed. My title would be lecturer, and the course a two-term, two hours weekly one.

On January 2, 1954, Irene and I gave a party in honor of Eliezer Livneh (formerly Liebenstein). This gave me the opportunity to talk to him about the suggestion made by some of my friends that I should be appointed president of Tel Aviv University. Livneh promised to talk to Hayyim Levanon, the mayor of Tel Aviv. On January 5, in Philadelphia, I discussed the chances I had of getting that position with Aharon Ben-Shemesh, an influential attorney from Tel Aviv who, although in his fifties, was my doctoral student at the Dropsie College. He promised to recommend me most warmly to Mayor Levanon, but ultimately nothing came of this either. On January 8 I asked my friend Robert Ehrich, professor of anthropology at Brooklyn College, to help me get a position there.

As shown by the above listing of the steps I took to find additional work, I was basically dissatisfied with my position at the Dropsie College. I had several reasons: the salary was poor, my course offerings were limited by the narrow framework of the college, the number of my students was small, and my future in the college was uncertain. This being the case, I always felt that my chief interest was not in teaching at Dropsie, but in research and writing.

While all this was going on in my professional life, my family life was no more tranquil. We received almost every week a phone call from Jack Pall, Irene's former husband and Emily's father, about his meetings with his daughter, to which he was entitled legally. These phone calls invariably deteriorated into arguments and recriminations between him and Irene, whose anger and bitterness often spilled over into her relationship with me.

On February 14, 1954, I gave a public lecture to the Jewish Community Center of Princeton, "The Cultural Problems of Israel." In the audience was Dr. Immanuel Velikowsky, author of *Worlds in Collision,* which I had read shortly before, and with which I was greatly impressed. After the lecture Velikowsky came up to me, and we had a long chat about the Israelites' passage through the Red Sea, which in his book he connected with the great planetary event he postulated.

Despite these and other distractions, I started to work on a new study, which I tentatively titled "Comparison of Cultures," and which, by February 1954, looked as if it would grow into a book. On March 1 I asked Harry Starr for a grant from the Littauer Foundation to enable me to finish it.

Also in February I met several times Rabbi Amram Blau, an old friend of mine from Jerusalem (of Hungarian origin), now chief rabbi of Argentina. I told him I would like to visit Argentina, and he readily undertook to arrange for an invitation to me to lecture there. I still remember that he was full of praise of Argentina and the Perons.

On March 3, 1954, upon the recommendation of Prof. Baron, I was asked by Dr. Simon Segal of the American Jewish Committee to prepare for their Ad Hoc Committee on Israel a thirty-forty page research paper on such Israeli issues as acculturation, minorities, educational trends, church and state, etc. I accepted the assignment, and delivered on June 1 a paper entitled "Acculturation in Israel," which they mimeographed and distributed. This study, which never appeared in print, still has value, I believe, because it paints a picture of Israel as it was seven years after its establishment.

On March 9 I had a long discussion with President Neuman of the Dropsie College on two issues. One was the appointment of a professor of Arabic to take the place of Prof. Solomon Skoss, who had died a few months earlier. I recommended my old friend Meir Bravmann, an outstanding Arabist, whom I had first met during my sophomore year in Breslau in 1930–31, when we were both students of the great Carl Brockelmann. In the event Bravmann did get the position. The other subject was my own status and salary at Dropsie. I told Dr. Neuman that my salary was inadequate, which he admitted, and added: "If I were in a position to pay you a full salary . . . , I would require that you live in Philadelphia." And there the matter rested, at least for the time being.

On March 29 I asked Dr. Paul Fejos, director of the Wenner-Gren Foundation for Anthropological Research (formerly the Viking Fund, a fellowship from which had brought me to America in 1947) to give me a grant of three thousand dollars for the completion of my study on comparison of cultures. He promised he would "push it" in the board of the foundation, but—nothing came of it.

All this while Irene, who had taken a leave from the New York City high school where she taught, was spending most of her time working on her Hosea novel. On April 1 she finished the typescript, and I delivered it to the secretary of Dr. Hiram Haydn of Random House, who had shown interest in the novel, and, as I was later to find out, in its author.

The same day I met Harold Weintraub of the Syosset Jewish Congregation, and discussed with him the possibility of taking a so-called "weekend rabbinical position" which involved nothing more than functioning as rabbi at their synagogue at the Friday evening and Saturday morning services. For this they offered a salary I could not accept; I asked for more—and there the matter rested.

On April 5, chatting with my Dropsie colleague Prof. Solomon Zeitlin, I found out that he was an old friend of Zalman Shazar (who later was to become the president of Israel). Thereupon I promptly asked Zeitlin to recommend me to Shazar for the position of director of the cultural and educational activities of the Jewish Agency in the United States, a position that was being relinquished by its incumbent. Next day I asked Mordechai Halevi, director of the American *Histadrut Ivrit* (Hebrew Association), to write to Shazar for the same reason. Both Zeitlin and Halevi promised to do as I asked, but without any result.

On April 9, at the weekly supper-conference of the Wenner-Gren Foundation, I had a long talk with Prof. F. S. C. Northrop of Yale about my planned study of a comparative evaluation of cultures. As I had expected from being familiar with Northrop's own studies touching upon this subject, he expressed doubts about the possibility of finding the absolute yardsticks that would have to be utilized in such an attempt. "How about general satisfaction with the culture in which people live?" I asked. His reply was a scathing "If you use that as a yardstick, you would have to conclude that the culture in which American businessmen live was the highest in the world!" Northrop's negative view of American culture, even in comparison with what he called "the rich culture of Mexico," was well known to me, so that his comment did not come as a surprise.

On April 19 I wrote to Mayor Levanon of Tel Aviv about the Tel Aviv University, and sent copies of my letter to several people in New York who had shown interest in it.

On May 18 Dr. Neuman finally agreed to raise my annual salary on condition that I would move to Philadelphia by the fall of 1955.

On June I wrote to the Geography Branch and the Human Relations Branch of the U.S. Office of Naval Research in Washington suggesting the publication of a series of monographs on Middle Eastern countries.

By the year 1954 the constant search for additional teaching positions and research assignments had become a regular part of my daily life.

8.

Reviews of *The Nazarene Gospel Restored*

O N JULY 16, 1954, I was surprised to read in the *New York Times* that *The Nazarene Gospel Restored* had been published by Doubleday. Although Jason Epstein had wanted to send me the galleys for review, he evidently had forgotten to do so. I sent him a note.

July 16, 1954

Dear Mr. Epstein:

I read in the New York Times *that the book of Robert Graves and Podro, The Nazarene Gospel Restored, was published by you yesterday. And this morning's mail brought me a request—which probably will be followed by other similar ones—from the Kansas State College, for a copy of my "Hebrew Installation Rites" on which, as the writer states, The Nazarene Gospel Restored "depends heavily in parts."*

You will recall that last fall you wrote to me that you would send me the galleys of the book so as to enable me to make my comments public when the books appears. I waited for this in vain.

Now that the book has been published, I am sure that my friend Don Robert will want you to let me have a copy. I am greatly looking forward to receiving this, and, needless to say, I shall seek the opportunity of publishing my comments on the book in one of the magazines to which I regularly contribute book reviews.

Yours sincerely
Raphael Patai

Jason Epstein replied:

July 19, 1954.

Dear Mr. Patai:

I am very sorry that the galleys of Robert Graves' book never reached you. I am sending you a copy of the book itself this after-noon.

I am very happy to know that you will contribute a review of this book to one of the magazines for which you regularly write.

Again I am apologetic.

Yours sincerely,

Jason Epstein

I no longer remember whether I tried to place a review in any of the scholarly journals, but the only review of which I can find a clipping in my files is the one published in the Fall 1956 issue of *The Chicago Jewish Forum*. Its editor, Benjamin Weintroub, had asked me quite some time earlier to contribute book reviews regularly to his quarterly and gave me a free hand in selecting the books for review. Since, on the other hand, I frequently received review copies of books from publishers and authors, about several of which I felt I had something to say, I did from time to time send in reviews to Weintroub, which he unfailingly published, even though occasionally only after considerable delay. My view of *The Nazarene Gospel Restored* was summed up in the first sentence of my review:

"Robert Graves, one of the greatest historical novelists of our times, has collaborated with Joshua Podro, a Jewish scholar, in producing this monumental book, which presents Jesus as a devout Jew who, with only minor reservations, held the Pharisaic attitude toward Mosaic Law, who never equated himself with God, and who, although he performed certain acts of faith-healing in God's name (as other Jewish rabbis of the period had done), neither did nor suffered anything that lay outside human experience."

After describing briefly my role in the development of the book, I observed that even though some disagreements were ironed out in correspondence between Graves and me, my careful perusal of the finished product revealed numerous instances of what I regarded as factual or linguistic errors. Then, moving on to general observations, I noted that the authors' most frequently employed method of interpretation was to show that passages in the Gospels were "*midrashim* on" passages found in the Hebrew Bible, and that "as a result the entire life story of Jesus appears as a series of conscious efforts to re-enact and dramatize the Old Testament," and primarily those prophecies which refer to the hoped-for Anointed (Messiah) of God, the expected spiritual and temporal Lord. This method, I observed, greatly helped the authors in restoring the original wording of the Gospel, since they assumed that its original text must have corresponded more closely than its later emendation to the Old Testament passage on which it is a *midrash*. I commended the authors on their solid scholarship, their competent utilization of Hebrew, Aramaic, Syriac, Greek, Latin, etc., sources, and concluded by saying that their approach "bursts the conventional restraints of commonplace, plodding and pedestrian scholarship," in which lies "the fascination of this volume."

As for the reviews issuing from the pens of New Testament scholars, their critical reception was, in general, not favorable. As Graves's biographer, Martin Seymour-Smith, put it, at that time "no bishop, whatever his personal view, could have dared to do other than condemn it as blasphemous."[1] After all, here was a book that propounded such heretical views as that Jesus was a grandson of Herod, that he was throughout his life a devout Jew, that he never made any claim to divinity, that he was lame, that he survived the crucifixion, and that his disciples, and in the first place Paul, "were guilty of falsifying Jesus's own doctrine by the publication of tendentious Greek Gospels."[2] A sampling of the reviews will show the indignation with which *The Nazarene Gospel Restored* was greeted in many circles.

The March, 1954, issue of the London *Journal of Theology* carried a largely negative review by C. S. C. Williams of Merton College, Oxford. He panned the book for reading "more like propaganda than argument," for speaking of the "Gnostic Trinity' but not giving any reference to what this "Gnostic Trinity" was, nor "any proof that if it existed it was more than a triad," and for not explaining "why if Jesus was no more than a misunderstood Pharisee anyone should have troubled to crucify him." Williams reproached the authors for refusing to "admit that Jesus was worshiped as Maran, our Lord, from the days of the primitive Aramaic speaking community," and for treating the four Gospels, the Talmud, the Apocryphal Gospels, and the Logia "as of equal value as evidence for the first century of our era." He concluded his review with a quote from the book, evidently to show the absurd lengths to which it went: "If these findings are accepted, historically minded Protestants will conclude that only one honest course is left for them: namely to revive Jesus' own form of Judaism, and subject themselves to circumcision and the law of ritual cleanliness in token of their sincerity."

The *Hibbert Journal* (52:315, April, 1954) termed *The Nazarene Gospel* a "misapplication of learning in defense of an extremely improbable thesis."

The *Kirkus Review* (22:308, May 1, 1954) fulminated: "The authors throw out of the window all of the work of Catholic and Protestant New Testament scholars. It is a controversial book which however is not apt to be taken seriously by Catholics or Protestants and will serve chiefly to provide faulty ammunition for attacks on Christian faith."

R. M. Grant, writing in the *Christian Century* (71:555, May 5, 1954), stated: "This fantastic book is the product of misdirected ingenuity unchecked by the faintest trace of common sense."

G. W. Wakefield, writing in the *Library Journal* (79:1049, June 1, 1954), admitted that the book was "undoubtedly a brilliant work of scholarship," but then followed up this compliment by saying that ''but the Gospel according to Graves and Podro will to most readers, I'm sure, seem hardly authentic enough to adopt.''

William F. Albright in the *New York Herald Tribune Book Review* (p. 8, July 18, 1954), opined that ''the book cannot be called an historical study; it is rather a novel rewriting of New Testament tradition, based largely on rabbinic sources,'' and took the authors to task for not evaluating critically those rabbinic sources but treating them instead ''as quarries from which to collect speculative building blocks.''

A bitingly sarcastic review was published in *Time* magazine (July 26, 1954). In its very first paragraph the reviewer wrote: ''When a crank has the reputation and writing ability of Novelist Robert (*I, Claudius*) Graves, publishers are glad to let him run on for page after page.'' Later in his review he stated: ''The foursquare Gospel discovered by Graves & Podro purports to be the Word as it was before the Gentiles began to monkey with it.'' And he concluded by quoting the same sentence from the book with which Williams had ended his review. Graves responded to the *Time* review with a brief letter in which he congratulated *Time* ''on a splendidly clean scythe sweep or hatchet job,'' and asserted that '' 'Crank' Robert Graves'' had not yet been ''caught out in any historical blunder'' which would have invalidated his findings, ''though he dared tempt British New Testament experts with valuable money prizes if they could spot one.'' Then he quoted from the review written by ''leading U.S. Protestant Theologian Dr. Reinhold Niebuhr'': ''The authors have labored so diligently and within the limits of their presuppositions so honestly, that the volume will be of great service to both Christians and Jews if they have the time to read so large a volume and the money to pay for it.'' *Time* duly published Grave's letter (in August, 1954), but tried to counterbalance it by another letter, printed right below it, which called the book a ''sacrilegious work.''

One of the first positive reviews of the book was written by Moses Hadas, John Jay Professor of Greek at Columbia University, recognized as doyen of American classical scholars, who was also an authority on Jewish studies (he had a rabbinical diploma from the Jewish Theological Seminary of America). In his review, published in the *New York Times Book Review* July 18, 1954), Hadas wrote: ''The argument is ingenious to the point of brilliance, sufficiently buttressed by wide learning to be plausible.'' Then he remarked: ''In its approach (though not in its close and systematic treatment,) [*The Nazarene Gospel Restored*] is analogous to that of Graves' 'Claudius' novels. There, too, evidence which professional scholars had rejected was made to support an ingenious reconstruction.''

Even more appreciative was the review written by Robert Weltsch in the August 16, 1965, issue of *Congress Weekly*, the organ of the American Jewish Congress. Weltsch was the noted former editor of the Berlin *Jüdische*

109

Rundschau, in whose April 1, 1933, issue he had written a spirited article titled "Tragt ihn mit Stolz, den gelben Fleck" ("Wear it with Pride, the Yellow Badge"), which had become the inspiring slogan for German Jews groping, after the assumption of power by Hitler, for their way back to Jewish values. In his review Weltsch found that *The Nazarene Gospel* "obviously [had] the most profound implication not only for Christians and the church, but for the Jewish people as well," because it had become overwhelmingly evident that all efforts to promote greater Christian-Jewish understanding must be founded on a revision of the crucifixion story which assigns the responsibility for Jesus' death to the Jews. This, Weltsch asserted was what Graves and Podro had undertaken. "From the point of view of establishing better relations between Jews and Christians, the book by Graves and Podro can serve as a most important tool."

Weltsch also referred to reviews of the book written by expert theologians who viewed it as "an attack on the whole framework of their profession," expressed his sympathy with the authors, and voiced astonishment that even the so-called "left" periodicals, such as the *Manchester Guardian* and the *New Statesman and Nation*, which had no religious ax to grind, attacked the book so vehemently. Weltsch himself took to task the hostile critics for focusing on minor details and ignoring the larger outlines, and emphasized that the main arguments of the book had not been demolished even by the most negative critics. Those arguments included: that the messianic sect led by Jesus was one of twenty-four sects mentioned in the Jerusalem Talmud and had nationalistic aspirations; that Jesus himself was a Jewish nationalist and an enemy of the Romans; that the Nazarene movement was faithful to Pharisee doctrine in every respect; and that the Gospels, in their extant form do not reflect the Nazarene movement, but its breaking up by Paul.

While this was going on on the literary front, Graves and Podro became involved in litigation with the London *Times*. This came about as follows. In the *Times Literary Supplement* of February 19, 1954, was published a lengthy, rather vicious, review of *The Nazarene Gospel Restored*. In it the anonymous reviewer attributed to Graves and Podro "tendentious alterations of the evidence," "misrepresentation of the evidence," "extravagant insinuations," and the like. Graves and Podro responded to this by a letter of protest which was published on March 6, and was followed, on March 12, by a rejoinder from the reviewer, which, in turn, led to another letter by the authors, published on March 26. Then on April 2 the *Times* published yet another response of the reviewer in which he implied that the authors, in their March 26 letter, by substituting an ellipsis for a crucial word in quoting the Greek text of Galatians 4:14, "behaved in a grossly unethical manner." (I put the last six words in quotes, because this is how the solicitors of Graves and Podro described the reviewer's statement.) Graves and Podro felt that what the reviewer had written was "a defamatory imputation" against their "ethical integrity," and

110

therefore they demanded a "suitable apology," or else they would litigate the matter. Since no such apology was forthcoming, on June 30, 1954, the solicitors of Graves and Podro entered a formal "statement of claim" at the High Court of Justice in London, in which they argued that the *Times Literary Supplement*, or, more precisely, its editor, proprietors, printers, and publisher, "falsely and maliciously printed and published" a letter from a contributor (the reviewer) claiming that Graves and Podro (the plaintiffs") "had acted dishonestly and dishonourably in suppressing" a certain Greek word in their argument against the reviewer. They claimed damages, as well as an injunction to restrain the *Times* from publishing the "said words" which the plaintiffs found damaging.

The legal wheels turn slowly in England (although perhaps not quite as slowly as in the United States), and it was not until a year later that finally the authors and the *Times* agreed on "an explanation," which was published in the July 22, 1955, issue of the *Times Literary Supplement*. In it the *Times* stated that it had not been their intention to charge the authors with unethical procedure, and conceded that "a certain small body of opinion in this country would support the authors' choice of reading" of the disputed passage. With this the matter was closed. As for damages, the authors did not pursue their claim, and, regrettably, despite the publicity provided by the exchange in the columns of the *Times*, the sales of *The Nazarene Gospel Restored* remained unsatisfactory.

Three years after the publication of *The Nazarene Gospel*, Graves and Podro published a small book titled *Jesus in Rome: A Historical Conjecture* (London: Cassell, 1957), which they characterized as "an Epilogue to *The Nazarene Gospel Restored*." In it they argue that twenty years after the Resurrection Jesus went to Rome, "where, according to prophecy, the Saviour of Israel must raise the standard of liberation in the enemy citadel." In the introductory part the authors, with evident and understandable disappointment, summarize the critical reception of *The Nazarene Gospel*: "Our *Nazarene Gospel Restored* was rudely rejected by almost every Protestant reviewer in Britain and the United States(a singular exception being Reinhold Niebuhr, the theologian); politely if cautiously received by Jewish scholars who preferred not to take sides in an argument on this, to them, painful subject; and wholly disregarded by Roman Catholics." I don't know whether Graves and Podro were aware of Robert Weltsch's review when they wrote these lines, but it would seem that they were not, otherwise they probably would have modified what they wrote about the reaction of Jewish critics.

Let me return for a moment to Graves's ingenious method of reinterpreting and reconstructing historical events, and comment on what I consider a constituent trait of all his historical studies, whether framed as fiction or scholarly writing. One unshakable conviction that (to adopt a phrase from his "In Her Praise") "straddles" Graves's neck throughout his writing career was that many ancient written documents contained either misunderstandings and misreadings or else intentional reinterpretations and reformulations of original narratives or pictorial representations of historically significant events or mythologically influential scenes. This is supplemented by the certainty that he, with his vast erudition and sharp, intuitive insight, was capable of digging up, reconstructing, and reestablishing the original versions of those ancient documents. Whether he wrote fiction or literary-historical studies, this conviction remained a major motivation in his approach, his analysis, and the theses he propounded. He did this most successfully in his Claudius novels in which he, as Moses Hadas put it in his review of *The Nazarene Gospel Restored*, rehabilitated "a pagan emperor whom the ancients had denigrated." Prompted by the same irresistible urge, Graves set out to do the same in his historical essays about the wheels of Pharoah's chariot, the creation of Eve, the Song of Songs, and, on a large scale, in the most ambitious of his undertakings in this area, *The Nazarene Gospel Restored*.

To be able to give free rein to his poetic imagination even when working with the constraints imposed by historical documents, Graves invented a novel theory he termed *inconotropy—from the Greek eikōn*, "image," and *trepein*, "to turn," or *tropē*, a turn—by which he meant the tendency to misunderstand and/or misinterpret ancient icons, pictorial or plastic representations of mythological scenes. As he put it in his *Adam's Rib*, iconotropy is "the misreading of ancient icons and sacred emblems to suit a new religious dispensation as the Greeks used when they substantiated the patriarchal Zeus cult at the expense of the hitherto sovereign Moon-goddess." To which he added a footnote: "For instance, they read a familiar icon, which happened to survive on a glass plaque, of the Cretan Goddess dominating the Minos Bull by riding on its back, as though Zeus, in bull-disguise, were carrying off the maiden Europa to ravish her at his leisure."[3]

In the same book he illustrates his "iconotropic method of narrative" by explaining the biblical story of the creation of Eve from a rib of Adam as having been "deduced from a picture of Agenor's driving a carved knife under Belus's fifth rib, with the connivance of the Goddess."[4] As we shall see in later chapters, I had quite a struggle in trying to keep explanations such as these out of the *Hebrew Myths*, or, at least, to keep them at a minimum.

However, Graves's interest in reconstructing or reconfiguring biblical stories dates back to a much earlier period in his life than the one in which he invented "iconotropy." As early as in 1931 he published a fragment titled "Alpha and Omega of the Autobiography of Baal" in his book *But It Still Goes On: An Accumulation*.[5] "The Autobiography of Baal" takes up only thirty-four pages in the book, and is described in the table of contents as "The First and Last Chapters of the Autobiography of Baal." In it Baal speaks in first person, identifies himself at the very outset as the author of the Pentateuch and of the Koran, and the editor of "the Septuagint translation of the

Bible.'' He further asserts that Baal was not his principal name, but ''a subsidiary and even somewhat invidious one, ''which he has not used for a number of centuries. Then Baal goes on to claim that he wrote *The Book of Mormon*, and that he had Mary Baker Eddy write *Science and Health with the Key to the Scriptures* in his name. He also takes responsibility for all kinds of other developments within various religious communities. Baal-Graves has some rather heretical observations to make on the Book of Genesis and other books of the Bible and the Gospels, and takes credit also for sanctioning the error based on the biblical narrative that the universe was created in six days in the year 4004 B.C.E., although, he says, he ''created time by simple Suns and Moons'' at about 15,000 B.C.E. Then Graves inserts an excursus on ''Lama''—Hebrew for ''why''—and puns on this ''Lama,'' which Baal identifies with himself, and the Dalai Lama, who, he says, ''is myself when I visit Tibet.'' The piece contains many references to, and explanations of, biblical passages, and flashes of typical Gravesian findings of connections between distant features, such as saying that ''Jacob's stone'' was ''cousin to the black stone of the Kaaba, the old rainmaker in my [Baal's] holy city of Mecca.''

All the above and much more is contained in the first part, titled ''Alpha.'' This piece was supposed to be followed by the body of the book which, however, was never written. In the book as printed it is followed by what was planned to be the concluding chapter, and is hence appropriately titled ''Omega.'' In it Baal-Graves has some unkind things to say about the Roman Catholic church and the Protestant and Dissenting congregations. On the other hand, in this concluding part, Baal admits that ''My God is, in fact, mind working independently of me, a human mind.'' Yet, at the end, Baal asserts, he will be recognized, and ''My people . . . will say . . . 'There is no God but Baal.' ''

I see in this fragment a satire of the interdependence of God and man, and, at the same time, a manifestation of Graves's own dependence on the biblical view of the deity, of the one and only God, whom he here rebelliously apostrophizes by the name of Baal, the Canaanite god, the greatest anathema of the Hebrew prophets and teachers of religion. This entire piece can, in fact, be considered a whimsical Hebrew myth created by the mind of the early Graves. It also constitutes an important preliminary excursion into, or reconnaissance of, a field that proved attractive enough for Graves to return to it repeatedly in later years for thorough explorations.

9.

On the Lecture and Research Circuit

I N 1954 AND 1955 I was even more busy than previously with teaching, lecturing, writing, and looking for income-producing employment in addition to my position as professor of anthropology at the Dropsie College. As an example of how full my days were let me list here my schedule for the ten days from November 28 to December 7, 1954.

On November 28 I attended the Tercentenary Conference on American Jewish Sociology at the Commodore Hotel in New York. On the 30th I took the train to Philadelphia to give my classes at the Dropsie College. Next day (December 1) I flew from Philadelphia to Buffalo, New York, to lecture that evening at 9:00 P.M. on the Jewish Indians of Mexico. On December 2 I attended a luncheon meeting with members of the sociology-anthropology department of the University of Buffalo, following which, at 2:30, I gave a lecture to a class of some one-hundred twenty students at that university on the culture of the Middle East today. At 4:55 I took the train from Buffalo to Syracuse, where I arrived just in time for my 8:30 lecture on the same subject to the Phi Kappa Lambda fraternity of Syracuse University. Next morning (December 3) I took a bus from Syracuse to Ithaca, N.Y., where from 4:00 to 6:00 P.M. I addressed at Cornell University the India Seminar of Prof. Morris E. Opler on similarities and differences between Middle Eastern and Indian village life. At 7:30 I flew from Ithaca to Newark, where Irene and her brother Bob met me at the airport and drove me home. After a quick dinner Bob drove me to Idlewild (later Kennedy) Airport, from where I took the 11:30 P.M. plane to Toronto, arriving there at 1:40 after midnight. I stayed overnight at the nearby Roseheath Airotel, and next morning took the 10:30 plane to Calgary, Canada, arriving there after a flight of close to ten hours, at

6:45 P.M. local time. Friends met me at the airport and took me to the Hotel Palliser, where I had dinner with some ten members of the Calgary Hebrew School Board. After dinner all of us adjourned to my hotel room to discuss what could be done to counter the machinations of the new young Conservative rabbi against the Hebrew school. Next morning (December 5) at 11:00, the president of the school board, Mr. Charles Waterman, and a young lawyer by the name of Joe Cohen, took me to the Calgary Zoo, to see what they said were the famous life-sized models of prehistoric animals, and then to a ride out to the Canadian Rockies to a point from where we could see in the distance the famous Banff resort hotel. Everything was covered with deep snow, and the air was invigoratingly fresh and cold. After lunch with the same two men, I was given a chance to rest, and then, at 6:00 P.M., Aharon Horowitz, former director of the Katzenelson Institute in Kfar Saba, Israel, and now principal of the Calgary Hebrew School, whom I had once met in New York in 1951, came, accompanied by Dr. Saffran, the school psychologist, to take me to the second annual dinner of the Hebrew School. The dinner was attended by some 350 people, a truly impressive number, considering that the total Jewish population of Calgary consisted of only 750 families. My address, "Heritage and Survival," was received with great enthusiasm. My host said, "You saved the Hebrew school!" After dinner there was a party at the home of one of the school board members, and then I was taken back to the hotel for a well-deserved night's rest.

Next morning (Monday, December 6) I went to the department store of the Hudson's Bay Company, and bought a pair of gloves for myself, and a pair of genuine Indian moccasins for Irene. At 10:30 A.M. Messrs. Waterman and Horowitz took me to the airport to catch the 11:20 plane back to Toronto. After a flight of some eight and a half hours I arrived at Toronto at 9:40 P.M., stayed overnight again at the Roseheath Airotel, and next day took a plane to New York. The plane was delayed for some two hours, and seeing that I would not be able to reach Philadelphia for my weekly Tuesday classes, I called Irene before boarding the plane and asked her to cancel my New York-Philadelphia flight for which I had made reservations, and to call Dropsie and say I was sick and could not give my class. I arrived home at 11:30 A.M.

This was a somewhat more than usually busy time. Normally all I did that winter was to give my courses at Dropsie, Columbia, and Yeshiva University, and, in addition, to deliver one or two public lectures a week to Jewish organizations and to universities, a schedule that left me just enough time for writing in the evenings and weekends. Much of my time that summer and fall of 1954 had been taken up by occasional meetings that had a semisocial and semiprofessional character, as shown by the following diary excerpts.

July 5. Lunch at Columbia University Men's Faculty Club with Prof. and Mrs. Halil Inalcik and Prof. Sinasi Altundag of Ankara University, in the course of which we discussed the possibility of an invitation for me to Ankara.

July 14. Met at the Waldorf-Astoria Dr. Abram Sachar, president of Brandeis University, and told him about my interest in becoming a member of the faculty of his university.

From August 15 to 22. Lectured at Camp B'nai B'rith in Starlight, Pennsylvania. Met there Rabbi Maurice Pekarsky, director of the Hillel Foundation at the Hebrew University of Jerusalem; Ludwig Lewisohn, the famous Jewish novelist (who was a fellow lecturer); the young philosopher, Dr. Sidney Morgenbesser; etc.

Aug. 27. Eldin Ricks, an instructor at Brigham Young University in Provo, Utah, came to see me to discuss his plan of becoming a doctoral student at the Dropsie College, and to suggest that I come to Provo to lecture at his university.

Aug. 30. My friend Rabbi Jay Kaufman asked me whether I would be willing to conduct High Holy Day services at Lorain, Ohio.

Sept. 8. Attended a luncheon meeting of the American Christian Palestine Committee, and participated in the discussion. After the meeting met an interesting character: the Rev. Martin P. Chworowsky, a minister of the Unitarian Church, who was born a Jew, and at the age of one was converted by his parents to Lutheranism. After serving for twenty-five years as a Lutheran minister, he converted to Unitarianism, and has become a great friend of the Jews and Israel.

Sept. 13. Met Prof. and Mrs. Louis Silverman of Dartmouth College, who are to sail a few days from now to Israel where Louis is to serve as visiting professor of mathematics at Tel Aviv University. We discussed affairs of the Tel Aviv University, including the chance of my being invited to its presidency.

Sept. 14. Rabbi Ben-Zion Bokser of the Forest Hills Jewish Center called to invite me to give one or more lectures to an adult group at his center.

Sept. 21. At 11:00 a.m. meeting with Dr. Everett R. Clinchy and Dr. Nehemia Robinson of the National Conference of Christians and Jews. They suggested that I conduct two seminars, one in Philadelphia and one in New York, on the role of religion in a culture with a technological-secular orientation. An hour later Miss Foster of the American Christian Palestine Committee came there to consult me about her plan of studying the adjustment of Arabs in Nazareth to life in

Israel. Later that day Dr. Simon Segal of the American Jewish Committee called to make an appointment with me about the paper they had asked me to write, "Acculturation in Israel."

Sept. 24. Delivered the outline of the planned seminars to Dr. Clinchy. I titled it "Religion in the Cultural Context of the Modern World." That afternoon went to the American Jewish Committee and worked there for about three hours with Mr. Goldblum on the edited version of my paper "Acculturation in Israel."

Sept. 28. Prof. Amira of the Hebrew University of Jerusalem came to see me. He is also connected with the Tel Aviv University, as member of its committee on academic appointments. He described Mayor Levanon's position as weak, because of political difficulties, but encouraged me to continue with my efforts for Tel Aviv University.

Oct. 1. Attended a meeting of the Conference on Jewish Sociology in the office of Marshall Sklar, at the American Jewish Committee. Present were also Dr. Werner Cahnman, Dr. Abraham Duker, Dr. Chain, Dr. Miller, and others.

Oct. 11. Was asked by Dr. Benjamin Schwadran, editor of the *Middle Eastern Affairs*, to prepare a research paper on slavery in the Middle East.

Oct. 13–15. In Chicago, attending the annual meeting of the American Anthropological Association. During those days also gave a lecture (Oct. 13) to the Chicago Anthropological Society; "The Dynamics of Westernization in the Middle East." [This was subsequently published in *The Middle East Journal*, 9:1:1–16.] Oct. 13 dinner with Prof. and Mrs. Sol Tax of the University of Chicago. Oct. 14 lunch with Benjamin Weintroub, editor of the *Chicago Jewish Forum*, and met several members of the Anthropology department of the University of Chicago, sat in in the class of Prof. Robert Redfield on "The Small Community," had dinner with Robert Tyroler, assistant to the dean, and in the evening read a paper to the AAA meeting, "The People of Israel Today." Next morning there was a hurricane warning, so got up early and caught the 8:00 A.M. plane back to N.Y.

Oct. 17. Attended an all-day meeting in New York of the *Histadruth Ivrith* ("Hebrew Association"). While there, Dr. Samuel Blumenfield told me that he wanted to arrange with the Brooklyn Jewish Center that I give a series of lectures, and Prof. Samuel K. Mirsky of Yeshiva University informed me that the proofs of the second part of my Hebrew study, "Birth in Popular [Jewish] Custom," were on the way.

Oct. 18. Worked all day on the slavery material, and after my 2:00 P.M. class at Columbia took out of the Columbia Library, with the help of my old friend Meir Bravmann, cataloguer of Arabic books, a number of books on that subject.

Oct. 20. Had a series of conferences with several people at the U.N. Secretariat, including Donald V. McGranahan, Gustavo Duran, and Edward Lawson of the Human Rights Department. Then worked at the U.N. library on the slavery paper. In the afternoon went to see Dr. Paul Fejos, director of the Wenner-Gren Foundation for Anthropological Research, who informed me, most regretfully, that my application for a grant to do a "Comparison of Cultures" study was not approved, because three of the four opinions he asked for were negative. He said he suspected personal bias, and suggested that I submit a new application, and ask in advance four anthropologists to support it, and then, when I submit it, let him know their names.

Oct. 24. In Philadelphia had dinner with the *Histadruth Ivrith* and the *Ivriyah* organization at Gratz College, after which, at 9:00 P.M., gave a lecture in Hebrew to the *Dukhan Ivri* ("Hebrew Forum"), on "Diaspora: Languages and Cultures." Managed to catch the 10:20 P.M. train back to New York.

Oct. 25. Delivered my slavery study to Dr. Schwadran, who told me on that occasion that a part-time position for such research might develop at his journal. That afternoon, after my weekly Columbia class, went to see Prof. Salo W. Baron to talk to him about the chances of giving next year a course on the anthropology of the Middle East. At 4:30 attended a meeting of the preparatory committee of the Conference on Jewish Sociology.

Oct. 26. After my class at Dropsie received phone call from Mr. Shevach of the Jewish Teachers College in Boston. He asked me whether I could give a Hebrew lecture at his college on Nov. 14, on the subject "Diaspora: Languages and Cultures." Answered in the affirmative.

Oct. 27. Dr. Schwadran called to ask me to prepare a research paper on "Polygamy, the Status of Woman, and Children in the Middle East." Deadline Nov . 17. The same afternoon Rabbi Max Schenk of the Brooklyn Jewish Center called to tell me that his center, in cooperation with the Zionist Organization of America, was planning a series of lectures on Israel; he wants me give a talk on "Israel and Its Neighbors."

Nov. 1. Attended a meeting at the Waldorf-Astoria organized by the Dropsie College in honor of the publication of the fourth volume of their Apocrypha series edited by Prof. Solomon Zeitlin.

Nov. 5. "Occupied the pulpit" of the union Baptist Church (a black congregation) in Philadelphia, whose chief minister, the Rev. James Kirkland, was my doctoral student at Dropsie. Spoke on "Religion in the Western World, the Middle East, and the Far East"—a brief, twenty-minute talk, a longer version of which was published in the autumn 1954 (10:3) issue of the *Southwestern Journal of Anthropology*. [This was the paper about which Dr. Leslie Spier, editor of the *SWJA*, told me, "I would give my right hand to have written that article."]

Nov. 8. Consultation with Prof. Charles ("Chuck") Wagley and Prof. Salo Baron about my next year's course at Columbia.

Nov. 10. Took the plane from Philadelphia to Kansas City, where, next morning, sat in classes, then addressed the Chapel Meeting and a class, and met several faculty members at lunch and in the afternoon. One of them was Prof. Ernst Manheim, who told me that he had been a student of my father at the Budapest high school he had attended, where my father taught Hungarian and German literature in the early 1900s.

Nov. 14. Attended in N.Y. a conference and luncheon of Jewish educators convened by the Department of Education and Culture of the Jewish Agency. After lunch took the train to Boston, where that evening gave a Hebrew lecture on "Diaspora: Languages and Cultures" at the Hebrew Teachers College. Stayed overnight in Boston, and next morning, after returning to N.Y., took the polygamy material, on which I had worked for some two weeks, to Dr. Schwadran.

Nov. 17. Dr. Schwadran asked me to prepare a similar research paper on health conditions and sanitation in the Middle East—again within three weeks. Undertook assignment. The same afternoon Prof. Samuel Mirsky called and asked me to give a course of eight lectures on "The Ingathering of Exiles in Israel" within the framework of the new Israeli Institute of Yeshiva University.

Nov. 18. Took plane at 3:00 P.M. from N.Y. to Boston, where Dr. Meir Ben-Horin met me and drove me to the Hebrew Teachers College. Sat in on two classes, then addressed the students' assembly (in Hebrew) on "Westernization in the Middle East," for which I had to coin a new Hebrew word, *hitma ʿaravut* ("Westernization"). In the afternoon Ben-Horin took me in a taxi from Brookline to Cambridge, where at 8:00 P.M. I gave a lecture on the same subject, but this time in English, to a group at Harvard. In the audience of some 120 was Prof. Philip K. Hitti of Princeton, who greeted me with warm friendship, and opened the question-and-answer period that followed my talk. They put me up for the night at the Eliot House in a guest apartment. Next morning at 8:00

Hitti called for me and took me to breakfast, and then to the Middle East Center. There I had a chance to talk to D. W. Lockard, who taught Middle Eastern anthropology at the center, and Prof. Gordon R. Willey, chairman of the anthropology department.

At 11:30 a student from Brandeis University came with his car to take me to Brandeis, located in Waltham, another suburb of Boston, where I met briefly the president, Dr. Sachar, and then had lunch with Profs. Ludwig Lewisohn, Simon Rawidowitz, Nahum Glatzer, and Robert Manners. Later also Prof. Alfred Kroeber, who served as visiting professor at Brandeis, joined us. Then Dr. Manners showed me around Brandeis's impressive campus. In the library I made use of the opportunity to ask Louis Schreiber, the librarian, to donate books they can spare to Tel Aviv University.

Because of bad weather flights to New York were canceled, so the same student took me and Dr. Max Lerner, chairman of the graduate department and columnist for the *New York Post,* to the train station. During the long ride to New York I discussed with Lerner the desirability of establishing at Brandeis a chair for the anthropology of the Jews. I mentioned that there was a good chance that Dr. Sachar could get money for this purpose from the Wenner-Gren Foundation for Anthropological Research, since that foundation wanted to repair the bad reputation its founder had among the Jews. That bad reputation, I explained to Lerner, was due to the fact that during the war the Swedish factories owned by the founder of the foundation, Axel Wenner-Gren, supplied arms and ammunition to Nazi Germany. At the 125th Street station I got off the train, and took a cab to La Quardia where I picked up my car and drove home. Reached home about 11:00 P.M.

Nov. 23. While I was at Dropsie I got a phone call from Mrs. Schen, of the *Histadruth Ivrith,* asking me to go to Calgary, Canada, to lecture for the Calgary Hebrew School Board, which resulted in my visit described in the beginning of this chapter.

The five months covered by the above excerpts were fairly typical not only of the two years of 1954 and 1955, but of much of the 1950s in general.

In the spring of 1955 I was approached by Dr. Brian Kay of the Human Relations Area Files (HRAF) of New Haven, Connecticut, with the suggestion that I edit for them three handbooks, one on Lebanon, one on Jordan, and one on Syria, as part of the large series of such country handbooks they were preparing under a U.S. Army contract. After protracted negotiations that involved repeated trips to New Haven, I reached an agreement with Milton D. Graham, Research Coordinator of the HRAF, and Fahim I. Qubain, its research associate for the Middle East, concerning the three handbooks. The ironing out of the financial and technical details took some more time, and then I began to recruit contributors to the projected books. This preparatory stage lasted several weeks, but finally, within a relatively short time, I managed to assemble a first-class group of experts who produced three highly creditable handbooks which were published (in xeroxed form) by the HRAF in the spring of 1956.

The completed handbooks—*The Hashemite Kingdom of Jordan, The Republic of Lebanon* (2 vols.), and *The Republic of Syria* (2 vols.)—all conformed, as they had to, to the same format, and were written by the same fifteen authors. Each of the books started with a chapter titled "General Character of the Society," written by me. Then followed a chapter on "Geographical Setting," also written by me. The chapters on "Historical Setting" were written by Prof. Philip K. Hitti of Princeton University; "Population Analysis," by Dr. Kingsley Davis, professor of Sociology at the University of California, Berkeley; "Physical Anthropology," by Dr. Robert W. Ehrich, professor of Anthropology, Brooklyn College; "Culture Groups," again by me; "Language," by Dr. Meir Bravmann, who by that time, at my recommendation, was visiting professor of Arabic at Dropsie College; "Social Structure: Introductory, Nomadic Life, and Sedentarization," by me; "Village Organization," by Dr. John Gulick, professor of Anthropology at the University of North Carolina, Chapel Hill; "The Town," by me jointly with Fahim Qubain; "The Family" and Social Values and Patterns of Living," by me; "The Theater and Cinema," by Dr. Jacob M. Landau, an old friend of mine from Jerusalem, now visiting lecturer in Near Eastern Studies at Brandeis University; "Music," by Toufic Succar, instructor at the National Conservatory of Music, in Beirut, Lebanon; "Literature," by Fahim Qubain; "The Arts," by Farid Aouad, art historian of Beirut, Lebanon; "Education," "Religion," and "Public Information," by Dr. Moshe Perlmann, lecturer in Semitics, Harvard University, and my colleague at the Dropsie College; "Forced Labor" and "Labor Relations and Organization," by Dr. Charles Issawi, associate professor of economics, Columbia University; "Health and Sanitation" and "Public Welfare," by me and Dr. Simon D. Messing, a former student of mine whom I employed as research assistant for the whole project; "Attitudes and Reactions of the People," by me; the political chapters, to wit, "The Constitutional System," "Structure of Government," "Political Dynamics," "Public Order and Safety," "Foreign Policies," "Subversive Potentialities," and "Propaganda," by Dr. Jacob C. Hurewitz, associate professor of government, Columbia University, and another colleague of mine at Dropsie; "Biographies of Key Personalities," by Perlmann; and the economic chapters, "Agricultural Potential," "Industrial Potential," "Taxation," "Banking and Currency System," and "Domestic Trade," by Issawi.

In addition to Simon Messing, who was my right hand throughout the duration of the work, I also employed a cartographer, Morton Kremer, and a

121

translator, Charles Wendell. I served as director of the project, and although officially the Dropsie College figured as project administrator, in fact all work was done in my home, including the extensive correspondence, the correcting, editing, and copying of all the articles, for which work I employed a secretary who also worked in my home. In addition to the editorial work and to writing myself a major part of the chapters, I had to spend that year an inordinate amount of time on technicalities and administrative details, discussing payment and control arrangements with the Army Audit Agency in Philadelphia, purchasing equipment, and arranging for my research assistant to be allowed to work at the U.N. Secretariat in New York and to be given use of facilities at the New York Public Library. However, when finally I held the five volumes in my hands I felt that the results were commensurate with the efforts that went into their production.

Also in the spring of 1955 I was elected president of the American Friends of the Tel Aviv University, with Dean James A. Pike of the Cathedral of St. John the Divine as honarary president, and some eight or ten persons as board members. I was subsequently reelected annually until 1968, when Dr. George Wise, the very active and energetic president of the university, wanted me to become a paid employee of the Friends and devote myself to raising funds for them, that is, for the university, which suggestion I felt unwilling to accept. So I resigned, although I remained a member of the board, and a paid, professional fund-raiser was elected president in my stead. I must admit that in the thirteen years of presidency the Friends under my leadership did not do much by way of fund-raising. But at least we took care of the legalities involved in setting up an American organization whose raison d'être was to support a foreign academic institution, we incorporated legally, obtained tax-exempt status (which at that time was becoming increasingly difficult), and employed a fund-raiser.

At the same time I was also asked by Prof. Baron to become a member of the editorial board of the quarterly *Jewish Social studies* of which he was editor, and also a board member of the Conference on Jewish Relations which was the sponsor of that journal.

That summer I, Irene, and the children spent two weeks (July 6–20) in Ellenville, New York, where I gave a series of lectures in Hebrew to the Seminar for Hebrew Teachers. Among the other lecturers were Dr. Simon Halkin of the Hebrew University of Jerusalem; Dr. Judah Pilch, executive director of the American Association for Jewish Education; Dr. Israel Mehlman, director of the department of education and culture in the Diaspora of the World Zionist Organization; and Dr. Elazar Goelman, executive director of the Buffalo Bureau of Jewish Education.

Later that summer, from August 15 to 26, I gave a lecture series at a seminar in Los Angeles organized by the American Association for Jewish Education. Irene came along, although her father had suffered a heart attack a few days before our departure, and was still in the hospital. From Los Angeles we went out to the Brandeis Camp, where I lectured, and then to a Habonim Camp for yet another lecture. On August 26 we flew over to San Francisco, which gave me the opportunity to visit the Berkeley campus of the University of California, and to meet again old colleagues and friends, among them Prof. Walter Fischel, who had been my friend in Jerusalem, and Prof. David Mandelbaum, who was doing the Pakistan handbook for the HRAF. On August 30 we flew back to New York.

In the fall my usual teaching routine began anew: a weekly course of two hours on Mondays at Columbia University, and two days a week (Tuesday-Wednesday) at Dropsie in Philadelphia. However, differences between me and Dr. Neuman, the president of Dropsie, sharpened: he demanded more and more insistently that I move to Philadelphia, which I was unable to do. Thus it appeared that my time at Dropsie was growing short, and I became convinced that I had to find another position.

These circumstances, sketched above in roughest outline only, explain in part why I neglected to write to Graves for about two years. However, late in November a concrete reason came up which prompted me to write to him: the Hosea novel on which Irene had been working for several years was now in galleys, and I thought I would approach Graves for an opinion.

10.

Irene's Novel

THIS IS WHAT I wrote Graves in November, 1955.

Dear Don Robert:

I am really ashamed of my long silence, and even more so since during the last two or three years I have derived repeatedly great enjoyment from your books published during this period.

To begin with, I read of course The Nazarene Gospel *from beginning to end with the Hebrew Bible in one hand and the New Testament in the other, and was filled with admiration for the painstaking thoroughness coupled with the great ingenuity manifested in its pages. Although I had read the New Testament several times and had a vague impression that much in it is based on the Old Testament, I never suspected what your book demonstrates now, that practically the entire story of the life of Jesus is based directly on Old Testament precedent. As I wrote to you in the course of our earlier correspondence about this book after reading part of the manuscript, there are numerous points and details in it with which I cannot find myself in agreement. To enumerate these would be a major scholarly undertaking in itself, and it will have to wait for a future occasion, or even better for a long hoped for personal meeting with you.*

Shortly thereafter I read your Homer's Daughter *and fell completely under its spell. This is the more of a compliment to your masterly hand since otherwise I do not feel any particular affinity with the Graeco-Roman world of myth. However, the worlds recreated by Robert Graves—as known to me from the pages of* Hercules My Shipmate *and* Watch the North Wind Rise *hold a special fascination for me.*

I myself have been pushed more and more into the modern Middle Eastern field as a result of which my historical-anthropological studies have had to suffer. There is a great and still increasing interest in this country in the modern Middle East, and I am one of the still all too few experts who have made this their field of specialization. As a result of this, I am frequently called upon to contribute articles to journals and to give lectures to learned and other groups. A few months ago I was entrusted by a governmental body with the writing and editing of three handbooks dealing with Syria, Lebanon, and Jordan. All this, in addition to my regular teaching schedules, keeps me more than busy.

I do not remember whether I mentioned to you in an earlier letter that my wife was working on a novel. She had been engaged in this for the last five years. Happily, some months ago the manuscript was completed and the novel accepted for publication by the first house to which she submitted it: Random House. It is an historical novel based on the scanty references contained in the first three chapters of the Book of Hosea. Around this skeleton Irene has built a story of flesh and blood, full of authentic historical detail, describing the life, thought, feeling of the period—the eighth century B.C. As you may well imagine, I had a share in supplying information for this aspect of the book, and have controlled carefully the scholarly accuracy and reliability of the background. As to the literary quality of the novel, I am not competent to judge, but Hiram Haydn, the editor of Random House, seems to be quite impressed by it. Haydn is regarded as a foremost critic in this country, but I would like the opinion of the man whom I regard as the greatest master of the historical novel. I therefore suggested (with the enthusiastic concurrence of my wife for whom you represent an idol and ideal) that a galley be sent to you, in the hope that you may find the time to read it and let us know your judgment of it. Needless to say, we both shall wait for your verdict with great impatience and trepidation.

Raphael

Graves answered immediately.

Dec 11 1955

Dear Raphael Patai

Always very pleased & proud to hear from you; I won't pretend I'm not disappointed at your temporary secession from the studies which were so illuminating to me—but I can understand the need for you in the other field, and as they say 'a man must eat.'

As for your wife's novel; let's be frank—I hate historical novels: my own among the rest, though it is great fun writing them. But I'll try to forget my

125

dislike in this case, since I know I can rely on the historical background—as for example one can't in the Hadrian *book by Mlle Yourcenar. (I have been helping Joshua Podro with a brief, scholarly and most touching biography of Rabbi Judah—who went on embassy to Hadrian—and either Mlle Y. has got the facts all wrong or else she is making Hadrian a liar!)*

So I shall read your wife's book as reconstituted history, which I expect it will be (though Hoshea is scanty), not as one of those annoying efforts to tell modern history in fancy dress, which I cannot think it will be. And if I can find anything to praise in it, will praise it, because you have been a good friend to me and your wife seems to be a good daughter of Israel.

One day will all meet.

About the Nazarene Gospel: *naturally the Protestants have been very angry about it; naturally the Jews have been polite but very cautious. Nobody has yet found a major flaw in the argument; and very few minor ones have come to hand. It is the greatest of pities that the few experts who could criticize particular passages in scholarly detail are either shy of doing so or overworked like you. It was of course far too ambitious a project for two persons to undertake; but we feel that the main argument is sound and are still hoping that someone will amend our argument where it is erroneous. The book was written from a sense of duty, not as a money maker. (It cost us about 6000 dollars overhead.) So I am looking forward to your sabbatical year and a visit to Majorca!*

> *Yours*
> *Robert Graves*

I responded without delay.

December 22, 1955

Dear Don Robert:

It was really good to get your reply so soon. In fact, your last sentence sent Irene and me to our atlas to see whether we could stop over in Majorca on our tentatively planned visit to Israel next summer. Our plans are still too vague, but I have a great yearning to see my mother whom I have not seen since 1951, and who has in the meantime sustained the loss of my father all alone in Israel. We are hoping for a windfall to make this trip possible. Since I am committed to teach a half-term at Ohio State University in the early summer, we could utilize only August and September for the voyage.

I suppose it is no surprise for you, but both your book of poems and your two volume Greek Myths *are being hailed by the critics over here. That your* Nazarene Gospel *has not received the critical acclaim it deserves can be attributed, I think, to the unfortunate mental habit of scholars to look with suspicion, or at least mistrust, at "intruders." Their reasoning goes something like this: "Here I have spent a lifetime in painstaking and meticulous research in this field, and this man from 'outer space' comes barging in and thinks he can show me the light." As for the clergy—their prime desire is to maintain the status quo. No scholarly journal has asked me to review the book, only a small Jewish quarterly magazine, and that too limited my space severely. I certainly wish I had the leisure to sit down and write a detailed study about the book. But I shall at least try to send you a few of my comments within the next few months.*

As to Irene's novel: it is really very generous of you to give it your time. I understand that the galley had just been airmailed to you by Random House. Incidentally, I think it will put your mind at rest to know that it is not actually a historical novel in the conventional sense. The scantiness of the data—a mere few sentences in the book of Hosea—precludes this. It is concerned with the man's interior struggle, the forces which brought him to prophecy, and the milieu of a semi-pagan Israel of the 8th century B.C.

> *Yours sincerely*
> *Raphael*

Graves's response quickly arrived.

> *Guillermo Massot, 73 pral. 2.a*
> *Tel. 5051*
> *Palma de Mallorca*
> *Spain*
> *Jan 7 1956*

Dear Rafael (sorry, I spelt it the Spanish way)

Just got your wife's book; but have an infected eye & am not allowed to read for a few days. This is a one-eyed scrawl of thanks. Looking forward to the book.

Funny to live in 'Puritan Hills,' a good Jewish family like yours! The man who named my street was a very inferior local opera-writer.

> *Now I must sign off.*
> *Yours*
> *Robert*

A few days later, after he had read Irene's novel, Graves wrote again, this time in some detail.

> *Jan 18th 1956*

Dear Raphael:

You should not really have sent me the novel, after I'd warned you that I disliked historical novels—and that includes my own—a misfortune which had prevented me from enjoying this one as it deserves. The plot, which keeps

127

close to the Hoshea story, moves well and ends very movingly, and there are splendid descriptive passages, e.g. of the marriage, or the Descent to Tammuz, and so on. But I am cursed with this continuous alertness to errors—not only in English (which does not seem to be Irene's mother tongue, or she could not make rams 'low' instead of 'bleat' or 'bill'; or horses 'bray' instead of 'neigh' or 'whinny') but also in historical anacronism. And this is very embarrassing to me because you should have guarded her against the suspicion of that; I have never been to Israel or studied Hebrew or Aramaic, and feel I have no right to make any objections.

Specifically, the cock is always being mentioned in the book, either for its crowing or its sacrificial use, but I can find no evidence for its existence in Israel for a century or so after Hoshea's day even if the creature "who likes to take up a quarrel" in Proverbs XXX 30 is a cock not a greyhound (as some say). There seems to be no evidence at all for coined money in Hoshea's day: gold, for Deborah to take in her purse; silver for Hoshea to pay for Gomer, and copper coins for the people of Bethel to pay Abiel all worry me. Ingots, buttons, beads, lumps; but not coins! As to the lost camel found eating cactus: all the cactus in Israel comes from Mexico, surely? I even doubt whether the 'cactus' of the Greeks, which is the cardoon, or wild artichoke, was found any further East than Sicily. I am old enough to have teased George Moore (that nasty old man) for the cactus in his Brook of Kerith *around 1917. Then again Beeri: I have been told that a prophet's father is never named in the scriptures (unless he too was a prophet); and I find that R. Simon in* Leviticus Rabba *15 makes this Beeri the author of the very appropriate prophecy in Isaiah (VIII 19 to end.) And why did Hoshea write to Gomer? Surely she could not read?— The later Asahel incident seems to prove she couldn't, and the Beth Din synagogue education for women hadn't yet been invented.*

Then I was surprised that Hoshea did not do anything when the dead son of Anak was found in the road; surely even a Rechabite or a High Priest was bound by the law to bury a dead man in such circumstances? Or were the Anakim not also God's creatures?

Finally I was disturbed by Irene's giving Israel credit for a loyal minority which would be spared, or deserved to be spared, the Assyrian invasion. Hoshea, as I read him, did not find so many as five just men in that Sodom, but condemned the whole nation impartially. (I admit that the common people weren't carried away; but still!)

Forgive me; I am what my own historical novel-writing has made me. The bad thing is that I am open to the same sort of criticism myself! The good thing is that I am prepared to offer a Temple shekel to a perutah *that nobody will notice these points except myself—so Irene needn't be aggrieved. And though Irene writes a little too well, in the sense of ascribing too civilized a sensibility to Gomer for a woman of that period, the final scene is very splendid and fascinatingly* Jewish, *or call it Israelite: no other nation in the world could*

have conceived anything so ironic, so human and so fanatic as Hoshea's ac-
tion. (Do you happen to know, offhand, the name of the Rabbi who tried to
discourage Sabbath breaking by deliberately picking sticks on a Sabbath—
trying to get stoned as an example? That's also really Jewish). Forgive me,
and praise me for my honesty!

> *Yours*
> *Robert*

To the top left-hand corner of the first page of his letter, Graves pasted a
slip of paper with a few lines into which he condensed his opinion of Irene's
novel, and which were intended for publication. He wrote:

> Moves well, ends movingly, and contains fascinating anthropological
> detail about life in early Israel. The final scene, in which the Prophet
> Hoshea buys back his adulterous wife from the idolaters, is most remark-
> able. No other nation in the world could have conceived anything so
> ironic, so human and so fanatically religious as that.
>
> Robert Graves

This letter is of considerable interest because its critical comments illustrate the thoroughness, care, and sense of responsibility with which Graves
approached the task of writing a historical novel. It also shows his interest in
the Bible and things Jewish, and his familiarity with midrashic exegesis of
biblical passages.

The letter was answered by both Irene and myself. Irene wrote:

> *January 28, 1956*
>
> *Dear Robert (if I may call you that?)*
>
> *You ask to be forgiven but I do not know what for. For having read the book*
> *with so much care? For having rescued me from error? As it happened, the*
> *day your letter came I had the page proofs in my hand and was able to make*
> *the changes then and there.*
>
> *Odd as it sounds, the "lowing" rams and "braying" horses were errors*
> *made by the printer. I substituted one animal for another on the manuscript,*
> *and he (the printer) paired the noun and verb forms wrongly. There was a*
> *strike at the plant and an inferior workman seem [s] to have been doing the*
> *script. Whole sentences were omitted, transpositions made, and so on. Actu-*
> *ally it had been our intention to send you bound corrected page proofs, but the*
> *strike postponed everything—even publication date from February to April.*
>
> *However, I must blushingly admit to everything else. I have now made an*
> *itinerant peddler read Hosea's letter to Gomer. The son of Anak is decently*
> *buried. Cactus has vanished from Israel. I shall ask Raphael to speak for the*
> *cock and the coins.*

129

*As for the loyal minority: I cannot believe in such complete social unifor-
mity as you suggest. How then can a man like Hosea arise? I find in his words
not the uncompromising condemnation which you see, but a great ambivalence which has him castigating one moment, imploring the next.*

*Gomer is perhaps a shade too modern, but then so is Hosea, so that I am
afraid one would have to toss out the entire book on those grounds. It is a very
tricky tightrope one walks trying to blend properly those traits which are cul-
turally derived with more basic human drives. If I have not succeeded too
well, perhaps I shall do better next time.*

For now—thank you, thank you, thank you!

With all my heart,
Irene

I added:

Dear Robert:

*Let me add my thanks to those of Irene for your friendly and critical pe-
rusal of her book. How well I know what it means for a man to put aside his
own work and read something he is not particularly interested in, which, in
addition, belongs to a literary genre he dislikes. The more I value what you
have done, and the words of appreciation you wrote on a separate slip. You
liked and praised the description of the wedding and the Descent to Tammuz;
yet there is no proof that these rituals took place in 8th century B.C. Israel.
Their acceptance by you and me is based on probability rather than certainty.
The same is my argument for the cock and the coins: the fact that they do not
happen to be mentioned in the Bible or contemporary documents merely
makes it impossible to prove that they existed; the probability of their existence
is not affected by the absence of documentation. I grant that coins in the sense
of minted pieces may not have existed, although the sheqel looks to me sus-
piciously like a piece of metal of a definite weight and shape. As to Beeri: I do
not think that one should put one's trust in a late midrash. The Biblical text
itself does nowhere indicate that the father of a prophet is named only if he
himself was also a prophet: Hosea ben Beeri; Isaiah ben Amoz; Joel ben
Pethuel; Jonah ben Amittai; Zephaniah ben Kushi—all these fathers are mentioned without any indication as to their professions. Jeremiah and Ezekiel
were sons of priests. In Zachariah 1, 1 the word ''hannavi'' (the prophet) can
be taken to refer to Zachariah or his grandfather, but not his father.*

*It is a general tendency of the midrash to identify persons named in the
Bible without any further data. The attribution of prophethood to the fathers
of prophets is merely one type of this general tendency. It certainly cannot
have any historical value. On general grounds one may assume, of course,
that it frequently happened that a son followed in the footsteps of his father,*

and that a man was a "prophet son of a prophet." This trend has survived in the Middle East to this very day in many professions. But all this does not prove that Beeri must have been a prophet.

I am sorry I do not remember offhand the name of the rabbi who tried to discourage Sabbath-breaking by picking sticks on the Sabbath trying to get stoned as an example. If you need the name for any reason, I shall be glad to search for it and let you know.

With best regards and gratitude
yours
Raphael

11.

First Meeting
with Graves

T HIS EXCHANGE OF letters was again followed by a long silence on the part of both Graves and myself. In the meantime I had occasion to read again parts of Graves's *The Greek Myths*, and was surprised to find that in it he referred—somewhat loosely—to my book *Man and Temple*. He stated that relics of the custom of performing an annual sacred marriage rite between the priestess of Anatha, "an orgiastic Moon-goddess," and the sacred king, for the purpose of ensuring good crops, "were found in Heracles's temple at Rome . . . and at Jerusalem where, before the religious reforms of the Exile, a sacred marriage seems to have been celebrated every September between the High Priest, a representative of Jehovah, and the goddess Anatha. Professor Patai summarizes the evidence for the Jerusalem marriage in his *Man and Temple* (pp. 88–94, London, 1947)."[1]

My irrepressible penchant for accuracy prompts me to make, even at this late date, a number of emendations to the above passage. I *did not* in my *Man and Temple* summarize "the evidence for the Jerusalem marriage" in the sense construed by Graves. What I did in the pages referred to by him was to show that traces of the idea that the Holy of Holies of the Jerusalem Temple was a nuptial chamber are found in ancient Jewish legends preserved in a number of Midrash collections which describe the Holy of Holies as a place where everything miraculously "was fruitful and multiplied." It was there that I first discussed the Cherubim in the Sanctuary, those two winged figures shown in marital embrace which symbolized the love of God for Israel stated to be "like the love between man and woman." Then I proceeded to show that in the classical kabbalistic sourcebook *Zohar Ḥadash*, which dates from the late thirteenth or early fourteenth century, the Holy of Holies is described as

132

the sacred bedchamber of God and His spouse, the Matron ("*Matronita*"), or the Shekhina. It takes considerable poetic licence to interpret this as constituting evidence of an annually celebrated sacred marriage between "the High Priest, a representative of Jehovah, and the goddess Anatha." Interestingly, in all the correspondence and discussions between Graves and me he never once mentioned that he had referred to my *Man and Temple* in his *Greek Myths*.

In the summer of 1956 I was involved in protracted negotiations about a part-time position as director of research of the Herzl Institute, the New York educational and cultural institution of the Jewish Agency, headed by Dr. Emanuel Neumann, a member of the agency's executive. The initiative came from Dr. Samuel Blumenfield, who proved a good friend and advocate, despite the fact that I had disappointed him a few years earlier when he invited me to teach at the College of Jewish Studies in Chicago of which he was then president. Now Dr. Blumenfield was head of the Jewish Agency's department of education and culture in New York, and it was in that capacity that he wanted me to become director of research of the Herzl Institute. My appointment came through on August 29, and I started work on September 10. This meant that from then on I was no longer dependent primarily on Dr. Abraham Neuman of the Dropsie College for my livelihood.

My work week was now fuller than ever. I worked on Mondays at the Herzl Institute, left Tuesday morning for Philadelphia, where I taught three hours in the afternoon at the Dropsie College and had an hour of consultations with students, then stayed overnight in Philadelphia. Wednesday morning I taught three additional hours at Dropsie, then took the train back to New York, at about noontime, and was at my desk that afternoon at the Herzl Institute, as well as all day Thursday and Friday. This meant that, in effect, all my research and writing had to be done in the evenings and on Saturdays and Sundays.

My schedule, however, was unrelated to a certain distance, even tension, that was developing between me and Irene. She had just at that time published her novel, had begun to be invited to give lectures, and had found interests outside the home.

In January 1957 I learned—I no longer remember from what source—that Graves was planning to come to America to lecture. Nor do I remember who informed me on February 1 that he had indeed arrived, or who gave me the address where he was staying in New York. In any case, on that day I wrote him a short note.

Dear Don Robert:

Welcome to America!
Is there any chance to get together with you? We would be happy to meet you finally eye to eye. Please phone to us at Liggett 4–1913 (in New York).

133

Regards

Raphael and Irene Patai

P.S. From Tuesday morning to Wednesday afternoon I am in Philadelphia and no one will be home.

I have no record of having received an answer to this note.

Graves's lecture took place on February 9, 1957, at the Young Men's and Women's Hebrew Association, the so-called "92d-Street Y." He spoke on "The White Goddess," the subject and title of one of his most successful non-fiction books, first published in 1948 and reprinted several times thereafter. Before the lecture Graves and I met in the lobby of the "Y." I was with Irene, and he with Alastair Reid, the young Scottish journalist and poet, whom Graves had first met in 1953, and who, by 1957, as Seymour-Smith put it in his Graves biography, had "pledged devotion to the Gravesian cause." Two years later, however, Reid "mortally offended him."[2]

Graves, as I remember him from that first brief encounter, was one of those men who make a great impression by their mere appearance. He was over six feet tall, just about an inch taller than I, with a robust body and a head that made one want to look at it again. A high forehead crowned with unkempt grey hair, a large Roman nose broken in the middle, generous mouth, jowly cheeks, and large grey eyes that darted from you to the distance just behind your back, as if focusing there on something only he could see. He did not speak much, clearly preferring to listen rather than talk, and when he did speak, it was typically in blurred, rapid phrases which yet conveyed the impression that he had much more to say than he cared to put into words. He had the uncanny knack of making you feel tense and, at the same time, putting you at ease. Much later I found that Seymour-Smith made a somewhat similar observation on the "presence" of Graves. He wrote, "Few English-speaking poets of the century have possessed [Graves's] poetic 'presence.'"[3]

At that first meeting of ours Graves was in a hurry and nervous—subsequently I found that he was always ill at ease before a lecture, even if it consisted of nothing more than reading out a prepared text. Thus all we did was to exchange a few words. I was disappointed that the tight schedule Graves had in New York did not enable us to have a longer meeting, to sit down and chat—we had, I felt, much to talk about, and I did not know when I would have another opportunity to meet him personally. This disappointment, coming as it did on top of my own overly full work schedule, may have been responsible for my not writing to Graves for almost three years after that meeting.

My schedule, as I just said, was extremely busy, because, in addition to the two jobs I held down, I felt I had to respond to the lecture invitations I received in growing numbers, so that traveling out of town took up much of my time. For instance, on Monday, March 11, 1957, I flew to Boston, gave there two lectures to two different audiences, then took a night train to Philadelphia, where I worked in the morning of March 12 in the Dropsie library on my new book, *The Kingdom of Jordan* (which was published in 1958). In the afternoon I gave my weekly classes at Dropsie, stayed overnight in Philadelphia, next morning had my usual Wednesday classes at Dropsie, then took the train back to New York and worked at the Herzl Institute. The next day (March 14), having taken a day's leave of absence from the Herzl Institute, I again flew to Boston to give two more lectures, then the same night flew back to New York.

On March 28 Dr. Emanuel Neumann and I agreed that as of June 1 I would work full time at the Herzl Institute. This enabled me to resign from the Dropsie College, where the situation had become too difficult for me (as well as for several of my colleagues, who also resigned at the same time).

On April 27 a heated altercation took place between me and Irene in connection with financial matters. Our arrangement had been that she deposited her earnings into a bank account of her own, while I put mine into a joint account from which she could, and would, draw for household use and other expenses she incurred. When the relationship between us deteriorated, I felt prompted to open an account of my own to parallel hers. When I told her that I had taken this step, she became enraged. In vain did I try to explain that this merely established a strictly parallel situation between her and me as far as finances were concerned, and that I would, of course, continue to defray all our joint expenses. A few days later she informed me, in the presence of her mother, that she wanted a legal separation. Then she called a cab and left with her mother and daughter. The same day or the next she withdrew all the money from our joint bank account, which I had left intact. I only found this out when a small check I wrote on that account was returned by the bank with the notation "insufficient funds." In the midst of the emotional upheaval that Irene's leaving meant for me I did not pay particular attention to this financial aspect of the breakup of our marriage, but I could not help remembering a line from Graves's poem "In Her Praise" (which I liked so much that I knew almost all of it by heart), in which he speaks of the "mortal woman" who leaves "you, / Her chosen lover, ever again thrust through / With daggers, your purse rifled . . . " The subsequent tribulations and litigation between me and Irene, which lasted more than three months, are best left unreported in this context. I felt wrecked emotionally, but continued to function as usual, and this time my busy schedule proved a boon instead of a burden. Also a great help were my two daughters, Ofra, now aged fifteen, and Daphne, thirteen, whose love and understanding far beyond their age gave me comfort and strength.

In the midst of all this I managed to finish the manuscript of my book *The Kingdom of Jordan*, and delivered it in July to Herbert Bailey, editor of the Princeton University Press, which had contracted for it many months earlier.

On September 27, 1957, Irene, in the company of her mother, flew down to Alabama and obtained a divorce, charging me with desertion.

In the ensuing months I worked hard on my book *Golden River to Golden Road: Society, Culture and Change in the Middle East*, and in March, 1958, I was delivered the typescript to Macmillan and to the World Publishing Company, both of whom had expressed interest in it. (By that time I had become impatient with the slowness of publishers in giving a yes-or-no answer, and had decided to disregard their objections to multiple submissions.)

About the same time I started to work on a study comparing sexual and family life as they can be gleaned from the Bible with the same areas of life in the modern Middle East, and elucidating the former by the latter. The resulting book was published by Doubleday in April, 1959, under the title *Sex and Family in the Bible and the Middle East*, a year later by McGibbon & Kee of London under the title *Family, Love and the Bible* (I was reminded of "No sex, please, we are British!"), in 1962 again by Doubleday in paperback, and in the same year by the Ner Tamid Verlag in Frankfurt a. M. in a German translation, as *Sitte und Sippe in Bibel und Orient*.

In November, 1958, I met Ann Drevet, a beautiful person of exceptional character. We fell in love, and after she officially converted to Judaism we married on June 14, 1959.

I want to insert here a brief reference to one of my literary efforts that had remained unpublished in English to this day. In 1957 I got in touch with the British author and seafaring expert James Hornell, and we agreed that I would send him an English translation of my 1938 Hebrew book *Jewish Seafaring in Ancient Times,* and that he would augment the text wherever he thought it needed supplementation in order to stand up as a contribution to the history of seafaring in general. In February, 1959, the completed manuscript arrived from Hornell, but I was too involved with other matters to devote the necessary attention to it, and put it aside. I never found the time to get back to it. James Hornell died soon thereafter.

Another book which never got beyond the planning stage was one on religion in culture or religion in its cultural context, an outline of which I drafted on March 1, 1959.

On July 19, 1959, Ann and I flew to Israel—my first visit there since 1951. All the members of family in Israel took to Ann instantly, loving her at first sight. At one point my mother (now seventy-three years old) took me aside and said, "Now, make sure you don't lose her, too!" This motherly admonition was to remain effective for seven years.

I enjoyed greatly "showing Israel" to Ann, including places such as Peki'in, Sa'sa', etc., where I had never been before, and the new towns and villages that had sprung up after the 1948–49 mass immigration. From Israel we flew on August 9 to Istanbul, where we met Prof. and Mrs. Halil Inalcik, who took us on a sightseeing tour of Bursa and the surrounding villages. On August 12 we flew on to Athens, then subsequently to Rome, Madrid, Granada, Tanger, Casablanca, Amsterdam. Finally we returned to New York on August 21.

In December, 1959, I started work on yet another book, which I tentatively titled "Pata: Traditional Jewish Culture and Its Relevance Today." I never completed the manuscript, but many of the ideas I had for it went into other books of mine.

When I got my first author's copies of *Sex and Family*, I mailed one to Graves, with whom I had not been in touch for almost three years. During that time Graves was busy winding up arrangements with Laura Riding, by which their two houses in Deyá were finally transferred to him; publishing two volumes of poems, his translation of Homer's *Iliad*, and other books.[4] He was also occupied with problems caused him by his current "Muse," and with efforts to have *I, Claudius* made into a film. This last-mentioned project did not come to fruition at that time.

In January, 1959, Graves visited Israel, where he met Ben Gurion. He described his visit in an article, "I Discover Israel," published soon thereafter in *Holiday* magazine. An abortive project in which Graves was involved at that time was a musical, to be titled "A Song of Sheba," for which he wrote the lyrics—unpublished to this day.[5]

In the summer of 1959 a new "Muse" appeared on Graves's horizon: Margot, a Canadian girl of striking appearance, whose influence on him caused considerable apprehension on the part of the friends of the sixty-four-year-old poet. In September, 1959, he had to undergo a prostate operation which necessitated a long postoperative stay in the hospital in London. While still in the hospital he got involved in the plan to make a film on T. E. Lawrence, the "Lawrence of Arabia," about whom Graves had repeatedly written in the past.[6]

These affairs kept Graves fairly busy after his return form London to Deyá, and it was not until December 17, 1959, that he acknowledged the receipt of my *Sex and Family*. On that day he wrote me:

Dear Raphael:

I had an operation in September which upset me and all my business for three months; I am now returning to myself and find hidden in a pile of unopened books your Sex & Family: *a real treasure trove!*

Thank you ever so much: I have always found your conclusions as sound as they are original.

I am just doing a piece on the new Gospel of St. Thomas. *What a mess! But there are some hidden treasures in it which will probably escape the ordinary Christian eye (having eyes they see not etc)*

I hope that your ex-wife and you are both equally happy in your new lives. I liked her.

Yours ever
Robert

I shall be briefly in New York in January, with my eldest daughter Jenny, and hope to see you if only briefly. I'm glad we have the same publishers. They treat me superbly.

The last paragraph of this letter (before the postscript) indicates that I wrote him telling him of my divorce from Irene. I must have written that letter by hand, for I am unable to find a copy of it in my archives.

12.

The *Hebrew Myths*— Conception and Inception

ON JANUARY 28, 1960, Graves phoned me from the apartment of R. Gordon Wasson, the "mushroom man," where he was staying, and suggested that we meet there on the 30th in the morning.

The day before that meeting was very hectic for me since that day all the offices of the Jewish Agency, including those of the Herzl Institute of which I was director of research, and of the Herzl Press, of which I was editor, were moved from their West Side location at 57th Street to their new premises at 515 Park Avenue in a fourteen-story building the agency had purchased and remodeled.

Even prior to receiving Graves's call, in fact ever since he and Joshua Podro had incorporated a substantial amount of the findings I had presented in "Hebrew Installation Rites," into their massive *The Nazarene Gospel Restored*, I had toyed with the idea that Graves and I jointly could produce a substantial book about the ancient myths whose residue is preserved in the Bible and in postbiblical Jewish literature. I had imagined that I would provide the Hebrew-Jewish material, and Graves would add elucidations from non-Jewish mythologies, and especially from the Greek world, which would throw light on the original meaning of the old Hebrew and Jewish myths. As I read one Graves book after the other, his *King Jesus* and *The White Goddess*, his essay on Pharaoh's chariots, his *Adam's Rib*, and, of course, *The Nazarene Gospel*, it became clear to me that he had an abiding interest in the mythical and comparative aspects of ancient Jewish lore, and I felt that his erudition, and especially his familiarity with Greco-Roman and old European mythologies, could be the basis for a most valuable contribution to the kind of book whose compass gradually took shape in my mind.

True, I also had misgivings about such a partnership. I was by then well familiar with the Gravesian way of presenting unproven assumptions as if they were generally accepted facts that only waited to be pointed out. This made me uneasy. From my reading of his books, and from the work I had put in correcting (or rather suggesting corrections, because they were not always accepted) what I *knew* were erroneous statements in *The Nazarene Gospel* (despite the collaboration of a Jewish scholar), I knew that for Graves what he believed to be a fact simply *was* a fact, and that he had a habit of stating matters as fact even if he had no proofs on which to base them.

But then, thinking over all this, I found reassurance in one circumstance: in his letters Graves repeatedly expressed his respect and admiration for my scholarship. I felt therefore that I could assume that if, in the course of a collaboration between us, I vetoed something he wanted to put into a book to be written by the two of us, and if I explained my reasons for so doing, he would accept it. Thus I could make sure that the book would be sound by scholarly standards. As it turned out, I was not always able to stick to this principle, and occasionally I became guilty of not checking thoroughly the factual basis of statements Graves added to subjects covered in the book.

In any case, when I went to that meeting with Graves, I planned to suggest to him collaboration on a book on Hebrew mythology, similar in approach and format to his *Greek Myths*. Ann accompanied me to the Wasson apartment at 1 East End Avenue at 11:00 A.M. on Saturday, January 30, 1960. I was impatient to hear Graves's reaction to my idea, and soon found an opportunity to broach my proposal.

Graves reacted to the idea positively, in fact, enthusiastically. He said that I was the only person with whom he would like to do such a book, and went on to praise my style, my clarity, my daring, my originality, etc. He even thought so far ahead as to say that since my contribution to the book would certainly be greater than his, the authors' names should appear as "Raphael Patai and Robert Graves," in this order. I was flattered, but countered by pointing out that whatever the proportion of our respective contributions, his name would sell many times more copies than mine, and that this was sufficient reason for putting his name ahead of mine. He then suggested that we should aim at a book of some five-hundred pages, do it in two years, and divide the proceeds half-and-half. I, of course, accepted. Then Graves said that fortunately Doubleday was the publisher of both of us, and that we should therefore offer the book to them. I concurred, whereupon he picked up the phone, called Ken McCormick (he reached him at his home), and told him about the projected book. Ken instantly agreed to publish it, and said that he would have his office prepare a contract as soon as we let him have some details about the book.

Once this was settled, we got down to discussing the division of labor between us, and the actual procedure of writing the book. We agreed that I

140

would prepare a first draft, chapter by chapter, gathering all the mythological material I could find in the Hebrew and Jewish sources, on one subject after the other. I would then mail him the draft chapter, and he would do with it what he thought had to be done: edit my draft as he saw fit, and add to it whatever material he thought should be added from other mythologies, and whatever explanations he felt were necessary in addition to those already contained in my draft. He would then return to me each rewritten chapter for my corrections, emendations, changes, and ultimate approval. We did *not* touch upon the question of what to do in case we could not agree on something— who would have the final say. We both took it for granted that such serious disagreements would not arise, and we were proven right. Before we parted Graves invited Ann and me to come to Deyá and stay in his guest house which, he explained, was located at a convenient distance from his own house.

Needless to say, I was elated by this development, and started to work on the *Hebrew Myths* without delay. I could not, of course, liberate myself from my work at the Herzl Institute and Press, nor could I cancel speaking engagements booked long before. But, almost miraculously, and in reversal of the well-known Parkinson's Law, time for me seemed to expand in relation to the increase of the work I undertook. The only nonwork distraction I had was searching for an apartment in Manhattan, for both Ann and I felt that our lives would be more comfortable if we lived within walking distance of our workplaces. On February 26 we signed a purchase agreement for a cooperative apartment at 135 East 71st Street, a mere eleven blocks from my office, and six from Ann's. On the same day I mailed the first sixty-three pages of the manuscript of the *Hebrew Myths* to Graves with this covering letter:

February 26, 1960

Dear Robert:

After our meeting I didn't waste much time and got to work. I am enclosing the first results. As you will readily see, this is a rough draft; especially the first introductory section is merely a sketch and you are free to do with it as you like. Although the number of pages I am enclosing is 63, this does not yet exhaust all the creation myths. There is more to say about Behemoth, the earth, the great mythological act of the separation of earth and the sky, other mythical animals (a dozen or so), and then, of course, the creation of Adam, his first wife, Lilith, his second wife, our good mother Eve and their breed both demonic and human. I am very anxious to get your comments on this material.

You told me you are a fast worker. I will try to match this and keep you supplied with additional chapters as I finish their first draft.

So much for the present. I look forward to hearing from you soon.

Cordially
Raphael

141

The same afternoon I went to the Metropolitan Museum of Art where, I remembered, there was a plaster cast of a relief from the triumphal arch of Titus erected in Rome in 70 C.E. to honor him for the capture of Jerusalem and the putting down of the Jewish rebellion. I had always felt it was ironic that the most accurate representation of the Menorah, the sacred candelabrum of the Jerusalem Temple, should be found precisely on the triumphal arch designed to commemorate an event that was a great victory for the Romans and a catastrophic defeat for the Jews. Now it dawned upon me that by destroying the Temple of Jerusalem (and then perpetuating its memory by depicting the Menorah and the other sacred vessels they looted from it) the Romans played a historical role in enabling Judaism to change from a religion centered on sacrificial temple ritual into a global faith in which that ritual survived only as a nostalgic memory. As I stood there in the museum, contemplating the Menorah, I wondered what would have happened if the Temple had not been destroyed: for how many more centuries would the antiquated ritual of slaughtering animals in honor of God have survived before the religious leaders of Judaism would have found a halakhic way of abolishing it as incompatible with the spiritual and ethical values of their religion?

Be that as it may, the arch of Titus shows the Menorah in full detail. Scrutinizing the plaster cast in the museum showing the Judean captives carrying the Menorah, I noticed that on its two-layered hexagonal base, of which the relief shows three-above-three panels, there are depicted what appear to be mythical monsters. Since the seven lights on top of the Menorah symbolized the seven stars—I had shown this in my *Man and Temple*—and the whole Menorah had cosmic significance, its base, I felt, *had to be* symbolic of the subterranean realm, the waters of the abyss, in which, according to biblical mythology, dwelt the primeval monsters. The only question I had to answer to my satisfaction was whether or not one could take those monster-reliefs as faithful copies of what was actually shown on the base of the original Menorah. After all, they could have been inventions of the Roman sculptor who supplied that entire relief for the arch. I pondered on that relief at great length and with concentrated attention, and found that the sculptor depicted all other details of the Menorah in strict accordance with what we know about its shape and decorations from the ancient Jewish sources. Hence, I concluded, it was not likely at all that only with the base of the Menorah the artist should have taken liberties. It must be assumed, I felt, that these reliefs, too, were faithful copies of those that decorated the actual Menorah taken from Jerusalem to Rome. If so, we had here a rare pictorial contemporary documentation of how the Jews in the days of the Second Temple, that is, prior to 70 C.E., imagined the primeval monsters of the abyss. I made a sketch of the panels then and there, and later, when the *Hebrew Myths* was published, a more careful drawing of mine of one of those monsters was used to decorate the front jacket of the book.

142

Next day I sent off another letter to Graves, and in it I reported of the Menorah.

February 27, 1960

Dear Robert:

Yesterday when I sent off the 63 pages to you I wrote only a few lines in a hurry, in the midst of all kinds of other business that I had to transact in my office. Today is Saturday which I can spend in my own modest fashion of imitatio dei—*resting, that is to say engaging in the studies I so thoroughly enjoy. Thinking back of the note I sent you yesterday I find that I omitted several things I wanted to tell you. ("Hurry is from the Satan" says the Arabic proverb.)*

First of all, I wanted to tell you how delighted I am at this collaboration between us. I am sure, or, more modestly, I should say I hope, that we shall produce a truly significant book. I have long felt that a scholarly analysis and a comparative presentation of Hebrew mythology has long been overdue, and I believe that you and I are just the right combination to do it. In fact, it has never even been pointed out as yet how much mythological material has been preserved in the Hebrew (and Aramaic) writings dating from 1000 B.C. to 1000 A.D. I shall gather it all and present it to you section by section.

Secondly I should have told you that I want you to treat the material I sent you yesterday as what it is: a collection of excerpts from the sources, arranged in a roughly logical order, but otherwise in a rather raw state. Please treat it as such, in other words use the stuff sent as you deem fit, elaborate upon it, shorten it, delete sections, add new material, interpret, compare with Greek mythology, etc., with complete freedom. This first installment should be regarded as a sample or a trial piece. When I receive it back from you after you put it through your treatment, I shall know better how to present subsequent chapters so as to reduce the amount of work you will feel you have to invest into them.

If you compare the translations of Biblical passages appearing in the MS with the standard translations, you will find that occasionally I deviated from them quite considerably. In a few cases I used my own judgment in interpreting the Hebrew text (once or twice even to the extent of changing the readings); in others I followed textual emendations suggested by Biblical scholars. However, I shall not be adamant with respect to these changes; so, feel free to suggest other translations wherever you wish.

I remarked in my letter of yesterday that the introductory section is merely a sketch. I should have added that also the pages dealing with the Apocalypse of John (pp. 49–54) are very sketchy. Herrmann Gunkel has treated Rev. 12 and related passages in his book Schoepfung und Chaos in Urzeit und Endzeit, *(Goettingen, 1895) in more than two hundred pages, discussing in great detail the mythical antecedents of John's vision of the dragon-fight. I shall peruse Gunkel carefully, and subject Rev. 12 etc. to a much more detailed analysis.*

There is one more thing: yesterday afternoon I went to the Metropolitan Museum of Art in which there is a plaster cast of the relief from the Arch of Titus showing, among other things, the seven-branched Menorah looted by the Romans from the Temple of Jerusalem in 70 A.D. The base of the candelabrum consists of six panels, each of which shows mythical monsters depicted in relief. Two of them are composite animals with lion's or tiger's head and fish tail, the third has a head like that of a lizard on top of a long S-shaped neck, with one front leg visible and a fish-tail; the fourth panel shows two Sphinx-like creatures with wings facing each other; the fifth is in very bad shape but seems to be identical with the fourth. The last one seems to show two eagle-like birds with intertwined wings (something like the traditional cherubs, but again the relief is very indistinct). I made sketches of each of these, and I think we should include a discussion of these pictures—which are contemporary illustrations of the ancient Hebrew mythical dragons—into the chapter dealing with Leviathan.

I hope to hear from you soon.

> *Cordially*
> *Raphael*

Graves responded by return mail.

March 5 1960

Dear Raphael

Just back from London where I was receiving an "Award" and visiting my children.

Your material is splendid, *and the only problem is: what will a logical order be? From the reader's point of view the order I used in* Greek Myths *seems best. The myths themselves are presented in separate chapters. e.g.* Leviathan *or* Lilith *or* Balaam *or* Elijah. *Each myth is told as a story with variants: "But some say . . . " The different parts of each myth are then referred to sources—these are quoted verbatim if important. The meaning, or peculiarity, of the myth is then treated in a commentary to each chapter, From the Creation to . . . the fall of the Second Temple—("Metabainōmen Enteuthen")?*

—I am very busy this year & can't make any promise of immediate collaboration. I don't want to start until my desk is clear of lesser jobs. But I propose to make it my next big job and am VERY HAPPY *to be collaborating with you. Send all you can and I'll be thinking hard. I must get the big Gins-*

berg. I already have the Jewish Encyclopaedia *which is a help, and the* Koran!

Best wishes to your wife.

Yours ever
Robert

As one can see from these two letters, I started working on the book before the final format had crystallized, and before Graves and I had reached a definite understanding as to the organization of the material. His suggestion that we follow the structure of his *Greek Myths* seemed a good one, and I readily accepted it. It is also apparent from the letters that at that point both Graves and I were thinking of a book that would encompass *all* Hebrew myths— hence his references to Balaam and Elijah, and to "from the Creation to . . . the fall of the Second Temple." Only much later in the course of our work did we both come to the conclusion that the myths contained, or rather alluded to, in the Book of Genesis alone were more than enough to form the subject of a volume.

The Greek phrase *metabainōmem entheuten*, quoted by Graves, means "we are departing hence." These words were heard, according to Josephus Flavius's *Jewish War* (6:300), by the priests at Pentecost in the Jerusalem Temple shortly before its destruction by the Romans. They took them to be a divine utterance telling them that God was about to depart from the Temple.[1]

The "big Ginsberg" Graves mentions is, of course, the seven-volume magnum opus of Louis Ginzberg, titled *Legends of the Jews*, published from 1909 on and reprinted since many times, which is the unrivaled classic of the subject to this day.

After receiving his letter, I followed Graves's suggestion, and sketched out the next chapter according to the format of his *Greek Myths*. It dealt with the birth of Adam, and I enclosed its draft with my next letter.

March 29, 1960

Dear Robert:

Thank you for your letter of March 5. After receiving it I got hold of a copy of your Greek Myths, *something I should have done long ago, and read enough of it to get a clear idea as to the way in which you want the material to be organized. After that, instead of going back to the creation story which I sent you and rewriting it I took the next subject, The Birth of Adam, and worked up whatever material I had on it, according to the order which you suggested. The results are enclosed. As you see, it tells first the myths themselves in a narrative form with the insertion of "but some say," or a similar phrase, wherever required. Then follow the sources and after them explanatory notes dealing with parallel myths in other ancient Near Eastern literatures*

145

and containing some other comments as well. I have not gone so far as to discuss the meaning or peculiarity of the myth. This, I think, should be done later when there is more material on which to draw and from which to make some general deductions.

As to your time schedule, I understand completely that you cannot put aside other commitments for the sake of this work. I shall continue to send you chapter after chapter as I finish them, and you feel free to either lay them aside until you clear your desk of other jobs or to let me have whatever comments you have to make upon first reading.

One more point. As you will notice, I made no comments on the connection between the myths treated so far and old Hebrew rituals performed in the Temple or outside it. I want you to know, however, that already at this early stage I am completely aware of such connections and that at a later stage I shall add whatever will seem important to elucidate the Hebrew myths as the legomena *to the* dromena *of the ritual.*

Let me know when you plan to be in New York again (will it be some time in May?) and whether you think you will have time to meet me. We would be happy, of course, to have you and your wife for dinner in our home one evening.

Yours cordially,
Raphael

The *legomena* and *dromena* to which I refer in my letter are technical terms popularized in the studies of myth and ritual by Jane Harrison and other students of Greek religion. *Legomena* are the "things said," and *dromena* the "things acted"; that is, they refer to the two aspects, the spoken and the acted, of religious performance that go together and complement each other, and are the essential modes of expression of the myth and the ritual respectively.

Again, Graves responded immediately.

Ap 7 1960

Dear Rafael:

That's a fine chapter about Adam.

In an early Welsh poem, Yr Awdil Vraith *(Diversified Song) there is a tradition that Adam was made by God at Hebron and that he lay without a soul for 500 years, until Eve was created, and that in his old age he fasted in Jordan with water to his chin. . . . This latter account comes from the early mediaeval* Life of Adam and Eve, *but the source is Jewish. (Hebron was the old Jerusalem.)*

Do you know the source?

Yours ever,
Robert

146

Could you get me a Stith Thompson? *I'll send you a prompt cheque. I want it for other work as well.*

In the Welsh poem there is a story of Eve stealing a tenth part of the seed God gave Adam to sow: when she planted it herself, it came up as black rye.

The reference to the early Welsh poem *Yr Awdil Vraith* was at Graves's fingertips: he remembered it from his *White Goddess*, in which he quotes it in full (in pages 151–55 of the 1966 New York edition). It states that God "made" Adam in "Hebron Vale," after which for

> five hundred years,
> Void of any help,
> There he lingered and lay
>   Without a soul.
>
> But she [Eve] then did hide
> Of the gift a tenth,
> And all did sow
>   In what was dug.
>
> Black rye then was found,
> And not pure wheat grain,
> To show the mischief,
>   Thus of thieving.
>
> When in his old age,
> To his chin immersed
> In Jordan's water,
>   He kept a fast.

I responded without delay.

April 14, 1960

Dear Robert,

Thank you for your letter of April 7. I inquired at a bookseller and found that the new edition of Stith Thompson Motif of Folk Literature *which comprises 6 volumes costs $81.00. I assume that Indiana University Press the publishers will let me have 25% discount. Do you want me to order the book for you? I shall be glad to do so. Just let me know.*

I am working on the chapter entitled Adam's Mates *which includes the following: (1) Lilith (2) the first Eve (3) the second Eve (4) miscellaneous demons. I hope you will like it.*

What about your planned trip to the United States in May? Will we have a chance to see you?

Yours cordially,
Raphael

P.S. I will try to track down the Jewish original of the legend according to which Adam was made by God in Hebron and lay without a soul for 500 years until Eve was created. I seem to recall that each of these details is contained in one or another of the Midrashim. I will let you know as soon as I find the source.

That Adam's body was formed by God at Hebron out of earth, or rather red clay, is an old Midrash, found in many Jewish sources, including Philo and Josephus.[2] Likewise midrashic is the notion that, after being formed, Adam lay prostrate, stretched immobile, although not quite lifeless. I do not know the origin of the motif about Eve having stolen one tenth of the grain God gave Adam. The motif of Adam in his old age having fasted and stood in Jordan's water immersed to his chin was originally quoted by Graves in *The White Goddess* (p. 156). Its Jewish source is the Midrash according to which, after Adam had sinned and been driven out of Eden, he waded into the Upper Gihon River, stood midstream with water up to his chin, and remained thus for seven weeks until the strong flow of the river made his body turn soft like a sponge.[3] In preparing this material for the *Hebrew Myths* I could have easily quoted, or referred to, additional variants of the same myth, but since my understanding with Graves was that we should present each myth briefly and rapidly, so as to keep the readers' interest alive, I did not even suggest the inclusion of more than was summarized under "The Fall of Man," section k, in the *Hebrew Myths*. Also, since the myth of Adam's repentance is given in its most complete form in the late (thirteenth-century) Midrash collection known as *Yalqut Shimʿoni*,[4] I quoted that source, although earlier sources would have demonstrated the great age of this myth.

To illustrate with a concrete example the problems involved in presenting old Hebrew myths in easily readable English, let me translate here verbatim some of the extant variants. The thirteenth-century text of the *Yalqut Shimʿoni* reads: "On the first of the Sabbath [i.e., Sunday] Adam entered the waters of the Upper Gihon, until the water reached to his neck, and he fasted seven weeks until his body became like his heart."[5] Two details contained in this passage are explained in the notes written by R. Abraham Abele Gombiner of Kalish (c. 1637–1683) and printed in the Warsaw Levin-Epstein edition of the *Yalqut*, as follows: "The Gihon river was chosen by Adam for the mortification of his flesh, because it is the strongest among the rivers, and its waters rush, as Rashi said; this is why Adam entered it, so that his pain should be great." And the expression that Adam's body "became like his heart" means that it became red and lean like the heart . . . "

148

In the *Pirqe diRabbi Eliᶜezer* (ch. 20), a Midrash dating from the eighth century, the same story is told, except that there the body of Adam is said to have become "like a kind of sieve" (*k'vara*), and the author adds that after Adam had suffered in that rushing water for seven weeks, he prayed: "'Master of all the worlds! Remove my sin from me and accept my repentance, and let all the generations learn that there is repentance, and that You [reading *'ata* instead of *ᶜata*] accept the repentance of those who return.' What did the Holy One, blessed be He, do? He stretched forth His right hand and removed Adam's sin, and accepted his repentance." This addition makes Adam act in a truly mythical fashion: what he did affected mankind for all eternity.

Interesting is the variant contained in the apocryphal *Books of Adam and Eve*, which state that Adam commanded Eve to stand up to her neck in the Tigris River, while he himself stood in the Jordan, and that Eve's body became like grass because of her long stay in the water.[6] This seems to go back to an old variant reading recorded much later in the *Pirqe diRabbi Eli'ezer*, where Adam's body is said to have become *k'min y'ruqa*, "like a kind of sponge." *Y'ruqa*, a Hebrew word for sponge, was misunderstood by the translator of the apocryphal book, who thought it meant *yereq*, i.e., "herb." In any case, the idea that Adam repented and mortified his flesh is very old: it appears in a statement by Rabbi Meir (c. 150 C.E.), who says that Adam separated himself from Eve for 130 years, during which time he covered his body with fig leaves which sting.[7] It is more than likely that a version of this myth somehow reached Gwion, the author of *Yr Awdil Vraith*, and the tenth-century author of the Irish *Saltair na Rann*, referred to by Graves.

My April 14th letter was answered by Graves on April 19th.

Dear Raphael:

Please send me the Stith Thompson at whatever price.

—I never knew Adam had so many wives: I hope he didn't exceed the Pharisaic royal limit of 18.

—Myself, I'm getting ready for N.Y., and busy on a piece which is embarrassingly close to Hebrew Myths—*namely the extraordinarily close parallels between the Paradises of Gilgamesh, Enoch, the Greek Hesperides, the Mexican Tlaloc, & the Polynesian one.*

The common factor seems to be a hallucinogene which produces the same bejeweled visions. It is a very speculative inference but has to be faced; though in the book only lightly touched on, if at all.

—I think that you should put the destruction of the Second Temple as a limit on the myth-making i.e. no historical events may be referred to later than that historically. The last Hebrew myth would be Josephus' story about God saying: "Arise, let us go hence!" It was Josephus, wasn't it? In the case of later myths (e.g. the turning-black of Ham as a punishment for his crime of unfilial

behavior) they should be included if interesting enough—that one I believe was invented by Sephardic Jews to excuse their traffic in black slaves after the Black Death: "Ham shall serve his brethren." Before that, Ham was really "Chnas," a Canaanite white. Hence Apartheid—justified by the Boers on that very text!

See you soon I hope.

Robert

The "Pharisaic royal limit of 18" wives, which Graves mentions in this letter is recorded in the Mishna Sanhedrin 4:2 as the anonymous opinion of the Tannaitic sages. Once I located the passage in the original, I could not resist reading on—ever since my father had taught me Talmud as a teenager, I had a weakness for the talmudic Aggadah. On the same page I found that the talmudic text appended to that Mishna (B. Sanh. 21a) also gives the view that the "royal limit" was twenty-four or even forty-eight wives. The aggadic fantasy, once unleashed, knows no limits, and the same page of the great folio contains a neat example of the wild exaggeration of numbers that was characteristic of some talmudic sages: Rabbi Yehuda quotes Rabh (third century) as having asserted that King David had four-hundred children, born to him by the beautiful women whom he captured in his military exploits. "They all let their locks grow long, all sat in golden chariots and went in front of the troops, and they were the men of power of the House of David." The Bible itself, of course, has David marry no more than six wives. In any case, I was impressed by Graves's erudition: few non-talmudists would have known and remembered the "Pharisaic royal limit" of eighteen wives.

The piece to which Graves refers as being "embarrassingly close to *Hebrew Myths*" was an essay on hallucinogenic mushrooms which, he believed, produced paradisaic "bejeweled visions." He read it to the Oxford University Humanist Society, and subsequently included it in his book *On Poetry: Collected Talks and Essays.*[8] It so happened that on the very next day after he and I agreed that we would collaborate on the *Hebrew Myths,* Graves, in the company of Gordon and Masha Wasson, "ate psilocybe," one of the mushrooms from which the hallucinogenic drug psylocybin is produced, and which were probably used by pre-Columbian Aztecs for ritual purposes. He recorded his resulting visionary experience and included the account of it into the essay "The Poet's Paradise," in which he argued that the largely similar descriptions of a "jeweled Paradise," found in Hindu, Babylonian, Hebrew, Icelandic, Irish, Greek, Chinese, etc. literature are derived from a common experience of visions resulting from ingesting that hallucinogenic mushroom. I read that essay carefully, but failed to discover in it anything "embarrassingly close to *Hebrew Myths.*"

However, reading on in Graves's book *On Poetry,* I found that the essay titled "Technique in Poetry" begins with an unacknowledged and only slightly recast quotation from the *Hebrew Myths*. In the chapter "Adam's Helpmeets" (10. f–g) Graves and I wrote, or, rather, he wrote—rephrasing the draft I had supplied—that after Lilith proved an unsuitable helpmeet for Adam,

> God tried again, and let him watch while he built up a woman's anatomy: using bones, tissues, muscles, blood and glandular secretions, then covering the whole with skin and adding tufts of hair in places. The sight caused Adam such disgust that even when this woman, the First Eve, stood there in full beauty, he felt an invincible repugnance. God knew that He had failed once more, and took the First Eve away. Where she went, nobody knows for certain. God tried a third time, and acted more circumspectly. Having taken a rib from Adam's side in his sleep, He formed it into a woman; then plaited her hair and adorned her, like a bride, with twenty-four pieces of jewelery, before waking him. Adam was entranced.

In "Technique in Poetry" (*On Poetry*, p. 397) this has become:

> God, according to a Hebrew myth, promised our father Adam the helpmate he needed, and invited him to watch while the divine fingers built up a woman's anatomy from primeval sludge. They extemporized bones, tissues, muscles, blood, teeth, brains and glandular secretions, wove them neatly together, co-ordinated their functions, covered the whole ingenious apparatus with the smoothest of cuticles, and embellished it with tufts of hair in selected places. This technical demonstration caused Adam such disgust that, when the First Eve stood up in all her beauty and smiled at him, he turned his back on her. God therefore removed the First Eve and behaved with greater circumspection: He formed the Second Eve from Adam's rib while he slept, then ordered the Archangel Michael to plait her hair and adorn her in bridal array. Adam woke and was enchanted.

What was Graves's purpose in placing this paragraph at the head of his essay on "Technique in Poetry"? Nothing intrinsic, except to be able to go on and say, "I inherit Adam's mistrust of creative technique," and thus to launch into his subject proper.

Whether we consider the first or the second Gravesian version, we have here a masterly recasting into a dramatic scene what in the original midrashic source is told in laconic and inelegant brevity. Here is a literal translation of the passage in *Genesis Rabba* (161, 163–64), the main source of this myth:

> In the beginning [God] created her [Eve] for him [Adam], and he saw her full of sinews and blood, and He took her away from him, and He then created for him a second time. This is why he said, "This now is bone of my bones . . . "
> He [God] adorned her like a bride and brought her to him . . . What did you think? That He brought her to him under a carob tree or under a sycamore tree? No, at first He adorned her with twenty-four ornaments, and then He brought her to him.

151

In the parallel sources, listed in *Hebrew Myths*, p. 67, the story is told in similar terms.

Hewing close to the original sources, Louis Ginzberg, in his classic *Legends of the Jews*, presented the story in a rather simple, prosaic form:

> God had created a wife for Adam before Eve, but he would not have her, because she had been made in his presence. Knowing well all the details of her formation, he was repelled by her. But when he roused himself from his profound sleep, and saw Eve before him in all her surprising beauty and grace, he exclaimed, "This is she who caused my heart to throb many a night . . . " God Himself, before presenting her to Adam, attired and adorned Eve as a bride.[9]

What Graves was able to do with this meager Midrash is truly remarkable. It also exemplifies how he treated all the material that went into the *Hebrew Myths*.

But, coming back to Graves's April 19, 1960, letter, his assumption that the myth of Ham's turning black was invented by Sephardi Jews "to excuse their traffic in black slaves after the Black Death" in erroneous on several counts. Most importantly, that myth appears first in the Babylonian Talmud which was put in its final shape about 500 c.e.—that is, some 850 years before the Black Death struck the Middle East and Europe. Secondly, the role of Sephardi Jews—or of any other Jews for that matter—in the slave trade was minimal; the lion's share of the African slave trade was held by Arabs—as is well documented in a number of impeccable historical studies. When Graves and I met again in New York three weeks later, I pointed this out to him, and he readily admitted his error. No trace of it was left in the final text of the *Hebrew Myths* which, in its chapter 21, "Noah's Drunkenness," deals with Noah's curse of Ham and the midrashic embellishments which tell of Noah having been emasculated by his son Ham, or his grandson Canaan, just as the Greek myths tell of the castration of Uranus, and Hittite myths of the emasculation of Anu, by their unfilial sons.

At the end of his letter Graves writes that the Greek *Chnas* refers to a Canaanite. This is well founded, although it is quite a complicated matter. The name Canaan (Hebrew *K'na'an*) appears in many cuneiform, Egyptian, and Phoenician inscriptions, from the sixteenth century B.C.E. to the Roman period, in the form *Inakhkhi* or *Kinakhna*. In the Tell el-Amarna letters it is *Kinakhni;* in Phoenician, *Kn'n;* and in Egyptian inscriptions *Kn'nw,* which, if vocalized, gives *Kin'anu.* In Greek it became *Chna* or *Chnas.* My old friend, the archaeologist Benjamin Mazar of the Hebrew University of Jerusalem, explained the name as meaning "merchants," derived from the Phoenician word *Kinakhkhu,* which means purple, i.e., woven cloth dyed with purple, which was the chief export of Phoenicia, and thus gave its name to the merchants dealing in it, and ultimately to their country as well. If so, the original meaning of *kn'(kana')* seems to have been the murex conch which secretes the purple dye.[10]

In his *Greek Myths* Graves states categorically: "Agenor is the Phoenician hero Chnas who appears in *Genesis* as 'Canaan.'"[11] While the equation of Canaan with Chnas is well founded, that of Agenor with Canaan is more tenuous. Agenor in Greek mythology was the king of Tyre and the father of Europē, whom Zeus, in the shape of a magnificent white bull, abducted from the Phoenician coast. Europē is probably no more than the eponym of the continent of Europe. Agenor's sons were Kilix and Phoinix, who are the eponymous ancestors of Kilikia (Cilicia) in southeastern Asia Minor and Phoenicia respectively. A third son of Agenor was Kadmos, who went in search of his abducted sister, and, unable to find her, founded a city called after himself Kadmeia, which, in historical times, became the fortress of Thebes. After killing a dragon, Kadmos, at the advice of Athena, extracted its teeth, sowed them, and—up sprung a host of armed warriors.[12]

Of Kadmos Greek mythology has a lot to say,[13] and his name, of course, bears a suspicious resemblence to the Hebrew-Phoenician *Qedem* and *Qadmon*, meaning "ancient" or "eastern." In Genesis *Qedma* appears as a son of Ishmael (25:15); *Qadmoni* as a Canaanite nation (15:19); and *B'ne Qedem* (29:1, etc.) as an ancient people.

Whatever the precise explanation of the Greek myths about Agenor, one thing seems certain: they speak, in typical mythical fashion, of the eastern Mediterranean, Phoenician, origin of a number of lands and city-states, including "Europe," and Minoan Crete. The identification of Kilix and Phoinix as sons of Agenor makes it plausible that the countries of Kilikia and Phoenicia were considered by the Greeks as having been founded by, or derived from, a country whose name they rendered as Agenor. The only country that comes into consideration is Canaan, although I would not make much of any linguistic connection between Canaan and Agenor. *In fine*, while I did not feel that any identification between Canaan and Agenor could be proven, I considered a connection between them a distinct possibility, and hence raised no objection to the statement that "Canaan was *Chnas* for the Phoenicians and *Agenor* for the Greeks,[14] although I would have preferred to see it stated as a possibility rather than as a fact.

13.

The *Hebrew Myths* Takes Shape

G<small>RAVES DID NOT</small> inform me of the exact date of his arrival in New York, so I sent two brief notes to Deyá dealing with his request that I obtain for him Stith Thompson's six-volume classic, *Motif Index of Folk Literature,* which I managed to do.

April 27, 1960

Dear Robert:

I am enclosing the chapter on "Adam's Mates."

I ordered the six volumes of the Stith Thompson for you. The Indiana University Press will mail it directly to you to Majorca and send me the bill so as to let us have the benefit of their discount. Hope to see you soon in New York.

In a hurry,
Raphael

April 29, 1960

Dear Robert:

I am enclosing the invoices from the Indiana University Press for the Stith Thompson set. As you can see they allowed a very nice discount. Please send me your check in the amount of $49.78, and I will pay them since they gave me this discount personally only as one of their authors.

Yours cordially
Raphael

These notes reached Graves only after his return from New York to Deyá, but on Saturday, May 7, 1960, in the afternoon, I quite unexpectedly got a phone call from him. He had arrived, he said, the day before, and wanted to see me to discuss our book. Two days later, on Monday, May 9, at 9:30 in the morning, I went to see him, again at the Wassons. The same evening I made what was for me an unusually long entry in my diary—as a rule I logged only a line or two, such as "Worked all day long in the New York Public Library," or "Gave lecture at the Herzl Institute on the cultural patterns of israel." This time I wrote:

> **9:30–12 A.M.** Long discussion with Robert Graves about our book. Agreed on many procedural details, including the Ham affair and documentation. He said that if he should put in less than half the work, he would insist on receiving a correspondingly smaller part of the royalties. He had already spoken to Ken McCormick of Doubleday about the book, and to many other people. "We shall finish it in two years," he said. His wife Beryl was present for the first half hour. We also agreed on publishing a chapter ("Adam's Mates") in advance in a magazine. His agent, Willis Wing, will handle it.
>
> After lunch I called [Clement] Alexandre [an editor at Doubleday]. An hour later McCormick called me back. Said they are ready to sign contract, and suggested an advance of $1,000. I agreed.

The above is, of course, a rather inadequate summary of a conversation that lasted two hours and a half. Even today, after thirty years, I remember much of it. The words "the Ham affair" refer to our discussion of the question of when the myth of Ham's descendents turning black originated (see Chapters 12 and 14). As for "documentation," I remember that much of our discussion that morning revolved around the amount of scholarly detail and references to sources that were to be included in the book. Trained as I was in the strict school of scholarly presentation of sources and cautious conclusions drawn from them, I was of the opinion that we should proceed in this fashion: whenever we made a statement of fact or draw conclusions, we should add footnotes listing all the sources on which they were based. Whenever we offered a conclusion not fully supported by the available evidence, we should qualify it by saying "possibly," "probably," or the like.

Graves countered that if we proceeded in this manner we *ab ovo* restricted the readership of our book to a small coterie of scholars, and would never reach a wide public. He felt that we should, by all means, make as sure as we could that everything we wrote was factually correct, but we could speak with authority, that is, we could make statements which the reader would have to accept, not because we spread out the evidence before his eyes, but because *we* were saying it. He was especially opposed to cluttering up our pages with too many bibliographic references, which, he said, few readers are interested in knowing, and which even fewer care to check. "Let us, in this respect," he said, "follow the style I used in my *Greek Myths*. Open that book anywhere, and you will see what I mean." He handed me the copy of the *Greek Myths* which was lying next to him on the table. Instead of opening the book at random, I turned to its first page, and read the first sentence of the introduction: "The medieval emissaries of the Catholic Church brought to Great Britain, in addition to the whole corpus of sacred history, a Continental university system based on Greek and Latin Classics."

"There," Graves interrupted me," you can stop right there. If I had followed what you suggest, I would have had to append several long footnotes to this one sentence: to list the sources or studies which show that the Catholic Church sent emissaries to Great Britain, that those emissaries brought along the whole corpus of sacred history, that there was a Continental university system, that it was based on Greek and Roman classics, and that those Christian emissaries introduced that Continental university system into Great Britain. With such scholarly apparatus appended, the *Greek Myths,* long enough as it is, would have grown to an unmanageable size and become unreadable. Instead, I made a brief statement, unsupported by footnotes and source references, but based on what I had read and knew about the subject."

It was a cogent argument, and I gave in. But I insisted that at least every statement in the first part of each chapter, which was to contain our summary of one particular Hebrew myth as it could be gleaned from the sources, should be documented with footnotes referring to the main sources so as to enable scholarly readers to verify the bases of our assertions. As far as the second part of each chapter was concerned, which was to consist of our interpretation of the myths presented in the first part, including conjectures, parallels from other ancient mythologies, and additional explanatory comments, there, I felt, documentation was not as essential, and we could follow Graves's method of stating things we both agreed were correct, without burdening the reader with a presentation of the evidence on which we based our conclusions.

This was agreeable to Graves, the more so since, by and large, this was what he did in his *Greek Myths*. This, as far as I remember, was the only time we had a disagreement about procedural matters, and it was resolved quickly and amicably to our mutual satisfaction. Thereafter, whenever a disagreement arose between us, it was on minor points contained in this myth or that, and in the great majority of cases my point of view was accepted by Graves, who being himself neither a Hebraist nor a scholar of Judaism, respected my judgment. On the other hand, when it came to adducing Greek (and to a lesser extent other non-Jewish) material, I generally accepted statements introduced by Graves, although I made an effort to check them for accuracy, as far as I could. Today, thirty years and twenty-five books later, I feel that I should have practiced stricter control over those materials as well, so as to modify or even delete some statements made, not by Graves the classical scholar, but by Graves the poet, whose intuitive insights occasionally showed him things not as they were but as he felt they should be.

I no longer remember whether I saw Graves yet another time during that visit of his to New York, nor whether I attended any of his public lectures. I don't think I did, because two weeks later, when I again wrote to him, I referred only to one meeting in New York:

May 24, 1960

Dear Robert:

You told me when we last met in New York that you found in some sources that the legend of Ham's turning black originates from the Middle Ages and that its intention was to justify the trade in Negro slaves engaged in by Sephardic Jews. I looked into the matter and found that the first mention of the black skin of Ham and his descendents dates from Tanaitic times and can definitely be dated at least as far back as Rabbi Hiya Bar Abba who lived in Palestine about 250–350 A.D. For your information I am enclosing several slips on which I copied a verbatim translation of the relevant sources. The explanations necessary to the understanding of the often elliptic texts are supplied by me and put in square brackets. I hope to be able to write up the chapter or section dealing with this question in the near future.

I received a call from Doubleday with the suggestion that we sign a contract with them concerning the book. I consented on my part in the assumption that this is agreeable to you as well. I believe I will get the contract for signature within the next few days.

I hope you had a pleasant trip back home and that you will soon find the time to write up the chapter on Adam's Mates for publication in a magazine.

Yours cordially,

Raphael

To my regret I kept no copies of the "several slips" I enclosed with this letter, but the material I sent Graves must have been the same summarized in *Hebrew Myths* 21.e, under footnote 5. (Incidentally, in the first source mentioned there there is a misprint: it should read B. Sanhedrin 70a–b, not 72a–b as printed.)

One more word on that chapter. Under 21.3 Graves added the statement that " 'Japheth' represents the Greek Iapetus, father by Asia of Prometheus," and goes on to make some additional comments on Iapetus. He has more to say on Iapetus in his *Greek Myths* (4, b, c; 39, a; 56, d), but as far as I can see does not mention there the identification Iapetus-Japheth. However, it seems more than probable that a connection does exist between the two figures. The cautious *Entziqlopediya Miqrait* (3:746) comments (my translation from the Hebrew): "The name *Yefet* [this is the original Hebrew form of Japheth] is similar to the name of the Greek god *Iapetos,* the son of Uranos (sky) and Gaia (earth), one of the Titans whom the Olympian gods with Zeus at their head removed from power. However, we do not know whether there is a connection between the names *Yefet* and *Iapetos.*" To this I would like to add that, in view of the large number of Greek mythological names which are derived from Hebrew-Phoenician originals (some of them are mentioned in the preceding chapter), it seems likely that Iapetus does, in fact, go back to *Yefet.*

My May 24 letter reached Graves with remarkable speed. A mere four days after I mailed it, he replied.

May 28 1960

Dear Raphael:

Safely back and recovering. Many thanks for the notes on Ham's blackness. It is surprising that the theme is Tanaitic; but I suppose that negroes in that era came to the knowledge of the Tanaim only as slaves of inferior quality.

The agreement with Doubleday must, so far as I am concerned, be approved by my agent, Willis Wing of 24 East 38th St, and there is the added complication that I am no long[er] I when it comes to contracts but "Co-Productions Roturman S.A" which is a means of mitigating the incidence of tax—it saves me about 25% of royalties. I think that you agreed to use Willis Wing too; my experience is that a good agent is worth five times his commission. But I don't want to force anything on you.

I have a small job to finish for Holiday *about mushrooms and paradise; then I'll get on with Adam's mates.*

Yours ever
Robert

By the time I answered this letter, two weeks later, I had finished the first draft of yet another chapter of the book, which I tentatively titled "Adam's Children." Subsequently this material was divided into two chapters, one called "The Birth of Cain and Abel," and the other "The Birth of Seth." In enclosed it with my letter of June 13, 1960.

June 13, 1960

Dear Robert:

Thank you for your last letter. I am happy to hear that you will start "doing" the article on Adam's Mates in the near future. As to your suggestion that I take Willis Wing as agent, I shall look into it. In fact, I called Mr. Wing's office and told his secretary (he himself was not in) that I would like to meet with him within the next few weeks. At the moment I don't see what precisely he could do for me. I work in a limited field—Jewish and Middle Eastern anthropology—and whatever I produce in these areas I have no difficulty in placing in the scholarly journals. Similarly, with the books I have been writing. However, I shall talk to Willis Wing and see what he has to say. Possibly he may suggest that I branch out somewhat into areas in which he can be of real help. In any case thank you for the suggestion.

I am enclosing a short chapter on Adam's Children which, I hope, I shall be able to follow soon with another one on the first fratricide.

I noticed a few days ago in the New York Post *an article about you and your* Food for Centaurs. *I am sending you the clipping enclosed. I would also like to tell you that I got a copy of* Food for Centaurs *from Doubleday and have already started reading it. I enjoyed very much the piece from which the volume takes its title, the comments you made on Ginzberg's* Legends of the Jews, *and the first two short stories. I shall go on reading the rest. I can tell you that to read anything written by you is stimulating, entertaining and enjoyable.*

Yours cordially,
Raphael

Finally, on June 26, 1960, Graves mailed me the first chapter as reworked by him. In accordance with his abiding interest in goddesses, queens, and women who had the mythical power to dominate men, he tackled first the chapter ''Adam's Helpmeets,'' which dealt with the First Eve, Lilith, and the Second Eve who became Adam's permanent helpmeet. His covering letter read:

June 26, [1960]

Dear Raphael

I find that I can help with this collaboration far more than I expected . . . I think we have now got the layout and process properly fixed to make the book both scholarly and readable. Tell me if you object to anything I have done with your work; and we won't quarrel, I think.

This chapter will, of course, be subject to alterations later—especially cross-references will be needed to, e.g., the Queen of Sheba, Job's children, etc.

The Jewish references I have inserted from various authorities need your checking. I guarantee the Greek ones. Could you be kind enough to find the place in Malinowski's Sexual Life of Savages—*someone has stolen my copy—to what I refer? And the Ras Shamra reference to Abdiepta?*

I foresee that we shall have to make a very big book: perhaps in two volumes. Creation to Exodus; Exodus *to the Destruction of Solomon's Temple. It's wonderful to have you as a collaborator in this book which I have long*

159

wanted to do, but lacked the solid scholarship for. This first chapter I think will be an eye-opener to many and I don't think we will have much difficulty in publishing it in some literary-historical quarterly or monthly.

I have started on 'Adam's Creation' but find little to add there.

Will you be responsible for keeping the conventions of reference the same in my authorities as in Jews? I should like you to adopt the Rabbinic conventions established in the English translation of the Talmud, e.g. Shabbath instead of Sabbath, Rabbah instead of Rabba, as I did in Nazarene Gospel; also the Biblical conventions of (e.g.) "II Kings XXVII 2–4," with the chapters in Roman letters. I wonder whether you can cut down the references a bit more? E.g. 34 and 36 notes seem too full.

Yours ever

Robert

Are you yet working on the Garden of Eden story? I have a good deal of material to add when you have dealt with the Jewish-Babylonian myths. And will you reconstitute the first Creation chapter which you sent me before we had agreed on the layout. Or are you expecting me to do that? In your letter of Feb 27th you say that you have still more material. But the chapter seems already overloaded.

A word needs to be said about "Abdiepta" mentioned in Graves's letter. We entered this name into the *Hebrew Myths* in two of the variant forms found in scholarly literature: *Abdu-Heba* (pp. 12, 150) and *Abdu-Khipa* (p. 155), meaning "Servant of Heba" or "of Khipa." This was the name of a prince of Jerusalem, who appears repeatedly in the fourteenth-century B.C.E. Tell el-Amarna cuneiform letters, written by Canaanite (or, rarely, Egyptian) scribes in Palestine, Phoenicia, and southern Syria, in vulgar Akkadian.[1] Heba or Hebat, a form of Ishtar in the Hurrian texts, also appears in Hittite myths as the wife of the Storm-god, while in Hittite god-lists she appears as "Hebat queen of heaven, Hebat of Halba, Hebat of Uda, Hebat of Kizzuwatna." In Hittite prayers she is addressed as "Sun-goddess of Arinna, queen of all the countries . . . in the land which thou madest the cedar land [Lebanon?] thou bearest the name Hebat," or, more briefly, as "Hebat, queen, my lady."[2] While in all this there is no proof that the biblical name Eve (*Ḥawwa* in Hebrew) is derived from or connected with the Hittite Heba or Hebat, it at least opens the possibility of such a connection. Hence I felt that we were justified in stating that Eve "may well be a Hebraicized form of the divine name Heba, Hebat" (*Hebrew Myths* 10.10), although in saying this we overlooked the discrepancy between the *b* which is the second consonant of the Hittite name Heba, and the *w* which appears in the corresponding place in the Hebrew name *Ḥawwa*. It should be mentioned here that most scholars, following the Midrash Genesis Rabba 20:11; 22:2, are of the opinion that the original meaning of the

160

name *Ḥawwa* is snake, *ḥiwya* in Aramaic, and *ḥayya* in Arabic. The explanation offered in the Bible itself, "And the man called his wife's name *Ḥawwa,* because she was the mother of all living (*ḥay*)" (Gen. 3:20), is discarded by all scholars as a typical example of folk-etymology.

The chapter on "Adam's Helpmeets" contains one of the few Gravesian references in our book to his favorite hypothesis of iconotropy. The comment in *Hebrew Myths* 10.9 to the effect that "Eve's creation from Adam's rib perhaps derives iconotropically" from a misunderstood or misinterpreted ancient relief repeats the argument Graves presented some five years earlier in his *Adam's Rib.* However, in that book he argued that "Jehovah's removing a rib from Adam's side and transforming it into Eve seems to have been derived from a picture of Agenor's driving a curved knife under Belus's fifth rib, with the connivance of the Goddess."[3] For the *Hebrew Myths* Graves rewrote this hypothesis and expressed the view that the story of Eve's creation from Adam's rib may have been based on an "ancient relief or painting . . . [which] showed the naked Goddess Anath poised in the air, watching her lover Mot murder her twin Aliyan; Mot (mistaken by the mythographer for Yahweh) was driving a curved dagger under Aliyan's fifth rib, not removing a sixth one." Although both "iconotropic" derivations are equally fanciful, as long as the qualifying "perhaps" was introduced I saw no reason to veto it.

Graves's June 26 letter manifests his increasing interest in the *Hebrew Myths.* He talks about a "very big book," about two volumes, about it being "an eye-opener." When he says that it is a book which he has "long wanted to do," he must have had in mind the several books and essays in which he nibbled at the subject of biblical myths: what he tasted evidently whetted his appetite, and when I suggested our collaboration he was more than ready to bite into it seriously.

14.

The First Two
Chapters Done

T HERE IS DOCUMENTARY evidence to show that Grave's interest in biblical
stories dates, at the latest, from the year 1923, when he published a
slight volume of poems titled *The Feather Bed*.[1] He gave this volume its title
from a poem contained in it, and wrote a preface to that poem in which he
looked on Lucifer "with warmth as a champion of Peace, and on Moses with
hatred as a bloody-minded charlatan." This is how Graves himself viewed
that preface two years later in the introduction to his first historical novel, to
which he gave the long descriptive title *My Head! My Head! Being the History of Elisha and the Shunamite Woman; with the History of Moses as Elisha
Related it, and Her Questions Put to Him.*[2] In that same introduction he states
that he changed his mind about Moses under the influence of "Isaac Rosenberg's magnificent play *Moses*."

Isaac Rosenberg (1890–1918) was an English poet and painter who died in
active service in World War I. His play *Moses* was printed privately in 1916,
but Rosenberg remained practically unknown until 1937 when his *Collected
Poems* were published by the Tate Gallery, London, with a brief but most appreciative foreword by Siegfried Sassoon, a longtime friend of Graves. In ret-
rospect Rosenberg appeared a figure of major significance and the first
important poet to emerge from Anglo-Jewry.[3] I am not able to ascertain
whether Graves read Rosenberg's *Moses* or saw it produced on the stage, but
it is evident that he got acquainted with it between 1923 and 1925, and was
greatly impressed by it.

In *My Head! My Head!* all the major features and literary devices of
Graves's subsequent famous historical novels are in evidence in a surprisingly

complete form: there is the introduction of a historical figure (in this case Elisha), who tells the story with another historical figure (in this case Moses) at its center. There is the irrepressible proclivity to "correct" the known historical record by reconstructing what *actually* happened, and, in the course of doing so, to present unique interpretations of passages in authoritative historical sources. There is also the insistence on mother-right or on other manifestations of the importance of women as actors and movers in historical events or situations. Concretely, there is the idea that the hero of the story was—this is unmentioned in the historical sources—the son of a king: in *My Head! My Head!* Moses is presented as having been the son of the son of Pharaoh (who later succeeded his father as King of Egypt) and Jochebed, the Hebrew concubine of that prince, just as in Graves's *King Jesus* (and also in *The Nazarene Gospel Restored*), Jesus is made the son of the son of King Herod and his secret wife Mary. There is the idea, moreover, that after the birth of the royal son, his mother was married to a nonroyal but noble personage: Amram the Levite in *My Head! My Head!* and Joseph, the scion of the House of David, in *King Jesus.* Incidentally, in making Moses an Egyptian, at least on his father's side, Graves anticipated by fourteen years Freud, whose *Der Mann Moses und die monotheistische Religion* was published in 1939.[4]

The framework of *My Head! My Head!* is the relationship between the Prophet Elisha and the "great woman" of Shunem, which, as Graves correctly maintains, is only sketchily and incompletely told in the Bible (2 Kings 4:8–37). Graves fleshes out the story, making its centerpiece a long historical narrative told the Shunamite women by Elisha, as only he, with his prophetic tradition and insight, knew it. The story of Moses, that is, of what "really" happened to Moses, fills most of the short novel. That he chose Elisha and Moses to write about in his first attempt to rewrite history shows the extent to which his interest was already, as a young author, focused on biblical history. This interest was to remain with him all his life, and to find expression in a series of novels and studies, culminating in the *Hebrew Myths.*

An interesting sidelight on Graves's reticence and modesty when it came to referring to his own writings is given by the fact that throughout our collaboration on the *Hebrew Myths,* and during our years of contact both before and after it, he never once mentioned any of his previous books dealing with related subjects. Not even when I, at one point, suggested that we follow up our treatment of the myths of Genesis with a volume on the myths of Moses did he mention that many years earlier he had written a novel about Moses. (Incidentally, he turned down that suggestion of mine. He said that a volume on Moses, whose life work was centered on his relationship with the male God Yahweh, and thus lacked the feminine element, could not interest him.)

Two days after mailing me his June 26 letter, having received my chapter "Adam's Children," he wrote me again.

June 28th 1960

Dear Raphael:

Thanks for your letter & Adam's Children. You have done it so beautifully that I expect my share in the book will be very small.

I don't think that brother-sister marriage was anywhere countenanced except among "the gods": meaning a dominant dynasty who were above taboos. The present Kubaka of Buganda (I think that's his title) is ritually entitled to sleep with his sisters but has shocked his people by actually doing so.

I like God and Michael's being substituted for Demeter and Triptolemus in the act of husbandry.

Yours ever
Robert

As the beginning of this letter shows, the more carefully I prepared my first draft of a chapter the less Graves felt he could significantly contribute to it. One June 26, 1960, he had started his letter by saying that he found he could "help with this collaboration far more" than he had originally expected. But only two days later he wrote the exact opposite: he now expected his share in the book to be very small. Today I wonder whether, recognizing this to be the case, I was not tempted to reduce somewhat my vigilance—especially over the material Graves contributed to the book.

The enigmatic sentence about "God and Michael's being substituted for Demeter and Triptolemus" refers to the myth fragment according to which an angel taught Adam how to plow, which Graves contrasted with the Greek myth of Triptolemus, whom the goddess Demeter taught the mysteries of agriculture and who, in turn, disseminated that art through out the world. He had dealt with Triptolemus in his *Greek Myths,* 24.m. The way we finally phrased the reference to Triptolemus in the *Hebrew Myths* (12. 1,6) was to call attention to the contrast between two Greek views: one reflected in the myth of Triptolemus, who is initiated into agriculture as a reward by Demeter, (which is parallelled by the Hebrew myth about the angel teaching Adam how to plow, and the other expressed by Hesiod, who regarded agriculture as an evil laid upon mankind by ruthless gods (this is also the biblical view that has survived in the Middle East into modern times.

While this was going on on the *Hebrew Myths* front, I was again almost overwhelmed with other concerns. I had undertaken to edit for Thomas Yoseloff and the Herzl Press the *Complete Diaries of Theodor Herzl,* the founder of Zionism and father of Israel, after whom the Herzl Institute and the Herzl Press were named. Dr. Emanuel Neumann, my boss at these two institutions, wanted to have the Herzl diaries published on the one hundredth anniversary of Herzl's birth, that is, in the summer of 1960. At my suggestion we entrusted Prof. Harry Zohn of Brandeis University with the task of translating the *Diaries* from the German original, and it fell to me to write the annotations, explaining the hundreds of names, references to events, etc., mentioned in the *Diaries*, with which the average intelligent American reader could not be expected to be familiar. Tracking down the names of often obscure individuals and other references was a difficult and time-consuming task, but it had to be done. *The Complete Diaries of Theodor Herzl* was published in 1960, in five volumes, of which the first four contained the text in Zohn's excellent translation, and the fifth my annotations. At the same time I also started work on a book entitled *Golden River to Golden Road: Society, Culture and Change in the Middle East.* It was to contain papers I had published in various scholarly journals in the course of the preceding dozen years, as well as several new chapters written especially for it. It was published in 1962 by the University of Pennsylvania Press, and went into subsequent expanded editions in 1967, 1969, and 1971.

Also in 1960 I edited, jointly with Francis Lee Utley and Dov Noy, a book of essays, *Studies in Biblical and Jewish Folklore,* for the Indiana University Press. Its introduction consists of a programmatic paper by me, and among its contributors were some of the foremost American and Israeli folklorists.

In June of that year we moved from our Forest Hills home to a cooperative apartment in Manhattan at 135 East 71st Street, which I had purchased some months previously. On the 29th I attended the graduation of my younger daughter Daphne from high school, and then took a brief but well-deserved vacation.

When I got back to the city Graves's letter of June 28 was waiting for me. Next day I responded.

July 12, 1960

Dear Robert:

Upon my return from vacation, I found the two revised chapters, The Birth of Adam and Adam's Helpmeets. I don't have to tell you that I was delighted to have these at so early a date.

I am in agreement with all the additions you made, as well as with the omissions. I shall try to check the references to Jewish sources, as well as the others, and shall then send back the chapters to you.

Do you think that Adam's Helpmeets could be published as it stands in a magazine? Doesn't it need some kind of introduction and possibly also, certain other changes, so as to make it an independent piece?

In a week or so, if I get rid of the burden of work accumulated during my vacation, I shall come back to answer, in detail, all the points raised in your letter.

Cordially yours,
Raphael

165

This letter of mine reached Graves in Majorca in three days, an almost incredible record considering the time it takes today for airmail to cross the Atlantic, not to mention the additional time letters need to get from Madrid to the island of Majorca, and, once there, to be sent from Palma to the village of Deyá some thirty kilometers away. Graves responded instantly.

July 15 1960

Dear Raphael:

I'm most relieved that you like my work on those two chapters.—I don't see why Adam's Helpmeets *can't be published more or less as it stands, if you O.K. it. The editor might insist on cutting out references but I don't think any introduction is needed. The* stories *are what people like, and the novelty of new light on an old subject . . . Eva Meyrowitz the authority on W. African queenships has written to me about Lilith: a possible explanation of the myth in terms of an affiliated matrilineal tribe moving out of Adam's confederation. I'll see whether it makes sense.*

Very busy, as you are; being the only person here besides Beryl who isn't on holiday.

Yours ever
Robert

Eva Meyrowitz (actually Meyerowitz) certainly was an "authority on W. African queenships." She was the author of several highly regarded books on the Akan, Ghana, and African divine kingship in general. I always regretted that her studies came too late for me to profit from them when writing my "Hebrew Installation Rites." Her view, referred to by Graves, about the political background of the Lilith myth, is in keeping with the frequently found approach of many anthropologists to myth: they tend to see in myth (or, at least, in some myths) a poetic condensation of the memory of major communal events. The view that Lilith's escape from Adam is a mythical reference to a historical incident found its expression in a modified form in the *Hebrew Myths* 10.10. Other examples of this type of myth interpretation are found, e.g., in *Hebrew Myths* 16.1–7.

The letter of Eva Meyerowitz to Graves, mentioned by him, was dated Cape Town, July 6, 1960, and most of it deals with Adam's helpmeets. She wrote:

Dear Roberto dear,

So happy to hear from you so soon again. I was thrilled to read that you have written about Adam and his three wives: I had forgotten about Lilith and do not think I ever knew of a second Eva. I wonder how you interpret this

166

myth. It is certainly an historical account, and the truth might have been something like this:

Lilith, queenmother of a matrilineal people, may have allowed Adam and his people to graze cattle on her land. When the latter made political demands, and she felt too weak to repulse these, she simply left with her people and settled elsewhere. Matrilineal people were always quick to do this, even to-day. I just got a letter from the chief and queenmother of Offuman, who informed me that they had left with their people their capital (no more than a village), because they had unpleasant quarrels with another chief. Now they are busy building themselves another one.

The first Eva may have been willing to create a state with Adam and his people. Doing it the matrilineal way it would have meant that a substitute of Adam would have been sacrificed and sewn into the skin of the totem animal of the goddess of the matrilineals. The patrilineals, who had none such customs, may well have been disgusted.

With regard to the second Eva: Eva listened to the snake (symbol for death and resurrection) i.e. divine ancestors, and converted Adam to matrilineal ways by seducing him, the apple may have symbolized the Earth goddess of the matrilineals. The god of the patrilineals, i.e. Adam's brothers, got angry and ousted Adam and Eva from the fertile land they lived in (paradise). Hence they had to endure hardships on barren land where the women had to work hard to survive.

All this is probably nonsense. I can not tell you how keen I am to know what you did with the story. I have read "Man and Temple" by Patai but had forgotten the title of the book, and I am afraid, much of the contents. I got the book again from a friend and am re-reading it.[5]

This letter is interesting because it shows the utter abandon with which even serious and responsible anthropologists approach the interpretation of early biblical myths, and read into them references to their own favorite subjects. For Eva Meyerowitz, all three mythical helpmeets of Adam—Lilith, "the first Eva" and "the second Eva"—were "queenmothers" of matrilineal peoples, and whatever is told about them must refer to struggles between the "matrilineals" and the "patrilineals." In making this connection, she becomes oblivious of the explicit content and intent of the Adam and Eve myth: to explain a number of extremely painful problems besetting the contemporary human condition by referring their origin back to the first ancestral pair and its improper conduct. Compared to Meyerowitz's flights of fantasy the poetically intuitive insights Graves brought to bear on his biblical exegesis must appear as but tame flutters of his Pegasus's wings.

Even before I received Graves's July 15 letter, I sent him another one with comments on the chapter "Adam's Helpmeets." That letter illustrates how meticulously both Graves and I approached our task, and the care that went

167

into each chapter before both of us were satisfied with it. No wonder the book could not be completed as fast as we had originally thought. Nevertheless, as seen from the following letter, in the summer of 1960 I still imagined that we should be able to finish the first volume within a year. As for the problem of footnotes, which had bothered us from the very inception of our work, we agreed that they should appear only after the first part of each chapter which contained our summary of the text of the Hebrew myths, and should consist of nothing but brief references to selected sources. I accepted Graves's suggestion that the second part of each chapter, in which we presented our observations, explanations, and indications of similar myths found in other cultures, should be left without source references or any other type of footnotes.

My letter of July 19, 1960, was quite detailed.

July 19, 1960

Dear Robert:

In the course of the past week I was able to devote quite some time to additional work on the chapter Adam's Helpmeets. I am returning to you your type script as well as a retyped copy so that you should be able to locate easily the changes and additions.

On page one, end of first paragraph (this and the following refer to your type script), I changed the wording in order to be in keeping with the Biblical text.

On page two, in the second paragraph I introduced a change so as not to put in something that is not contained in the sources. I should have done the same with the words you put in the mouth of Lilith "how can I return to the house of Adam and live like a decent housewife" etc., but I simply did not have the heart to do so. This simply is too good to be omitted.

Section d on page three has been transferred to the end of the chapter because I think it disrupts the story.

The word "vexed." I changed this to "undismayed." It is somewhat more respectful.

On page four, line six, I introduced a change because, as it is stated three lines later, God forbade Adam and Eve to have intercourse and therefore the impossibility of intimacy could not have been one of the reasons for sawing the androgyne in halves.

On page nine, I substituted a much longer section for the original number IX. Similarly, on page ten, a new section eleven has been substituted.

On page eleven, the first few lines in section twelve have been expanded and the precise spelling of Heba or Hebat substituted.

On pages fourteen and fifteen, changes have been made in the source references. The Malinowsky reference was checked and changed somewhat so as to conform to his statements.

In checking the references to Jewish sources which you added, I found that they were repeatedly inaccurate. This is to be expected, however, when one works with these sources at second hand. You would be surprised how many times wrong references are given, for instance, in that standard work of Samuel Krauss, Talmudische Archaeologie.

I completely agree with you that perhaps two volumes will be necessary. We might aim at finishing the first volume (From Creation to Exodus seems to be the right material to be covered) in about a year. I shall be glad to keep track of the conventions of reference. I have nothing against adopting the ones you suggest.

If you feel very strongly about keeping the references short (for instance old-34 and 36 = new-41 and 43), I shall acceed to your wishes. I myself feel that I like to put in references to all the sources which I actually consulted and in which I found quoted material.

I have not yet started on the Garden of Eden story. I am trying to proceed chronologically. I shall soon get back to the first chapter and rewrite it so as to conform to the layout on which we agreed and which I think is fine.

I have a question in connection with the layout, however. As the "Adam's Helpmeets" chapter now stands, it consists of a text section subdivided by lower-case letters. Then follow the footnotes containing sources of references of this section. Then follows another text section subdivided by Roman numerals, and this again is followed by footnote references. I think that it makes no sense to divide the footnotes into two parts in this manner. Why don't we relegate all the footnotes to the end of the chapter and number them throughout consecutively? Or do you feel differently about this?

Lastly, as to the publication of "Adam's Helpmeets" in a magazine: Don't you think that it requires, for that purpose, a brief introductory paragraph? If so, do you want to write it?

Once we have this chapter in final shape, will you send it to Willis Wing or do you want me to do this?

Kindest regards,
Raphael

This letter remained unanswered, and I wrote again five weeks later.

August 23, 1960

Dear Robert:

I haven't heard from you for some time. I hope that everything is alright with you. I myself was very busy during the last few weeks with the finishing touches on my book Golden River to Golden Road, *which is scheduled for publication within a year by the University of Pennsylvania Press. I had some difficulty with this manuscript and it made the rounds of several publishers*

169

until finally the University of Pennsylvania Press decided to take it. As it usually happens when a manuscript remains unpublished for a number of years (I completed this one in 1956), upon rereading it one finds quite a lot to change, to omit, or to add. In fact, I added a completely new section dealing with the problem of dividing the Middle East into "culture areas." In earlier years I tried to solve the problem presented by such an attempt but never felt that I had enough knowledge of all the details to be able to do it. Now the pieces of the jig-saw puzzle fell into place almost by themselves. I drew up a map of the whole area from Rio de Oro to Samarkand (you remember Flecker's "Golden Road to Samarkand"?), and mapped out some 23 distinct culture areas within this huge "culture continent."

I am now practically done with this work and can return with renewed zeal to our Hebrew Myths. *I shall send you new material very soon.*

As soon as I receive from you the final O.K. to the "Adam's Helpmeets," I shall hand it to Willis Wing and I hope he will be able to find a suitable outlet for it.

> *Yours cordially,*
> *Raphael*

Graves answered by return mail.

> *Aug 27 1960*

Dear Raphael:

Thanks for your letter. I have been very busy myself on film-business and poems, so please don't apologize for your own distractions.

Your work on Adam's Helpmeets *is admirable. I have an addition to suggest on page 20 end of para 2.*

On Sept 15 I move for three months to London where I will be separated from my books, but will be able to use Joshua Podro's library & get him to check the Talmudic & other texts. The address will be: 128 Kensington Park Road, London W. 11.

I suggest that when you have approved or omitted or amended my insertion, you should ask Willis Wing to try the piece on Commentary *or whatever other journal he thinks fit, and ask them to suggest what introduction is needed.*

I favour the keeping of footnotes in two sections, simply because if you run both lots together it means more renumbering work if we make last minute additions to either section. I learned this in my Greek Myths *work.*

> *Robert*

As you can see from the last paragraph of this letter, the problem of the footnotes continued to bother us. But I did not come back to it in my next letter: Lilith interested me more.

September 1, 1960

Dear Robert,

Just a line to let you know that I received your letter dated August 27th, and that I am very happy that you like my last work on the chapter "Adam's Helpmeets."

As soon as Willis Wing is back from his vacation I will get in touch with him and talk to him about placing the article as you suggested.

I have to give careful thought to your suggested insertion. The idea strikes me as most plausible, but I would like to find at least some documentary allusion to it so as to make Lilith's supersession by Hebat not merely a possibility, as you phrased it, but a probability.

Raphael

Since I was unable to find any "documentary allusion" to Lilith having been superseded by Hebat, the insertion made by Graves to that effect was ultimately deleted from our manuscript.

On September 9 Ann and I took Daphne to Bloomington where she had been admitted as a freshman at Indiana University. The distance from New York to Bloomington is some nine hundred miles, and I drove leisurely, stopping twice en route for overnight stays. While in Bloomington I visited my old friend David Bidney, who in 1947–48 had done a lot to facilitate my adjustment to the New York environment—not an easy thing for a newcomer from Jerusalem—and who now was professor of anthropology at the university. I also went to see Richard Dorson, who had contributed an article to the volume *Studies in Biblical and Jewish Folklore,* which was published that year by the Indiana University Press. Then I went to pay my respects to Stith Thompson, dean of American folklorists, who had written the first of the two introductory chapters to that book. Talking to these people, and getting a whiff of the scholarly atmosphere that surrounded them, I felt reassured that Daphne had made the right decision in going to Indiana University rather than one of her other choices. On the return trip I was impatient to get back to my desk, so we stayed overnight only once in a motel about halfway, and next afternoon arrived home. Both my daughters being now away in college, the house felt empty, and Ann and I were alone for the first time since our marriage.

15.

The Biblical
Encyclopaedia—An Attempt

I N SEPTEMBER, 1960, I was busy, in addition to all my other works and duties, with a grandiose plan. By that time the first three volumes of a new Hebrew biblical encyclopaedia, titled in Hebrew *Entziqlopediya Miqrait,* had been published in Jerusalem by the Bialik Foundation of the Jewish Agency for Palestine (Israel), under the editorship of the foremost biblical scholars, linguists, archaeologists, and other specialists, most of them affiliated with the Hebrew University of Jerusalem. Some time earlier I had approached the people in Jerusalem who administered this multivolume project (originally six volumes were planned, but eventually this expanded to eight), and got from them a tentative agreement to represent them in negotiations with a large commercial publisher in New York for the publication of the encyclopaedia in an English translation in cooperation with the Herzl Press.

I contacted, first of all, McGraw-Hill, the largest encyclopaedia publisher in America, and found them receptive to the idea. On September 20, 1960, I went, together with my friend Sam Bloch, who served as business manager of the Herzl Press, to see Curtis Benjamin, chairman of the board of McGraw-Hill, and Carl Nagel, its vice-president, and had with them an intensive, and what I considered fruitful, discussion of the project. After a silence of several weeks, in November Nagel called me and asked me and Sam Bloch to have lunch with him. We met on November 10, and Nagel told us that McGraw-Hill was willing to sign a contract for the *Biblical Encyclopaedia* with these provisions: the Herzl Press was to take care of its translation and printing, and McGraw-Hill was to purchase from the Herzl Press ten thousand sets for 35% of the list price, which was to be between $120 and $150. This, as Sam and I saw it, was a very attractive offer, since it meant an income from McGraw-

Hill alone of some half a million dollars, which would be enough to cover all the translation, editorial, and printing expenses.

However, in the weeks that had elapsed between our first meeting with McGraw-Hill and the second meeting with Nagel, two developments had taken place which prompted me to propose to McGraw-Hill an alternative plan. One was that, despite my urgent letters and phone calls to Moshe Gordon, executive director of *Mossad Bialik* (Bialik Foundation), which was the legal owner of the encyclopaedia, I had received no formal consent from him to enter into an agreement with McGraw-Hill, or with any other American publisher for that matter, about the English edition. Knowing as I did the creaky machinery that turned the wheels of the Bialik Foundation, I understood that the executive of the Jewish Agency, of which the Bialik Foundation was a subsidiary, was unable to reach agreement on such a weighty issue as the publication of the encyclopaedia in English was for them. Part of this inability, I suspected, may have been due to the less than total harmony between the executive of the Jewish Agency in Jerusalem and its New York office, in which Dr. Emanuel Neumann, the president of the Herzl foundation, was a central figure.

The other development was that, encouraged by the positive reception I found at McGraw-Hill, I devoted much time to reading the available volumes of the Hebrew encyclopaedia. Up to that time I had relied on the considerable scholarly reputation the editors and contributors enjoyed; it was on that basis that I had no hestitation in suggesting to McGraw-Hill the publication of the encyclopaedia in an English translation. Now, however, I wanted to see for myself whether my confidence in the quality of the encyclopaedia was not misplaced, and whether this major scholarly undertaking which, after all, was produced in Israel with a Hebrew-reading scholarly public in mind, was in fact suitable for a wider English-reading public ignorant of Hebrew. As I spent evening after evening reading the entries, I got the impression that the *Entziqlopediya* as it stood devoted far too much space to archaeology, topography, the flora and fauna mentioned in the Bible, and other such subjects usually subsumed under realia. Furthermore, it became evident that it allocated relatively little room to the social and cultural life of the ancient Hebrews and the neighboring peoples reflected in the Bible, to religious ideas and trends, and, indeed, to the whole spiritual world of which the Bible was the product.

For instance, in the very first volume, the article "Elohim" ("God") was twenty-four columns in length, while the very technical article "Alefbet" ("Alpha-Beth") covered forty-four, almost twice as much. The article "Apocalypse" was given a mere two columns of text, while the one on "Urwah" ("Stable") got five. Involved as I was in working on the *Hebrew Myths,* which dealt with a largely neglected aspect of bibilical religious development I was especially sensitive to these disproportions and to what appeared to me a one-sided approach. Realia, I felt, have of course their place

173

in a biblical encyclopaedia, but its emphasis should be on the Bible as the most important religious sourcebook in the world.

Once I became convinced of this, and that therefore the Hebrew encyclopaedia as it stood would not have a sufficient appeal either to the general public or to the American scholarly community, I decided that I would modify my original proposal to McGraw-Hill, or, rather, substitute for it a new alternative: that my task, instead of merely supervising the translation of the Hebrew text into English, should rather be to edit it, which would enable me to shorten the technical entries dealing with realia, and to expand those devoted to anthropological, social, cultural, and, above all, religious subjects.

As another alternative I thought of an entirely new biblical encyclopaedia which would have nothing to do with the Hebrew one published in Jerusalem, but would be an original and important large-scale publishing venture for McGraw-Hill. Still, when I met Nagel on November 10, I felt that on that occasion I should only listen to what he had to say, and not come out with any new proposal.

However, a day or two after that meeting I thought there was no sense in procrastinating, and called Nagel for an additional meeting. This took place on November 15, with the participation of both Benjamin and Nagel. I explained to them what I had in mind, and why I thought that the English edition should not be a translation but a revised version of the Hebrew, or, alternatively, we should plan for an entirely new biblical encyclopaedia. Most of the discussion thereafter revolved around how such a new biblical encyclopaedia should be structured, what type of scholars should be invited to contribute entries to it, who should constitute the editorial committee, and the like. Benjamin and Nagel's reception of my suggestion was entirely positive, and, in fact, I gained the impression that they were more favorably inclined to these new proposals than the original one.

Two days later I got another call from Nagel. He told me that they wanted to get more details about my two new plans, and suggested that I make an oral presentation a few days later to a group of eight or ten McGraw-Hill executives.

On November 30 Nagel called to inform me that the meeting was set for December 2, in the afternoon. When I arrived at the appointed time I found in the boardroom the entire high command of McGraw-Hill: Harold McGraw, president; Curtis Benjamin, chairman of the board; Carl Nagel, vice-president, and some five or six others whose names I did not get, or, in any case, cannot remember. I made a fifteen-minute presentation, going into an analysis of the differences between the alternatives on the table.

The ensuing discussion, which lasted an hour and a half, was intensive and covered a wide range of issues, from editorial problems to marketing outlook, possible competition from other, similar projects, etc. It was most interesting to me becaue, among other things, it gave me an insight into the working of a major publisher, in which, I learned right there at the source, the major consideration, when all was said and done, was the business angle. Although nobody said so explicitly, it was nevertheless clear that the decisive factor was whether or not McGraw-Hill would make money on the planned encyclopaedia.

On December 13, Carl Nagel called and informed me that McGraw-Hill had decided to go ahead with the translation of the Hebrew biblical encyclopaedia. This meant that now the whole plan again depended on Jerusalem, which was not a propitious situation. In fact, the consent of the Bialik Foundation was never given, and the Hebrew biblical encyclopaedia has to this day not been published in an English translation.

16.

Work Intensifies

I N THE FALL of 1960 I began to make inquiries with a view to placing a chapter or two from the *Hebrew Myths* in a magazine to be published in advance of the appearance of the book itself. In September I called my old friend Gertrude Samuels of the *New York Times,* told her about the book, and asked her whether she thought she could publish a chapter of it in the *Times* Sunday Magazine. She showed interest, and I sent her the chapter "Adam's Helpmeets." A few days later she returned it with regrets: it was, she wrote, "much too specialized for the magazine." About the same time I also sent a copy of the same chapter to Willis Wing, the literary agent, but he, too, found it unsuitable for magazine publication. I reported this to Graves on October 3, 1960.

Dear Robert:

As I wrote to you in my last letter I sent "Adam's Helpmeets" to Mr. Willis Wing. Today I got a note from him in which he writes:

> *I have read with the greatest interest the ADAM'S HELPMEETS chapter from yours and Robert Graves' HEBREW MYTHOLOGY. The material is fascinating but I think it would have to be radically recast to provide an article a magazine could expect to use. You may not want to invest the time at present and first to let me see other chapters as they are ready; it might be we could then show several chapters as they are including this one on Adam to editors likely to be interested and would then learn whether we could draw some definite interest which would give us some specific line to go on. Can you give me an idea when other chapters might be available? Meanwhile I will hold this here if I may.*

What do you think of this?

I am enclosing my retyped copy of the chapter "The Birth of Adam," as well as the original which you sent me and in which I made the few corrections which I thought should be introduced. I supplied the source reference to footnote 8 on p. 8 of your copy. There seems to be some confusion with regard to footnotes 13–19 on the same page, but I hope that I shall be able to clear this up.

I have just completed the chapter "The Fratricide" and placed it into the trustworthy hands of my secretary. I hope she will have time to type it in a few days, after which I shall immediately send it to you.

> *Yours cordially,*
> *Raphael*

Graves responded three days later.

> *128 Kensington Park Road*
> *London w. 11*
> *[October 6, 1960]*

Dear Raphael:

I fear that Willis may be right: the ordinary editor of a magazine would find it indigestible, though readers *would not. Maybe the* Hudson Review, *which does not cough at difficulties, would like it? Apart from University magazines there is a continuous decline in boldness among editors. But when the book is published, everyone will say how fascinating it is.*

Don't apologize for delays. Here I find myself called on to doctor the script of the Col Lawrence film (proposed successor to The Bridge over the River Quai, *by the same team) for which my agent will demand enormous sums of money in return for my availability until Christmas. But at least I'm not taking on any other writing job to conflict with the Myths.*

I have made a few verbal emendations to your admirable additions to the Birth of Adam *chapter & will return this when I have shown it to Joshua Podro who will be greatly interested.*

Chamai & Erichthonius *are O.K. and help the argument. I look forward to the* Fratricide.

> *Yours ever*
> *Robert*

The Lawrence film Graves mentions was a project of Sam Spiegel the producer, *Lawrence of Arabia,* for which at first Alec Guinness was considered in the role of T. E. Lawrence. Ultimately the role went to Peter O'Toole. Graves did, in fact, serve as adviser, but all he was able to do in that capacity was to help O'Toole in his characterization of Lawrence.

Of Chamai and Erichthonius only the latter survived in the *Hebrew Myths* (14). In his *Greek Myths* Graves refers to Erichthonius repeatedly: he was a son of Mother Earth, of the seed of Hephaestus, entrusted by Athene to Aglauros, eldest daughter of the Athenian King Cecrops who, was himself a son of Mother Earth. Subsequently Erichthonius was brought up by Athene herself, and became king of Athens.[1] The argument in the *Hebrew Myths* Graves thought would be helped by a reference to Chamai and Erichthonius pertained to the midrashic interpretation of Gensis 3:1ff., according to which the serpent in the story of the Fall of Man was none other than Samael in disguise. We made the comment that snakes were identified in some ancient Near Eastern and Greek myths with the spirits of dead heroes, who were portrayed as snakes, or half-snakes. It was in this context that we mentioned Erichthonius.

When I received Graves's October 6 letter I had just finished my draft of the chapter "The Fratricide," and mailed it to him on October 12, with this letter.

Dear Robert:

I am enclosing the chapter on "The Fratricide." I have a new secretary and I forgot to give her precise instructions as to how to type the footnotes. This is the reason for the footnotes appearing all at the end of the entire chapter instead of divided into two, one after the narrative part of the chapter and the other after the explanatory part. However, we can correct this when we retype the chapter in its final shape.

It does not often happen that I cannot read a word in your letters. However, I am defeated in trying to decipher the first of the two words in the name of the review which you thought could be interested in our "Adam's Helpmeets." Would you kindly give me again the name of this journal and then I shall communicate it to Willis Wing.

It was interesting to hear about your work in connection with the Lawrence film. Do the producers of the film have an expert who takes care of those little details in costuming, scenery, behavioral traits, gestures, speech manners, etc. which can make all the difference between true and false when a film tries to portray people who are the products of a non-Western culture, such as the Arabs?

I would not mind at all going over to England for a limited time in order to take care of these matters and make sure that the only difference between real Arabs and those appearing in the film will be that the latter will speak English.

I am looking forward to receiving back "The Birth of Adam," and I am greatly interested in Joshua Podro's comments.

> *Yours cordially,*
> *Raphael*

Graves responded on November 7.

Dear Raphael:

Have been over the Cain & Abel *piece but can't finalize my version until I get back to my books. I agree with you on principle but want to take the argument a little further on general anthropological principles. There seem, I agree, to be three levels of the myth and a lot of accretions.*

1) An incident of a herdsman farmer conflict: the herdsman always wins.
2) Royal religious fratricide.
3) The general war between desert & sown.

Cain seems in one sense to be Agenor *(Chnas, Canaan) and Abel to be* Belus *(Baal) who were a pair of twins from Libya who quarrelled—as also did Belus's twin sons. I agree that the Esau-Jacob quarrel is a parallel.*

This is to reassure you that I'm not dead, though harassed by urban life.

> *Yours ever*
> *Robert*

My answer, too, was prompt.

November 17, 1960

Dear Robert:

I am glad that you are in agreement in principle as to the three levels of the Cain and Abel myth. I am very curious to see in what way you plan to take the argument further on general anthropological principles.

I quite understand, of course, that you will not be able to do this until you return to your own library.

In the meantime, I am sending you herewith three more chapters: the first one is a rewriting of the chapter on "The Creation of the World"; the second states how the world, once created, was imagined to be constructed; the third discusses what probably is one of the most outspoken myths preserved in the Bible, even though in a cruelly abbreviated form.

Take your time with these, and let me hear from you at your leisure.

> *Yours cordially,*
> *Raphael*

Not long afterwards I got back the "Cain and Abel" chapter with this letter:

> *128 Kensington Park Road*
> *W. 11*
> *[c. December 10, 1960]*

Dear Raphael:

This is a tentative version of Cain & Abel. Please disagree where necessary.
There seems no point in putting the references in their right order until we stabilize the text.

179

I'll work on the other long piece next.
Good luck & I'm enjoying this a lot!

Yours ever
Robert G

I responded on December 22.

Dear Robert:

I am very happy *with the work you did on our Fratricide chapter. I notice that this time you practically rewrote the entire text, and the result is a version far beyond anything I alone could have written.*

There is nothing in your version that I would disagree with, the exception being two statements. The first is at the bottom of p. 12 (your typescript), where you suggest a connection between Cain and Abel and Agenor and Belus. However, in the very same sentence you state that Agenor is the Greek form of Canaan, and Bel or Belus, the Greek form of Baal. It seems to me that the two identifications cancel out each other. If Agenor is Canaan, how can he also be Cain? If Belus is Baal, how can he also be Abel? I think we should confine ourselves to pointing out that Canaan has its Phoenician counterprart in Khnas, who became Agenor in Greek mythology. This identification was proposed by Buttmann, Mythol *I, 232 ff., and although it was refuted by Movers,* Phönizier, *2, 1, 131 f., I think we can go along with it. According to one version of the myth, (recorded by Schol. Eur. Phoen. 247) Agenor and Phoinix were brothers, the sons of Belos and Io. Translated back into the probable original Canaanite context this means that the god Baal was regarded as the father of both Canaan and Phoenicia. The mother Io, who appears in the form of a white cow in the Greek myth, fits quite well into the Canaanite context in which Baal appeared in the form of a bull.*

My second comment concerns your p. 14, the letter "T." The letter "T" in the Hebrew myth is explicitly stated to have been the "tet" (ט). The castemark connected in mythology with the crucifiction could have only been the letter "tav" (ת), which, in the ancient Hebrew and Phoenician alphabets was represented by a cross, + or ×. Therefore, this paragraph will have to be rephrased accordingly.

However, these two little details did not detract from the pleasure I had in reading your fine version of the chapter.

The following seven additional chapters are ready:

The Fall of Helel
The Fall of Man
How Man Learned About Sex
The Death of Cain

The Flood
The Drunkenness and Castration of Noah
The Giants of Old

*Please let me know whether you want me to send these chapters to you in
London or to Mallorca? How long will you be in London, and when do you
plan to return to Mallorca?*

> *Yours cordially,*
> *Raphael*

Graves responded after the New Year.

> *Jan 3 1961*

Dear Raphael:

*Back in Majorca and just got your Dec 22 letter forwarded. So relieved you
like the fratricide, and of course I accept your emendations. I'll get on with
the job as soon as I've settled down. All the children are here for the vacation
and the house is in a turmoil.*

> *Best wishes to you both*
> *Robert*

And the very next day he wrote again:

> *Jan 4 1961*

Dear Raphael:

*Perhaps the substitute of Ṭeth for Tav, in Cain's case, was due a recollec-
tion of Tav's use (Ezekiel ix, 4,6) as a brand to safeguard the faithful at
Jerusalem?*

The Greek Tau is taken from Tav and Lucian in his Court *of* Vowels *connects it with crucifixion: "his shape they imitate when they set up the erections on which men are crucified", and curses Cadmus for this.*

I'm so relieved you approve of my work. I trust you to check on Hebraica!

> *Yours ever*
> *Robert*

*Busy with Tehom, Leviathan & Co. The workings of the rabbinical mind
fascinate me.*

Checking Lucian's "Court of Vowels" which Graves mentions in this letter, I found that it was not Lucian himself who cursed Cadmus, but anonymous "men" to whom he refers. This is what he says: "Men weep, and
bewail their lot, and curse Cadmus with many curses for introducing Tau into

181

the family of letters; they say it was his body that tyrants took for a model, his shape that they imitated, when they set up the erections on which men are crucified." Cadmus is identified by Lucian as "Cadmus the islander," and "one of our first legislators."[2]

I replied to Graves on January 9.

Dear Robert:

I was glad to receive your note of January 3rd, and to know that you are back on your home base.

In the last few weeks I found myself able to devote quite some time to work on our book and I am enclosing the result.

I am somewhat uneasy about the chapters dealing with Abraham. My feeling is that much of the material contained in these chapters can be regarded as mythological only by using the term in a rather loose sense. While writing these chapters I felt increasingly that the time has come when we must clarify first to ourselves, and then to the readers of the book, what is our understanding of myth, *and how we distinguish between myth and legend.*

At this time I have only one preliminary observation to make on this subject: I am inclined to regard as myths all those stories in which there is a supernatural element. By this definition the Abraham stories are myths because God, angels and Satan constantly interfere. However, I am not quite sure as to the validity of this criterion because the supernatural element forms part of those stories as well which, by general consensus, are regarded as legends. On the other hand, I have the impression that such a story taking place in a "pagan" context is regarded a myth, while the same story within a Christian (or other monotheistic) context is usually taken to be a legend. For instance, Hercules and the Hydra is regarded by everybody as a myth, but St. George and the Dragon as a legend. Siegfried and the Dragon would be a border case because the whole Niebelungenlied *retains its distinctly pagan flavor under the superficial Christian varnish.*

I personally would be inclined to be unconventional, and regard and treat as myths all the stories contained in the Hebrew sources which have a supernatural element in them.

All the above is purely tentative, and if you feel differently, please let me know. Also, if you should feel that the Abraham material or parts of it should not be included, let me know, and since I myself am uncertain about it, I shall, in all probablility, accept your decision without argument.

Yours cordially,
Raphael

Graves replied promptly.

182

Jan 15 1961

Dear Raphael:

I regard myth as referring to people like Cain or Abraham who were not historical in the sense that, say, Jehu or Ramases II were, but represented nations or tribes or dynasties and lived on intimate terms with a deity or deities. Myth is also, always, a traditional religious charter confirming laws or customs. Exodus is highly mythical, most of it. But not much of Joshua.

—A legend is by definition an idle invention of monks which provides morally improving literature: *e.g. the Joseph & Cherry tree legend borrowed from pseudo-Matthew.*

—George & the Dragon is a myth under a Christian veneer, not a legend, just Marduk & Tiamat again. I think some rabbinical legends *should be included; but not too many.*

—I have had a very difficult time with the Creation—wrestled 6 days with it, like my illustrious Maker trying to banish Tohu wa Bohu—but finally got it into 5 chapters of the required length. It needs a lot of work on it still—yours in amendment of mine. I am now resting for a while. Karl (my Jewish secretary) types it clear. The difficult[y] is what to omit as not of interest except to grammarians.

It is odd how your knowledge & mine complement each other so neatly. It's going to be an exciting book for Jews and *Christians.*

When the foundation has been laid in these five chapters I shall think more clearly about those we have already done, putting them in more topical order. Until this is accomplished I think it best to leave the new material alone. As I say, I am in favour of cutting down on references where these are not essential; but here I must leave the decision to you.

I'll send those 5 chapters along in a week or two. I hope they won't prove too strong meat for the Children of God. But you pointed the way in your Man and Temple & Hebrew Installation Rites.

Yours ever
Robert

I answered on January 30.

Dear Robert:

Thank you for your recent letter. I am in agreement with you as to your definition of myth, and the distinction between it and legend. We will, I think, have to return to this later. In the meantime, I am expecting the chapters on Creation which you rewrote.

In yesterday's New York Times Book Review, *I came across the enclosed article which you may not have seen yet. Should you be elected to the Chair of Poetry at Oxford, let me be the first to congratulate you.*

Yours cordially,
Raphael

The article I referred to was Walter Allen's "London Letter," in which he tells about Graves's candidacy to the highly prestigious Oxford chair of poetry. In the event, among the several candidates it was Graves who was elected.

On January 29, Graves wrote me again.

Dear Raphael:

Sending Creation Myths *herewith.*

Now that we have the start in what I consider the right style (and it meant five drafts of every page) we can go on to the next incidents, if you agree.

Where is the Garden of Eden? I don't seem to have got it?

If you think that I am being too wilful, please tell me. One thing I do know: what is readable *by the general intelligent public & what isn't except by a few dozen scholars. That is my trade.*

It looks as if the first volume will go as far as Joseph & the next start with the Captivity & Exodus.

Yours ever
Robert

To this letter I responded on February 9.

Dear Robert:

I received the five chapters dealing with the Creation a few days ago, and so far was able only to give them a cursory reading. What I saw filled me anew with admiration for your mastery of English, and your ability to express tersely and effectively what I tried to say in fumbling loquaciousness. The first parts of the chapters containing the body of the myths are magnificent indeed. My first cursory reading revealed practically no point of disagreement. As to the second part of the chapters—I will buckle down in a few days to going over them critically, and if I should find statements with which I cannot agree, I shall let you know, and at the same time give you my suggestions. In any case, I think I shall have the completed chapters retyped with all the footnotes put in their proper places, and then send them to you for final approval.

Mentioning the footnotes, I noticed that in the second part of the chapters you refrained, in most cases, from giving references to sources. Was this done advisedly, and, if so, why? Or was it your intention to leave to me the insertion of the source references in these second parts of the chapters?

I agree with you as to how far the first volume should go. The death of Joseph would be a fine breaking point, marking as it does the end of the patriarchal period.

The question of the introduction begins to occupy me now. I think it should contain a general statement about what we regard as myth, and about the historical background of the ancient Hebrews and the cultural influences to which they were exposed. The point in discussing the cultural influences will have to be two-fold:

1. To demonstrate that Hebrew mythology has its root in ancient Near Eastern mythologies, which, in some cases, are older by two, or even three millennia.

2. To justify the frequent presentation in the book of ancient Near Eastern "parallels."

So much for the moment. I shall write to you again soon.

Yours cordially,
Raphael

True to my promise I wrote again a week later.

February 16, 1961

Dear Robert:

I am enclosing retyped copies of chapters 2–5. Chapter 1 requires more thought and work, and I want to return to it after finishing the chapter on Paradise, on which I am working at present.

In the following I want to give you my reasons for making the few changes which I felt were necessary in chapters 2–5.

Chapter 2, pp. 11–12:

I introduced a few chages in the Biblical references which, I believe, need no explanation.

On p. 12 *I omitted the closing words of point I, (because the Creatrix whom he [God] displaces, is a goddess of fertility, and, therefore, of water), and substituted instead several lines which now appear in the middle of my p. 4, and which, I believe, describe the reasons of God's fight against the watery elements more accurately and more in the spirit of the Midrash itself. I hope you will accept this.*

P. 13, point IV: *I rephrased the entire paragraph for reasons similar to the above, as well as in order to refer to Sumerian material which I have just found. In* point V *on the same page, I would like to add source references, unless you object to this. My general feeling is that when we refer to a straight fact, we should mention its source so as to enable the readers to distinguish between data adduced and our conclusions or explanations. I changed the last sentence of this point—(you wrote "in Greece she (Baau) was Eurynome who took the Serpent Ophion for a lover") into "her true Greek counterpart is Eurynome" etc. Because I feel that to say that Baau was in Greece Eurynome is too elliptical, besides, it wasn't really Baau who was Eurynome in Greece, but rather both Baau and Eurynome seem to be similar prototypes of ancient mother goddesses. The identification of the two is done by us, but should not be stated as a fact.*

P. 13, point VI, 1st line: *I changed your "Jewish Ophites" into "anti-Judaistic Ophites," because I found no trace of the Ophites having been Jewish, while, on the other hand, they were known to be opposed to Jewish doctrines.* Same point: *Could you add the source of the statement about the Sanhedrin having "distinguished this false material creation," etc.?*

P. 16, point XII: *I rewrote this paragraph (see my pp. 9–10), and expanded it somewhat.*

Chapter 3, p. 17, line 2 from the bottom:

I changed "heavenly spirits" to "Gods" because the Hebrew original of Job 41, 17, has "Elim" which clearly means "Gods" and not "heavenly spirits," nor "the mighty" as the word is usually translated.

On p. 21, point S: *I changed the last line so as to conform wih the original source.*

I rewrote the whole of points III and IV on p. 23, without, however, introducing any substantial changes. Bodenheimer's book just reached me, and I found interesting data in it about both the crocodile and the hippopotamus.

P. 24, point VII: *(which has now become* point VI). *I hope you will find yourself able to agree with my substitution of "Middle-Easterners with predominantly cereal diets" for your "poor synagogue Jews."*

Same page, point VIII: *I suggest that we delete these three lines because the Egyptian etymology of Behemoth is purely fantastic.*

P. 26: *I added a few lines to the end of your* point XII *(now* point X), *which strengthened the argument.* Last two lines on the same page: *I changed somewhat the wording of the identification of the* Book of Raziel.

Chapter IV, p. 27, section 3, last line:

I changed "privy" into "cesspool," because the latter is what the Hebrew description suggests.

P. 30–31, point II: *I suggest that we omit these four lines because of the comparison of the primeval chaos to a cesspool is so appropriate that it seems far-fetched to read into it an allusion to male and female prostitution and other abominations practiced in the Temple.*

On p. 32 (p. 7 of Chapter IV in *the enclosed* retyped copy): *I added a new point which I believe speaks for itself.*

The changes I introduced in your point VIII, *are minor, and if you can give me the sources for God's secret name being written in six or eight letters, we can restore them.*

Chapter 5, p. 34:

Slight correction—Topheth was not another name for the Valley of Hinom, but was located in it.

I hope you agree with me that all the above changes are few, and minor in comparison with the major and many areas of agreement between us. In fact, I am very happy about the way our collaboration on the book is developing, because I imagined that there would be much more disagreements and difficulties. The main thing is that we have a basically similar approach to and understanding of the ancient Hebrew mythical material.

> *Yours cordially,*
> *Raphael*

This letter, more than the others, affords an insight into the painstaking scrutiny to which I subjected every line Graves contributed to our book. He on his part considered just as carefully the changes I suggested, and adjusted them to his version of the text. It might be of some interest at this point to show how and to what extent my emendations were incorporated into the final text of the *Hebrew Myths* (hereafter *HM*). I list here the items page by page as they appear in my letter above.

P. 12: In response to my comments Graves restored the phrase about the Creatrix I wanted deleted, but added the lines I wanted to be substituted for it (*HM* 2.1).

P. 13, point 4: My Sumerian reference was added (*HM* 2.4).

P. 13, point 5: Graves insisted that his phrasing remain, and so it did.

P. 13, point 6: Where Graves had originally written "Jewish Ophites," which I amended to "anti-Judaistic Ophites," the agreed phrasing became "the heretical Ophites of the first century." The reference to the "Sanhedrin having 'distinguished this false material creation' etc." was deleted (ibid.).

In chapter 3 (which became chapter 6 in the final version), the reference to "heavenly spirits" was deleted. The book by Prof. Frederick Simon Bodenheimer, to which I refer in my comment on points 3 and 4 (of chapter 6) was his *Animal and Man in Bible Lands*, published in 1960, a year after the death of the author, who had been a good friend of mine while I lived in Jerusalem.

P. 24, point 7: My emendation of Graves's "poor synagogue Jews" into "Middle-Easterners with predominantly cereal diets" was rephrased by him to read, "The poor of the Middle East have always hungered for flesh feasts to supplement their predominantly cereal diet" (*HM* 6.7). The Egyptian etymology of Behemoth cited by Graves was deleted as I suggested (*HM* 6.5). On p. 26, my description of the *Book of Raziel* was introduced (*HM* 6.12).

187

In chapter 4, section 3 (which became *HM* 4.2), both the term "privy" and its possible reference to male and female prostitution were retained at Graves's insistence.

In chapter 4, point 8, the mention of God's names consisting of twelve, forty-two, and seventy-two letters was retained with an added reference to Graves's *The White Goddess*, chapter 16, where they are discussed in great detail.

In chapter 5, point 3, my correction with regard to Tophet (2 Kings 23:10) was introduced.

As can be seen from the above list, in most cases my emendations were accepted by Graves and included in the final text. Of course, this brief list conveys no idea of the many items, comments, explanations, suggestions, parallels, etc., which Graves added to my original drafts of each chapter, and with which I found myself in agreement.

Next, I sent Graves the draft of the chapter on Paradise, with a brief covering letter

February 27, 1961

Dear Robert:

I am enclosing the chapter on Paradise. As you will see, I am sending you this chapter in a rather rough form. All I did was to collect (under points a.–s.) the source material on the subject; point g. etc., I presented in a verbatim *translation so as to enable you to get as accurate a picture as possible of the original wording of the myths. Then, under 1–4, I gave you a few points of comparison. I did no more, because I remembered that you had stated that you would have quite a lot to say about paradise. I therefore thought that it would be sufficient to supply you with raw material so to speak, from which you can build the chapter as you see fit.*

Now that I finished this, I am going back to chapter 1 (the opening chapter of the book dealing with Genesis 1 and 2), and hope to be able to send you that, too, within a week or so.

I hope this letter finds you well. Does your election to Oxford mean that you will move there, or will you retain your residence in Mallorca? And where will you be in August?

Yours cordially,
Raphael

I followed this up a few days later with another brief note.

March 1, 1961

Dear Robert:

Due to an inadvertence, I omitted any reference to a Sumerian myth in which scholars have found a resemblance to the Biblical paradise story. At

188

this stage, I think the best I can do is to enclose a summary of the entire myth so that you can use it in any way you see fit.

Yours cordially,
Raphael

My letters elicited this response from Graves:

March 4 1961

Dear Raphael:

I am in such a jam with work that I fear I'll have to let the material you send pile up while I harshly deal with priorities. Forgive me. The Oxford job isn't serious: three lectures and a term's residence. I won't be away from here much. In May (16–24) I come very briefly to N.Y. to give an address & some poem readings; hope to see you. Between the 16th & 24th.

—I know about Paradise, because I have been there by the hallucinogenic back door: have written my account for Holiday, *not yet out. The Paradises are all the same—Assyrian, Greek, Jewish, Mexican, Polynesian—and* RE-ALLY *entrancing.*

The "Knowledge of good and evil" means universal rather than critical knowledge, which the paradisal state grants (or seems to grant) to entrants. But one is so euphoric that one doesn't worry about any particular item of knowledge.

Yours ever
Robert

189

17.

A Photographic Session
at Doubleday

I RESPONDED TO GRAVES'S letter of March 4 (in which he informed me that he was coming to New York in May) with an invitation to stay with us. By that time we lived in Manhattan, on East 71st Street, a very convenient central location just three blocks from the Frick Collection (my favorite small museum). I wrote to Graves on March 9.

Dear Robert:

Your planned visit to New York is good news. I certainly count on seeing you and having a chance to discuss some of the problems in connection with our book. In fact, when I told my wife about your planned visit, she suggested that we invite you to be our house-guest. If your wife plans to come with you, this invitation, of course, is extended most cordially to her, as well. We now live in the city (135 East 71st Street), in a location which is more central than that of the Wasson apartment where you stayed last time. Both our daughters are away in college, and their room can serve as a convenient guest room.

In any case, let me know when and where you will speak in New York so that if the event is open to the public we can attend.

I hope that the other work which you mention in your letter will not keep you away too long from our book. I myself am making a special effort to finish before the summer the first draft of the material which has to go into volume 1. It would be great if by the fall we could send this volume to press.

I am enclosing my rewritten version of chapter 1, "The Creation according to Genesis." As you will see, I omitted several pages which were contained in your version of this chapter, and which dealt mostly with the question of early

*matriarchy and the Creatrix, the mother goddess. I did this not as if I would
be in disagreement with the ideas expressed, but because I think that this general argument should rather be included in the introduction. Please give me
your frank reaction to this suggestion.*

Yours cordially,
Raphael

The chapter "The Creation according to Genesis," to which I refer in this
letter was, I remember, one of the most difficult to write. I still have among
my papers two early drafts: one comprises no less than sixty-three typed
pages and has an introduction, followed by sections on Tohu waBohu, Darkness, Tehom, Male and Female Waters, The Gathering of the Waters, Apsu,
Leviathan and Company, The Monsters in the Apocrypha and the New Testament, and the Midrashic Myth of Leviathan. The other draft, which, I
think, is the later one, is organized after the Gravesian pattern and has a total
length of forty-nine pages. Its first part comprises sections, numbered alpha-
betically, on What Happened prior to Creation? The Creation of Heaven and
Earth, The Waters, The Sea, The Shetiyya Stone, Tohu and Bohu, Tehom,
Leviathan, The Dragon *(Tannin), Aphsayim,* and Behemoth. This is followed
by source references, after which come the explanatory sections, numbered
one to thirteen, again with source references. I am no longer sure whether I
sent either of these two versions to Graves, but neither of them could have
been the one I referred to in the foregoing letter, because in it I speak of rewriting a chapter Graves sent me. Ultimately the materials covered in these
two early versions, or parts of them went into the first seven chapters of the
book. Other parts were omitted because we agreed that their inclusion would
make the beginning of the book much too cumbersome.

Graves responded to my letter on March 13, 1961.

Dear Raphael:

*Thanks very much for the invitation to be a house guest; but I will be with
my friends the Lyes in Bethune Street, as promised two years ago, so can't
accept, though yours is a more central situation.*

*—I am sorry about having to go slow with the book for awhile but this
Oxford business (three lectures to deliver in the autumn) and a lot of other
previous commitments have priority—especially the Terence edition—and I
have been plagued with a spate of poems which since they are my main excuse
for existence on this planet I cannot oppose. But I am taking on no other main
work and beg your patience! I think you have done a very lucid, bold and
sensible recasting of the* Creation *story; and this proves that if this is going to
be the really important book which I know it can be, we mustn't hasten it.
(Here I quote various Biblical texts about putting in the sickle when the corn*

191

is green, and plucking the unripe grape and unripe perfume.) I don't care how long it takes myself, and promise you that it will be my central prose work task until it is completed to our common satisfaction.

I am already appalled by the thought of the people I'll have to see in New York in the course of business, and without Beryl to protect me! I am too many different characters in one, and my daily mail never contains less than ten letters which require careful answers.

Yours ever

Robert

I had thought of postponing the Terence—a 3 months job—but would feel better with it out of the way and am starting at once.

The first three addresses on poetry Graves delivered at Oxford after he was elected to the highly prestigious position of professor of poetry were given in the fall of 1961 and early in 1962, and published by Cassell in London and Doubleday in New York. The "Terence edition" he mentions in his letter is *The Comedies of Terence,* edited and translated by him, and published in 1962 by Doubleday, and in 1963 by Cassell. In 1961–62 no fewer than five volumes of his poems were published in England and America, as well as five more volumes of his prose writings. He was a busy writer indeed in those days, and had no choice but "to go slow with" the *Hebrew Myths.*

As for me, I was no less busy. In addition to my teaching, editing, writing, lecturing, and many social engagements, I was still producing fresh ideas for new literary projects. One of them was a project to edit an *Encyclopaedia of Peoples and Tribes,* which, after the biblical encyclopaedia plan foundered, I discussed, on March 20, 1961, with George Hoy, Jr. and Robert Kendall, two editors at McGraw-Hill. Nothing came of this either. Other literary plans I discussed (still in March of 1961) with Schocken Books and, on March 24, I had lunch with Webb and Dennett of the Macmillan Company to present them with the idea of editing a book about the position of women in the modern world. This resulted in *Women in the Modern World,* which I edited and which the Free Press (affiliated with Macmillan) published in 1967—proving how long it can take for a literary project to come to fruition.

On March 21, 1961, I wrote to Graves.

Dear Robert:

I am sorry that we came too late with our invitation. Please put it on your waiting list and let me know whenever its term of acceptance comes.

I am very glad that you liked my last revision of the Creation story. I agree with you that such a book cannot, and should not be hastened. On the other hand, I would hate to see it postponed for too long a time. I think, in view of

192

all the circumstances, that we should suggest to Doubleday that the first volume should be published when ready without waiting for the completion of the whole work. This procedure may be best from the publisher's point of view, as well.

I just spoke to Ken McCormick, and he told me that Doubleday would like to have a photograph taken showing you and me together. They will want to use this for the backside of the jacket, as well as for other publicity purposes. Since it is uncertain whether we can get together again after your May visit to New York, and before the first volume goes to print, I think we should let Doubleday's photographer take the pictures during your week in New York in May. I am, of course, aware that your schedule will be very tight during that week, but I hope you will be able to squeeze a few minutes in for this. McCormick suggested either the 25, 26 or 29th of May. Please let me know so that I can tell him in time to make the arrangements.

I am sending you enclosed a number of additional chapters.

> Yours cordially,
> Raphael

Graves answered by return mail.

March 25th 1961

Dear Raphael:

On arrival at New York on the 16th May I'll first get rid of my two 'away' engagements (on 17th and 18th) and be back on the 19th. Then I'm free until the 22nd. (A last engagement on the 24th; then back here on the 25th.) Please tell Ken McC.

Thanks for the additional chapters: they look fine.

I find that the Terence will not take nearly as long as I feared and may even have it done by the time we meet; but that's working really hard.

> Yours ever
> Robert

I continued to work on the *Hebrew Myths,* and was able to enclose two more chapters with my letter of April 4, 1961.

Dear Robert:

Just a line to let you know that Ken McCormick is arranging for us to be photographed together at the Doubleday offices (575 Madison Avenue, between 56th and 57th Streets), on Friday, May 19th, in the afternoon—probably around 4 P.M. I hope that this meets with your approval, and your schedule.

193

Would you give me the name and address of the people with whom you will stay during your visit in New York. Did I read correctly that their name is Lye?

I am enclosing three more chapters. I would especially like to call your attention to the chapter "Esau Sells His Birthright," and would like to have your reaction to my explanation of the myth given on pages 8–13.

Cordially,

Raphael

My explanation of the biblical story about Esau selling his birthright to Jacob (Gen. 25:29–34) was that it mythically justified the conquest of the Edomites, the descendants of Easu (Edom), by their junior kinsmen, the Israelites, the offspring of Jacob (Israel). Then, I argued, when Herod the Edomite became king of the Jews, this new situation had to be explained mythically. Hence the rabbinical myth that Esau's exemplary love for his father Isaac was rewarded, many generations later, by his progeny achieving domination over Israel in the days of Herod (see *HM* 40.3).

Graves response was positive and appreciative.

Apr 12 1961

Dear Raphael:

Thanks for letter: good, lets be photographed together on Friday May 19th at 4 P.M. But this time I don't want to be photographed by a German. Can't it be a Hungarian? I refuse to be photographed by a German because they always make me look like one & I don't mind being mistaken for a Hungarian.

Yes: Len & Anne Lye is the name. 41 Bethune St. Greenwich Village.

I should have handled the birthright question in the same way; though forced to look up the facts which fortunately you have. But although Herod was an Edomite etc, the prophecy in Genesis about Esau breaking his brother's yoke from off his neck is pre-Roman by centuries. I prefer to think that the prophecy refers to the rebellion in the time of Jehoshaphat's son Joram, though afterwards explained in the Roman sense.

Yours ever

Robert

I replied on April 25.

Dear Robert:

Thank you for your letter of April 12th. The date for picture taking at Doubleday's on Friday, May 19th, at 4 P.M. is set. Let us meet in Ken's office. I passed on your stipulation that the photographer should not be a German. This they understood. But when I added that he can, or should be a Hungar-

ian, they were surprised at such loyalty which I seemed to hold to my twice-removed homeland.

Do you think your schedule will allow you to spend some time with me? We have dinner engagements on Friday the 19th and Sunday the 21st in the evening, but would love to have you dine with us on Saturday the 20th, in the evening. Or, if this is impossible, let me take you out for lunch any day during your stay in the city. If this, too, is not feasible, perhaps we can spend some time together either before or after the photographing session. Let me have, please, word about this in time. Also, where will you lecture in the city? We would like to attend.

I am enclosing five new chapters, all dealing with Jacob, who emerges as a much more important character than the mere Biblical sketch of him would allow us to guess.

> *Yours cordially,*
> *Raphael*

Graves responded by return mail.

> *May 1 1961*

Dear Raphael:

Thanks for the Jacob chapters. I'll be through with Terence *before I come over.*

—Lets arrange a time for a long talk when we meet: suggest lunch and afternoon on the 20th. I have been asked to address the Hillel Foundation in London on Hebrew Myths *on Oct 17th and have consented: but this is the only extra-Oxford job I've taken on. I'll be the first goy to be chosen for that annual talk, & want to make it good.*

Yes: of course I know you're a Magyar!

I'll be reading poems at the YMHA on May 22nd at 8:30 P.M. It will be quite an occasion, I promise you: the best audience in America and the craziest poet.

> *Yours ever*
> *Robert*

My answer, dated May 16, was addressed care of Mr. L. Lye.

Dear Robert:

Welcome again to these shores!

The Lyes seem to have an unlisted phone, so that the only way I can get in touch with you is by writing.

This is merely to remind you that we have the following appointments:

195

1) Friday, May 19th, 4 P.M., in Ken McCormick's office at Doubleday's, 575 Madison Avenue (between 56 and 57 Street): photography session.

2) Saturday, May 20th, 1 P.M., in my home, 135 East 71st Street, (corner Lexington Ave.): lunch and discussion session.

My telephone numbers are:
Office—PLaza 2–0600
Home—YUkon 8–1319

> *Cordially,*
>
> *Raphael*

The photographic session at Doubleday took place as scheduled, partly in Ken McCormick's office, and partly on the terrace fronting it, high above the city. The photographer, a young woman named Leni Iselin, was not German, but neither was she Hungarian. She snapped dozens of shots, most of them while Graves and I were engaged in discussion, or were looking at some manuscript. Several of the pictures turned out excellently, and they are among my cherished mementos of that meeting. One of them shows Graves as I remember him from that meeting and some others: he is looking into the distance, as if he were seeing something there that we others could not see. It was, I always felt when I saw that look of his, as if the poet that Graves was had reverted momentarily to the ancestral *vates,* the seer, carrying the burden of the double gift: to see what others cannot see, and to be compelled to clothe it in words of magic and power.

Next day, Saturday, May 20, 1961, Ann and I had Graves over for lunch in our apartment. There were no other guests, and after lunch we had a long discussion of our book, part of which I taped. What follows in the next chapter is a verbatim, uncorrected transcript of the tape, which so far has been published only in Spanish, in the translation of Graves's daughter Lucia, in the March 16, 1987, issue of *Bitzoc,* the Majorcan literary journal.

Graves and Patai at the photographic session at Doubleday. (Photo courtesy of Leni Iselin.)

18.

A Conversation Taped

Patai: I jotted down a few points which I think should be discussed in the introduction. First of all, some general characteristics of Hebrew mythology as compared with Greek mythology primarily. After all, the idea of mythology is a Greek idea, the very term "mythology" is Greek, and the science of mythology grew up on the basis of the study of Greek myths. I don't know if you will agree with me, but I find that one of the basic differences between Hebrew and Greek mythology is that in Hebrew mythology other Godlike beings outside God play a much more subordinate role than in Greek mythology.

Graves: Not allowed to appear.

Patai: That's right.

Graves: Although they are present, although they are potent, they are very strong, and the God is fighting for his whole tribe—but that is the great difference, yes. But we have in Hebrew mythology both Lilith and Eve, both goddesses, but later both reduced to an ordinary human level.

Patai: Right. But you have the so-called "princes" of the elements, such as the Prince of the Sea, that is, the celestial patron of the sea who is a force opposing God, and at least in one case God has to kick him and finally kill him in order to be able to create the world.

Graves: And there is the Goddess of the Sea, Rahab; you have the Lord of the House who is Baal Zevuv (Zevul) but, specially, I think, you have the seven planetary powers combined in Jehovah as a single character, who in Greek, Egyptian, or Babylonian mythology are separate characters. So this limits myths in a way.

Patai: Yes, you don't have that colorful situation as in Greece, where two or three gods or goddesses of equal power . . .

Graves: . . . fight each other or are scheming . . .

Patai: In Hebrew mythology it is a foregone conclusion that God wins out. There can be never any doubt about that.

Graves: There is always Samael, who is the devil, who is still allowed a certain potence, although he is destined to be beaten.

Patai: In fact, I often have the feeling that if the Hebrew myths would stop before they reach the end, that inevitable end which always tells about the opponents of God being beaten, they would be much more colorful. Then you would really have the feeling of an equal contest.

Graves: Another thing is that Greek mythology is very much circumscribed by being attached to particular localities, and each god or hero has a particular state, and Greek mythology consists of a number of charters of particular states or cities, whereas in Jewish mythology it's all centered at Jerusalem. Just about.

Patai: Not all.

Graves: Not all. There is the mythology attached to the Northern Kingdom but that happens to be destroyed by the Captivity.

Patai: Even more than that. There is for instance that myth cycle of the Amorite Wars, which I mentioned to you yesterday. Those myths come very close to the Homeric myths of the battles between the Greeks and the Trojans. Jerusalem does not appear in them at all. They all deal with the original conquest of the territory of Ephraim by the sons of Jacob, and the territory is an actual area which can be found on the map. It is the area which later became the tribal territory of Ephraim. So there you have a cycle of myths which have nothing to do with Jerusalem.

Graves: Well, that's splendid.

Patai: Yes, I had the same feeling. I had the same feeling because of the wars described in it, which are so rare in Hebrew mythology.

Graves: Where do they occur?

Patai: Well, they start with the Apocrypha, in the Testament of Judah, because Judah is the main hero in those wars.

Graves: Judah is a very queer character, isn't he? And even in the story of Joseph he has a very important and rather equivocal role because he is against and yet he is for Joseph.

Patai: It's not quite clear what he wants. He wants to save Joseph and yet at the same time he wants to eliminate him.

Graves: And Reuben is still more equivocal. Reuben is the hero in one sense, and in another sense he is the devil who got into his father's bed and seduced his father's wife. Very, very strange, Reuben. When did Reuben disappear?

Patai: Historically, he seems to have disappeared soon after the conquest of Canaan.

Graves: The first to disappear was Gad, wasn't he? He was overwrought. I think then Reuben and the other Transjordanian tribes disappeared. The most interesting tribe, it seems to me, was the tribe of Dinah.

Patai: There is no such tribe, of course. Actually there is no trace of a tribe of Dinah. There is only . . .

Graves: . . . the tribe of Dan.

Patai: Yes.

Graves: There were two Dans, weren't there? There was a Dan right up on the top. Wasn't there another Dan?

Patai: But Dinah is a very interesting figure mythologically.

Graves: Because she doesn't occur in the story of Joseph at all and yet she is there. Dan means judge, doesn't it?

Patai: Yes, it means judge.

Graves: And Dinah means judge, too—female judge. I should say that on anthropological principles Dinah was a queendom among various kingdom tribes, and she represents a very early Palestinian entity.

Patai: Of course, the story of the rape of Dinah . . .

Graves: Who raped her?

Patai: Shechem, which of course must be interpreted as an intermingling between Dinah and the Canaanites.

Graves: That's right. If Dinah was a queendom it wouldn't be an actual rape. It would mean that she, that is, the priestess of the tribe, took her lovers from among the Canaanites.

Patai: But you know that the story goes on to say that the child born of that union was Asenath, who later became the wife of Joseph. Asenath was merely the foster daughter of Potiphar, and her actual mother was Dinah and her father was Shechem. This is very interesting because it involves these two tribes. And later Dinah was supposed to have married Simeon.

Graves: Simeon, her own brother?

200

Patai: Yes. According to one myth all the twelve sons of Jacob married their own twin sisters. Each one of them was born with a twin sister.

Graves: How splendid. How absolutely right. Like Cain and Abel.

Patai: Yes, exactly the same story. A repetition of the same principle.

Graves: Do you know what that means? It means that they had a bisexual deity, like they do in West Africa, and like they do in Haiti among the Loa. I didn't realize that. A bisexual deity, meaning that a man can be possessed by the same deity as a woman.

Patai: Do you think that the myth about the original creation of man as an androgyne, which exists in Hebrew sources as well, may have something to do with it?

Graves: I am sure it has. We'll have to go into that. It will be very helpful.

Patai: The second point I think we should discuss in the introduction is that as far as I see there is a much greater preoccupation in Hebrew mythology with Creation and related subjects than there is in Greek mythology. In Hebrew mythology you have cosmogony, cosmology, many stories about the layered structure of heaven and earth, about the underworld, paradise, hell, and so forth. Simply quantitatively it takes up a much larger space than in Greek mythology.

Graves: Quantitatively, but myths of origin are just as important in Greece, and in Greece you have the very strong sense of the geography of heaven and hell. The supernal heights take up so far that the infernal ones are just as varied so you don't have so much in depth, more in . . .

Patai: Do you have anything in Greek mythology which would be comparable to those Hebrew myths which talk about several successive creations? About eons which preceded the creation of this world, about what God did prior to having created the present world?

Graves: The point is that in Greek mythology it all talks about the goddess, and so it does in pre-Jewish mythology. The god comes into the story very late in Greek mythology. You see, this is how I look at it: there are two cultures, the cattle culture and what I call the bee culture. In the cattle culture, the god, the whole social system, is based on the cattle. Among cattle the bull is the boss, and he has lots of subservient cows and heifers, and he disciplines the young bulls with his horns, until eventually he is ousted. In the same way as Zeus ousted Kronos, and as Zeus

201

was fated to be ousted by Apollo, although it never came to that. It was always said that Apollo would emasculate Zeus with the same sickle with which Zeus emasculated . . .

Patai: . . . Kronos, his father.

Graves: In that culture the women are cows, they have no particular fertility rites. You have a nomadic movement. All you do is go from pasture to pasture and there is no question of having to plant anything because it is already there. The head of the tribe is the strongest, meanest, and most egocentric male. And the women are his subjects. He keeps the younger men in order. He exercises complete discipline. His daughters are merely milkmaids. The word "daughter" means milkmaid, do you know that?

Patai: No, I didn't.

Graves: Well, now, at some time or other in the third millennium B.C. something happened, some climatic change happened in central Asia which dried up the pastures and sent the cattle people going west towards where the water came from, which was Europe. Well, now, so far as we can make out there were no gods at all in Europe before these cattle people came with their three gods, three joint gods of different names, Indra . . .

The queendoms were agricultural queendoms and the symbol of the goddess was the bee. The queen bee takes what drone she likes and then destroys him. All holiness was in the possession of women. All domestic culture, all arts, were in the possession of women. She was a potter, she was a goldsmith, she was everything. The men were just hunters. They belong to animal fraternities and they protected the frontier. She chose the most distinguished among them to be her lovers. Every year there was a holocaust of all the male animals in her honor. She was the lady of the wild bees, as well as the queen of heaven. The men lived in terror of her. On the other hand they had no responsibilities, there was no fatherhood. The children which were born, if they were girls, came under the supervision of the mother; if they were boys, after a time they passed into the hands of the mother's brother. These huntsmen lived a very free life and occasionally they had the sexual orgies which satisfied them but there was no question of responsibility.

When the cattle people impinged upon these queendoms all hell broke loose. They pleaded: let us in, we are starving, and so on. Sometimes they were allowed to come in, and they were allowed because obviously there was value in having beef. They pleaded: let us pasture our cattle on your grass. And for a time

202

they behaved themselves. Then, gradually—they obviously were much tougher, stouter, and better-looking men—they were chosen as lovers against the hunters. Then you had a transitional setup in which you had a marriage between the priestess—the queen mother, the bee mother—and the bull king. The earliest thing is that you have a sort of stasis in which you have equal representation between the six gods and the six goddesses, making twelve.

Then gradually that breaks down. The women still keep all their prerogatives, as planting, and so on, but gradually the men sneak in and take it over. First of all they take over things like pottery, which only women were allowed to touch earlier. Athene ceases to be a potter very early. Then they have this tremendous contest for farming rights. In the story of . . . , you have that, and how the women try to keep the men out by parching the corn so that it won't grow. And then gradually the men get in and the women slowly fade out and then finally you have Zeus destroying Hera, so that there is revolution, and he suspends Hera by her hands with an anvil at her feet. Then at one time finally you have Hestia ousted and replaced by Dionysus so that you have seven against five, and that brings it down. And then the women go down, down, down until by Hellenistic times women are just bought and sold like chattel.

Well, the same thing happened in Israel, but quite late [he meant early] I don't think it happened later than about the sixth century B.C., and you had the Queen of Heaven still being worshipped, I believe, until the time of the Exile.

Patai: That undoubtedly is correct. We have it in Jeremiah. But the question that comes to my mind is whether the worship of the Queen of Heaven really implies all this, or whether she was simply one of several deities just as there was Baal and Astarte— there were both male and female deities in historical times. So that the mention of the Queen of Heaven does not in itself prove that this is the last stage of a matriarchal society, or of a religion that centered on the Queen of Heaven.

Graves: But you have evidence of matriarchy in the Book of Genesis in which man is said to have to cling to his wife and leave his father and mother. Then you have all the naming of the children done by the mothers. Then Samson, that's matrilocal marriage, isn't it?

Patai: Definitely.

Graves: You have lots of vestiges, and the question is how much more has been suppressed by the editors of Genesis. I am under

203

the impression that you had coexisting patriarchal and matrilineal states as you did in Greece. But in Greece you had certain tribes in which the women would put on a beard for certain functions in order to appear as a man. And African parallels are very close.

Patai: I can add another parallel. Among the Arabs, the favorite tattooing pattern of the women is nothing but an imitation of the men's beards. They tattoo dark blue dots on the chin and the upper lip. It is actually an imitation of the beard.

Graves: That would give a woman chieftain the right to function in a male council.

Patai: We shall have to touch on this whole question in the introduction. The question is to what extent we should commit ourselves to one or the other point of view.

Graves: All we can say is that there are definite vestiges in the Scriptures of matrilineal descent . . .

Patai: And of female deities, of course, which go together, and of matrilocal residence. But I think we should leave the question open whether all this sums up to a matriarchal society.

Graves: Well, it should. No doubt at all. No, I never discussed it. You know, Solomon's Temple. Jehovah's house was very small. The House of the Forest of Lebanon and the House of Pharaoh's Daughter were very much bigger, and I regard those as the Houses of Anatha and Ashima, corresponding with the Elephantine setup in which, we know, about 400 B.C., that the goddess had twice as much money paid to her as the other deity.

Patai: This again is merely a clue showing that those goddesses had a great importance.

Graves: But they were obviously Palestinian and not Kassite, not Hittite, if you like.

Patai: I still don't know how to handle this problem. I don't feel myself, on the basis of all the evidence that I know of, that I can commit myself to a point of view, one postulating a definite matriarchal stage . . .

Graves: Matriarchal goes right back . . . there are several modifications of matriarchal order in which you have the king as a vizier, or you can have an executive king who derives all his power through the mother.

Patai: Isolated features like, for instance, the naming of children, can survive for millennia without any other trace of mother-rule. To this day in the Arab villages it is the custom that the mother names the child, exactly as reported in the Bible. And, of course, for the last two or three thousand years there was no matriarchal society in the Middle East. But this isolated feature survived.

Graves: But on the other hand we do know that there were goddesses at Jerusalem. We know that much.

Patai: That we know.

Graves: And you don't have goddesses unless there is some . . . goddesses originally represented a social setup in which . . .

Patai: . . . women are predominant.

Graves: . . . women are predominant. That's all we can say. But what their powers were in biblical times is impossible to say.

Patai: Well, I found here in my work that there are indications that certain old customs as far as religion is concerned were preserved by women more than by men. For instance, this whole question of the *teraphim*. *Teraphim* were definitely a female affair in the times of the patriarchs, and even in the times of the kingdom. We have the story of Rachel, who took the *teraphim* . . .

Graves: They were her father's *teraphim,* weren't they?

Patai: Yes.

Graves: Or were they really her mother's *teraphim?*

Patai: Her father's, it says.

Graves: Well, I ask you, were they really her mother's?

Patai: The mother doesn't appear at all. But we know from a later story which concerns Michal, the daughter of Saul, who took a *teraphim,* a statue, and put it into her bed so as to make the people believe that David was there. So, again, it is a woman who had in her room—it was her bedroom, her chamber—a statue, an idol, which, to my mind, means that the women preserved this form of worship at a time when in the outside world there was a prophet like Samuel who thundered against it.

Graves: Samuel the prophet . . . the sons of the prophets seem to have been a minority group, probably of Egyptian origin. It seems to me that the whole mainstream of Jewish religion was not prophetic. And only very very late that prophetic people really got control, and they did it in order to preserve the nationality of the Israelites, of the Jews, which were being threatened by extinction by different nations around them.

Patai: This really leads us into the question of the place of prophecy in Israelite history, and that is a very complicated one.

Graves: The important thing is that the prophets were always represented as shepherds, as agriculturalists. Weren't they?

Patai: Not always. Jeremiah was a priest, Ezekiel was a priest.

Graves: Yes I know, but symbolically . . .

Patai: Yes, originally the prophet was a. . . .

Graves: . . . a herdsman, and therefore he was not local.

Patai: Yes, he came from somewhere else.

Graves: What I mean to say is that they came from the north, all herdsmen came from the north. What I mean to say is that the herdsmen concept is a patriarchal concept. The fact that the prophets were originally herdsmen and that God is the supreme male seems to be of importance. The *teraphim* were connected with the high places, with growth, with trees. Up in the north from where the herdsmen come there are no trees.

Patai: Well . . .

Graves: And it's true that when the wind marches in the mulberry trees, it is really a sycamore, isn't it?

Patai: Sycamore.

Graves: That is a local Amorite oracle, not a Hittite oracle. And when Saul sits under a pomegranate tree, that is an Amorite and not a Hittite thing. You have a tremendous diversion, but on the whole . . . one thing I have been interested in is this: the African gods have two things: one is called a *Kraa,* which means the divine essence; the other is called *Tsumsum,* which means a personality. Now, if you have in Greek myth heroes ridden by gods in battle, the way they fight represents exactly the personality of the god in whose service they are. If you have Athene, she behaves like an American woman of good family who rides a fast car and does dangerous things, and actually her timing is magnificent. And Athene always won when she was fighting a stupid,Thracian swashbuckle like Ares.

    When Paris is ridden by the goddes Aphrodite he behaves exactly like a woman. He is mean, he is clever, he is cowardly, and when he is fighting Menelaos, who is under the control of Poseidon, I think, Paris runs away, runs home to his wife, they have a wonderful time in bed together, and Hector comes and says, "You dirty coward . . . better come home and have a good cry!" Then he comes out, he fights Diomedes, who is under the [protection] of Athene. Remember that Athene was an enemy of Aphrodite because of the judgment of Paris. He is in the top of his form in killing Tojans right and left . . . Paris gets behind a pillar, and he gets a little bird, and he pins his foot to the ground. It was a very neat . . . Diomedes shouts at him:

"You dirty coward, how dare you," and so on, but he had to go off the field. Paris wins. And it's Paris eventually who kills Achilles. So you have the exact personalities of the gods represented by the *Tsumsum*.

Now the question is whether the Hebrew prophets had really the *Kraa*, the divine power of Jehovah, or whether they had his personality? I believe that the fact that they were not allowed to take any drugs, they had to live very rugged lives, shows they were not imitating *Tsumsum*, they were just clear *Kraa* . . . whereas I think all the Amorites spoke in the *Tsumsum* of the gods.

Patai: Well, of course, this is not very exactly applicable to the Hebrew prophets, because their God was so much farther away than were the Greek gods . . . but nevertheless you have in the case of the prophet Hosea, you have the idea that he acts in a way which represents what God did; he takes a harlot for wife as God took Israel, and the relationship between Hosea and his wife is exactly the same as that between God and Israel. In other words, he actually represents and personifies, if not God himself, at least God's acts and God's relationship with Israel.

Graves: Yes, that is a very good parallel.

Patai: There is one additional point I want to bring up. I find that in the Hebrew myth there is a remarkable awareness of the historical significance of the acts of these mythical characters. In modern mythology we try to explain, in historical terms or in terms of the historical significance, the acts of mythical characters in general. You can apply this principle to Greek mythology as well. But you don't find in Greek mythology that the people who tell those myths are themselves completely aware of the historical effect those acts have on posterity. Let me give you an example to show how in Hebrew mythology this is so pronounced. Whatever Jacob does—let's take him because he is one of the most important characters in Hebrew mythology—whatever he does, the rabbis who tell the myths about him emphasize that Jacob did so-and-so, therefore his children to the end of time will have this-and-this happen to them. In other words, what this ancient mythical character does affects the entire fate of all his progeny, his children. Here we get a sort of an insight not only into our own interpretation of the myth but the interpretation of the myth by the people who themselves made up the myths and believed in them.

Graves: The trouble about Greek myth is that there were so many different cities, and yet I think within the cities the same thing, if

207

we are talking about the tribes . . . the descendants of Perseus, all looked to him as their great exemplar, and all the descendants of Erechtheus in Athens also looked to him. I admit that the moral emphasis in Judaism is entirely different, there is no morality in the same sense.

Patai: I am talking not only about morality, I am talking about any action by the mythical characters which has automatic results, which go on and on for many generations. For instance, it says there that when Jacob and Laban set up that cairn, the pile of stones, as a boundary mark between them . . . later when David wanted to conquer Aram (Aram was identified with the descendants of Laban), he was unable to because the cairn stood there. So, what he had to do before he was able to conquer Aram was to demolish the cairn and thereby break the magic power—it must have been magic power, if it can be broken by demolishing the cairn—and after that he was able to conquer Aram. So the simple act of Jacob, of setting up that cairn as a boundary mark, affected the fate of the descendants of Jacob for many generations.

Graves: You had the same sort of taboo in Greek myth about the—I am talking without the book—at any rate the rights of the Ilians in the Olympic games, according to some traveler, was affected for hundreds of generations, and you had the extraordinary story of the rape of Cassandra, that for a thousand years the Locrians were forced to send priestesses to Troy and they could be killed by the inhabitants if they were caught. You have the same consequences of ancient myth, but it is now somehow different in that. . . .

Patai: I'd like to give you another example from a somewhat different area. It says that when Abraham was ready to sacrifice Isaac, in the last minute God said, "Don't touch the boy," and then he took a ram, he found a ram, and sacrificed the ram instead. In the Midrash it says that this happened on the first of Tishri, on New Year's Day, and because Abraham sacrificed the ram, therefore when the children of Abraham take the ram's horn on New Year's Day and blow into it, that reminds God of the great piety of Abraham, and he forgives them all their sins. In other words, it has a moral, a sort of a saving, effect for all future generations.

Graves: Well, the story of the ram caught in the thicket, and the story of Jephthah's daughter, they both occur in Greek myth, and there are a lot of consequences, such as certain people are not allowed to eat asparagus, because of a certain woman whom Theseus tried to rape hid herself in wild asparagus. Historically the consequences are the same, but the moral tone is wholly Jewish. Morality is a Jewish invention, or rather it exactly comes from the Greeks but from the Orphics. I think it is an Orphic thing which the Jews caught . . .

Patai: You said somewhere, I think in the introduction to *Greek Myths,* or maybe in your introduction to *The Larousse Encyclopedia of Mythology,* that myth is the spoken part of the ritual. My feeling is that this is too narrow a definition of myth.

Graves: It's a Greek definition. It may not be a definition of Hebrew myth.

Patai: Let's put it this way: that it does not fit precisely the Hebrews. In Hebrew mythology there are many myths for which you find no rituals, with which there is no ritual connected. But, on the other hand, what I do find in my study of Hebrew myths is that each Hebrew myth serves as an explanation of a situation which was somehow puzzling or bothersome, or which later Jews found was unjust or difficult to understand. So they told the myth, a story which we call a myth, and which explained it to them. For instance, the subjection of the Jews to Rome was explained in terms of the relationship between Jacob and Esau, who was Edom, and this was a helpful thing to know. This is not something which is unjust . . .

Graves: But of course, the trouble here is the limit because Rome comes long after the destruction of the First Temple.

Patai: But it is a myth talking about Jacob, it interprets what Jacob said to Edom, and as a consequence of which Jacob's descendants were fated to undergo this and this from the hands of Edom's descendants.

Graves: I think that the Hebrew myths were ecclesiasticized in a popular way, whereas Greek myth is purely royal and aristocratic. That is a difference, I am sure. Among the Hebrews, by the time of the Pharisees every man was equally royal, apart from the king. Among the Greeks, the ordinary man . . . his spirit went to a wretched place, he had no right . . . he was no good. Every Jew had equal rights in paradise, and that is the whole difference. Greek myth is aristocratic, and Hebrew myth, after the first original, is democratic—well, theocratic. I think that is the difference. Nobody is interested in anybody in Greece, except in the dynastic set-up. You see, the Athenians were so crazy that they murdered a whole lot of mixed-marriage peoples. They

209

murdered something like two thousand people who came to Athens and were only half-and-half.

Patai: Nothing like that ever happened in Jewish history. The worst they did was to force them to divorce their non-Jewish wives, as Ezra did. But they did not kill anybody. They did disinherit them, but never killed them. But what I am driving at is that there is a sort of historical consciousness in this . . .

Graves: In both, but implied. I don't think there is any actual difference. In one case it is for the benefit of the Jews as a whole, and in the Greek case it is merely for the benefit of merely a certain ruling class. It gives the authority for a certain class to behave in a certain way.

Patai: Especially I am fascinated by these projections into the past of what was at that time present-day situations.

Graves: Well, look at the attachments to the twelve patriarchs, what could go further than that?

Patai: In Roman times when the Jews suffered under Roman subjection they asked: how is it possible that Edom, who was so evil, his descendants should rule over the Jews, who were so pious? And they answered that Edom had one good feature in his favor: he loved his father, and in this he excelled over Jacob. For Jacob went to Mesopotamia and stayed there for twenty years and didn't serve his father as is the duty of a good son. Whereas Esau did serve . . .

Graves: I know, it was Rebecca who put him up to the dirty job.

Patai: For this reason, they say, since Esau served his father, his descendants get the upper hand over the Jews, the sons of Jacob. So that actually the myth helps not only to explain a present-day situation but also to put up with something which otherwise would be quite unbearable.

Graves: But of course the original myth refers to that breakaway of Edom from under Judean rule, when the Edomites became independent under Joash, isn't it?

Patai: Yes, a few kings after David. Well, in every successive new historical situation, of course, they reinterpreted the original myth, and they always found in it some kind of indication or explanation for the present situation.

Graves: The Greeks didn't do that. They kept the story . . . if there is a change in dynastic rule, they naturally incorporated it by making new myths, but not in the Jewish way. I think it is because . . . If you would have this typed out it would be wonderful.

Patai: I think I will have it typed out, and then I will send it to you, and I will use it actually in writing the introduction.

Graves: I can make it as the basis of this Hillel lecture, giving you full credit.

Patai: I am sure you will. I think another typical characteristic of Hebrew mythology is that they attribute a full historical awareness to the mythical heroes themselves. When Jacob or Abraham do something, they know that "I by doing this herewith determine the fate of my descendants in all eternity."

Graves: And to me the most extraordinary characteristic of Hebrew myth is that it is actually timeless, that everything coexists, the foundation of the Temple coexists with Creation, that Abraham, Isaac and Jacob know each other as it were, and that in Greek myths the historical continuity is kept to successive generations, and the idea of Hercules ever conferring with his great-grandfather Perseus is ridiculous. In Hebrew myth the telescoping is most extraordinary.

Patai: On the one hand, they telescope history; on the other, they extend the life span of a man to one thousand years or more. There is the story, you know, of Judah and his friend in Adullam called Hirah. They say that this Hirah was the same as Hiram, king of Tyre, who lived in the days of David, and that Hiram again was the same as the king of Tyre who was killed four hundred years later by Nebuchadnezzar. So they figure out in the Midrash that Hiram lived 1,200 years. No one bats an eye. But to give you an example of this awareness of historical significance: when Jacob—it says in the Midrash—when Jacob divided his family into groups before he met Esau, because he was afraid, and when he sent several groups of his servants with presents to Esau, he said: "Put a space between you, so that one should arrive first, the second a little while later, and so on." Then he said to God: "Master of the Universe! When afflictions will come over my children, don't allow the afflictions to come one after the other, put a space between one affliction and the other, just as I did."

Graves: Yes, the Babylonian captivity, and then the Roman captivity.

Patai: So that the troubles don't appear one after the other, which the people would not be able to take. They must have a breathing space.

Graves: By the way, have you seen Joshua Podro's book *The Last Pharisee?*

Patai: Yes, I have it here.

Graves: I think it's wonderful, the whole thing of what to do about the sacrificial sheep, sacrificial lambs, with no Temple in which to offer them. Most extraordinary.

Mrs.
Patai: Is he a very well-known scholar?

Graves: No, he's not, but . . .

Patai: I hadn't heard about him before the appearance of *The Nazarene Gospel Restored.*

Graves: He lectures in London . . . but nobody reviewed his book.

Mrs.
Patai: What do you think the psychological significance of all these myths is? What gives rise to them, what do they reveal about the human psyche?

Graves: In Greek myths it is the authority for a certain clan to rule a certain piece of land in a certain way, and you have certain feasts which are acted out to commemorate the past history of these people, and the very fact that it goes on year after year confirms the ruling people in their jobs.

Mrs.
Patai: In other words, it is a practical matter.

Graves: For a practical purpose, but the difference is that in the Hebrew myth it is not a particular clan, it's the whole people you're concerned with, they're all sons of Jacob. Not every Greek could claim to be son of Perseus or the son of Pelops, that was only given to a very narrow range of . . .

Patai: I think that the Hebrew myth is definitely a charter for many things. Some Hebrew myths are a charter for the possession of Canaan, others are a charter . . .

Graves: . . . for the possession of slaves . . .

Patai: . . . for the possession of the Torah, the law. Again others are charters for occupying the position of the "Chosen People." Others are charters for Jewish morality, which was in contrast to the morality of the whole world outside the Jewish people.

Mrs.
Patai: So it is a practical thing.

Patai: Not merely practical, it really helps to live.

Graves: Yes, it's a way of life . . . Eventually the belief in Europe was that anybody was allowed to go to heaven; in the Greek thinking only certain people were allowed to go to heaven, and that, of course, Christianity had taken from the Jews. And what's more the mysteries, which were the only part of religion that the Jews took seriously, were restricted to people who had a clean conduct sheet. Anybody who'd committed incest, who'd killed a man, who'd done anything, was not allowed to take part in the mysteries. Well, in Christianity, anybody who repented could go in and was allowed to take part in the sacramental feast. You had to be a free man, not merely a freed man, to take part in the mysteries.

In the Christian thinking . . . this was taken over from Judaism and, of course, what happened was that the lower classes came gradually pushing upwards, and by the time of Constantine the entire Roman army, all the NCO's were Christians . . . the officers were pagan, so they wouldn't fight the Goths, they had a sit-down strike until the queen, the empress Theodora, told Constantine, "Look here, the armies won't fight unless you proclaim Christ." So he put up the *"in hoc signo vinces"* and all the army went to it like lions. And apart from the attempt of Julian the Apostate—his attempt to bring back paganism, he was a very strenuous person—that was the end of the old gods. It's a democracy, and it was the Jewish myth really which killed the Greek myth. Wasn't it? Wouldn't you say? The Jewish mythical way of thinking.

What I regret is that Judaism was turned into Christianity by such a rotten, wretched, lying, desperate character and turncoat as St. Paul. If any decent person had taken it over, and there were decent Christians, who would feel quite different about Christianity. But the fact that it was taken over by a man who was the very lowest of the low—liar, a hypocrite, a murderer, a coward—that has made Christianity stink ever since. I have a whole dossier.

Patai: In Judaism, to come back to that for a moment, definitely there is a democratic basis, anchored in the idea that all the Jews are ultimately the descendants of Abraham, and it lives and effects the lives of Jews to this day, as can be seen, for instance, from the very fact that if a gentile converts to Judaism he receives a Hebrew name and the second part of his name is "son of Abraham." The same idea exists in Islam. All the Moslems are brothers.

Graves: The effect of Judaism on Islam is terrific. Were these Karaite Jews who influenced the Moslems?

Patai: Originally Mohammed was not influenced by Karaite Jews. He was influenced by Rabbanite Jews who lived in Arabia. In those days there were many large Arab tribes who were Jewish, in the

213

sixth or seventh century. Mohammed had contact with them, and he heard from them stories of the Bible and absorbed ideas from them.

And I have one last point, which is really not so important as the previous ones, and that is that in Hebrew mythology there is the idea of reward and punishment both in this world, in subsequent generations, and in the world to come. Therefore if a man does something, something wrong, for instance, he is not necessarily punished by God in his own person, but he may be punished in his children after many generations, in the sense that his evil deeds influence the fate of his children.

Graves: Oh, that's commonplace in Greek, when Zeus says, "Do not destroy me, o dreadful curse of my father's!" The curse of Pelops goes right through that family. As to rewards and punishments, you have the classical hell in which you have the Danaids and their sins; you have Theseus, who stuck to a rock because he tried to seduce Persephone; you have Tantalus who has eaten the fruit of the gods and he can't eat or drink; you have Sisyphus and the rock—a lot of types of people who committed crimes and are punished there by the three judges of the dead. You have the same punishment both in this world and the next nether one. Of course, you have the curse on one dynasty of David, don't you, which Jesus escaped by belonging to one branch of the House of David, by belonging to Nathan.

Patai: This is one aspect of it, but there is another aspect which works involuntarily. For instance, the example that comes to my mind is that when Jacob is told that Joseph has been killed and he puts on sackcloth and ashes, and then the Midrash remarks that since Jacob put on sackcloth and ashes, sackcloth and ashes will never be removed from his descendants. This is not a sin, it is not something for which the children are responsible, it is an act which he did spontaneously, but which nevertheless automatically sort of affects the fate of his children. They will always have to repent, they will have to suffer, they will always be sad, and so forth.

Graves: What I am interested in very much is the carob tree as a symbol for repentence.

Patai: I think that that is based on a misunderstood word, *harub* for *arbeh*.

Graves: It is a joke between Herod [?] and somebody else.

Patai: *Harub* and *arbeh*.

Graves: But then also they say that when Israel will not repent they will eat carobs, in other words till times are so hard that they will be forced to eat these damn things.

Patai: I believe that the original meaning was there locust, because locust was an accepted food, as it is to this day among the Arabs, and what they actually ate was locusts. Are you talking about St. John? That's why it is called St. John's bread, isn't it? Isn't carob called St. John's bread?

Graves: But you can't eat locust the whole time, can you? Because very rarely you can get it, and they don't keep very well. But carobs you can eat all the time, and it is very bad for you, has a bad effect on you. In our island they had to live on carobs because of the wars. It's caustic, binding, and makes you very bad-tempered, as St. John was.

Mrs. Patai: How close are you getting to the end of your book now?

Graves: Well, the point is that I have written another book in the last two months and gotten it out of the way so that I can get back to this one, and concentrate on it.

Patai: What I would like to do, if it is possible, if your schedule permits it, to see this book finished and go to print in the fall. Not possible?

Graves: I know how long the thing should take and you can't hurry a thing like that. We can get a lot done, but the process of tidying up and cleaning . . . If we were together it would be different, but having to send these back and forth I don't think it's possible. I wouldn't like to promise anything like that. We'll get as far as we can. Then again, in the fall I've got to go to London, and I can't do any work there, for two months. I am not doing anything else apart from a week in Greece. My secretary is a Jew.

Patai: Well, I think that as far as the individual chapters are concerned we can very nicely go on by correspondence. There is no great difficulty.

Graves: No, it's not as if we disagreed. Have we ever disagreed about anything?

Patai: No, not on anything . . .

Graves: . . . on anything important.

Patai: As far as the introduction is concerned, I think that that has to be ironed out between us, and maybe if we really can manage to get

	over to Mallorca, I would definitely prepare the introduction before we come there, and we may finish it up there.
Graves:	That will be very nice. When do you hope to come?
Patai:	Well, we are taking our vacation from the middle of August to the middle of September, so we can go first to Paris or Italy, the last two weeks of August, and then come to Mallorca.
Graves:	Well, I can engage our house we have for our friends for that part of September if you will tell me you are coming.
Patai:	We don't want to . . .
Graves:	No, no, no, no, we have a house in the village, a beautiful house, more beautiful than ours, it's not as elegant as this, in fact it's rather crude, but the woman who would look after you talks French.
Mrs. Patai:	We can go to a hotel.
Graves:	Oh, no, you will be much happier in the house.
Mrs. Patai:	You have people living there, don't you?
Graves:	No, we lend it to a succession of friends, you see. When you'll come to town you'll have it. But I'd like to know it beforehand so I can make out a schedule.
Patai:	We can come there on the first of September.
Mrs. Patai:	Are you sure it's not inconveniencing in any way?
Graves:	If it was I wouldn't say so. Let's turn this off—it makes me nervous.

So I turned off the tape-recorder and we continued our conversation without it.

19.

Problems with the Introduction

A s ONE CAN SEE, in much of our conversation (which was the first lengthy face-to-face exchange of ideas between Graves and me), we did not so much speak *to* each other as engage in something like two parallel monologues, each of us pursuing his own ideas, taking up his thread of thought after it was interrupted by the other. I had a definite program for that meeting: I wanted to tell Graves what I felt were the main features of Hebrew myths, and wherein they differed from Greek myths and the myths of other peoples. I wanted to get his reaction, so as to be able to present a concise characterization of Hebrew myths on the basis of a consensus, however tentative, which I hoped we would reach in the course of that conversation. I was so intent on doing this that I doggedly came back again and again to my ideas and, in most cases, did not respond at all to the points Graves made.

Graves, on the other hand, wanted to speak of favorite ideas he had formulated long before and expressed in his *King Jesus, The White Goddess, The Greek Myths,* and *The Nazarene Gospel Restored,* as well as in several other shorter writings. He emphasized the "Goddess of the Sea, Rehab"; "the tribe of Dinah," which was a "queendom"; the "bisexual deity"; the goddess as dominant in early Greek and "pre-Jewish mythology"; "cattle culture" and "bee culture"; all [the] arts "in the possession of women"; etc. From his comments it became evident that he still firmly believed that prior to patriarchy there was a matriarchal society—about this, for him, there was "no doubt at all." As for me, not wanting to be drawn into discussing an issue that was far from central to a book on Hebrew myths, instead of marshaling arguments against these contentions, I registered only mild objections: "We should leave the question open," "merely a clue," and the like, and tried to keep our conversation focused on what I felt were the basic issues before us: namely, the essential characteristics of Hebrew myths.

A few days after our meeting I listened to the tape, and had to conclude that Graves and I had not reached anything like a general agreement as far as the cardinal features of Hebrew myths were concerned, and that therefore I would not be able to present my planned portraiture of Hebrew mythology in the introduction to our joint book. Hence I decided that I would write a separate essay on the subject and publish it elsewhere. (Ultimately I did write such a paper, titled it "What Is Hebrew Mythology?" and read it to the New York Academy of Sciences on October 26, 1964. It was published in the November 1964 issue of the academy's *Transactions*. At my request my friend Prof. Harry Zohn translated it into German (although I have spoken German quite fluently ever since childhood, I did not trust myself with the intricacies of German academic style), and I read it in that language to the University of Munich and the Frobenius Institute of Frankfurt a. M., and then published it in the Wiesbaden *Paideuma*.)

Still, the May 1961 conversation with Graves was useful. Each of us glimpsed the working of the other's mind, got a live impression of what the other considered important, and learned to weigh the ideas of, and accept corrections from, the other. Although concretely not much of what we discussed that day found its way into the introduction, that conversation cleared the way toward an understanding of what should and could go into it. One can say that our discussion was for us an introduction to the introduction.

Three days after the taping of our conversation, I was again together with Graves at a party given in his honor by Max Gissen, an editor of *Time* magazine, and his wife Louise Thomas, director of the public relations department at Doubleday. There was quite a crowd there, so that Graves and I did not have much of an opportunity to talk to each other. However, the party was useful as a publicity affair: pictures were taken and we were asked questions by quite a number of people.

The next day (May 24) I went to the American Academy of Arts and Letters to attend the induction of new members and the awards ceremony, at which Graves gave a talk titled "The Word *Baraka*." As was his wont, he had written out the lecture and read it from his typescript. Graves started his lecture by saying that the Arabic word *baraka* meant "the sudden divine rapture which overcame either a prophet or a group of fervent devotees," which "can therefore stand for the blessedness acquired by holy shrines and other places where the spirit of God has been plainly mainfested." While this definition fell somewhat short of the true meaning of the word, my major disagreement with Graves was not about this but about his subsequent statement that *baraka* was derived from "a Semitic root *BRK* present in the Biblical name *Barak* and in the Phoenician *Barka*," which meant lightning. He went on to explain that

218

"since lightning is a phenomenon everywhere attributed to the gods, *baraka* means the sudden rapture," etc., and added that "the Jews prefer to derive *baraka* from a root meaning 'knee' and therefore devotion to a god whose worshippers kneel."

As far as I can remember, there was no question-and-answer period after the lecture; instead everybody repaired to the courtyard to socialize, and it was there, standing about with drinks in our hands, that Graves and I discussed the conclusions he had drawn. I refrained from pointing out to him that there was no such thing as a *Jewish* derivation of a word as against a Muslim or Christian one, but told him as gently as I could that Arabic *baraka* and its Hebrew equivalent *b'rakha,* both meaning "blessing," are spelled *BRK,* and that this form is derived from the verb *baraka* in Arabic and *barakh* in Hebrew, whose primary meaning is "to kneel," but which in a different conjugation in both languages means "to bless," since the person who received the blessing knelt before him who gave it. This, I explained, was the origin of the Arab concept of *baraka,* which means, as Westermarck had pointed out, "blessed virtue."[1] The word for lightning, on the other hand, has a different k-like phoneme, usually spelled in English scholarly transliteration as ḳ or *q.* In pronunciation it has a deep guttural sound which is so different from the k of *baraka* that it can never be confused with it. This word, *barq* in Arabic and *baraq* in Hebrew, is derived from a verb meaning "to shine, glitter, sparkle," and hence to emit lightning. It is from this root, I added, that the name of Muhammad's fabulous winged horse, *al-Burāq,* is derived, because it flew with the Prophet at lightning speed from Mecca to Jerusalem, and from Jerusalem up into heaven and back again, all in a single night. Also from this root is derived the Arabic name of Cyrenaica, *al-Barqa.*

Graves was not the man to give in easily and he insisted that there must be some connection between the two words or groups of words, since it made good sense that blessedness was something that descended from above like lightning.

"No," I countered. "In Semitic languages similarities of sound do not necessarily denote common origin. Take, for instance, the Arabic words *kalb* ("dog"), and *qalb* ("heart"). The difference between them exactly parallels the difference between *baraka* and *baraqa,* but they are two entirely different words, with different meanings and without any connection."

I no longer remember whether Graves continued to defend his equation, but there is proof that he did not consider my argument important enough to change that introductory paragraph of his lecture. He repeated it unchanged in his address to the Oxford University Poetry Society, and let it stand in two later printed versions.[2]

In recording this episode it should not be left unmentioned that the lecture was nonetheless a delightful one. In it Graves showed how the concept of *baraka,* that is "blessedness," appeared in many walks of life, survived in modern Western culture, and was "of the utmost importance"—this is how he put it—in literature and the creative arts. He took to task the editors of *The New English Bible,* who "are now trying to supplant the King James version with . . . a translation carefully purged of all *baraka.*" It is *baraka,* he said, that "in poetry can cast an immortal spell on the simplest combination of words." On the other hand, there is also "anti-*baraka* in poetry." All in all, I felt, as I still feel, that the *baraka* of Graves lay in his poetic intuition rather than in his scholarly analysis.

But, to return to our taped conversation of May 20, I had it transcribed, and sent a copy of the typescript to Graves with the following covering letter, dated May 31, 1961.

Dear Robert:

I hope you arrived safely and soundly back home. It was a real pleasure to meet you several times during your short visit to the U.S., and to discuss with you some of the problems of our book.

I am enclosing the transcription of the tape made in my home. It is uncorrected, and, as you will see, on several pages some of the words could not be understood. On p. 12 you said quite distinctly "late," but I assume your intention was to say "early." On pp. 17 and 18 I believe it would be more correct to say that the herdsmen came from the East; it is to the East of Palestine that the treeless steppe lies which was suitable for grazing.

Upon reading through the transcript Ann thought that it might be suitable for publication in the New Yorker. *Possibly, they might publish it as an unedited transcript. However, even in that case I would like to make some of my sentences more grammatical, and you, too, may want to introduce certain changes. If so, make whatever corrections you want, and return to me the transcript which I then will put into the trustworthy hands of Willis Wing.*

> *Yours cordially,*
> *Raphael*

Graves responded on June 9.

My dear Raphael

Thanks very much for the transcription. But I can't agree with Anne that the New Yorker *would publish it,* however neat our revision: you and she don't know them! Also: ever since I called Shawn 'lily-livered' (and worse) they and I are through with each other.*

As a document it is interesting as showing how complementary our approaches are; and it can be the basis for our Introduction; and meanwhile I can get some of it into shape for this Hillel Foundation address.

. . . The New Yorker *selection is made by a council who read everything offered and have to arrive at unanimity; one black ball rejects anything. And nothing with character, unless commissioned from a staff-writer, gets through. I am now starting work again after answering 200 accumulated letters.*

Yours ever,
Robert

Love to Ann.
*It really is no good as it stands: too rambling.
Have been at it all day.

The man Graves refers to as "Shawn" was William Shawn, editor of the *New Yorker.* I am unable to check whether Grave's characterization of Shawn as " 'lily livered' (and worse)" was published.

I replied on June 20, 1961.

Dear Robert:

You are right in thinking that the transcript of our discussion might not be suitable for the New Yorker, *quite apart from your tiff with it's editor. Nevertheless, I am very glad that we had a chance for this dialogue. I reread it a few days ago, and share your opinion that several points discussed in it can be incorporated in the introduction. In fact, I have started a few days ago to work on the introduction because I want to have it ready at least two-three weeks prior to our visit to Mallorca, and mail it to you. In this manner, you will have, I hope, a chance to read it and do some work on it by the time we arrive there. (Our plans now are quite definite. We shall arrive on the 1st of September, and leave on the 11th). In this manner we can put it into final shape during the few days when we shall be directly accessible to each other.*

I have by now a fair idea as to what I want to discuss in the introduction. I should start with a very brief sketch of the views of poets and philosophers of antiquity on what myth is. This should be followed by an equally brief discussion of the various schools of thought on myth from the 18th century to the present time. Thirdly, I should like to present our own views about myth (and I pray to all the deities that you and I don't come to blows about this). Fourthly, I should try to bring to bear the conclusions of the previous section upon the interpretation of Hebrew mythology, the distinction between myth and legend in the Hebrew field, and the characterization of Hebrew myth.

I am enclosing now eight new chapters, as well as three pages which have to be inserted as marked into chapters you already have.

Yours cordially,
Raphael

221

Two weeks later, on July 3, I followed up this letter with another one.

Dear Robert:

I made a special effort putting aside everything else, to finish the introduction. Here it is, of course, only in very rough first draft. I am quite certain that you will have much to change, delete, and add. Please do whatever you feel is necessary, and during the few days which we can spend working together in Mallorca, we shall, I am sure, iron out whatever differences remain between us, and settle on a final version.

Especially, I suspect, that you will find the first half or so of the introduction, which discusses various approaches to mythology, too detailed. If so, do not hesitate to use the blue pencil. The work and time I devoted to these summaries will not be lost—I shall, in that case, use them in an essay I intend to write for the American Anthropolgist, *or the* Journal of American Folklore.

We shall be leaving New York on August 13, and, as I mentioned, in my previous letter, plan to arrive in Mallorca on September 1st.

Cordially,
Raphael

The draft of the introduction which I sent to Graves was a very long piece: it ran into no fewer than eighty-eight triple-spaced pages, some eighteen thousand words. Apart from its inordinate length, it was, as I subsequently recognized, more suited to serve as an introduction to a theoretical book on myth than to one on Hebrew myths which was supposed to prove of interest to the general intelligent public. As I indicated in my June 20 letter, I started with a survey of what scholars, philosophers, anthropologists, psychologists, and historians of religion considered myth to be. This part took up more than half of the total length. It was followed by a presentation of our own views (where I presumed to speak in the names of both authors), and then came some methodological comments on how to reconstruct ancient Hebrew myths, on the characteristics of Hebrew myths, and on related issues. In this latter part I included many of the explanations I gave in the course of my May 20 conversation with Graves. Since this piece of writing of mine has never been published—the introduction to the Hebrew Myths as put in final shape by Graves is fewer than four thousand words—I am appending it, in its original form, to the end of this volume.

Of all the analyses of myth which I gathered in preparation for my long Introduction, the one that impressed me most was that of Walter F. Otto of the University of Tübingen. In fact, I was so moved by it that I not only translated several pages of it for inclusion in my introduction, but wrote him a fan let-

222

ter—one of the extremely few such letters I have ever written in my life. I wrote it in German, and give it here in my English translation.

June 27, 1961
Prof. Walter F. Otto
Mörike Strasse 8
Tübingen, W. Germany

Dear Professor Otto:

Permit me, first of all, to introduce myself. I am an anthropologist who has devoted himself to the study of the cultural anthropology of the Jews, the Arabs, and other Mediterranean peoples of ancient and modern times, and has published several books and studies in these fields. Up to a few years ago I taught at various universities as professor of anthropology, and am now director of research of the Herzl Institute in New York.

About almost two years ago I began to work on a book on Hebrew mythology in collaboration with the renowned English poet Robert Graves. Recently I embarked on writing the Introduction, and in that connection it was necessary for me to deal with the major trends of modern mythological investigations. While doing this I encountered your extremely valuable work, Die Gestalt und das Sein: Gesammelte Abhandlungen über den Mythos und seine Bedeutung für die Menschheit *["Form and Being: Collected Studies on Myth and Its Significance for Humankind"], whose chief conclusions I intend to summarize in ca. ten pages in the Introduction (provided my friend Mr. Graves will be in agreement).*

What you say about myth and ritual ("Kultus") has impressed the more since I myself had come to similar conclusions on the basis of my studies of biblical, talmudic, and midrashic literature. If you are interested, I shall be glad to send you our Introduction, as soon as it is in final shape, for perusal and possible comment.

It so happens that on August 18 my wife and I shall pass through Tübingen on our way from Stuttgart to Switzerland. Should you be at home on August 18 (ca. 10 A.M.), I would be glad to make use of the opportunity to pay you my respects and to make your personal acquaintance. Would you be so kind as to let me know whether this would be convenient for you.

Yours sincerely,
Raphael Patai

Two weeks later my letter was returned with the note on the envelope: "Addressee deceased. Return to sender."

My July 3 letter was answered by Graves by return mail.

223

July 8th 1961

Dear Raphael:

I have been idle this last month: that is to say I have felt obliged to get my Oxford lectures ready, also my address to the Hillel Foundation. And I have been undergoing a sort of poetic crisis which unfortunately takes priority of everything: the oldest rule in my book. The results are at least there to remind me & the world, if interested, of its violence . . . But the Myths are on my conscience.

I'll send (am sending) the Hillel Address for you to judge our incompatibilities.

I have nothing against your Introduction *and a great deal of satisfaction in it: except that it contains a great deal too many words; and cites from too many dull writers. Me, I don't mind that sort of thing because I garner wheat from any chaff-heap; but I do understand reader psychology and there mustn't be a dull paragraph in our book or it may as well not be written.*

It will be fine having you both here from Sept 1st to 11th.

Yours ever
Robert

Graves's Hillel lecture, which he enclosed with this letter, is reproduced in the next chapter page by page and line for line in order to facilitate the iden-tification of the passages to which I referred in my comments contained in my July 25 letter. The text Graves sent me had neat corrections (are) in the hand of Kenneth Gay, to whom Graves liked to refer as "my Jewish secretary"; is addition, on almost every page there (were) also corrections entered by Graves himself in his rather difficult hand.

20.

Graves's Hillel Lecture

Hebrew and European Myth Contrasted
Address to the Hillel Foundation, October 23rd, 1961

I AM AT present engaged on a study of Hebrew Myths, in collaboration with Dr Raphael Patai of the Herzl Foundation, a leading authority on this difficult subject. Though this address is based on a tape-recorded conversation of ours in New York last May, I do not wish to make him responsible for all the views I am about to express. Our book is still in its preparatory stages.

The word 'myth' is Greek, mythology is a Greek concept, and the study of mythology is based on Greek examples. I have heard Jews denying that the Bible contains any myths at all; and, in one sense, they are justified. Normally, myth implies belief in a number of gods and goddesses who take sides in human affairs, each favouring rival heroes; whereas the Bible acknowledges one God alone, and this turns myth into theology. But despite the severe editing undergone by Israel's sacred traditions, from perhaps the sixth century B.C. onwards, the Bible still harbours mythical accounts of ancient gods and goddesses—disguised as men, women, angels, monsters or demons. Nor is this the sole hidden source of such myths. The Talmud and Haggada contain others of venerable antiquity; and some occur in Moslem and Judaeo-Christian legends.

Lilith and Eve are two Palestinian goddesses with whom the Hebrews had dealings early in the second millennium B.C. Both were later described as Adam's wives. Yet Eve can be identified with the goddess Hepa, Hipta, Hepatu, or Hebat, wife of the Hittite Storm-god, who rode naked on a lion's back and, among the Greeks, became the goddess Hebe, Hercules' bride. A prince of Jerusalem in the Tell Amarna period (fourteenth century B.C.) styled himself Abdu-Heba— 'servant of Eve'. Lilith has been wholly exorcized from Scripture, though her children the Lilim are held up to reproach by Isaiah. She seems, from accounts of her sexual promiscuity, to have been a Canaanite fertility-goddess; and figures in Babylonian spells as

1

'Lilitu', a wind-spirit.

We also find mythical references to the angel Samael, 'Celestial Venom', who first appears in history as Samal, the patron-god of Harran Abraham's Mesopotamian city; but is likely to have come there from Samal, a small Hittite-Aramaic kingdom lying to the east. The Zohar mentions Samael's former divinity; though by then he had already become a fallen angel, Chief of all Satans, and was to rank among the Moslems as Shamāl ('head of the Jinn'). Another faded god of Hebrew myth is the Prince of the Sea, who unsuccessfully defied Jahweh—much as the Greek god Poseidon defied his brother Almighty Zeus. Jahweh, according to Isaiah, also killed the Sea-monster Rahab, with a sword; and 'Rahab' is a title of the goddess Tiamat, similarly killed by the Babylonian god El, or Marduk. The Bull-headed God of Tabor, Baal Zevul, or Atabyrius, still existed in Roman times. He was originally a Hittite god, and had another oracular seat in the Island of Rhodes; the Galileans accused Jesus of traffic with him.

Nor must we forget the seven planetary deities, borrowed from Babylon and Egypt, whose powers according to *Zechariah* iv. 10, and Josephus, are commemorated in the seven branches of the Menorah; these seven were, in fact, combined into a single transcendental deity at Jerusalem—as among the Heliopolitans of Egypt, the Byblians, the Gallic Druids, and the Iberians of Tortosa. Scornful references are made to gods of enemy tribes humiliated by Jahweh; such as the Philistine Dagon, Chemosh of Moab, and Milcom of Ammon. Dagon we know from Philo Byblius to have been one of the planetary powers.

Greek gods and goddesses could play amusing or dramatic parts by their intrigues on behalf of favoured heroes, if only because the myths arose in different city states which wavered between friendship and enmity. Yet among the Hebrews, once the Northern Kingdom had been destroyed by the Assyrians, myths became monolithic, and

2

centred almost exclusively on Jerusalem. A rare exception is the tale of the Amorite wars, which has much in common with the Trojan cycle and occurs in the apocryphal *Testament of Judah*; it describes the conquest of Palestine by the Sons of Jacob, especially the area which fell to Ephraim.

Jacob's twelve 'sons' stood, it seems, for independent petty kingdoms, with local gods and populations not necessarily of Hebrew race, though ruled by a Hebrew priesthood. That these 'sons' are said each to have married a twin-sister suggests a matrilinear system of law— inheritance even under patriarchal government. It is not always remembered that Israel, like Edom, consisted of thirteen tribes: for Jacob had a daughter, Dinah—'Dinah' is the feminine form of 'Dan', meaning 'judge'. She does not figure in the story of Joseph, but is best understood as a tribe attached to the Israel confederacy—with semi-matriarchal government.

The account in *Genesis* of Dinah's rape by Shechem suggests that her small queendom was overrun by the Canaanite Shechemites, and that the tribes of Simeon and Levi took revenge by massacring them. Afterwards Dinah married Simeon; meaning that Dinah's tribe was for awhile incorporated with his. But when Simeon forfeited its tribal lands, and the remnants were affiliated to Judah as a sub-clan—which may explain why Simeon has been omitted from Moses' Blessing in *Deuteronomy* xxxiii—we read that Asenath, Dinah's daughter by Simeon (rather than Asenath, the High Priest of On's daughter, as in *Genesis*) married Joseph. In other words, her lands were absorbed by Ephraim.

These petty kingdoms will have acknowledged the over-lordship of Israel, a line of sacred kings, representatives of Jahweh, whose seat was Hebron. It may well be that the king made a royal progress from tribe to tribe, marrying in turn all the local princesses as a symbolic means of fertilizing their lands. This habit, well attested among the peoples of East Africa, is implied

3

in the Biblical account (2 *Samuel* xx) of a general rebellion
against David, when he made Jerusalem the seat of government, by
all the tribes except Judah. In retaliation David locked away
his ten wives in the palace, and ceased to do his marital duty by
them—ten, I suppose, because they were in fact tribal princesses,
and because the Judahite princess, the eleventh, was omitted from
this ban. So was the twelfth, the Simeonite princess; if,
indeed, the clan possessed one of the required dignity.

Other vestiges of an originally matriarchal culture occur in the
Bible: such as the right of a mother to name her sons, still
exercised among the Arabs. Also the matrilocal marriage mentioned
in *Genesis* ii. 24: 'Therefore shall a man leave his father and his
mother and cleave unto his wife.' This custom is proved in the
account of Samson's marriage to Delilah; and was perhaps
the reason why Abraham sent his servant to buy Isaac a bride from
his own kinsmen at Harran, rather than let him marry a Canaanite
woman. To have done so would have meant losing Isaac's services;
nor had Abraham any daughter to attract a son-in-law capable of
taking Isaac's place. Matrilocal marriage is the rule in early
Greek myth: one mythographer records that the first to defy
this tradition was Odysseus, who carried Penelope with him
from Sparta to Ithaca.

David's decision, after quitting Hebron, to concentrate the
tribal princesses in his new, strategically chosen capital, and
convert them into an Oriental harem, was more likely the cause
than the sequel, of this revolt; it was led by Benjamin, Saul's
tribe. David apparently omitted the ritual precaut-
ions which the abandonment of matrilocal marriage should have
prompted. Such as, for instance, the British King Arthur (not
the fifth-century A.D. Arthur, but his shadowy predecessor of the
fifteenth century B.C.) took when he married 'Gwynevere'. Geoffrey
of Monmouth records that the enchanter Merlin brought the 'Giants'

4

Dance' to Stonehenge; and this is now identified with the horse-
shoe of blue sarsen stones known to have been transported overland
from Prescelly in South Wales. As I read the story, 'Arthur', a
High King of Britain, representative of the Sun-god Bel, who
ruled the sacred places of Salisbury Plain, and had subjugated all Southern Britain, disdained to restrict his powers by matrilocal marriage to
the High Priestess of an ancient religious cult established in South
Wales. Nor could Gwynevere leave the sacred stone circle at
Prescelly—in Palestine called *gilgals*—without forfeiting her royal title. So, on Merlin's advice, Arthur brought the gilgal to Stonehenge;
and she accompanied it. (Gwynevere's association with Stonehenge is
confirmed in the *Morthe d'Arthur* by her retirement, after Arthur's
death, to a near-by nunnery.)

Patriarchal and semi-matriarchal cultures co-existed in ancient
Greece. At one time the High Priestess of Argos could claim an
inherited seat in an otherwise all-male council, but had to assume
a beard at the meeting. Worship of a
sovereign goddess points to an original matriarch; and (with all
deference to the Bible) just how powerful goddesses were in ancient
Israel is shown by the comparative size of the three temples on
Mount Zion recorded in *Kings*: 'the House of Pharaoh's Daughter'—
presumably the temple of the Dove-goddess Ashima or Ashera, whose
title Ya-Hu, 'Exalted Dove', Jahweh is held by some commentators
to have borrowed; and 'the House of the Forest of Lebanon'—presumably that of the Love and Battle-goddess Anatha, *alias* Hebat, or Eve,
—were both much larger than Jahweh's.
Records of the late fifth-century Jewish temple at Elephantine
show that these two goddesses, worshipped side by side with him, together enjoyed richer revenues than he though he is styled 'King of
Heaven'. Not for nothing did Jeremiah reprove his co-religionists' cry:
'Let us once more worship

5

the Queen of Heaven, as our fathers did before us.' Anatha's
name occurs in 'Bethany', the village on the Mount of Olives. Ashima
was the Creatrix, the Dove who hatched the World Egg; and it was as
a dove that the King of Babylon, Marduk's representative, symbolically
cut Tiamat in two with his sword at the New Year Rites. In Ugarit myth,
as Ashera, she is styled the 'Mother of the Gods', and 'the Lady Ashera
of the Sea'.

The fact is that every ruler who reforms national institutions,
or, like King Josiah, has reforms pressed upon him, must either write a
codicil to the old religious charter, or produce a new one; and
this involves the manipulation or complete re-writing of myths.
It became clear that if Judaea, a small buffer state between Egypt
and Assyria, was to keep its political independence, a stronger
religious discipline must be inculcated, and the people trained
to arms. Hitherto most Israelites had clung to the orgiastic
Canaanite cult in which goddesses played the leading rôle, with demi-
gods as their consorts. This, though perhaps admirably suited
to peaceful times, could not steel the Jews to resist the invading armies
of Egypt and Assyria. One of the last surviving societies, by the
way, in which all domestic handicrafts are still left to
women, where the men are concerned only with hunting, and where
wars are never fought, was the Eskimo before the missionaries came.
No gods appear in Eskimo mythology, but only a Goddess who has
charge of the Happy Hunting Grounds, and controls the movements
of seals and reindeer.

The prophets knew that the one hope for national independence lay in
the benignant patriarchal monotheism they preached— a cult perhaps
originally brought from Egypt by Akhenaton's
fleeing priesthood—and urged that Jahweh repudiate his two powerful companion deities. The demise of the Davidic crown at
Babylon had converted the exiles to this view.
When Zerubbabel rebuilt Jahweh's temple, he left the House of Pharaoh's Daughter and the House of the Forest of Lebanon in ruins.

Ezekiel points to Israel's double inheritance: 'Thy mother was

6

a Hittite, thy father was an Amorite.' Strange, that he did not
reverse this genealogy! The dour, righteous, witty, practical
Kassite herdsmen who came from the North-East with the Hittite
hordes, were sons of the hero Abraham; the humorous, artistic,
gay, eloquent, agricultural Amorites were children of Sarah—
Sarah, 'Queen', was another of Anatha's titles. These two strains
still combine and separate unforeseeably among Jews; which makes
them so difficult a people to generalize about. On one extreme are Hillel, John the Baptist, Maimonides, Spinoza, Karl Marx; on the other
Heine, Mendelsohn, Chagall, and the Marx brothers. The Hebrew
prophets were dour sons of Abraham, for ever at odds with the
laughter-loving children of Sarah.

Two main social traditions can be distinguished here: I call
them the Bull-culture and the Bee-culture. Bull-culture society,
imported to the Mediterranean area from Central Asia, is modelled
on the cattle herd. The herd is led by the strongest, fiercest,
most cunning bull, lord of all cows and heifers. He disciplines
his sons, the young bulls, until one of them dares challenge and
oust him. In a
Bull-culture, women are treated as cows, chattles of the dominant
male. Since cattlemen rove from pasture to pasture, there is no
question of the women's planting corn or tending trees. Hence the
chieftain's daughters are mere milkmaids—which is the meaning of
the word *daughter*, or *tochter*. Towards the close of the third
millennium, some climatic change dried up the central Asian steppes
and sent the nomad herdsmen moving west and south towards areas of
greater rainfall, towards the agricultural queendoms of Syria and
Europe.

In these queendoms, because the principle of fertility was held

7

to reside in woman, the Moon-goddess's representatives were credited
with her holiness and given charge of crops, trees, springs, bee-
hives and all domestic arts, including pottery and goldsmithing.
They owned the land and its rivers. The men (hunters and fisher-
men) belonged to totem fraternities, kept their tribe in meat
foods, and protected the queendom against wild beasts and raiders.
The Queen was their Mother, the Lady of Wild Things, and
they made her an annual holocaust of totem animals. She chose totem
leaders as her lovers; and sacrificed the King, her favourite of
the year, to fructify the lands. Her symbol was the bee: because
of the queen-bee's sovereignty, energy, and callous treatment of
the drone. There were no gods.

When the cattlemen reached these queendoms, they pleaded, if
we can trust West African analogies: 'Let us in; we are starving;
we will pay for our lives with milk and beef.' If the Queen
agreed, the nomads behaved for awhile in orderly fashion. And
bull-men, being tougher and better-looking, displaced the hunters
as her lovers. But once the nomads had consolidated their position, the chieftain would demand monogamic marriage with the Queen,
and refuse to die at the end of his term. She naturally stopped
her ears, and resorted either to murder or suicide.

This cultural conflict accounts for several Greek myths: particularly that of Zeus' courtship of Hera as a bedraggled cuckoo
on whom she took pity, but who suddenly assumed his true shape and
overpowered her: later depriving her of all her powers except
that of child-bearing and prophecy. Men gradually usurped women's
ancient prerogatives of agriculture and art. The myth of King Athamas
illustrates women's defensive tactics in this sex-war: when he
dishonoured the Corn-goddess Ino, her devotees parched the seed
corn in an oven, so that it would not sprout. Other incidents
are the murder by the Danaids (the Goddess Danae's priestesses) of
husbands forced on them by the invading 'sons of Aegyptus';

8

and the Lemnian women's revenge on their husbands for marrying
foreign wives. The gradual reduction of women from sacred beings
to chattles, provides a main theme of Greek myth. Similarly,
Jahweh's punishment of Eve for causing the Fall of Man is the
first human crisis recorded in the Bible. Further to disguise
Eve's original godhead—her title 'Mother of All Living' survives in *Genesis*—later mythologists represented her as formed
from Adam's rib (as monstrous a birth as Athene's from the head
of Zeus), which is an anecdote based apparently on the word *tsela,*
meaning both 'rib' and 'a stumbling'. Still later mythologists
say that she was formed from Adam's barbed tail. . . And even
the earliest commentators on *Genesis* reject the Biblical explanation
of Hawwa (Eve), preferring to connect it with *Hiwya*) ('serpent').
According to Rabbi Aha, Adam said to the woman: 'The serpent is
your serpent, who led you astray, and you are my serpent who led me
astray.' The Greeks, too, made woman responsible for man's unhappy
lot, by accepting Hesiod's fable of Pandora's jar from which a Titan's
foolish wife let loose the combined spites of sickness, old age,
and vice. 'Pandora', ('all gifts'), it should be observed, was
once a title of the Greek Creatrix.

The Cain and Abel myth records how the agriculturist Cain—
presumably Canaan, a goddess-worshipper—murdered the herdsman
Abel in a fit of jealousy. Although Abel had broken God's command
'In the sweat of thy brow shalt thou eat bread', his flesh sacrifice was preferred to Cain's 'sober' offering of corn and fruit.
This suggests that Abel, a chieftain of invading Kassite nomads,
seized control of Eve's tribal oracle, and that her Canaanite
agriculturists thereupon killed him. (One post-Biblical mythographer actually records that Cain and Abel fought for the
favours of Eve: which makes good historical sense.) As a result,
Cain's agriculturists were expelled from their lands, and built a
new city elsewhere. The legend of Lilith, who quarrelled with

9

Adam about their sexual relations and left him, suggests that the
herdsmen had similarly seized another Canaanite queendom. Lilith
being a typical Bee-culture representative. El, the head of the Semite
Pantheon, was a Bull-god; and Jahweh figures as a bull-god in *Kings*
xxii, where Zedekiah impersonates him by wearing iron horns and cry-
ing: 'Thus shalt thou push the Assyrians!'

As for the Bee-goddess, it is significant that a censorship
imposed by post-Exilic editors banned all favourable reference to
bees in the Scriptures; though honey remained in constant meta-
phorical use. The word of Jahweh, the speech of friends, the
memory of a good man, Wisdom herself, are all likened to honey;
but where is the Queen-bee who rules the hive and the constant bandy-
ing about of whose *mana*—an exudation now named 'Royal Substance'—keeps the community together? She occurs nowhere, except
in a curse pronounced on Israel by Isaiah (vii. 18): 'The Lord
shall hiss for the Bee that is in the Land of Assyria'—namely
for the Battle-goddess Beli or Belili, wife of Ashur, a type of
the Amazonian Cybele, whose emblem was the bee. (Beli occurs
disguised in the phrase 'Sons of Belial'—a cacophemism, *beli ya'an*,
meaning 'that from which nothing comes up', i.e. Hell.) In
Deuteronomy i. 44, *Psalms* cxviii. 12, *Maccabees* xiv. 19, bees are
mentioned for their stinging powers alone. In the story of
Samson, they breed in a lion's carcase, which would make the honey
unclean. Of two favourable references to bees, one occurs in
Ben Sirach's *Ecclesiasticus* xi. 3: 'The bee is little among such
as fly, but her fruit is the chief of sweet things.' Ben Sirach,
however, was a Hellenist of High Priestly family, and wrote in Egypt
beyond reach of Jerusalem censorship. The other reference, contained
in the Egypto-Greek text of *Proverbs,* is a continuation of 'Go to
the ant, thou sluggard, consider her ways and be wise . . .'

> . . . Or go to the bee and learn how delightful she is, and how holy
> is the work that she doeth. Whose labours kings and lesser men
> employ for their health, and who is desired and reverenced in the
> eyes of all . . .

That the Massoretic text omits this convincing poetic balance to

10

the ant-metaphor suggests a reluctance to praise any matriarchal society; indeed, apiculture, an art practised throughout the Middle East from very early times, gets no mention in the Bible. This story of Samson is paralleled by the Greek myth of Aristaeus— for whom bees bred in sacrificial carcases. He also received divine honours for his invention of bee-hives, and lived under the patronage of the Muse-goddesses. Athenians, of course, lavished praise on their Battle-goddess Athene who always proved herself more than a match for the War-god Ares himself. Yet they make her subservient to Zeus; and in the famous criminal trial of Orestes, she gives her casting vote against mother-right, as represented by the avenging Furies.

Let me repeat: monotheism, as opposed to the worship of two supreme goddesses and their male companion, was for centuries confined to an Israelite minority led by the Guild of Prophets who, as we know from Zechariah and other sources, made a point of dressing as shepherds or herdsmen in honour of their pastoral God. (Where pasture is too thin for cattle, as in most of Judaea, the Ram-god appears: and it was to a Ram-god that Abraham sacrificed his totem beast on Mount Moriah.) The prophets ceaselessly declaimed against Goddess-worship in the Canaanite sacred groves; and *Deuteronomy* bans numerous Canaanite rites, among them the hanging of sacred kings from trees. Yet the censors have been careless about excising all favourable mention of tree-worship: in *2 Samuel* v. 24, for example, the rushing noise of wind through sycamore (or perhaps acacia) trees is given divinatory meaning. Tabernacles, a Canaanite vintage feast, could not be suppressed but only purged of sexual abandon, and converted to the joyful worship of a Supreme God; even so, the light-headedness of women worshippers continued to trouble Pharisee sages.

Hebrew myths were edited with moralistic intent. Greek myths, granted, account for curses and taboos still in force after a

11

thousand years; and the Greek Hell contained warning instances of criminals punished, like Tantalus, for eating forbidden food; like the Danaids, for husband murder; like Sisyphus, for betraying divine secrets; like Peirithous, for the attempted seduction of a Goddess. But the Greeks never glossed their myths with pietistic comment, such as that Abraham's attempted sacrifice of Isaac took place on the First of Tishri; and therefore all Israel blows a ram's horn on that day to remind God of Abraham's piety and implore forgiveness of their sins. Although the Isaac myth is paralleled in the Greek account of Athamas' attempted sacrifice of his son Phrixus—a sacrifice interrupted by the arrival of Hercules and the divine appearance of a ram—the occasion was remembered only because this Ram supplied the Golden Fleece for which Jason's Argonauts eventually went in quest.

Some Greek myths are chronologically inept. Thus Theseus runs off with lovely Helen two generations before Paris follows his example. But the mythographers do not try to reconcile this anachronism by explaining that at the age of ninety Helen remained miraculously young: which was the Biblical way of explaining how Sarah could be Isaac's mother after having married Abraham so long before. The Greeks leave the reader to assume that Paris' Helen was merely a namesake of Theseus' Helen. In the myth of Judah, again, Hiram of Adullam is said to be the same as Hiram of Tyre, who exchanged riddles with Judah's remote descendant Solomon and provided material for the first Temple; and also as the King Hiram killed by Nebuchadnezzar after the lapse of four centuries. A midrash therefore decides that Hiram lived twelve hundred years: thus easily beating Methuselah's record.

Nor did the Greeks use myths as texts for political sermonizing. The account of Esau's ill-treatment at Jacob's hands was later rounded off by a prophecy that he would one day break Jacob's yoke from off his neck—an addition clearly intended to justify a revolt of

12

Esau's Edom from Judaea, in King Joram's reign. This was given a
new meaning when the Roman invaders crowned Herod the Wicked, an
Edomite, King of the Jews: Edom then became a synonym for Rome,
and the Pharisees counselled the Jews to make no armed rebellion,
but to expiate their ancestor's ill-treatment of Esau with
patience and forbearance. A full historical prescience was
attributed to Israelite heroes; and whoever in the Scriptures
performs any solemn act is understood to be thereby determining
the fate of his descendants for all eternity. Thus when Jacob
on his way to meet Esau, divided his household and cattle into
three groups, sending gifts with each at intervals, he was warning his
descendants of the Diaspora that they should always prudently guard
against the worst. According to a midrash, Jacob prayed: 'Lord of the
Universe, when afflictions descend upon my children, pray leave an in-
terval between them, as I have now done!' And the apocryphal *Testament of the Twelve Patriarchs* credits these patriarchs with a precise
knowledge of later history.

Jacob is a useful character for judging the difference between
Greek and Hebrew myth. He steals flocks and herds from his kinsman by altering their colour and appearance; the Greek hero
Autolycus does likewise, and the legends have the same Palestinian
source. Autolycus is a clever thief, and no more; but since Jacob,
re-named Israel, was to become the saintly ancestor of all Jews,
his deceit has been justified on the ground that Laban had twice
cheated him. And, instead of using magic, as Autolycus did, on animals
already the property of others, he conditions their colour and
establishes their ownership by pre-natal influences. The moral
being that Jews may defend themselves against their oppressors by legitimate means only, never by magic.

The Greeks drew no such conclusions from the great deeds of their
ancestors, unless it might be a warning against the fickleness of fortune.
The fall of Troy brought ill-luck on every important Greek leader

13

responsible for its capture. Heroes of an earlier generation,
Theseus, Jason and Bellerophon, were all destined to end miserably,
victims of divine nemesis; whereas Abraham, Isaac, Jacob and
Joseph died in contented old age and were honourably gathered to
their fathers. This contrast is sharpened when we recall that
the story of Joseph and Potiphar's wife Zuleika is identical with
that of Bellerophon and his step-mother Anteia—both being based
on the Egyptian *Tale of Two Brothers.* Major Hebrew prophets were
equally blessed: Elijah and Enoch rose staight up to Heaven;
but the Greek prophet Teiresias foresaw the doom of Thebes and died in
ignoble flight. Moses, who rescued his people
from the Pharaonic Sphinx, had to expiate a particular fault on
Mount Pisgah, but was honourably mourned by all Israel, and buried
by God Himself; whereas Oedipus, who saved his people from the
Theban Sphinx, and had enjoyed much the same nativity as Moses,
died banished and poor, hounded by the Furies of Mother-right.

Perhaps the main difference between Greek and Hebrew myths—
apart from this glaring contrast in the rewards of virtue—is that
Greek myths were royal and aristocratic: accounting for certain
religious institutions in particular city-states, presided over by
aristocratic priests who claimed descent from the gods or heroes
concerned. Only the hero, or his descendants, could hope for a
pleasant after-life in the Fortunate Isles or the Elysian Fields;
and his moral conduct did not matter in the least. The vile
Odysseus, the vindictive Achilles, the overbearing Agamemnon, took
Elysium as their right; thievish Autolycus, reputedly Odysseus'
real father, will have done the same. Yet the souls of slaves and
foreigners, however exemplary their lives, were relegated to a
dismal Tartarus where they flew blindly about, twittering like bats.
Among the later Jews, on the other hand, every righteous observer
of the Mosaic Law, whatever his birth or station, was made free of
a Heavenly Kingdom which would arise from the ashes of our present

14

world. The later Greeks took no such democratic step; for
though they excluded from the Mysteries, which gave initiates an assur-
ance of Paradise, all persons with criminal records, they still
confined admission to the free-born.

The Sadducees, it is true, rejected the Prophets and the Pharisees' Millennial Paradise. Yet a text in *Deuteronomy*—
'Thou shalt not seethe a kid in its mother's milk!'—proves the
Orphic Mysteries to have reached Jerusalem by King Josiah's reign.
That the Sadducees, who were Hellenistic Levites, maintained a
secret cult from which the Essenes derived their Classical Paradise,
is more probable than that they altogether abandoned the Orphic
hope of an after-life.

Greek myths, in fact, are charters for certain clans—descendants of Perseus, Pelops, Cadmus, or whoever it may have been—to
rule certain territories so long as they placated the local gods
with sacrifices, dances and processions. Annual performance of
such rites confirmed their authority. Hebrew myths are national
charters: the myth of Abraham for the possession of Canaan; the
myth of Jacob for Israel's status as a chosen people; the myth of
Ham for the possession of Canaanite slaves. Others confirm the
supreme sanctity of Mount Zion against the rival shrines of Hebron
and Shechem; and the eternal persistence of the race.

This sense of national destiny is absent from Greek myth, as it
also was from Roman myth, until inculcated by gifted members of
Augustus' ministry of propaganda—Virgil, Livy and the rest.
Professor Hadas of Columbia University has pointed out close cor-
respondences between the *Aeneid* and *Exodus*—the divinely-led
exodus of refugees to a Promised Land—and I accept his conclusion
that Virgil must have borrowed from the Jews. I am equally certain
that Livy's moral anecdotes of Ancient Rome, which are quite
unmythical in tone, were written under Jewish influence. Of course,
Roman morals differed sharply from the Jewish: Livy had to rate

15

courageous self-sacrifice above truth and mercy. For the Augustans, Rome was the sole legitimate object of worship; not their Divine Trinity of Juno, Diana and Juppiter. And though the early Emperors had prudently extended the citizenship to Latin and Gallic allies, it still remained a class privilege. Not until the Hebrew myths, borrowed by the Christians, gave subject peoples an equal right to salvation, were the Olympians finally dethroned. Granted, some of these drifted back to power disguised as saints, and perpetuated pagan rites in the form of Church festivals, yet the aristocratic principle had been securely defeated by the democratic one. Granted also, Greek myths continued to be studied, because the Church took over schools and universities where the Classics were required reading; and the Constellations, which illustrated these myths, were too well established to have their names changed. But the moral quality of Hebrew myths, patriarchal and monotheistic, has established the ethical principles of Western civilization—however laxly they are now followed; and the Goddess is still dethroned.

16

Within about ten days after the receipt of this typescript I was ready with my comments and suggestions for corrections. In them I touched upon only a few of the many points with which I disagreed, but in several cases I went so far as to suggest even the phrasing for my recommended emendations. I do not know to this day to what extent Graves used my suggested corrections when delivering the lecture the following October.

July 25, 1961

Dear Robert:

Your letter of July 8 received and here are my comments on your Hillel address:

My first comment is that it occasionally contains statements of fact where scholarly caution would permit only conjecture. E.g. on p. 1 you say "Lilith and Eve are two Palestinian goddesses with whom the Hebrews had dealings in the second millennium B.C.*" I would have formulated this sentence, and the following ones, thus: "Eve figures in Genesis, and Lilith in the Midrash, as the two wives of Adam. Yet it seems probable that in their origin they both go back to ancient Near Eastern goddesses familiar to the early Hebrews. The name Eve* (Hawwah) *may be taken as a late variant of the name of the goddess Hepa, etc . . . ."*

On p. 3, par. 2, line 5ff., I would suggest the following phrasing:

"Twelve was the round figure in the ancient Near East, and any self-respecting people had to maintain the tradition that it was composed of twelve parts or tribes, and thus be a properly constituted representative in its land of the great natural phenomena, such as the signs of the zodiac, the months of the year, the hours of the day, all of which numbered twelve. This is why, even against more concrete historical reminiscences, the duodecimal system was asserted for Israel, Aram, Edom, etc.

"In reality, of course, there may have been either fewer than 12 tribes (if Levi is not counted), or more (if he, as well as Ephraim and Manasseh are counted). Moreover, there was Jacob's daughter Dinah, who may have represented a tribal group as much as any of her twelve brothers. In fact, the account in Genesis *of Dinah's rape by Shechem suggests a matriarchal tribe or a queendom, overrun by the Canaanite Shechemites and subsequently avenged by its brother-tribes of Simeon and Levi. If the Midrash states that, following this incident, Dinah married Simeon, this can be taken to mean that subsequently the weakened Dinah tribe was incorporated into the tribe of Simeon. The daughter of Dinah and Shechem, says the Midrash, was Asenath who became Joseph's wife: this may be the mythical formulation of the historical process by which the lands of Dinah and Shechem, i.e. the neighborhood of the city of Shechem, were ultimately absorbed by the strongest Joseph-tribe, Ephraim."*

241

On p. 4 lines 1–8: There is no basis for the assertion that the ten concubines of David were from ten different tribes. David ceased to do his marital duty by them (2 Sam. xx. 3) simply because, following Ahithophel's counsel, Absalom publicly cohabited with them (2 Sam. xvi. 22) in order to demonstrate that he had succeeded his father David, and as a royal installation-rite; as far as David was concerned, these women thereby became defiled once and for all, and unfit to serve as his concubines. Moreover, apart from these concubines, David had at the time several wives.

Page 4 middle: The assumption that if Isaac had married a Canaanite woman, Abraham would have lost his services, seems to me unwarranted. On the contrary: in the family of Abraham, Isaac, and Jacob, patrilocal residence was the rule. The sons remained with their father. This is why Abraham had to "send away" his sons by his concubines (Genesis xxv. 6), when he did not want them to inherit with Isaac. This is why Esau's Hittite wives were "a bitterness" to Isaac and Rebekah (Gen. xxvi. 34–35; cf. xxvii. 46; xxviii. 8–9): they lived with them.

Page 4, last par.: The revolt against David was led, not by Benjamin, Saul's tribe, but by Absalom, David's son (2 Samuel xv.).

Page 5, line 11 from bot.: Where is it stated that the House of the Daughter of Pharaoh was larger than the House of the Lord? In 1 Kings vii. 8 no measurements are given. And what is the basis of the statement that this, and the House of the Forest of Lebanon, were temples? As I read the text, it only states that these two were the palaces for Solomon, and his wife, the daughter of Pharaoh. And where is the basis for the identification of Anath with Hebat? I would suggest that these conjectures be omitted and that you say instead: "How powerful goddesses must have been in ancient Israel can be surmised from their ability to maintain positions at least equal to that of Jahweh as late as the fifth century, in the remote Jewish temple at Elephantine where they were worshipped side by side with him and enjoyed richer revenues than he, though he is styled 'King of Heaven.' " (I had no chance to check these last two points.)

Page 6 top two lines: the name of Anath (this is more correct than Anatha) occurs, primarily, in the name of the village Anathoth (literally: "Anaths"), the priestly village north of Jerusalem, the home of Jeremiah (Jer. i. 1).

Page 6, lines 6–7 from bot.: couldn't you forego the clause between the dashes? It is highly problematic, in the best case.

Page 7, line 6: Sarah means princess. Queen would be malkah.

Page 9, last par.: It is, to my taste, too daring to identify Cain with Canaan. In fact, there is ony one single letter identical in both names, the n: Qyn is the Hebrew spelling of Cain; Kn‘n of Canaan (the ‘ stands for the guttural ‘ayin).

Page 10, line 4: that Jahweh was a bull-god is correct. But instead of arguing from Kings xxii (correctly: 1 Kings xxii) which simply describes a sym-

bolic act (such as the wearing of a yoke by another prophet), why not refer to the fact that whenever the Hebrews represented Jahweh in a statue, they made the image of a calf, i.e. a young bull (the Golden Calf of Aaron; the Calves of Jeroboam).

Page 10, 2nd par.: You could add that the name of the bee is preserved in the name of the amazon-prophetess Deborah (= bee). Correct the spelling beli ya'an *to* beli ya'al, which can also mean "that which is of no use," i.e. useless, valueless.

Page 12, line 10 from bot. correct Hiram to Hirah.

In conclusion let me say that, in spite of these disagreements, I thoroughly enjoyed reading your paper, and certainly have no quarrel with its general argument.

Both Ann and I are greatly looking forward to seeing you on September 1.

> Cordially,
> Raphael

Graves responded by return mail, on July 29.

Dear Raphael:

Thanks so much for your amendments, most of which I accept. But when you come I'll justify the rest of my statements with the appropriate texts. e.g. relative size of temples; the difference between Sheba's and Absolom's revolts, etc. I know that you can take anything, if the evidence leans that way. You are almost unique in that of your scholarly correligionists.

—I have had an extraordinary time lately: working on poetic problems of an entirely new sort, so that I'm way behind with the Myths. This you must forgive; it is as bad as an illness or domestic upheaval when poetry suddenly insists on my attention. But it clears the mind for other jobs; and is the only excuse for my existence.

I'll be in Greece from Aug 16th–25th with my daughter.

I fear you'll be sweltering in N.Y. Me, I can't have it too hot for my taste.

> *Yours ever*
> *Robert*

Love to Ann

21.

To Majorca!

THE SUMMER OF 1961 was no less busy for me than the preceding academic year had been. Later in the afternoon of the very day I attended Graves's lecture on *baraka,* I went to a dinner at the Statler-Hilton Hotel given by the American Zionist Council in honor of Dr. Nahum Goldmann, the Zionist leader, who at that time organized the Conference of Presidents of Major Jewish Organizations, and about whom I was to write a book many years later.

On June 7 took place the presentation of the *Complete Diaries of Theodor Herzl,* which I had edited in five volumes, to Dr. Abba Hillel Silver, another important Zionist leader, president of the Central Conference of American Rabbis and, incidentally, a longtime opponent of Goldmann within the Zionist movement. The focal point of this gathering was my work as editor of the *Diaries,* and I gave a talk on the significance of this publication, which contained, for the first time in any language, *everything* Herzl had written in his *Diaries.*

From that affair I went directly to a dinner at the Gotham Hotel given by the Conference on Jewish Social Studies. After this we adjourned to the nearby Temple Emanuel, where a meeting organized by the conference took place. Chaired by Prof. Salo Baron, its subject was "Africa and the Jews." The speakers were Eliahu Elath, former Israeli ambassador to the United States; Prof. Joseph Greenberg, the African linguist of Columbia University; myself; and Prof. Hugh Smythe of Brooklyn College. In my talk I presented the gist, with additional conclusions, of my 1947 study on the similarities between the biblical Hebrew and the Sudanese royal installation rites as an example of Hebrew-African cultural contact. My lecture was subsequently published in the April 1962 issue of *Jewish Social Studies.*

At this time of my life I was still hoping to be able to return to Israel, and next day (June 8) I had a long talk with my friend S. Z. Abramov, the attorney and member of the Israeli Knesset, about steps I could take to be appointed editor-in-chief of the *Encyclopaedia Judaica,* which was then in the planning stage in Jerusalem. By sheer coincidence, a week later Dr. Emanuel Neumann told me that he had budgetary difficulties with the executive of the Jewish Agency, and did not know "how long we shall be able to continue with the Herzl Press."

On June 20, my elder daughter Ofra, having finished her college studies at Cornell University, left for a visit to Israel. She returned on August 7, sunburned, full of exciting stories, but with no desire to settle in Israel. Instead, she was determined to begin graduate work in genetics at an American university.

On July 7 I gave a lecture on "Society and Culture in the Middle East" to the Stern College for Women (a subsidiary of Yeshiva University). On July 18 I placed an order for a Mercedes-Benz car, for a total price of $3,864.77, to be picked up by me at the Stuttgart factory.

On July 19 I got a call from Lew Schwarz of Abelard-Schuman Publishers informing me that they were ready to sign a contract for the publication of a two-volume anthology I had planned to edit, *Women in the Modern World.* I no longer remember why I did not take up their offer.

Throughout this time I utilized every free moment to work on the *Hebrew Myths,* which I was impatient to advance as much as I could before our planned visit to Graves in Majorca. I was becoming increasingly dissatisfied with the limitations on the time I was able to devote to my scholarly writing, which, of all possible occupations, has always been the most attractive and most satisfactory to me. Concretely, I felt that, in order to be able to finish the *Hebrew Myths* within the time frame Graves and I had envisaged when we embarked upon the project, I should be freed of my responsibilities at the Herzl Institute for at least one year. Since the institutions under the aegis of the Jewish Agency had no such thing as a paid sabbatical, I could afford to take a leave of absence only if I could secure a grant from a foundation to replace the lost income. What I needed was the amount of ten thousand dollars, and I made up my mind to apply to several foundations.

Accordingly, in June of 1961 I composed what I believed was a persuasive letter, describing briefly the literary-scholarly project I was engaged in with Robert Graves, and requesting a grant of ten thousand dollars to enable me to devote a year exclusively to the *Hebrew Myths.* Within the ensuing few weeks I sent this letter to some fifteen foundations, and asked references from several scholars who, I knew, were familiar with my published writings. Among them was Prof. Erwin R. Goodenough, the author of the magisterial multi-volume *Jewish Symbols in the Greco-Roman Period,* in which he had quoted me several times. In response he wrote me a most flattering letter ("I found your work on Rain Magic in the Feast of Tabernacles fascinating"), but declined, pleading insufficient familiarity with my work. I also asked Prof. Emil Lengyel, an old friend of mine—he once told me that he remembered meeting me as a teenager in my father's house in Budapest—and he responded most graciously and generously.

Bracha Habas, the Israeli novelist (one of whose books the Herzl Press was publishing at that time in an English translation) and her husband David Hacohen (the well-known Israeli diplomat, politician, and member of the Knesset) put me in touch with David E. Levitt, president of the DCA Food Industries, Inc. I went to see Levitt on August 11, but it turned out that he had an idea of his own which he wanted me to realize. As I wrote to Bracha Habas on the same day (in Hebrew):

> Mr. Levitt did show a certain interest in the subject of a book on Hebrew mythology, but instead of discussing the substance of that book and ways in which he could be of help in obtaining a grant for this research, he told me that for several years now he had been trying to find a researcher-writer who would be willing to write a book on the prophets of Israel. And not simply a book, since there is no dearth in books on this subject, but a book that would create a spiritual revolution in this world of ours, and, in addition, would also be a "best seller." Such a book he would be ready to finance. He expressed the opinion that Robert Graves and I would be the ideal authors to write such a book. I promised him that during my visit with Graves in a few days time I would talk to him about this idea, and we shall see how he will react.

A few days later Levitt wrote to Rabbi Wolfe Kelman of the Rabbinical Assembly of America, calling his attention to the *Hebrew Myths,* and Rabbi Kelman, in reply, came up with some suggestions which Levitt duly forwarded to me. Upon my return from Majorca I wrote Levitt (dated September 28):

> As to your idea of a book on the Hebrew prophets: I discussed it repeatedly with Robert Graves, but I found him somewhat lukewarm about it. Nevertheless I believe that if I put to him a concrete and attractive proposal, he might agree to collaborate with me on such a book. On the other hand, I have some ideas about possible collaborators which I would like to discuss with you personally.

I have no record or recollection of any further meeting between me and David Levitt.

Also in the summer of 1961 it occurred to me that a preface from the pen of a recognized authority on biblical archaeology and religious history would be a considerable asset to the *Hebrew Myths.* I knew precisely the person who would have been ideal for this purpose: Prof. William F. Albright of Johns

246

Hopkins University, widely respected as dean of American biblical archaeologists. I had met Albright the first time in 1933 in Jerusalem. I still remember that soon after my arrival there I attended a meeting of the Hebrew Society for Palestinian Archaeology, and at one point in the discussion period, a tall, sparsely built, bespectacled man with short-cropped blond hair rose to make some remarks. Prof. Samuel Klein, under whom I was preparing my doctoral thesis, and who had taken me to the meeting, whispered to me: "That is Prof. Albright." It was the first time that I heard a non-Jewish scholar speak fluent modern Hebrew, even though with a recognizable American accent—the accent that characterized the Hebrew speech of all American Jews as well.

Albright was at the time director of the American School of Oriental Research in Jerusalem. Years later, he very favorably reviewed the two volumes of my Hebrew book, *Man and Earth in Jewish Custom, Belief, and Legend*, in the April 1943 and October 1944 issues of the *Bulletin of the American School of Oriental Research* (known in scholarly circles as *BASOR*). In the course of the years I had encountered Albright from time to time, and had formed the highest opinion of his books on biblical archaeology, which remain classics in the field. I could think of no better man to endow the *Hebrew Myths* with scholarly respectability and help its acceptance in academe.

So, on July 25 I placed a long-distance call to Albright. I found him in his Baltimore office, and after identifying myself—he remembered me well and was glad to hear from me—I told him what I wanted. His response was outright and emphatic refusal. He even warned me, I remember, not to undertake the writing of a book in partnership with Graves. "You will ruin your reputation," he said. Evidently, he shared the negative opinion many scholars had of Graves's excursions into their domain—an opinion that was amply evidenced by their reaction to *The Nazarene Gospel Restored*. I was downcast, but I don't think I would have listened to him even if I had had the benefit of his opinion before I had started to work on the book with Graves.

After my phone call I felt that I had not sufficiently explained to Albright what the book was about, and so the next day I wrote to him.

July 26, 1961

Dear Professor Albright:

Your opinion of my work is of such importance and value to me that I feel I must try to correct the impression you may have gained in yesterday's hasty telephone conversation about the character of the book on Hebrew Mythology I have undertaken to write jointly with Robert Graves. For this reason (and not in order to make you change your mind about sponsoring my application for foundation support), I decided to write to you, and to send you the table of contents of vol. I of the book as well as five completed chapters (completed, that is, with the exception of some checking of sources and such changes that thereupon may become necessary).

247

The material within each chapter is organized in the following way: The first section contains wherever available, the Biblical version of the myth; then follow in several sections, and in narrative form, the Talmudic and Midrashic versions, variants, amplifications, etc.; these are followed by source references; lastly come the critical, comparative and analytical comments on the myth (or myths) contained in the earlier sections.

As to what constitutes Hebrew myths, this question will be dealt with in the Introduction, which will also provide the theoretical framework for the study of Hebrew mythology. Also discussed in the Introduction will be the problem of the function of myth in general and of Hebrew myth in particular, as a motivating force in social, cultural and individual life.

My share in writing the book is to extract material from the sources, arrange it topically, make my comments, and thus to prepare the first draft of each chapter. These drafts then are sent to Graves who adds whatever observations he has to make; adduces occasionally Greek parallels; suggests ideas which, although often intuitively reached, have repeatedly proved to be sound upon investigation; and rewrites the whole chapter in his masterly English style. When I receive the chapters back from him, I use my critical judgment as to what to accept and what to change or to excise altogether; having thus established what I regard as the final version of the chapter, I send it to Graves a second time for his formal acceptance. So far, he has in every case deferred to my views. He is aware, as he has told me repeatedly, that I am the senior, and he the junior partner in this venture. It is our endeavor thus to produce a book which will be sound from the point-of-view of scholarship, yet at the same time interesting for the average intelligent reader.

I hope that your interest in the subject matter of the planned book will make all this seem less of an intrusion upon your time than it would otherwise appear to be. Please return to me the enclosures at your convenience.

> *Yours sincerely,*
> *Raphael Patai*
> *Director of Research*

I have no record of any response from Albright.
On August 3 I wrote to Graves.

Dear Robert:

I am enclosing:

1) The last five chapters of volume I, taking the story to the death of Joseph and the very last verse in the book of Genesis.

2) Notes to eighteen chapters which I sent to you earlier. These notes either have to be simply added to the end of the chapters, or, when so marked, substituted for certain pages.

I still have notes to some eight chapters, on which I am working now, and which I may be able to mail to you in a week from today, just before Ann and I leave for our vacation.

As I wrote to you before, we shall arrive in Mallorca in the morning of September 1 with the overnight boat from Barcelona. I have made arrangements for a car which I will take along on the boat. Upon arrival, we shall spend some time with Ann's relatives in Palma, then shall drive over to Deya and shall arrive at your home at about 3 P.M.

A few weeks ago Ken McCormick kindly sent me a copy of your new Collected Poems. *We have been reading them with great enjoyment. As I read them they brought into sharp focus the difference between you and me in relation to myth: I may have an understanding of myths and be able to write about them; but you live them and breathe them. In view of this, it is quite remarkable that we have so few differences about our* Hebrew Mythology.

Looking forward to seeing you soon,

Cordially yours,
Raphael

I just received your letter of July 29. Shall be greatly interested in seeing your documentation of the statements I disputed in your Hillel lecture. Also what you write about your poetic attack makes me very curious as to its results.

On August 7 I wrote again.

Dear Robert:

As indicated in my last letter, I am enclosing the last few notes to eight chapters in volume one. With this material you now have in your possession a complete copy of the entire first volume of our book. Whatever additional work I will do on this volume will have to be in response to your comments, criticisms, deletions, additions, or other changes.

I know that you are very busy and that you have many other commitments and projects, and that this makes the date of the completion of the MS of the first volume questionable. I, on my part, shall always, I hope, manage to devote the necessary time to working on the chapters as they come back to me in your formulation. If possible, I would like to work with you during our short stay in Mallorca on the Introduction. I shall certainly be willing to spend as much time as you will be able to spare on this.

Whatever free time I will have left I would like to utilize for the purpose of talking with a few older members of the Chueta community in Palma, in order to find out whether they have retained any knowledge of their Jewish ancestry, any Jewish religious or popular customs, or anything else from their Jewish past. This might not be an easy task because I assume that few, if any, of them will be willing to talk on this subject. But perhaps I shall succeed in explaining to them that my interest in this matter is purely scholarly and historical, and that I shall undertake not to publish in print anything that in any way can harm them or can be unpleasant to them. In connection with this plan, I shall need your help to put me in touch with a few of them, and to find for me an interpreter, since my Spanish is only good enough to read but not to talk. If need be, I shall be glad to pay the interpreter an appropriate hourly fee.

One more word on this subject:

According to all the published studies I could obtain, the Chuetas have insisted as far back as the 1930's that they remember nothing and know nothing of the Jewish past of their ancestors. This to me seems impossible in view of the fact that the last auto da fe took place as recently as 1691. Can it be that in 250 years every trace of their ancestral faith for which some of their forefathers died on the stake should have been obliterated?

I remember you told me that you have never been to Greece. I am sure that your forthcoming visit to that country will be a great experience. I myself stood under the columns of the Parthenon only two years ago for the first time. I don't know how to express the experience. You probably will be able to, in poetry.

Yours cordially,
Raphael

Ann and I left New York on August 13 in the evening, and after stopovers at Shannon and London, reached Paris next afternoon. I must have written Graves another letter of which I have no copy, in which I gave him the address of the hotel in Paris where I had made reservations, for when we arrived a letter from Graves was waiting for me. It was dated August 12, 1961.

Dear Raphael:

Thanks for Dinah.

Your Chueta project is hopeless. All that I could glean myself I incorporated in my piece "A Dead Branch on the Tree of Israel" (Food for Centaurs, Doubleday) and that wasn't much. They are the devoutest Catholics in Majorca and have erased all their Jewish memories. On Holy Thursday they even go in their own copadia *in procession, wearing the traditional dress of the Inquisitors! Even if you could talk Spanish you'd get nothing from them unless they sold you a watch or a string of Manacor pearls. Also Palma is 17 miles from here and there is no bus or train service. Forget it, I beg. Scores of historians have followed the same dead scent.*

See you soon.

Yours ever
Robert

Graves's essay, "A Dead Branch on the Tree of Israel," traces briefly the history of the Jews of Majorca from Roman times to the present day, when they, or rather their long-converted descendants the Chuetas (Graves spells it Xuetas), occupy a couple of narrow streets in the center of Palma and monopolize the gold- and silver-smith trades. He quotes the explanation of the name Xueta (from the French *chouette*, "screech owl"; from *xua*, Majorcan for "pork chop"), and adds that it seems to come from "Jeu-ete," "a playful diminutive of "Jew." After the 1492 Spanish expulsion of the Jews, those of them who lived in Majorca pretended to adopt Christianity, while continuing to adhere to Judaism in secret. The Inquisition persecuted them, and some were put to death by burning. The others eventually became Catholic in heart as well as in word, and in 1773 they sent a deputation to King Charles III, who, at their request, ordered that they should be given equality with the rest of the population. The royal order was, however, disregarded, as was the 1782 order of King Charles, which only created a backlash resulting in the strict exclusion of the Chuetas from all aspects of Majorcan life and society. In the last few pages of his article Graves tells of the contemporary situation of the Chuetas: they still constitute a closed, separate group in Palma, marrying only among themselves, though they observe Catholic ritual scrupulously, attending the Montesión Church which was once their synagogue. He reprints the letter the Chuetas sent to Ben Gurion in which they declare that they "yearn to return to our people," and ask for permission to enter Israel. However, when Graves consulted his Chueta acquaintances, they denied that they wanted to leave Majorca.

At the time I went to Majorca I had not read Graves's essay, and, as I shall tell in the sequence, despite his warning I did some research and wrote an article about the Chuetas.

Ann and I spent three days in Paris, mostly visiting museums. On August 17 we flew over to Stuttgart, where I picked up my Mercedes-Benz 220S at the Sindelfingen factory, and then drove to Tübingen for an overnight stay and a visit to its famous university. Next day we drove on and out of Germany into Switzerland. When we arrived at the German-Swiss border and handed our passports and the car papers to the German guard, he pointed at the brand-new car and said proudly, *"Deutsche Prezision!"* Reaching Swiss soil I breathed freely, suddenly realizing how depressed and apprehensive I had been during the twenty-four hours I had spent in Germany. My God! It was only some sixteen years since Auschwitz, Mauthausen, Bergen-Belsen!

We drove through Switzerland to Milan, where we stopped just long enough to have a look at the Dome and at Leonardo's *Last Supper,* which I had last seen many years before, and then drove on to Bergamo for an overnight stay. Next morning we went on through Salo on Lake Garda and Verona to Venice, where we stayed two days. This gave me an opportunity to see, in addition to the usual tourist attractions, also the *Gheto* (sic) *Vecchio,* the

251

Sephardi synagogue, and the Jewish Old People's Home. On August 23 we drove on to Florence, where we had dinner on the Piazza de la Signoria, facing and staring all the time at Michelangelo's *David*. (Next day I learned that it was a copy put in place of the original, which had begun to be damaged by the weather.) The two days in Florence remain in my memory primarily for the rapture I felt seeing for the first time some of the masterpieces of Michelangelo whom, ever since my childhood, I had considered the greatest of all sculptors and painters. I remember standing in the Accademia in front of his *David* (the original), the *Deposition from the Cross,* and the unfinished *Slaves,* not wanting to move on. But our plans were set, and on we moved.

Our drive led us through Pisa, Lerici, Sanremo, Montpellier, and Nice, where we bought a case of Chambertin as a present to the Graveses. Then on to Llansa on the Costa Brava, to Ampurias, and to Barcelona. On the evening of August 31 I delivered the car at the pier, and then we boarded the ship for Majorca, where we arrived next morning. At Palma the car was lifted out of the ship's hold and let down on the pier in a net of heavy rope, and after the longshoremen detached the net from the crane and let it fall to the ground around the car, they motioned me to get into it and drive away. In my impatience I started up too fast, so that some of the ropes got caught and wound around the axis. The stevedores shouted, "Ho! Ho!" I stopped instantly, but they had quite a job untangling the ropes from the underside of the car.

We were met at the pier by Ann's relatives, John and Tinka Covey, who were staying in Palma at the time, and spent the morning with them. After lunch we drove on to Deyá, a distance of some seventeen miles from Palma.

22.

Guests of Graves

DEYÁ TURNED OUT to be a very small village with only one main street running through it. I had no difficulty in finding the Graves house, called, as I well knew from his letters, "Canellun."

We were warmly welcomed by Graves and his wife Beryl, a charming woman still beautiful in middle age. After Graves took us to the house where we were to stay, we went back with him to Canellun where we all had dinner. Present were Graves's secretary Kenneth Gay, whom everybody addressed as "Karl," his wife, and the Graveses' youngest son Tomas, aged eight. What I remember from that dinner is, peculiarly, a trivial detail: Graves behaved with total informality. He drank amply (evidently our choice of Chambertin was a good one), and exhibited a hearty appetite. When he saw that one of those sitting around the table had left some food on his plate, he reached over with his fork, speared it, and ate it.

I don't remember much of the Graves house, except that it was a middle-sized, square, two-story building, faced with roughly hewn grey stone, and surrounded by a spacious, rather wild, garden. It made a rustic impression, as did the furnishing of the rooms inside.Graves's study on the ground floor was cluttered with books, which not only filled the shelves lining all the walls, but overflowed and covered almost the whole of his desk, and lay around even on the chairs and the floor. Seeing all these books I asked him what he did if, notwithstanding his extensive library, he needed other books for his work. For me, I said, the accessibility of the New York Public Library was one of the chief attractions of living in New York. His answer was, "I buy the books I need, and once I no longer need them, I sell them. Thus my library always reflects the book I am working on."

The house in which Graves puts us up was even more rustic than his own. Called "La Posada," it was located at a distance of perhaps five hundred yards from his own house, adjoined the back of the village church, and gave the impression of being half-ruined. It was built of even rougher stone than Graves's own house, and the walls of the ground floor rooms were unfinished, unplastered. On the second floor two good-sized rooms—a bedroom and a living room—were finished, and furnished with the same kind of rustic Spanish furniture as was Canellun. There was a bathroom equipped with a tub and a washbasin, but I no longer remember whether it had hot- and cold-running water. Neither do I remember whether the kitchen was on the first or the second floor. Beyond the habitable and quite pleasant part of the house there were several more unfinished rooms on the second floor. Toilet facilities were represented by an outhouse containing a primitive latrine with a board of unpolished wood with a round hole of requisite size in its middle serving as a seat, and under it a large, malodorous pit. What was unusual about this outhouse was that it was surrounded by only three walls, also made of rough wood, while the fourth side had boards only up to a height of some three or four feet. The upper part of this side opened onto an adjoining shed which was the home of a friendly donkey. Each time I entered the outhouse, the donkey would come to the partition and stick its head across to see, I suppose, who was its visitor. (Twenty-seven years later, in May 1988 to be exact, when Graves's daughter Lucia came to visit me in Forest Hills and we chatted about my sojourn in her father's house in 1961, she reminded me that the donkey's name was Isabella, and that the village postman took care of it.)

Graves explained that they had a maid, a Majorcan woman, who would come to La Posada every morning to clean house and cook for us, and who spoke French—a language in which Ann was fluent. He also informed us that he had a standing arrangement with the village grocery store about all purchases made by his guests: we should buy whatever we wanted, and the grocer would put it on his bill. This, he said, was nothing more than standard Graves hospitality. We, however, had our own standards of seemly behavior as guests, so each time we bought groceries or anything else, we instantly paid and did not allow any part of our bill to be charged to the Graves account. Likewise, we insisted on paying the maid.

The very day after our arrival (September 2), Graves and I got down to work. I went over to his house, he made me comfortable in the study—that is, he removed several books from a chair—and we discussed the introduction. It did not take him much of an effort to convince me that the draft I had sent him could not be used in anything resembling its actual form, but would have to be drastically abridged and rewritten. I was rather unhappy about this, because I knew I had done a creditable piece of work in sketching something that, to the best of my knowledge, had not been done before: what amounted to a brief history of scholarly myth interpretation. But I had to bow to

Graves's clinching argument that it was extremely important to have an introduction which would not only interest the general reader, but, more than that, would whet his appetite for further reading. Graves undertook to use my draft as the basis for a new, much shorter, introduction, and said he planned to write it while I was still in Majorca.

Apart from our conversation in May in my home in New York, which dealt largely with generalities, this was the first opportunity Graves and I had to come to grips with concrete details in a face-to-face exchange of views and approaches. I could not help feeling that I was to some extent at a disadvantage vis-à-vis Graves: I was somewhat intimidated by his reputation as one of the greatest living poets and novelists in the English language as well as by his personality, which I somehow associated with what I had read about Michelangelo's famed *terribilità*. Also, I was his guest, and as such I felt I had to beware of hurting his sensibilities. Nevertheless, when it came to scholarly issues connected with Hebrew myths, I was convinced that I had a much better grasp of them, that I was the expert where he was an amateur, and that my judgment was balanced and always based on objective evaluation of sources and data and reached by a sound deductive method. Graves readily recognized that I was in this respect in a stronger position—he often made statements to this effect in his letters, and on one occasion when we worked in his home in Deyá he even said that although I could have written the book without him, he could not have done it without me.

Still, there were fixed pivotal points in his mind about "iconotropy," matriarchy, the goddess, and other issues touching upon the man-woman relationship from which no amount of argument, let alone gentle persuasion, could make him cast off. This being the case, the phrasings on which we settled often represented a compromise with which I was, occasionally at least, not totally satisfied. The preceding chapters contain several examples. Later, when the reviews of the *Hebrew Myths* began to come in, I regretted that I was not more insistent on having my way, but in the circumstances I was unable to argue more energetically than I did.

All this is not to say that the contribution Graves made to the book was in any sense less important than mine. His share in it had many aspects. One consisted of references to, and comparisons with, Greek myths and, to a lesser extent, ancient Near Eastern parallels. Another was his uncanny ability to intuit, that is, to recognize hidden meanings in biblical stories, not by patiently sifting the evidence and carefully weighing information—that was *my* way—but by illuminating them with a lightning stroke. Once he did this, it fell to me to scrutinize the image that appeared to see whether there was substance to it or if it was merely a chimera. And it goes without saying that Graves's mastery of English style and great storytelling talent were invaluable assets to our book. Yes, Graves was right, I *could* have written a book on Hebrew myths without him, but it would have been a different book, more prosaic, more pedestrian, poorer in style and presentation—perhaps less con-jectural here and there, but certainly less interesting and less enjoyable.

In the afternoon of the very first day after our arrival, Graves took us down to the sea to swim. The village of Deyá was located on a hillside, perhaps two hundred or so feet above the sea. A steep footpath led from the paved road between Graves's two houses down to the sea. Graves led the way, and he proceeded at such speed that, trying not to fall behind, I was soon out of breath. He was sixty-five at the time, and I fifty, but he was clearly in a much better physical condition—which became even more apparent when, after a short swim, we climbed up the same precipitous path.

Near the waterline there was a small cove surrounded by rugged rocks, and at some distance in the water there were more rocks jutting out of the waves, forming something like a small partly-sheltered bay. Facing this stretch of wa-ter there was a sandy patch of beach, not more than a few square yards in size, and from it a small concrete jetty protruded into the water. Graves used this jetty as a diving board, hurling himself into the waves headfirst, like a veri-table champion swimmer. Ann and I, being less sportive, waded into the wa-ter from the shore.

Among the rocks there was a small cave with an opening framed in rough concrete. In it was kept a tiny rowboat, just big enough to accommodate two children. Graves's youngest son Tomas and a friend of his of the same age were with us and Graves, with the help of the two boys, carried the boat down to the water, where the boys got into it and paddled about happily, while we adults swam—Graves well, I much less so.

In the evening the Graveses took us to a party given by a friend of theirs (his name escapes me), a professor of Spanish from McGill University who, Graves told us, spent his summers in Majorca, where he had developed quite a business for himself. He would buy old houses, fix them up, and rent them to summer guests or on a year-round basis. I drove all four of us in my new car to a point on the road from where we had to climb up a footpath to reach the professor's house. We left the car on the roadside and set out: Graves lead-ing the way followed by Beryl, Ann, and me. It was pitch-dark, and none of us had thought of bringing a flashlight. It was slow going, uphill, and we stumbled more than once, but reached the house without any mishap. The party was crowded and noisy, the rooms smoke-filled—and this is all I re-member of it.

Next day (September 3), Graves and I again spent the morning together working, this time on problems that still remained in the early chapters of the book. Then we had a picnic lunch prepared by Beryl, and then again down to the sea for a swim. In the afternoon, Graves's secretary Karl and his wife Renée drove with us to Palma to see the bullfights which took place every Sunday afternoon. The *toreros* must have been second- or third-rate, for the bullfight was a sorry spectacle indeed. The *matadors*, despite their awe-inspiring appellation of "killers," had considerable trouble dispatching the poor animals. At one point one of the *matadors,* trying to deliver the coup de grâce, thrust his sword, not into the bull's heart, which would have put an end to it instantly, but into its lungs, so that the animal started to vomit a stream of blood. This was too much for Karl: he jumped up from his seat and started yelling, "Butcher! Butcher!"—which English word, however, nobody seemed to understand.

On the drive back to Deyá we were overtaken by a storm. It was the *sirocco,* Karl informed us. When we arrived at La Posada we found that the wind had shattered two windowpanes. So next morning we drove to Soller, a small town not far from Deyá, to buy new ones, making use of the opportunity to buy postcards also and to exchange some travelers' checks at the local bank for Spanish money.

In the afternoon Graves and I had another long work session, in the course of which I brought up the question of a book on the Hebrew prophets. Would he be interested in collaborating with me on such a book? His answer was no, because the subject was "too orthodox" for him.

The following day (September 5), Graves and I continued to work, going over the drafts of several chapters which I had sent him but which he had not yet returned to me in his rewritten version. However, we did not consistently focus on this work, but instead discussed, in a rather haphazard manner, various subjects touched upon, or to be touched upon, in the *Hebrew Myths.* I became apprehensive that the book was growing too big—as had happened with *The Nazarene Gospel Restored*—since by that time the manuscript, as I figured it, ran into some 1,000 pages, or about 300,000 words. I suggested that we should perhaps divide into two the material that we had planned to include in the first volume, so as to make it in this respect, too, comparable to Graves's *Greek Myths.* Graves said we should consider the idea later, when we had a more concrete idea of the actual length of the book. As it happened, Graves continued to "tighten" the manuscript (his word), and in the end the *Hebrew Myths* turned out to be one medium-sized volume of about 150,000 words, or some 300 printed pages.

The same afternoon we again went down to the sea. Graves encouraged me to practice swimming, which, he said, was equally good for the body and the soul.

Although Graves was very negative about the possibilities of research about the Chuetas (as he had indicated in his letter of August 12, 1961), I did not give up so easily. On September 6 I drove with Karl and Renée Gay to Palma to find out what I could about that "dead branch on the tree of Israel," as Graves phrased it. The Chuetas interested me in particular because only a few years earlier I had studied, and written about, another Marrano group, the *Jedīd al-Islām* (New Muslims) of Meshhed, Iran, with whose members in Jerusalem I had conducted lengthy interviews. Karl took me to Señor Fulgencio

Mir, a non-Chueta Majorcan, and I questioned him intensively (Karl acting as interpreter) about what he, as an outsider, knew about the Chuetas. Then we went to the Spanish governmental archives and library in the city, where I glanced through the collection of books and studies on the Chuetas. I also attempted to speak to the Chuetas themselves. Despite the relative scarcity of data I managed to dig up about the Chuetas, I felt I had enough material to write a paper on them, which I did. It was published in the spring of 1962 issue of *Midstream* and in the June 1963 issue of *Le Judaisme Sephardi* of London. In 1983 I included it, together with my studies of the Marranos of Meshhed and the Jewish Indians of Mexico, in my collection of essays, *On Jewish Folklore*.

In my article I spoke only very briefly on the history of the Jews of Majorca, but pointed out that in 1435 they were forced to choose between death and Christianity, and that, with the exception of a few who managed to escape from the island, all the rest, some two hundred families, converted. Thereafter, and until modern times, no Jew was allowed to live in Majorca. For about two-and-a-half centuries the *Conversos* (as they were called) preserved their Judaism in secret, that is, were Marranos, crypto-Jews, and during this period "only" about a dozen of them were burned or otherwise put to death by the Inquisition for the capital sin of Judaizing. Toward the end of the seventeenth century the inquisitorial zeal increased, and some forty *Conversos* were condemned to die. Thereafter, it would seem, the knowledge of Judaism among the *Conversos* rapidly diminished, and during the last century of the existence of the Inquisition (which was abolished in 1834), no trial of *Conversos* took place.

After this introductory part of my paper, I dwelt on the stereotypes that characterized the attitude of the Old Christian Majorcans vis-à-vis the Chuetas, as the descendants of the *Conversos* came to be called. These negative stereotypes found expression, e.g., in the teasing behavior of Old Christian children toward the Chuetas, while the adult Old Christians firmly believed in the existence of a number of unpleasant physical and mental traits that, according to them, characterized the Chuetas.

As I had expected, direct interviews with the Chuetas themselves revealed little. Accompanied by Karl, I looked up several of them in the *Calle de Plateria* ("Street of Silversmiths") where they had their stores. As soon as they understood what I sought—information about the Chuetas—they froze, and said either that they knew nothing about them, or that there were no differences between the Chuetas and the Old Christians.

I found only one single Chueta, an intelligent man, well-read in both Castilian and Catalan, and a deeply religious Catholic, who was willing to admit that he was a Chueta. He had, in fact, what amounted to a certain racial pride in his Jewish descent. His analysis of the Chueta personality, although amateurish, was most interesting. According to him, the pressures and dangers amid which the Chuetas had lived for centuries had shaped their person-alities: they tended toward insecurity, timidity, and a measure of avarice or frugality. Also, they were either extremely talkative or extremely taciturn. They loathed waste, tended to be hoarders, and were conservative by tem-perament. There were no drunkards among them, but they liked to eat well. They were much more musical than the Old Christians. The large number of children they had was interpreted by some—this opinion my informant did not share—as a sign of their greater sensuality compared to the old Chris-tians. They were a hard-working lot, but liked to be their own bosses, and hence went but rarely into government employment, the army, or civil ser-vice. Many of them were in the professions. Apart from this, the Chuetas dif-fered in no way from the Old Christians.

As for the name "Chueta," I was, and still am, inclined to accept the ex-planation that it is derived from the Majorcan word *Xua,* meaning "pork-chop," or rather "suet," the fatty tissue of the pig's body. That is, it was the Majorcan equivalent of the mainland Spanish word *Marrano,* which means "pig." After giving a brief list of the concrete, objectively observable dif-ferences between the Chuetas and the Old Christians, I referred in my article to some historical attempts made by the Chuetas to escape from the island, and concluded that because of increased intermarriage their days as a separate ethneme were numbered.

The same evening Graves came over to La Posada for a while, and there-after Ann and I went over to the Gays, where Señor Mir and his wife Conchita were also present, and we spent most of the evening talking about the Chuetas.

On September 7 we followed what had become more or less a routine: in the morning I worked with Graves, and in the afternoon we went swimming. These repeated working sessions and joint periods of relaxation gave me a chance to observe Graves closely. At home and when going out into the street of Deyá he dressed most informally. Most of the time he wore khaki shorts, a white short-sleeved tricot shirt with open neck, and short, ankle-length socks. When the sun shone, he put on a loosely woven straw hat with a dome-like top and a broad, disk-shaped brim. Despite the strong summer sunlight, I never saw him wearing sunglasses. On his left arm he wore a wristwatch with a metal strap. His hair, almost totally white by that time, was never groomed or combed down, but stood up on top of his head in unruly tufts. Later, in 1963, in New York, I saw him put on black-rimmed glasses for read-ing. As far as I can remember, in Deyá he used no glasses. He smoked cig-arettes, but I don't know whether he was a heavy smoker. Physically he was in good shape, with a lean, muscular body and not a trace of embonpoint. His rugged visage was a perfect human counterpart in miniature of the rocky Ma-jorcan coastline.

I spent the following day in Palma, and in the evening we reciprocated the Graveses' hospitality by having them over for dinner at La Posada.

259

Graves at La posada, his guest house in Deyá. (Photo Raphael Patai.)

Saturday, September 9, Graves and I again put in several hours of work in his study, and then toward evening he again came over to La Posada for a lengthy chat, which we continued at a local café-restaurant to which Graves, Beryl, Ann, and I repaired for dinner. Then again we stopped by at the Graveses for short while.

Sunday, September 10 was the day of our departure from Deyá. In the morning Graves and I worked together for the last time. We summed up what we had accomplished up to that point, and what still remained to be done. Then we said good-bye to Robert and Beryl.

Were the ten days spent with Graves useful for finishing the *Hebrew Myths?* They undoubtedly were, although they were not quite as productive as I had hoped they would be. There were too many distractions. The Graves house was open at all times to sundry visitors who would drop in unannounced and make us waste precious minutes of our limited time. Added to this was the fact that Graves tended to wander off in conversation in all directions—a tendency well familiar to me from our taped discussion of May 20. Also, it so happened that during those days Graves was rather distraught over problems having to do with a young woman who, as Karl caustically remarked to me, was Graves's latest White Goddess. When I said good-bye to Graves, he gave me a letter addressed to her with the urgent request that I mail it as soon as I got ashore at Barcelona.

Quite apart from the work we accomplished, to get to know Graves at close quarters in lengthy meetings over ten days was a rare experience. He was open, frank, and uninhibited. He spoke of his beliefs in ghosts, of experiences not amenable to natural explanations, of his conviction that in World War I he had actually died and then miraculously came back (or was brought back) to life. He told me of his unshaken belief in an ancient matriarchal period which, when overthrown by rough and rude men, was superseded by an age of troubles not yet ended. He revealed fascinating details about what it was for him to write poetry, when he felt that some external power forced his neck into an iron yoke.

What I learned in those days with Graves was that beyond the world of mental exertion, rational judgment, events that could be observed and categorized, results that could be reached by deductive processes, there was another world that revealed itself only to a chosen few, a world in which logic was not king, and certainties were reached by an intuitive grasp akin to revelation. While I sat there on the periphery of the magic aura that emanated from the personality of Graves, when I saw that faraway look come into his eyes which made me sure that he was seeing something in the distance behind me, I felt that my mind opened up to a better understanding of what it must have been to be a *Vates,* a foreteller and seer—nay, a prophet—who saw, heard, and spoke in the name of a higher power.

261

It was, I believe, this insight into the world of Graves the poet-*vates* that made me less insistent on the factual underpinning, the documentation by reference to sources of each and every statement that he introduced into my drafts while reworking and recasting them. Most interesting in this connection was that Graves himself in his letters, and especially in those he wrote me after my visit with him in Deyá, repeatedly emphasized that we must be careful to present in our book only facts and legitimate conclusions based on facts, and was totally unaware that quite often what he considered statements of facts were actually surmises his intuitive imagination clad in the garb of fact.

After leaving Majorca we drove through Barcelona, in whose crowded streets I was involved in an accident. A dog jumped in front of my car and I slammed my foot down on the brake, managing to stop in time without hitting the animal. But a bicyclist who followed too closely behind my car was not as fast, and ran into my rear bumper. The car was not damaged, but the front wheel of the bicycle was twisted, and its rider hurt in a sensitive part of his body. A policeman at the scene ordered me to take the cyclist to a nearby clinic, and he himself got into my car, either to show me the way, or to make sure that I did not simply drive away. After depositing the cyclist at the clinic, the policeman got back into the car and directed me to the nearby precinct house, where he made his report, and I was asked to produce my passport. I did not understand much of the exchange between the policeman and the sergeant at the desk, but I do remember one phrase the policeman uttered: *"El Señor no es culpable,"* which reassured me and secured my instant and honorable discharge.

Some three hours later we reached the French border, and drove on to Quillan, Carcassone, Cordes, and Gramart. Next day we visited the famous Lascaux caves with their wonderful prehistoric paintings. (The caves were soon thereafter closed to the public because in the few years since they had been opened the paintings had deteriorated more than they had in the twenty thousand years up to that point.) We made brief stops at Blois, Chambord, Orleans, Chartres, and Versailles, and after reaching Paris I delivered the car for shipping to New York. On September 16 in the morning we went out to Le Bourget Airport from where our plane was supposed to leave at 11 A.M. Instead, it left at 1:30 the next morning, stopped over in London for four hours, and finally arrived in New York at 9 P.M. on September 17.

23.

The Hillel Affair

A LONG NIGHT'S SLEEP was enough to restore me to full working order, and next morning I was at my desk at the Herzl Press, where I found the galleys of my book *Golden River to Golden Road* waiting for me. This meant that whatever time I could spare from my permanent commitments had to be devoted to proofreading. Once done with that I wrote to Graves and Beryl.

> *September 22, 1961*
>
> *Dear Beryl and Robert:*
>
> *Just a brief note to let you know that we are safely back home, and to thank you both most heartily for your very kind hospitality. It was indeed a wonderful experience for us to be with you and to enjoy together with you all the things Deyá has to offer.*
>
> *I hope you, Robert, will soon begin to send me redone chapters of the book and that we shall, before long, have the first part completed.*
>
> > *Yours,*
> > *Raphael*

By the time this letter reached Deyá Graves must have left for London, where he was scheduled to give his lecture to the Hillel Foundation. This took place on October 23, 1961. (The full original text is reproduced in Chapter 20, above.) It was the annual Hillel Foundation lecture, held at Friends House, Euston Road, N.W. 1, London. Prof. David Daiches of the University of Sussex was in the chair, and it was attended by an unusually large audience. According to a letter sent me the next day by my friend, the Zionist historian

Joseph Fraenkel, there was an audience of some thirteen hundred Jewish students. Also on October 24 the London *Times* reported of the lecture under the title "How Democracy Toppled the Olympians—Prof. Graves Traces Reward of Virtue." In its four hundred-word article, the *Times* gave a brief account of the contents of Graves's lecture, emphasizing such points from it as "Hebrew myths were edited with a monotheistic intent, and the prophets knew that the best hope for national independence lay in the benignant patriarchal monotheism they preached, though vestiges of an originally matriarchal culture occurred in the Bible," and "It was not until the Hebrew myths, borrowed by the Christians, gave subject peoples an equal right to salvation that the Olympians were dethroned and the aristocratic principle defeated by the democratic one."

Were one to judge from this report, Graves's lecture should have given great satisfaction to its Jewish audience: he extolled the moral superiority of the biblical myths and presented them as the source of Western democracy. Ah, but the orthodox among the Jews were not satisfied with this; on the contrary, they found the lecture execrable.

The record of what transpired after the lecture is contained in several issues of the *Jewish Chronicle,* the central organ of British Jewry. In its October 27 issue, the *Chronicle* printed a prominent article titled, "The Bible Is Full of Myths—Robert Graves." An unsigned article—its author is identified only as a reporter of the *Jewish Chronicle*—it opens by stating that Robert Graves, professor of poetry at Oxford University, who is working together with Dr. Raphael Patai of the Theodor Herzl Foundation of New York on a book on Hebrew myths, gave the annual Hillel Foundation lecture. Then it goes on to give a brief summary of the talk, and ends by quoting part of the concluding sentence: "the moral quality of Hebrew myths, patriarchal and monotheistic, has established the ethical principles of Western civilization."

In a letter of December 18 to me, Graves stated that the lecture "was a resounding popular success," which I took to mean not only that he was warmly applauded, but also that no critical comments were made by the audience. A week after the lecture, however, the storm broke loose. In letters to the editor of the *Jewish Chronicle*, conservative rabbis and other correspondents gave vent to their ire at what Graves had said, and also to their indignation over the Hillel Foundation having invited him at all, and over the *Jewish Chronicle* having given his lecture front-page coverage. In the November 3 issue, one letter writer characterizes Graves's lecture as "a monumental example of superficial pseudoscholarship" which was "irresponsible" and nothing but "higher hooey." Another writes, "I must vigorously protest against the front-page publicity and the unusually extensive coverage you have chosen to give to the lecture of Professor Robert Graves," adding, "That 'the Organ of British Jewry' should give pride of place and extraordinary detail to nauseating misinterpretation of the holiest treasure of the Jewish people is really surprising."

A week later the *Jewish Chronicle* published five more letters, one of which contained this sentence: "Prof. Graves was only echoing the monstrosities which the Egyptian Apio uttered in Egypt nearly two thousand years ago, and which Josephus in his masterly "Contra Apionem" conclusively refuted." Another week later (the issue of November 17) several more letters were published, this time defending Graves, and the November 24 issue printed one pro-Graves and one contra-Graves letter. Finally, in the December 1 issue, Graves wrote a brief reply to his attackers, in which he presented such a measured and reasonable position that it deserves to be quoted in full.

> Sir:
>
> If in my recent address at the Hillel Foundation I made any unhistorical statements I shall be glad to have it corrected.
>
> When I showed that the historical links between Hebrew and other Mediterranean mythologies are close ones, and that the Hebrews treated their myths—the Greek word does not mean "falsities" but "sacred traditions or utterances"—as moral stories of universal application rather than as charters for particular aristocratic institutions, the audience made no protest at any point and were even good enough to cheer. I also said that this un-Greek treatment of ancient legend created the ethical system which now rules the Western world.
>
> That the lecture was given at the Hillel Foundation should create no dismay. I hope that I will not cause further offence to my rabbinic critics by pointing out that Hillel was no petulant Shammai, and that, in expounding the Torah to a Gentile, he put love of one's neighbour before all theological disputation. A religion that obstinately disputes historical fact can have no future in the world today: true Jewish faith transcends historical fact.
>
> Robert Graves

A few weeks later Graves briefly recounted the controversy in a letter to me.

Dec 18 1961

Dear Raphael:

Just back from England where I had a wonderful time. Had Hebrew Myths *on my desk but too many engagements and interruptions to do a handstroke on it. Now I am back, & after Christmas my desk is clear at last. To work!*

My Hillel lecture about the difference between Greek & Hebrew myths was resounding popular success: but I was fulminated at from a number of synagogue pulpits, & a bitter correspondence appeared in the Jewish Chronicle. *I finally replied saying that Hillel being no Shammai, would not have been in the least worried by my lecture, since he put love of one's neighbour (including the Goyim) above history or theology, & that Jewish religious teachings transcended history, & that the Jewish treatment of myths had stabilized the ethics of the whole Western world.*

It was a trial balloon & I think very encouraging. All we must be careful of is our facts.

Love to you both
Robert

Please return this if you approve. Roturman *will pay you 50% of the net royalties.*

(The postscript refers to the contract for the publication of the *Hebrew Myths.*)

While (as shown above in chapter 20) I was not in agreement with everything Graves said in his Hillel lecture, I was impressed, again, by his capacity to appreciate the moral stature of the talmudic sages, who stamped Hebrew mythology with a character fundamentally different from that of Greek mythology. In relation to this basic accolade unstintingly given by Graves, his lapses in interpretation of detail must appear insignificant. And, of course, my own position coincided with his: I was, and still am, convinced that by studying biblical and rabbinic stories *qua* myths we can uncover the moral power informing them and the secret of their influence down the ages. For the religious fundamentalist minority among the Jews and Christians, the treatment of the Bible as a storehouse of myths remains offensive, reprehensible, and even heretical. But then, tied as they are to the tenet—unassailable for them—that the Bible is literally the word of God, they neither need nor can tolerate attempts at revealing the deeper meaning of biblical stories. As Habakkuk (2:4) put it, "The righteous lives by his faith." But for the rest of us, who constitute the overwhelming majority in the Western world, the presentation of biblical stories as myths reendows them with a value they had long lost for us, because it shows that despite the widespread agnosticism that characterizes our age, the Bible remains the eternal guidebook of humanity, even if in a sense different from that which the ancient rabbis believed. Such were my thoughts when I embarked upon writing the *Hebrew Myths* with Graves, and today, some thirty years later, they still represent my view of the Bible and my judgment of our book.

Thus I felt indignant at the attacks launched by the Jewish *religiosi* against Graves, and I responded to his December 18 letter with complete sympathy.

January 4, 1962

Dear Robert,

I was very glad to get your letter of December 18th, and to hear that you were satisfied with the reception of your Hillel lecture.As to the storm your lecture aroused on the pages of the Jewish Chronicle—*I was well aware of it, and followed it with great interest week after week. I cannot hide that my reaction to the short-sightedness and narrow-mindedness displayed by several of my conservative co-religionists filled me with dismay. I can well imagine what will be the reaction and the outcry of the same elements (echoed, of course, among their counterparts in the various Christian denominations) once our book appears.*

As to the agreement between Roturman and Cassell—whatever satisfies you will be fine for me as well. To make sure that I am in the clear with Doubleday, I called Ken McCormick's office, and was told that the contract should be ready for signature within 2–3 weeks. (High time, after a delay of 18 months!) Since I have not yet seen our Doubleday contract, I think I should wait with the Cassell contract until after I sign the Doubleday contract, so as to be sure that the two are mutually compatible. Also, since Roturman does not represent me, don't you think that it would be more advisable that either Cassell make a direct contract with me, or that Roturman and I agree that Roturman represent me in connection with this book? Finally, the agreement, as it now stands, does not provide any advance against the royalties, and in my present finances an advance of a $1,000 within the next few weeks would be very welcome. Is it all right with you if I hold the copy of the agreement you sent me until I sign the Doubleday contract?

To come now to the really main issue, I very greatly hope that now you will be able to get down to working on our Hebrew Myths, *and that I shall soon begin to get from you chapter after chapter. Before long we should have the Ms. of the first volume in final shape.*

Cordial regards and happy New Year wishes from both of us to all of you.

Raphael

Graves responded by return mail.

Jan 9 1962

Dear Raphael:

How complicated all this contract business is! It would certain[ly] seem simpler if Roturman acted for us both and paid us our respective shares; but it's as you please. The Roturman boss is Thomas Roe Esq. C.B.E.; Roturman S.A. 2 Avenue de la Rasude, Lausanne and Switzerland. An English lawyer with a good record. If you need an advance from Doubleday, demand it.

—I have now got out of the way, and into print or final typescript, all the cows on the line, books contracted for that were on my conscience—three in all, Terence's Comedies, *90,000 words;* Six Oxford Addresses, *50,000 words;* The Siege & Fall of Troy, *30,000 words (Juvenile). Also two volumes of poetry; one new, the other (early rejects) poems revised. The last two add*

267

up to, I suppose 5000 words, but have taken about three months in all of con-
tinuous work.—Poetry is forced on one by fate! What I mean is: my desk is
now clear, and tomorrow our servants come back from olive-picking, and all
our Christmas guests are out of the house. I have rejected scores of offers of
other work from publishers & editors: have a Protestant conscience. So—
*   Now to work.*

> *Best wishes from us both*
> *Robert*

*   The sentiment in favour of that lecture was enormously stronger & more*
general than the complaints. So no dismay; but let us keep strictly to facts and
accepted anthropological theory.
*   Enclosed may interest you—is he on the right track? And what is his ad-*
dress so that I may thank him? Please return. The sense of words blossoming
out from the same ancient root seems of as great importance in Hebrew as in
Arabic.

The "enclosed' referred to in Graves's postscript was a letter he had received from a certain Mr. Israel Shahab. Since I returned it to Graves as he
asked me to do, and made no copy of it for myself, I no longer know what it
was about, except for the general comment I made at the end of my January
23, 1962 letter. (See the following chapter.)
    I was heartened by Graves's assurances that he had at last "got out of the
way" his other commitments and projects, and could work with me on the
Hebrew Myths in earnest—as indeed proved to be the case.

24.

More Chapters
in the Works

HE YEAR 1962 was the period of our most concentrated work on the *He-brew Myths* and, consequently, that of the most intensive correspondence between us. We exchanged that year alone some fifty letters, many of them quite long, and most of them containing detailed discussions of our book. In addition, we mailed drafts of chapters back and forth several times. On January 17, 1962, Graves sent me a batch of chapters he had rewritten, with the following covering letter.

Dear Raphael:

Here's ten days' work in separate package. I have used my discretion in omitting what seems to me boring, and this has of course spoilt the footnote sequence. I do hope you approve. I also feel that the sources of the information supplied by the notes should either be omitted or contained in the text: as in Greek Myths.

My next piece on which I am working is the Fall of Man, *then follows* The Act of Love *(then* The Fratricide *already done). But I'm not yet sure about the order of the earlier pieces; it's difficult.*

Maybe it will be better for you to keep the source lists of each chapter on ice until the final draft, to prevent renumbering.

Above all: this is a book for the general reader & the student, not for the Rabbinic experts.

It may not take so long as I feared, now my table is cleared.

Love to you both
Robert

My response contained the usual comments on minor details.

January 23, 1962

Dear Robert:

I received your letter of January 17th and the four chapters yesterday. I worked late into the night comparing your rewritten version with my original draft, checking your additions, omissions, etc. I can say that I am very happy with the way you handled these chapters which, I feel, can stand by and large exactly as they are. I wish that all the future chapters should also go as smoothly as these.

I completely agree with you that the sources of the information supplied by the notes should be kept to a minimum, and be contained in the text, as in your Greek Myths. *As to the order of the first ten or so chapters—let us decide on it once they are in proper shape.*

I have only a very few comments to make on your text. In fact, none on "Mythical Cosmology." In "The Reem and the Ziz," do you want me to check and supply the page references for Doughty's Arabia Deserta *on p. 4, 1st para., and that for the* roc *or* rukh *of the* Arabian Nights *(bottom of same page)? Or do you feel that these, and similar references should be left in their present general form, i.e. without giving volume and page numbers?*

In the chapter "The Fall of Helel" (p. 3 line 12) there seems to be a slight misunderstanding: the line should read "Observe, now Adam will foresee all his descendants and give each his own name." P. 5—from where did you take the information that (line 9) the Hittites called Mount Zafon Mount Hazzi, and regarded it as the broken body of Ullikummi? On p. 6, section 4, *I suggest the following change: "The name watchers . . . seems to be the Greek rendering of two Aramaic words* Irim *and* Kadishin."

Chapter "Paradise" page 1, line 9—I do not recall that Adam is stated in the Bible as having been allowed by God to attend the Divine Assembly. P. 6, section 2—What is the basis of the identification of two of the four rivers of Paradise with Chospes and the Pallakopas Canal? And of the identification of Havilah with Northern Syria?

To be on the safe side, on p. 6, bottom, and the top of p. 7—*I would prefer something like " . . . is of a younger age among the Jews than among the Greeks whose Homer in Odyssey . . ."*

And this is the last of my remarks.

And now as to Israel Shahab's letter (which I am returning herewith). Such ideas of postulating a common origin for Hebrew words which have three or only two common root letters crop up every few years. They suffer from a common shortcoming: ignorance of other Semitic languages derived, with Hebrew, from a common "Ursemitisch." In Hebrew several originally different phonemes have converged and become one. No distinction, for instance, is made between Ayin *and* Ghayin. *As a result of this process words which in the ancient Semitic mother tongue were completely different, may appear in Hebrew as similar or identical. Incidentally, Mr. Israel Shahab is not listed in any of the New York phone books.*

Yours cordially,
Raphael

A comparison of my comments on Graves's version of the chapter "The Fall of Helel" (chapter 8 in the book, retitled "The Fall of Lucifer") shows that my objections were accepted by Graves. As for Mount Saphon or Zaphon (*Tzafon*) being called Mount Hazzi by the Hittites, Graves was right: its name in Hittite and Akkadian documents is *Khaz(z)i,* from which is derived the Greek *Kasios oros* and the Latin *Mons Casius.* But his statement that Mount Saphon was regarded "the broken body of Ullikummi" was deleted and replaced by a brief summary of the Hittite "Song of Ullikummi," which tells of the battle between the Storm-God and the stone-giant Ullikummi, which ended with the defeat of the "diorite man" (*Hebrew Myths* 8.3).

My suggestion as to the phrasing of our comment on the "Watchers" was incorporated into *Hebrew Myths* (13.4) as I formulated it. The identification of two of the four biblical rivers of Paradise with Choaspes and the Pallakopas Canal was modified so as to state (11.2) that the terrestrial Paradise was, in one version, thought to have been located "at the head of the Persian Gulf—a delta watered by four main streams: Tigris, Euphrates, Choaspes, and the Pallakopas Canal." The identification of Havilah with Syria was deleted, and replaced by a parenthetical "Havilah (Northern Syria?)" The fact is that to this day the identity of the "Land of Havilah" and the river Pishon which waters it, according to Genesis 2:11, is unknown: all that is said about them is mere guesswork. (Incidentally, in that paragraph in *Hebrew Myths* 11.2 the river Gihon is misspelled as Gihor.)

In his reply Graves responded to my strictures.

Feb 1 1962

Dear Raphael:

I've been back to the start and got all the difficult early chapters in a semi-final state.

In answer to your letter of Jan 23

1) I accept all your amendments
2) The Hittites called Mount Zafon 'Mount Hazzi' according to Gaster Oldest Stories in the World *p. 118. Ullikummi's body comes from the same book. (God, how badly he writes!) Hazzi = Casius.*
3) If you accept the Persian Gulf Delta ltheory of a Babylon Eden, those are or were the four streams of the Delta.

Meyer identifies 'Havilah' with N. Syria of which the Orontes is the only large river.

Sending you a large batch very soon. The book gets more and more fascinating.

Am now coming to the Flood. *That is about ⅓ of the first book, and by far the worst part to write. It is going to be an indispensable reference book, & the only one.*

—There are five of my new poems in the Jan 27th New Yorker, *there were several more in a recent* Sat[urday] Eve[ning] Post, *and another batch appears soon in* Encounter. *They explain, I hope, my neglect of the* Hebrew Myths. *(The spell is, I think, now over.) Poems always get priority.*

> *Love to you both*
> *Robert*

I'm afraid that you will have some trouble reallocating references; and eventually I'll put the cross references in—a tedious but important job.

My response went out quickly.

February 6, 1962

Dear Robert:

I have just received your letter of February 1st, with the enclosed chapters. I have had no time as yet to go over the chapters, which I will do within the next few days, and then I will write you about it.

I am very happy to see that you have really buckled down to the job. If we can continue at this rate, we shall certainly have the first volume ready quite shortly.

You remarked in your P.S. that you were afraid that I would have some trouble reallocating references. This matter could be greatly simplified if, in rearranging the material, you would keep the original reference numbers. These would, of course, not be in the proper order (1, 2, 3, etc.) but, when I go over the chapter, I would, in this manner, have no difficulty in appending the corresponding footnote to each reference number, and then renumbering them consecutively.

Another suggestion which would simplify procedure is the following: Since you seem to be in agreement with me that in the second part of each chapter (the one containing the comparative and explanatory notes), whenever we mention a fact we should document it by adding immediately thereafter the source in parenthesis, it would greatly simplify matters if you would do this whenever you redraft a chapter and add such elucidating comments. To take a random example from the last batch of material you sent: in the chapter The

Fall of Man, *on page 6, point 5 is an example to show how these references should be made; on the other hand, point 4 immediately preceding it, should conclude with a parenthetical source reference containing author, title of book, place and date of publication, volume and page number. If you would supply this in each case, it would save me the trouble of asking you from where you took the statement, and would save you the trouble of having to look it up later. It would also make it easy for me to check the source in the library whenever I feel that I should do that. In the final version we may abridge these references to a bare minimum, and give a key to abbreviations, following the preface, or in some other place.*

I am making this suggestion not only in order to facilitate our work, but also because I agree with you wholeheartedly that the Hebrew Myths *"is going to be an indispensable reference book and the only one." In order to make it such a book, we must, I believe, supply source references to each and every factual statement we make.*

I have been so busy during the last few weeks that I had no chance to see the New Yorker, *and so I missed your poems, but I will look up the January 27th issue now. What kept me busy more than usual was that some months ago the Collier Books (a part of the Crowell-Collier publishing company) asked me to edit two volumes for them: one on* Women in the Modern Western World, *and the other on* Women in Modern Afro-Asia. *These volumes will contain twenty chapters, each on one of the major areas of the world, and it is quite a task, involving intensive correspondence with friends and colleagues scattered all over the world, to secure twenty competent contributors. This job is finished now, and I have some respite until June 1st, when the MSS will begin to come in. Then I shall have to edit them and to write the two introductions.*

In the meantime, I am returning to the Hebrew Myths, *and shall try to carry them on from the Exodus onward, as far as I can. I am keeping in mind that our tentative understanding was that we would go as far as the destruction of the first Temple.*

> *Yours cordially,*
> *Raphael*

This time Graves allowed over two weeks to elapse before he replied.

Feb 25 1962
Dear Raphael (sending 6 chapters under separate cover):

This goes well. The difficulty is having at times, for economy of statement, to interrupt one version of a narrative with elements borrowed from another: confuses the references.

It's curious how different our interests are, and how complementary.

(I have a set of books in the Posada called Women in all Ages *or some-thing—full of miscellaneous information. Would it be worth the trouble & ex-pense to send them to you? I'd gladly do it, if so.)*

Am now on the Ishmael story, where you're very good in the notes. I always examine every story and ask myself "What questions will readers of this or that ask?" and then try to answer. That's my function.

—I think "Hebrew Myths: Book of Genesis" is the right title. Makes a cer-tain unity & many readers (the non-Jewish ones) are not interested in the more parochial myths of what happened to Israel during & after the Exodus.

> *Love to you both*
> *Robert*

Even before I received this letter I had sent off another one to Graves.

> *February 27, 1962*

Dear Robert,

I worked over nine of the chapters you sent me, and I hope they are now in an almost final shape. I am enclosing retyped copies of each chapter for your final inspection and approval.

As you will see, I made very few and minor changes. Only in one point, did I introduce what can be regarded as a major change: I divided the chapter "The Fall of Helel" into two. The title of one remains "The Fall of Helel," and is based mainly on Isaiah *xiv. 12–15; the other, which I named "The Fall of the Jewelled Cherub," is based on* Ezekiel *xxviii. 2, 6, 16–19. To this chap-ter I added a general comment (pp. 3–4) which, I hope, you will approve. I made this decision because, upon reconsideration, I became convinced that these two myths were originally separate, and remain separate as treated by the two prophets.*

Apart from this, my changes are so minor that I don't think I have to com-ment on them. In several places I added the word "source" on the margin, which means that I would like you to indicate the source from where you took the preceding statement. Also, wherever I added a sentence or a paragraph, I marked it with a vertical line on the left-hand margin.

One more small point: I would prefer that we spell all names (mostly names of women) ending in Hebrew with a he, *without an "h" in English translit-eration. Let us write Ada and not Adah, Zilla and not Zillah, etc. I feel that this will make the names simpler and less strange to the English reader.*

I hope that this finds you and yours well, and that I shall soon get more material from you.

> *Yours cordially,*
> *Raphael*

Graves's response was:

March 8th 1962

Dear Raphael:

I'll be sending you another six chapters soon—I think its' six—which takes us to <u>Sodom</u>, a chapter I'm interested in. I have had to quarry harder in these chapters than I expected. Our readers will ask constant questions and we have to supply the answers. E.g. "why 318 retainers of Abram?" Answer: "318 was the numerical equivalent of Eliezer's name & he was said to be as strong as them all put together." But I am enjoying myself, and our interests complement each other.

—I have just heard from Watt, enclosing your correspondence with Bryan Gentry at Cassell's. He writes: "Dr. Patai seems chary of paying our commission on his share, though ready to take advantage of the agreement we have made for you . . . I don't think Cassell are likely to advance him some £300 on the signature of the agreement; and I don't see why he should have an advance if you don't. All the royalties would go against his advance, and you would receive nothing until it had been earned." Please treat this as confidential and tell me at once what you think; I don't want to rob either you or myself, as Abram said to the King of Sodom (with a mention of threads, . . . & shoe-latchets.) And I don't want to give Watt the notion of any disagreement between us: which obviously cannot be. Watt is under the impression that our arrangement was that I would sell the book & give you half the proceeds—since I understood this particular market better than you did, from my Greek Myths *experience. This is how it started I believe; but then your accountant gave you advice which separated our names in the Roturman contract. The sooner we get this cleared up the better, don't you agree? It is holding things up.*

> *Love to you both from us, & best wishes from Karl*
> *Robert*

Again, Graves's letter and mine crossed in the mail.

March 9, 1962

Dear Robert:

Thank you very much for the 6 chapters (#20–25). I looked through them, and find the barest minimum to comment. In other words, I feel that we have reached a stage where we not only complement each other, but do it in a mutually agreeable and congenial manner. I shall have these 6 chapters retyped within the next few days, and then return to you a copy for your final approval.

275

I am enclosing today another few earlier chapters which I carefully reread and then had retyped. Everything seems to be proceeding now in the best order, and the only remaining problem is that of source references in connection with statements of facts added by you to the second part of the chapters. It would greatly facilitate the putting of the chapters in final shape if, whenever you add such statements, you would follow it with a parenthetical source reference. In many cases, I see that you have done this. In others, you confined yourself to a general reference, such as on p. 7 of the chapter on The Fall of Man, *where you only say "Works and Days," without mentioning chapter and verse, or on p. 8 of the same chapter, where you give no source reference to your statement about the Greek myth of Triptolemus.*

In the Paradise *chapter, I got the impression that you went into too lengthy a description of the Mexican mushroom. I hope you will agree with me that considering that this is merely a hypothesis for which the Mexican Tlaloclan is external supporting evidence by analogy only, it is sufficient to devote to it some 250–300 words. I therefore retained in the enclosed retype, on pp. 11–12, only those parts of your exposition which I felt were essential. In checking this part, please make sure whether the spelling is Tlalocan or Tlaloclan, Tepantitla or Tepentitlan, and the spelling of the name Chalchiuthlicue, Psilocybin, etc.*

I am also enclosing a page which has to be inserted into the chapter The Birth of Noah, *into p. 2. I will take care of the corresponding changes in the footnotes.*

Now I come to the weighty question of the overall division of the book. I am in agreement with you that the first volume should be titled Hebrew Myths: The Book of Genesis. *However, if we put the entire material pertaining to the book of Genesis into one volume, we shall get a very large and rather unwieldy (from the marketing point-of-view) volume. In my original draft of the chapters, this volume would comprise something like 300,000 words. Let us assume that after you recast these chapters, abridge or omit what you feel should be so treated, and add your comments and notes, this material will be reduced from 300,000 to 200,000 words. Even this length, however, is much too much for a handy, easily marketable volume. May I suggest, therefore, the following:*

Let us divide this material into two volumes, each of which will be 100,000 words in length. The first volume would deal with the early ages up to, and including, the death of Abraham. This volume could be called Hebrew Myths: Genesis, *or, perhaps,* Hebrew Myths: The Earliest Times, *or by some similar title. The two main figures, taking up most of the second volume, would then be Jacob and Joseph. Accordingly, the second volume could be called* Hebrew Myths: Jacob and Joseph. *Then would follow the third volume, on which I am working at present, and which would in its entirety be dominated by the figure of Moses. This could, therefore, be called* Hebrew Myths: Moses. *The fourth*

276

and last volume would contain the myths from Joshua to the destruction of the First Temple by Nebuchadnezzar. Its main protagonists would be the judges, kings and prophets of Israel. The title of this volume could be Hebrew Myths: Rulers and Prophets.

Each of these volumes would be roughly of the same length, ca. 100,000 words. If you are in agreement with this suggestion, we can have the first volume ready for print in a relatively short time. There would be no hurry, however, in letting Doubleday know that our plan now calls for four volumes. We would have time to tell them of this after we deliver the MS of the second volume. Once the four volumes have been on the market for a year or so, they will, undoubtedly want to produce a paperback edition which could be issued in two volumes.

Yours cordially,
Raphael

[P.S.] I have asked a friend who is now in Rome photographing ancient monuments to let me have a really good close-up of the dragons on the base of the Menorah of Titus' arch. Such a picture could be used for the dust jacket of our first volume.

Thank you for your offer to send me those books on women you have there; but please don't bother. I don't need them at present, and if I should in the future I can always obtain them here in the library.

Graves's ''business'' letter of March 8 called for a separate response.

March 12, 1962

Dear Robert;

Thank you for your letter of March 8th. I am glad at the prospect of receiving from you another six chapters in the near future.

Now as to the contract with Cassell. I wrote my letter to Cassell a few days after I received the contract from Doubleday. As you know, this Doubleday contract was in the making for approximately a year and a half. I, therefore, felt that it embodied the best possible arrangement settled on by ''Roturman S. A., c/o Willis Kingsley Wing (in conjunction with A. P. Watt and Son, London, England)''—this is how it reads—and myself as ''the author'' on the one hand, and the publisher on the other. Moreover, this Doubleday contract was dated December 29th, 1961, and I therefore assumed that the form in which it embodies the double authorship has superseded the Cassell contract, which is dated December 6, 1961. It was on the basis of this assumption that I wrote to Cassell suggesting, in effect, that three simple changes be made in order to bring the draft of the Cassell contract in line with the subsequent Doubleday contract, which was actually signed by all the parties.

I fail to understand why a form of contract which was arrived at by "Willis Kingsley Wing (in conjunction with A. P. Watt and Son, London, England)" should be regarded as unsatisfactory by "Messrs. A. P. Watt, and Son . . . (acting in conjunction with Willis Kingsley Wing . . .)."

One more detail: In the draft of the Cassell contract, Roturman S. A. figures as the "proprietors" of the book, and the contract stipulates that all royalties from Cassell are to be paid through Watt to Roturman. However, Roturman represents, in fact, only you and not me. In order to make the contract valid, I would, therefore have to enter into an agreement with Roturman, appointing him as my representative, with reference to my share of the royalties. I have nothing against this in principle, but in practice this would mean that after Watt receives his commission on my share of the royalties, he would pay over the remaining part to Roturman, Roturman, in turn, would deduct his share of the royalties, and then forward to me whatever is left over. This would not only be rather expensive for me, but also cumbersome, and cause, foreseeably, considerable delays between the date of royalties due and the date of their arrival into my hands.

In view of this, I feel that the contract, as worked out between us and Doubleday, is better, simpler, and more efficient. I hope that Watt will admit this.

However, I do not wish to deprive Messrs. Watt and Son of their commission. Let them, therefore, arrange for the changes in the contract as I suggested in my letter of January 25th, and get their commission on whatever royalties will be due to me from Cassell.

As to my suggestion with reference to an advance—I wrote explicitly: "I would like you to pay me an advance of $1,000 against my 50% of the royalties." What Watt writes, that "the royalties would go against his (i.e. my advance) and you would receive nothing until it has been earned" is therefore incorrect. However, I shall not insist on this detail. If you receive no advance against the royalties, I also shall be content with receiving none.

I hope that this clears up the whole issue. I absolutely concur with your feeling that there is no disagreement between us and obviously there cannot be.

Yours cordially,
Raphael

Graves's next letter to me was written before he received the above. It is one of the only three letters to me that were not handwritten by him, but typed, presumably by Karl Gay. It contains a few corrections and additions in Graves's own hand.

March 15th, 1962

My dear Raphael

Thanks for chapters. I'll keep the going-over until the end.
The overall division of the book—yes, a weighty question. The most

278

important considerations are: 'For whom are we writing?' and 'What is myth?'

The answer to the first is: 'For the intelligent public, the emancipated public, not restricted either to Protestants (Catholics aren't interested at all), or to Jews; and not the scholarly few who have the Talmud, all Greek literature, all German Biblical commentaries, and the cuneiform corpus on their shelves.' As a Protestant with strong interest in Jewish problems, I count myself able to decide at what point boredom sets in; Karl, a typical example of our public, is far less patient of the Meah Shearim pietistic atmosphere than I am. . . . In the Sacrifice of Isaac, *at least, two thirds of your material (excellent though it is for rabbinic students) is lacking in* mythical *as opposed to devotional interest; and the same goes for a great deal of wanton midrashic exaggeration elsewhere about size, height and so on. I* don't want *to cut out altogether the later myth-making about the events in* Genesis; *but we must use a crispness of statement, and no laborious appearance of scholarship. So 150,000 words is not an unfair estimate for* Genesis.

I certainly can't afford to do four volumes of 100,000 words; it would cost me too much in time, nor could they be sold popularly. And to be honest, as soon as Joshua invades Canaan my interest wanes. Myths then become parochial and too closely bound up with reformed Temple worship, on which you have already written in a masterly way. A 100,000-word book about Moses would be highly unappetizing; though the Exodus *is a very good myth for historical dissection, I should hate to see it run into more than from 30,000 to 50,000 words.*

Let us be content for the moment with Genesis. *I can see that finished, tightened, polished, indexed, and selling like hot cakes. But when it's done, I don't intend to plunge into the second book at once; I want to be free for other things, particularly for thinking about the arcana of poetry.*

Today I suddenly realized that Hagar and Sarah's quarrel was behind the binding of Isaac: persuaded by a close mythical parallel with the ram of the Golden Fleece myth, and by your own arguments from Hamurabi. Strange, that nobody else seems to have noticed it!

The question of reference is one that worries you more than me. For example, I remember reading about the equitation of the phallus in Hippodrome society under the Emperor Justinian, when I wrote Belisarius; *but that was in 1938, and I sold my source books, and haven't the least idea where it occurred. The main reference book is the Bible, and everyone can get hold of that.*

Thanks very much for your statements about the contract which couldn't be fairer; I'll tell Watt. But the mathematics are on his side. If you get 1000 dollars as advance on 50% of the takings, and I do not ask for any advance, then if (say) the net takings are 1500 dollars, there will be only 500 left for me. However, this is too gloomy a prospect to be considered; so I'll tell him to forget it.

279

*Have now got Keturah straightened out, with the very interesting Spartan claim to Descent from Abraham (confirmed by Maccabees). Tomorow Isaac's marriage. Query. *Can Atham or Etham mean a 'sacrificial knife' in Hebrew as it does in a N. African Arabic dialect?**

Yours ever
Robert

Even before I received this letter I wrote:

March 20, 1962

Dear Robert:

I am enclosing six chapters which you sent me in recent weeks, and which I had retyped with very minor changes or corrections.

In the Deluge chapter on p. 10, I marked with a vertical line on the left hand margin the paragraphs I rephrased. Similarly in the chapter the Severed Carcasses on p. 5, the chapter Ishmael on p. 5, and the chapter Abraham in Gerar p. 2. Once you approve of these, and supply the source references missing here and there, this material, I believe, can be regarded as in final shape.

Yours cordially,
Raphael

After sending off the above letter I received Graves's letter of March 15, which required a detailed answer. So I wrote again on March 26.

Dear Robert:

Thank you for your letter of March 15th. I am in complete agreement with you as to our procedure after we finish the Genesis material. In fact, I think that I, too, will want to wait a while before plunging into the Exodus and subsequent periods. The Exodus itself, of course, has been the central myth-cycle of Judaism throughout the ages: the miraculous redemption from slavery, the passage through the sea, and the revelation from Sinai are unequalled in their significance for Jewish life to this day. They are constantly referred to in prayers, form the basis of morality, and are the most powerful mythical charter for survival ever devised by any people. However, let us wait with all this until we have Genesis out of the way, and in press.

I also find myself in agreement with the way you prune the draft chapters. When you will look through the chapters which I have been returning to you in the last few weeks, and five more of which are enclosed herewith, you will see that I suggest in practically no case that any story or detail which you had deleted should be restored. In this respect I let myself be guided completely by

*you. Your understanding of what interests the "intelligent, emancipated pub-
lic" is much deeper than mine can ever be. Where I do suggest changes from
your text is in places where it touches upon factual details. I believe that here
I am right in insisting that references to facts should be impeccable so that no
critic should be able to accuse us of unreliability or even imprecision. This is
why in the enclosed chapters I rewrote a few sections (The Fratricide, p. 14;
Noah's Drunkeness, pp. 4–6; The Tower of Babel, pp. 5–7; Abraham's Birth,
p. 7). In each case I marked the rewritten lines by a vertical pencil line on the
left margin.*

*In this connection, I want to tell you that although I rewrote the comments
made by you, in order to substitute e.g., for the more than 100-year-old study
of Knobel, on which you based yourself, the results and findings of the latest
research, what you did was invaluable, because your original comments
covered areas which I had completely overlooked. Thus, although the precise
formulation of the identification, e.g. of the ten generations between Noah
and Abraham is mine, the idea that such an identification should be included among the comments is yours, and remains an important enrichment
of the book.*

*I am most curious to see what you mean by Hagar and Sara's quarrel being
behind the binding of Isaac. Will I get this chapter soon?*

*I cannot deny that I am worried by the question of references. My feeling is
that if we make a statement of fact, it has to be supported by a source reference. I tried to find a trace of the equitation of the phallus in Hippodrome
society under Justinian. No luck. But, I found that the custom as a marriage
rite was practiced in Rome with images of Priapus or Mutunus (see Augustine,
de civ. Dei VII. 24, and Lactantius Div. Inst. I. 20.) Same custom survived
until recently in India with the lingam taking the place of the Roman deity
(Ploss-Bartels-Reitzenstein, Das Weib, 11th edition, ii. 43). Perhaps these
data could be substituted for the reference to Hippodrome society?*

*I tried to find the answer to your query whether Atham or Etham (is this
the spelling?) means "sacrificial knife" in Hebrew, as it does in North African Arabic dialect. The answer is negative. No such word in Hebrew; or
did you have in mind a Hebrew word which has this form and its meaning
is uncertain?*

*I am glad that you found my statement about the contract satisfactory. As
we both said earlier, there can be no difference between us with reference to
this. Where we might get into each other's hair is in the area of the interpretation of the myth. However, since this has not happened so far, I am confident
it will not in the future either.*

> *Regards and love to you all*
> *Raphael*

A few days later I had more to write.

April 6, 1962

Dear Robert:

First of all I want to acknowledge the receipt of chapters 32–37. As I read these chapters, and so far I have given them only a cursory first reading, I am more and more impressed by the value of your contribution to our book.

In addition to calling my attention to the need of explaining many things overlooked by me (I mentioned this in my earlier letter to you), I was especially gratified by your comparisons with Greek myths. Your comparison of the Abraham-Sara-Hagar-Isaac-Ishmael story with the Cadmean story of Athamas-Nephele-Ino-Phrixus-Melicertes is so striking, that when reading it I asked myself: is it possible that nobody else has noticed this? Just a few days ago an item was published here in the papers about the decipherment by my friend, Prof. Cyrus H. Gordon of Brandeis University, of the ancient Cretan script Linear B. His contention is that these inscriptions are in a language almost identical with Phoenician which, in turn, differs only dialectally from Hebrew. If his thesis proves to be correct, and knowing his scholarship I think it will, this will prove the close cultural connection between pre-Israelite Canaan and Crete in the early 2nd millennium B.C. Viewed against this new scholarly breakthrough, your comparisons of Hebrew with Greek myths gain added significance. They are proofs of a cultural connection between the two peoples of the type one would have to postulate once the linguistic connections are established.

My detailed comments on these chapters 32–37 will follow within a week or so, after I have a chance to work them over.

Today I am enclosing the last three chapters of those which you sent me earlier. In chapter 23, as you will see, I rewrote comments 1 and 2 on pp. 2–4, on the basis of the latest available scholarly studies.

In chapter 27, on p. 3, I inserted section F, which I would like to retain. Please consider this. Also, in pp. 4–6 and 8, I rewrote the comments. In chapter 31, on p. 3, I added a section F. I believe that this is mythological material interesting enough to be retained. On pp. 4–5, I rewrote comment 3.

Cordially,

Raphael

The comparison between the biblical story of the sacrifice of Isaac and the Greek one of the sacrifice of Phrixus, added by Graves to my draft, is included in chapter 34, points 5–7 of the *Hebrew Myths*. The similarity of the two myths of a father being commanded by a divine voice to sacrifice his son, and then, in the last minute, being ordered to desist, is remarkable indeed, as is the appearance of a ram in both. The reconstruction, on this basis, of a hypothetical "original myth" underlying the Genesis story, as suggested by Graves, while it of necessity must remain conjectural, can serve as an example of how much farther poetic intuition can go than scholarly step-by-step deduction.

On April 9 Graves sent me another batch of chapters reworked by him with this covering letter.

Dear Raphael:

Sending you another seven chapters, and most relieved that you think well of the others. I'll not look at your amendments until I have finished the whole job, and then go through them chapter by chapter.

Yes I saw the "Eteo-Cretan" business myself, and particularly liked the occurrence of David's name in Crete, since he had a Cretan bodyguard. And a Semitic script was likely because of various pointers such as the late Dynastic Egyptian school exercise book in which the answer to "What Cretan name do you know?" was "Achish"—a name connected with David by the way. (I think that the Semites came before Aeolian Greeks but after the Libyo-Thracians).

Also, there's the new Jerusalem inscription just found.

Am now having fun with the mandrakes . . . I once saw a mandrake: rather like a dahlia root in its exterior.

Have accepted the Little lectureship at M.I.T. in May 1963 for a fortnight.

> *Love to you both*
> *Robert*

My reply was dated April 27.

Dear Robert:

I was glad to hear that you have accepted an invitation by M.I.T., and plan to be in America a year from now. Will Beryl come with you? It would be fine if she would, but in any case, we would like to have you, i.e. either both of you or you alone, as our guests. We have just bought a house in Forest Hills, which is at a distance of about 10 miles from midtown Manhattan, and although we cannot offer you a separate guest house, we can let you have a separate floor consisting of bedroom, study and bathroom. The neighborhood, although, again, it cannot vie in beauty with Deya, is one of the most attractive garden sections of New York. I hope that this invitation comes early enough before you accept others.

I am enclosing chapters 32–44. I followed the customary procedure of marking on the margin whatever I changed or added. As you will see, there isn't too much of this. In many cases, I was struck by your fine insights. Your explanation of the sacrifice of Isaac with the help of the Cadmeian story is excellent, as is the piece on Jacob's figure in the myth (41:3, p. 7). There

283

are several other places where I could stop and praise, but there is no need for that.

I hope everything is well with you, and that I will soon get more material from you.

Cordially,
Raphael

While engaged in working intensively on the *Hebrew Myths,* I turned my thoughts again and again to the question of a jacket picture for the book. As I had written to Graves on March 9, I believed that the reliefs of the dragons shown on the base of the Menorah of the Arch of Titus in Rome would be most suitable. After I received a clear photograph of that part of the relief with the help of my friend Prof. Tullio Tentori, I sent a copy of it to Ken McCormick with this covering letter.

April 30, 1962

Dear Ken:

Although it might be too early to think of the cover picture for the jacket of Hebrew Myths, *I wish to make a suggestion which, if accepted, may take quite a long time to execute, and, therefore, I am making it already now.*

Enclosed photograph (made at my request) by the German Archaeological Institute at Rome, shows a detail from a panel on the Arch of Titus in Rome. The captives are shown carrying the menora, *the seven-branched candelabrum, looted from the Jerusalem Temple. The six little panels at the base of the* menora *contain reliefs of dragons and other mythical animals. Both Robert and myself are in agreement that these must be true copies of the reliefs which adorned the* menora *in the Second Temple in Jerusalem, and which, in turn, went back to a much older original. In fact, to the best of my knowledge, these panels contain the only extant visual representation of ancient Hebrew mythological ideas.*

If you agree with me that this menora *base would make a fine cover picture for the jacket, I would suggest that either you or I write again to the German Archaeological Institute (via Bocca di Leone, 78, Rome) and ask them to have a close-up made of the* menora *base, so as to show more clearly and sharply all the details than would be possible if we would be satisfied with a blow-up of the enclosed picture. For the enclosed picture the Institute charged me 300 lires (which is 48¢), and on this basis I assume that their charge for a close-up of the* menora *base would also be very reasonable. If you want me to proceed, have your secretary call me, and I shall write to the Institute explaining to them exactly what I want.*

As to the MS—⁴/₅ths of it is ready in an almost final draft. Robert is working at present on the last few chapters, after which he will go over the entire MS.

Yours cordially,
Raphael

Ken's response was enthusiastic.

May 8, 1962

Dear Raphael:

Thank you so much for your April 30th letter. I'm currently at a Sales Conference, and I can't wait for the next one, when I'll be telling the men about HEBREW MYTHS. I'm absolutely enchanted with the picture you sent me and with the possibilities for jacket art. Our art department will go to the Institute and ask for the shot that you suggest.

Best personal wishes to you and to Daphne when you write her.

Sincerely,
Ken

My daughter Daphne had, a year or two earlier, worked for a while in the Doubleday editorial offices; she was at this time a student at Indiana University in Bloomington, Indiana.

I wrote to Graves next on May 4.

Dear Robert:

Thank you for chapters 45–51, which I read for the time being only superficially. Their thorough study will have to wait until I can unpack my books in our new house.

I like your approach very much. Your treatment of the twelve patriarchs, Dinah, etc., as standing for tribes is convincing to me, but I think we better explain this whole matter in the introduction. Otherwise, many of our readers will think us arbitrary. Our argument, I think, should run, more or less, as follows:

Archeological evidence has demonstrated irrefutably that the ten generations leading from Noah to Abraham are but the mythical-traditional reflection of city kingdoms, or peoples, located in the middle Euphrates. It is, therefore, reasonable to assume that also the subsequent four or five generations (descendants of Abraham) have to be understood in a similar manner. Moreover, comparison with other peoples, both contemporary and present-day, supports this view. For instance, the nations of Moab and Ammon lead to the assumption that they were the descendants of two individuals called Moab and Ben-Ammi. Among the present-day Arab tribes, the existence of the great Aneze tribal confederacy in the Syrian desert led to the creation of their ancestor figure, called eponymously Annaz. The name of the people of Israel led to the story of Jacob's change of name to Israel, etc.

This, it seems to me, is the basis of regarding stories about such figures as Dinah, and her brothers, as hiding tribal occurrences behind the apparent individual guise. Do you think some such argument should be included in the introduction? I am for it.

Query: On page 3 of chapter #50, Reuben and Bilhah, you write that there is a Reubenite geneaology given in Judges *V, which reads: Phalek-Rubel-Serug-Abiram. There must be some mistake in your source reference. I cannot trace this geneaology in* Judges, *nor anywhere else in the Bible. Could you answer this at your earliest convenience?*

Another matter: The dragons depicted on the base of the Menora of the Arch of Titus in Rome are, I believe, the only more or less authentic pictorial representations pertaining to Hebrew mythology in antiquity. I think, therefore, that a good close-up of the Menora-base would make a fine picture for the dust jacket of our book. How do you feel about this?

> *Cordially,*
> *Raphael*

This letter crossed Graves's, dated May 5.

Dear Raphael:

Good again.

The Amorite Wars, and the Patriarchs' Marriages *I am cutting down (as not true myths but fictions) and making notes to certain chapters.* Esau's Death *I have also cut down a lot but kept your useful notes.*

Now I'm at Joseph at last. I don't think that mythologically much can be said about him, but I'll do my best to supplement your notes.

The book will be of manageable size, and I expect to complete the chapters before June 25th when I have to interrupt work with a visit to Oxford. Then I'll go over the others as amended by you.

Curious: I expected to be bored with the job, but it has been great fun, and I hope that this pleasure that we have shared communicates itself to the reader.

> *Yours ever—*
> *Robert*

I hope your Women book goes well.

After he got my May 4 letter, Graves sent me another one.

May 8 1962

Dear Raphael:

I apologise for my slip in the Reuben piece: it was a careless reading of the too speculative Reuben *article in the* Encyclopedia Biblica. *I must rewrite it.*

Yes: the Introduction must have all that sort of argument in; but first the book must be written to get everything clear so that we can quote examples.

Yes: you sent me those Menora Beasts: good for the cover.

Yours ever
Robert

Melvin Lasky of Encounter *came to call & wants to publish 6 chapters from the early part of the book. I told him 'good'; but to wait.*

I have now got Kramer's Sumerian mythology which will make a few changes necessary in those chapters: Lilith, the Deluge, Cain & Abel etc.

The entry under "Reuben" in the *Encyclopaedia Biblica* (4:4094) to which Graves gave "a careless reading" was written by Hope W. Hogg, professor of Semitic languages at Victoria University in Manchester. In a footnote (on p. 4094, n. 4), Hogg speculates inconclusively on possible Reubenite genealogies, including the hypothetical Reuben-Phaletz-Reubel-Serug b. Hezron-Abiram quoted by Graves in his original redrafting of chapter 50. After the receipt of Graves's May 8 letter I excised that reference from our text. But what is most interesting in our exchange on this issue is that Graves did not rely on my draft chapters alone, but consulted the *Encyclopaedia Biblica* which, although many of its articles were antiquated by the 1960s, was still a valuable storehouse of information on many aspects of the Bible. Although Graves had complete confidence in my scholarly reliabilty when it came to biblical, talmudic, midrashic, etc. materials, he still felt that he could contribute something even to these parts of our book by going to a standard source, and felt impelled to do so.

That summer Graves worked persistently and intensively on our book, as can be seen from our correspondence. By early June he had mailed me his revised versions of all the sixty-one chapters with the exception of chapter 17, "The Birth of Seth," which somehow went astray. On June 10, 1962, he wrote:

Dear Raphael:

I have had back from you up to chapter 44, Jacob's Marriages. *In collating the two versions (your quarto & my folio) I find that I have not got a copy of chapter 17, which is the* Birth of Seth. *Would it be a bother to send me a new copy, or did you never have the original?*

Chapter One *had to be retyped.*

I'll now start final work of revision in both versions, with cross-references where needed; and then, when the Introduction has been composed from our two drafts, I'll send both versions for you to put the references in, and make your own corrections of my revision.

Yours ever
Robert

Even before receiving the above letter I wrote to him.

June 13, 1962

Dear Robert:

This morning's mail brought chapters 52–61. This brings us to the end of the first volume, and I don't have to tell you how happy I am that we have reached this stage. From now on it will, I hope, be all clear sailing. I shall work over the last chapters and send them as I have hitherto done, and you, as you wrote to me, will start going over the chapters which I already returned to you. If I remember correctly, I have returned to you about 45 chapters, and I hope that by the time you finish your last revision of those I will be able to send you the remaining 16 chapters.

At the moment, we are still busy with alterations in our new house in Forest Hills, painting, etc. For a change I am working on building bookshelves instead of working on the stuff which goes into them. But by now I begin to itch to return to my desk.

I suppose this letter will be sent after you to England. I hope you are having a pleasant sojourn there.

Yours cordially,
Raphael

After I received his June 10 letter I wrote him again.

June 14, 1962

Dear Robert:

Only yesterday I wrote to you expressing my gratification over having received from you the last chapters of Volume I.

In accordance with your letter of June 10th, which reached me today, I am sending you, enclosed, copies of both your and my versions of chapter 17, The Birth of Seth.

You write that you are about to start final work of revision in both versions. Since my quarto version, of which I sent you so far up to chapter 44, is in its entirety based on your folio version, and deviates from it only where I felt either that I cannot agree with a particular statement made by you, or where

I wanted to add some new material, I think that you could save time and labor by concentrating on "my" version only. But perhaps this is what you had in mind?

Let me again emphasize how happy I am that we have reached this concluding phase of our joint effort.

Raphael

Yes we had reached the "concluding phase of our joint effort," but by no means the actual conclusion of our work. For months we were busy tying up loose ends and ironing out remaining differences of opinion. On June 21 Graves wrote me the second of his typewritten letters, again with some handwritten additions.

My dear Raphael:

My trouble is that I'm a perfectionist, and don't let anything get out for publication with which my name is associated until it has gone through several versions and is all of one piece; and I don't stop to calculate expense of time or money. So I am now re-writing and re-typing the earlier chapters with the help of your additions.

There is one single disagreement between us, which is the identification of Helel with the 'Jewelled Cherub'. That they are the same mythic character, seems proved to me by the connexion made by both Isaiah and Ezekiel with the Mount of Meeting, which is also Paradise; both emphasize the angel's vaunt of his Power and God's delegation to him of authority over the nations. And many Biblical commentators agree with me that they are the same character. Taken apart from each other, the stories make poor sense and inadequate chapters.

The later chapters are probably in more or less final form, and some of them may not need re-typing; but the early ones have certainly needed heavy revision on stylistic grounds to make them agree with the rest. At first (last year, I mean) I was working blindly, confused with too much material; by this Spring I got into my stride. I think you'll realize how well worth the work, this revision has been.

*If you can send me back my own version as well as yours, it may save a good deal of re-typing. You can count on me to incorporate all your scholarly amendments. But the main trouble is references. Here and there I have had to cut out or compress, so that the reference numbers are again thrown out of gear. It is a great pity that we can't meet and work together; but I can think of no alternative, as it is, to sending you back the reference pages from your typescript and, when I eventually send you back both copies of my typescript in final form, ask you to amend these reference pages, attach them to the copies, and give both completed copies to Willis Wing for handing over to Doubleday and Cassell.**

289

*Please forgive me being such a bore, but I want this book to be as ser-
viceable and readable and perfect as possible: an example of how a Jew and
a Gentile can work together and produce something that won't be just another
book about the Bible, but something new and exciting and useful for the general reader, regardless of his religious (or non-religious) upbringing. What
first encouraged me to work with you was your fearlessness in your pursuit
of truth; and I hope that the readers will realize that I am not merely not anti-
Semite but very much at home in Jewry, however little respect I may seem to
pay the chroniclers of* Genesis.

Love to you both
Robert

**In the circumstances, it would be best if you now merely attached your
comments to my version, and save trouble and expense that way.*

My reply went by return mail.

June 27, 1962

Dear Robert:

*Thank you for your letter of June 21st. I quite understand how you feel
about the book, because I too want to see it in as perfect a shape as the two
of us can give it.*

*As to the question of the identity of Helel with the jewelled cherub—I don't
feel too strongly about this problem. I was inclined to regard the two as two
separate myth fragments, because Helel seems to have been, as his name indicates, the mythical representation of the morning star, whereas the jewelled
cherub was an angel set by God into His garden. The sin of Helel was that he
wanted to establish himself on the Mount of Assembly. The jewelled cherub
was set by God himself on His holy mountain. These features indicate, to my
mind, that we have to do here with the fragments of two originally independent
myths. However, I have an open mind about the possibility of interpreting the
two fragments the way you are inclined to do, and if you feel that you are
right, I am willing to go along with it.*

*As to the manner in which I should handle the final version on which you
are working at present, including the problem of the reference numbers, I
shall in every way follow your suggestions. Far from thinking you a bore, I
feel, at least as strongly as you do, that this book will be a truly significant
one. It will, I feel, take the Bible altogether out of the narrow religious realm
into which it has been pressed by Jews on the one hand, and by Christians on
the other, and will establish it (or, to be modest, make a contribution to establishing it) as an all-human source and guide book for Jew and Gentile,
religious people and agnostics, the happy and unhappy, the problem-ridden*

and the contented. It certainly is worth our best effort, and I, on my part, can assure you that however much additional work it will demand of me I shall be glad to invest it into it.

A piece of news that might interest you: A few days ago Doubleday arranged for me to have lunch with Lewis Nichols who writes the "In and Out of Books" column in the New York Times *weekly Book Review magazine. He found the things I told him about our book very interesting, and we can look forward to seeing some of it in one of the forthcoming issues of the magazine.*

Raphael

This was followed in July by two short notes of mine.

July 11, 1962

Dear Robert:

I am enclosing five chapters (45–49). This leaves me with only 12 more chapters (50–61) which I hope to send you in a week from today.

Having completed this work I am now ready to receive the final version on which you are working at present.

Love to you all,
Raphael

July 18, 1962

Dear Robert:

Herewith chapters 50–58.
The last three chapters will follow within a week.

Regards and love to you all,
Raphael

Although busy with the *Hebrew Myths,* my work on other books, articles, and lectures (all this, of course, over and above my regular job at the Herzl Press), I still found time to think up new literary projects. On January 22, 1962, I suggested to Clement Alexandre, at the time editor of Jewish and Protestant religious books at Macmillan, that I would like to write for his house a book on the Negro Jews of Harlem. He liked the idea, but ultimately nothing came of it. Next day I had a meeting with Mrs. Latifeh Yarshater, who was contributing the chapter on women in Iran to my book *Women in the Modern World,* and suggested to her that we collaborate on a book on "Iranian Women: Between Old and New."

On February 2 I noted in my diary: "Last night I had an idea for a new book more or less along the lines of the two volumes on women. Tentative title: *The World Moves West: A Survey* (or: *Highlights) of the Global Impact of Euro-American Culture.* It would be written by 20 area experts, and I would write the Introduction. I may ask F. S. C. Northrop to write the Preface.'' Although for several years thereafter I made desultory attempts to find a publisher for this book, in the end nothing came of it.

I also renewed my efforts to be appointed managing editor of the new *Encyclopaedia Judaica,* which was still in the planning stage. On February 26 I spoke about it to Dr. Nahum Goldmann, who was about to provide the financial basis for that encyclopaedia from the German Reparations. He was very receptive, but in the end nothing came of this, either.

In September 1962 I met two other authors of my ''Women'' book: Prof. Tullio Tentori of Rome, who was working on the Italian chapter, and Prof. Helge Pross of the University of Tübingen, who wrote the German chapter. These meetings were important because the personal contact with my authors facilitated the writing of my introduction to the book.

Also in the winter of 1961-62 Ann and I were busy house-hunting. We were not happy with our city apartment, and wanted to move again into a one-family house. After looking at quite a number of houses both in the city and in Forest Hills, we decided to purchase a pleasant seven-room house in the Forest Hills Gardens, at 39 Bow Street, and there I still live. Once this was settled, I sold our cooperative apartment at 135 East 71st Street, and we moved into the house in May.

As we neared completion of the manuscript, I made modest efforts to help Doubleday publicize the forthcoming *Hebrew Myths.* On June 18, 1962, Linda Cohen of Doubleday invited me and Lewis Nichols of the *New York Times Book Review* for lunch at the Pompei to discuss the book and supply Nichols with material for an advance note on it in his column, ''In and Out of Books.'' In the July 1 issue of the *Times Book Review* he published the following chatty piece:

Collaboration

For better than a year, the airplanes have been running copy between Mallorca, Spain, and here in a long-distance collaboration on a book about Hebrew myths. At this end is Raphael Patai, author, scholar, research director of the Theodore Herzl Institute. At that end is Robert Graves, poet, mushroom fancier and authority on myths in general. At the moment the copy is in Mallorca, being given a final once-over by Mr. Graves. A plane is expected to bring it back in time for late winter publication.

It seems that the Messrs. Patai and Graves have known one another casually for years, talking Hebrew myths, and a couple of years back decided to set them down, with commentary. (One myth every badgered man knows is that Eve was carved from Adam's rib.) Being the Hebrew scholar, Mr. Patai is ''in control of the sources,'' so he sets down the myth in New York. This raw myth then goes to Mr. Graves, who works it over, supplying comment and related myths such as from the Greek. Mr. Patai then gets a second crack at it before it is returned to Mr. Graves for final polishing. Sixty-one myths, all from the Book of Genesis, will be in the book. After a breathing spell, the collaborators may do a second volume, starting with the myths of Exodus.

Fine collaboration, says Mr. Patai. No airmail sulking or pummeling. When Mr. P. said he thought a description of the hallucinatory mushrooms of Mexico a little long for a book on Hebrew myths, Mr. Graves cut it cheerfully. When Mr. G. wished time out to listen to the voice of The White Goddess (poetry), that was O.K. this side. The mails went through without hitch. That business of the postman not being stayed by snow or gloom of night is no myth.

In addition to all this, in August of 1962 Dr. Emanuel Neumann asked me to take charge of the directorship of the Herzl Institute to fill in for Dr. Emil Lehman, who was taking a year's leave of absence. Although I was less than enthusiastic about shouldering this additional burden—it meant being responsible for arranging and supervising a dozen or so lectures every week, over and above my work as editor of the Herzl Press—I felt I could not refuse. Of course, the additional salary was also a consideration I had to take into account.

But by now, August, the *Hebrew Myths* was uppermost in my mind, for the text of the MS was nearly completed (except for the inevitable polishing insisted upon by both Graves and myself): we were ready to tackle the introduction and conclusion.

25.

———

Introduction and Conclusion

M Y JULY 18 LETTER was answered by Graves on August 13:

My dear Raphael:

The book is now being retyped in its final version. Occasionally the paragraphing has had to be altered, which has sent the notes out of order. That is your job now. I have incorporated all your new material. It now reads smoothly all through: this damn perfectionism about prose will be the death of me! Every chapter has now gone into at least six drafts.

—It remains to do the Introduction *by a weaving together of your notes & mine; but I'm in favour of keeping it short and unaggressive. Only the small, shrill orthodox minority will object to the book: they do not matter. The more liberal & enlightened will rejoice that the Jewish myths are part of the general E. Mediterranean & Mesopotamian & Syrian culture, however pruned & trimmed.*

Once this book is published, it won't be overlooked. The only chapter now missing from the file is the first of all, which had to be completely recast: you have it. Please send!

Love to you both.
Robert

It would be fun to dedicate the book to David Ben Gurion: he'd love it, wouldn't he? I like him.

I answered this letter on August 17.

Dear Robert:

It was good to hear from you after relatively a long silence. I am delighted to know that the book is now being retyped and, you can imagine, that I am looking forward impatiently to seeing this final version. As to the Introduction, I agree with you that it should be unaggressive, but, I think, it should contain a clear statement as to our understanding of the nature of myth in general, of Hebrew myth in particular. I do not know whether one can do justice to this, rather difficult subject, and yet keep the Introduction short. In any case, I feel that a definition of myth should be included in the Introduction. On page 53 of my draft for the Introduction which I sent you several months ago, I suggested a definition which I thought was adequate. I would very much like to see it, or something to the same effect, contained in the Introduction.

Only a few days ago I had an opportunity to read out this definition to an Orthodox Rabbi friend of mine and his reaction was:

"Well, if this is the definition of myth, then I certainly have no objection to the idea of Hebrew Mythology." Don't misunderstand me—I would not deviate an inch from expressing my convictions in order to placate Orthodox Jews or Christians. But, if it so happens that the definition of myth which I reached on the basis of purely scientific considerations satisfied the Orthodox, well so much the better.

This is Friday, and I am writing this letter from my office. My copy of the first chapter is at home, I shall dig it up and mail it to you on Monday.

As to your idea to dedicate the book to David Ben-Gurion, it is intriguing. But, we have time to decide when we have the book in galleys.

> *Love to all of you.*
> *Raphael*

As one can gather from the last paragraph of this letter, Graves's suggestion that we dedicate the book to Ben-Gurion did not strike a responsive chord in me. I considered Ben-Gurion a great historical figure whose role in the establishment of Israel was greater than that of any other Zionist leader. But he was a statesman and political leader, not a scholar, and I therefore felt that a scholarly book such as the *Hebrew Myths* was to be, and especially a controversial one as I knew it would prove to be, should rather be dedicated to a scholar of great renown whose work had some relationship to what we were trying to do in our book. True, I was aware of Ben-Gurion's scholarly interests, his studying of the Bible, Greek philosophy, and Buddhism, but my admiration for him on this count was diminished by his ruthless handling of the "Lavon affair" in 1960-61. In any case, as far as I can remember, the question of dedicating the *Hebrew Myths* to somebody never again arose in my contact with Graves.

In response to my letter of August 17, Graves sent me the typescript of his corrected version of all the sixty-one chapters, with this covering letter.

Aug 24 1962

My dear Raphael:

Here's the lot except for the Introduction, *which we can tell the publishers will be 3000 words, and supplied before the New Year.*

I have incorporated almost all of your new material, but compressed it. The book is now readable *by the same sort of general audience that read* Greek Myths, *& it may be assumed that they will be content with the references given to the text, and not ask for a huge* apparatus criticus *to the notes.*

May I ask you to see to the maps? The index of names and places can safely be left to the publisher.

It remains for you to see whether I have misinterpreted you or slipped in anything which you know to be historically false; and to send me typed copies of the reference lists, numbers from 1 to 61 which I can include in my copy here; you pasting a similar series into the typescript I enclose here. When this is done, I can offer some of the chapters to Encounter, *(they will take copies) and then give Cassell the whole lot.*

As you may see, this last go-over meant thousands of small changes in the wording, to assist readability; so any further changes you feel must be made, please submit to me for style. *Every chapter has now gone into at least six drafts. The whole policy is to instruct without being pedantic.*

—It has been a hell of a task, but worth it, I hope.

I found the second copy of Chapter I after all; & return yours. So sorry! What matters is not what Rabbis and Bishops say about the book; but the conviction of truth-telling which we give, and our sympathy with the chroniclers & commentators.

—In the proofs we will probably find a lot of small errors but that won't be until next year, I guess.

> *Love to you both*
> *Robert*

The extravagant inventions of the later midrashim has had to be toned down; it is a bit too strong for the early myths.

I'm here [at this address] until Oct 1st—Then at St John's College Oxford; or % Wm Watt 10 Norfolk St, Strand, W.C.2.

In the event, *Encounter* of London, edited at the time by Stephen Spender and Melvin J. Lasky, published sample chapters from the *Hebrew Myths* in two installments under the title, "Some Hebrew Myths and Legends." In its February 1963 issue they printed the entire introduction, deleting only the parenthetical references it contained to chapters in the book, and transposing its last paragraph to the first page, into an editorial box. This was followed by chapters five, six, seven, nine, and ten: "Earlier Creations," "The Primeval Monsters," "The Reem and the Ziz," "The Birth of Adam," and "Adam's

Helpmeets." This last chapter was illustrated by a woodcut showing Lilith, and on the cover of the magazine there was another woodcut, by "Barlach," depicting God himself—not his "spirit"—"hovering over the face of the waters." The subsequent issue of *Encounter* (March 1963) presented chapters eleven, thirteen, fourteen, and fifteen: "Paradise," "Samael's Rebellion," "The Births of Cain and Abel," and "The Act of Love."

Graves's August 24 letter with the typescript of the whole book reached me within three days, and I answered it immediately.

August 27, 1962

Dear Robert:

I hurry to acknowledge the receipt this morning of the big batch of typescript containing all the 61 chapters of the book. I have begun reading from the very beginning and find it not only immensely readable but, in fact, fascinating, although it cannot have for me the attraction of newness which it will have for our readers.

It will take me about two weeks to go over all the chapters, settle whatever questions your last reworking raises in my mind and put the source references in proper shape. You can therefore, count on receiving all this by the middle of September.

As to the introduction, since you set your mind on making it short (3,000 words) I shall no longer press for a longer one. Besides, seeing what you can do by way of expressing ideas in utter conciseness, I am sure you will be able to put all that has to be stated in the Introduction within the compass of the 3,000 words.

The time element, however, bothers me. When I last spoke to Ken McCormick several weeks ago, before he left on an extended European trip, he told me that he would like to aim for a Spring 1963 publication. Unless we can give him the Introduction within a relatively short time, Spring publication will be ruled out. Do you think it would be possible for you to write the Introduction before you leave for Oxford on the 1st of October? This would be very desirable for another reason as well: once you are in Oxford, you will, I am afraid, not have time to do it and it would have to wait until after your return to Majorca. When all the factors are figured out, this may mean a difference of a whole year in the date of publication.

To return for another minute to your text: after having read the first three or four chapters, I am filled with admiration for your patience and persistence in going over the text again and again and making improvements in it. When reading your text I shuddered to think how this book would have looked if I had done it alone!

Do you think it is worthwhile to make an attempt to submit some of the chapters to a good magazine in this country? I am thinking of Harper's or Commentary.

If I have any questions as I go on reading the typescript, I shall write to you again,

Raphael

In response Graves sent me this note.

Sept 9 1962

Dear Raphael:

I'll do my best with that Introduction. *It's so familiar a subject to me now & I have your material to help me shape it tactfully; and I don't want to delay publication.*

Don't worry.

Yours ever
Robert

It took me longer than I had estimated in my letter of August 27 to go over the entire typescript. So when the two weeks were up I wrote to Graves:

September 11, 1962

Dear Robert:

I received your letter of September 9th and hurry to let you know how delighted I am that you intend to have the Introduction finished before long.

I, in the meantime, am doing my best to finish the last check of the MS. I am afraid however, that this will take longer than the two weeks I over-confidently estimated in my previous letter. Especially the early chapters seem to contain a number of details which I feel I must check, although I am willing to go along with you in omitting practically all the source references from our comments. Precisely because of this, I feel, that I have to be absolutely sure that every factual statement made in them has a reliable basis.

Today, I can send you for the time being the adjusted source references to chapters 2 through 30. In most cases I was able to leave unchanged the numbers in the text which refer to these source references. In a few instances however, it was inevitable to change them. The changes are as follows:

In chapter 9, (The Birth of Adam): please erase all the present footnote numbers from the text beginning with #4; replace 9 by 5; 10 by 6; 13 by 7; 14 by 8; 15 by 9; 16 by 10; 19 by 11; 22 by 12; 23 by 13; 25 by 14; 26 by 15; 28 by 16; 29 by 17; and 30 by 18.

In chapter 11, (Paradise): on page 72, insert footnote #14 at the end of the second line of section g. after the words, exceptional piety, erase #14 from page 73, end of paragraph 2.

In Chapter 12, (The Fall of Man): on page 80, erase all the 4 lines of section 3., because I am unable to locate any source for this statement. This

*makes section f. into e, etc. and footnote 6 into 5, 7 into 6, 8 into 7, 9 into 8,
10 into 9, 11 into 10, erase footnote #12 and substitute 11 for 13, 12 for 14,
13 for 15, 14 for 16, 15 for 17, and 16 for 18.*

In Chapter 16, *(The Fratricide) erase footnote numbers 4 and 5, change 6
to 4, 7 to 5, erase 8 and 9; change 10 to 6; erase 11 and 12, change 13 to 7;
erase 14, 15, 16 and 17; change 18 to 8; 19 to 9; erase 20 and 21; change 22
to 10; erase 23, change 24 to 11; erase 25, and change 26 to 12.*

In Chapter 19, *(The Birth of Noah) insert footnote #1 in page 125, section
c. third line after "Consolation in him" change #1 into 2 and 2 into 3.*

In Chapter 26, *(Abraham In Egypt) on page 173 section d. after the end of
the poem, insert footnote #3; change 3 to 4, 4 to 5, and 5 to 6.*

In Chapter 27, *on page 179, please insert the section enclosed herewith. I
feel that this is interesting material which should not be omitted. Since this
section will end with footnote #3, the following section which now will be
changed from f. into g. will end with footnote reference #4.*

You may be interested in the reason for these changes. It is quite simple. In
Chapter 9 *for instance, to take the first example: you put in footnotes 4 to 9
into section b. However, all the material contained in this section is a composite and a summary of statements repeated in many versions in the sources
whose enumeration takes six lines. If we would retain the footnote numbers as
appearing in your typescript, we would have to repeat this long list of sources
six times, or repeat the words "sources same as in preceding footnote" five
times. Instead, it is much simpler to provide only one single footnote reference
number for this whole section.*

*I shall go on working as much as I can on the MS and shall let you have
the material as I get through with it.*

> *Yours cordially,*
> *Raphael*

Finally, on September 14, Graves sent me the introduction with this
brief note.

Dear Raphael:

*This was deduced from our original tape recording plus your long intro-
duction, which I hope you'll use elsewhere, and things that occurred to us
while writing the book.*

I hope it pleases you.

> *Yours ever*
> *Robert*

The introduction did indeed please me, but still I had quite a few comments
to make. However, before I could get to that, I had first to straighten out a
number of minor points in several chapters. I wrote to Graves:

September 18, 1962

Dear Robert:

First of all let me acknowledge your Introduction *which came this morning and which I am most happy to have. This means that the book is almost ready to go to press—sooner than I hoped. I shall read the Introduction within the next few days and then write to you about it in greater detail.*

Today, I am sending you enclosed the adjusted source references to chapters 31 to 61. Only a very few of the reference numbers in the chapters themselves have to be changed to fit these source references. The required changes are as follows:

Chapter 31. *I would suggest that you allow section f. to stand as you did when you first reworked this chapter. In that case section f will end with footnote reference #6, the corresponding footnote to which is included on the enclosed page containing the footnote references to chapter 31.*

Chapter 36, *page 232, please transfer footnote reference number 4 from the end of the first paragraph to the end of the second, and footnote reference number 6 from its present place at the end of section d to the end of section e to replace number 7.*

Chapter 44, *page 267: insert footnote reference number 1 into line 11, after the words "throughout his stay." On pages 268–271 there is a mistake in the reference numbers: 3 appears twice, the second 3 should be changed to 4, 4 into 5, etc.*

Chapter 46, *page 285, insert the omitted reference number 3 at the end of section c.*

Chapter 54, *page 329, insert the missing reference number 4 to the end of section d; on page 330, change 4 into 5 and 5 into 6.*

Now to a much more serious matter. This is my final revision of chapter 1. (I finished the going-over of several more chapters, but I found that this one contains the most numerous differences between us. Once we straighten these out, the rest will be smooth sailing.) I am enclosing both your folio typescript and my retyped version. In order to prevent any possibility of misunderstanding, let me give herewith my reasons for each change:

On Page 1, *line 3, I changed "brooded" into "hovered," because the term used in the Hebrew original clearly means hovered, the same verb being used in* Deut. *xxxii. 11 where God is compared to "an eagle hovering over her young." (Reference to this will be made in chapter 2).*

On Page 2, *bottom: the name of the god is corrected according to the latest and the best reading.*

On Page 4, *the words "possibly of Edomite origin," are added on the basis of the very plausible theory of Professor Robert Pfeiffer.*

On Page 9, *section 15 has been omitted for the following reasons: In* Kings *vii .8 it is explicitly stated that the house of Pharaoh's daughter was built* for her *by Solomon: it is therefore very doubtful whether this building and the House of the Forest of Lebanon were Temple buildings. Even if they were, it remains doubtful that they were Temples of Anath and Asherah precisely, for why should a Temple of a* Canaanite *goddess be named after an Egyptian princess? The Elephantine documents, it is true, mention Anath-Bethel and Asham-Bethel, but the tributes paid to these deities were* smaller *than those paid to Yahu (I checked the original text). Asham-Bethel is by all scholars taken to refer to a* Male *deity not a goddess. Moreover, it is probable that these two gods were not venerated by the Jews of Elephantine, but by the non-Jewish population of the island. More importantly, however, I strongly feel that this whole argument is not really relevant to chapter 1. We are here discussing the Creation story and not goddesses who probably were worshipped by the Jews in Jerusalem or in Elephantine. The point that goddesses were worshipped by the Hebrews down to 586* B.C.*, is made with sufficient clarity in the preceding section 14.*

In section 16, (which now becomes 15,) I changed the names of the goddesses to Astarte and Asherah, because these two are the ones singled out repeatedly in prophetic reproaches, and the name Anath does not appear at all in the Bible.

On Page 11, I erased seven lines because I was unable to trace their source; because the consensus of scholarly opinion sees no connection between Yahweh *and* Ia-hu; *and because, again, the argument is irrelevant to the discussion of the Creation. Pp. 12–13 I erased because of the same reason, and because we have ample opportunity elsewhere to refer to the Ugaritic myth mentioned here.*

A final point: the name of the goddess is Anath, *and not Anatha; on this all authorities are unanimously agreed.*

I regret very much that I have to insist on these surgical steps in connection with this chapter. However, I feel that both of us should have the right to veto: I acquiesced in the omission by you of passages of considerable length, and I hope that you, too, will accept these omissions which I feel are necessary. As I mentioned above, in the subsequent chapters the changes will be minimal.

Both Ann and I just read your Oxford lectures and enjoyed them immensely. My next letter will go to you in Oxford.

> *Love to you both*
> *Raphael*

This was the strongest and most censorious of all the letters I wrote to Graves, and I was somewhat apprehensive as I waited for his answer. It was quick in coming, and although it betrayed some irritation with my insistence on the excisions, Graves accepted my corrections graciously.

301

Sept 23 1962

Dear Raphael:

All right: I play fair, as you have done, and agree to the excisions in Chapter One. Actually the account at Elephantine was $12^k 6^s$ for Jahveh as against 12^k & $7^k 2^s$ for the girls—$19^k.2$ = to $12^k.6^s$—but indeed, some say "Ishum Bethel" was a boy! Nonsense! And Jeremiah was a queer man to collect for Jehovah and the other deities. I must reject the exclusion of the argument about the Temple complex. Pharaoh's Daughter for me means the Goddess of Pharos, who was patroness of the Minoan confederacy based on the huge port there. But O.K. What the hell!

Karl is putting the references straight & I'm sending the early chapters to London for Encounter *to choose what they like to print serially.*

Am off on Oct 1st—address c/o A. P. Watt 10 Norfolk St Strand, London W.C. 2 until I have a better one.

Hope Introduction *is O.K. or thereabouts. Enclosed rewriting of that Abram paragraph—merely a matter of style, not sense.*

All the best
Robert

This looks like a happy ending: no arguments ever.

Just got the second lot of references. May I exercise my veto on the iron citadel of Keturah's sons? it is ungeographical and unmythical in our sense, just an itsy bit of midrashic fancy.

The mysterious numbers in the first few lines of this letter refer to the amounts donated to the three deities worshipped at Elephantine in the year 419 or 400 B.C.E. The relevant passage of a letter written by a temple official states that Yedoniah (Graves wrote "Jeremiah' in error for "Yedoniah"), the son of Gemariah, priest and head of the Jewish military colony at Elephantine, a Nile island in Upper Egypt, had the following amount in "cash on hand;" a total of 31 *karash*, 8 *shekels* (1 *karash* equaled 20 [light] *shekels*), which comprised: "for Yaho 12 k., 6 sh.; for Ishumbethel, 7 k.; for Anathbethel, 12 k." Despite Graves's assertion, Ishumbethel was a male deity; Anathbethel, of course, was female. The monies were donated by 123 contributors of both sexes. Evidently, most of the money was given to Yaho (=Yahweh); almost as much to Anathbethel; and considerably less to Ishumbethel. Most scholars answer the question of how Jews could make donations to two pagan deities in addition to Yahweh by maintaining that they did not: the monies for the other two deities were contributed by non-Jews and handled by Yedoniah in his capacity as treasurer or banker for all the Aramaeans in Elephantine. These considerations make it unlikely that Graves was correct in his argument about the deities Ishumbethel and Anathbethel.

In any case, once he accepted my emendations and excisions, there was no point in carrying on the argument. So this is what I answered him by return mail:

September 27, 1962

Dear Robert:

Thank you for your letter of September 23. I am glad that you accept my excisions in Chapter I. I was somewhat worried on this count, but I see that it was groundless. We shall always be able to come to an understanding whatever the differences in our original approach to a problem.

I shall be glad to see some of the early chapters published in Encounter. *However, so as not to let any error slip in, I would like them to use the final MS, that is the one which emerges after I have a chance to comment on the typescript which you recently sent me.*

I am working hard on ironing out the last questions raised by this version. I can send you today my comments to chapters 2–8 inclusive and hope to be able to send the rest very soon.

When reading my emendations, please do not think that I am a stickler for detail. The procedure I adopted in general was that wherever you included a statement without giving a source reference for it, I tried to locate the source. In most cases I was successful in doing so and I left the statement standing. In a few cases however, I was unable to locate the basis for a statement, and since I have here, in the New York Public Library, the best collection of books, articles, etc. available, I assumed in these cases that somehow an error slipped in among your notes, and therefore, I either excised the statement or changed it so as to conform with the sources I was able to consult. I should like therefore to ask you to accept these few omissions and emendations.

I had my comments to each chapter typed on a separate page to facilitate their use. In a few cases it seemed simpler to have an entire section or even a page retyped. In such cases the retyped parts are appended to my comments on the chapter.

I feel that this work should have preference before the Introduction. So I want to finish this first and then get to the Introduction, which will be a simple matter.

Love to you both
Raphael

Four days later I sent off another epistle, addressing it c/o A. P. Watt in London.

October 1, 1962

Dear Robert:

I am by now almost finished with the last checking of the MS, but I find a number of statements for which I am unable to locate any source or basis. I hope you won't mind if I raise a number of questions which you may be able to answer from memory, whereas I would have to spend many days searching for the answer and may still not find it.

On page 69, section 7, you state "and it [the superior posture] occurs in early Sumerian representations of the sexual act, though not in the Hittite." Could you tell me on what source this statement is based?

On page 136, second paragraph from the bottom, you say that an element in the flood story was the autumnal new year vintage feast of Babylonia, Syria and Palestine, where the ark was a crescent-shaped moon-ship containing sacrificial animals. What is the basis of this statement? Would you remember in what book did you see pictures of such Babylonian, Syrian and Palestinian crescent-shaped moon-ships containing sacrificial animals?

On same page, bottom, you say that a "strange ark-like rock structure on Ararat—Mt. Judi near Lake Van—recently investigated by American archeologists." Same question: what is the source of this statement?

On page 139, section 11, I do not understand the last sentence: "The belief that broken glass, is an ostrich's sole food, rather than a convenience for dealing with the contents of its crop . . . " *What do the underlined words mean?*

On page 211, end of section 6, you say that "sexual orgies in honor of Jus, a pre-Islamic love-goddess, are still celebrated on the Yemen border." Please supply the source for this statement. Jus must be a Latin attempt to transcribe the original form of the goddess's name. I cannot find any trace of such a pre-Islamic goddess. Is this perhaps taken from a modern traveler's account?

On page 273, who was David of Edessa? When did he live and what is the title of his book which mentions the oracular use of mummified human heads? And what is the title of Chwolson's collection of tales where reference is made to the same custom?

Page 289, section 5, what is the source of the statement that the Hebrew method of planting asphodel roots along boundaries is traditionally ascribed to the time of Joshua?

On Page 297, what is the source of the reference to the Arab human sacrifice, called nahia? I just found this, in Robertson Smith, Rel. of the Semites. It is naciᶜa.

Page 313, section 3, you say that Reu was a well-known Mesopotamian god. I checked Jastrow's standard 3-volume book on the religion of Babylonia and Assyria and found no trace of a god by this name. What is your source?

Page 319, what is the source of the statement that Apollo of Delos was the son of Lat? How can a Greek god be regarded as the son of a pre-Islamic Arab goddess?

Let me repeat that I am reluctant to have to trouble you with these questions. Believe me, I have spent several days in the Oriental Division of the New York Public Library, which is one of the best collections in the world on this subject, looking up all possible references, and checking hundreds of statements of this sort contained in the comments added by you. In most cases, I was able to find the sources and leave the statements unchanged. In a few, I felt constrained to introduce some corrections, part of which you find on enclosed pages (others will follow soon). In a few cases, however, I was completely stymied which left me no choice but to write to you for help. This is what I have done above.

Love to you both
Raphael

Eight days later I found it necessary to write again.

October 9, 1962

Dear Robert:

In order to expedite the completion of our MS, I put aside everything else and devoted the last weeks exclusively to checking and rechecking every questionable detail in it. My comments are contained in the enclosed bulky pages which, I hope, are clear enough to enable you to insert them or the corrections indicated by them into the text.

All that remains now is the Introduction on which I am working at present. My comments and additions will be sent to you within a week or so.

I have just talked with Ken McCormick and the magazine man of Doubleday's, John Mong. They would like to offer some of the chapters of the book to a magazine here, such as Harpers *or* Atlantic *for publication prior to the appearance of the book. In order to be able to do so, they want to know which chapters will be published in London in* Encounter. *You will probably hear from them directly but since I am interested in this anyway, would you let me know which chapters will appear in* Encounter?

Another matter: while Ken McCormick carefully refrained from saying that he would like to have the MS at an early date, he did say that if they received the MS by the first of November, they would schedule it for summer 1963 publication—the summer appears to be, on the basis of Doubleday's recent experience, a particularly good time for publication.

One more word: I cannot suppress a certain feeling of apprehension, lest you be annoyed by the amount of minor changes contained in enclosed pages. All I can say is that I feel most keenly that we have to do our best to make this book as perfect as possible. And I feel I would not do my share, if out of consideration for you, I would refrain from suggesting even a single correction.

Yours as ever
Raphael

My next letter followed two weeks later.

305

October 24, 1962

Dear Robert:

I am enclosing a copy of the Introduction. As you will see all I did was to add two sections to it which I marked by a horizontal line on the left hand margin.

The first addition (pp. i–iv) deals with the lost ancient Jewish literature which must have been a rich repository of myths, and with the relative lack of restraint with regard to mythical material in the post-Biblical Jewish literature.

The second addition (pp. xii–xiii) deals with the problem of the negation of time which, I believe, is a very important factor in Hebrew mythology and should therefore be pointed out. I also added the names of two people to whom I owe thanks because of bibliographical help. I hope you won't object to all this.

I hope you received my two previous letters which I addressed c/o Watt and Son and that before long I shall get from you your reaction to the comments to the chapters which were attached to those two letters.

You should also be in possession of a letter written to you by Doubleday inquiring about the chapters which will be published in Encounter. *As they explained to me they want to know this in connection with their plan to have some of the chapters published in a magazine here.*

Yours as ever
Raphael

Graves's reply to the four foregoing letters came from London.

39 Montagu Sq
London W. 1
Oct 31 1962

Dear Raphael:

I have just sent you back by air your comments with my replies, also my Cassell copy. I have accepted almost all your amendments, though sometimes altering the English. All three are now incorporated in the Cassell copy which please return when you have corrected the Doubleday copy with it. Have been very hard at work & no Karl beside me.

It has been difficult, being away from my books, but you can rely on all the source material you question, except where I agree (after e.g. looking up Reu) *that it isn't good enough, or accept your doubts on faith.*

Joshua Podro is very ill indeed or he'd have helped me.

I believe, however, that some explanation should be offered as a speculation wherever possible for mythological cruces: even if not insisted upon. I happen to have studied the royal lameness at length for some years, & hope you can include my material in its modified form. In some places I can see that you were hurried and working against time.

I await your comments on the Introduction.

The Encounter *editors, both of them, are off to foreign parts without taking any decision—characteristic of those sons of apes. So try to place what you can in the U.S.A.*

Desperately busy.

Love to you both. I don't think that any outstanding disagreement still exists between us. The facts *are what makes us form judgements; & they aren't hard to establish.*

Yours ever

Robert

Graves's replies to my comments and his "Cassell copy" of the typescript mentioned in the first sentence of this letter reached me on Wednesday, October 31. Regrettably, both the replies and the typescript are lost. I acknowledged their receipt on November 2.

Dear Robert:

Your letter and the MS reached me Wednesday morning and since then I have done nothing else but worked on it. I have not even slept but spent the last two nights struggling in order to reconcile the few remaining differences. In general, I am very *happy with the book as it now stands, and in the cases where you objected to the changes suggested by me, I was able mostly to accept your arguments. There are now in the whole MS not more than some half-dozen cases where I was simply unable to follow you. I have explained each of these on the pages containing your remarks which I inserted next to the pages to which they pertain. It was in these cases that I most keenly felt the drawback of having to work with you at such a distance. I believe that if we had a chance to sit down and argue out the differences, we could reach an agreement easily and quickly. As matters stand however, all I can do is to ask you to consider that in every case my objection is directed to hypothetical points and that their omission will not detract from the value of the book as a whole, while their retention might expose us to justified scholarly criticism. I would certainly not insist on the excision of anything unless I felt very strongly that its retention would be wrong.*

I greatly hope you will see my point and that we shall not have to get embroiled in protracted arguments at this late stage. My hope is that you will be able to glance through the MS and then, after possibly suggesting stylistic changes, give me the go-ahead signal to deliver the MS to Doubleday's who are quite impatiently waiting for it.

307

I hope you received the Introduction which I returned to you a few days ago. I liked very much what you wrote and added only two sections of what I believe is interesting material.

Yours as ever
Raphael

A few days later Graves sent me the corrected version of the introduction. In my response, dated November 8, I referred to it as the "foreword."

Dear Robert:

Thank you for the corrected and amplified version of the Foreword *which I am returning to you herewith. The only change I introduced was the addition of a few words at the bottom of page 2 and on page 5. I hope you will accept these minor points. I think that the* Foreword *as it now stands is excellent and I am grateful to you for having insisted on a short statement instead of the lengthy* Introduction *I originally intended for the book.*

I am also enclosing a list of "Abbreviations, Sources, and Annotated Bibliography." Since we intend this book to be read by many general readers rather than by a few scholars, I think that an explanation of the sources quoted is essential. I therefore made a brief statement of the date and origin of each of the Jewish sources quoted, as well as more briefly listed also the other, non-Jewish, sources. Printed in small type, all these should not take up more than perhaps ten pages which should come at the end of the book but before the index.

In connection with this list I have one or two questions:

On page 20, bottom, I was unable so far to find anything about the Tanis Papyrus. *Perhaps you could ask somebody to trace it for you in the British Museum Library so that we could have a complete bibliographical reference to it.*

On page 21, I left unfinished the entry referring to the book by Mgr. Terhoorst. *In the catalog of the New York Public Library no such name appears. Could you, again with the help of somebody in the British Museum, give me the bibliographical data of this book to which you refer in the text?*

Apart from the above everything seems to be fine and we seem indeed to be nearing the end of our labors on this book. I only hope that we will be able to overcome the last remaining differences between us which are now in your hands together with the entire MS which I returned to you on November 2nd by Registered ship mail, *addressed c/o A. P. Watt.*

Love to you all
Raphael

A few days later I had to write him again.

November 13, 1962

Dear Robert:

In my letter of November 8th I listed two questions in connection with the Bibliography. I found the answer to one of them. Please paste in the enclosed slip on page 20 bottom.

I am expecting to hear from you soon.

Yours as ever

Raphael

The bibliography I mention appeared in the *Hebrew Myths* under the title "Abbreviations, Sources and Annotated Bibliography." It stands exactly as I compiled it, but it turned out to take up more than thirteen closely printed pages, not ten as I had estimated. Graves's reply, dated November 17, was detailed and contained his reaction to each of my suggestions, almost all of which he accepted.

My dear Raphael: thanks a lot. I think that all's well now.

Chap. 23. section 2. I accept your version but please let it end is indicated. . . . *by a ten-fold, hundred-fold, or thousand fold multiplication of their reigns or ages.*

Section 6. omit and *in 3rd line from bottom.*

Chapter 27. Section 4 five from end should read "castration and consequent supersession as God's priest."

Please insert in Section 9, line 7 after together: *"It should be observed that the numerical equivalents of the letters in ELIEZER add up to 318". Whether this is accidental or not, the Midrash records it.*

Last line of 10. "a neighbouring hill" not "a hill near Hebron."

Chapter 30. Section 2. Last sentence should read

An increasing number of scholars, however, incline to the view that the 1200 B.C. Philistine invasion was not the first (just as Joshua's was only the concluding phase of a protracted process of Hebrew immigration into Canaan) and that some Philistines may well have been established in Gerar by 1500 B.C.

Section 3. Line 3 omit Aegean *(which is not a 'sphere')*

Top of p 200. read

. . . . coast is the location in Caphtor of Kothar-wa-Khasis's workshop. He was the divine craftsman of 14th century B.C. Ugaritic mythology, known to the Greeks as Daedalus.

line 4. for their warriors with *read them wearing*

Chapter 32. Please keep the Jus *reference in Section 6. I will append my testimony before closing this letter. [The foregoing sentence is struck, and the following added:] All right: leave it out. 'Jus' is a conceptual conflation, used*

309

down in Yemen of the spirit of the goddesses Maanat, Lat & Uzza, who are regarded as idols.

Chapter 35. Section 3. line 5. for "names of individuals" read "personal names"

I have left 294ff to the last

You will see that I have met all your main objections remembering that you are more vulnerable than I am—in your position of trust with the Institute—and that you have been very generous to me.

Have pasted in the Tanis *papyrus reference. The Terhoorst can wait for the proofs or simply be omitted.*

Yours ever

Robert

p 294 line 1. sentence should end:
or occupies a new country.

line 3 remove end of sentence from because *to* junctures

lines 6–8 should read: position: hitherto he had been a hired servant of Laban, his father-in-law; now he was an independent chieftain, ready to enter etc.

line 9. for secure in his trust in the etc *read* secure in a parental blessing & a divine promise

Remove last sentence of para with which I disagree.

Section 7: after line 7 add: like that attributed by Homer to the God Hephaestus

line 9. omit perhaps connected with this belief or a similar one which is reflected in the Peniel myth was *and replace by* perhaps a memory of the limping *The text should then continue:* performed by devotees who believed themselves possessed by a god, like the prophets of Baal on Mount Carmel etc.

Last two lines should read: near Jericho may have been so called for this reason, *because*

p 295 line 1. after hop *read:* and both Jerome and Eusebius call Beth Hoglah, 'the place of the ring-dance', The Tyrians performed such limping dances in honour of Hercules Melkarth. It is possible therefore that the Peniel myth originally *accounted for a limping* ceremony that commemorated Jacob's triumphal entry into Canaan after wrestling with a rival.

p 296 line 2.

Add after: the Rachel tribes:
that were to be

line 3 should read: account of a struggle for supremacy over tribal territories

Introduction

ii/ last line but one, for
originally *read* once

310

III top line: for confederacy *read* federation
Insert at p 6 line 5:— remove the *before* Astartes
and before Anaths;
for as far as *read* so far as
para 2 line 2 should read mention even of human sacrifice

FINIS

Received your typescript only yesterday: you should have airmailed it, as I did; but I guess its O.K.

Only a very few comments are required to clarify some of the points made by Graves in this letter.

In stating that "the numerical equivalents of the letters in ELIEZER add up to 318," Graves moved into the orbit of the traditional Jewish *gematria,* the method of adding up the numerical values of the letters in a word and either equating that word with another whose letters give the same total, or inferring some other connection between the two words. In the Hebrew alphabet each letter stands for a number: *aleph* = one, *beth* = two, etc.; *yod* = ten, *kaf* = twenty, etc., *qof* = one hundred, *resh* = two hundred, *shin* = three hundred, and *tav* = four hundred. The Hebrew spelling of "Eliezer" is ʾLYʿZR (the first letter of the Hebrew alphabet, *aleph,* is transliterated as ʾ, the letter ʿayin as ʿ: the six letters of ʾLYʿZR have the numercial values of 1, 30, 10, 70, 7, and 200, for a total of 318. This, in the *gematria* system, became the basis of the Midrash, according to which Eliezer himself was the equivalent of the 318 men who constituted the retinue of Abraham (see *Hebrew Myths* 27.9).

When Graves says that Kothar wa-Khasis was the divine craftsman of fourteenth-century B.C.E. Ugaritic mythology "known to the Greeks as Daedalus" (*HM* 30.3), this is his terse formulation of the idea that Kothar wa-Khasis was the divine craftsman in Ugaritic mythology whose *equivalent* in Greek myths was the craftsman Daedalus.

As for *Jus,* the mention of which was deleted with Graves's consent, a quick check I made in the *Encyclopaedia of Islam* did not disclose any reference to such a pagan goddess in pre-Islamic Arabia.

The *Tanis Papyrus* is mentioned in *HM* 14.1. "Terhoorst" was deleted.

The limping dance at Bet Hogla was dealt with above, in chapter 1 (Cf. *HM* 47.7.)

On November 27 I replied.

Dear Robert:

Let me thank you most heartily for your last letter and your generous acceptance of the last changes I suggested. I am really very glad that the book

311

is finally finished. I introduced all the corrections contained in your letter into my copy of the MS and then delivered it to Doubleday. Now it is up to them to set a publication date.

*It is my feeling that this book might sell quite well. I spent last week-end in St. Louis and appeared there on a radio program Saturday morning. After a ten minute interview, in which it was brought out that three of my books will be published shortly (*Hebrew Myths *and the two books on Women), questions were received from the audience by telephone which I was supposed to answer. The questions and the answers were broadcast. There was time for 12 questions. The first questioner asked why husbands so often lose interest in their wives. The second, mistaking me for an M.D., asked what to do about his persistent morning cough? The remaining 10 questions pertained all to the* Hebrew Myths. *This is definitely an indication of general interest in the subject.*

Incidentally, if in the near future the sales of your The Nazarene Gospel Restored *should increase in Catholic circles, don't be surprised. The purpose of my going to St. Louis was to conduct a seminar on Israel and Judaism under the auspices of St. Louis University and Webster College, two Catholic institutions. The audience consisted of about 50 nuns, all of whom were professors of history or social sciences in Catholic girls' colleges all over the country. In the course of the proceedings, the discussion inevitably touched upon the Jewish background of the New Testament, and since I saw that the Sisters were greatly interested in this issue, I dwelt upon it to some extent and suggested that they read* The Nazarene Gospel Restored *in order to get a complete picture of the dependence of the words and acts of Jesus on the Old Testament and on his Jewish environment.*

Love to you all
Raphael

PS: In your letter you said that a sentence in chapter 27, section 4, should read "Castration and consequent supersessions as God's priest . . ." I could not find the proper place for this sentence. In chapter 35, page 294, section 7, line 9; you said this should read: "perhaps a memory of the limping . . ." I think the context requires: "perhaps a memory of this belief was the limping dance . . ."

Graves's answer was late in coming, it was undated and it contained no reference to my queries.

Dear Raphael

Kenneth Parker of Cassell's is asking for the two maps we promised. One should be of the World of Genesis—*from Babylonia to Egypt, and down south to Arabia. The second of Palestine at the time of the patriarchs, including Damascus and the Dead Sea & Edom.*

Could you possibly see to this? It is your field rather than mine & you have better maps. And write to Kenneth Parker?

I airmailed you the first Encounter. *We get only 160 between us for the two issues; but it is very good propaganda, so I don't mind, & I hope you don't either. Nobody else would have paid more.*

I guess you're both pretty cold, but at least N.Y. is built for cold weather. England isn't. Nor is Majorca.

> *Yours ever*
> *Robert*

My next letter went out to Graves before I received the above.

> *February 5, 1963*

Dear Robert:

I am sending you this letter in two copies, one to Mallorca and one to London, because I do not know where it will reach you.

The immediate reason for my writing you today is to tell you about my gratification over the publication of the lengthy excerpt from our book in the February, 1963, issue of Encounter. *I tried to read the printed pages with as much detachment as possible, and I can say that they read extremely well. On the basis of this advance publication I hope that the book will sell well in England. How it will sell in the United States, I do not know. So far, Willis Wing has not been able to place any chapters in an American magazine for advance publication. But, he is still trying. However, it is my impression that he does not try too hard, and I do not know what to do in order to motivate him to a more active interest. Perhaps, if you would drop him a line and emphasize that you regard it as very important that one or two pieces from the book should be published in advance in an American magazine, this may impress him sufficiently to make a special effort.*

I noticed a few misprints in Encounter, *and therefore would like to have a chance to proofread the British as well as the American edition of the book. I hope that Cassell's printing schedule will permit them to send me the proofs which I shall return within two or three days.*

This is all for the moment. How are your plans for your visit to the United States coming along? Will you spend some time in New York? Don't forget that you and yours have a standing invitation to stay with us.

> *Love to both of you*
> *Raphael*

Two days later I wrote again.

February 7th, 1963

Dear Robert:

Your letter which I received today and mine which I wrote to you a few days ago dealt with the same subject: the forthcoming publication of the book and the chapters published in Encounter. *As far as the royalties for the latter are concerned, I agree with you that in view of the publicity value of this publication we must be satisfied with whatever royalties we can get.*

Now, as to the two maps: I shall be glad to prepare them. I shall do rough sketches of the two maps and send them to Doubleday who will give them to their Art Department to put them in final form. Then, a copy of the final two maps can be sent to Cassell, attention Kenneth Parker. I also want to tell you that, in reply to a letter I received recently from Cassell, I suggested to them that they use one of the pictures taken of the two of us in Ken McCormick's office. I also suggested that they use the picture of the base of the candelabrum on the Arch of Titus with the Dragons on it for the front of the jacket. I hope these suggestions meet with your approval.

Thank you very much for sending me a copy of Encounter. *As I told you in my previous letter, the pieces read extremely well. However, I missed the source references which they omitted. Without them, I must admit, I myself would not believe that all those things are actually contained in the Talmudic and Midrashic sources. I can well imagine the reaction of my (and possibly your) Conservative or Orthodox co-religionists!*

Yes, the weather has been miserable here and we were longing for the gentle clime of Mallorca. Today, for a change the thermometer hit 50°.

Yours ever
Raphael

And again five days later:

February 12, 1963

Dear Robert:

I am enclosing three maps I made. One and two would be printed on the front end papers and three could be placed over the two back end papers. The maps could also appear inside the book.

I am sending copies of the same maps to Ken McCormick with the same suggestions. If Cassell wishes to cooperate with Doubleday in producing the final shape of the maps, let them get in touch with Ken McCormick.

If you have any suggestions as to changes, omissions, or additions to any of these maps, please mark them and return them to me. If not, would you send the maps on directly to Cassell?

Yours ever
Raphael

Graves answered my February 7 letter on February 13.

Dear Raphael:

Thanks for your letter of Febr 7th. I'm glad of the maps: a great relief!

I've spurred Willis Wing to have some more chapters placed; but it will be difficult.

The Cassell *edition will be the master one:* Doubleday *will use photo-offset, I understand. So of course you* must *read the Cassell proofs, & then send them here: to be incorporated in one set. Karl & I are wizards at finding misprints. Fortunately, no rewriting necessary!*

I'll be in New York very briefly indeed, Boston being very adhesive. May 10th and 11th is the only time I'm sure of, & I have promised to stay with Gordon Wasson (my old mushroom-friend & banker) as before. But will surely see you!

> *Love to you both*
> *Robert*

Yes: without references, it's no use at all, I agree.

26.

Preparations for the
Y Lecture

AFTER RECEIVING GRAVES'S February 13 letter I took the initiative to arrange some public appearances for the two of us as advance publicity for the *Hebrew Myths.* On February 25 I called Channel 13 and suggested that they should have Graves and me in an interview program in May. Next day I called Dr. William Kolodney, director of education of the 92d Street Poetry Center of the YM-YWHA (Young Men's-Young Women's Hebrew Association), told him about our book and Graves's impending visit, and suggested that Kolodney schedule a discussion evening between us at his center. Kolodney liked the idea and said we should meet to discuss details. On February 28 we had lunch at the restaurant of the Metropolitan Museum of Art, at that time still a very pleasant eating place with the pool and water-sprouting statuary in the middle.

I thought I would make use of the opportunity of being at the "Met" to have a look at Leonardo's *Mona Lisa,* which was on loan from the Louvre. So I went to the museum an hour early, and gazed—for the fifth or sixth time in my life—at the famous enigmatic smile, after which I still had just enough time for a quick look at the Greek gallery, the great sixteenth-century Persian carpets, and Rembrandt's *"Artistotle Contemplating the Bust of Homer,"* which the "Met" had acquired shortly before for what was then a record sum.

At our lunch Kolodney and I worked out the details of the *Hebrew Myths* evening, set the tentative date for May 15, and agreed about the fee. I undertook to prepare a draft for the invitation which the Y would mail out to its members.

The same afternoon I wrote to Graves.

316

Feb. 28, 1963

Dear Robert:

I just had lunch with Dr. Kolodney, Director of the 92nd Street Young Men's Hebrew Association. He would like us (that is, you and me) to appear jointly at his institution to discuss The Hebrew Myths *on Wednesday, May 15th in the evening. Since the season is quite advanced, most of his budget is already exhausted and all that he can offer you is $200 plus round trip expenses from Boston. I told him that I myself shall be satisfied with a fee of $100, so as to make this event possible.*

I hope you will agree with me that such a discussion evening will generate considerable interest in the book, which, of course, will be of great importance for its success in this country, especially since it seems that Willis Wing is unable to place chapters from it for advance publication in an American magazine.

I would therefore like to ask you to accept this invitation if at all possible. Please let me know soon, so that I can report back to Dr. Kolodney.

What you write about reading of the proofs is fine with me. I can promise you and the publishers to return the proofs within 3 days.

> *Love to you all*
> *Raphael*

Graves answered by return mail.

March 4th 1963

Dear Raphael:

The 15th May was the day I intended to fly home; but this is a request I can't turn down. I don't see why you should get less than I do, however.

—Cassells are pleased with the maps.

—Very well, I'll fly back on the 16th.

—I hope you're good at answering questions; I'm not afraid of anyone but New York Jews have needle sharp minds.

> *Love to you both*
> *Robert*

After receiving Graves's letter, I sent a copy of it to Dr. Kolodney with the following note.

March 8, 1963

Dear Dr. Kolodney:

I am enclosing the correspondence between Robert Graves and myself, of which you wanted to have a copy. Although with this the matter is settled,

317

nevertheless I think that you might send him a note acknowledging the arrangements.

As I promised you, I shall have the text for the leaflet by Monday. It occurred to me that a picture showing Graves and myself engrossed in an animated discussion, might be used to illustrate the leaflet. Printing it offset would not add at all to the cost.

I am also enclosing six pictures from which you could choose one. However, I must ask you to return them all to me including the one which you select.

Yours sincerely
Raphael Patai

Kolodney introduced a few changes into my draft of the invitation, and had it printed as a four-page flyer with the picture of Graves and me on the front page. It was one of the photographs Leni Iselin took of us in Ken McCormick's office.

On March 12 I wrote to Graves.

Dear Robert:

I was very glad to have your consent for the joint appearance at the 92nd St. Y on May 15. I informed Dr. Kolodney and he too expressed his great satisfaction over this.

Although we have ample time to decide how we should organize the evening, I might as well jot down some ideas as to the subjects we could discuss. The following come to my mind:

What is Hebrew Mythology?
The Paradox of Mythology in a Monotheistic Religion.
How do Hebrew and Greek Myths differ?
How was Hebrew Myths *written?*
What were the main contributions of each author?
What were the areas of agreement and disagreement between them?
The Problem of a Hebrew Goddess.

I think the best way would be to talk to each other in an informal manner, as we did over two years ago in my home when we recorded our conversation. How do you feel about this?

You ask whether I am good at answering questions. I think I will be able to manage. Incidentally, I don't share your opinion about the "needle-sharp

318

ROBERT GRAVES and RAPHAEL PATAI

will discuss

"THE HEBREW MYTHS"
the subject of their forthcoming book

Wednesday, May 15, 1963, at 8:30 o'clock

$1.50

The Poetry Center, YM-YWHA, 92nd Street and Lexington Avenue,
New York 28, New York   ATwater 9-2400

**First page of the announcement of the joint lecture by Robert Graves and Raphael
Patai at the 92nd Street Y. (Photo courtesy of Leni Iselin.)**

*minds" of the New York Jews. My experience with question and answer pe-
riods following lectures is that the majority of the questions betray dullness
rather than sharpness.*

*In any case, I know that I shall enjoy immensely such a "public" dialogue
with you.*

Love to you all
Raphael

Graves's answer again came by return mail.

March 17 1963

Dear Raphael:

*—The Y is rather a large hall for an informal discussion; but the audiences
are good. I think the fees they offer are pretty poor; but never mind! (When
Betty Kray was in charge we'd have got $300 each; but they foolishly quar-
relled with her)*

—I think your topics for discussion are all right.

*—And we ought to emphasize that the same distortion of history for ethical
reasons is found in Christian myth and myths of the American Revolution; as
in historical drama & historical films for dramatic reasons. I could enlarge on
these points.*

"Historical distortion in myth" could be a subject heading.

Yours ever
Robert

I'll be at 1 East End Av. with Gordon Wasson.

Even before receiving this letter I wrote again to Graves to invite him to a
cocktail party Ann and I wanted to give in his honor.

March 19, 1963

Dear Robert:

*Ann and I would like to give a cocktail party for you in our home on the
occasion of your visit to New York. You wrote to me that you plan to be in New
York on May 11th, Saturday. Would 5:30 on that day be convenient? I would
come and pick you up wherever you will be at, say, 4:30 P.M., drive you out
to our house (30 minutes from Manhattan), and later drive you back. If May
11th is not convenient for you, would you tell me what other day would be?
(Preferably another weekend day.) We would be grateful if you would let
us know soon, because we would like to send out the invitations as soon
as possible.*

320

The May 15th discussion evening is all set. I expect quite a lot of people will attend. The lecture hall of the 92nd Street "Y" holds, I believe, 850 seats.

I just spoke to Ken McCormick. They are planning the publication of the book for November. They want me to prepare the index, which I shall be glad to do. They decided, incidentally; to typeset the book here, because it is cheaper than in England. Incredible! Cassell will offset it from the Doubleday type, presumably after introducing the required changes to conform to the British spelling.

I also spoke to Willis Wing's office about magazine publication of chapters. They told me that the MS is now in the hands of Show *magazine; then it will go to* Horizon. *I cannot escape the impression that Wing handles this matter somewhat negligently.*

Love to you all
Raphael

Graves answered by return mail.

March 22 [1963]

Dear Raphael & Ann:

On May 11th I'll be at Washington. I hate cocktail parties, if only because I don't like cocktails and don't drink except at meals; and don't really get to know anyone at cocktail parties before he or she is whisked away. But if my presence at one in your house will be of any use, sure I'll come & behave properly. Say Sunday the 12th at 5:30 P.M. Really I'd much rather have a quiet time with my friends Raphael & Ann. I'll be pretty tired by Boston & Washington. But I'm at your disposal.

I'm glad Doubleday will do the printing: far more accurate than Cassell's. But Cassell's have the cleanest copy & Doubleday should use it. Willis Wing is far from negligent: he knows markets well; but if you can help him with this problem, please do.

How good of you to undertake the Index.

Yours ever
Robert

Am Haseffer of Tel Aviv *want to publish the* Hebrew Myths. *I am referring them to Watt who will send you a copy of the letter.*

Attached to this Graves forwarded to me a letter he had received from the Israeli publishers ʿAm waSefer expressing interest in publishing a Hebrew translation of the *Hebrew Myths*. I thereupon wrote to Aharon Amir of ʿAm waSefer, telling him that when the original edition came out I would send him a copy, and thereafter we could discuss conditions. At the urgent request of

321

Amir I mailed him a copy of the manuscript on April 24. Ultimately, however, 'Am waSefer withdrew, and Massadah published the Hebrew edition.

My response to Graves's March 22 letter was tardy.

April 11, 1963

Dear Robert:

Both Ann and I appreciate that you are willing to accept our invitation, in spite of your general dislike of cocktail parties. We promise to try to make it as painless for you as possible. In fact, we hope that you will definitely enjoy to meet at least some of the people invited. Moreover, whenever you will indicate to me that you had enough, I shall whisk you away, to whatever place you wish to go. So—we will see you on Sunday, May 12. I shall call you at Wasson's about lunchtime, to find out what time you want me to pick you up.

The discussion evening at the 92nd Street "Y" is all set. In whatever form you want to conduct the discussion will be all right with me. Perhaps it would be advisable for us to meet a little in advance of the time, say in the afternoon of May 15, and settle some of the details. In any case, the subject you suggested, "Historical distortion in myth," will be included among the other topics we shall discuss.

The enclosed letter will interest you. I am not convinced by Prof. Janson's argument, because I don't think that one can draw a sharp line between a Lamia-nightmare and other types of erotic dreams. A Lamia nightmare would not be devoid of pleasurable aspects, while a dream of a "symplegma" with a siren would have nightmarish, frightening aspects as well. However, I shall postpone my reply to Janson until I have your reaction.

Love to you all
Raphael

The art historian Horst Woldemar Janson was chairman of the department of fine arts at New York University and the author of the classic *History of Art*, among many other books. His letter to me read as follows:

New York University
Washington Square College
of Arts and Science
Washington Square, New York 3, N.Y.
Department of Fine Arts
Area Code 212 SP 7–2000
April 6, 1963

Dear Dr. Patai,

Some weeks ago, I wrote to you for information about a Hellenistic relief showing a Lamia-Nightmare, which was referred to in the first of the two ar-

*ticles by Robert Graves and yourself in ENCOUNTER. You were kind enough
to inform me that the work in question is reproduced in Erich Neumann's THE
GREAT MOTHER.*

*With that as my starting point, I have looked further into the problem of this
puzzling relief, and I thought you might be interested in what I have found out.*

Neumann's plate is taken from an older publication, Schreiber's Hellenis-
tische Reliefbilder *of 1890; it shows a drawing after the relief, not a photo.
Unlike my archaeological colleagues, I always distrust such drawings, so I
tried very hard to locate the relief itself. As luck would have it, the panel
turned up very recently, after being hidden in private collections for many
years, and was bought by the Boston Museum, which provided me with a
photo. It turns out that the draughtsman who copied the panel for Schreiber
suppressed one important detail, which is clearly visible in the photo: the
sleeping man's phallus. The scene, in other words, is not a nightmare but a
symplegma of a siren and a Bacchanalian celebrant—a mythological event
that happens to be unrecorded in classical literature. This conclusion is further borne out by a second relief of the same scene, found a few years ago in
Beghram, Afghanistan and now in the Museum at Kaboul. Here the composition is inscribed in a roundel, and is somewhat earlier in date than the Boston relief. Also, it is complete, while in the Boston relief the upper left corner
is missing. In the latter area, as the Beghram roundel clearly shows, there
must have been a Cupid—hardly a figure one would expect to assist at a nightmare. This was pointed out in the 2nd volume of the Beghram excavations, by
Hackin, which has a commentary on some of the finds by Otto Kurz of the
Warburg Institute, London.*

*I am afraid, therefore, we must relinquish the Lamia-nightmare interpre-
tation of the scene.*

With kindest regards
H. W. Janson

As I wrote to Graves, I was not convinced by Prof. Janson's argument, but
thought it would be impolite to leave his letter unanswered for more than a
month. So I replied on April 19.

Dear Professor Janson:

*I forwarded a copy of your letter of April 6 to Robert Graves who sent me
the enclosed answer.*

*I, on my part would like to add that the original presence of the phallus in
the relief does, to my mind not prove that the scene is not a nightmare but a
"symplegma" of a siren and the Bacchanalian celebrant. The position of the
reclining body of the man is clearly that of a sleeper. If so, the scene probably
shows what the man experiences or sees in his sleep. What he dreams is that*

323

a non-human female has coitus with him in a superimposed position. This is precisely the position in which the Lamiae were supposed to seduce sleeping men.

As to the figure of a Cupid—from what you say it seems that it is not clear whether such a figure actually appeared in the upper left corner of the Beghram roundel.

But even if there is a Cupid there, I agree with Graves interpretation which reconciles it with the Lamia nightmare view of the relief.

> *Yours sincerely*
> *Raphael Patai*

Graves's view of the subject was expressed as follows:

Easter Monday [April 15] 1963

Dear Raphael

It was always obvious to me from the sketchiness of the treatment in the plate that the recumbent bloke had a phallus. The children of Lamia who used to seduce weary travellers by the roadside were called the Empousae *('forcers-in.') and you need a phallus for the process; but Miss Jane Harrison was a Victorian, and left this to the imagination of her readers. Cupido, or Eros, was the natural character to appear at this 'symlegma', not yet having attained the arch-sentimentality of the Lace-Valentine period, but signifying simply sexual desire. He would have assisted unblushingly at the Pasiphae-Bull 'symplegma'. The Lamiae destroyed children exactly as Lilith did, as well.*

Why should a Siren (usually bird-headed, and a death figure) seduce a Bacchanal? That the liason happens to be unrecorded in Classical literature does not surprise me. Nor is the figure a Bacchanal.

Yes: we should meet in advance of the time to marshal our forces for the night of the 15th.

And we'll contact each other about the May 12th party. I'd like to see Norman Podhoretz again. And do you know Jason Epstein and his wife?

> *Yours ever*
> *Love to Ann*
> *Robert*

What are your phone numbers?

I believe that Graves's reference to Jane Harrison as "a Victorian," with the implied reproach, was not quite justified. Only recently, while working on the present book, I fell into the habit of reading as a bedtime relaxation studies of ancient Greek religion. Among these studies was Jane Harrison's classic *Prolegomena to the Study of Greek Religion,* in which I came across a reproduction of the Lamia-Nightmare relief (p. 203). It is a line drawing, it too lacks the phallus of the sleeping man. Jane Harrison describes the scene as follows: "Some peasant or possibly a wayfarer has fallen asleep. Down upon him has pounced a winged and bird-footed woman. It is the very image of obsession, of nightmare, of a haunting midday dream. The woman can be none other than an evil Siren." When working on the *Hebrew Myths* I had not remembered this passage. It gives me some satisfaction to find now, years later, that Jane Harrison's interpretation of the relief closely paralleled mine.

Even before receiving Graves's letter of April 15 I had reason to write again.

April 17, 1963

Dear Robert:

I just received a call from television channel 13 (the educational channel, which has most of the serious programs in this city and carries no "commercials" i.e. advertisements). They got wind of our discussion-evening at the 92nd Street "Y" and would like us to appear on their program a short time, some two or three weeks, thereafter. I told them that you won't be here that long, and they suggested that a conversation between us should be taped in advance in their studio for broadcasting at a later date. In the hope that this will be agreeable to you, they reserved studio time for us on Monday, May 13, from 7:30 to 9:30 in the evening. The program will take at least 30 minutes, at most 60, with 45 minutes the preferred length. No third person would appear on it, only you and I, chatting informally on all or some of the subjects we agreed upon for our May 15th discussion evening. Such a TV appearance would be excellent publicity for the book; in fact the channel plans to rebroadcast it in November, immediately following the publication date of the book.

I told them I would write to you and ask you whether you are willing. Please let me have your answer as soon as possible.

Love to all of you
Raphael

This letter reached Graves in the astonishingly short time of two days. He replied immediately.

Ap 19th 1963

Dear Raphael:

Sorry: but I have to be at M.I.T. on the 13th: the President has a party or something for me that evening. (The May 15th date involves me already in staying longer than I intended.) and on the 14th I give the 'Little' Lecture for which I'm hired. I'm very sorry but that's how it is. No way out.

Not for publication. *I have just had to decline the Charles Eliot Norton professorship at Harvard (24 000 bucks for six months) because it conflicts with my job at Oxford, for which I get 240 bucks annually when tax & fares have been cleared.*

Yours ever
Robert

Thank Ann for her letter
I have no names to add to the list

I have no copy of Ann's letter mentioned by Graves. The list Graves mentions must be a reference to a list of the guests I planned to invite to the May 12 cocktail party in his honor. I replied:

April 23, 1963

Dear Robert:

I told Channel 13 the sad news that you are busy at the time they suggested for taping the discussion between us. They were extremely sorry, and asked me to return to you with the following suggestion: Let me know whether there is any time *during your stay in this country when you could drop in at their midtown studio for the taping (I shall free myself at whatever time suits you)—and they will try to make studio-time available, if at all possible.*

Please don't misunderstand: I am not trying to persuade you in any way; I am simply transmitting the TV station's request.

Too bad about the conflict between Oxford and Harvard! Would no compromise between the two be possible? The fee they offer you at Harvard is extraordinary even for this country and even for Harvard. Not to mention the contribution you would make to raising the status of poetry and of the humanities in general at Harvard!

My phone numbers are: office: PL 2–1234. Home: BO 1–4259. Please call me when you arrive. Or, if you let me know in advance, I shall be glad to fetch you from the airport.

Yours
Raphael

The three weeks prior to our lecture happened to be a hectic time as well as a time of anxiety and troubles in my private life. On April 27, 1963, my brother Saul arrived from Jerusalem on his first visit to America, and I was busy showing him around and going with him to his publisher, John Wiley, for

*whom he was editing a huge series of books titled The Chemistry of Func-
tional Groups.* (As he only recently told me, this series filled by now a shelf
space of more than ten running feet!) On May 2 Saul got a letter from his wife
Lisl, informing him that her father had died of a heart attack. Next day my
wife Ann was told by her doctor that he had found a lump in her breast which
would have to be removed as soon as possible, and that only in the course of
the biopsy would they know whether it was benign or not, and accordingly
whether a mastectomy would be necessary.

Despite this cloud hanging over our heads, our social life and my professional activities had to continue, and on the afternoon of May 12 we had, as
planned, our cocktail party for Graves. As I offered in my letter, I drove in to
fetch him from the Wassons' apartment at 1 East End Ave., and after the
party (at about 7:30) I drove him back, taking along also Prof. and Mrs.
Moses Hadas of Columbia University, my daughter Jennifer, and my brother
Saul. We had some fifty guests at the party: professors, scholars, editors,
writers, poets, artists, lawyers, bankers, etc., and the crowd spilled over into
the garden in front of our ground-floor living room. (I took some pictures, but
they did not come out too well. One of the pictures taken by my brother
Saul—a better photographer than I—is shown here.) Graves was, of course,
right: he had no chance of really getting to know anyone. However, the party
was, as they say, "a success," and the guests were pleased and honored to
meet the famous author.

I admired Ann: she was the perfect hostess, although next day she was
scheduled to enter the hospital for breast surgery. We had a caterer taking care
of the food and drinks, but it was Ann who made sure everything went without a hitch, and no guest was left standing alone even for a minute.

Next morning I drove Ann to the Hillcrest General Hospital. The surgery
took place the following morning. I shall never forget the anxious, fear-filled
hours I spent in the waiting room and corridors of the hospital, until finally
the doctor came out to tell me that no malignancy had been found. Ann was
pale, her face drawn, but she said she felt okay. She had to stay in the hospital
for another three days; every day I visited her and sat at her bedside for an
hour or so.

Ann was still in the hospital when the Graves-Patai discussion took place
at the 92nd Street Y on May 15. I met Graves about an hour in advance in Dr.
Kolodney's office to straighten out some last-minute details, such as how to
handle the questions. Then, accompanied by Kolodney, we crossed the lobby
to enter the big Kaufmann Auditorium. As we neared the entrance door, a
woman who had been seated nearby stood up, approached us, said to Graves,
"I am Irene Patai," and went on to say that she wanted, even though belatedly, to thank him personally for the kind lines he had written about her novel.
Graves, always sensitive to feminine charm, reacted in a kind and friendly

327

Patai and Graves examining an antique at Patai's Forest Hills home. (Photo courtesy of Saul Patai.)

way—I remembered that he had once written me that he "liked Irene"—but time pressed, and we had to proceed to the auditorium.

The hall was crowded. As Graves and I came out on the stage, we were greeted by prolonged applause. We sat down on the two chairs set in the middle, and as I scanned the sea of faces, I saw, in the fifth or sixth row, Irene sitting between her parents. When the applause subsided, I stepped up to the lectern, and opened the proceedings.

The Discussion at the Y

T HE FOLLOWING IS a verbatim transcript of what Graves and I said about the Hebrew myths in our joint appearance at the 92d Street Y on May 15, 1963.

Patai: I am Raphael Patai. Let me tell you, first of all, the order of this evening. I will sit down in two minutes. Mr. Graves will come up here, and will read an introductory statement. After that we both will discuss a number of those questions which you saw in the published announcement. Then we will have a brief intermission. In the course of our discussion, if you have any questions, please jot them down on those little cards which you got as you entered. During the intermission those cards will be collected and passed on to us, and we will try to do our best to answer them—if not all of them, at least some of them.

And now I wish to introduce Mr. Graves. Introducing Robert Graves means to praise him. And there is a saying in the Talmud to the effect that *"omrim miqtzat shivḥo shel adam b'fanav,"* which, roughly, means, "One should not praise a man to his face more than a little." [laughter] Therefore, I will not praise him more than a little, will not tell you what the man Robert Graves is, what the name Robert Graves stands for. I will merely tell you that in the course of this collaboration beween him and myself I learned to appreciate two qualities in him. One, his extraordinary erudition. His erudition, I found again and again, is really remarkable. He is thoroughly at home in many literatures of ancient times, medieval times, and, unnecessary to say, modern times. Secondly, I found that he has, in scholarly matters—now, I am not talking about poetry—but in scholarly matters, a wonderful intuition. This intuition, which Professor Moses Hadas just a few days ago characterized as his "famous nose" . . . [laughter] Problems on which I worked for weeks and months and was unable to solve he, with his famous nose, just sniffed at them and found the solution. And this combination of erudition and intuition was invaluable for our collaboration, and, I am sure, its mark is felt in every line or every page of our book. Now, Robert! [prolonged applause]

Graves: It is very nice talking here today. It's the first place in New York I have talked. And Miss Betty Cranes, in charge then, had a ticklish job in deciding whether or not my presence would fill sufficient seats to bring back the necessary income for the Y. And, I am glad to say, she, they, pulled it off. [laughter] And I always feel at home here, especially as I am the only *goy* here among so many Israelites. Now, this is . . . I am in a very delicate position. Although I have Dr. Patai here to back me up with the authority of his position at the Theodor Herzl Institute, I feel rather awkward about talking to Jews about the Scriptures which are holy things to them. And, last year, I was invited by the Hillel Institute in London to talk on this sort of subject, and although I must say the audience was very warm, charmingly warm, yet the letters which afterwards appeared in the *Jewish Chronicle* [laughter] was so fierce [laughter] that I . . . The fact is, let's face it, that there are certain hard core of believers in the Bible, literal believers, who are as impossible to convince of the historical nature of the text as Roman Catholic priests are about the historical nature of Christian texts . . . And it's very difficult to know at what point one should be tender to them and say nothing. [laughter] And I sincerely hope that anybody who feels too strongly about what we are saying will just shut his ears, walk out, and forgive us. Because what we are doing is trying to show that Hebrew myth, although very different in its emphasis, does belong to the same general comity of nations, not only in the Middle East but actually in Greece and Egypt, which . . . This body of myth which is accepted without question as the basis of European education. The connection between Greek and Hebrew myth is far closer than it seems.

One thing more. How we came together was that I read a book of Dr. Patai called *Man and Temple,* and he's the only Hebrew scholar that I met who's really come clean about what

331

happened in the Temple [laughter] before they reformed religion. And I was so pleased that when he asked me to do this job, I said certainly, although I had other things to do. Right. [laughter] Now I'll begin to read this introduction which we wrote together, and . . . We never fought, you know, but sometimes one or the other seemed to be a bit silent, you know [laughter] . . . It was very much give and take . . . right . . .

[At this point Graves put the typescript of the introduction to the *Hebrew Myths* on the lectern in front of him and read the full text of it, deleting only a very few paragraphs, making a very few minor changes, and adding a very few impromptu asides. This took about half an hour. Since the text he read was very familiar to me, in listening to his reading I could concentrate on his English pronunciation, and was struck by a few peculiarities. He pronounced the "y" in "mythology" and "Mythographer" as in "why." His pronunciation of some biblical names was, I thought, unusual: Shamgar ben Anath became "ben Eyneth"; Rehab, "Reyheb"; El-Zebub, "Il-Zeebab"; Baal-Zebub, "Beyl-Zeebab"; Dagon, "Deygon"; Chemosh (Khemosh), "Cheemash"; Shechem, "Sheekem"; Tishri, "Tishray."

After reading the sentence which tells about Sarah that she suckled all her neighbors' children as well as her own (*Hebrew Myths*, p. 18), Graves added; "Showing off!" which provoked hilarious laughter. When he finished reading the sentence about Og, who survived, according to the Midrash, from the days of the Deluge to the days of Moses, he read from his script:]

> The heroes of ancient Hebrew myths not only leap across lands and deserts, visit the farthest ends of the world, explore the seven heavens, inspect seven hells, they also annihilate time spans, all through their extraordinary longevity.

[For some reason Graves deleted this sentence from the final version of the introduction, which after "Time is telescoped" continues with "Adam sees all the future generations . . . " (*Hebrew Myths,* p. 18) As against this he deleted the sentence, "Indeed, the hero of Hebrew myth is not only profoundly influenced by the deeds, words, and thoughts of his forbears, and aware of his own profound influence on the fate of his descendants; he is equally influenced by the behavior of his descendants and influences that of his ancestors." (*Hebrew Myths,* p. 18) Instead he read:]

> What is much more difficult to grasp is the complementary idea that reciprocally, the acts of future descendants in the time distance may have a direct effect on the lives of the hero, and that his own acts influence the lives of his ancestors who preceded

him on earth by many centuries. It is this idea and the underlying belief in retroactive influence—back through time—are basic to Hebrew mythological thinking, which thus overcomes time in much the same manner—but on the spiritual plane—as Wells's time machine did on the technological level.

[Then he added: "Well, I'm just coming to the end of this. One last thing about the Greek myths," and continued as in the printed text from "Greek myths show no sense of national destiny" to "patriarchal and monotheistic Hebrew myth had firmly established the ethical principles of Western life" (*Hebrew Myths*, pp. 18–19). Then he ad-libbed the concluding sentence:]

That just about is all. I was discussing the point of Livy the other day with somebody . . . This is really a relief . . . [laughter] I'll leave something there . . . [applause]

[Now it was my turn.]

Patai: Well, I think the first point we should discuss is to elaborate somewhat on this very brief statement of what is myth. And I think this is really important to do because I know from my conversations with people on mythology in general and Hebrew mythology in particular, that most of the people have a very erroneous idea about what myth is. They usually equate myth with fairy tale, with something told for entertainment, or to put children to sleep. And this is wrong. In fact, it is my understanding, and I think Robert thinks likewise, that myth differs from fairy-tale precisely in this point: that the myth is always something very significant, something weighty. It is never told for the sake of entertainment. It is always puzzling, something which is difficult to understand. It makes a situation, which otherwise would be intolerable, tolerable, by explaining how it came about. It is a charter validating existing customs, laws, explaining the meaning of rituals, of festivities, and so forth. So by saying—and I want to emphasize this in particular—that there is such a thing as Hebrew mythology, we do not by any chance demean ancient Hebrew literature, or desecrate, *has w'halila* (which means "God forbid") the Bible; on the contrary, it is my serious conviction that by pointing out the mythical significance of these stories we give an added importance to these stories in the Bible, especially to the stories in the Book of Genesis, which tells, par excellence, of the mythical age of the Hebrews. Now this, I think, also answers to some extent the question of

333

how can there be mythology in a monotheistic religion? Or, rather, the paradox of mythology in a monotheistic religion. The paradox is only apparent. Because, evidently, if a religion is extremely, strictly, monotheistic, it can have no mythology. But Hebrew religion, as it is reflected in the Bible, and especially in the early books of the Bible such as Genesis . . . that book catches the development of Hebrew religion precisely at the stage when it was on the way to monotheism, and was not yet a hundred percent monotheistic. So that we see that there are, in addition to God himself, there are all kinds of other divine powers who are able to oppose God, whom God occasionally has to fight. And the moment we reach such a situation, of course we are in the very midst of the matrix, of the material, of which mythology is made, and which is familiar to us from Greek myths. [Turning to Graves] I think that this, more or less, coincides with your thinking about this particular subject.

Graves: Yes indeed. And Genesis is not the only storehouse of myth. The Psalms, for instance, contains remarks about a pre . . . precreation creation which had to be included in this, what we have written, to make it more complete. And it refers to the fight of God against the mythical monsters who seem to be portrayed, as Raphael points out, on the Arch of Titus.

Patai: That's a very interesting thing which you, incidentally, can verify just by going to the Metropolitan Museum of Art. In the basement of that museum, you know, there is a small collection of plaster casts, of ancient Roman statues. And there is a plaster cast of a relief from the Arch of Titus which shows the Judean captives carrying the sacred vessels of the Temple. Now, as you know, Titus destroyed Jerusalem and the Temple in the year 70 A.D., and carried off the sacred objects, one of which is the Menorah, the seven-armed candelabrum. On the base of the Menorah there are six little panels, each of them showing one, or even two, mythical monsters, dragons, animals. One of them has a head like a lion, or tiger, and a tail like a whale. Another has all these features plus wings added. Now, these monsters evidently were copied, together with the entire pattern of the Menorah, from the original which Titus took away from Jerusalem. That Menorah was probably made by Herod. But Herod, in turn, must have copied an earlier Menorah which was made under Zerubbabel when the Jews returned from the Babylonian captivity. And that, in turn, was copied from the Menorah made by King Solomon, and that takes us back to the year . . . around the tenth century B.C. Why can we assume that these were copied? Because they were sacred objects, and no artist would have dared to take liberties with a sacred object. That had to be copied exactly because of its sanctity, and because of its great historical significance. So in these six little panels on the base of the Menorah we have the only extant representation of any ancient Hebrew mythical image which is contemporary, more or less, with the period from which Hebrew myths stem. [Turning to Graves] Do you think we should take a rest?

Graves: We'll take a rest in a minute.

Patai: There is the question of Jacob. And I would like you very much to say something more on this problem of the relationship between Jacob and Esau. This is, at least as far as I am concerned, my favorite subject in the whole book.

Graves: And mine too.

Patai: And yours too. Very good. Agreement! [laughter] Now, you probably all know the biblical story of Jacob and Esau. Esau is not represented in the Bible as an evil character. He only has shown . . . Actually, he is a fool, who sells his birthright, who allows his blessing to be stolen, and who consequently is doomed, by the words of his own father, to servitude, to the Jews, to the Hebrews. Now, this is a myth. And since it is a myth, it is not an idle tale but explains something. What does it explain?

It explains how it came about that the Edomites, who were regarded as the sons of Esau, were subjugated by the Hebrews. Now there was only one period, one historical period, when the Edomites were actually under Hebrew rule, and that was from the rule of King David to that of King Joram. King David was the one who conquered Edom, which was a country to the southeast of Palestine, on the other side of the Jordan. So, this really fixes the date of the writing of this myth, and it's biblical. [Turning to Graves] Do you want to add something to this?

Graves: I feel very strongly about it. Because to Protestants who read the Bible—and I don't know to what extent to Jews—Jacob is a thoroughly unpleasant character, and Esau is a hero. And it's very unusual. I know of no other case in which the hero of the race or tribe is made such a scoundrel. Because the ordinary hero, King Arthur, or Aeneas, or whoever it is, is a fine chap, he fights dragons, he . . . you know . . . And there is this . . . Jacob who behaves in a way which would be impugned today among all of you, I hope, who are here. [laughter] And yet you have to call yourselves the children of Jacob. Now, one thing is

335

that Jacob never fought. He always ran away. This was repaired in a midrashic story of how Jacob conquered . . . Shechem with great heroism. But it smells all wrong. Now, the point about the Jews is that they are hells of fighters, when they fight. In their wars of liberation they fought against the Romans, in the time of Titus, and again in the time of Bar Cochba, and whenever they had a chance, in the '48 war . . . There is no . . . They fight, you see. And Jacob is all wrong as a hero. Now the interesting explanation of this is, it seems to me, I've written it down, and I'll, or we have written it down, and I'll read about it. I say that the biblical story consistently favors Esau.

[At this point Graves read from the typescript an early version of the first paragraph of chapter 48, section 1, of the *Hebrew Myths,* which to some extent differed in phrasing from the final version. He read:]

I say that the biblical story consistently favors Esau at Jacob's expense. Not only according to modern ethical standards, but according to those of ancient Palestine. Esau refrains from vengeance and fratricide, he honors his parents by remaining dutifully with them, worships now the God of Isaac and, no longer a wild and improvident hunter, makes such a success as a pastoralist that he can afford to refuse an enormous gift of livestock in compensation for the theft of his blessing. Moreover, instead of repudiating the sale of the birthright, forced on him long before, when he was starving, he peaceably evacuates the Canaanites' pastures to which the agreement entitled Jacob, calls this cowardly wretch "brother," weeps with pleasure at his return, and though Jacob's guilty conscience prompts him to shameful obsequiousness, forgives him wholeheartedly. Then he rides back to prepare a royal welcome on Mount Seir—an invitation which Jacob studiously neglects.

[A comparison of this passage with the printed version in *Hebrew Myths* shows only minor stylistic improvements introduced by Graves at the last minute. As for the harsh condemnation of Jacob contained in it, although I would have preferred a milder alternative, I did not think the matter was worth arguing about. For a while I was thinking of adding a paragraph or two of psychological explanation to show that a character of Jacob's ilk corresponded to a certain type of ideal hero found elsewhere, too, in ancient Near Eastern literature, as well as in early Arab legend, and that, measured by those yardsticks, he was neither a "cowardly wretch" nor "shamefully obsequious." But on second thought I refrained, for the clearing of such an addition with Graves would have caused considerable delay in publication.

336

When he finished reading this passage, Graves lay down the typescript and prepared to make some additional comment on the subject. But I interrupted him.]

Graves: Now . . .

Patai: Let me ask . . . Let me interrupt you and say something about this . . .

Graves: Yes. Fine, fine . . .

Patai: I think, quite apart from the question of morality involved, you have here an explanation of a situation which prevailed, say, from the tenth to about the eighth or the ninth century B.C., when the Hebrews were the overlords of the Edomites, subjugated them, subjected them. This is . . . this situation, when the Edomites are the servants, the slaves, of the Hebrews, is validated by this mythological story: the Edomites are subject to the Hebrews *because* Isaac ordained it in this manner in his blessing. Now, a few hundred years later, the situaton radically changed. Now the Edomites . . . became the lords of the Jews. King Herod himself was an Edomite. Then, about the same time, the Romans were identified by the Jews—not historically but mythologically—with the Edomites. So a new situation was in existence in which the Hebrew, or the Jews, were the subject people, and the descendants of Edom, now in the shape of the Romans, were the overlords. Now this had to be explained somehow mythologically. And then comes the Midrash, and tells quite a number of stories about why Edom was destined, after all, to prevail. And they were at great pains to find indications, in the biblical story, to underpin, to establish, this supremacy. And they said, for instance, in the Midrash, that Esau was a better son to Isaac than Jacob. Jacob left Isaac, he went away for twenty years to Mesopotamia and became rich, while his old father was almost left alone. Were it not for Esau, who remained with his father and who loved his father very much, who visited him every day, who always . . . The Midrash even states that he always put on festive clothes whenever he entered the tent of his father—in other words, he fulfilled the very important commandment of "Honor your father and your mother." And because of this pious deed his descendants were rewarded by becoming the overlords of the Hebrews. And another point in the same direction is that when Esau and Jacob met, after Jacob came back from Mesopotamia, Jacob, in keeping with his character, behaved obsequiously. He called Esau "my lord," and

337

bowed down before him. And then, the Midrash says, God said to Jacob: "Because you called Esau 'my Lord,' I will actually make him your lord." In other words, this situation also has its foundation and its validation in the myth.

Graves: Well now, let's go over it, well and fine. But it doesn't explain the point I made [laughter]: that Esau is a hero in the original story. And my view is this: that the myth originated in Edom, about their ancestor Esau, and was brought to Jerusalem by Calebite and Kenizite clansmen, who were incorporated into Judah. Judah was a very mixed tribe. It had . . . a brief . . . Philistine, Edomite . . . all sorts of mixtures. But the Kenizite and Calebite tribes seem to be extremely important. [Here Graves read from the *Hebrew Myths* 48.2.] "Judah was the son of Leah, traditionally opposed both to Benjamin, a Rachel tribe whose royal dynasty he overthrew, and whose territory he swallowed, and the other four Rachel tribes, Ephraim, Manasseh, Gad, and Naphtali, which formed the hard core of the Northern Kingdom. Genesis admits Leah's hatred of Rachel, and the tradition of Israel as originally consisting of Rachel tribes with which the Leah tribes made uncomfortable alliance, will have encouraged the Edomite aristocracy of Judah—Caleb held Hebron and the ancestral shrine of Machpelah—to glorify their ancestor Esau at Israel's expense." So you couldn't say, since you don't . . . Only very few of you can be the descendants of the Northern tribes, most of you come from the Southern Kingdom, that you are also the descendants of Esau, and you can be proud of him as an ancestor. [laughter]

Patai: Horrible thought! [laughter] Well, whatever the origin of the Jacob and Esau myth, the fact remains that the Jews accepted it, and accepted Jacob as their ancestor. And they made efforts to whitewash him. You see, at the time when the biblical story was written down, a character like that of Esau, and like that of Jacob, was all right. I mean, to cheat, to be clever, to outwit an adversary—this is Middle Eastern, primitive Middle Eastern, and traces of it can be found to this day . . . [laughter]

Graves: Only when you are under the Turks, or the British, or some other . . .

Patai: Yes . . . Or one Arab tribe against the other . . .

Graves: Yes, yes . . . it's a defeatist . . . a defeatist thing . . .

Patai: In talmudic times this already went against the grain . . .

Graves: Yes . . .

Patai: So in the Talmud there is a story how this came about that Jacob stole the birthright. He didn't want to do it, it was . . . it was his mother, Rebecca [laughter] who forced him. It was the beginning of Jewish mamism. [laughter] So Rebecca said to him: "You just do as I say." And Jacob said to her: "What if my father discovers . . . the ruse, and will curse me, instead of blessing?" She says, "I will take the curse upon myself, my son. Just as"—and this is interesting: a mythical precedent within a myth—"just as, when Adam sinned, God cursed *adamah*, the earth, which was his mother, the same way I will take upon myself the curse which you may receive." The poor fellow couldn't say anything against his mother . . . And, also, a few angels took him under the arm and pushed him before Isaac, and finally he had to accept the blessing . . .

Graves: He hated it . . . [laughter]

Patai: Well, I think we should make a break now, for about three minutes, and if you have any cards, any questions, somebody will come to collect them . . . Three minutes . . . [applause]

[In the intermission the questions jotted down on cards were collected and handed up to the speakers.]

Patai: All right. [To Graves] Do you see anything there? . . . Well, we have here a very large number of questions, some of them completely outside our own respective fields of competence, others may be within those fields but transcending the time limits which we put ourselves in this book. We deal here only with myths based on stories in the Book of Genesis. So it's very difficult at this stage to answer questions about Moses, and about later figures.

Graves: Another thing I find that the . . . the names of tribes and . . . which I think clouds the issue . . . we don't appear in . . . they're not in our field, really. [laughter]

Patai: Right. You want to start?

Graves: One question was: "Why did . . . Why are we so beastly about Jacob [laughter] when Odysseus was even a greater stinker?" Well, the answer is that . . . the Greeks took a rather severe view of Odysseus, and in the original story of Odysseus, not the *Odyssey*, which is later rewriting . . . In the original story of Odysseus, the Greek heroes who offended against the gods protecting the tribe were punished either by being shipwrecked and

339

drowned, by going home and being . . . finding their wives living with someone else, and then having to . . . to . . . escape abroad, or by some other horrible fatality . . . Well, now, Odysseus is shipwrecked and finds his wife living with someone else. He escapes. Little . . . Ajax is . . . is . . . drowned. Odysseus is . . . has . . . spends twenty years at sea, in a miserable time. And when he finally returns, he finds his wife is living, not with one man, but with fifty. [laughter] She was . . . But Odysseus is given the worst punishment of them all. He is eventually killed by Telegonus's spear.

Patai: I really wonder whether we can't generalize on the basis of these examples and say that this is another basic difference between Hebrew and Greek mythology: that in Greek mythology the typical hero comes to a miserable end. He is killed, he . . . he never reaches high old age, and when he's "satisfied with days," as the Hebrew phrase goes. And the typical Hebrew hero reaches that. Whatever the vicissitudes which he undergoes while he is alive, he lives until he is ready to die: 150 years, 900 years, [laughter] in some cases a paltry 120 years. But they always live to a ripe old age, and then they are peacefully "gathered to their fathers." So it seems it was a better business to be a Hebrew hero than a Greek hero. [laughter] [turning to Graves] Shall . . . I'll take this question about the Hebrew goddess. All right. There's a question: "What do you know about the myth or ritual of the Hebrew goddess?" Well, we know a lot about it. The Hebrew goddess seems to be a little older than the Hebrew God. There is . . . there are traces in the Bible of a number of Hebrew goddesses who, of course, later were denied. They were regarded as just idols, as pagan deities. But there is the goddess Anath, whom Robert mentioned in the introductory statement, and after whom a township was named near Jerusalem, Anathot, in plural . . . And this answers, parenthetically, a question, another question: "Why is *Elohim* in plural?" Because all these original ancient deities were *numina* who appeared in many places, and the people were not certain whether they are the same or different deities who appear in similar shapes, and therefore they called them in plural. So there is *Elohim,* which means gods, there is *Anathot,* which . . . in feminine, which means Anaths, and there are the *Baalim,* which means Baals, and so forth . . . There are many other goddesses: there is Astarte, who was a good and honorable Hebrew goddess in the early times, and then she just went astray somehow. [laughter] And by the time the Bible was canonized and the sacred text es-

tablished, direct references to these goddesses were mostly ex-
orcised [excised], and only incidentally, by oversight as it were,
do a few names or references remain, like that incident reported
in the Book of Jeremiah where the Jews, when they went to
Egypt, said to him: "All this calamity, the destruction of Jerusalem, came about because we forsook the ways of our forefathers, and ceased to worship the Queen of Heaven." The Queen
of Heaven, she was probably Anath, the goddess Anath. And
Jeremiah tried to persuade them to see sense, but they would not
listen to him and continued to worship the Queen of Heaven.
And then, later, during talmudic times, the Hebrew goddess
went underground, as it were, and she appears only in a very
faint shape in the form of the *Shekhina,* which is ususally translated as "the Presence of God," and which is a female form by
grammar, and also a female entity. But then, still later, in the
Zohar, she comes back with a vengeance. In the *Zohar* the *Shekhina* is usually referred to as the *Matronita,* which is the Aramaic form of the *Matrona,* and the Matron is there described, in
the *Zohar,* as the wife of God, and all details about the love of
God and the Matron are described in the *Zohar* in a very outspoken form, and, there she is, the Matron . . . There are other
female deities, too; there is Lilith, who was a female deity, although according to one story, one legend or myth, she was created by God. But according to the *Zohar,* when God allowed the
Temple to be destroyed, and thereby He divorced the Matron,
who was His lawfully wedded wife, He had union with Lilith:
God had union with Lilith according to the Zohar. But these are
very mystical . . . things, and let's not go so far into new . . .
We are interested only in things that are at least two thousand
years old. [laughter] Seven hundred years . . . the *Zohar* is only
seven hundred years old, that's really too new for . . . for
mythology.

Graves: There is a question here about the sons of God and the daughters
of men, which is . . . has been puzzling not only Jewish but also
Protestant divines for a very long time. The story is that for lack
of other female company [here Graves read from his typescript]
"the angels known as the Sons of God found wives among the
Daughters of Men. The children of these unions would have inherited eternal life from their fathers, but that God decreed, 'Let
not My spirit abide in flesh for ever! Henceforth the years of
man are limited to one hundred and twenty.' These new creatures
were the giants, known as *Nefilim,* the 'Fallen Ones,' whose evil
ways decided God to wipe out both mankind and their gigantic

341

corruptors from the face of the earth.'' [This is an earlier version
of *Hebrew Myths* 18. a, b.] There is a whole lot of . . . talmudic
comment about . . . about what these angels did . . . [Here
Graves again took up his typescript and read an earlier version of
what became *Hebrew Myths* 18. m–q.] ''Some views are that
the Sons of God won that name because the divine light, out of
which God had created their ancestor Samael, the father of Cain,
shone from their faces. They say that the Daughters of Men were
the children of Seth, whose father was Adam, not an angel, and
their faces were therefore like ours. But others said that the Sons
of God were the sons of Seth, and the Daughters of Men were
the sinful descendants of Cain, explaining that when Abel died
childless, mankind soon divided into two tribes: namely the
Cainites, who were wholly evil, and the Sethites, who were
wholly righteous. These Sethites occupied the summit of the sacred mountain in the far north, near the Cave of Treasure—
which some take for Mount Hermon. The Cainites lived apart in
a valley westward. On his deathbed Adam ordered Seth to keep
his tribe separate from the Cainites; and each Sethite patriarch
repeated this order publicly, generation after generation. The
Sethites were extraordinarily tall, like Seth himself, and by living so close to the Gate of Paradise, they won the name 'Children of God.' Now, many Sethites took vows of celibacy in
emulation of Enoch, and led lives of anchorites. By way of contrast, the Cainites practiced unbridled debauchery, always keeping at least two wives apiece: one to bear chidren, and the other
to gratify their lust. The first lived in poverty and neglect, as if
she were a widow. The second was forced to drink a potion
which made her sterile, rather anticipating the modern contra-
ceptual pill, after which, decked out like a harlot, she luxuri-
ously entertained her husband. The punishment of the Cainites
was characteristic. They each had a hundred daughters born to
every son, [laughter] and this led to such hunger-husband
[Graves evidently meant to say husband-hunger] among the
women that they began to raid houses and carry away men.
[laughter] For different reasons the same happened to . . . One
day it pleased the Cainites to seduce the Sethites. These Cainites, they daubed their faces with rouge and powder, they
touched their eyes with antimony, and their feet with scarlet,
they dyed their hair, they put on golden earrings, golden anklets,
jewelled necklaces, bracelets, and many-colored clothes. In their
ascent to the holy mountain they twanged harps, blew trumpets,
beat drums, sang, danced, clapped hands. Then, having ad-

dressed 520 anchorites in cheerful voices, each caught hold of her victim and seduced him. These Sethites, after once succumbing to the Cainite women's blandishments, became more unclean than dogs, and forgot God's laws. Even the Sons of Judges, the *Bne Elohim,* began corrupting the sons of the poor. Whenever a bride was beautified for the bridegroom, one such would enter the chamber and enjoy her first.'' The mythical comments on these . . . these mysterious early, early, early myths . . . lots of them are extremely . . . puritanical, wouldn't you say? . . .

Patai: Yes, yes . . .

Graves: At the same time they have all the puritan gory [?] in detail as they perceive nature. [laughter]

Patai: Well, let me take up another question: "What has Hebrew mythology to say about race differences?" It has something very interesting to say. Let me first tell you what Arab, or Muslim, mythology has to say about race differences. According to Arab myth, God took black earth and made out of it black man, brown earth and made out of it brown man, white earth and made out of it white man, and this is how the three major races which were known to the Arabs came into being: the white, the brown, and the black. In other words, according to this myth three different races were created by God. According to Hebrew myth it's quite different. According to the Hebrew myth all mankind is ultimately derived from the sons of Noah, from one father. Now . . . they were all white. He had three sons: Shem, Ham, and Japheth. They were all white. And then happened . . . that story, that incident, when Ham, one of the sons, castrated his father. When Noah woke up—he was drunk at the time, so that he did not feel the pain of the operation—when he awoke, he cursed Ham and said: ''You and all your descendants should be black.'' And also he cursed Ham that he and his descendants should be the slaves of the descendants of his two brothers. So here you have a somewhat different concept, where slavery is regarded as an evil, something which came about as a punishment for sin. And therefore it is implied in it that there is a chance for redemption, and for liberation. [Turning to Graves:] Would you want to comment?

Graves: That the . . . why the . . . this idea of . . . of . . . of Ham being slaves, why slavery is connected with black, is that most of the slaves coming into Palestine came through Egypt, from the . . . from the south, and . . . being a rather poor type of

343

Negro . . . if they had Negroes from the west of Africa, the story would have been different. Black would have been a glorious color. As it was, the . . . you had rather bad quality, and they were treated badly, and had the same sort of . . . slaves get of whatever color.

Patai: Incidentally, this is another example to show a myth is really a charter for the validation of a situation. The question arose in the minds of the ancients, why are the black people slaves? Or, why are all the slaves black? And the answer is supplied by this myth: because their father, Noah, cursed them, and condemned them to slavery.

Graves: Here is the actual . . .

Patai: That's right, the actual text . . .

Graves: Text . . .

Patai: [here read from an early version of *Hebrew Myths* 21.e]: "Others report that Ham himself unmanned Noah, and that Noah, awakening from his drunken sleep and understanding what had been done to him, cried, 'Now I cannot beget a fourth son whose children I would have otherwise . . . I should have ordered to serve your children and those of your elder brothers. For this reason, it must be your own son, Canaan, whom they enslave. And since you have now prevented me from doing things which are unseemly unless done in the blackness of the night, Canaan's chilren shall be born ugly and black as coal. Moreover, because you twisted your head around to see my nakedness, your grandchildren's hair shall be twisted into kinks, and their eyes shall be red. Again, because your lips jested about my misfortune, theirs shall swell. And because you neglected my nakedness, they too shall go naked, and their male members shall be shamefully elongated.' " Here you have a detailed explanation in the myth of the typical appearances of that type of Negro which was brought from the south, from Africa, into Palestine, and sold there into slavery.

Well, I think . . . It's ten o'clock now, and we have a curfew . . . We have to close, and, in closing, I wish to thank the audience and my friend Robert, and tell you all that I personally very much enjoyed this evening [prolonged applause]

Looking over the foregoing transcript today, almost thirty years after that discussion, I am struck, first of all, by the pronounced difference in style, cogency, and formulation between the way Graves and I expressed ourselves in writing and the manner in which we put things orally, in impromptu delivery. The pieces we read from our manuscript bear all the marks of Graves's mastery of English style, his economy of phrasing, his power of expression. Compared to them, the comments we made without the benefit of a prepared text lacked style, were poor in phrasing, and weak in expression. As the transcript shows, they were interspersed with frequent false starts, unfinished sentences, and much hemming and hawing. True, when one listens to oral delivery, these featues are not necessarily disturbing. On the contrary, they can even contribute to the liveliness, the immediacy and spontaneity, of the talk. Still, I wish that instead of what I said, for instance, in response to the question about the Hebrew goddess, I had said this:

We know quite a bit about the Hebrew goddess. First of all, it can be established that she was widely worshipped by the Hebrews in monarchic times before the worship of Yahweh became general. Secondly, when I say "Hebrew goddess" I generalize: in fact, there are traces in the Bible of several goddesses who were worshipped with great devotion, although, in later days, the Hebrew prophets execrated them as pagan idols, together with the male deities.

One of them was the goddess Anath, whose name survives in the Bible as that of the mother of one of the judges, Shamgar ben Anath (i.e., "son of Anath"), and in various place names, such as Anathot near Jerusalem, which was the hometown of Jeremiah. *Anathot* is the plural of *Anath,* and this brings me to another question put by somebody here in the audience: "Why is *Elohim* in plural?" There are two answers. One is that *Elohim,* despite its apparent plural form, is singular in biblical usage, as can be seen from all the passages in which the verbs associated with God are in the singular. The very first verse of the Bible reads: *"B'reshit bara Elohim . . . "* ("In the beginning God created . . . "). The verb *bara* ("created") is in the third person singular (the plural would be *bar'u*), which proves that for the ancient Hebrews *Elohim* was a singular noun. Only when speaking of other gods is the noun used in the plural sense, as shown by the adjective in *"Elohim aherim"* ("other gods").

The second answer is that originally—and I emphasize *originally*—*Elohim* did have a plural meaning, because the ancient gods were *numina,* divinities who, as they appeared in many different places, were considered manifestations of the genus "deity," of the *numen,* just as was the case with the *lares et penates* of ancient Rome. Since there was uncertainty as to the individual identity of a *numen* encountered, he (or she) was considered, and referred to, as one of the *numina,* one of the *Elohim,* or, briefly, as an *Elohim.*

Likewise, the ancient Hebrews spoke of *Anathot,* that is, "Anaths," and *Baalim,* i.e., "Baals." The typical recurrent prophetic reproach was that the backsliding Israelites "served the Baals and the Asherahs." (Asherah was the name of a goddess whose worship was extremely widespread, as attested by the ubiquity of her figurines found in the excavations of ancient Israelite dwellings.) The name of yet another goddess worshipped in biblical Israel, Astarte, also appears frequently in plural: *Ashtaroth*. And just as there was a locality called *Anathot*, so there was one named *Ashtaroth*, that is, "Astartes."

Down to the days of Jeremiah the worship of these goddesses, and especially the one called Queen of Heaven, was considered by the Hebrews proper and legitimate.

This is how I would have liked to formulate what I had to say.

28.

Work on the Proofs—
First Copy in Hand

A FEW DAYS AFTER his return to Deyá, Graves wrote to Wolcott Gibbs of Doubleday about the proofs of the *Hebrew Myths*

May 25th 1963

Dear Mr. Gibbs:

If you can airmail me the proofs, express, I'll deal with them at once but Patai must see them first, for matters of fact and I'll see to the English: which has been our rule all along.

I should have brought a typescript back with me, but what I need is the one from which you are setting—folio, not quarto, with additions made in London last November. Dr Patai's secretary (I notice from the copy I returned to you) has made a number of typing errors.

Yours sincerely
Robert Graves

Next day he wrote me, expressing his satisfaction with our joint appearance at the Y.

May 26th 1963

Dear Raphael:

Well: that was all right, wasn't it? And very many thanks to you and Ann for my party: it was marvellous to meet your friends, and especially your splendid brother, and Moses Hadas who is so wise and so funny. But I liked them all.

347

—About galley proofs. I have told Doubleday I want you to have them first to check facts, spelling of proper names & so on. Then you'll send them here & I'll correct any small points in English that occur to me, but promise not to alter the sense—which has now been established by treaty as it were. Then I'll send them back to Doubleday, express.

How's that?

Yours ever

Robert

On May 29 Wolcott Gibbs forwarded to me a copy of Graves's May 25 letter, with this covering note:

Dear Dr. Patai:

Here is a letter from Mr. Graves about the problem of the galley proofs.

Since Mr. Graves wants to see the galleys, he certainly ought to, especially in view of the amount of his handwriting on the setting copy of the manuscript. If there are any problems in the galleys, Mr. Graves' handwriting is apt to be the cause.

I will see if we can gain some time elsewhere in the schedule.

Regards,

Wolcott Gibbs, Jr.

In response I called Gibbs and discussed with him how to handle the proofs. Then I wrote to Graves.

May 31, 1963

Dear Robert:

Thank you for your letter of May 26. I too had the impression, reinforced by spontaneous expressions of appreciation from numerous members of the audience, that our joint appearance at the "Y" was all right, and in fact more that that; quite successful.

As to our party, I was glad that Moses Hadas was there—were it not for him, I am afraid, those would have been two trying hours for you. As to our other guests, they were all greatly impressed, indeed, somewhat awed, by your presence.

Now to business. I have discussed with Wolcott Gibbs the question of the proofs. The only difficulty is that I am leaving on July 4 for a six-week holiday in Israel and other countries, and the galleys will be ready only on June 17th. This leaves me only a little more than two weeks for the combined job of reading the galleys and preparing the index. I therefore have the following suggestion which I cleared with Gibbs; let Doubleday prepare two sets of galleys

348

and send simultaneously, and as soon as possible, one to you and one to me.
I shall confine my corrections to catching printer's errors only and shall ab-
solutely refrain from making any changes. You, in reading your set of galleys,
therefore, do not have to bother about printer's errors but read them only for
the English, then airmail them back to Doubleday. If it were possible for you
to do this in time for the galleys to reach Doubleday on the 2nd or even 3rd
of July, this would still allow me sufficient time to look at them before leaving
on my trip on the 4th. If this should not prove feasible, I shall simply have to
let it go and accept your corrections sight unseen. How does this strike you?

> *Love to you all*
> *Raphael*

PS: Mr. Shlomo Katz editor of Midstream, *the quarterly magazine pub-*
lished by the Theodor Herzl Foundation, has asked me to inquire whether you
would be willing to write an article for Midstream? *The desired length is 6 to*
7,000 words, the honorarium $275. If, in principle you are inclined to do this,
I am sure it will not be difficult to find a suitable subject, since Midstream
publishes articles not only of Jewish, but of general literary and social inter-
est. Mr. Katz is sending you simultaneously two recent issues of Midstream.

Graves responded immediately.

> *June 4 1963*

Dear Raphael:

Have a nice time in Israel & best wishes to your splendid brother.

—As for the proofs: good, but it is impossible for me not *to attend to print-*
ers' errors, which you may well miss, especially in passages that were mainly
supplied by myself. I'll work at full stretch on them and send them back ex-
press air mail.

—As for Midstream: *sorry, but the fee is inadequate and I am very busy.*
Nothing I write now for serial publication is paid less than 250 dollars a thou-
sand words: my agents forbid it! Books are different because they are tasks
undertaken for self-education.

Love to Ann.

> *Yours ever*
> *Robert*

By May 25 Ann was well enough to come with me and my brother Saul on
an outing. We drove to the Cloisters, then down to Chinatown for lunch, and
then to Greenwich Village and Washington Square to see the outdoors art
show. On June 9 Ann and I drove to Ithaca to attend the graduation at Cornell
of my elder daughter Ofra (she had changed her name to Jennifer), and bring
her home.

349

On June 5 Wolcott Gibbs sent me the jacket copy for the *Hebrew Myths,* which I read carefully and returned with some minor suggestions.

Finally, on June 24, I received the galleys of the *Hebrew Myths* and, putting aside all other work outside my office, I immediately went to work on them. Next day I wrote to Graves.

June 25, 1963

Dear Robert:

I have just received the galleys of the Hebrew Myths *and started working on them. I am confident that I shall be able to finish both the proof reading and the index within a week, that is to say, just prior to my departure for Israel.*

As I wrote to you in my previous letter on the subject, I am making no changes whatsoever in the galleys as compared to the MS. All I am doing is checking the text for printer's errors.

I understand from Doubleday that they sent out yesterday another set of the galleys to you by airmail. Since I assume that you will not be able to finish reading your galleys in time to return them to me by July 2 or 3, I suggest that you airmail them instead to me to Israel where I shall be from July 5 to July 18. My address there is:

Raphael Patai
6 Patai Street
Givataim, ISRAEL

Doubleday informs me that July 10 is the deadline set by their production department for the return of the galleys. This is very close but I hope we can make it, if you send the galleys to me to Israel in time and if the airmail from Mallorca to Israel and then from Israel to New York does not leave us in the lurch.

Needless to say that I am very glad that we reached this *stage and shall soon see the finished product.*

Love to you all
Raphael

The day after I wrote again.

June 26, 1963

Dear Robert:

In the letter I sent you yesterday I forgot to mention one important detail.
In the set of galleys which I received and on the basis of which I am preparing the index, the page numbers have been introduced by Doubleday's proof reader. It is this feature which enables me to prepare the index now.

However, this being the case, I have been warned that stylistic changes should not be of a nature requiring the addition or subtraction of paragraphs or even single lines because this, of course, would result in a dislocation of the pagination. Since I assume that stylistic corrections which you may wish to introduce into the galleys will be of a minor extent, I hope that the above restriction will not cause you inconvenience.

I spent all day yesterday and today working on the index. This seems to be a more difficult and more time-consuming job that I imagined. Nevertheless, I shall finish before leaving on my trip.

> *Love to you all*
> *Raphael*

Graves replied by return mail.

> *June 29th 1963*

Dear Raphael:

My experience of airmails between here & Israel or U.S.A. is that the proofs will be at least a fortnight late. The only cure is for me to make my few corrections, avoiding any changes that will upset page-proof, and send them to Doubledays. Doubledays will then reconcile the two proofs; they have admirable continuity & research girls. Any small errors can be caught in a second edition. (There will be a lot of editions I hope.)

Have a good time in Israel. Love to Ann & a firm handclasp to your splendid brother.

> *Yours ever*
> *Robert*

I received this letter just a day or two before leaving for Israel. I had devoted many hours daily to reading and correcting the galleys, and I was able to return them to Doubleday before July 4, the day we set out on our trip.

The many things I did in Israel during our four-week visit, and the feelings I had seeing the developments in the country to which I was still tied by many unbreakable emotional bonds, do not belong here. However, I must mention one matter. While there, I happened to find in the library of my sister Evi a copy of the Hebrew translation of Graves's *I, Claudius,* which she had received from its publishers, the Massadah Company. Mrs. Brachah Peli and her son Alexander, the owners of Massadah, were good friends of my sister and her husband, George Koigen. I read the translation and, since I found in the Koigen library also a copy of its original English edition, I made random comparisons of the original with the Hebrew version. What I found was nothing less than disconcerting. On the first page, for instance, where Graves had written, ''My readers must not therefore be surprised at my practised style,''

351

the translator had rendered it (I am retranslating it here verbatim from the Hebrew): "Therefore, the reader should not be surprised at my practical style." The last sentence of the book reads in the original: "Even the mature historian's privilege of setting forth conversations of which he knows only the gist is one that I have availed myself hardly at all." This became in the Hebrew: *"And believe me,* even that special right, *given to* the mature historian, *to explain one thing from the other and to develop and amplify* conversations of which he knows only their abstract—*even that right* I almost did not use at all." (I have put in italics the phrases gratuitously supplied by the translator.)

These findings considerably cooled my desire to have the *Hebrew Myths* published in a Hebrew translation by Massadah—incidentally, one of the largest and most respected publishing houses in Israel. Nonetheless, when during my stay in Israel Mrs. Peli called me to tell me that she would like to publish the *Hebrew Myths* in Hebrew, I responded in the affirmative, but insisted that I be given the opportunity to check over the Hebrew translation before publication. Mrs. Peli readily agreed, and some time later the contract between us was signed. For a long time thereafter I heard nothing from Massadah, until one day, without any advance notice, I got a copy of the published book. I started to read it, but found, to my consternation, that the translator had taken so many liberties with our English text that, utterly discouraged, I had to stop reading it after a few pages. To quote only one example, the very first sentence in the Introduction reads in the original: "Myths are dramatic stories that form a sacred charter either authorizing the continuance of ancient institutions, customs, rites, and beliefs in the area where they are current, or approving alterations." This became in the Hebrew translation (I am again giving it here in my literal retranslation into English, with italics added): "The myths are stories *pertaining to plots* which constitute a sanctified *support* for the continuation *of the existence* of institutions and custom and ancient rituals, in the place where those are current, *as well as for the continuation of the existence of* ancient beliefs, or an authorization *and confirmation* for changes *in all of these."* I was at a loss to understand (I still am) why the translator found it necessary to introduce so many changes and additions into our text. I was reminded, *mutatis mutandis,* of the old Jewish joke about the Yiddish translation of Goethe's *Faust,* which said on its title page, *Fartaycht un farbessert fun Hayyim Yankel"* (i.e., "Translated and improved by H.Y.").

After leaving Israel we stopped over in Rome, where on July 31 I met my friend Prof. Tullio Tentori. I gave him a copy of the manuscript of the *Hebrew Myths* and he willingly undertook to find an Italian publisher for it. I in turn promised to find an American publisher for an English translation of his fine anthropological study of the village of Matera. One day in the course of that visit to Italy (on August 7, to be exact), I went to the Forum to have another look at the original of the relief on the Arch of Titus which shows the Menorah and the dragons on its base.

We returned home on August 20. It took me about three weeks to take care of accumulated work, and then, on September 13, I wrote to Graves.

Dear Robert:

I wrote to you several weeks ago that the Massadah Publishers were interested in bringing out a Hebrew translation of Hebrew Myths. *Today I got a letter from them in which they specify the conditions as follows:*

They offer the authors $100 for a 1st edition of 3,000 copies; 7½% for all copies sold from 3,000 to 10,000 copies, and 10% royalties thereafter. May I have your reaction to this offer? Shall we accept it, or shall I try to negotiate better terms? Incidentally, Massadah told me orally that the above were the precise terms under which they published your I, Claudius *and* Claudius the God. *Is this true?*

As to the galleys of Hebrew Myths, *after a number of mishaps I finally got them. What happened was that after Doubleday received the galleys back from you, they sent them to my address in Israel, although I explicitly left instructions that after July 28 the galleys should be sent to me to Rome. The galleys arrived in Israel about a week after I had left and, for some reason which I could not yet elicit, the package was left lying at the Givataim post office and not delivered to the house of my sister where it was addressed. On August 21st, when I arrived back to N.Y. and found that the galleys were not here, I sent a cable to Israel to my nephew asking him to airmail the galleys immediately to me. A week later I received a letter from my family in Israel which made it clear that they did not know what the telegram referred to. So on Aug. 28 I put through a phone call to Givataim and thus finally succeeded in clearing up the matter. On the same day the galleys were finally airmailed to me and arrived here on September 3.*

In going over your corrections, I could not help admiring the meticulous attention which you gave to stylistic improvements even at this late stage, and, of course, I accepted wthout question your few substantive emendations as well.

I hope this finds you and yours well. For us, it took quite a few days to recuperate from the exertions of this last trip, in the course of which we drove from Naples down to Paestum and then up across Italy, Switzerland, France, and Belgium.

Yours ever
Raphael

In September of 1963 Rizzoli of Milan, one of the biggest Italian publishers, expressed interest in an Italian edition of the *Hebrew Myths* (I believe this was in response to Prof. Tentori's initiative). However, nothing came of this connection, so I wrote (in the late spring of 1964) to the Casa Editrice

Valentino Bompini of Milan, who responded with a request for an option of three months. Ultimately, though, the Italian translation was published by Longanesi of Milan in 1969.

Still in the fall of 1963 I tried to interest German publishers in the *Hebrew Myths*. I contacted two major houses, the S. Fischer Verlag of Frankfort, and the Kindler Verlag of Munich, but both declined. A German edition was not published until 1986, when Rowohlt brought out simultaneously a hardcover and a paperback edition with Graves's name listed as "Robert von Ranke-Graves" (Graves's mother was born a von Ranke, but to the best of my knowledge he was never called by this double name, except on the German editions of his books).

In the meantime the publishing process of the *Hebrew Myths* continued, and we were expecting the page proofs. On October 9, 1963, Graves wrote:

Dear Raphael:

Busy summer. I was promised page proofs five days ago. Today I go to St. John's College, Oxford; which makes a further delay, & I won't have Karl to help me. The bigger the publishers' house the slower its methods.
Love to Ann.

> *Yours ever*
> *Robert*

I have no record of precisely when I received the page proofs, but it must have been in October of 1963. While reading them I also finalized the index, and sent it to Doubleday together with the corrected page proofs.

Once I had thus finished the technical winding-up process of the *Hebrew Myths*, I started working in earnest on my next book, whose theme had slowly crystallized in my mind while I put the finishing touches on the *Myths*. It was to be a study of the role played in Jewish religion by female deities and by the concept of the feminine in the godhead, beginning with the earliest references found in the Bible, and concluding with the resurgence of the image of the "Matronit," the mystical spouse of God, in the medieval Kabbala. As I completed chapter after chapter, I submitted them to scholarly journals. Thus, in the course of 1964 "Matronit: The Goddess of the Kabbala" was published in *History of Religions;* "Lilith" in the *Journal of American Folklore;* "The Shekhina" in the *Journal of Religion;* and the following year "The Goddess Asherah" in the *Journal of Near Eastern Studies.* The book itself, titled *The Hebrew Goddess*, was published in 1967.

Once it was clear to me that I would write such a book—and I wish to state that had I not worked on the *Hebrew Myths* I probably never would have conceived the idea—I began to look for illustrative material, which is extremely scarce when it comes to the conceptual aspects of biblical and later Jewish religion. On October 5 and 6 I was invited to give a number of lectures in Toronto, among them one on the subject "What Is Hebrew Mythology?" In it I utilized some of the material which I had assembled for my long Introduction to the *Hebrew Myths* and which ultimately was not included in the final, much shorter, version as rewritten by Graves. Being in Toronto I made use of the opportunity to visit the Royal Ontario Museum, where I found an Arslan Trash ivory plaque showing a winged Cherub with a palm tree. I obtained a photograph of it and printed it in *The Hebrew Goddess,* in the chapter dealing with the Cherubim.

Upon returning to New York I found waiting for me in my office the proofs of the index of the *Hebrew Myths.* It was a tedious job to check it over, as I described it in my next letter to Graves.

January 20, 1964

Dear Robert:

I have just finished proof-reading the index of Hebrew Myths. *I had quite a difficult time with this index. I originally prepared it several months ago and delivered it to Doubleday. They, however, proceeded to change the pagination, in consequence of which they also had to change most page numbers appearing in the index. This, in turn, as you can imagine, made it quite difficult for me to check whether the index is correct. However, it is now done and the book is scheduled for early March publication.*

Do you remember that last May, Channel 13, intended to arrange a television interview for the two of us, centering on the Hebrew Myths, *but it did not materialize because your schedule was too tight? When they learned that you will be again in this country towards the end of February, they again brought up the same suggestion. I very much hope that this time you will find the half-hour or so needed for preparing the tape for such a broadcast. The actual broadcasting would be timed to coincide with the publication of the book which would be an excellent and effective publicity for it. If you think you can manage this, would you please let me know when you will be free.*

On this occasion let me tell you something about a book in the writing of which I have been engaged in the last few months. This is a study of the concept and worship of the female deity beginning with the earliest Biblical times and ending with the 16th century Palestinian Kabbalists. The material presented in the book will, I hope, be original and interesting throughout. The most remarkable part, however, will be the one presenting the Kabbalistic concept of the Matronit, who appears in the Zohar as the sister and wife of God the King, and whose life history—which can be pieced together from hundreds of scattered fragments—rivals that of any of the ancient Near Eastern virginal yet promiscuous, motherly yet bloodthirsty, love goddesses.

355

Ann joins me in sending you best regards,

> *Yours cordially,*
> *Raphael*

Graves responded by return mail.

> *Jan 24 1964*

Dear Raphael:

I'll be in New York (Greenwich Village) briefly between Febr 23rd and 29th.

I don't know about "Channel 13"; but why not ask Louise Thomas of Doubleday to arrange with "Martha Deane" for her weekly book-discussion. She & I got on so well last time. Or is Channel 13 better?

—I'll be free any morning from the 24th to the 28th.

—Sorry you had all that index trouble.

—Most interested in your studies of the Goddess. I think the Kabbala one is a distortion of the Black Goddess of Wisdom, who goes back to the Orphic figure of Night. I shall be talking about this in my last lecture at N.Y. Univ.

My chief difficulty in N.Y. will be avoiding entanglement with people I don't want to see.

Love to Ann.

> *Yours ever*
> *Robert*

I responded without delay.

> *January 29, 1964*

Dear Robert:

Thank you for your letter of January 24. I got in touch, as you suggested with Louise Thomas at Doubleday. She will take up the matter of a joint interview for you and me with the Martha Dean Program *as well as Channel 13. For your information, Martha Dean is a radio program whereas Channel 13 is a television program, and in fact, the best and most serious T.V. Channel in the city. Our appearance on this program is of greater importance than on any radio program.*

Please let me know where you will stay (address and phone number) so that I should be able to get in touch with you and tell you the hour they will have set aside for us for taping both programs.

Your comment on the "Black Goddess of Wisdom" is most intriguing. I would very much like to attend at least that lecture of yours in which you touch upon her.

> *Yours cordially*
> *Raphael*

356

P.S. I am sending you in a separate envelope the chapter on the ''Ma-tronit—the Goddess of the Kabbala'' . . .

Graves was again quick to reply.

Feb 4th 1964

Dear Raphael:

The Matronit *is astonishing to me, and I am very grateful for this peep at your typescript.*

—I think virginity *means merely that the woman, or goddess, is wholly in control of her sexual affairs; not bound to any male. Thus Aphrodite used to* renew *her virginity yearly in a ritual bath at Paphos. Athene was originally Anatha; but her promiscuous role then was delegated to Aphrodite. See my* Greek Myths.

—I don't know where I shall be yet, but probably at 41 Bethune St N.Y. 14 with Len Lye.

—My new poems have one section devoted to the Matronit, *or White Goddess; one to her successor the Black goddess—viewed as an eventual solution to the ambivalence of the white.*

You should read Idris Shah's The Sufis, *just out, to which I contribute an introduction—(Doubleday)—for a discussion of Black in that sense. It is a most important book.*

Love to you both
Robert

Graves's unhesitating identification of Matronit of the Kabbala—of whom he first learned from reading my paper—with the White Goddess was typical of the working of his mind.

Finally, on February 17, Ken McCormick sent over to my office the first copy of the *Hebrew Myths*. I thumbed through it, and then right away air-mailed it to my mother in Givatayim, Israel.

The Martha Deane Interview

O N FEBRUARY 24, 1964, Louise Thomas of Doubleday called me to say that the taping of my appearance with Graves on Channel 13 had been set for the 26th, at 6:15 P.M., and asked me to inform Graves, who had arrived in New York a few days earlier. I called Miss Emily Laraçuen, who handled Graves's schedule in New York—I could not reach Graves himself—and she thought the date would be okay. She also offered to let me have two tickets to Graves's February 27 lecture at the Guggenheim Museum. The same afternoon Louise Thomas called me back to tell me that Channel 13 had cancelled the February 26 taping due to lack of studio time. I made several phone calls to the powers that be at Channel 13 to convince them to reschedule the taping within the few days Graves was staying in New York—but it was of no avail.

The interview with Martha Deane was taped on February 25. Graves and I arrived at the studio of WOR accompanied by Louise Thomas and Jean Booth of Doubleday, and learned that the interview was scheduled to be broadcast on March 20, at 10:15 in the morning. I did not think this a very good time slot, but the broadcasting industry has its own iron rules. During the taping Graves was his usual self: witty, rambling, somewhat disconcerting, but visibly (or, rather, audibly) more at ease than at the Y, where he had had to face a large audience. What follows here is an uncorrected literal transcript of the Martha Deane interview.

Deane: . . . and now here are Robert Graves and Dr. Raphael Patai. I am delighted to have both of you here, and I am glad I had a chance to read the book which you have written together, *Hebrew Myths,* and I wonder whether it might be a good idea for me to read the first sentence in the introduction of this book: "Myths are dramatic stories that form a sacred charter either authorizing the continuance of ancient institutions, customs, rites, and beliefs in the area where they are current, or approving alterations."

Graves: Okay. You see. I am a Protestant, an Irish Protestant, and, also, my mother was a Lutheran, so black Protestant on both sides, and Dr. Raphael Patai is a Jew, he's been brought up in the Scriptures. And as the Bible was first presented to us, it was something straight from the hand of God, and we weren't allowed to question it, and we had to accept the stories as true historic . . . The stories in the Bible are still of extreme importance to . . . not merely to us, but to the whole of civilization. They are the basic stories, and . . . it's really what they . . . how they're understood which is far more important than how they originated. But how they originated is also of great interest because it's not enough to say, "The Bible is false, because it can be proved that these stories come from sources . . . so-and-so and so-and-so, and not directly from the hand of God." It's important to realize that those stories have value still, and the way they are interpreted is of still immense importance.

Patai: I think it's very good that you started by reading this definition of . . . of what a myth is, because we both, Robert and myself, ran against this question: How is it possible that a monotheistic religion, such as Judaism, should have myths? People usually don't know what a myth is. They think myth is a love story between Venus and Adonis, or something like that . . . Nothing else can be a myth. That a monotheistic religion nevertheless can have myths has to be first pointed out, and in order to be able to do that you have to give a comprehensive, true definition of what myth is. And this is why we started the book, in the introduction to the book, with this definition. It wasn't easy to reach a definition like this . . .

Graves: We never quarrelled. But there was a certain difficulty about arriving at the exact phrase which would satisfy both of us . . .

Deane: Did you come to quarrelling? All by letter . . . ?

Graves: I never quarrelled with him, because . . . all you have to agree about is about facts. Once you have an agreement about facts then sensible people don't quarrel. Interpretation is a different matter. If you agree about facts . . . And in . . . we've concentrated on Genesis . . . we haven't gone on to Exodus and so on. Because that is the most packed with myth. And . . . Genesis,

359

curiously enough, is a very much later book than most people think. It's about, what's it about, seventh century?

Patai: Oh, even later than that. Probably in its final form it was put about the fifth century B.C.

Graves: Which is . . .

Patai: Very late. But it doesn't mean that there are not a lot of old myths, stories, old traditions, incorporated in it.

Deane: I think, in order to give our listeners who have not had a chance to read the book—after all, this is publication date—an idea of how you handle some of the myths and how it goes along, because it's . . . it's so good to read . . . I enjoyed it simply as a book to read, not something to read because I wanted to be able to talk to you two about it. And I want, sort of, give them an idea of what's it like. And perhaps if we pick the . . . the Flood, the story of . . . starting with Noah . . . maybe . . . and turn to something that I marked, which rather explains, I think, of why woman's place in the world is a secondary place . . . God said, you said in the book, to Noah, If the male is lording it over the female of its own kind . . .

Graves: That's with the animals . . .

Deane: With the animals, and they came two by two into the Ark, both are to be admitted. Otherwise not. So then, at the time of the Flood . . . women were supposed to be in a secondary place, otherwise they wouldn't have been here at all, they wouldn't have been admitted. All females. I just wonder . . .

Graves: Well, that, of course . . . the Flood comes a great deal after the Fall, and the Fall is the same story of . . . of Eve having been subservient to . . . to . . . Adam . . . It comes very early in the story indeed . . .

Patai: In fact, it's very interesting to observe how these myths about the position of women reflect the patriarchal society, which means in Middle Eastern time-perspective that they are relatively young. Older myths would speak about a situation where the woman is either equal, or possibly even the superior of man.

Graves: That's why that whole business about Creation . . . how God creates the world. And, there's no question about it, anybody else can certainly . . . But in the earlier myth it's a woman who creates it. Then it gets on to a man who creates it with a woman's help. Then gradually the woman disappears.

Patai: So what they did, they actually took the physical conditions, and disregarded them, reversed them, and instead of telling a story

360

about how man is born out of the body of woman, they told a story in Genesis of how God creates a woman out of a part of the body of man. Eve . . .

Graves: Adam's rib . . .

Patai: Adam's rib, that's right.

Graves: You see . . my side of the thing . . . I am not a Hebrew scholar . . . I never knew the Bible well . . . I can say without boasting . . . But I know more about the Greek and . . . other Oriental sides of the story, so I very much rely on Raphael to help me out a bit. But he tells me that the word for a rib and word for stumbling or making to stumble, are the same. So the thing is really a pun about how Eve is the woman who made man to stumble. And the same story . . . we have the same story in the Greek myth of how Pandora let . . . opened her . . .

Patai: Box . . .

Graves: Not box. It was originally a vase . . . It became a box . . . Never mind, it became a box later. And she opened the vase, and she let loose on mankind all the spites and all the troubles which afflict him. And they blame the woman for doing it. And, curiously enough, those two myths are written within a hundred years of each other. They . . . Hesiod and the author of Genesis. But it's the same myth in different . . . different ethnic . . .

Patai: You know, Robert, now that you mention this, let me say that it is . . . recently . . . it has been recognized more and more clearly that there was an old connection between Hebrew, or generally Near Eastern, societies and cultures, and those of ancient Greece. There are more and more similarities being discovered . . .

Graves: I am very much amused by that, because it seemed impossible, in old days the Bible was a sort of great rock, set apart, you know, and then, when we knew about the Greeks, but the idea of any connection between the two was fantastic. And now, of course, some people say that Hebrew in its ancient form has a lot in common with Greek . . . It has the same . . . has the proponent verbs . . .

Patai: I really don't know about that. But there are ancient inscriptions which were found on the island of Crete, the so-called Linear A and B, the oldest of them seem to be nothing but an old Semitic language which was very, very close to Hebrew. So that in this case the cultural diffusion seems to have proceeded from Palestine across the sea to Crete, and then from Crete to the mainland of Greece.

Deane: Do you still find people who seem a little upset, a little per-
turbed, when you begin to talk to them about stories from the
Greek, or myths from some other culture, being so closely related to Bible stories? Do they seem a little disturbed that there
can be any other word except The Word?

Graves: Yes. But . . . they are upset. And I think the Jews are equally
upset. Because they like to think that they have the . . . that it's
all up to them . . . Yet there are a great many Jews who are very
pleased to realize that Judaism is a very part of a big culture, of
Near Eastern culture, in which they . . . For instance, where
David is found in . . . King David's name occurs in these Cretan
inscriptions, so that he's not a local boy, he belongs to Mediterranean culture. And we found, actually, five or six of these
Hebrew myths which link up with the most ancient of the Greek
myths, especially of the ones concerned with Corinth, and a
couple concerned with Cadmia. Cadmia is an old name of what
is now called Boeotia. And the Cadmeans were supposed to have
come from a place called . . .

Patai: Kedem or Kedma . . .

Graves: Right . . .

Patai: Which in Hebrew actually means "east," or it can also mean
"old home" . . .

Graves: Old home . . . And Ishmael, Abraham's son by Hagar, he had a
son called Kedma . . . and you can . . . it's as straight as
that . . .

Patai: You know, what you are touching here upon is a question of
whether a treatment like this is not a desecration of the Bible.
And many of my orthodox Jewish friends, and I may say many
of my orthodox Protestant and orthodox Catholic friends, also
asked me, "How can you treat the Bible in this manner?" And
I, I am convinced that this is a very reverent way of approaching
the Bible, and if we discover in the Bible myths, we do not de-
crease, but in fact increase, its sacredness, its holiness. Because
these myths have a very great relevance to life today, which the
Bible, interpreted literally, in a traditional sense, has already
lost. A myth in the Bible can be a guideline for our lives to this
day. And this is what I think this book will make clear. I think
I should add something lest a false impression is gained—that,
namely, we do not base this book entirely and only on stories
contained in the Bible, the Book of Genesis . . .

Graves: Yes . . .

Patai: It deals with stories outlined in the Book of Genesis, but the material is taken from the entire ancient Jewish literature, which, in addition to the Bible itself, contains the Apocrypha, the New Testament, the Mishna, the Talmud, and the Midrashim, which are collections of legends woven by ancient Jewish sages around biblical subjects. And this type of reinterpretation of biblical stories, in fact, has started, not with Robert Graves and myself, but with the sages and the teachers who were among the teachers of Jesus, in fact, like Hillel . . .

Graves: Yes . . .

Patai: They, in fact, started to reinterpret the biblical stories in the light of their present-day, that time present-day, experience.

Deane: And this book is interpreting biblical stories in the light of present knowledge . . .

Patai: Well, in the light of present knowledge, yes, but in the light of anthropological and mythological insights into these old stories. I think we best take an example . . .

Deane: I do too! . . .

Graves: Let's have the Deluge . . .

Deane: All right, let's have the Deluge.

Patai: Well, in the case of that little vignette, or story, which you mentioned, Miss Deane, about animals being admitted to the Ark only if the female of the species showed due reverence, or, what is it, deference, to the male: this is a myth which actually validates, explains and validates, an existing social situation. At the time when this was written, which is about, let's say, fifteen or sixteen hundred years ago, this particular story, women were in a subordinate position with regard to men. And the question arose, just as today, in the minds of women: Why are we in this position? And this was their answer: Because this is how God instructed Noah, and thereby God gave His stamp of approval to this social situation—woman must defer to man.

Graves: And anybody alive now, according to the story, was in the Ark, in the persons of Shem, Ham, and Japheth and their wives and children.

Patai: And the animals . . .

Graves: Yes, and the animals too . . .

Patai: That's right . . .

Graves: And then the . . .

Deane: Excuse me . . . When questions come up, would you answer them earlier?

363

Graves: Yes, when questions come up, you see, the disciple says to the rabbi, How's the . . . how did they feed the animals? . . .

Deane: How did Noah keep that much food on hand? . . .

Graves: Yes, And so the rabbi says, My boy, he was working . . . away the whole time . . . day and night, because some animals had to be fed at three o'clock in the morning, given barley, and the ostrich had to be given . . . And the . . . the awful trouble it was . . . And another rabbi would give another answer, he'd say, Well, you know, it wasn't so difficult really because they gave them all the same food, they gave them fig-bread, you know, figs rolled in the hand . . . and they could all eat that, they could get along. And the boy said, But what about the lion here? You can't give a lion fig-bread? No, he said, but the lion was sick . . . [laughter]

Patai: The lion was sick, so he had lost his appetite for meat, and all the other animals in the Ark were safe, for the time being.

Deane: And a good thing he did, he would have eaten all the other animals in the Ark . . .

Graves: Then there's the dear old phoenix. And the phoenix somehow was an animal, a bird, which the . . . Jews believed to exist . . . Whether they believed it didn't matter, it was a sort of nice thing to talk about, and the . . . why did the phoenix last so long? You see. And so, what was the story about the . . .

Patai: Well . . .

Graves: The Garden of Eden, how did that go? . . .

Patai: I really . . .

Deane: Well the phoenix was the only, the phoenix bird was the only living thing in the Garden of Eden who refused to eat the forbidden fruit.

Patai: That's right.

Deane: Everything else took a bite, but the phoenix bird said no.

Patai: All the other animals followed Adam and Eve, and ate of the forbidden fruit, except the phoenix.

Graves: The darling phoenix. He comes into the Ark, and he sits in the corner, and . . . Noah is terribly busy with trenches of food for the different animals, and he sees the phoenix and he says, You're being served? and he says, Noah, you are so busy . . . [laughs]

Patai: He was very considerate.

Graves: But the phoenix, you see, it's not really a bird, he represents the spirit of illumination that you get from the . . . It's really an eagle from the city of On where Moses came from. And he represents illumination. And so that tradition of the phoenix remained with the Jews for a long time.

Patai: In fact, he represents three related things: rejuvenation, illumination, and immortality. All the three.

Graves: That's right.

Deane: The phoenix represents all . . .

Patai: So he is a very important, high symbol.

Graves: Then, of course, they said, Why isn't the phoenix alive now? And they said, He was killed by the Emperor Augustus. Why? Well it's like this: You see, originally it's a difference between the solar year and the lunar year. And you tried to fix the calendar, which is very difficult. Then you find that a year is not 365 days, but 365 days and a few minutes.

Deane: That's why there is a leap year in four years.

Graves: That's why there is a leap year. Well, the story about the phoenix was this: that each of those little bits of time left over in each year mount up, mount up, In the old days they made no provision for that in the calendar, so gradually midsummer, the midsummer feast, came a bit later, and a bit later, and a bit later, until in fourteen hundred years it came right around to midsummer again. You gained a year. And that's the phoenix year. Well now, this particular calendar went on for thousands of years, until the Emperor Augustus, following his granduncle Julius Caesar's recommendation, abolished the old, what's called the Sophic year, namely the phoenix year, and that way killed the phoenix. Because by adding leap years and things like that, it's . . . the midsummer always came at the same time.

Patai: There is one comfort in this situation: that he killed the phoenix only for the Western world. Among the Arabs, who retained the lunar year, it remained . . . In fact, the phoenix became the *rukh,* that huge . . .

Graves: The *rukh,* yes . . .

Patai: That huge bird, you know that huge bird . . .

Graves: I'm so delighted that he is still alive, the phoenix . . .

Deane: What do the Arabs do with that whole year that accumulates every fourteen hundred years?

Patai: Actually, the Arab, the Muslim, calendar is shorter than the European calendar by ten days, it has only 355 days, and it goes around merrily without taking into account any leap year or anything . . . So that every fixed feast in the Arab, in the Muslim, calendar falls every successive year ten days earlier.

Deane: That's a great gambit for a conversation, isn't it? To say, who killed the phoenix? And the answer is, the Emperor Augustus.

Graves: But he only killed it in the West.

Patai: That's good . . . There's a symbol in this: that Greek and Roman scholarship passed on to the Arabs.

Deane: Dr. Patai, do you think we have given our listeners a pretty good idea of how you handled material in this book, and how it explains Hebrew myths?

Patai: No, I don't think so. [laughs]

Deane: Do you think they need one more example? Do you want to stay with the Deluge, or do you want to move on to . . .

Graves: Then, you see, you have to talk about the Deluge itself. Was it a natural deluge? I say, did the . . .

Deane: Did it rain for forty days and forty nights?

Graves: . . . and was the whole earth covered? You see . . . Well, the answer, of course, is that the whole earth is not covered in that way, never has been covered in that way, since tens or several hundreds of millions of years. What happened at the dawn of creation, we don't know. But those are . . . there are various flood stories, all over the world, and the Hebrew flood story seems to come from a story of, when was it, about two thousand B.C.?

Patai: There is the Sumerian flood story . . .

Graves: No, there was a tremendous cloudburst in Armenia, and all the rivers came rushing down and flooded the whole plain, and everything was destroyed except one or two cities which were built upon mounds, and that is the basis of the story . . . It's mixed up with all sorts of other things. And there was another flood in the . . . in the . . . in the Sahara, there was another flood in Greece . . . All these stories have been mixed up . . .

Patai: In other words, what you have here is a local flood which has been magnified in the story into an universal flood . . .

Deane: People who were reporting, they knew only about just a tiny section of the world . . .

Patai: That's right. People were isolated. They only knew their own little environment.

Graves: Yes, but then, you see, then the idea of the people being saved who believed in getting into the Ark becomes very important as a moral . . . as a moral story, for teaching people that . . . the . . . destruction which awaits if they behave in an evil way. And the story, the old story, which has no moral implications at all, is used for moral ends.

Patai: That is, virtue reaps its reward. And in order to make this sure, they impressed the audience, whether the audience lived three thousand, or two thousand, or a thousand years ago, or today, they used this story: that this was ordained by God. He decided that all the sinners in the generation of the Deluge have to be . . . have to die . . .

Graves: There was, you see, there was originally this Babylonian story of the flood, which is caused in quite a different way. It has to do with a quarrel between a goddess and a god . . .

Patai: It was a competitive situation between two gods, and those poor people sided with the wrong god, so he sent them a flood and killed them all.

Graves: But the . . . but the interesting thing is what different use is made of the same story by different people.

Deane: And you had done many of these in your book on the Greek myths . . .

Graves: Well, the Greek myths . . . the only connection between the two books is that we used the same layout, the same way of . . . of . . . of telling the stories, the comments, the quotations . . . Apart from that it's very different . . .

Deane: It must have been difficult to work all this out since you didn't live in the same place while you were doing it. Weren't you in Majorca all the time?

Graves: When I wasn't elsewhere. [laughs]

Deane: Well, when you were lecturing on poetry in Oxford . . .

Patai: Often I had the feeling that we were keeping the United States and the Spanish post offices busy with sending our manuscripts, chapters, back and forth . . .

Graves: And by airmail, which is very expensive . . . [laughter]

Patai: I think I can say that each chapter, each paragraph which is contained in the book, crossed the Atlantic at least eight times.

Deane: You mailed it back and forth?

367

Graves: Yes, and it comes to about fifty cents a throw . . . Never mind . . . [laughs]

Deane: Well, all that's deductible . . .

Graves: All right.

Patai: Good.

Deane: Then . . . the story . . . you ended the story of the Deluge in the book with the different interpretations of men have thought of the rainbow. In the Old Testament God says, Despite man's evil disposition I will never again use water to destroy him. And when you see a rainbow in the sky after a storm, you're reminded of God's promise that the earth will never again be destroyed by flood.

Graves: There's a popular song that says . . . it can rain no more, no more . . . how in the world . . . no more, no more . . .

Deane: Very popular . . .

Graves: How in the world . . .

Deane: That isn't from the rainbow, though . . .

Graves: It is! Excuse me, you don't know your popular songs. It's something like . . .

Deane: I forgot you're an authority . . .

Graves: The Lord God said to Noah, I set the rainbow in the sky, and it can rain no more. That's the first verse there . . .

Deane: Oh God, that's funny!

Graves: In the song it is . . . yes . . . He was the . . .

Patai: What is the Hebrew equivalent of "ain't"?

Graves: How do you say that in Hebrew?

Patai: It would be too difficult. [laughter] But of course the ancient Hebrews were convinced that God spoke in Hebrew, and they had very interesting proofs for that: in all other languages "man" and "woman" are two different words. But in Hebrew, the word for "woman" is simply the feminine form of "man." In other words, "man" with the addition of the feminine suffix. And this proves that God spoke in Hebrew. Who can object to this explanation?

Graves: Well, I think that the early Christian fathers proved that in heaven only Latin is talked.

Deane: I thought that it has been proved somewhere along the line that in heaven only impeccable English is spoken.

Graves: That is the Episcopalians' view. [laughter]

Patai: So you have the Episcopalian version, the Catholic version, the Protestant version, and the only true version is the ancient Hebrew one. [laughter] After all, is there another holy tongue in addition to Hebrew?

Deane
and
Graves: No.

Patai: Therefore Hebrew is the language in which . . . Can you imagine that God spoke any other language than the holy language? He *must* have spoken Hebrew . . .

Graves: May I tell you . . . Do you know the story of God and the angel? You know the story of how the American aircraft carrier was paid off? Well, first of all they sent away this head man, and then various lots of draft, you see, according to seniority, and finally there was nothing . . . to sort of prepare people, and people in charge of this . . . these ships . . . and the last people to go was the Catholic padre and the Protestant padre, and the Jewish rabbi. And then they have a site celebration, at the end, you know, and they say good-bye to each other, very politely, and the Protestant said, ''You know . . . '' The Catholic spoke first, and he said, ''I think you've been . . . you behaved very, very well, you haven't tried to steal any of my flock, you know, and really I am quite surprised how well we got on together.'' And so the Protestant got up and said, ''You know, I am very grateful to you chaps who allowed me to be in charge of the welfare, you know, let me take care of . . . arrange all these football games, and so on, and I'll always remember how we stood shoulder to shoulder . . . '' And then the Jewish rabbi got up, and he said: ''My dear friends, it's been very interesting, being here with you, watching you,'' to the parson, ''worshipping God in your way,'' and to the Catholic, ''and you in your way, and I in His . . . [laughter]

Deane: A nice story. Our time is about run out. And if there is anything that either of you would like to say about this excellent book, *Hebrew Myths,* before we go, we have just a few seconds . . .

Patai: Well, let me say just one word about a very interesting figure, who appears, and plays a great role in Hebrew mythology, and in our book too, and that is Lilith, who is a . . .

Graves: Adam's first wife . . .

Patai: . . . the first wife of Adam, who was created by God of earth, just as Adam was, and who was incompatible with Adam. She left him, and then God tried again and created a second

369

> woman . . . He didn't succeed either, and the third time He created Eve, and she remained with him and she became the mother of all living. Now this Lilith, although she left Adam, she had a very interesting life, in all parts of the world . . .

Graves: Especially by the Red Sea . . .

Patai: . . . by the Red Sea, which was a very disreputable place . . . and she seems to be around even to this day, I must say, and if you want to know what to do about her, against her, you can read something about it in this book. [laughter]

Deane: Since we have to end, let's have an amusing way to end . . . I want to tell all again the book we have been discussing is *Hebrew Myths* by Robert Graves and Raphael Patai.

Here our conversation with Martha Deane ended. She was a delightful hostess indeed, who knew how to put us at ease from the very first moment. In our conversation we touched upon many subjects that could, and perhaps even should, be elaborated, but I want to confine myself to only a few points.

Graves's reference to the phoenix being an eagle from the city of On (that is, Heliopolis in Egypt) is correct in the sense that in Egyptian mythology the phoenix symbolized the sun, suffered death by immolation once every five hundred years on the Ben-ben, a mound in the Temple of Heliopolis, and rose again. Others believed that the phoenix burned itself every five hundred years in its nest, and out of the ashes arose a new phoenix. Nowadays there is agreement among scholars that the phoenix is the Greek transmogrification of the Egyptian mythical *bennu* bird, which represented the resurgent sun and rose daily from a flaming tree at Heliopolis. Zoologically, the phoenix has been variously identified with the egret or flamingo, said to be native to Arabia.[2] I do not know from where Graves took the statement that Moses came from On, or that the phoenix was "killed" by Augustus.

As for the *rukh* (whose name entered the English language in the form "roc"), I was off the mark. The *rukh* in Arab folklore is not the phoenix, which has no Arab equivalent, but another mythical bird: one of such huge dimensions that its egg, seen by Sindbad the Sailor of *Arabian Nights* fame, measured no less than fifty paces in circumference. The *rukh* itself carried off elephants (or, in another version, rhinoceroses) to feed them to its young. Sindbad escapes from the desert island by tying himself to a toe of the *rukh,* who flies with him to an inhabited land.[3]

In saying that God spoke Hebrew I was merely restating an old talmudic view first voiced by R. Simon (R. Shim'on ben Pazzi), a Palestinian Amora of the second half of the third century C.E., who was one of the great Aggadists. The passage I had in mind is found in Genesis Rabba 18:4, and reads as follows (in my literal translation): "She shall be called Woman (*ishah*) because she was taken out of Man (*ish*) (Gen. 2:23). Hence you learn that the Torah was given in the Holy Tongue. R. Pinhas and R. Hilqiyyah in the name of R. Simon [said]: Just as it was given in the Holy Tongue, so the world was created in the Holy Tongue. Have you ever heard [anyone] say [in Greek] *gyne—gyniah*, [or in Aramaic] *ita—it'ta*, [or in Greek] *anthrope—anthropia*, [or in Aramaic] *gavra—gavr'ta*? But, *ish* and *ishah*. Why? because this word is derived from that word.'' In other words: Adam must have spoken Hebrew, because only in Hebrew does the sentence, ''She shall be called Woman *because* she was taken out of Man'' make good sense. In the other languages known to the talmudic rabbis, the word for ''woman'' was not the same as that for ''man'' with the addition of the feminine suffix. Since this proved to the Aggadists that Adam spoke Hebrew, it followed that God too must have spoken Hebrew, both to Adam, who otherwise would not have understood Him, and to whatever heavenly company He addressed in the first chapter of Genesis.

371

30.

The Black Goddess and the Hebrew Goddess

IN THE EVENING of February 27, 1964, I went with Ann to listen to Graves's talk on "The Black Goddess" at the Guggenheim Museum. The audience was much smaller than the one we had addressed nine months earlier at the 92d Street Y, but no less receptive. It was a typical Gravesian talk, comprised of several loosely connected parts, touching upon some of his favorite subjects, and interspersed with readings of no fewer than sixteen of his poems.

He began by comparing the biblical prophets, inspired by God, with the true poets inspired by the "Muse-goddess." In talking about the Hebrew prophets he presented, as he often did in his writings, some highly personal views as if they were established facts. He said, e.g., that "the prophetic age ended for Israel early in the second century B.C., when her Guild of Prophets was disbanded by the Sanhedrin."[1] This single brief sentence is a veritable collection of problematic statements. If by "prophetic age" he meant the period in which the Hebrew prophets lived (and what else could he have meant?), then the prophetic age ended with Haggai, Zechariah, and Malachi, who lived in the late sixth century B.C.E., and not in the second. As for a "Guild of Prophets"—true, there were "bands of prophets," variously termed in the books of Samuel and Kings *ḥevel n'vi'im, lahaqat n'vi'im,* and *b'ne n'vi'im*—but these groups of prophets had an ecstatic character, and seem to have disappeared by the time of the onset of the classical period of Hebrew prophecy, that is, by the eighth century B.C.E., from which time on the prophets always appear alone. Hence there is no historical basis for speaking of a "Guild of Prophets" existing down to the second century B.C.E. Again, as far as the Sanhedrin, the supreme Jewish religious court, is concerned, there is no historical datum for its existence prior to the first century C.E.

372

Incidentally, that the age of prophecy had come to an end with Haggai, Zechariah, and Malachi was a generally accepted tenet among the talmudic masters, who taught that with the death of those three prophets "the Holy Spirit departed from Israel, and they were served only by the *bath qol*" (literally "daughter of a voice"), that is, an indistinct divine voice, in response to their need for divine guidance.[2]

The issue of prophecy aside, prominence was given in Graves's talk to his favorite conviction that there was "a revolution in early historical times that upset the balance between male and female principles: namely the supersession of matriarchy by patriarchy" (p. 429). There were also references to another favorite subject of Graves—which he most beautifully and powerfully expressed in his poem "In Her Praise" (he read it as part of his talk)—that the Goddess chooses a woman, enters into her, or "rides" her, for a period of time, during which the love bestowed by that "Muse-possessed woman" on a poet "however briefly . . . , heightens his creative powers to an unparalleled degree" (p. 430). Almost the entire talk revolved around the White Goddess, and it was essentially a presentation of a selection of Graves's muse-poems with connecting and explanatory notes.

Only at the very end of his lecture did Graves introduce the "Black Goddess" with the enigmatic statement that "at Hierapolis, Jerusalem, and Rome" Ishtar (whom he identifies with "the Goddess Anatha" and with Eurydice—all three being for him manifestations of the White Goddess) "acknowledged a mysterious sister, the Goddess of Wisdom." It is this Goddess of Wisdom whom Graves calls the "Black Goddess," because, according to "an ancient tradition," Wisdom was Blackness, identified with Night, which "throughout the Orient was regarded as a positive power." Having made this quasi-oracular statement, Graves announced that Wisdom as Blackness was the basis of the "Black Virgins" venerated in Provence and in Sicily (I could add many other places where the Black Virgin is or was venerated); Wisdom as Blackness, he asserted, was Sufic in origin. Then, returning to the ancient Jewish world with which he'd begun his talk, Graves spoke of "the Jewish Wisdom-cult, also apparently of Orphic origin" (p. 445).

In an aside he gave his own exegesis of the passage in the Canticles, "I am black but comely"; it meant, he said, "Though comely, I am as wise as any crone." He went on to add some likewise original explanations of the myth of the phoenix, and concluded his talk with a brief adumbration of the three stages of what could be called the poet's progress: from vestal love of affection and companionship, through the experience of death and re-creation at the hands of the White Goddess, to a certitude in love given him by the Black Goddess, who "promises a new pacific bond between men and women, corresponding to a final reality of love."(p. 447).

After the lecture we went with Graves and several others to a party at the home of Miss Rena Johnson, a commercial artist and friend of Emily

Laraçuen. Emily (or Aemilia), it appeared, not only fulfilled secretarial functions while Graves was in New York, but also seems to have been his White (or Black?) Goddess, that is, his "Muse," for a time. She was, I remember, a striking-looking young woman (Seymour-Smith says she was Mexican-American), and Graves was visibly smitten with her. He was at the time in his sixty-ninth year, and she could not have been older than thirty-five. I remember clearly walking down Fifth Avenue from 89th to 83d Street, in the cold evening, I on the curbside, Emily in the middle, and Graves on her left. He wore his favorite black Spanish hat with the wide, straight brim, and she a very similar hat fastened with a chin-strap. Graves was elated—after a lecture he always felt better than before it. But I could not help noticing that once or twice Emily gave me that certain look which few men do not recognize—however, I loved my wife Ann, and so wore an invisible coat of arms which no feminine allure could penetrate. But I was seized with pity for the aging poet, caught in the web of a fickle Muse.

Early the next morning (Friday, February 28), Graves appeared live on the "Today" program of NBC, but, to my regret, I overslept and missed it.

After these meetings I had no contact with Graves for several months. He was busy and troubled with both financial losses and with the unhappy poet-muse relationship between him and Laraçuen.[3] Yet it was in those months that he prepared the publication of several volumes of poetry: *Man Does Woman Is, Ann at Highwood Hall* (a book for children), *Love Respelt*, and *Collected Poems 1965*. He also put the finishing touches on his *Collected Short Stories* and completed his *Majorca Observed* and *Mammon and the Black Goddess*.

As for me, I was busy as usual with my work at the Herzl Press and with my public lectures, but I devoted every free moment I had to finishing my new book, *The Hebrew Goddess*.

In the spring and summer of 1964 I was also kept busy with affairs of the Tel Aviv University. On June 23, in my capacity as president of the American Friends of Tel Aviv University (AFTAU), I flew down to Washington in the company of Dr. George Wise, president of the university, to sign papers, for a two-million-dollar loan to the university which Dr. Wise had negotiated with the State Department's Agency for International Development. The same evening I drove out to Kennedy Airport with a signed application for the issuance of the money, which Dr. Wise was to take to Israel to present personally to the Israel Discount Bank for processing.

From July 15 to August 14 I was in Mexico with Ann and her friend Rosalie Berkowicz. I revisited all the places I had been sixteen years earlier, looked up old friends, spent again some time in the village of Venta Prieta and in Mexico City with the Licenciado Baltasar Laureano Ramirez, who in 1948 had been most helpful in connection with my studies of the Mexican Indian Jews. After my return to New York I wrote two papers on the basis of that short field trip, one of which, titled "Venta Prieta Revisited," was published in *Midstream*; the other, titled "The Iglesia de Dios and Zionism," I included in volume six of the *Herzl Year Book*, of which I was editor.

In the fall of 1964 I gave several lectures on "What Is Hebrew Mythology?" based partly on my unused introduction to the *Hebrew Myths*. The one I gave to the New York Academy of Science on October 26, 1964, was published that November in the academy's *Transactions*. When giving these lectures, I always expected to encounter negative reactions similar to those elicited by Graves's lecture to the London Hillel Foundation, but I can state with satisfaction that my lectures never provoked adverse comment.

In November I mailed Graves offprints of my articles "Matronit," "Lilith," and "Shekhina," which appeared in various American scholarly journals (these were chapters from my planned book *The Hebrew Goddess*). He acknowledged them on December 16, 1964.

Dear Raphael:

Your admirable three pamphlets make me proud of our collaboration in Hebrew Myths: *what industry, courage & perception! And the excitement of discovery has tightened up your English style worthily!*

I shall be in N.Y. in Feb. for awhile; hope to see you.

The whole problem of man and woman in this sense is what is engrossing me at the moment. I know the Matronit only too well; I was born under LEO.

Love to Anne

> *Yours ever*
> *Robert*

Being ignorant of astrology, I had to go to handbooks of that—for me— esoteric subject to try to understand what Graves meant by his reference to Leo. I found that astrologists consider those born under Leo to be proud, generous, creative, self-reliant, enthusiastic, warmhearted, positive. Possessed of a strong element of selfishness, Leos are supposed to be great dominators of those around them, projecting their personalities powerfully, and inviting others to admire and flatter them.[4] Some of these traits were certainly characteristic of Graves, but I fail to find in them a clue as to why, as a Leo, he should have felt that he knew the Matronit "only too well."

Even before receiving this letter I considered the manuscript of *The Hebrew Goddess* ready to be submitted to a publisher, so I mailed it to Ken McCormick, editor-in-chief of Doubleday. In due course Ken informed me that he and his readers liked the book very much, and that he wanted to give it to Prof. Moses Hadas to read. This I welcomed. I was, however, less happy with the suggestion Ken made at the same time, namely that he would like to find a coauthor, or a "with" author, who would give the book a more popular slant. I did not quite see how the contribution of a rewrite man could be great enough to warrant coauthorship. Decision on this issue was postponed until Ken got the opinion of Moses Hadas, but once Ken had raised this matter I had the feeling that in the end Doubleday would not take the book, and I was proven right. *The Hebrew Goddess* was ultimately published in 1967 by Ktav Publishing House, a New York publisher specializing in Jewish scholarly books. It got a good critical reception, but did not achieve wide distribution until 1978, when Avon Books published an enlarged paperback edition of it. (This second edition coincided with the appearance of another book of mine, *The Jewish Mind*, published by Scribner's. In between I had published four other new books, as well as six older books of mine in new, enlarged editions, and edited another five volumes.) A third, again considerably enlarged, edition of *The Hebrew Goddess* was published in 1990 by Wayne State University Press of Detroit, Michigan.

Because I consider *The Hebrew Goddess* one of the most original and most important of all my books, and because, as I have already indicated, it was a direct outgrowth of my work on the *Hebrew Myths*, I think it will not be out place here to state what I set out to do in the first edition of *The Hebrew Goddess*.

My intention in that book was to give a diachronic review of the role played by female deities and numina, as well as by the feminine element in the god-concept in general, in the religious history of the bibilical Hebrews and their heirs, the Jewish people. In the introduction I argued that the goddesses Asherah, Astarte, Anath, and the Queen of Heaven, although of foreign origin, were accepted in ancient Israel, or, as I put it in my text, these goddesses "adopted the Hebrews as their children, and allotted them all the benefits man finds in the worship of a goddess." The first two chapters, dealing with Asherah and Astarte-Anath (I held that these two were identical), traced the worship of these old Canaanite goddesses in Israel down to the end of the first Hebrew commonwealth in the sixth century B.C.E.

In chapter 3 I discussed the significance of the Cherubim, those two most sacred winged figures in the Holy of Holies of the Jerusalem Temple (both the first and the second Temple), one a man and one a woman, shown in marital embrace and symbolizing, according to talmudic sources, the love of God and Israel.

Chapter 4 dealt with the Shekhina, the feminine manifestation of God on earth, who, from talmudic times on, played a central role in the Jewish god-concept as the loving, rejoicing, motherly, suffering, mourning, and, in general, emotion-charged aspect of the deity.

Chapter 5 discussed the kabbalistic tetrad, the four *personae* in the godhead postulated by medieval mystical Jewish doctrine. In kabbalistic literature the four are most frequently referred to as Father, Mother, Son, and Daughter, and I argued that the author of the *Zohar*, Moses de Leon, was influenced by Hindu mythology, in which a divine tetrad played an important role.

Chapter 6 traced the further development of the Shekhina-concept in the medieval Kabbala, in which the Shekhina is frequently referred to as *Matronita*, Aramaic for "the Matron," the spouse of God the King. She also symbolizes the Community of Israel, and I included in that chapter verbatim translations of wonderful passages from the *Zohar* which describe quite explicitly the intense love relationship between God the King and His Matron, the Shekhina, which came to a tragic end when their bedchamber, the Temple of Jerusalem, was destroyed.

Chapter 7 dealt with Lilith, the most dangerous she-demon ever to haunt Jewish imagination, whose role as the original helpmeet of Adam is discussed in the *Hebrew Myths*. The career of Lilith reached its pinnacle after the destruction of the Temple and the exile of God's spouse the Shekhina-Matronit, when Lilith usurped her place and became God's consort.

Chapter 8 discusses the Sabbath, personified in Jewish folk-tradition as a queen in whose honor the pious are supposed to have union with their wives at midnight on that holy day. The coupling of man and wife here on earth was (and in traditional Hasidic circles still is) believed to bring about the achievement of a mystical marital reunion between God and His Matron.

In sum, I intended—and I believe succeeded, at least to some extent—to add a new dimension to the Jewish god-concept: the feminine dimension. The central biblical commandment, "Thou shalt love the Lord thy God with all thy heart" (Deut. 6:5), I still believe today, becomes more meaningful and is easier to fulfill if it is recognized that God corresponds to the human condition by comprising in Himself both a male and a female aspect.

With both Graves and I intensely involved with our respective new literary projects, the plan for a second volume of the *Hebrew Myths* was quietly forgotten. Neither Graves nor I ever mentioned it again. As far as I was concerned, a book treating biblical material from Moses to the Exile *qua* myths had lost its attractiveness. After the appearance of *The Hebrew Goddess* (1967), I again turned to studying the modern Middle East, and most of my subsequent books dealt with that subject. Not until the late 1970s did I return to Jewish legends, in my two books *The Messiah Texts* (1979) and *Gates to the Old City* (1980).

In 1965 I continued to give lectures on the two related subjects of Hebrew mythology and the Hebrew Goddess, e.g., at Indiana University in Bloomington (April 1, 1965); at Newberry College, South Carolina (April 22); at the University of Munich (July 20); at the Frobenius Institute of the University of Frankfort (July 21). But my main work that year and for five years thereafter was the *Encyclopaedia of Zionism and Israel*, of which I was editor-in-chief.

When my *Hebrew Goddess* was published in 1967, I sent a copy of it to Graves, who reviewed it in the May 24, 1968, issue of the *Jewish Chronicle*. His review was long and rambling and contained no analysis of the book; it

377

was, rather, a summation of the contents with the addition of some original Gravesian observations. On a personal note, he remarked:

> I have admired Professor Raphael Patai, a scholar of Hungarian-Jewish stock, ever since the early 'fifties when he was working as an anthropologist at Jerusalem University. [In fact, I had left Jerusalem in the fall of 1947.] He follows the truth wherever his researches lead him, even though its publication may occasionally offend the Orthodox beliefs equally of Christianity and Judaism. And he has always buttressed his findings with impeccable annotations, not only from the Hebrew Bible, the Apocrypha, the Talmud, the Midrash and Cabalistic literature, but from a vast storehouse of Middle Eastern archaeological and anthropological material.
>
> Enemies lie in wait for him everywhere, and a single major error could have ruined him long ago. But he has always escaped public persecution and is still Director of Research of the Theodor Herzl Institute, and editor of the Herzl Press.

I was somewhat taken aback by the assertion that enemies lay in wait for me everywhere, a circumstance of which I had been blissfully unaware. But then I explained it to myself by assuming that in writing this Graves attributed to me a situation in which he had found himself ever since the publication of *The Nazarene Gospel Restored*.

Of course, after reading his review I wrote to Graves to express my thanks, but I can find no copy of that letter in my files.

31.

Reviews and Translations of the *Hebrew Myths*

I T IS TIME NOW, before bringing these recollections to a close, to insert here a brief survey of the reviews and translations of the *Hebrew Myths*, which were not long in coming. Regrettably, at the time I was not very methodical in preserving the reviews, although quite a number were sent to me by Doubleday, the journals in which they appeared, or the reviewers themselves. Looking over those reviews of which I do have copies, I note that they ranged from openly enthusiastic to sharply critical. Among the positive ones was that which appeared in the prestigious *Kirkus Report*. The review, published several months prior to the book's publication, was sent to me by Ken McCormick of Doubleday on November 27, 1963.

Dear Dr. Patai:

Following is the famous Kirkus report, the first advance review on Hebrew Myths:

> All the laconic scholarship and lightning sharp interpretations and insights which have made Graves' studies of the Greek myths one of the most seductive source books of the decade are here brought to bear with equal effectiveness on the Book of Genesis. True, the mating of religious matters with myths can offend the orthodox, for after all Hellenic polytheism is a far cry from Jewish monotheism. But Graves, along with his co-author Raphael Patai, makes short shrift of objections in a succinct, satin-tongued introduction. The offering frequents both the canonical and apocryphal tracts, and thus sheds light on much Biblical obfuscation. Among the touchier items: how Adam and Eve were initiated into the act of love; why Noah took to drink and how Ham "unmanned" him; what was what with Sodom, Potiphar, Behemoth and Leviathan; and the

> *possibility that an earlier matriarchal culture was done in by the later patriarchy (elsewhere a consistent concern of Graves). Pietistic glossings, rabbinic expansions and multi-references are treated all over from the creation and cosmology through the Fall, the Flood, the stories of Abraham, Isaac, Jacob and Joseph. Important for any literate home or library.*

It is very good, and should certainly suggest to the libraries and book stores that they must stock the book.

My best to you, and give my best wishes to Daphne.

Sincerely,

Ken

The next review I got to see, in chronological order, was written by Ursula Schoenheim of Queens College, and appeared in the March 15, 1964, issue of the *Library Journal.* It read, in part:

> Robert Graves needs no introduction. Raphael Patai has published widely, chiefly in matters concerning Judaism . . . Graves is his old individualistic self, with his old knack of digging up obscure bits of information under the old protection of "the White Goddess." The result is a well-written, illuminating, often humorous account, particularly strong in putting things into historical, geographical, etymological focus, and in comparative mythology and religion. "All pre-Biblical sacred documents in Hebrew have been either lost or purposely suppressed" and "the Bible itself allows us only brief hints of its mythological riches." In spite of that and the limitations of scope, the harvest is surprising. One hopes for equal treatment of Books other than *Genesis.*

A typical example of the rave reviews was Carl Alpert's short note published in the March 20, 1964, issue of the *National Jewish Post*, one of the most widely read Jewish weeklies in America. It read, in full:

> The world's most distinguished writer on matters mythological and the greatest of scholars on Jewish legendary [matters] have joined to prepare the ultimate work on the myths in and deriving from Genesis. They have fashioned a comparative study, embodying the variegated knowledge of all cognate narratives known to the authors. Definitely, they have added thousands of generally unknown and unpublished facts to a literature formerly considered definitive. The authors have chosen wisely and rendered their extraordinary opus as attractive to the general reader as to the student.

A more restrained, but still very laudatory short review was published a few days later in the *New York Times* (March 31, 1964) from the pen of Lisa Hammel. She concluded by saying: "Although the research is scholarly, the result is clear, straightforward and animated by that rare and delightful phenomenon, imaginative reasoning."

Before publishing Lisa Hammel's short note, the *Times* had planned to accord the *Hebrew Myths* a full-size review. They asked Prof. Samuel Sandmel, provost of the Hebrew Union College-Jewish Institute of Religion and an out-standing scholar of the Bible, Hellenistic Jewish literature, and early Jewish-Christian relations, to review it. Dr. Sandmel sent in his review about March 1. As he himself informed me, he was less than delighted with our book. He wrote me on April 17, 1964.

Dear Dr. Patai:

The New York Times asked me to review the new book by you and Mr. Graves and I sent that to them some six weeks ago. This is the first of the many things you have written which I read with less than delight. Your previous books I found fascinating, informative and authoritative. This one impressed me principally as inordinately difficult to maintain an interest in. I read two reviews, one by Gaster and one by Rowley, which I suppose differ from mine, not only in severity but also in this, that it seemed to me that they were re-viewing a book that wasn't written rather than the book that was before them. I suppose also that Mr. Rowley, who is a wonderful gentleman, did not quite escape his religious conservatism. Having read reviews of my own books which persuaded me that the reviewer was more interested in a book that he could have written on the subject and which, of course, would have been a better book, I don't take reviews as seriously and I hope you won't—includ-ing mine.

> *Cordially yours,*
> *Samuel Sandmel*
> *Provost*

I responded by return mail.

April 20, 1964

Dear Dr. Sandmel:

Thank you for your letter of April 17th. What you write about reviews and reviewers is only too true—I know this from my own experience in the past.

I am of course curious to see what you have written about Hebrew Myths, *if the* New York Times *will still come back to publishing your review after so many weeks.*

With Professor Rowley's review I was able to sympathize, although it was somewhat difficult to make out whether his paragraphs contain strictures or merely informative statements. As to Gaster's review, I think it was simply malicious.

Did you notice a very fine review Professor Moses Hadas wrote in the Re-porter *magazine some weeks ago?*

> *Yours sincerely,*
> *Raphael Patai*
> *Director of Research*

This was acknowledged by Dr. Sandmel on April 28.

Dear Dr. Patai:

If the review is not printed in the Times by the middle of May, I'll be glad to send you what I wrote.

> Cordially,
> Samuel Sandmel

P.S. No, I did not see the review in the Reporter magazine.

Our exchange was concluded by my note of May 4.

Dear Dr. Sandmel:

Thank you for your note of April 28th.
I am enclosing a copy of the review by Professor Hadas which was published in the April 9th issue of the Reporter.
I certainly would be interested in seeing the review which you prepared for the Times.

> *Yours cordially,*
> *Raphael Patai*
> *Director of Research*

Sandmel's review was never published in the *Times*, nor did he send me a copy of its manuscript.

On May 1, 1964, the Detroit *Jewish News*, in an unsigned review, described the book and called it "an important work." Two years later, when the book was published in a paperback edition by McGraw-Hill, the same paper returned to it (in its October 28, 1966 issue) and stated that "these collected myths add immeasurably to the scholarship which has become so eminent in the gathering of legendary material about ancient times."

Hadassah Magazine, in its September, 1964, issue devoted a total of seventy-five words to the book, which, I felt, was slighting it, even though the last sentence read: "Students of all ages will find this an exciting and eye-opening book."

The *New Statesman* of London, in its October 23, 1964, issue, carried a 550-word review by M. I. Finley, which was so carping in tone and insignificant in content that I find nothing worth quoting in it.

Encounter of London published in December, 1964 a long (eleven hundred words) review by Frank Kermode, in which he said, among other things, that the *Hebrew Myths* "was scholarly work, thoroughly documented . . . The evidence is economically presented in that athletic prose with which Mr. Graves confers plausibility upon his more arcane speculations. His learning, and that of his collaborator, is expressed with a sober clarity which makes the whole book eminently gravesian and a model of exposition."

The *Intermountain Jewish News* of Denver, Colorado, took its time, but when it finally came around to publishing its (unsigned) review (in its June 4, 1965, issue), it was effusive in its praise. "This fascinating volume, conceived of encyclopaedic research and monumental learning, owes much to the all-embracing Midrashic knowledge of Patai, editor of the Herzl Press. The result of these combined operations and the pooling of resources from Shem and Japhet, that is Hebrew and Greek mythology, is a work which will please as well as educate an ever-growing circle of readers to whom the Bible is the staff of life."

The reviewer also summarized what he considered the most important differences between Jewish and non-Jewish myths, as pointed up in the book. "Non-Jewish legends reflect a society dominated by clans, swayed by the fickleness of fortune and ruled over by gods and goddesses with very human failings. The Midrash reflects the essential characteristics of Judaism and monotheism, a central place of worship, the uniformly virtuous life of our patriarchs and national heroes, and a picture of Paradise to which all good men, regardless of creed and rank, may attain."

Scholarly reviewers, of course, delved more deeply into the book, and in many cases found in it details with which they disagreed. The *Saturday Review*, in its March 21, 1964, issue, printed a very negative review from the pen of my old Dropsie College colleague, Theodor H. Gaster. "This time Mr. Graves is accompanied on the safari by a well-known Jewish anthropologist presumably more familiar with the terrain. Nevertheless, the net result of their joint expedition to date amounts, one has regretfully to report, to little more than going around in circles and getting lost . . . It is difficult to speak with restraint of the mischief that is done to serious scholarship and research by such works as this."

Another negative review was by Prof. H. H. Rowley, the renowned biblical scholar of the University of Manchester. Rowley argued in the April 16, 1964, issue of the *New York Review of Books* that many of the stories of Genesis which we treated as myths were actually not myths at all but stories from real life, as could be seen in surviving documents from Nuzu, which summarize legal cases parallelling, e.g., the sale of the birthright by Esau to Jacob, and other customs reflected in the biblical patriarchal narratives. (As we shall see below, precisely the opposite comment was made by Prof. E. R. Leach, who criticized us for treating the mythical figures in Genesis as if they were real historical persons.) Rowley even found fault with the "misleading" title of the book, since many of the myths, or stories, we dealt with are found not in Genesis but come from rabbinical literature dating from much later ages, and are, in addition, "without Scriptural authority." He also reproached the authors for not emphasizing "the fact that Abraham shows a singular loftiness of character . . . or that Joseph rises to a very high ethical plane." The conservative Protestant theological-ethical point of view of Prof. Rowley was evident when he said that when Adam sinned "he was conscious that his sin shut him out from fellowship with God, and that it was his act and not God's that did this. Here is something more profoundly perceptive than anything in the mythology which the authors present."

My reaction when reading this statement was that attributing to Adam a consciousness of having shut himself out from fellowship with God is surely reading a twentieth-century Christian theological concept into a three-thousand-year-old myth! I was particularly pained by Prof. Rowley's censorious review because it was he who in 1945 recommended my book *Man and Temple in Ancient Jewish Myth and Ritual* to Thomas Nelson of Edinburgh (who published it in 1947), and it was that book which led to my friendship and collaboration with Graves.

In contrast to the above two reviews, Prof. Moses Hadas of Columbia University had nothing but praise for the *Hebrew Myths*. He wrote in the April 9, 1964, issue of the *Reporter* (this was the longest review, 1650 words, which came to my notice): "This particular merit of the book is that it is at once pioneer and popular . . . It may be the duty of a reviewer to warn the uninitiate that prudent scholars will demur at some of the approaches and conclusions of Hebrew Myths, but it is also his duty to invite them to look at an illuminating and attractive work of creative scholarship."

I derived much satisfaction also from the review of Prof. Omer C. Stewart of the University of Colorado (published in the April, 1965, issue of the *American Anthropologist*). He started off by saying that "a book by two famous scholars, one the author of more than 90 books, the other of more than two dozens, must be important," and went on to observe that "Graves and Patai appear to belong with those who postulate a widespread, ancient, and persisting culture common to those countries within the Fertile Crescent for several millennia and shared with adjacent peoples since 1000 B.C." Stewart also found that "the authors demonstrate that the function of myths among the Hebrews was always different from their function among other eastern Mediterranean peoples. Uniquely, Hebrew myths sermonized on national unity and destiny and otherwise revealed special Hebrew values." And he concluded: "For its information and insight *Hebrew Myths* should be popular and valuable among anthropologists."

A likewise very favorable scholarly review was written by E. J. Duschinsky and published in the February, 1965, issue of the Johannesburg *Jewish Affairs*. Duschinsky stated that "all readers must be impressed by the wealth of material covered, by the range of sources from which the authors drew, by their superb mastery of the scientific armory in a variety of lores and doctrines, and by the artistic balance they found between the meticulous demands of the scholar and the need for pleasant readability by the intelligent reader."

384

He guessed—it so happens correctly—that "the text of the legends (the authors would have it 'myths') is Robert Graves', the Hebrew research may be attributed to Professor Patai." Dr. Duschinsky took exception to our discovery of "vestiges of an Ugaritic or Accadian water-goddess myth in the second verse of Genesis," but applauded us for stressing "the basic difference between Greco-Roman mythology and Rabbinic-Aggadic literature, pointing to the moral superiority and religious significance of the latter."

By far the most delightful review was written by Prof. Francis Lee Utley, the noted folklorist of Ohio State University, with whom, only a few years earlier, I had edited a volume titled *Studies in Biblical and Jewish Folklore* (Bloomington: Indiana University Press, 1960). True, he was somewhat hard on Graves, but his good-natured humor made his review (published in the October-December, 1965, issue of the *Journal of American Folklore*) a fine endorsement of our book. He started by saying that "the riches of rabbinic commentary have saved Robert Graves from some of the invention and conflation which mar his treatment of Celtic myth in *The White Goddess*; and the restraining hand of a competent Talmudist and anthropologist, Raphael Patai, saves him from some of the sins he committed in his equally rich domain of *Greek Myths*."

Then he went on to say that "the authors' comparison of Greek and Hebrew myth is sound" and summarized the differences we pointed out between them: "Greek myth is aristocratic and centered on the cult of separate city-states, whereas Hebrew myth is democratic and national; Hebrew myth blurs the time element by ancestral identification; Greek myth lacks the sense of national destiny, the chain of history, the *Heilsgeschichte* which Jew and Christian share." He called our explanation of the Cain and Abel myth "imaginative but plausible anthropological reconstruction," and commended the authors for "quite properly using historical time-depth in exegesis of exegesis" in dealing with the Jacob and Esau myth. He pointed a critical finger at the one facet about which I had the most struggle with Graves: "Much too prevalent is a tendency to treat hypothesis as fact," and remarked that the *Jus primae noctis* was much more popular among post-medieval savants than it was among the medieval lords themselves."

I was much amused by Utley's comment: "An analyst of folktales is tempted into strata identification himself, into an attempt to dissect the Pataian layers from the Gravesean." He chid Graves for "his bubbling enthusiasm for the Matriarchy," and concluded: "Strong minds can skim over such evidences of the unquiet Graves kept in leash on the whole by his mentor Patai." Well, how could I not chuckle at being made the "mentor" of Robert Graves!

I have left purposely to the last the anonymous review published in the December 31, 1964, issue of the London *Times Literary Supplement*, because it leads me to quite a number of comments. The *Times* review stated that the

Hebrew Myths "is the product of two kinds of immense and curious learning, but it is not what we might have expected." and went on to reproach the authors for making no reference to the structural analysis of myth, "i.e. Dr. E. R. Leach's 'Levi-Strauss in the Garden of Eden' (1961), and 'Genesis as Myth' (1962)." This criticism, since I was the anthropologist in the Graves-Patai team, was clearly directed at me, and I feel it calls for comment even at this late date.

I was, of course, well aware of the work of both Claude Lévi-Strauss and Edmund Ronald Leach, including the two papers of the latter mentioned by the *Times* reviewer. In fact, I had even had some contact with Lévi-Strauss. When I started to work on my original introduction to the *Hebrew Myths*, I began by making notes of what I thought were the most important schools of, or approaches to, the study of myth. Among those notes, which I had preserved for many years, were jottings based on my reading of Lévi-Strauss and Leach. However, once I started working up my notes—and they were quite voluminous—into the text that was to be the introduction, I decided to confine myself to discussing those approaches that, to my mind, pointed the way to an understanding of what myths meant for the society in which they were current and for whose life they constituted vital assets. Because of this self-imposed limitation, the structuralist interpretation was among those I decided not to include in the introduction nor, further, to make reference to in the body of the book.

As for Lévi-Strauss, I can still recall struggling with the French text of his *Structural Anthropology* (published in 1958), which contained a chapter on "The Structural Study of Myth." I remember jotting down some of the more oracular pronouncements of the famous French anthropologist on the essence of myth, and asking myself, "Do these statements in any way help in understanding the Hebrew Myths which are the subject of our book?" Among his pronouncements were such as these (I give them here in the English translation published in 1963): "The purpose of myth is to provide a logical model capable of overcoming a contradiction" and "Myth is an intermediary entity between a statistical aggregate of molecules and the molecular structure itself."[1]

Reading declarations such as these, I formed the opinion that the Lévi-Straussian approach to myth could be of little help in answering the central question that preoccupied me—namely, what did the stories contained in Genesis mean to the ancient Hebrews? I did not think that in the great biblical myths of the creation of the world, of the primeval monsters, of the birth pangs imposed on Eve and all her daughters, etc., etc., one could find "statistical aggregates of molecules." Could one really believe (or accept) that the purpose of the ancient Hebrew myths was "to provide a logical model capable of overcoming a contradiction?'' The whole approach, I still remember it quite vividly, just rubbed me the wrong way, and I felt that the best solution for me was simply to make no references to it in our book.

As for Leach, there too I found myself in basic disagreement with some of his cavalier reinterpretations of the biblical text, and it was primarily because of this that, rather than entering into an argument with him, I preferred to let him, like Lévi-Strauss, join those scholars to whom I made no reference. But, since the London *Times* reviewer reproached me for not referring to Leach, let me discuss his approach now, albeit belatedly and briefly.

In an essay published in the May, 1962, issue of *Discovery*, Leach speaks of "the theme of homosexual incest in the Cain and Abel story," although in the biblical text there is not the slightest basis for such an interpretation. He also asserts that this theme "recurs in the Noah saga when drunken Noah is seduced by his own son Ham"—again, the biblical text supplies no basis for such an interpretation.[2] Quite to the contrary: in a midrashic embellishment of the story, which, as we pointed out in *Hebrew Myths* 21.a–e, is actually a reconstruction of what the original, unexpurgated version of the myth must have told, the atrocity committed by Ham on his drunken father was not "seducing" him but emasculating him, the Oedipal crime familiar to us from the Hittite myth of Kumarbi and Anu and from the Greek myths of Cronus and Uranus and of Zeus and Cronus.

Leach seeks support for his interpretation of the Ham and Noah myth in Leviticus 18:6–19, which contains a list of incest prohibitions phrased, "thou shalt not uncover the nakedness of . . . '' However, the analogy he draws between these prohibitions and the Ham-Noah myths is false. In the latter, the text says explicitly that Noah in his drunkenness uncovered *himself* (Gen. 9:20–23), and that, when Ham "saw the nakedness of his father" he "told his brethren without,'' whereupon Shem and Japheth covered the nakedness of their father, walking backward: "and their faces were backward, and they saw not their father's nakedness.'' This repetition of the phrase shows clearly that the issue here was not the "uncovering of the nakedness'' of the old man in the sense of "seducing'' him sexually.

As for Leach's paper (originally a lecture) on "Lévi-Strauss in the Garden of Eden,'' in it he resorts to even more freewheeling reinterpretations of biblical myths. There is the well-known myth of the seduction of Eve by the serpent, to understand which one does not have to be an expert myth interpreter or mythologist. It explains why woman has to suffer birth pangs, why man must work hard to make a living, etc. (See *Hebrew Myths* 12.a–c). In Leach's recasting this becomes: "If 'the seed of the serpent' be here read as 'the semen of the father,' while 'the seed of the woman' be read as the son of the father by his impregnated wife, the curse refers to the opposition between man and woman and the hostility between father and son. It might even be taken as a 'charter' for circumcision."[3] I was (and still am) at a loss to understand why the explicit enumeration of the divine curses put on the serpent, on the woman, and on Adam (Gen. 3:14–19) should mean not what the text says, but refer instead to hostility between man and woman, and between father and son, not to mention the enigmatic "'charter' for circumcision." Leach himself felt that this type of interpretation may be thought to be "too like a conjuring trick" (p. 395), which, however, did not keep him from asserting self-assuredly that, after having shown in his paper that "the component elements in some very familiar stories are in fact ordered in a pattern . . . , no one will ever again be able to read the early chapters of Genesis without taking this pattern into account" (p. 395).

The passage of years did not bring about a modification in Leach's views of biblical myth. Seemingly unaware of the overwhelming archaeological evidence bearing on later biblical history (and especially on the period of the divided Hebrew monarchy), he takes exception to the view that "Moses (probably) and Saul and David (certainly) were real people who actually existed in the period 1250 to 1000 B.C.": "Personally, I find this most implausible . . . I regard all the personalities of biblical narratives, both in the Old Testament and in the New, as wholly fictional."[4] How a responsible scholar can make such a blanket statement is hard to understand. Leach may be unfamiliar with the many references to Old Testament personalities found in archaeological excavations, which prove beyond doubt their historicity, but can he really "regard as wholly fictional" such New Testament personalities as Jesus, Paul, Herod, Pilate?

I regret that I had to point out these shortcomings in the work of an astute scholar such as Leach, with whose views on myth I often find myself in general agreement. I consider, for instance, his criticism of Lévi-Strauss entirely justified and well taken, including his objection to Lévi-Strauss's usage of the term *myth*. (It so happens that despite his own structuralism Leach is one of the sharpest critics of Lévi-Strauss.)

Before closing my one-sided polemic against Leach, I want to offer a rejoinder to what he has to say about my own approach to myth. As we have just seen, Leach is opposed to the view which considers some biblical characters as "real people." To that statement he appends a footnote, which reads:

> The uncertainty is shared by anthropologists. A striking case is provided by the work of Raphael Patai, who is knowledgeable both as an anthropologist and as a biblical scholar. In Patai (1960) [*Sex and Family in the Bible and the Middle East*][5] every incident in the biblical narrative is treated as a record of historical fact and as evidence that "in the days of the Hebrew patriarchs" such and such behaviour was "a binding custom." On the other hand Graves and Patai (1964) [*Hebrew Myths*], which is mainly concerned with non-canonical Hebrew sources, includes sub-

stantial parts of Genesis under the category of myth. Correspondingly the definition of myth given at Graves and Patai (1964) p. 11 is an uncomfortable compromise between the "sacred tale" and the "impossible tale" view.[6]

In my *Sex and Family* I analyzed folk-customs and mores (such as marriage between first-degree relatives, cousin marriage, polygyny, concubinage, bride-price, etc.) as they are reflected in the biblical narratives about the patriarchs and later figures. Nowhere in that book did I state that these biblical characters were historical, but assumed that the stories told about them exemplified actual customs and mores as they existed among the biblical Hebrews. I still believe that this procedure was legitimate and scholarly sound, and especially so since I showed that many of the same customs and attitudes have persisted in the Middle East down to modern times.

Take as an example the custom of serving for a wife. This custom is well-attested in the story of Jacob and Rachel (Gen. 29:18), as well as in twentieth-century Arab Palestine. Stating this, however, did not mean that I considered Jacob a historical character. Even an entirely mythical character can be, and often is, described as acting in a way which is in accordance with traditionally observed custom. Hence the observation that my work provides a "striking case" of the "uncertainty" between historicity and what can be called "mythicality" is totally unjustified. Or does Leach think that when, e.g., a scholar says that the biblical story about Noah having built the Ark and planted a vineyard indicates that the society in which this story was current knew something about ships and viticulture, this means that he considers Noah a historical figure?

As for our definition of myth being "an uncomfortable compromise between the 'sacred tale' and the 'impossible tale' view," I simply fail to see how a definition which is as close to his own can be considered so by Leach. Let me put the two definitions here one after another:

> *Graves-Patai, 1964:* Myths are dramatic stories that form a sacred charter either authorizing the continuance of ancient institutions, customs, rites, and beliefs in the area where they are current, or approving alterations.[7]

> *Leach, 1983:* I use the word *myth* to mean "a sacred tale about past events which is used to justify social action in the present."[8]

Not only is there no reference at all in our definition to the " 'impossible tale' view" of myth, but the basic agreement between it and Leach's definition leaps to the eye.

Now a few words about the editions and translations of the *Hebrew Myths*. The original edition was published in 1964 simultaneously by Doubleday in New York and Cassell in London. Two years later a paperback reprint was issued by McGraw-Hill in New York. When I was told by Doubleday that a paperback edition was in the works, I asked McGraw-Hill to make sure that two irritating printer's errors, which I had overlooked when reading the proofs of the original edition, would be corrected. One was in the introduction, p. 13, where King Ahaziah was said to have, not "consulted" the god Baal-Zebub (2 Kings 1:2ff.), but "insulted" him. The other was in chapter 1.5 (p. 24), where the "creation of the heavens" was listed as having taken place on the first day instead of the creation of light (Gen. 1:3). I duly submitted the corrections to McGraw-Hill, and on February 16, 1966, Miss Ednamae La Bue of its paperback section sent me the proofs of the corrected lines with a brief note saying that there was "no need for these to be returned." Imagine my consternation when, a few weeks later, I got my author's copies and found the two errors uncorrected.

In 1969 *Hebrew Myths* appeared in Italian, Croatian, Hungarian, and Spanish translations. None of the publishers of these foreign-language editions sent me the manuscripts of the translations, so that it was only when I received my author's copies that I first saw what was in them. I have spoken in chapter 28 about what I found when I looked at the Hebrew translation. Now, in glancing through the Italian translation, I found a real howler. In the introduction (p. 12) we referred to the Israelite judge "Shamgar ben Anath who smote of the Philistines six hundred men with an ox-goad . . . (Judges 3:31)." In the Italian this became "che sconfisse seicento Filistei servendosi del dio-toro," that is, it attributed the smiting of the six hundred Philistines to Shamgar's using the ox-god"! I sent off an indignant letter to the publisher, Longanesi of Milan (incidentally one of the biggest Italian publishing houses), and urged that the page in question be replaced by a corrected page. I sent a copy of my letter to Graves and asked him to send off a similar letter to Longanesi—regrettably, I retained copies of neither of the two letters. Graves responded:

Sept 14 1969

Dear Raphael:

I agree with you in principle but one can do nothing with Italians—in fact all they could be persuaded to do would be to publish an errata *slip and fix it in every copy not yet sold. They are impossible . . .*

I have been very busy and around the world since I last saw you . . . There is a chance of the republication of Joshua Podro's and my Nazarene Gospel Restored *by Cassell and Doubleday. Its a question of expense and of course the book is also in the Catholic* Index. *If you can do anything to show Ken McCormick that the Jews are in favour of the book which shows Jesus as a left-wing Pharisee who happened to be picked as the Jewish Messiah and got framed and crucified by the Goyim, it would perhaps help. I hope you ap-*

proved of my review of your splendid Hebrew Goddess *in the* Jewish Chronicle. *Love to your wife.*

> *Yours affectionately*
> *Robert*

Went to Hungary last year—what a tragic nation! But the expatriots are active everywhere & real leaven.

Longanesi's response was even less helpful than Graves had anticipated. They wrote that they were sorry but nothing could be done at this stage about the unfortunate error; however, they would correct it if and when a second edition was published. (A second edition was, in fact, published in 1980, but the "ox-god" remained in place. This time I did not even bother to write to Longanesi about it.)

The lack of attention some translators pay to their work was amusingly, and at the same time annoyingly, illustrated by another passage in our introduction. I mentioned above the error of "insulted" for "consulted" in referring to King Ahaziah's turning to the god Baal-Zebub. The Hungarian translator noticed the error and corrected it—that translation was supervised and checked by my old colleague at the Budapest Rabbinical Seminary, Dr. István Hahn, who in the 1960s was a professor at the Budapest University and a respected scholar. The French translation (published in 1987) also corrected the error, and added a footnote stating that "insulted" in the English edition is "certainly a mistake for 'consulted.'" The German, Hebrew, Italian, Croatian translations, and the first two editions of the Spanish, retained "insulted," although that way the sentence does not make good sense, and the source reference (2 Kings 1:2ff.) included in the quote made it easy to check the biblical text.

In the late 1980s, the *Hebrew Myths* was well and thriving. In addition to the editions mentioned, a new Spanish edition was published in 1986 (with the translation revised by Graves's daughter Lucia), an Italian in 1988, and two new paperback editions in 1989, one in London and one in New York. (The former retained the "insulted" error, but the latter finally corrected it to "consulted." As I am writing these lines a Greek translation is in the press.

I do not want to close this section without stating that most of the translations which I was able to read were, by and large, satisfactory, which is significant praise in view of the difficult nature of our book and what one of its reviewers called Graves's "athletic prose."

32.

The Hebrew Goddess in
Graves's *Song of Songs*

I N 1973 GRAVES published his *The Song of Songs: Text and Commentary.*[1]
This beautifully produced book, with the very attractive, refined erotic
drawings by Swiss artist Hans Erni, contains Graves's free translation of the
Song of Songs, based, as he himself states, not on the original Hebrew biblical text but on "whatever informed readings seem to make both poetic and
historical sense" (p. 16). The translation is preceded by a sixteen-page introduction, written in the typical Gravesian freewheeling style, replete with references to the Bible, the Mishna, and the Talmud, as well as Greek, Egyptian,
and other sources, including R. Gordon Wasson's identification of the hallucinogenic mushroom fly-agaric (*amanita muscaria*) "with the Indian ambro-
sia called Soma" (p. 10), one of Graves's favorite subjects.

The occasion for this last-mentioned reference is given in explaining Song
2:15, "Take us foxes, little foxes that spoil the vineyards, for our vineyards
are in blossom." Graves connects this passage with the three hundred foxes
Samson is said to have captured, "turned them tail to tail and put a torch in
the midst between every two tails. And when he had set the torches on fire, he
let them go into the standing corn of the Philistines." (Judges 15:4–5). Graves
points out that this story lacks verisimilitude, and suggests that what actually
may have happened was that Samson gathered a battalion of young Israelite
warriors (he mentions in this connection that General Dayan had told him,
"We had a battalion of guerrillas in the 1946 [*sic*] War of Liberation called
Samson's Foxes"), dosed them with fly-agaric and wine and sent them out in
pairs, carrying torches, to set fire to the enemy's fields (p. 10). The fly-
agaric, Graves adds, "is said to induce reckless courage, sexual lust, and superhuman energy" (p. 10).

392

Then Graves goes on to say that the meaning of Song 2:15 seems to be that the Bride was encouraging the Bridegroom "to match her in reckless passion like the little foxes with fire in their tails" (p. 10). This is not the place to examine the tenability of these explanations of Samson's foxes and of the "little foxes" referred to in the Song of Songs, but let me point out that what Graves says on this subject in his *Song of Songs* is but a brief recapitulation of the more detailed argument he had presented in his *Food for Centaurs* a dozen years earlier.[2]

What surprised me most, therefore, when reading Graves's *Song of Songs*, was not his original exegesis of that biblical book but the fact that the only modern author whose works he cites or quotes is Raphael Patai. In fact, he refers to me repeatedly and in quite some detail. On p. 2 he writes:

> Dr. Raphael Patai in his carefully documented works *Man and Temple* and *The Hebrew Goddess* shows that out of the three hundred and sixty years for which Solomon's temple-complex lasted at Jerusalem, the matriarchal Canaanite Goddess Ashera, who represented the old farming population of Israel, had been worshiped there for two hundred and forty as Jehovah's bride and sister, with her wooden image publicly displayed. The tribe of Asher had originally been named in her honour. Dr. Patai points out that when Elijah slaughtered the four hundred priests of Baal on Mount Carmel he left the priests of Ashera unmolested; Baal was then Jehovah's rival male deity and therefore, like Molech, Milcom, Chemosh (1 KINGS xi. 7) and all other male gods, had to be suppressed.

Graves here takes some liberties in citing me. I did *not* say that Asherah (as I spelled the name) "represented the old farming population of Israel," but that she was a goddess widely worshipped by the population of Israel throughout the centuries of the existence of Solomon's Temple in Jerusalem. I never called Asherah "the matriarchal Canaanite Goddess," nor said that she was considered "Jehovah's bride and sister." What I said was that "Asherah was the chief goddess of the Canaanite pantheon," that she was "the wife of El the [Canaanite] chief god," and that her worship was introduced into Jerusalem by Solomon.[3] In fact, for lack of evidence I was not able to establish whether or not Asherah was considered Yahweh's bride and sister, hence I never stated that she was. I did not state as a fact that "the tribe of Asher had originally been named in her [Asherah's] honour," only that the name Asher, Jacob's and Zilpah's son, "may have been derived from Asherah" (p. 280–81). Apart from these liberties, and the error of speaking of "priests" of Asherah and Baal where the biblical text has "prophets," Graves used my findings correctly, and based on them legitimately his conclusion that Asherah was widely worshipped in Israel in the First Temple period.

For some reason unknown to me Graves preferred the form "Anatha" to "Anath," although the sources are consistent in giving the name of this goddess as "Anath," and this is how I put it throughout *The Hebrew Goddess*.

When Graves and I worked on the *Hebrew Myths* I insisted on "Anath," he accepted it, and this is how the name appears in our text. However, later, while working on his *Song of Songs*, he returned to his favored "Anatha."

A few pages later in his introduction to *The Song of Songs* he writes: "Dr. Patai's recent *The Hebrew Goddess* emphasizes the vast importance that Ashera-Anatha maintained throughout Jewish history under various pseudonyms such as 'The Shekhinah,' 'The Matronit' and 'The Sabbath' (p. 7). Here it appears that Graves considered Ashera and Anatha as two alternative names of one and the same goddess. But he was not consistent in this, and later on the same page he says that "Anatha . . . honors her mother Ashera." This latter alternative is, of course, the correct version of the relationship between these two goddesses: Anath was Asherah's daughter. On the other hand, as I argued in my *Hebrew Goddess* (pp. 42–45), she was called either Anath or Astarte.

Even at this late date I must take serious exception to Graves's statement that I considered the Shekhina, the Matronit, and the Sabbath pseudonyms for Anath. I made it quite clear, I believe, that the Shekhina (referred to in kabbalistic literature as the "Matronit") is a talmudic term denoting the visible and audible manifestation of God's presence on earth, and that the Shekhina was, "if not by character, then by function and position, a direct heir to such ancient Hebrew goddesses of Canaanite origin as Asherah and Anath" (p. 99). "Heir by function and position" is something very different from identity "under various pseudonyms." Elsewhere I even emphasized that "the numinous images" I discussed in my book "were originally either foreign goddesses and demons (Asherah, Astarte, Anath, Lilith, Naamah), *or had their beginnings in Jewish divine attributes* which were conceptualized and personified (Shekhina, Matronit)" (italics added). This either-or proposition clearly shows that I could not have considered the Shekhina or the Matronit identical "under various pseudonyms" with Asherah or Anath.

As far as the Sabbath is concerned, such an imputation is even more unfounded, since I state clearly that "the Sabbath is a unique example of a day of the week—or more precisely the name and idea of such a day—having been developed into a female numen and endowed with the character of virgin, bride, queen, and goddess" (p.226).

Once more in his introduction to *The Song of Songs* Graves refers to me when he speaks about the royal shields which were stored in the Jerusalem Temple and had a role in its ritual. He writes: "Dr. Patai has shown that the guards also used them [the royal shields] in an annual race" (p. 11). The reference here is not to *The Hebrew Goddess*, but to my 1947 *Man and Temple in Ancient Jewish Myth and Ritual*, which had first brought me and my work to the attention of Graves. In that early book I discussed the great annual celebration in the Jerusalem Temple, and quoted a late Midrash to the effect that ten thousand youths of the quick-footed tribe of Naphthali took part in the races that were held in Solomon's Hippodrome on the last day of the month of Kislev and on the first two days of the following month of Tebheth, each carrying a golden shield.[4] I explained that "the shields carried in these races symbolized the sun, which begins its victorious race through the sky on the day of the winter solstice."[5] The connection between these purely legendary races and the point Graves makes about "the sixty valiant warriors who had protected Solomon from night attacks" (p. 11) is not clear.

The foregoing comments may seem nitpicking in relation to the broad, sweeping approach of Graves to the Song of Songs. I jotted them down only in order to set the record straight. As I have stated elsewhere in this book, Graves's nonfiction writing—of which *The Song of Songs* is a good, albeit late, example—is a unique combination of great erudition and poetic insight *cum* licence. Whenever erudition is about to shackle him, he breaks loose, jumps off the broad back of the heavy-set lumbering Mecklenburger which he had to ride while pulling the weighty impedimenta of scholarly argument and, changing mounts, swings onto the back of his waiting, snorting Pegasus to fly with it unhampered toward the envisaged goal.

Indeed, in presenting interpretations of features from the past—whether of events, actions, processes, or developments—Graves was never able to keep fact and fiction strictly apart. In both his novels and his scholarly books and essays he mixed a vast array of facts, which his erudition put at his disposal, with assumptions that simply "smelled" right to him. Perhaps the best example of the manner in which he proceeded, in which he could not resist proceeding, is found in the early part of his novel *King Jesus*, written in the early 1940s. In a fascinating scene, the high priest Simon, son of Boethus, tries to convince Antipater, the son of King Herod, to marry Miriam, that is, Mary, who subsequently becomes the mother of Jesus. The conversation between the high priest and the prince takes up several pages in the book, and in its course Simon makes reference to a huge amount of data culled from the Bible, from Egyptian, Greek, and Roman history, and from the Jewish Midrash, as well as to matters invented but presented as fact—and all this in order to persuade Antipater that it is his duty as the future king of the Jews to marry in secret that particular virgin.[6] Although the argument is based on what Graves as the author terms "a most unorthodox historical theory" confided by Simon to Antipater (p. 56), it is unmistakable that, in effect, it is Graves himself who speaks through the mouth of Simon, and that he believes in the correctness of Simon's presentation of historical data even more than does Simon himself, who, we suspect, is not above coloring his accounts in order to make them more convincing to Antipater. That "most unorthodox historical theory," which Graves makes Simon confide to Antipater, is fully in line with what Graves himself believes concerning an early phase in human history: there was a matriarchal age which preceded the establishment of patriarchal rule in many (or even all) ancient cultures. Applying this Gravesian theory to the early history of Israel, Simon explains to Antipater that "in Israel every ancient chieftain or king had ruled by woman-right: namely by marriage with the hereditary owner of the soil" (p. 56). In adducing historical examples to bolster this theory, Simon (that is, Graves) boldly reinterprets historical references in the Bible, and then, to further strengthen his argument, proceeds to show that "it was the same once in Crete and Cyprus and Greece. It was the same in Rome under the Kings." While we follow with interest Simon's "feminist" interpretation of ancient Hebrew and classical history, we cannot help hearing Graves's voice issue from the mouth of the learned Jewish high priest.

The mix of fact, reinterpretation, and fiction in what Simon-Graves says is in itself fascinating. He refers, for instance, to the incident of Judah and Tamar: according to Genesis 38, Tamar, the childless widow of Judah's son Er, and then of his second son Onan, disguises herself as a harlot, seduces Judah, and bears him the twins Perez and Zerah. In Simon's account this becomes "Judah's rape of his daughter-in-law Tamar," which he explains by adding a seeming non sequitur: "For Tamar the palm-tree is another title of the ancient Goddess of Hebron." Furthermore, Simon asserts that "the identification of Tamar with Rahab [the harlot of Jericho] is made in the same chapter of Genesis, the thirty-fourth [correctly: the thirty-eighth], where she plays the harlot, bears twins to Judah and ties the scarlet thread of Rahab about the wrist of Zarah, who is supplanted by his brother Pharez" (p. 4)— and so forth, reciting a long list of unproved and unprovable assumptions as if they were known facts.

Incidentally, in making Tamar tie the scarlet thread "of Rahab" around the wrist of Zerah, Graves, unknowingly perhaps, proceeded in true midrashic fashion. The Midrash, as I pointed out in the *Hebrew Myths* (p. 18), disregards the time element, and has, e.g., Jacob study the law of Moses, who lived ten generations after him, in the House of Study of Sem, who lived ten generations before Jacob. Graves likewise has Tamar use the scarlet thread of Rahab, blithely disregarding the fact that Rahab, the harlot of Jericho, lived some five hundred years after Tamar.

As long as Graves speaks through the mouth of a fictional character—in this case the high priest Simon ben Boethus—he, of course, cannot be faulted for unsound scholarship, or cavalier disregard of explicit biblical statements. A novelist, even in a historical novel, is free to make his characters say, think, feel, imagine, or experience whatever he wants. He cannot be called to account for anything his creative imagination makes him write. But in Graves the creative novelist (and, of course, the creative poet) was so powerful that even when writing scholarly essays—in which the author is supposed to present as fact only that which can be established as fact, and to draw from it his conclusions in a logically impeccable step-by-step process—he was unable to rein in his Pegasus. Thus a typical Gravesian scholarly essay (or book) contains both a rich array of factual observations, and an occasionally bewildering variety of statements presenting as fact things that are not known to be facts, or are even known to be contradicted by facts. But for him they are what he liked to term "poetic truths."

33.

Last Letters

As soon as I received Graves's letter of September 14, 1969, I wrote to Ken McCormick of Doubleday about *The Nazarene Gospel Restored*. Although I could not "show . . . that the Jews are in favour of the book," because I was not in a position to speak in the name of "the Jews," I did the next best thing I could, and gave Ken my opinion—a very positive one—of the book.

September 23, 1969

Dear Ken:

I understand from Robert Graves that the republication of his and Joshua Podro's Nazarene Gospel Restored *is under consideration by Doubleday and Cassell.*

I am prompted to write to you because I have felt for a long time that this book should be published in a new edition. Since its original publication the name and fame of Robert Graves have spread in this country, and after the publication of the book Hebrew Myths, *which he wrote jointly with me, it can be expected that both in Jewish circles and in those interested in the Bible there will be increased receptivity for his* Nazarene Gospel Restored.

I, for one, would greatly welcome the reissuance of this significant opus.

> *Yours cordially,*
> *Raphael Patai*
> *Director of Research*

The same day I sent a copy of this letter to Graves with a brief note.

398

Dear Robert

I don't know how much weight my opinion carries with Ken Mccormick and the powers that be at Doubleday. But I sincerely felt what I said above.

Regards
Raphael

Graves answered a few days later.

Dear Raphael

Thanks a lot for your note to Ken McCormick. It may swing the decision.

Between you & me this Catholic Church is in such distress now, because its dogma was frozen before the age of modern science, that to keep alive it must eventual[ly] also accept modern views of history. Its survival depends on having a historical, dependable and more sympathetic Jesus than the Pauline one. And the Naz[arene] Gosp[el] R[estored] ought to show them the way to acquiring him. I think in fact that by the next twenty years the leading cardinals will have come round to it under pressure from the young (and by that time married) priests.

Your Hebrew Goddess *now! Ten years ago you could never have got away with that. Now I am allowed, though a Goy, to give it a big write-up in the* Jewish Chronicle! *How rapidly times are changing.*

Affectionately always
Robert

I had a wonderful time in Buda Pesth this year & because I have so many royalties there I am now allowed to give a huge money prize (the Robert Graves Prize) for an annual poem in Magyar!

I have no copy of my reply to this letter, although I am sure that I did reply, because I would not have left unacknowledged the friendly review Graves wrote of *The Hebrew Goddess*. (I quoted from his review above, in chapter 30.)

My next letter to Graves of which I have retained a copy is dated some eighteen months later, and it has to do with a permission I needed to quote five lines from one of his poems in my new book, titled *Myth and Modern Man*. In that book (published by Prentice-Hall in 1972), I examined the ways in which the life, the thinking and the outlook, of modern man was influenced by myths, and analyzed such powerful new myths as those of the Marxist world and of Nazi Germany, as well as the Madison Avenue myth, the "God is Dead" myth, the suicide myth, the myth of planetary escape, the new sex myth, and more. I discussed the mythical images of "Jerry," "Whitey," and "Baby," and argued that the subordination of individual events or persons to generalized types offered a simpler, easier, and more convenient way of relating to them, and that this was one of the factors which made for the ready popular acceptance of this mythical process. It is, I pointed out, always easier to deal with one than many, which explains the tendency to overlook individual differences, to emphasize the common features to the exclusion of personal traits, and to focus on one single, generalized image, the image of a type, instead of taking into account the innumerable variations. I wrote: "It is easier to feel that one is having yet another encounter with Venus, whom one has already met several times before and with whose effect on one's emotions one is quite familiar, than to face up to the problematic possibilities inherent in a new, never-before-experienced, relationship." Then I went on to say that Graves expressed this idea explicitly and with great poetic force in his poem "In Her Praise," of which I then quoted five lines, the same lines I quoted above in chapter 7. Then I explained: "The goddess whom Graves finds possessing one after the other the women with whom the poet falls in love is, of course, the same Venus whose earthly manifestation, according to Ovid, the youthful Attis blithely, and, as it turned out, unsuccessfully, foreswore, with fateful consequences to himself." I went on to assert that "the tendency to consider all members of a certain human aggregate as sharing identical mental traits—this is what stereotypes basically do—has mythological antecedents or overtones.[1]

For quoting even a few lines from a poem one needs permission from the copyright holders and so I wrote to Ken McCormick of Doubleday, the publishers of Graves's poetry, and asked their permission. But, as a matter of courtesy, I also wrote to Graves.

March 8, 1971

Dear Robert,

I just wrote to Ken McCormick to ask Doubleday's permission to quote five lines of yours in my forthcoming book Myth and Modern Man *to be published this spring by Prentice-Hall). Assuming that I get Doubleday's permission, may I have yours as well? To show you in what context I am quoting you, I am enclosing a copy of the entire page.*

These days I received the first copy of the two-volume Encycl. of Zionism and Israel *which I edited and on which I worked for seven years. It was an exhausting job, and although the result is impressive, I am glad it's over.*

I hope this finds you and yours well. When are planning your next visit to America?

Yours as ever
Raphael

Graves responded by return mail.

March 12 1971

Dear Raphael:

How good to hear from you again—
—It seems to be my fate to meet splendid friends in various countries and
to discover that they are all Magyars. A Magyar called Felix Gluck is pub-
lishing my translation of, and introduction to, the Song of Songs *with litho-*
graphs by Hans Erni. Magyars (1956 vintage) in Australia have saved my
daughter's life and my grand-daughter's. And the Magyars are printing the
Na. Gospel Restored *in a revised version in Budapest, by order of a man who*
read my poems in jail and invited me to open the Poetry Congress there last
year: none other than the Gen. Sec. of the Party—who began life as a
Shakespearean actor, I'm told. I had a wonderful visit to Budapest, and when
I had an hour and a half interview with "Big George" (all about poetry), the
British Ambassador & all his staff got diplomatic grippe, fearing the worst
and were unable to entertain me.
Went to Jugoslavia later & that is the most bourgeois country in Europe.
Of course quote my poem—am honoured.

Yours ever
Robert

Not *coming to U.S.A. while Nixon and/or Agnew is still in power. Congrat-*
ulations on your new books. I hope that the Hebrew Goddess *got the praise it*
deserves. Soon off to London for a fortnight in hospital on a massive sinus
operation to repair damage done in May 1916! Hope you are both surviving
the pollution and purse-snatching of N.Y.

Yours affectionately
Robert

The man Graves identifies in this letter as ''the Gen. Sec. of the Party,''
appears in later letters of his as ''Big George'' and ''George Astel.'' His correct name is George (Hungarian György) Aczél (b. 1917), a member of the
Central Committee of the Hungarian Socialist Workers' Party, who in 1957
became first deputy minister of culture, and was considered the cultural boss
of Hungary.

My response to this letter is not extant. But when my *Myth and Modern
Man* was published, I sent him a copy (on January 15, 1972 by ship mail), and
he acknowledged it without delay.

March 11th 1972

Dear Raphael

Very many thanks for your admirable Myth & Modern Man *and your kindness in quoting me.*

401

Have been in hospital a lot lately, and losing my memory not for ancient, but immediate, names and faces. But I have written a good many poems and a prose-collection of answers to historical problems, and will soon be in my seventy-eighth year.
Patience!
I have been adopted by the Hungarians as their favourite British Author, & have a standing invitation to visit there from "Big George" who is the Party Secretary for Culture and once read my poems in prison. It is extraordinary how many Hungarians have been my friends. It started with Kordaly (spelling) who taught me sing his songs in English translation in 1912

All the best
—Robert—

"Kordaly" is, of course, none other than Zoltán Kodály (1882–1967), the famous Hungarian composer, who was a close friend and collaborator of Béla Bartók. The words "losing my memory" and "Patience!" touched me deeply. I knew what was happening to Graves because I had seen the same illness destroy my father. It was some time before I was able to answer him.

April 21, 1972

Dear Robert:

It was good to hear from you and to know that you received, and liked, my Myth and Modern Man.
I was saddened by what you write about your illness and loss of memory. When men of great mind lose their memory it strikes me as the vengeance of the gods—they cannot tolerate that a human should be like them for more than a brief allotted span, and jealously damage him at his noblest. I saw this happen many years ago to my father who suffered from it the worst way. It is wonderful that you can remember things long past and can continue to create. I would be most interested in seeing your new poems and your essays on historical problems.
I don't think I told you that this past summer I too visited Hungary—for the first time since 1936. This was also the first time that I set foot inside a Communist country, and I must say I was rather disappointed. The city of Budapest which I remembered as a gay, beautiful place, with well lit streets, luxurious shops, elegant women, and a live, sophisticated atmosphere, now appeared to me drab, dirty, the houses in a very bad shape, the streets half dark, the stores poor, the people shabbily dressed, many of them disgruntled. Everybody has to work hard, long hours, and after work spend more hours lining up and waiting in stores, at street car stops, everywhere. But, perhaps the memory of my youth paints my native city in much too brilliant and rosy colors compared to which the present must appear grey and ugly. However, quite objectively,

we went to Budapest from Vienna, and my wife too found that the difference between the two cities was striking.

I have just finished my latest book, entitled The Arab Mind, *for Scribner's. I am afraid that just as my "Jewish" books have brought down upon my head the wrath of many Jews so this book will arouse the ire of many Arabs. Seriously though, I am convinced that if, in analyzing the Arab character, I occasionally deviate from strict objectivity, it is in the direction of a romantic sympathy with the Arabs which has been with me ever since my early youth. In the very personal preface that I wrote to the book I tried to show the various roots of this incurable Arabophilism*

Yours as ever
Raphael

This brought the following rather quick response:

[No date, Mailed May 1, 1972]

Dear Raphael

Sorry you didn't like modern Hungary. They treated me with wonderful warmth—especially as I knew Kordali (spelling?) when I was a boy and could sing his songs in my father's translation.

—I must go to Balaton in August to open a Hotel in honour of Claudius who had a victory there in what was Pannonia.

—But Hungary is alive in a sense denied to the other Russian-overcast countries. Jugoslavia I found fearfully bourgeois.

I hope your Arab Mind is successful. My two closest friends, Sufis, are in direct senior descent from the Prophet (from whom I am also descended, like most of us English gentry, including the Queen, via Edward III and the Spanish Alfonso line). So I have a love and sympathy with Arabs especially the mediaeval ones who civilized S. Europe and introduced the romantic love-motif. I am glad that you are similarly attached.

Do you know the great Arabic dictionary's definition of SUFI? It is the absolute truth: "A Sufi is a Sufi." But of course that means that only others can award this distinction to a would-be Sufi.

Yours ever
Robert

I am becoming too famous: I hope you can avoid this disagreeable happening.

When I received this letter I was completely involved in finishing my book *The Arab Mind*, the writing of which was an extraordinary challenge for me. In it I felt called upon to sum up all that I had learned about the Arabs in the course of four decades, and to present the gist of my understanding of their culture, personality, talents, and mental traits. It was a formidable task to which, I felt, I had to devote not only all my abilities, but also those hours of my working day in which I was the freshest and hence most likely to do the best I could. Never before did I feel as burdened by having to hold down a full-time job as editor of the Herzl Press, which meant that I could do my research and writing only in after hours and on weekends.

Added to this was the fact that my views of the Arabs were not as clear-cut as my view of the Jews. My Jewish identification had always been so strong, I always had such deep roots in Judaism, that I never felt the slightest hesitation when it came to publishing the results of my researches dealing with the history of Jewish religion, even if I knew that some, or even many, Jews would find them unpalatable. Graves had recognized this in me very early, when he wrote me, after reading my study "Hebrew Installation Rites," "I think you are a very brave man not to 'pull your punches'''(see above, chapter 2), and again many years later, in his review of *The Hebrew Goddess*: "[Patai] follows the truth wherever his researches lead him, even though its publication may occasionally offend the Orthodox beliefs equally of Christianity and Judaism" (see above, chapter 30).

As for the Arabs, despite my lifelong interest in their language, religion, and culture, my approach to them had to remain, of necessity, that of an outsider. Despite my familiarity and fascination with the Arab world I could, of course, never be an Arab but only an "Arabist." True, ever since my student days, when I started to learn Arabic—it was my seventh language, coming as it did after Hungarian, German, Hebrew, Latin, Aramaic, and English—I loved it. The better acquainted I got with the Arabs, the more I learned about their history, culture, and personality, the more I liked them, too, the more I fell under their spell.[2] In the fifteen years I spent in Jerusalem, one of the best friends I had was Shaykh Aḥmad al-Kinānī—I described my sentimental reunion with him after a separation of twenty years in the preface to *The Arab Mind*, and years later I was to dedicate to his memory my 1986 book, *The Seed of Abraham: Jews and Arabs in Contact and Conflict*.

Yet—and a great "yet" it is–in the course of my personal contact with the Arabs and my continuing study of them, I also learned to recognize their faults, and in writing a book about the Arab "mind" I had, of course, to present what I knew about them irrespective of whether it was positive or negative, whether it showed the bright or the dark side of their character. And there a difficulty arose, the like of which I had never felt when writing about the Jews. By the time I was working on *The Arab Mind*, there had developed an implacable political antagonism on the part of the Arab states and the Arab religious, political, and intellectual leadership to Israel and, by extension, to

404

the Jews in general. This, I was afraid, could tend to color my perception of the Arab "mind," and make me present it more critically than I would have had I written the book while I still lived in Jerusalem. Consequently, I felt that I had to be more than ordinarily alert to the possibility that my portraiture would be unduly weighted on the negative side as a result of the inevitable resentment I, as a Jew and a Zionist, could not help feeling against this Arab position. Hence, throughout the hundreds of hours I devoted to researching and writing *The Arab Mind*, I always felt that whenever I wrote something negative about the Arabs I had to examine carefully whether my judgment was not influenced by my almost atavistic Jewish reaction to the anti-Semitic manifestations of the Arab attitudes on Zionism, Israel, and Judaism. Occasionally, even when I concluded after such an inner examination that my criticism was justified by objective criteria, I still felt prompted to quote what Arab authors had said on the issue rather than present the criticism as my own conclusion. Because of these factors—and there were others as well—I was more preoccupied with the problems attendant on writing *The Arab Mind* than I had been with those I encountered in writing my "Jewish" books. These circumstances explain, to some extent at least, why I was remiss in answering Graves's May 1, 1972 letter.

Finally, I was prompted to write by a news item about Graves I saw in a Hungarian illustrated magazine. So I wrote Graves on November 18, 1972.

Dear Robert:

I just received the Sept. 2, 1972, issue of the picture-magazine Magyar Hirek *(Hungarian News) which is published in Budapest by the "World Federation of Hungarians" and is being sent free of charge to thousands of Hungarians all over the world. I am enclosing the last page (pp. 15–16) of the issue which contains your picture. The caption says: "Following an invitation by the Hungarian Pen Club, English writer Robert Graves met with his Hungarian colleagues in Budapest at the writers' headquarters."*

I hope this finds you well and busy as usual.

I have just finished the six-hundred-page MS of my book The Arab Mind, *to be published by Scribner's in May 1973, and have immediately embarked on a new venture, a book on the Jewish "race." I am doing this book, also for Scribner's, in co-authorship with my daughter Jennifer who has a Ph.D. in biology and genetics. She will write the genetic chapters, using the most modern computer technology; I—the historical-anthropological chapters. Between the two of us we should produce what the blurb will undoubtedly describe as the "definitive" book on the subject.*

Yours ever
Raphael

*I remember I wrote the same thing to you in April. However, at that time I only thought I had finished the book. It soon turned out that I had to work on it for several more months. But now it is really done, and in the hands of the printer.

In your last letter you mentioned that you, like most of the English gentry, are descended from the Prophet Muhammad. This is a most intriguing statement. On what do you base it? Is there any historical evidence or documentation?

Graves replied right away.

Nov 27th 1972

Dear Rafael—

It is very good to hear from you again. I have stopped visiting the States for the last four or five years: something went so badly wrong when Nixon came to power that I refused all invitations to lecture there. Instead I go to Hungary. I was much surprised in 1968 when I was invited to open a poetic congress at Balaton. The invitation came from the poet Devesceri and through him I got the friendship of 'big George' George Astel, the party member for culture and education, who had read my poems in prison. I now go to Hungary every year. A Hungarian named Felix Gluck is publishing a book I have written about the Song of Songs *in which I present a theory about who the writer was and his links with Sicily and the Lebanon—he was obviously an Alexandrian Jew. For me it is a book of enormous importance—I mean the Song, not my translation. Both your books sound extremely important, as usual. Unfortunately the word 'Arab' covers a multitude of sins—the Egyptians, for instance, are described as Arabs, but are a fearful mixture of races of whom the only decent lot are the Copts . . . It must be wonderful having a daughter who can work with you. My daughter Lucia is content to translate my books into Spanish.*

I will always feel enormously indebted to you for my instruction in Hebrew and Arabic traditions. The Mohammadan descent of most of the English nobility and gentry comes through the Beauforts descended through John of Gaunt from the Spanish Royal Family—the second Alfonso married the daughter of the Mohammadan King of Cordoba who traces his descent directly to Ali.

Let me know if there is any chance of seeing you—in England, Spain or Hungary.

Beryl sends her best wishes, your ever—

Robert—

This year I opened a Hungarian hotel in SAVARIA, called the "Claudius Hotel" As you know he added this part of Hungary to the Roman Empire.

This letter requires a few comments. "'Big George' George Astel" is, as I stated earlier, George (György) Aczél. "Devesceri" is Gábor Devecseri, a well-known Hungarian poet and translator. I am unable to identify Felix Gluck.

Graves's derivation of "most of the English nobility and gentry" from Muhammad is rather difficult to follow. The Beauforts were a well-known noble family in England, descended from John of Gaunt, Duke of Lancaster, and Catherine, the widow of Sir Hugh Swynford. John of Gaunt was a son of Edward III (1312–1377), whom Graves mentions in his May 1, 1972, letter as a link between English gentry and descent from the Prophet Muhammad. From 1386 to 1389 John of Gaunt was engaged in strenuous diplomatic and military efforts to gain the crown of Castile and Leon, which he claimed belonged by right to his wife Constanza, the daughter of the Castilian King Pedro I the Cruel. It is not clear to me whom Graves had in mind in saying that "the second Alfonso married the daughter of the Mohammadan King of Cordoba." Both Alfonso II (759?–842), the king of Asturias, and Alfonso II (1185–1223), the king of Portugal, fought the Moors. A third Alfonso II (1265–1291), was the king of Aragon. I must leave it to historians of Spain to find which of these three Alfonsos II, if any, married a daughter of an Arab king of Cordova who traced his descent to Muhammad.

I have no record of any letter I may have written to Graves in response to this communication.

Two years later, quite unexpectedly, I got a brief note from Graves.

Nov 11th 1974

Dear Raphael

I haven't been in your country for a long time but you are frequently in my thoughts. Beryl and I have just come back from Hungary and Poland where they are promising to publish Hebrew Myths shortly.

I enclose a letter from one Marion P. Cox in case it means anything to you. I don't feel equal to answering it myself.

Yours ever
Robert

This was the last letter I was to receive from Graves. Marion P. Cox's letter (which I cannot locate among my papers) raised a question about the *Book of Yashar*, and I answered her:

December 7, 1974

Dear Miss Cox:

Our publisher forwarded your letter of Sept. 3 to Robert Graves, and he, in turn, passed it on to me.

The solution to the problem you raise is really quite simple. In various passages in the Bible there are references to a "book of Yashar." This book has been lost in antiquity. We have only a very vague idea as to what it contained from the references to it in the Bible.

About the 12th century A.D., *either in Italy or in Spain, an unknown author wrote a book in Hebrew which he called "Book of Yashar" and in which he presented legendary material covering the period from Genesis to Joshua. This book was first printed in Naples in 1552. This book is, of course, not identical with the ancient lost book of Yashar. You can find more details about this medieval Book of Yashar in the Jewish Encyclopedia, s.v. Yashar, Sefer ha-.*

Yours sincerely
Raphael Patai

The same day I also wrote to Graves:

Dear Robert:

It was good to hear from you. By one of those strange coincidences, your brief note of Nov. 11 arrived just on the day on which I finished re-reading (purely for my enjoyment) your delightful novel Watch the North Wind Rise *whose title in the original British edition was, I believe,* Seven Days in New Crete.

I am glad to know that you liked Hungary so much that you again returned to visit it. There is a chance that I may be going there next summer as a guest of the Hungarian National Academy of Sciences.

I answered the query of Miss Marion P. Cox. She confused the lost Book of Yashar mentioned in the Bible and referred to in our Hebrew Myths *with the medieval book of the same name which is nothing but a late midrash—in fact the latest midrash, dating from the 12th c.*

Let me tell you in brief what I have been up to recently. My last published book was The Arab Mind, 1973. This will be followed in March 1975 by *The Myth of the Jewish Race* which I wrote jointly with my older daughter Jennifer who is a Ph.D. in genetics. At present I am engaged in two projects: a book on The Jewish Mind, *and a new translation of the* Koran *richly annotated. I am trying to do all this over and above my teaching of 12 hours weekly at Fairleigh Dickinson University in Rutherford, New Jersey, where I serve as professor of anthropology. However, I am planning to retire from teaching soon after reaching my 65th birthday which will occur next November.*

Please give my best regards to Beryl.

Yours most cordially
Raphael

This letter was not answered by Graves. However, in the summer of 1975 I received a printed invitation from Beryl to a celebration of his eightieth birthday. I responded by addressing a congratulatory letter to Graves.

July 15, 1975

Dear Robert:

Upon our return from Israel we found here your invitation. To our regret it will not be possible to comply with it—to cross the Atlantic once a year back and forth is all we can manage. But in spirit I shall be with you on the occasion of your 80th birthday celebration. According to Talmudic tradition 80 is the age of strength ("g'vurot" in Hebrew), and, as you know, Moses was 80 years old when he undertook the great task of liberating the Children of Israel from Egypt and leading them for forty years through the desert to the gates of the Promised Land. The first 80 years of his life were nothing but preparation for this one great feat. You certainly have this over Moses: in your first eighty years you produced—to switch from the Hebrew to the Latin realm—a monumentum aere perennius. I shall be most curious to see what great works you will accomplish now that you have reached the age of g'vurot.

Let me conclude with the traditional Jewish birthday wish—"To a hundred and twenty years!"

In true friendship and affection

Yours
Raphael

My comment about future works by Graves came true at least in the sense that his books continued to be published after his eightieth birthday. In 1975 and 1977 the last volumes of his poems were published, and in 1980 a book of fiction, *An Ancient Castle*, was brought out by Peter Owen in London. Also, Graves experienced the appearance of his final Muse in the shape of a very young girl called Julie. He wrote poems to her, but even in them he began to be aware of the irresistible approach of death.[3] In 1976 he gave his last TV interview in connection with the airing of the serial *I, Claudius*. In 1977 he ceased writing even letters.

In the spring of 1979, when I planned to go to Paris to conduct interviews with Nahum Goldmann, another octogenarian, about whom I was writing a book, I considered making a side trip to Majorca to visit Graves. But then, in the April 1, 1979, issue of the *New York Times Magazine*, I saw John Wain's sensitive, and for me very sad, article, "The Lion in Winter," in which he described his visit to the Graves home in Deyá and the condition in which he found the eighty-four-year old Graves. When I read that "nowadays the poet does nothing much except sit in the house," and that he "sits, for the most part, in silence,'' I knew that my wish to have a meeting with Graves—a last one—came too late. John Wain's article told me that Graves was, as the Talmud says about Ben Zoma, one of its great sages, ''already on the outside''— outside and beyond ordinary human contact and conversation. I don't know whether my visit would have meant anything at all to Graves—probably not—but I knew that for me it would have been too painful an experience. I still vividly remembered the anguish I had felt when I last saw my father, the man who had been most dear to me of all men, in a similar condition two years before his death. So I gave up the plan of going to see Graves. I could not allow the image of the human ruin that he was to overlay the memory I had of him, the poet, the *vates* and visionary, the Leo, the man of Michelangeloesque *terribilitá*. I mourned for him six years before physical death took him, on December 7, 1985, at the age of ninety.

APPENDIX

Myth and Hebrew Myth

T HIS IS THE original, uncorrected version of what I had planned to serve as the introduction to the *Hebrew Myths*. It was not used, and has remained unpublished until now.

1. INTRODUCTORY

The combination of the noun "mythology" with the adjective "Hebrew" will undoubtedly appear strange to many readers. Those familiar with mythology primarily as a concomitant of polytheistic Greek religion will ask, What place can mythology possibly have in Hebrew (or Jewish) religion, monotheistic in its doctrinal aspect and centered around a deity, believed to be not merely the only God who exists or who can possibly exist, but also regarded as being everlasting and ever-present, omnipotent and omniscient, and devoid of any physical shape, appearance, or function, of any and all human or quasi-human need, desire, and volition, and having only the noblest and loftiest attributes imaginable? How could, they will ask, such a God be involved in any way in mythological situations or happenings? And, conversely, how could any mythology exist side by side with this God-concept?

These are serious questions and require considered answers. In fact, the answers have to be more than considered; they have to be elaborate, and will be reached by following a circuitous route. The first leg of the journey will be to clarify what groups and individuals of various descriptions have meant by "myth." The second—what the present authors understand by myth. The third—what they regard as Hebrew myths and how they explain the existence of such mythical materials within the general context of the historical development of Judaism.

2. WHAT IS MYTH?

The question "What is myth?" has been asked for at least twenty-five centuries, but to this day there is no consensus as to a generally valid answer. One of the reasons for this remarkable longevity of disagreement is that the problem of myth has attracted the attention of men of greatly varying interests and orientations, which, of necessity, are reflected in the answers they came up with.

The very formulation of the question "What is myth?" presupposes a certain detachment and critical approach. For millennia before it was first asked, men had accepted myths unquestioningly as important traditional lore which was imparted and learned at various stages of the human life cycle, and thus transmitted from generation to generation. To early man, myths were true accounts of significant, mostly primordial, or at least remote, happenings which had to be known in order to make life in the human group possible. Just as man had breathed air for ages before first asking the question "What is air?" so he had lived with myths for ages before asking "What is myth?" And just as the air made it possible for the physical man to live, so the myths sustained the emotional man in his confrontation with society, nature, and what he perceived as the supernatural.

Nor, when the question finally was asked, did this come about suddenly or abruptly. Gradually there arose a kind of men, a "tribe" the ancients would say, who took a more intense interest in myths than the average elder. These men, later to become known as poets, began to gather myths, to put them in rhythmically or otherwise pleasing form, to recite them repeatedly, and thus make the others accept and remember their versions rather than the earlier, simpler ones.

Whether the ancient Sumerian, Akkadian, Hittite, and Canaanite poets—all sharing a largely common ancient Near Eastern mythical and religious heritage—believed the myths they incorporated into their epics and other poetic writings or merely used them for themes, as was done later by Greek and Roman poets, is a moot question. In either case, our indebtedness to them is great, for it was almost exclusively due to this early poetic interest that the enormously important ancient Near Eastern corpus of myths has been preserved to this day.

3. THE GREEK HISTORIANS AND PHILOSOPHERS

The historians, who came somewhat later, inaugurated the process—which has not ended to this day—of *reinterpreting* myths. In general, this took the form of rationalization. Thus Herodotus (c. 485–425 B.C.) himself, the father

412

of historians, took myths, and, by ingenious rationalizations, turned them into historical accounts. For instance, the original myth told about Cyrus, the great king of the Persians, that he was brought up by a bitch, just as Romulus and Remus were said by the Latin myth to have been brought up by a she-wolf. But Herodotus says instead that the infant Cyrus was brought up by a herdsman's wife named Spako (in Greek, *Kyno*), meaning "bitch."

Still later came the philosophers, whose stand on the truth of myth was invariably critical or even skeptical. In Greek philosophical thinking myth was scrutinized from the vantage point of rational truths, which, however, at one and the same time allowed only of a very narrow and one-sided view.

The Greek Sophists attempted to reinterpret the traditional myths or theogonic tales as allegories revealing naturalistic and moral truths. Plato criticized this allegorical reinterpretation, but the Neoplatonic and Stoic philosophers of the Hellenistic period, who saw in it a method of preserving the authority of tradition, approved of it. The historian Sallustius (86–34? B.C.), and four centuries later the emperor Julian the Apostate (332–363) regarded myths as divine truths and mysteries, while the Epicurean philosophers considered them fabrications which were introduced primarily to bolster the authority of the priests and the rulers. Euhemerus (third century B.C.) formulated this approach, and Euhemerism has become the term for the historical explanations of myth.

As David Bidney put it, "Both the Neo-Platonists and Stoics, as well as the Epicureans, agreed that the myths were not to be taken literally, but the tender-minded conservatives saw in them eternal, allegorical, religious, and philosophical truths, while the tough-minded reformers explained them away as fictions designed to mislead the credulous, superstitious multitude."[1]

4. FROM THE RENAISSANCE TO MAX MÜLLER

Following the outburst of interest in the meaning and truth of myth which was part of the Hellenistic controversy with Judeo-Christian monotheism, the problem was swept into the background and remained quiescent throughout the centuries dominated by Christian dogmatism. It seemed as if myth had definitely become a thing of the past, dead and buried as far as its ability to move and motivate was concerned.

Then, with the Renaissance, came a revival of interest in all things classic, including mythology, which became anew a motivating power, first in the fields of visual arts for which it became an inexhaustible source of subject-matter, then also in philosophy. In the latter, although at first nothing startlingly new was added, the preoccupation itself with the meaning of myth was the significant factor. For instance, Francis Bacon (1561–1626) interpreted, in his *Wisdom of the Ancients,* the classic myths of Greece as moral allegories.

Perseus, for Bacon, was a symbol of war; when Perseus attacks only the mortal one among the three Gorgons, this to him meant that only practicable wars ought to be attempted.

In the following century the interest in mythology flared up in full force. The controversy between opposing schools as to the interpretation of myth continued right where it had been cut short by the victory of Christianity, as if only a few years, and not fifteen centuries, had intervened.

The Epicurean argument was taken up by the rationalistic philosophers such as Voltaire (1694–1778), who attempted to establish reason as the foundation of all belief and of all rules of conduct, and who therefore tried to discredit the classical myths, together with the Hebrew-Christian Scriptures, either as irrational superstitions or as deliberate fictions foisted upon the multitude by crafty priests. Arrayed against such thinkers were the heirs of the Neoplatonists and Stoics, represented by the German Romanticists of the late eighteenth and early nineteenth centuries, for whom poetic myth became a subject of veneration, and who saw in it the mainspring of human culture. This renewed controversy as to the *value* of myth prepared the ground for the ensuing discussion about its *meaning*. The main protagonists of this fight, however, were no longer poets and philosophers, but anthropologists, psychologists, and linguists.

The first of these was Edward B. Tylor (1832–1917). He maintained that at a certain stage of cultural evolution and "with a consistency of action so general as to amount to mental law . . . among the lower races all over the world the operation of outward events on the inward mind leads not only to statement of fact, but to formation of myth."[2] This being the case, Tylor asserts, "myth is the history of its authors, not of its subjects; it records the lives, not of superhuman heroes, but of poetic nations" (1:416). His thesis is that there was a "myth-making stage of the human mind" and that "myth arose in the savage condition prevalent in remote ages among the whole human race . . . [and] it remains comparatively unchanged among the modern 'rude' tribes who have departed least from these primitive conditions, while even higher and later grades of civilization, partly by retaining its actual principles, and partly by carrying on its inherited results in the form of ancestral tradition, have continued it not merely in toleration but in honour" (1:283–84).

As to "the causes which transfigure into myths the facts of daily experience," Tylor assigns the chief role to "the belief in the animation of all nature, rising at its highest pitch to personification . . . To the lower tribes of man, sun and stars, trees and rivers, wind and clouds, become personal animate creatures, leading lives conformed to human or animal analogies" (1:285). Among the "lower races" these analogies are "real and sensible"; only in "more advanced periods of civilization" is there "the great expansion of verbal metaphor into myth." Therefore, "material myth" or "myth founded on fact" is "the primary, and verbal myth (or 'myth founded on word') the secondary formation" (p. 299).

Only a very brief reference need be made to the "solar" mythology of Friedrich Max Müller (1823–1900). This scholar, the leading Sanskritist of nineteenth-century England, maintained from 1856 (when his long essay "Comparative Mythology" was published) to his last publication in 1897 (the two bulky volumes of his *Contributions to the Science of Mythology*) that all Aryan mythologies, including Hindu, Greek, and Germanic, tell about the sun and the natural phenomena occasioned by it—such as dawn, day, night, the seasons, and the like. The ingenuity that went into this solar mythology was quite impressive. To take a single example, according to it the tale of Hercules's death by the shirt poisoned with the blood of Nessus was derived from the sun setting amid red clouds.

Solar mythology was soon followed by a number of offshoots such as lunar mythology, wind mythology, storm-cloud mythology, and sky mythology. It also stimulated research into biblical mythology, such as A. Smythe Palmer's book, *The Samson Saga and Its Place in Comparative Mythology* (London, 1913), and an excursion into Hebrew solar mythology undertaken by that great Islamic scholar, Ignaz Goldziher (1850–1921), in an early book entitled *Der Mythos bei den Hebräern* (published in 1876, and in English translation the year after).

Today, solar mythology is memorable only for the uncommon interest aroused by the truly gigantic battle between Max Müller and his bitter opponent, Andrew Lang (1844–1912), a representative of cultural evolutionism in anthropology. "The giants slew each other," wrote Richard M. Dorson,[3] "although the corpse of cultural evolutionism bled more slowly than the dismembered torso of solarism."

5. WILHELM WUNDT

It has generally been overlooked by mythologists who summarized the development of various mythological theories that the first scholar to postulate an intrinsic relationship between myth and ritual was not Jane Harrison (see below), but the German psychologist Wilhelm Wundt (1832–1920). Miss Harrison's *Themis,* in which she made the point that myth is the spoken correlative of the acted rite, was published in 1912. Four years earlier, however, Wundt, in his monumental *Völkerpsychologie,*[4] devoted a subchapter, *"Mythus und Kultus"* ("Myth and Ritual"), to a discussion of precisely this subject.

Nature myth, Wundt observed,

in its basic forms, including, above all, those forms which lend it the character of a *believed reality,* finds its expression in *acts* which eliminate all doubt as to its origin out of emotion (*Affekt*) . . . The acts which stem from mythological motives are accompanied by specific characteristics which are as significant for the general connection of the acts of will with the feelings and emotions as they are expressive of the unusual intensity of precisely those emotions which belong to the realm of myth and religion. The acts which belong to this realm are termed *Cultus,* the name introduced by the Romans for the system of their religious feasts and sacrifices . . . Inasmuch as the *Cultus* comprises those acts which the community believes to be calculated to secure for it the protection and help of the gods, it endows the more narrowly delimited circle of mythical views which relate to this protective relationship and the duties imposed by it upon man with a special, augmented value, not shared by the mass of other myth components. This value itself, however, is founded upon two characteristics of the mythological view which form the basis of the ritual; one of these is of a practical, the other of a theoretical nature. Practically, the value of ritual lies in the reliance on the protective and helping might of the gods or also on the expectation that a misfortune which the gods threaten to bring upon man can be averted by means of magic acts. Theoretically, the significance of myth-structures carried by the ritual consists in the truth-content which is atributed to them. A witness of this belief-form, intensified to a conviction, is contained precisely in the ritual acts themselves: performances, which dominate the acts and deeds of man in all vital situations, and which often consist of the surrender of his most precious goods or even his own life, can have their origin only in motivations whose reality is undoubted. Therewith, however, the content of those conceptions of beliefs by which the ritual is carried, is elevated, with respect to both value-content and external validity, high above the circle of the other component parts of mythological thinking which continue much more unsteady and exposed to destruction or transformation.[5]

The beginnings of ritual, Wundt continues, reach back into the primitive stages of myth-development. The ritual acts attest to the validity of the mythical belief-contents, and express confidence in protection and help. The gods themselves receive a certain truth-content in the ritual dedicated to them. Both the ritual acts proper and the conceptions of belief connected with them are endowed with the attribute of holiness. On the earliest levels of mythological development, each custom which spread to any, even limited, extent had a ritual value. For the belief in magic which permeates primitive mythology renders each act of some importance an integral part of a magic ritual. When the gods of the nature myths are added to the primitive magic ritual, which itself originates in animistic beliefs, there ensues the development of higher ritual forms, as well as a dichotomy of myths into a part consecrated by the cult of the gods, and another, more profane, part (5:25–27).

Moreover, says Wundt, there are three forms in which mythological thinking concerned with nature expresses itself: firstly, in statements about the meaning of single natural objects; secondly, in stories in which natural events or occurrences interfering with natural events play a decisive role; and thirdly, in acts which refer back to natural-mythological motives and which consist of rites (*"Kulte"*) or rudiments of rites (5:86–87).

As to the interrelationship between myth and ritual, Wundt observes:

> Although every ritual refers to certain mythological ideas, not so in reverse: not every myth-construction has some connection with ritual. At the early stage, when as yet no doubts have been implanted into religious thinking, everything that belongs to the solid substance of belief finds its expression in ritual, and with its compelling force determines thereby also the way of acting. There are, however, myth-constructions which are less significant secondary components, or which belong to that realm of poetic fantasy which, whether admitted from the outside or produced independently, has no deeper relationship to those emotional needs which give rise to the doctrinal convictions (*"Glaubensüberzeugungen"*) nurtured by custom. These myth-constructions, as a rule, stand outside the ritual or have only a loose and more variable relationship to it. Among many African and West Indian native peoples one finds that the beliefs in magic, rooted in a primitive animism, has developed into an orderly, well-regulated ritual which stands under the protection of common custom. (4:316–17)

Translated into modern terminology, the gist of what Wundt says is that (1) there is an intimate connection between myth and ritual; (2) mythical beliefs give rise to rites; (3) the rites, in turn, validate the beliefs expressed in the myths; (4) all rites have their associated myths; but (5) not all myths have their associated rites; however, (6) the most important myths are those which are associated with rites. Thus Wundt, to say the least, adumbrates the pivotal features of the myth-and-ritual theory.

6. THE PSYCHOANALYSTS

Close on the heels of the *Völkerpsychologie* approach followed that of psychoanalysis. According to Freud, myth is a daydream of the race; it symbolizes a psychological and ethnohistorical reality. An important slice of this reality is symbolized in the Oedipus myth, most familiar to us as formulated in Sophocles's famous tragedy. In fact, this myth expresses a traumatic ethnohistorical experience which resulted, on the one hand, in the introduction of two basic taboos—in-group murder and in-group marriage—and, on the other, in the incessant outcroppings of the repressed wish to commit precisely these two crimes.

The Freudian school of psychoanalysis has spread its web of interpretation actually over many, and potentially over all, myths. The favorite, though not exclusive, "keys" have remained sexual: persons, objects, acts, situations, etc., figuring in myths are taken to express in symbolic form the subconscious processes of the human psyche. The story told in the myth stands for what the individual experiences in his own life and especially in his relationship with his parents. The myth of the birth of the hero, for instance, tells of the greatest heroic deeds—the emergence from the mother's womb and the survival of the birth-trauma.[6] Similarly, all myths stem from the dark pool of the subconscious into which we must delve if we want to reach down to their true psychological meaning.

In view of this interpretation of myth, common among psychoanalysts, it is remarkable that Géza Róheim (1891–1953) (who was an anthropologically oriented psychoanalyst, or a psychoanalytically oriented anthropologist), in his definition of myth gave no room at all to the subconscious. According to Róheim, myth is a narrative in which the actors are mostly divine and sometimes human; there is a definite locale; the story is part of a creed; and it is believed by the narrator. In comparison, in a folktale the dramatis personae are mostly human; the hero frequently battles with supernatural beings; the actors are nameless; the scene could take place anywhere; the story is purely fiction; and is not intended to be anything else.[7]

7. THE MYTH AND RITUAL SCHOOL

The myth and ritual school, which still commands the adherence of many students of myth, started out on its conquering career with Jane E. Harrison's *Themis*, published in Cambridge in 1912, in which she made three important points: (1) that myth arises out of a rite rather than the reverse; (2) that it is the spoken correlative (*to legomenon*), of the acted rite, the thing done (*to dromenon*); and (3) that it is not anything else, nor of any other origin.[8]

It should be noted that Miss Harrison based her observations on Greek material, and that her conclusions, too, referred to the Greek context. Similarly, all the others who developed the myth and ritual hypothesis in its early stages were classical scholars who specialized in the study of Greek religion: Gilbert Murray, A. B. Cook, F. M. Cornford, to name only a few of its most outstanding contributors.

However, it did not take long before the myth and ritual approach was applied to other fields as well. The diffusion of the theory proceeded in several directions simultaneously. In one direction it led to its application to many areas of Greek culture itself, outside the religious field proper but connected with it in their ultimate origins, such as art, drama, and comedy. In another, it broke out of the confines of ancient Greece and struck out boldly first into European folklore, and then into the vast and insufficiently explored fields of ancient Near Eastern cultures.

In the latter, S. H. Hooke became the foremost spokesman of the myth and ritual theory, supported by a number of specialists in Egyptology, Assyriology, biblical studies, and related fields. The results of their inquiries were assembled by Hooke in two successive collections of essays, whose impact on the study of ancient Near Eastern religions was as strong as that of Miss Harrison's *Themis* on the study of Greek religion two decades earlier.[9] From the theoretical point of view, however, Hooke's collections represent no advances as against the position reached earlier by Jane Harrison, Gilbert Murray, and other Greek scholars.

In his introductory essay to *Myth and Ritual,* Hooke reiterates that the early ritual patterns of the ancient Near East "consisted not only of things done but of things said. The spoken word had the efficacy of an act . . . In general, the spoken part of a ritual consists of a description of what is being done, it is the story which the ritual enacts . . . The original myth, inseparable in the first instance from its ritual, embodies, in more or less symbolic fashion, the original situation which is seasonally re-enacted in the ritual" (p. 3). Or, as reformulated in Hooke's introduction to *The Labyrinth:* "Together with the ritual and as an essential part of it there was always found, in some form or other, the recitation of the story whose outlines were enacted in the ritual. This was the myth, and its repetition had equal potency with the performance of the ritual. In the beginning the thing said the thing done were inseparably united, although in the course of time they were divorced and gave rise to widely differing literary, artistic, and religious forms" (pp. v–vi).

The position of the myth and ritual school can be rephrased succinctly as follows: myth is the spoken part of the ritual. There is no myth without ritual and there is no ritual without myth.

In the 1940s the tidal wave of ritualism continued, conquering many new realms, from the culture of the Stone Age on the one hand to the modern theater on the other. Although its main domain has remained to this day the Old World, it made occasional forays across the Atlantic, nibbling even at such typically American cultural phenomena as the Negro blues.[10]

8. LORD RAGLAN

The most extreme exponent of the myth and ritual theory among modern anthropologists is Lord Raglan. His definition of myth is "simply a narrative associated with a rite."[11] In support of this definition, Lord Raglan quoted a number of anthropologists who have recorded their views on the nature of myth. Malinowski is quoted by him to the effect that "Myth fulfills in primitive culture an indispensable function: it expresses, enhances, and codifies belief; it safeguards and enforces morality; it vouches for the efficiency of ritual and contains practical rules for the guidance of man."[12]

Next, Lord Raglan quotes C. von Furer-Haimendorf, who says of the Gonds, an Indian jungle tribe:

The social norms regulating the tribal life of the Gonds are firmly rooted in mythology. They derive their validity from the rulings of culture-heroes and from the actions of deified ancestors recounted in epics and countless songs. The myths that tell of the origin of the Gond race and the establishment of the four phratries are more than history or folklore; they are the pragmatic sanction for institutions that determine the behaviour of every Gond towards his fellow-tribesmen, they are the vital forces inspiring the performance of the great clan feasts, and they define and authorise man's relations with the divine powers on whom his welfare depends. A relationship of mutual enlivenment links myth and ritual: as the myths lend power to the ritual acts, so the symbolic enactment of mythical occurrences during the cardinal rites of the clan feasts endows the myths with reality . . . It is in the sacramental rites based on the clan-myth that the unity of the clan attains realisation.[13]

Next follows a quotation from W. J. Culshaw, who observed of the Santals, a tribe of northeastern India, that

many of the social activities of the Santals are based on myths, and the strength of their clan organisation is due in no small measure to its foundations in mythology . . . When for any reason a piece of ritual associated with a myth falls into disuse, knowledge of the myth begins to die out; conversely, when the myth is looked upon as outmoded, the activity with which it is linked begins to lose its hold on the people's imagination . . . The decay of the ritual is leading to the disappearance of the ancient myth. It is nevertheless true that these stories do reveal the Santal view of the world. When they are told they call forth assent, and frequently in ordinary conversation the myths are cited in order to point a moral or clinch an argument."[14]

Finally, Raglan quotes M. Fortes, who reports of the Tallensi of the Gold Coast that "the complementary functions of chiefship and *tendana*-ship are rooted directly in the social structure, but are validated by myths of origin and backed by the most powerful religious sanctions of the ancestor cult and the cult of the earth."[15]

Following the above four quotations, Raglan says: "Other examples could be given, but these should suffice to show that myth and ritual are as closely linked among modern savages as they were in the ancient civilizations."[16]

An unbiased perusal of the four passages in question reveals that the authorities quoted are unanimous in refraining from stating, or even implying, that myth is a narrative associated with a rite, or that, as Raglan puts it on the subsequent page (p. 459), "it seems legitimate . . . to regard as myths such narratives whether quasi-historical or quasi-fictitious, as suggest a ritual origin."

On the contrary, the authorities quoted by Raglan state explicitly that myth "expresses, enhances, and codifies belief; it safeguards and enforces morality; . . . it . . . contains practical rules for the guidance of man" (Malinowski); that "the social norms regulating . . . tribal life . . are firmly

420

rooted in mythology . . . They are the pragmatic sanction for the institutions" (Furer-Haimendorf); that "many of the social activities . . . are based on myths"; that "the strength of . . . clan organisation is . . . [founded on] mythology" (Culshaw); and that certain social functions are "validated by myths" (Fortes). It is clear that all the four anthropologists quoted by Raglan attribute a much wider range of functions to myth than does Raglan himself.

9. DAVID BIDNEY

A new approach to myth has recently been developed by David Bidney. His interpretation of myth hinges on the question of the truth value contained in it. He states that "myths are, psychologically, charters of belief for those who accept them and live by them. Belief is essential to the acceptance of 'myth' and accounts for its effectiveness in a given cultural context, but the very fact of belief implies that subjectively, that is, for believer, the object of belief is not mythological."[17] Here Bidney seems to accept the modern anthropological interpretation of myth (exemplified by the four authorities adduced by Raglan) with one difference: he maintains that "for the believer" these myths are not really myths but truths. Then he goes on to say that, "Hence, nonbelief in a given narrative, tradition or explanation is essential for its evaluation as myth, just as belief in its truth and validity is essential for its acceptance as an effective element of culture." In other words, for Bidney, there is no such thing as myth in itself. The use of the term myth implies, according to him, that the narrative, tradition or explanation believed in by the society within which it exists, is, in fact, falsehood from the point of view of the user of the term.

The arbitrariness of equating the meaning of the term myth with false narrative, tradition, or explanation becomes evident when Bidney denies the applicability of the term within the context of Greek culture in which it originally arose. "What we now regard as myths," he says, "were not myths to the Greeks at all, but traditional religious narratives which were accepted literally and formed the validation for their rites and religious institutions" (p. 310). Here it becomes clear that Bidney chooses to use the term myth in a sense diametrically opposed to the one in which it was coined and used by the ancient Greeks. To them it was *precisely* the traditional religious narratives which were meant by the term myth. Bidney's argument, since it ultimately hinges upon the two adjectives "true" and "false," can be restated as follows:

1. The ancient Greeks used the term myth to denote certain types of traditional religious narratives which they believed to be true.
2. Our analysis shows that the term myth can be applied properly only to types of religious narratives which we know are false.

3. Therefore, what the Greeks termed myths were not myths.
4. Ergo, the Greeks had no myths.

Since Bidney equates myth with false doctrine, he also regards it as an evil. Accepting a parallel development between culture and myth in a manner reminiscent of Wundt, he maintains that "in precritical cultures animistic tales of culture heroes and of magic and epic cosmogonic and theogonic myths tend to prevail. In critical, prescientific cultures myths of the miraculous and supernatural gain currency. In scientific thought there is a tendency to discount narratives of the miraculous and supernatural, but to accept secular myths instead. In our so-called scientific culture we have the secular beliefs of pseudo-science, such as the myth of racial superiority and the stereotypes of racial and national character (p. 325).

Having unmasked myth as an evil, Bidney finds that it has to be combated: "That is why the struggle of man against myth demands such ceaseless vigilance . . . Myth is most potent when it is assumed complacently that one is free from it . . . Normative, critical, and scientific thought provides the only tested, self-correcting means of combating the growth of myth (pp. 325–26).

10. MALINOWSKI

Of the anthropologists with extensive field experience, the one who devoted most attention to the theory of myth was Bronislaw Malinowski (1884–1942). Malinowski's thesis on myth, as stated at the very outset of his Frazer Lecture, entitled "Myth in Primitive Psychology,"[18] is that "an intimate connection exists between the word, the myths, the sacred tales of a tribe, on the one hand, and their ritual acts, their moral deeds, their social organization, and even their practical activities, on the other" (p. 96). His own studies of "living myths among savages" satisfied Malinowski that myth "is not an idle rhapsody, not an aimless outpouring of vain imaginings, but a hard-working, extremely important cultural force" (p. 97). The most important services performed by myth within the context of a primitive culture "are done in connection with religious ritual, moral influences, and sociological principles" (p. 98).

The reason for myth being such a highly potent cultural force is that "it is not of the nature of fiction, such as we read today in a novel, but it is a living reality, believed to have once happened in primeval times, and continuing ever since to influence the world and human destinies. This myth is to the savage what, to a fully developed Christian, is the Biblical story of Creation, of the Fall, of the redemption by Christ's Sacrifice on the Cross. As our sacred story lives in our ritual, in our morality, as it governs our faith and controls our conduct, even so does his myth for the savage" (p. 100).

422

Consequently, Malinowski goes on, myth "is not symbolic, but a direct expression of its subject matter; it is not an explanation in satisfaction of a scientific interest, but a narrative resurrection of a primeval reality, told in satisfaction of deep religious wants, moral cravings, social submissions, assertions, even practical requirements. Myth fulfills in primitive culture an indispensable function: it expresses, enhances, and codifies belief; it safeguards and enforces morality; it vouches for the efficiency of ritual and contains practical rules for the guidance of man . . . It is . . . a pragmatic charter of primitive faith and moral wisdom" (p. 101). It "comes into play when rite, ceremony, or a social or moral rule demands justification, warrant of antiquity, reality, and sanctity" (p. 107).

Therefore, Malinowski asserts, every important magic, ceremony, or ritual has its associated belief which is spun out into accounts of concrete precedent which are myths. But, like Wundt, he does not maintain that every myth is associated with magic, ceremony or ritual. On the contrary, he assigns myth a much wider, much more variegated role. He stresses and reiterates as "perhaps the most important point" of his thesis on myth that "there exists a special class of stories (namely the myths), regarded as sacred, embodied in ritual, morals, and social organization," and looked upon by the natives as statements "of a primeval, greater and more relevant reality, by which the present life, fates, and activities of mankind are determined" (p. 108).

Elsewhere Malinowski formulates the same thought even more explicitly. After discussing the relationship between myth and magic, he states: "Myth, it may be added at once, can attach itself not only to magic but to any form of social power or social claim. It is used always to account for extraordinary privileges or duties, for great social inequalities, for severe burdens of rank, whether this be very high or very low" (p. 84).

When, following his theoretical introduction to myth, Malinowski next proceeds to a more detailed discussion of the myths of the Trobriand Islanders, he treats them under three headings: myths of origin, myths of death and of the recurrent cycle of life, and myths of magic. He does not say that this threefold division is exhaustive, but it is clear that each of the three he found to be representative of a major type of Trobriand mythology.

The main function of the first type is to supply the traditional precedent and charter in such areas as the totemic clan system, its ranking order, etc. The second myth type fulfills the same function with reference to aging, epidemics, death, the underworld, and so forth. These two types of myths, therefore, are not narratives associated with rites, but their function is to express, enhance, and codify beliefs, or to safeguard and enforce morality, or, again, to serve as guideposts in communal and individual life. Only in the third type of myths, the myths of magic, do they function as narratives associated with rites.

11. WALTER F. OTTO

A position on myth similar to that reached by Malinowski from an anthropological point of view was taken recently by the German philosopher Walter F. Otto in his book whose title can be translated as "Image and Existence: Collected Essays on Myth and Its Meaning for Mankind."[19] In fact, Otto carries the argument considerably farther than Malinowski in his emphasis on the importance of myth for mankind as a whole. His prefatory remark sets the tone for his inquiry, and stakes out its limits: "The existence (*Sein*) of the things themselves reveals itself to man in the primeval phenomena of image (*Gestalt*) and myth, in contrast to thought processes and moods of feeling; to wit, it reveals itself, as expressed by the myth, as something divine."

Otto begins his examination by stating that "myth is understood in general as a story about fabulous things which may contain a deeper meaning but which is not essentially true" (p. 66). The Greek word *mythos*, he says, assumed this meaning relatively early, when the Greeks began to subject the transmitted stories about the gods and the primeval world to intellectual criticism (pp. 66–67). But the original meaning of the word *mythos*, as used by Homer and other ancient Greek authors, was "word," "thing," "matter," "fact," "story," and primarily an "account" of what actually had happened in the past. The older and the more venerable the "story" contained in the *mythos*, the smaller the possibility of a mistake or purposeful falsification, the greater therefore its truth value (pp. 66–71).

Similarly, Otto goes on, the primitive peoples, too, distinguish explicitly between the old and sacred stories regarded as "true," and the newer ones, full of imagination, regarded as "false." The sacred seriousness with which the true myths are received manifests itself among other things in that they must not be recited at will and to any audience, but often only to a very few, with the exclusion of women, and only at certain times of the day and the year. Only these old stories, regarded as sacred, about the origins, the primordial days, and the gods, are therefore myths in the proper sense (p. 72). They are claimed to be true; in fact, to represent the ultimate and most sacred truth, and regarded as the most precious property.

Next, Otto turns to the problem of the evaluation of myth by outsiders, and especially by students of mythology: The nearest thing seems to be simply to deny the claim to truth which the myth makes so decisively. And this is what actually is being done under the naive assumption that our own worldview is the only true one and must constitute the yardstick for the evaluation of all others. Then, it remains to explain how could the age of myth reach such peculiar views as to what was true. One must postulate a mode of thinking which, since it does not conform to our logic, is called "prelogical."

And all this is done, says Otto, without as much as first asking ourselves seriously whether myths could possibly be based upon true experiences

424

(p. 73). This approach is unjustified, Otto continues, for are we, in fact, so fashioned that we can allow ourselves unquestioningly to pass judgment on the world of ideas of early man? While we attribute to him a mode of thinking which is foreign to reality, so to speak artificial, it never occurs to us that we ourselves live and gather our experiences in a throughout artificial world. We have long ago banished primeval nature from our circle of vision. Those few who have not only fleetingly passed through one of the wildernesses so far removed from us, but actually experienced it, can still tell of the shudder of the awesome in whose face the oldest myths suddenly appear true.

And not only we, men of the technical age, live in an environment that lacks the prerequisites for an understanding of myth. Already the cultures of antiquity had become more and more removed from the form of existence of the generations for whom myth meant truth. This, and not merely the awakening of independent thinking, is the reason that already in the sixth century B.C. Theagenes of Rhegion felt that he had to justify the Homeric myths by declaring the names of the gods to be poetic designations for the elements, and that Xenophanes could so fiercely ridicule Homer and Hesiod for the human-likeness of their gods. He who wants to attempt an immediate understanding of the ancient myths would have to be able to transport himself into the environment in which prehistoric man lived and thought. Researchers, of course, feel that they can do this by collecting and interpreting as many survivals of the oldest cultures as possible, and by trying to disregard everything that man has experienced and learned in the course of centuries. That this is impossible is quite apparent. Thus we must give up any attempt at a direct understanding of the myths, and this is, in fact, the opinion of all those who know what true belief is.

While thus the direct road is closed to us, we can proceed indirectly; instead of asking about the meaning of the myths, let us inquire into the *effect* emanating from them.

> I do not mean primarily the effect of myth upon later generations throughout many centuries. This effect is unmeasurable: without it no Homer, no Pindar, would have sung, no tragedy been written, no statues carved, no temples built . . . Even as late as modern times, it has stimulated the spirits to always new efforts. One must therefore say: myth, whatever its origins and content, is the creative, the arouser to creative activity . . .
>
> But let us speak of a much more immediate effect of the myth, the one exerted by it on the posture of man himself, as long as it was held true and sacred . . .
>
> There was a time when it seemed self-evident that myth gave the acts of the ritual their meaning and form, and that therefore it was older, more original, than the ritual. However, once it has become clear how unthinkably old most ritual acts are, it seemed proper to reverse the relationship,

425

especially since the ritual acts appeared to be so called magic purposive acts which needed no such interpretations as those given by the myth, and, in fact, excluded them. This view has many adherents to this day.

But more thorough studies among precisely those peoples who were regarded as the chief witnesses for the magic origin of ritual acts made it evident that there is no ritual without myth, and never has been . . .

To this was added recently the important finding that the whole existence of primitive tribes is dominated by a single, great myth of primeval events, and that their entire ritual is carried out with conscious reference to that myth . . .

Thus, myth and ritual cannot be separated. But the statement that ritual demands myths is not sufficient. Of greatest importance is the other, that the *myth demands the ritual.*

That true myth is not without ritual is shown in that it in itself is a recital, a kind of ritual act. Myth is, as the Greeks designated it, the "word," that is to say it is only what it is in a spoken form. Its recital constitutes a special act amidst the observances of the ritual feast: it takes place in the intermissions between individual rites. It is expected that the ritual acts will result in beneficial effects, and the same is expected of the myth . . .

If, as in the ritual recital of myth, a word must have the power to perform miracles, it must be a word of a special kind, a word which is more than the words spoken every day or in which one expresses something witty or delightful . . . It must be the kind of word which not merely designates the thing, but *is* the thing itself. This, as we have seen, is the word originally understood by the Greek *mythos* . . . If the word *is* the thing itself, in a manner which, of course, simply remains incomprehensible to the rational scholarly way of thinking, then it cannot be but that it is effective in the realm of things. And of this kind is the word of the myth which the ancient peoples designated as the true one.

It is the word as living image (*Gestalt*) which has this significant quality. As everywhere where creative things happen, the image comes as a miracle to him who creates, so that he believes in revelation, and no longer distinguishes between thinking and being—thus did the word of the myth come to early man, and it had to be true and powerful because it was not a thought-out word but an experienced one: the being (*Sein*) of the things themselves." (pp. 73–78)

With reference to the interrelationship between myth and ritual, Otto emphasizes that primitive peoples declare that they carry out their ritual feasts in a manner which corresponds to the prehistoric event described in the myth. The same holds good for old rituals in general. That is, the ritual act is, or pretends to be, the repetition of a divine primeval happening, but a special kind of repetition. In it the meaningful event of early days is supposed to *happen* anew (pp. 79–80).

This is precisely what is supposed to take place at the performance of the Passion Play and the ritual of the wine and the host. They are highly charged repetitions of the events of the Redemption. But these repetitions are performed not merely for the purpose of bringing about a beneficial effect:

426

If they can achieve this, as we believe, this is rooted in their being much more than, and of a character quite different from, all purposive acts. They possess this power only because in an essential sense they *are* that event itself. They are, after all, always performed at the moment when the divine with its truth is immediately present. The salvation-bringing divine happening takes place at that time anew, and this miracle represents itself in the festive proceedings which to the superficial on-looker appears as mere imitation. The ritual act is nothing less than the revelation of the divine and its presence itself. This is how the rituals of the ancient peoples represent a sacred happening of early days and recite the mythical word about it, not in order to make this happening take place again through the force of magic, but because the divine of the sacred happening requires a manifestation in which it can be present itself. (p. 80)

In this sense, the ritual act is the necessary answer of man to the presence of the divine. But this answer is not a self-evident, freely willed action of man. In it the divine presence itself expresses itself, creates itself witness, in-carnates itself. That is to say, the ritual act itself is the revelation of divine truth. The divine, when it is truly near, wants to encounter itself in this human formulation (*Gestaltung*). The original ritual act, which repeats itself in all the subsequent ones, did not have to be preceded by a belief in the divine: it was immediately present in the ritual postures and acts.

Ritual, therefore, is not only inseparably connected with myth, but is essentially identical with it. As we recognized above that the true ancient myth is a kind of ritual, so it now transpires that the true ancient ritual is a kind of myth. The two are one in that in both the divine proximity re-veals itself formfully: in the ritual as posture and act, in the myth as the true word . . . The deeper difference between the two is that in the ritual man is elevated up to the divine, and in a way acts together with it; while in the myth the divine descends, incorporates itself as word in human or quasi-human form, and acts in a human-like fashion . . .

Thus we reach the conclusion: the most original and genuine myth, wherever and however it appears, is *true*. More than that: it is not merely true next to other truths, but is *the truth*, because it brings to light not only that which is temporarily right, or for the time being just and proper, but the being (*Sein*) of the things as image, to wit, as the form of all forms, the Divine.

If this be so, we have all reason to approach with respect also the ac-tual content of the myths. They tell us of divine or godlike beings and of acts performed by them. The locale of the events, attested to by the myth, is not a mysterious distance, but the very nature and world in which we live. (pp. 86–87)

Commenting upon the broader significance of myth for human culture in general, Otto observes that, although myth shows it's most immediate and powerful effect in the transformation of man into the image of him who be-haves and acts ritually, it remains creative in other realms as well. For under its aegis stand not only all works of art, but also the arrangements of communal life, the forms of spiritual and practical activity, the fashioning of characters.

While Otto thus recognizes and declares myth as the mainspring of all human cultural achievement, it is in the spiritual realm that he considers myth—together with ritual—as having its most fundamental role. Myth and ritual, he reiterates, constitute a dual bridge between man and God. Both myth and ritual are, each in its manner, manifestations of one and the same process, which takes place between the finite and the infinite, between man and God. Myth brings the infinite nearer to man. The infinite does not thereby lose its awe-inspiring magnitude, but it transforms itself and shows man a human face, talks to him in a human tongue. How this became possible, we do not learn from the myth itself. But the ritual, connected and related to myth, allows us to obtain some notion of it. Ritual, too, does not completely eliminate the distance between the eternal and man. The eternal remains in its magnitude, but man is transformed; ritual presents to man a god-like face and speaks to him in the tongue of the gods. The humanization of the divine in the myth, and the divinization of man in the ritual meet together in one single act (p. 254).

12. OUR DEFINITION OF MYTH

Having thus answered the first question we posed at the outset, it is time now to pass on to the second: to state what the present authors understand by myth.

We feel we can go along with Malinowski's thesis with reference to the sociocultural function of myth. We also find that Otto's interpretation of myth as a primary cultural force and a humanization of the divine reveals a deep insight, although we would prefer to leave open the question of whether in the myth the divine actually "descends and incorporates itself as word" and "the divine proximity reveals itself," or whether myth is merely the verbalized expression of human imaginings about the divine and the supernatural in general. Either of these two alternatives amounts to the attribution of a high value-content myth.

Thus we are led to a definition which both takes into account the sociocultural function of myth and reckons with its value-content. A third point, we feel, of a satisfactory definition of myth must be a reference to the concrete features contained in it. On these bases we reach the following definition:

Myth is a traditional religious charter validating laws, customs, rites, institutions and beliefs, or explaining human situations and natural phenomena, and taking the form of stories, believed to be true, about divine beings and heroes.

This definition, although applicable to myth in general, is phrased in particular with the ancient and more recent Mediterranean mythologies in mind. As far as its applicability to Hebrew mythology is concerned, this is best demonstrated by a number of examples. First, however, two points have to be clarified in connection with the foregoing definition.

Firstly, it must be pointed out that, although myths are, by definition, narratives which constitute traditional religious charters validating laws, customs, etc., this does not mean that all the details contained in any given myth likewise have some reference to or association with a corresponding detail in a law, custom, etc. On the contrary. The connection between myth and the cultural features of which it is the validating charter is often rather loose. A myth, once in existence, has the tendency to burgeon, to become elaborate and involved. In this respect it parallels ritual, which displays the same tendency. The old Hebrew ritual law, for instance, which prohibited the cooking of a kid in its mother's milk, has developed into the complex system of regulations which make it unlawful to use the same plates, or even the same refrigerator, for meat and milk dishes, or to taste milk for several hours after having eaten meat. Similarly, a myth such as that of Joseph and Potiphar's wife, which in its original biblical form was a charter validating the prohibition of adultery, has subsequently undergone detailed novelistic elaboration, and presents at considerable length the emotions and maneuvers of Mrs. Potiphar. It would be as futile to look for the mythical validation of all the details of the meat and milk regulations as it would be to search for features in the laws of sexual morality which could be said to be validated by the midrashic embellishments of the Joseph story.

Secondly, some remarks are in order about the heroes whose deeds often form the subject matter of myth.

13. THE HEBREW HERO

A comparison of the Hebrew hero with the Greek will point up important features specific to Hebrew mythology. The Greek hero is usually descended from a divine father and a human mother. Thanks to this semidivine descent, he has exceptional qualities, and is able to perform great feats. But he is mortal, and dies at the end, unless, in one way or another, he succeeds in gaining immortality.

The typical Hebrew hero, by contrast, is an ordinary mortal who becomes a hero by divine election. This takes the form of God addressing him and informing him that he has been accorded a special status. Thus were Noah, Abraham, Moses, and others made heroes. Alternately, the divine selection may take place in early childhood, or even before the hero's birth, in the form of an annunciation to his future mother and/or father (Samson, Samuel).

Throughout his life the hero retains the special qualities which distinguish him only as a result of the divine will or grant. It is his reliance on God, his acceptance of God's will, which make him prevail against adversaries stronger and more numerous. Thus physical prowess, although possessed by many Hebrew heroes, is an unimportant, secondary concomitant, contingent upon the primary factor of Hebrew heroism: the chosenness by God.

Hebrew mythology, like Greek, also knows of half-human and half-divine beings who issued from unions between divine fathers and human mothers. In fact, one Hebrew mythical cycle tells of an entire race that sprang up from the union of the sons of God with the daughters of man. But, typically, Hebrew mythology has very little to say about these semidivine heroes: they barely exist as individuals, but remain instead an undifferentiated crowd of gigantic and evil anonyms whom the great Flood soon washes off the face of the earth.

On the other hand, some Hebrew heroes, although of purely human descent, also succeeded in attaining immortality. But this, too, was allotted to them as a divine gift, in reward for exceptionally meritorious conduct in fulfilling, during their life span, the exacting moral and ritual demands of Hebrew herohood. Thus pious Enoch becomes the chief archangel Metatron; Eliezer enters Paradise alive; Abraham is translated into the eternal gatekeeper of Gehenna; Elijah continues to roam heaven and earth; and the Messiah—a flesh-and-blood descendant of David—sits in chains awaiting the blast of the great shofar of liberation.

The typical Hebrew hero is not a historical figure; or, to put it more cautiously, his historicity cannot be attested. In this sense not only Adam and Eve, Cain and Abel, Noah and his sons are typically mythical heroes, but also Abraham, Isaac and Jacob, Moses and Aaron, Joshua and Caleb.

On the other hand, also historical figures can, and not infrequently do, become heroes of myths. Solomon or Jeroboam, Isaiah or Zerubbabel, were undoubtedly historical characters, yet so much mythological material has been woven around them that their myth-suffused figures differ in no way from those of the typical heroes of the primordial ages.

14. TYPES OF HEBREW MYTHS

Now for our examples illustrating the various types of Hebrew myth.

A myth validating a legal precept is the account of Jacob's encounter and fight with the angel at the Ford of Jabbok. The ancient Hebrew ritual prohibition of eating the *nervus ischiadicus* in the top portion of the hind legs of animals is validated by this myth, which tells of Jacob having suffered an injury in the corresponding part of his body as a result of his nocturnal fight with an angel—who was none other than Yahweh Himself. The story of the divinity's touch of the hollow of the thigh establishes the unquestionable basis for the holiness of the sinew running along it and renders it taboo.

A myth validating a custom is the account of Abraham's visit to Ishmael in the desert. Although this myth differs from that of Jacob's fight—inasmuch as it presupposes the existence of the value of hospitality instead of establishing it—it nevertheless supplies the sanction and validation to the custom and thereby removes it from the realm of free choice and stamps it with the distinctive mark of obligatory observance.

A myth validating a rite is the account of the ʿAqēdah, of the "binding" of Isaac on Mount Moriah. It contains a message about the abolition of child-sacrifice and its replacement by animal sacrifice; it establishes the basis for the use of the *shofar,* the ram's horn, in the New Year's ritual; it conveys the certainty that on that great and annually recurring Day of Judgment God will have compassion on His children and forgive them. It is a part of the ritual, being read in full on the second day of New Year, and referred to explicitly on both the first and the second day.

A myth validating an institution is the account of Ham's castration of Noah. As a punishment for this unspeakable crime, his descendants turned black and were condemned to slavery—this is the mythical statement. Thus the use of black slaves receives its mythical sanction.

A myth validating a belief is the account of Isaac's blessing, for which his twin sons so keenly competed. The belief in the power and efficacy of the blessing, especially the paternal one, is validated by the demonstration of the supreme value attributed to the blessing by the ancestral heroes of the nation.

A myth explaining a human situation in the political and social order of things is the account of the strife between Jacob and Esau and of the relationship between the twins and their father Isaac. Rome, which is Edom, gained ascendancy over Jerusalem, which is Israel, because Esau, who was Edom, had certain merits in relation to Isaac in regard to which he excelled over Jacob, who was Israel.

A myth explaining a natural phenomenon is the story of the creation of the world. It explains the existing order of nature by describing how the constituent parts of the universe were created or established by God.

In sum, as shown by the above examples, the various types of Hebrew myth are, in their totality, expressive of Hebrew-Jewish ethos, that is, of the characteristic and distinguishing attitudes, habits, values, aspirations, and outlooks of the people. The connection between *ethos* and *mythos* is intrinsic and manifold. For not only does the *mythos* express the national *ethos,* but the latter, in turn, is influenced, molded, and shaped by the national *mythos.* This interdependence of *ethos* and *mythos,* incidentally, is a subject which could bear closer scrutiny by both mythologists and social psychologists, and which has hitherto been largely overlooked even by those anthropologists who have studied national character, modal personality, or basic personality structure.

431

15. THE RECONSTRUCTION OF HEBREW MYTHS

A word is now in order about the problem of reconstructing the earliest versions of Hebrew myth. Such a venture is of considerable importance, since it could open an avenue to the understanding of primitive stages in the development of ancient Hebrew religion. But the difficulties are considerable. In fact, the problem is much more difficult than any comparable reconstruction in the mythologies of other ancient peoples, as a brief consideration of the different circumstances will indicate.

In the study of the mythologies of the ancient Near Eastern and Mediterranean peoples, the central difficulty is that the early layer of mythographic activity reflecting a matriarchal order of society lies, as a rule, buried deep beneath younger superimposed strata which represent the later, largely patriarchal, phases of social development. What is often required, therefore, is to peel carefully away the patriarchal encrustments before one can reach the old substrata dating back to the prehistoric or protohistoric days of early matriarchy.

The same task, when one wants to perform it in the realm of Hebrew mythology becomes much more complex. In tracing the development of other ancient Near Eastern and Mediterranean mythologies, one has to account only for a unilateral change: that of the replacement of what can be called *matri-myth* with the younger *patri-myth*. The divine family figuring in the myths remains largely of the same composition: gods and goddesses of several successive generations, called in most cases by the same old names, even though the power relationship between the sexes has been reversed. The pantheon is now headed by a male god, and the goddesses take the same subordinate positions with which the human members of their sex had to be satisfied following the patriarchal breakthrough, but there they are, nevertheless, to serve as a starting point for the historical reconstruction.

Not so in Hebrew mythology. Here the development proceeded in a twofold direction simultaneously. There was the shift from the *matri-myth* to the *patri-myth* familiar from other contemporary cultures. But then there was the specific Hebrew shift from polytheism to monotheism, as a result of which the ancient female goddesses not only had to abdicate their leading positions but, to all intents and purposes, disappeared altogether.

To what an extent this complicates the process of arriving at the original form and meaning of a myth can be illustrated by a relatively simple example. In Akkadian mythology there is the incident of the fight of Marduk, the young male creator-god, against Tiamat, the old, primeval goddess of the salt-watery chaos. The myth relates that Marduk vanquished and killed Tiamat, and that out of her body he formed the heaven and the earth. It is the task of the mythologist to find the older version of the creation myth which was probably replaced by this one. This younger myth regards the original state of the universe (that is, society) under matriarchal rule as having been chaotic. The creation of the cosmic order (heaven and earth, etc.) came about when the young male god (or king) vanquished the old matriarchal goddess (queen) and killed her. The old goddess is reduced to bodily serving as the building material out of which the cosmos is formed. In the older, matriarchal version of the myth (not extant), the primal queen of chaos probably brought forth the cosmos out of her own body by spontaneous generation.

In the corresponding Hebrew creation myth, to which only allusions are found in the Bible, not only the female point of view has been firmly supplanted by the male one, but, in addition, the polytheistic elements of the pre-creation theomachy have also been excised to a degree where it is only by a lucky chance that they can at all be surmised to have originally been comprised in it. The lucky chance is represented by the term used in the Genesis account to denote the primeval chaos: it is *Tehom,* linguistically identical with *Tiamat.* On this basis, one is able to speculate that what in the extant form appears in the Genesis version of the Creation story as a series of unchallenged, autocratic creative divine acts must have contained, also in the original Hebrew formulation, an account of a primeval combat between the creator-god and opposing deities. It so happens that allusions found in some prophetic and poetic books of the Bible, as well as more ample mythical material that survived in the Talmudic and Midrash literature, support this assumption to the fullest.

As to the femininity of *Tehom,* all that we have to go by, as far as the biblical references are concerned, is the grammatical gender of the word, which is, as a rule, feminine. In Hebrew myths recorded much later, but undoubtedly going back to very ancient origins, instead of *Tehom* there appear the "Lower Female Waters," who opposed God at the time of creation, who yearned to reunite with the "Upper Male Waters," and who, at the time of the Flood, destroyed the world.

Equally little has survived in the Hebrew sources about other female deities. That the simple folk of Judaea worshipped the Queen of Heaven down to the last days of the First Temple (destroyed in 586 B.C.), we know from a few brief references in Jeremiah. Nor can there be any doubt as to the familiarity of the Hebrews in the biblical period with other female deities, such as Astarte, Anath, and Asherah. These goddesses were worshipped with tenacity in spite of the prophets' battle against them for nearly three centuries.

Yet it is impossible to say anything with certainty as to an early period of Hebrew matriarchy in which—corresponding to the leading position of women in human society—female deities may have headed the divine family. Direct proofs are lacking. The indirect evidence is too fragmentary to base any definite hypothesis upon it. The question of the old goddesses thus remains one of the great enigmas of Hebrew mythology.

433

16. THE CHARACTER OF HEBREW MYTHS

We reach safer ground when we proceed to an analysis of the main characteristics of Hebrew mythology. One of these is the subordinate role played in Hebrew myths by divine or superhuman beings other than God. This becomes apparent especially when Hebrew myths are compared with other ancient Near Eastern and with Greek myths. The chief reason for this specificity lies, of course, in the monotheistic reworking to which ancient polytheistic or polydemonistic mythical material had been subjected before attaining the form in which they were finally incorporated into the Bible, the Talmuds and the Midrashim. In the ancient Near Eastern and Greek worlds, as far as the development of belief is concerned, those who wrote down the myths were not far removed from those among whom the myths originally gained currency. The written account of the Marduk-Tiamat fight, for instance, although unquestionably younger by many centuries than its original oral version, nevertheless reflects a largely identical religious atmosphere and a highly similar belief system.

With Hebrew mythology the situation is different. By the time the earliest parts of the Bible were written down, official Hebrew religion was monotheistic. The populace as a whole still retained numerous features of its old polytheism or polydemonism, but the compilation of the sacred writ was done not by them but by the learned few whose outlook conformed to the monotheistic orthodoxy of the time. Thus, grossly polytheistic features or references were ruthlessly excised from any mythical piece included in the early compilations upon which the final canon and other collections were to be based.

There can thus be little if any doubt that the Bible, Talmud and Midrash, in their extant form, preserved but the palest remnants of early Hebrew mythology, those myth-fragments only which, because of their relatively innocuous character, escaped censorship. The few allusions, for instance, to God's fight with the Dragon (variously named Leviathan, Rahab, Tehom, or the Prince of the Sea) found in the Hebrew sources cannot be more than the last faint echoes of an original elaborate ancient myth which must have dwelt lustily on all details of the Primeval Combat. Moreover, we may assume that, in accord with the general mythical tendency to develop themes toward poetic perfection,[20] that full version must have comprised the description of a phase in the combat in which the hero-god was almost vanquished by his monstrous opponent, before he rallied and arose to deal the Dragon the final, mortal blow.

Of all this, of course, practically nothing has been left after repeated monotheistic scrutinies and excisions. This is why in its *extant form* Hebrew mythology differs from those of other nations. Other mythologies are polytheistic; in them, equally—or almost equally—powerful deities figure and

434

act, fight and make love, create and procreate, kill and destroy. Hebrew mythology is monotheistic; there is only one God in it, although there are also other divine beings, demons and dragons, good and evil angels, celestial patrons of nations, and princes of elements. But instead of engaging God in mortal combat, all that these superhuman beings can do is to oppose Him, rebel against Him, threaten Him, and occasionally even physically tangle with him. However, be the form of their opposition to Him what it may, it is a foregone conclusion that, in the end, God always prevails, and this, of course, takes away much of the excitement and fascination inherent in the non-Hebrew divine-combat myths.

Still, one recognizes that in Hebrew mythology God does not yet have the absolute power attributed to Him in the subsequent development of the Hebrew and Jewish God-concept. He is not yet powerful enough to prevent the other superhuman beings from trying to pitch their strength against His. But He is already elevated so far above them that they can proceed with their rebellious attempts only as long as He pays no attention to them or takes no action against them. Once His attention is caught, His ire aroused, He has no difficulty in frustrating their knavish tricks and bringing about their downfall. God's rule in the stage in which Hebrew mythology shows Him is comparable to that of a powerful sheik who holds sway over his unruly and restless family with promises and threats, rewards and punishments, persuasion and cajoling, and, in the last resort, physical force, against whom sons or nephews may plot and rise, but who, in the end, always succeeds in maintaining his autocratic but benevolent rule.

17. THE ORIGIN OF THE SUPERHUMANS

A specific question in Hebrew mythology pertains to the *origin* of the superhuman or divine beings. In the earliest stages of which literary traces have been preserved, the divinities opposing God have an existence independent of Him. They are, in fact, present at the time God begins His great work of creation. What the precise nature and character of these primeval divinities was we cannot tell on the basis of the extant Hebrew sources alone. These convey to us nothing more than toned down reflections, watered down versions, in which very little except their mere existence is stated, or, even less than that, alluded to. Thus Genesis 1 tells about the precreation existence of Tohu and Bohu, Darkness, Tehom and Water, but nothing more. That these were, originally, mythical divinities or entities is, however, hinted at in other parts of the Hebrew sources, and more firmly established by comparison with other ancient Near Eastern mythologies.

The independent origin and existence of these mythical divinities harmonizes with the myths of combat which tell about their objections to God's creative intent and their subsequent attacks on Him. But at a later stage of Hebrew mythical thought, the independent, that is noncreated, existence of these mythical divinities or superhuman beings came to be regarded as offensive, because incompatible with the more advanced monotheistic ideas, and they were therefore said to have been created by God, in most cases prior to the creation of the present physical world. This change at once established the overlordship of God in the superhuman realm as in the human and physical ones, for entities created by God must, of course, be subordinate to Him. This new power relationship, however, introduced of necessity a change also into the tone and content of the combat myth. Whatever fight between God and other divinities was still allowed to be told of, was now no longer a combat between two originally independent opponents, but the result of a rebellion started by subordinate divinities against God, who created them and who thus *a priori* had the assigned status of overlordship over them. The younger combat myths, therefore, are paler, more restrained, and less outspoken, than the old ones. They are nothing more than short but repetitious accounts of how certain divinities, one after the other, made unsuccessful and halfhearted attempts to rise up against God, their Creator, or merely to assert themselves in His face by disobeying Him.

An additional consequence of this development was that while the distance between God and these subordinate divinities increased, the distance between the latter and man decreased. Man, too, it was now remembered and reported, occasionally tried to disobey God and to act against His will—with, of course, the same poor results. Where man stood a better chance to succeed and to prevail was in his occasional encounters with one of those downgraded divinities, whose powers barely—if at all—exceeded those of heroic humans. To make the matter even more acceptable to monotheistic orthodoxy, the divine opponent of the hero was called "a man" (not even "an angel"), and his divine status was not stated as an established fact but only allowed to be guessed or surmised by the hero. Thus Jacob, we are told, fought "a man" at the Ford of Jabbok; only subsequently did he conclude that his opponent, who, in fact, proved weaker than he, must have been an *Elohim,* a divinity. Similarly, in later mythical accounts which tell about how a king or a sage got embroiled with a demon of either the male or the female sex (as Solomon with Ashmodai, or Hanina ben Dosa with Igrat the daughter of Mahalat), it is usually the flesh-and-blood hero who bests his superhuman opponent. When, as it rarely happens, a clash is reported as having taken place between a hero and God Himself (as in the awesome nocturnal encounter of Moses and Yahweh, Exodus 4:24–26), we can be sure that we are faced with an inadvertently preserved myth-fragment of extremely great antiquity.

18. THE MYTH OF CREATION

Another characteristic of Hebrew mythology is its great preoccupation with Creation. In this respect, Hebrew mythology shows itself to be of one kind with other ancient Near Eastern mythologies, and of a hue different from Greek mythology. Among all ancient Near Eastern peoples the concern with Creation was so great that around it was centered the myth and ritual complex which had by far the greatest importance in their religious life and which had to be performed annually in order to secure the well-being of the community—and, indeed, of the whole world—for the ensuing year. This myth and ritual complex, or "pattern," as Hooke and his associates called it, in which the priest-king was the central figure—incarnating as he did in his person the fortune of the state—followed the same broad general lines in all ancient Near Eastern religions.

> This pattern consisted of a dramatic ritual representing the death and resurrection of the king, who was also the god, performed by priests and members of the royal family. It comprised a sacred combat, in which was enacted the victory of the god over his enemies, a triumphal procession in which the neighboring gods took part, an enthronement, a ceremony by which the destinies of the state for the coming year were determined, and a sacred marriage.
>
> Together with the ritual and as an essential part of it there was always found, in some form or other, the recitation of the story whose outlines were enacted in the ritual. This was the myth, and its repetition had equal potency with the performance of the ritual.[21]

This general pattern constituted, in all probability, the basis of the great annual feast among the ancient Hebrews, as well. However, among them the pattern has become gradually modified, beginning with early historic times, so as to conform with the general religious development, which inexorably marched toward increasingly stricter monotheism. As a result, the pattern was successively divested of its polytheistic features, the deification of the king became more and more muted, the figure and concept of God more and more exalted, and the sacred marriage—which to the rigidly monotheistic taste smacked too strongly of idolatrous fornication—altogether dropped. What remained were a number of inoffensive rites: Temple furnishings and paraphernalia such as the booths, which originally were, in all probability, nuptial chambers for the sacred marriage; the "levity" in the Temple courtyard, which probably was a popular survival of the sexual licence accompanying the sacred marriage; the fight around and with the *lulabs* and the priestly footrace, in which one can see a survival of the reenactment of the primeval combat; the water libation, which symbolized and brought about the union of the Upper Male Waters with Lower Female Waters; the divination, by means of the altar smoke, of the extent of the ensuing year's fertility; and other such ritual traces.[22]

Much clearer and more outspoken traces survived of the spoken part of the "pattern": that is, of the myth associated with it. In the Bible, but even more so in Talmud and Midrash, the mythical references to Creation abound. In fact, the creation myth underwent that elaboration which is always an unmistakable sign of continuing interest in the subject matter dealt with by a myth. Hebrew creation myths, significantly, are rich and detailed, not in their early, biblical forms, but in their later Talmudic and Midrashic ones. In fact, in Talmudic times speculations about the creation of the world were in vogue to such an extent that they constituted a special subject of study called *"Ma'ase Merkavah"* ("matters of the chariot"), into which to delve was regarded a highly dangerous undertaking.

Inevitably, the question arose as to what God had been doing prior to the creation of the world, and this subject, too, was seized upon and elaborated. Only a few traces survive of the speculations on this problematic subject, barely enough to indicate that a thousand successive creations were postulated preceding that of our present world. In a different direction, mythical thinking became preoccupied with the structure of the universe, the dimensions, interrelationships, and movements of its component parts, and thus mythical cosmogony branched out into mythical cosmography and cosmology.

The latter topics, again, tied in with fantasies about the abode of the dead, and about storehouses filled with souls waiting for their incorporation into the bodies of the newborn. The mythical descriptions of the world thus dealt with matters of direct concern for everybody, for it was, of course, as vital to know what region of the invisible world would be assigned to one as the *post mortem* abode, as it was to know how to conduct oneself in this life in order to escape the seven regions of Gehenna and to secure oneself a satisfactory seat in The World to Come.

19. THE HERO AND TIME

A further important characteristic of Hebrew mythology is the great awareness evinced by it of the historical and cosmic significance of the words, acts, and attitudes of the mythical heroes. Without using the modern terminology, the Talmudic sages in their interpretations and elaborations of biblical myths operate freely and frequently with the idea that certain myths are charters validating human situations, power relationships, rituals, customs, etc.

Take, for instance, such a figure as Jacob, one of the most important characters in Hebrew mythology. He succeeded, we are told, in obtaining the blessing from his father Isaac, and therefore his descendants were to conquer Edom and defeat the Edomites, the sons of Esau. However, all this happened only because it was willed by God: He sent Satan to detain Esau in the field and thus enable Jacob to secure the paternal blessing. When Isaac said, "The

438

voice is the voice of Jacob, but the hands are the hands of Esau," he predetermined thereby the relationship between Jacob and Esau (that is between Israel and Edom or Rome) for all times: as long as Jacob raises his voice in prayer and the study of the Law, Esau's hands have no power over him. As to Esau, his possession of Italy was likewise predetermined by Isaac in his blessing. As to the subjugation of Israel by Rome, this was due to the greater respect Esau had paid to his father than Jacob: Esau served his father with filial devotion throughout those twenty years which Jacob spent away from his father in Mesopotamia, building up his own family and fortune.

Moreover, and this is possibly of even greater significance with regard to the awareness of the "charter" character of myths, in Hebrew mythology the heroes themselves are fully conscious of the indelible historical effect their acts or words have upon the fate of their descendants. For instance, when Jacob, upon his return from Mesopotamia, prepared to meet Esau, he instructed his servants (with whom he sent propitiatory gifts to his brother): "Put a space between drove and drove." In truth, the mythical elaboration of this passage asserts, Jacob was addressing himself to God and had the future fate of his children in mind. "Master of all the worlds," he said, "if troubles come over my children, let them not come one after the other, but let there be a breathing spell in between!"

Thus the typical Hebrew hero, while acting in response to an actual situation, is aware at the same time that his acts, words, and even intentions are of irrevocable historic significance; that they predetermine what will happen to his descendants to the end of time; that therefore his behavior and very being are of more than ordinary mortal dimensions. This, too, is, of course, a result of having been spoken to and elected by God; but whatever its source, the responsibility is heavy on his shoulders and compels him to act circumspectly, to move ponderously.

Connected with this feature of Hebrew mythology is another one—the unmistakable moral-spiritual character inherent in it. A basic underlying idea, expressed in many myths, is that the hero's success or failure in any important venture depends, in the first place, upon his moral-spiritual merits. The merits, if one has them, either through one's own good deeds or those of one's ancestors, form a claim which, in the crucial moment, God will not fail to honor.

Thus when Jacob was about to meet Esau, he was sore afraid, but not because he suspected that Esau commanded a stronger army. In Jacob's view, the outcome of the expected battle between Esau and himself depended on the relative weight of the two antagonists' merits; it was, therefore, a question of spiritual considerations. At that moment he became aware of the merits Esau had unquestionably accumulated in the twenty years he, Jacob, had spent in Mesopotamia: Esau remained all that time in the Land of Israel, and honored his father and his mother. These merits, he feared, could assure Esau of

439

victory over him. Although at the time, as it transpired, Jacob's fears proved groundless, in the long run, some fifteen centuries later, it was precisely this circumstance—Esau's special filial merits—which resulted in Edom-Rome gaining the upper hand over Israel.

While the relationship between the mythical hero and his late posterity is thus, as a rule, expressed in the ancestral hero's influence upon his descendants, occasionally at least the influence proceeds in the opposite direction: from the descendants back to the forefather. Thus, when Jacob and Esau fought in their mother's womb and some angels helped Esau, God said to them: "Do not help the wicked; rather, help the righteous, Jacob, whose children will offer up sacrifices for their sins . . . therefore be charitable to him! But wicked Esau [i.e., Rome] will in the future oppress the earth, therefore prepare for him, already now, roads leading to hell!"

In Hebrew mythology, therefore, not only does the past influence the present and the present determine the future, but also the future influences and determines the present. Psychologically, this can be explained by saying that those who are convinced that they foresee the future inevitably let their assumed knowledge of the future influence their present thoughts and deeds. Morally, it means that past, present, and future, in both projective and retroactive relationship, are tied together into one inseparable unity of responsibility. Ancestors must act with an eye to posterity, and descendants must equally be aware that their deeds determine the fate of their progenitors. This consciousness was implanted by the Hebrew myths into the hearts of each successive Jewish generation, and in this manner the Hebrew myths became a psychological and moral force for Jewish survival.

Notes

CHAPTER 1

1. Paul O'Prey, ed., *Between Moon and Moon: Selected Letters of Robert Graves 1946–1972*, London: Hutchinson, 1984, p. 51.

2. Raphael Patai, *Man and Temple in Ancient Jewish Myth and Ritual*, Edinburgh: Thomas Nelson, 1947.

3. Raphael Patai, *Man and Temple in Ancient Jewish Myth and Ritual*, 2d ed., New York: Ktav, 1967, pp. 220–22.

4. Apollonius of Rhodes, *Argonautica*, trans. with an intro. by E. V. Rieu, Harmondsworth, Eng.; Baltimore: Penguin Classics, 1959, p. 193.

5. Robert Graves, *The White Goddess*, London: Faber, 1948. In the revised edition (New York: Farrar Straus, 1966) I used, it is on pp. 327–29.

6. However, cf. 1 Macc. 9:63.

7. Paul de Lagarde, *Onomastica Sacra*, 2d ed., Göttingen: Dieterich, 1887, p. 121, ll. 15–19. My translation from the Latin.

8. See Epiphanius, *De pon. et mens.*, § 62, ed. Paul de Lagarde, *Veteris Testamenti ab Origine recensiti fragmenta apud Syros reservata quinque . . .* , Göttingen: Kaestner, 1880, p. 65. My translation from the Syriac.

9. William Robertson Smith, *The Religion of the Semites*, 3d ed., London: A. C. Black, 1927, p. 191, n. 1.

10. Gustaf Dalman, "Die Ausflüge," in Deutsches Evangelisches Institut für Altertumswissenschaft des heiligen Landes, *Palästinajahrbuch* 9 (1913): 25; Albrecht Alt, "Das Institut im Jahre 1925," *Palästinajahrbuch* 22 (1926):35; Wilhelm Borée, *Die alten Ortsnamen Palästinas*, Leipzig: E. Pfeiffer, 1903, p. 77.

11. *Entziqlopediya Miqrait*, Jerusalem: Mossad Bialik, 1954, 2:72.

12. See talmudic and midrashic examples of this meaning in Marcus Jastrow, *A Dictionary of the Targumim . . .* , New York-Berlin: Choreb; London: Shapiro, Vallentine, 1926, s.v. ḥagal.

13. Raphael Patai, "The 'Control of Rain' in Ancient Palestine," *Hebrew Union College Annual* (Cincinnati) 14 (1939): 251–86.

14. Hedwig Jahnow, *Das hebräische Leichenlied im Rahmen der Völkerdichtung*, Giessen: Töpelman, 1923, p. 75, n. 6, citing Wetzstein, "Die syrische Dreschtafel," *Zeitschrift für Ethnologie* 5 (1873): 297.

15. See Stanley A. Cook's note in William Robertson Smith, *Religion of the Semites*, pp. 671–72.

16. Hermann Gunkel, *Genesis*, 9th ed., Göttingen: Vandenhoeck & Ruprecht, 1977, pp. 364–65; William O. E. Oesterley, *The Sacred Dance*, New York: Macmillan, 1923, pp. 117ff.

17. Solomon Mandelkern, *Concordantia*, 2d ed., Berlin: Schocken, 1937, p. 963, s.vv. *pasaḥ, pisseaḥ;* Jastrow, *A Dictionary of the Targumim*, s.v. *pisseaḥ.*

18. William Robertson Smith, *Religion of the Semites*, p. 432; and the instructive note of Cook, pp. 471–72.

19. Robert Graves, *The Greek Myths*, 2 vols., Baltimore: Penguin Books, 1955, 12.c, 92.1. See also the long entries "Perdix" and "Talos" in W. H. Roscher, *Ausführliches Lexikon der griechischen und römischen Mythologie*, Leipzig: Teubner, 1884–1937.

20. Graves, *White Goddess*, pp. 325, 327.

21. *Entz. Miq.*, s.v. *Yaᶜaqov*, and literature there.

22. Cf. *Entz. Miq.*, s.v. *Qore*. See also 1 Sam. 26:20, where the same word is translated by the Septuagint as *nuktikórax.*

23. Patai, *Man and Temple*, pp. 36, 56–58, 71–72, and sources on pp. 50–51, n. 51.

24. Raphael Patai, *The Hebrew Goddess*, 2d ed., New York: Avon Books, 78, p. 38.

25. Raphael Patai, *Society, Culture and Change in the Middle East*, 3d ed., Philadelphia: University of Pennsylvania Press, 1971, pp. 205, 207.

26. *Entz. Miq.* 4:113.

27. For more information about the *q'deshim*, see *Entz. Miq.* 7:35–36.

28. See also 2 Chron. 3:15–17, and numerous other biblical passages. For midrashic sources see Patai, *Man and Temple*, pp. 108–9, 113–14.

29. Cf. Herodotus, *History* 2:44.

30. Patai, *Sex and Family in the Bible and the Middle East*, Garden City, N.Y.: Doubleday, 1959, pp. 190–94.

31. *Entz. Miq.* 2:282, s.v. *Boᶜaz*. For other suggested explanations of the name, see T. K. Cheyne and J. Sutherland Black, eds., *Encyclopaedia Biblica*, London: Adam and Charles Black, 1901, II:2304–5.

32. Patai, *Man and Temple*, pp. 108–9.

33. *Entz. Miq.* 3: 682, s.v. *Yakhin.*

34. See various attempts at explanation in *Enc. Biblica* 2:230–35; *Entz. Miq.* 3:525–26.

35. Stanley A. Cook in William Robertson Smith, *Religion of the Semites*, pp. 487–88.

36. Patai, *Man and Temple*, p. 34.

CHAPTER 2

1. Published in the *Hebrew Union College Annual* (Cincinnati) 20 (1947): 143–225.

2. Published as Memoir No. 67 of the Memoir Series of the American Anthropological Association, October 1947, 48pp.

3. *Encyclopaedia Biblica* 1: 526–27, s.v. *Belial.*

4. See also *Entziqlopediya Miqrait* 2: 132–33, s.v. *B'liyyaᶜal.*

5. James B. Pritchard, *Ancient Near Eastern Texts*, 2d ed., Princeton, N.J.: Princeton University Press, 1955, p. 109.

6. *Entz. Miq.*, loc. cit.

7. This is the translation in the English Bible of the Jewish Publication Society of America. It is found already in several medieval Jewish commentaries.

8. Patai, "Hebrew Installation Rites," pp. 160–62.

9. Robert Graves, *The Greek Myths*, 2 vols., Baltimore: Penguin Books, 1955, 57.2, 82.6, 86.2, 95.5. Cf. Pliny, *Historia Naturalis* VIII: 57 (many editions). On Ker see also H. J. Rose, *A Handbook of Greek Mythology*, London: Methuen, 1933, p. 23; Roscher, *Ausführliches Lexikon*, s.vv. *Carmenta, Cerus, Keren (Keres).*

10. A. M. Hocart, *Kingship*, Oxford: Oxford University Press; London: Humphrey Milford, 1927, p. 102.

11. Patai, "Hebrew Installation Rites," p. 143.

12. See the review of the various interpretations of the name Israel in the *Entz. Miq.* 3:938–40.

CHAPTER 3

1. Richard Ellmann, *Oscar Wilde*, New York: Alfred A. Knopf, 1988, p. 339.

2. Martin Seymour-Smith, *Robert Graves: His Life and Work*, New York: Holt, Rinehart, and Winston, 1983, p. 16.

3. The story of this incident from the apprenticeship of Hillel is interesting enough to be quoted in full from its sources, the Babylonian Talmud, Yoma 35b (my translation): "It is told about Hillel the elder that by working he earned daily one tropaikos [a coin of little worth], half of which he gave to the janitor of the House of Study, and used the other half to sustain himself and his family. One day he found no work, and the janitor did not let him in; thereupon he climbed up onto the roof and sat on the skylight to hear the words of the living God from the mouths of Shemaya and Avtalyon [the heads of the academy]. They say that it was on a Friday, at the winter solstice, and snow fell upon him from the sky. When the morning broke, Shemaya said to Avtalyon: 'Brother Avtalyon, on every other day the room is light, but today it is dark; is it that the day is so cloudy?' When they looked up and saw a figure of a man in the skylight, they went up and found him covered with three cubits of snow. They brought him down, washed and rubbed him with oil, and set him in front of the fire, for, they said, he deserved that the Sabbath be desecrated for his sake."

4. Sydney Musgrove, *The Ancestry of 'The White Goddess'*, English Series, no. 11, Auckland, New Zealand: University of Auckland, 1962, p. 3.

5. *Entziqlopediya Miqrait*, s.v. *Elohim*.

6. See Raphael Patai, *The Hebrew Goddess*, 3d ed., Detroit: Wayne State University Press, 1990, pp. 165, 172, 195, 198.

CHAPTER 4

1. *Transactions of the New York Academy of Sciences*, ser. 2, 10, no. 6 (1948): 200–209.

2. Robert Graves, *Occupation Writer*, New York: Creative Age Press, 1950.

3. See *Entziqlopediya Miqrait*, s.vv. Lot, Lotan, Moab; *Encyclopaedia Biblica*, s.vv. Ammon, Moab.

4. See *Entz. Miq.*, s.v. ʿAmmon.

5. In the *Enc. Biblica*, s.v. Ammon.

CHAPTER 6

1. Statement by Graves as quoted in Martin Seymour-Smith, *Robert Graves: His Life and Work*, New York: Holt, Rinehart, and Winston, 1983, p. 360.

2. Seymour-Smith, *Rober Graves*, p. 428.

3. Paul O'Prey, ed., *Between Moon and Moon: Selected Letters of Robert Graves 1946–1972*, London: Hutchinson, 1984, p. 66.

4. I argued in that paper that 1 Sam. 19:18–24 could not have formed part of the original narrative. See Raphael Patai, "Hebrew Installation Rites," *Hebrew Union College Annual* (Cincinnati) 20 (1947): 203. W. O E. Oesterley and T. H. Robinson, *Introduction to the Books of the Old Testament*, London: Society for Promoting Christian Knowledge, 1934, p. 85, n. 1, regard

that section a "late midrash," as does W. A. Irwin, "Samuel and the Rise of the Monarchy," *American Journal of Semitic Literature* 58 (1941): 128, 129.

5. Patai, "Hebrew Installation Rites," pp. 202–4.

6. "The Indios Israelitas of Mexico," *Menorah Journal* 38, no. 1 (Winter 1950): pp. 54–67.

7. *Talpioth* (New York) 5, nos. 3–4 (1952): 828–44.

8. *Mult és Jövö* (Paris) 35, no. 4 (April 1952): 88–89.

9. O'Prey, *Between Moon and Moon,* p. 74, letter by Graves to T. S. Eliot, dated May 14, 1950.

10. Joseph Klausner, *Yeshu Hanotzri,* Jerusalem: Stiebel, 1922; *Jesus of Nazareth,* New York: Macmillan, 1929.

11. Joseph Klausner, *MiYeshu ʿad Paulus,* Tel Aviv: Hotzaʾat Maddaʿ, 1939–40; *From Jesus to Paul,* New York: Macmillan, 1943.

12. Robert Graves, *Adam's Rib,* New York: Thomas Yoseloff, 1958, p. 8.

13. Raphael Patai, *The Hebrew Goddess,* New York: Ktav, 1967, pp. 19, 52, 54–56.

14. Elizabeth Bacon, "The Culture Areas of Asia," *Southwestern Journal of Anthropology* 2 (1946): 117–32; Raphael Patai, "Nomadism: Middle Eastern and Central Asian," *Southwestern Journal of Anthropology* 7, no. 4 (Winter 1951): 401–14.

15. *Hadoar* (New York) (May 7 1954).

16. Patai, "Hebrew Installation Rites," pp. 169–70, quoted in Robert Graves and Joshua Podro, *The Nazarene Gospel Restored,* Garden City, N.Y.: Doubleday, 1953, pp. 94–95.

17. Patai, "Hebrew Installation Rites," pp. 215–16; reprinted in *Nazarene Gospel Restored,* pp. 106–7.

18. Patai, "Hebrew Installation Rites," pp. 216–17; reprinted in *Nazarene Gospel Restored,* p. 107.

CHAPTER 7

1. Robert Graves, *New Poems,* Garden City, N.Y.: Doubleday, 1963, p. 35.

2. Robert Graves, *The White Goddess,* New York: Farrar Straus, 1966, p. 490.

3. Martin Seymour-Smith describes the relationship between Graves and Judith with tact and restraint, on pp. 440–47 and 453–56 of his biography *Robert Graves: His Life and Work,* New York: Holt, Rinehart, and Winston, 1983.

4. Robert Graves to Ken McCormick, as quoted in Seymour-Smith, *Robert Graves,* p. 450.

5. *Talpioth* (New York) 6, nos. 1–2 (1953): 226–68; 6, nos. 3–4 (1955): 686–705; 9, nos. 1–2 (1965): 238–60. Many years later I translated it into English and included it in my volume *On Jewish Folklore,* Detroit: Wayne State University Press, 1983, where it takes up more than a hundred pages, pp. 337–443.

6. *Middle East Journal* (Washington) 6, no. 1 (Winter 1952): 1–21.

7. Wolfgang Weissleder, ed., *The Nomadic Alternative: Modes and Models of Interaction in the African-Asian Deserts and Steppes,* World Anthropology Series, ed. Sol Tax, The Hague: Mouton, 1978, pp. 3–39.

8. *Islamic Culture and Contemporary Life,* published in Cairo, 1956, with the cooperation of Franklin Publications, pp. 195–202.

CHAPTER 8

1. Martin Seymour-Smith, *Robert Graves: His Life and Works,* New York: Holt, Rinehart, and Winston, 1983, p. 429.

2. Seymour-Smith, *Robert Graves,* p. 429.

3. Robert Graves, *Adam's Rib,* New York: Thomas Yoseloff, 1958, p. 1.

4. Graves, *Adam's Rib,* p. 15.

5. Robert Graves, *But It Still Goes On: An Accumulation*, New York: Jonathan Cape & Harrison Smith, 1931.

CHAPTER 11

1. Robert Graves, *The Greek Myths*, 2 vols., Baltimore: Penguin Books, 1955, 141.1.
2. Martin Seymour-Smith, *Robert Graves: His Life and Work*, New York: Holt, Rinehart, and Winston, 1983, p. 463.
3. Seymour-Smith, *Robert Graves*, p. 467.
4. The title of Graves's *Iliad* translation is *The Anger of Achilles: Homer's Iliad*, New York: Doubleday, 1959.
5. Seymour-Smith, *Robert Graves*, 486–89.
6. *Lawrence and the Arabs*, London: Cape, 1927; also published as *Lawrence and the Arabian Adventure*, New York: Doubleday, 1928; *T. E. Lawrence to His Biographer Robert Graves*, New York: Doubleday, 1938; London: Faber, 1939.

CHAPTER 12

1. I wish to thank Prof. Roger Bagnall of Columbia University for deciphering this Greek phrase and locating its source. He also kindly indicated that the preferred reading is *metabainōmen entheuten* (i.e., with an omicron instead of the omega), meaning "We are departing hence."
2. *Hebrew Myths* 9.b and sources in note 5; 9.i and note 18.
3. *Hebrew Myths*, "The Fall of Man," 12.k and 14, where, however, Graves (for this was evidently his contribution) referred to the tenth-century Irish *Saltair na Rann*, and not to the Welsh *Yr Awdil Vraith*. Many additional sources containing references to Adam's repentance and self-mortification in the waters of the Gihon River are brought together in Louis Ginzberg, *Legends of the Jews*, Philadelphia: Jewish Publication Society, (1947), 5:114–15.
4. So called after its author Rabbi Shim'on haDarshan, "Simon the Preacher," who lived in Frankfurt a. M.
5. *Yalqut Shim'oni*, Gen. 34.
6. See "The Books of Adam and Eve," in R. H. Charles, *The Apocrypha and Pseudepigrapha*, Oxford: Clarendon Press, 1913, II:134–37.
7. See B. Erubin 18b; Gen. Rab. 20:11 and 24:6; Tanh. Buber 1:20; Num. Rab. 14:12; and Ginzberg, *Legends of the Jews* 7:106.
8. Robert Graves, *On Poetry: Collected Talks and Essays*, Garden City, N.Y.: Doubleday, 1969, pp. 367–82.
9. Ginzberg, *Legends of the Jews* 1:687.
10. See *Entziqlopediya Miqrait*, s.v. *K'na'an*.
11. Robert Graves, *The Greek Myths*, 2 vols., Baltimore: Penguin Books, 1955, 58.1.
12. H. J. Rose, *A Handbook of Greek Mythology*, London: Methuen, 1933, pp. 149, 183–84; Graves, *The Greek Myths* 58, etc.; and especially the long entry "Agenor" in W. H. Roscher, *Ausführliches Lexikon der griechischen und römischen Mythologie*, Leipzig: Teubner, 1884–1937.
13. Rose, *Handbook*, pp. 122, 183–86; Roscher, *Ausführliches Lexikon*, s.v. *Kadmos*.
14. *Hebrew Myths* 21.2.

CHAPTER 13

1. James B. Pritchard, *Ancient Near Eastern Texts*, 2d ed., Princeton; N.J.: Princeton University Press, 1955, pp. 487–89.

445

2. Pritchard, *Ancient Near Eastern Texts*, pp. 89, 124, 206, 393, 398.
3. Robert Graves, *Adam's Rib*, New York: Thomas Yoseloff, 1958, p. 15.

CHAPTER 14

1. Robert Graves, *The Feather Bed*, published in Surrey, England, by the Hogarth Press of Leonard and Virginia Wolf, 1923.
2. Robert Graves, *My Head! My Head!* New York: Alfred A. Knopf, 1925, 141 pp.
3. See Isaac Rosenberg's brief biography in the *Encyclopaedia Judaica*, Jerusalem: Keter Publishing House, 1972.
4. Its title in the 1955 English translation is *Moses and Monotheism*.
5. I am grateful to Beryl Graves for having sent me a copy of this letter by Eva Meyerowitz.

CHAPTER 16

1. Robert Graves, *The Greek Myths*, 2 vols., Baltimore: Penguin Books, 1955, index, s.v. *Erichthonius*.
2. *The Works of Lucian of Samothrace*, trans. H. W. and F. G. Fowler, Oxford: Clarendon Press, 1905, 1:27, 30.

CHAPTER 19

1. Edward Westermarck, *Ritual and Belief in Morocco*, London: Macmillan, 1926, 1:35–261.
2. *Oxford Addresses on Poetry*, Garden City, N.Y.: Doubleday, 1962, pp. 109–19; also published in *On Poetry: Collected Talks and Essays*, Garden City, N.Y.: Doubleday, 1969, pp. 359–66.

CHAPTER 29

1. Graves included a longer and more literary version of this anecdote in his lecture titled "To Be a Goy," which he delivered at the Zionist Organization of America House in Tel Aviv on January 19, 1959, to the Israel and Commonwealth Association. See Robert Graves, *Food for Centaurs*, Garden City, N.Y.: Doubleday, 1960, p. 153.
2. *Encyclopaedia of Religion*, New York: Macmillan, 1987, 10:78, 14:135.
3. Edward William Lane, *A Thousand and One Nights*, London: C. Knight, 1841, 3:90–91, n. 22, "On the Rukh"; Kazwini, as quoted in Joseph Catafago, *An Arabic and English Dictionary*, 3d ed., Beirut: Librairie du Liban, 1975, p. 159, s.v. *rukh*.

CHAPTER 30

1. Robert Graves, "Intimations of the Black Goddess," in *On Poetry: Collected Talks and Essays*, Garden City, N.Y.: Doubleday, 1969, p. 428.

2. Babylonian Talmud, Yoma 9b.
3. Martin Seymour-Smith, *Robert Graves: His Life and Work,* New York: Holt, Rinehart, and Winston, 1983, pp. 533–49, for a description of the role Laraçuen played in Graves's life.
4. See, e.g., Fred Gettings, *Dictionary of Astrology,* London: Routledge & Kegan Paul, 1985, p. 177, s.v. *Leo;* Carl L. Sargent, *The Astrology of Rising Signs,* London: Rider, 1986, p. 79.

CHAPTER 31

1. Claude Lévi-Strauss, *Structural Anthropology,* New York-London, Basic Books, 1963, p. 229.
2. Edmund Leach, "Genesis as Myth," in *Genesis as Myth and Other Essays,* London: Jonathan Cape, 1969, p. 19.
3. Edmund Leach, "Lévi-Strauss in the Garden of Eden: An Examination of Some Recent Developments in the Analysis of Myth," *Transactions of the New York Academy of Sciences,* ser. II, 23, no. 41 (February 1961): 395.
4. Edmund Leach, "Anthropological Approaches to the Study of the Bible during the Twentieth Century," in Edmund Leach and Alan Aycock, *Structural Interpretations of Biblical Myth,* Cambridge: Cambridge University Press, 1983, p. 10.
6. Leach and Aycock, *Structural Interpretations,* pp. 29–30.
5. Raphael Patai, *Sex and Family in the Bible and the Middle East,* Garden City, N.Y.: Doubleday, 1959. Leach cites the British edition of this book, *Family, Love and the Bible,* London: McGibbon and Kee, 1960.
7. *Hebrew Myths,* p. 11.
8. Leach and Aycock, *Structural Interpretations,* p. 8. In note 4, appended to this definition, Leach quotes Malinowski's definition of myth, which largely coincides with his and ours.

CHAPTER 32

1. *The Song of Songs,* text and commentary by Robert Graves, illustrated by Hans Erni, New York: Clarkson N. Potter, distributed by Crown Publishing Co., 1973.
2. Robert Graves, *Food for Centaurs,* Garden City, N.Y.: Doubleday, 1960, pp. 272–73. For the variety of attempts to explain Song 2:15, see Marvin H. Pope's monumental *Song of Songs: A New Translation and Commentary,* The Anchor Bible, Garden City, N.Y.: Doubleday, 1977, pp. 402–5.
3. Raphael Patai, *The Hebrew Goddess,* 2d ed., New York: Avon Books, 1978, pp. 19, 23.
4. I quoted this from a late Midrash titled "The Throne and Hippodrome of King Solomon," ed. Adolph Jellinek, *Beth HaMidrash,* 2d ed., Jerusalem: Bamberger & Wahrman, 1938, 5: 38 ff.
5. Raphael Patai, *Man and Temple in Ancient Jewish Myth and Ritual* Edinburgh: Thomas Nelson, 1947, p. 76.
6. Robert Graves, *King Jesus,* New York: Farrar Straus Giroux, 1981, pp. 52–65.

CHAPTER 33

1. R. Patai, *Myth and Modern Man,* Englewood Cliffs, N.J.: Prentice-Hall, 1972, p. 267. Incidentally, this is the only one of my books to have been published in a Portuguese translation (São Paulo: Editora Cultrix, 1975).
2. Incidentally, in the preface to *The Arab Mind,* I mentioned Walter de la Mare's "hauntingly beautiful poem on Arabia," which, in my youth, had made a great impression on me. When I wrote that sentence I relied on what I had remembered of that poem. Recently, prompted by

curiosity, I looked it up in de la Mare's *Complete Poems*. I should not have done so. What I found only went to prove to me once again how false can be the basis of an old memory cherished for decades. It is tempting to analyze the poem "Arabia" in detail, in the manner of the French *explication de texte*, but I shall confine myself to mentioning that the "loveliness" that constitutes "the spell of far Arabia" for de la Mare consists of "verdurous vales and thickets," "flowers in the forest," and "gliding streams" with "green banks"—all features less than characteristic of that arid country.

3. Martin Seymour-Smith, *Robert Graves: His Life and Work*, New York: Holt, Rinehart, and Winston, 1983, p. 565.

APPENDIX

1. David Bidney, "Myth, Symbolism, and Truth," *Journal of American Folklore* (October–December 1955): 379.

2. Edward B. Tylor, *Primitive Culture*, 1871. Reprint. New York: H. Holt, 1924, 2:446.

3. Richard M. Dorson, "The Eclipse of Solar Mythology," *Journal of American Folklore* (October–December 1955): 415–16.

4. Wilhelm Wundt, *Völkerpsychologie*, Leipzig, 1908; 2d ed., Leipzig: W. Engelmann, 1914. The source references above are to this 2d edition.

5. Wundt, *Völkerpsychologie*, 5:23–24. My translation of this and all subsequent quotes.

6. See Otto Rank, *The Myth of the Birth of the Hero*, Nervous and Mental Disease Monograph Series, no. 18, New York, 1914. Originally published in German in 1908.

7. Géza Róheim, "Myth and Folk-Tale," *American Imago* 2, no. (1940) 3: 266.

8. Jane E. Harrison, *Themis*, Cambridge: The University Press, 1912, pp. 13, 328, 331.

9. S. H. Hooke, ed., *Myth and Ritual: Essays on the Myth and Ritual of the Hebrews in Relation to the Culture Pattern of the Ancient East*, London: Oxford University Press, 1933; *The Labyrinth: Further Studies in the Relation between Myth and Ritual in the Ancient World*, London: Society for Promoting Christian Knowledge, 1935.

10. Stanley Edgar Hyman, "The Ritual View of Myth and the Mythic," *Journal of American Folklore* (October–December 1955): 465, 470–71.

11. Lord Raglan, "Myth and Ritual," *Journal of American Folklore* (October–December 1955): 454; Lord Raglan, *The Hero*, London: Methuen, 1936, p. 145.

12. Quotation from Bronislaw Malinowski, *Myth in Primitive Psychology*, London: K. Paul, Trench, Trubner, 1926, p. 13. Note that in quoting the above passage in "Myth and Ritual," p. 457, Raglan omitted the crucial words "of ritual."

13. Christoph von Furer-Haimendorf, *The Raj Gonds*, London: Macmillan, 1948, p. 99, as quoted by Lord Raglan in "Myth and Ritual," p. 457.

14. Wesley J. Culshaw, *Tribal Heritage*, London: Lutterworth Press, 1949, p. 64, as quoted by Raglan, ibid.

15. M. Fortes, *The Web of Kinship among the Tallensi*, Oxford: Oxford University Press, 1949, p. 3, as quoted by Raglan, ibid., pp. 457–58.

16. Raglan, "Myth and Ritual," p. 458.

17. Bidney, "Myth, Symbolism, and Truth," p. 294.

18. Originally published in 1926; reprinted in Malinowski's *Magic, Science and Religion*, New York: Doubleday Anchor Books, 1948, which edition is quoted in all the subsequent page references.

19. Walter F. Otto, *Die Gestalt und das Sein: Abhandlungen über den Mythos und seine Bedeutung für die Menschheit*, Düsseldorf-Köln: Eugen Diederich's Verlag, 1955. All the subsequent quotes are my translation from the German.

20. Kenneth Burke, "Myth, Poetry and Philosophy," *Journal of American Folklore* (October–December 1960): 287.

21. Hooke, *The Labyrinth*, p. v.

22. Raphael Patai, *Man and Temple in Ancient Jewish Myth and Ritual*, Edinburgh: Thomas Nelson, 1947.

Index

449